MULTICULTURAL EXPERIENCES, MULTICULTURAL THEORIES

MULTICULTURAL EXPERIENCES, MULTICULTURAL THEORIES

Mary F. Rogers

The University of West Florida

Consulting Editor

George Ritzer

University of Maryland

The McGraw-Hill Companies, Inc.

New York St. Louis San Francisco Auckland Bogotá Caracas
Lisbon London Madrid Mexico City Milan Montreal New Delhi
San Juan Singapore Sydney Tokyo Toronto

for
Michael James Russell

McGraw-Hill

*A Division of The **McGraw-Hill** Companies*

This book was set in Times Roman by ComCom, Inc.
The editors were Jill S. Gordon and Katherine Blake;
the production supervisor was Denise L. Puryear.
The cover was designed by John Hite.
Project supervision was done by Tage Publishing Service, Inc.
Quebecor Printing/Fairfield was printer and binder.

MULTICULTURAL EXPERIENCES, MULTICULTURAL THEORIES

This book is printed on acid-free paper.

2 3 4 5 6 7 8 9 0 FGR FGR 9 0 9 8 7 6

ISBN 0-07-053560-4

Library of Congress Cataloging-in-Publication Data

Multicultural experiences, multicultural theorizing / Mary F. Rogers,
consulting editor George Ritzer.
    p.   cm.
ISBN 0-07-053560-4
1. Pluralism (Social sciences)   2. Multiculturalism.   3. Social
sciences—Philosophy.   I. Rogers, Mary F. (Mary Frances), (date).
II. Ritzer, George.
HM276.M72   1996
301 '.01—dc20   95-25248

PERMISSION ACKNOWLEDGMENTS

Jane Flax, "Women Do Theory" from *Quest: A Feminist Quarterly,* vol. v., no. 1 (Summer 1979), pp. 20–24. Copyright © by Jane Flax. Reprinted with permission of the author.

Maria C. Lugones and Elizabeth V. Spelman, "Have We Got a Theory for You! Feminist Theory, Cultural Imperialism, and the Demand for the Woman's Voice" from *Women's Studies International Forum,* vol. 6, no. 6 (1983), pp. 573–581. Copyright © by Maria Lugones. Reprinted with permission of the authors.

Patricia Hill Collins, "Learning from the Outsider Within: The Sociological Significance of Black Feminist Thought." Reprinted with permission of the publisher and author from *Social Problems,* vol. 33, no. 6 (December 1986), pp. 14–32. Copyright © by University of California Press.

bell hooks, "feminist theory: a radical agenda" in *talking back: thinking feminist, thinking black,* pp. 35–41. Copyright © by South End Press, 1989. Reprinted with permission of the publisher.

Molefi Kete Asante, "The Afrocentric Metatheory and Disciplinary Implications" from *The Afrocentric Scholar,* vol. 1, no. 1 (May, 1992), pp. 98–117. Copyright © by the Center for Black Culture and Research. Reprinted with permission of the publisher.

Alan Banks, Dwight Billings, and Karen Tice, "Appalachian Studies and Postmodernism." Reprinted with permission of the publisher from Alan Banks, Dwight Billings, and Karen Tice, "Appalachian Studies, Resistance, and Postmodernism," pp. 288–301 in Stephen L. Fisher (ed.), *Fighting Back in Appalachia: Traditions of Resistance and Change.* Copyright © by Temple University Press, 1993.

Donald Morton, "The Politics of Queer Theory in the (Post)Modern Moment." Reprinted with permission of the author and publisher, from "The Politics of Queer Theory in the (Post)Modern Moment," by Donald Morton in *Genders,* vol. 17 (Fall 1993), pp. 121–127 and 142–144. Copyright © The University of Texas Press, 1993.

Wendy Rose, "The Great Pretenders: Further Reflections on Whiteshamanism" in M. Annette Jaimes (ed.), *The State of Native America: Genocide, Colonization, and Resistance,* pp. 403–21. Copyright © by South End Press, 1992. Reprinted with permission of the publisher.

Michelle Fine, "Coping with Rape: Critical Perspectives on Consciousness" in Rhoda K. Unger (ed.), *Representations: Social Constructions of Gender,* pp. 186–200. Copyright © by Baywood Publishing Company, Inc., 1989. Reprinted with permission of the author and publisher.

Alan J. Bishop, "Western Mathematics: The Secret Weapon of Cultural Imperialism." Reprinted courtesy of the Institute of Race Relations, London from *Race & Class,* vol. 32, no. 2 (October–December, 1990), pp. 51–65. Copyright © The Institute of Race Relations, London, 1990.

Barry D. Adam, "The Holocaust." Reprinted with permission of Twayne Publishers, an imprint of Simon & Schuster Macmillan, from Barry D. Adam, "The Holocaust," with slight deletion (pp. 45–55), Chapter Notes, p. 168, and selected entries from References (pp. 174–191), *The Rise of a Gay and Lesbian Movement.* Copyright © 1987 by G.K. Hall & Co.

Carroll Smith-Rosenberg, "Captured Subjects/Savage Others: Violently Engendering the New American." Reprinted with permission of the publisher from *Gender & History,* v. 5 (Summer, 1993), pp. 177–180 and 190–192. Copyright © 1987 by Basil Blackwell, Ltd., Oxford, 1993.

W. Roger Buffalohead, "Reflections on Native American Cultural Rights and Resources" in *American Indian Culture and Research Journal,* vol. 16, no. 2, pp. 197–200. Copyright © by W. Roger Buffalohead, 1992. Reprinted with permission of the author.

Clovis E. Semmes, "Religion and the Challenge of Afrocentric Thought." Reprinted with permission from the publisher, from *The Western Journal of Black Studies,* vol. 17, no. 3, pp. 158–163. Copyright © by Washington State University Press, 1993.

Ellen Swartz, "Emancipatory Narratives: Rewriting the Master Script in the School Curriculum." Reprinted with permission from the author, from *Journal of Negro Education,* vol. 61, no. 3, pp. 341–355. Copyright © by Ellen Swartz, 1992.

Judith Lorber, "Believing is Seeing: Biology as Ideology." Reprinted with permission of Sage Publications, Inc., from *Gender & Society,* vol. 7, no. 4 (December, 1993), pp. 568–581. Copyright © by Sage Publications, Inc., 1993.

Linda Gordon, "Women's Agency, Social Control, and 'Rights' among Battered Women" from Linda Gordon, "Women's Agency, Social Control, and the Construction of 'Rights' by Battered Women," pp. 128–44 in Sue Fisher and Kathy Davis (eds.), *Negotiating at the Margins: The Gendered Discourse of Power and Resistance.* Copyright © by Rutgers University Press, 1993. Reprinted with permission from the author.

Nicola Gavey, "Technologies and Effects of Heterosexual Coercion" in Sue Wilkinson and Celia Kitzinger (eds.), *Heterosexuality: A Feminism & Psychology Reader,* pp. 93–98 and 115–119. Copyright © by Sage Publications, 1993. Reprinted with permission from the publisher.

Wendi Hadd, "A Womb with a View: Women as Mothers and the Discourse of the Body." Reprinted with permission from the publisher, from *Berkeley Journal of Sociology,* v. 36, pp. 165–175. Copyright © by the Berkeley Journal of Sociology, 1991.

Karlene Faith, "Institutionalized Violence." Reprinted with permission from the publisher and the author, from Karlene Faith, *Unruly Women: The Politics of Confinement and Resistance.* Copyright © by Press Gang Publishers, 1993.

Elizabeth Martinez, "Beyond Black/White: The Racisms of Our Time." Reprinted with permission from *Social Justice,* Vol. 20, Nos. 1–2; P.O. Box 40601, San Francisco, CA 94140. Copyright © by Social Justice, 1993.

Mariana Valverde, "Bisexuality and Deviant Identities." Reprinted with permission from the publisher, from Mariana Valverde, *Sex, Power and Pleasure.* Copyright © by New Society Publishers, 4527 Springfield Avenue, Philadelphia, PA 19143, 1-800-333-9093, 1987.

Larry Gross, "Identity Politics, Coming Out, and Coming Together." Reprinted with permission from the publisher, from Larry Gross, "Identity Politics," "Roles or Realities," and "Coming Out and Coming Together," pp. 106–121 and 319–331 in *Contested Closets: The Politics and Ethics of Outing.* Copyright © 1993 by the Regents of the University of Minnesota.

Sandra Lee Bartky, "Feeding Egos and Tending Wounds: Deference and Disaffection in Women's Emotional Labor." Reprinted from *Femininity and Domination: Studies in the Phenomenology of Oppression* (1990), by permission of the publisher, Routledge, New York.

Audre Lorde, "The Uses of Anger: Women Responding to Racism." Reprinted by permission from the publisher, from "The Uses of Anger," pp. 127–133 in *Sister Outsider: Essays and Speeches.* Copyright © 1984 by Audre Lorde, The Crossing Press, Freedom, CA.

Christine Sypnowich, "Some Disquiet about 'Difference' " from *Praxis International,* vol. 13, no. 2 (July, 1993), pp. 99–112. Copyright © by Blackwell Publishers, Ltd., 1993. Reprinted by permission from the publisher.

Anndee Hochman, "What We Call Each Other." Reprinted by permission from the publisher and the author, from Anndee Hochman, "What We Call Each Other," pp. 257–62 in *Everyday Acts & Small Subversions: Women Reinventing Family, Community, and Home.* Copyright © by Anndee Hochman (Portland, OR: The Eighth Mountain Press, 1994).

Bonnie Thornton Dill, "Fictive Kin, Paper Sons: Women of Color and the Struggle for Family Survival." Reprinted by permission from the publisher, from Bonnie Thornton Dill, "Fictive Kin, Paper Sons, and *Compadrazgo:* Women of Color and the Struggle for Family Survival," pp. 149–58 and 164–69 in Maxine Baca Zinn and Bonnie Thornton Dill (eds.), *Women of Color in U.S. Society.* Copyright © by Temple University Press, 1994.

Reva Landau, "On Making 'Choices'." Reprinted by permission from the publisher, from *Feminist Issues,* vol. 12, no. 2, pp. 47–72. Copyright © by Transaction Periodicals, Rutgers, The State University of New Jersey, 1992.

Paula Gunn Allen, *"Hwame, Koshkalaka,* and the Rest: Lesbians in American Indian Cultures." Reprinted by permission of Beacon Press, from *The Sacred Hoop: Recovering the Feminine in American Indian Traditions.* Copyright © 1986, 1992, by Paula Gunn Allen.

William Wei, "Reclaiming the Past and Constructing a Collective Culture." Reprinted by permission from Temple University Press, from William Wei, "Reclaiming the Past" and "Constructing a Collective Culture," pp. 54–71 in *The Asian American Movement.* Copyright © by Temple University Press, 1993.

Cheryl Townsend Gilkes, " 'If It Wasn't for the Women . . .': African American Women, Community Work, and Social Change." Reprinted by permission from Temple University Press, from Cheryl Townsend Gilkes, " 'If It Wasn't for the Women . . .': African American Women, Community Work, and Social Change," pp. 229–46 in Maxine Baca Zinn and Bonnie Thornton Dill (eds.), *Women of Color in U.S. Society.* Copyright © by Temple University Press, 1994.

Dorceta E. Taylor, "Environmentalism and the Politics of Inclusion." Reprinted by permission from the publisher, from Dorceta E. Taylor, "Environmentalism and the Politics of Inclusion," pp. 53–61 and 211–239 in Robert D. Bullard (ed.), *Confronting Environmental Racism: Voices from the Grassroots.* Copyright © by South End Press, 1993.

Steven Seidman, "The Politics of Subverting Identity and Foregrounding the Social." Reprinted by permission of the publisher, from Steven Seidman, "[The Politics of Subverting Identity and Foregrounding the Social]," pp. 127–139 and 142 (partial essay) in Michael Warner (ed.), *Fear of a Queer Planet: Queer Politics and Social Theory.* Copyright © by the Regents of the University of Minnesota.

Denise A. Segura and Beatriz M. Pesquera, "Beyond Indifference and Antipathy: The Chicana Movement and Chicana Feminist Discourse." Reprinted by permission of the authors, from *Aztlan,* vol. 19, no. 2, pp. 69–92. Copyright © Denise A. Segura, 1992.

R.W. Connell, "Men and the Women's Movement." Reprinted by permission of *Social Policy,* from *Social Policy,* v. 23, pp. 72–78. Copyright © 1993 by Social Policy Corporation, New York, NY 10036.

bell hooks, "feminism: a transformational politic." Reprinted by permission of the publisher, from bell hooks, "feminism: a transformational politic," pp. 19–27 in *talking back: thinking feminist, thinking black.* Copyright © by South End Press, Boston, 1989.

Cornel West, "The New Cultural Politics of Difference." Reprinted by permission of the publisher, from Cornel West, "The New Cultural Politics of Difference," pp. 19–36 in Russell Ferguson et al. (eds.), *Out There: Marginalization and Contemporary Cultures.* Copyright © by MIT Press, 1990.

CONTENTS

PREFACE

Working with the papers you will be reading has been uplifting yet taxing. Because much of our collective future, many of our democratic prospects, and a hefty portion of our selfhood hinge on the issues aired here, I sometimes felt weighted down by the challenge of doing any justice to them. At other times I felt exhilarated by the energy and creativity afoot among multiculturalists. I hope that in these materials you will find similar cause for consternation and inspiration. Above all, I hope you find strong nurture for your consciousness of self, others, and community.

I owe many people many thanks. George Ritzer heads that list. As consulting editor, he gave me the opportunity to bring these readings together and then served as a caretaker of this project. Jennifer Lehmann and Becky Thompson were two of the reviewers whose theoretical savvy and multicultural awareness helped me fashion a collection both ambitious and lean. Susan Chase, also a reviewer, infused this project with her indefatigable spirit and critical consciousness, tempered as always by her kindheartedness. I am honored to call her friend as well as colleague.

Among friends near and far whose very lives inspire and encourage me, I can only mention names where I would rather tell stories of stamina, courage, and compassion. Those friends include Dorothy Juhlin, Sue Foley, Fran White, Helen Koster, Viola Caprio, Neil Riordan, Arline Riordan, David Patriarca, Lola Buonanno, Maurice Natanson, Lois Natanson, Dallas Blanchard, Art Doerr, Dale Doerr, Mary Hood, Louise Weston, Gloria Mattingly, Claudia Rogers, Ira Cohen, Reggie Cohen, Catherine McVey, Cheryl Thomas, and Wendy Luttrell. Named in the order of their appearances in my life, these friends are my family just as my "family" comprises friends like my sisters Kathy, Martha, and Sharon and my mother Gen.

I have left two people unnamed because saying how much they sustain me is flatly impossible. The first person is Phillip Lott who worked on this project as a research associate ready to change hats as quickly as circumstances shifted. Phil's energies are not tireless, but he consistently acted as if they were; his research, computer, and inter-personal skills are not endless, but they felt that way to me; his good humor and kindness of heart cannot be limitless, but they seemed so. Unable to say how much he poured himself into this project, I say only that working with him was reason enough for under-taking this effort.

The other person is Christy Garrett. No one in my circle of loved ones has taught me more about dignity, social justice, and the inestimable value of education aimed at empowering people. No one has listened more patiently to my rantings and ravings, and no one has spoken more passionately to the issues these readings address. Only she knows the span of my indebtedness to her, yet she knows it with a modesty and gen-erosity that leave me free to go into further debt.

Finally, I want to mention six young people. Five are too young to have indebted me to them but just the right ages to have inspired me in diffuse ways. My five youngest nephews—Ian, Stewart, Noah, Sam, and Jarrett—have been frequent guests in my con-sciousness throughout this project. Awash in innocence and growing in dignity, they face a future at once uncertain and hopeful. I wish for them the kinds of awareness expressed in these readings and the kinds of community with others that will satisfy their spirits while enhancing the planet. The sixth person is also a nephew. Just entering young adulthood as a high school graduate and first-year college student, Mike has come of age during difficult times for American preadolescents and adolescents. Triumphing over those difficulties, he has remained true to his big heart and keen consciousness. His is already a multicultural awareness, and I take inspiration from him.

Mary F. Rogers

INTRODUCTION

Multiculturalism has to do with whose perspectives figure in our consciousness. When we think about American society, do we envision only members like ourselves? When we talk about homelessness or abortion-clinic violence, do we consider only the perspectives of groups that have won our allegiance? Multiculturalism challenges such limits. It illuminates the cultural diversity and multiple standpoints shaping people's experiences as neighbors, workers, students, citizens, parents, worshippers, and consumers making and sharing a world in common. It asks who masterminded past decisions in our society, whom they thus benefited and deprived, and how our social structure perpetuates those inequalities. Multiculturalism promotes our sense of common humanity without reducing its richness to a white blur of privilege or a masculine presence that goes unnamed. Its overriding purpose is to acquaint us with perspectives and experiences "different" from our own while helping us grasp how "differences" get socially created and reinforced.

Multiculturalism as a movement is distinctively, though not exclusively, American. It emerged as the second wave of the civil rights movement that shaped American society during the 1950s and 1960s.[1] Like that movement, multiculturalism grows out of the realization that the " 'price of admission' to the bourgeois civil societies of the West" remains indefensibly high for many groups of people and out of reach for other groups. Full admission entails assimilation.[2] It requires "different" people to compromise or even abandon their distinctiveness by conforming their public behavior to bourgeois tastes and to act as if they fully shared the culture of straight men in the white Protestant middle classes. Unwilling or unable to pay such prices, members of many groups get cast as our society's "Others."

Today many of those "Others" are multiculturalists of one sort or another. Whatever else they favor, most multiculturalists advocate schooling that affirms cultural diversity.

1

They emphasize that students come to school with identities anchored in historically specific, psychologically comfortable subcultures. Besides seeking equal access to and equal distribution of educational resources, multiculturalists want social-psychological equity. Such equity necessitates textbooks, classroom guests, laboratory manuals, and field trips offering each student a mirror wherein his or her own face sometimes makes an unmistakable appearance. Giving diverse students equal opportunities to learn requires inclusive curricula that pay detailed attention to the history, arts, and customs of all those groups in our society whose subcultures are misunderstood or widely maligned.

American higher education has been moving toward multicultural curricula since the days of "free" or "open" universities in the 1960s. In those student-run, loosely structured, alternative "universities" students learned about women's bodies and women's history, about colonialism and its aftermath, about how to make peace instead of war. As early as 1984, more than forty percent of American colleges offered Women's Studies courses; more than a third offered courses in Black Studies; a quarter offered Asian and Pacific American Studies courses; nearly a quarter offered Hispanic Studies courses.[3]

Perhaps you bought this book in connection with such a course. You may be enrolled in a Women's Studies course this term, or maybe you are taking a course in multicultural education, social stratification, or social theory. Then you are a participant in multiculturalism. With many other actors, you are standing on a panoramic stage where a historical play is taking shape. This drama, which is about cultural diversity, is a morality play concerning power, dignity, and social structure. Its plot revolves around the close connections among diverse kinds of subordination in society, a plot informing or even centering many fields of study today.

Sociology courses from race relations to the American class structure, for instance, widely focus on social inequalities. We have long known through wrenching expressions of social unrest, failed social policies, and false starts at substantial social progress that race, money, power, and privilege densely intertwine in our society. By now, we are beginning to see that gender, age, sexual orientation, and much else inform the dynamics of race and class in American life. In practical terms that generalization means that many women are socially positioned to feel the weight not only of their sex, but also of their race or ethnicity; it means that many lesbians, gay men, bisexuals, and other sexual minorities feel the weight of their race or social class as well as their sexual orientation; it means that many impoverished and working-poor people feel the weight of their skin color, national origins, or sexual orientation as well as the weight of their class position. During the past several decades we have come, in short, to recognize that social inequalities not only take shape as structured systems but also gain force as *interlocking,* albeit distinct, systems. Thus, how individuals experience gender depends substantially on how they are positioned within hierarchies other than the sex/gender system and how they experience their heterosexuality or their middle-class position depends on their gender, age, and ablebodiedness.

On their way out, then, are what Jean-Francois Lyotard calls "totalizing grand narratives." Also on their way out are essentialist or essentializing theories implying that one dimension of individuals' identities—gender, sexual orientation, or race, for instance—is capable of rendering their "situations or experiences . . . essentially the same in all social, cultural, and historical contexts."[4] Such essentializing entails a denial of diversity and difference. In its stead stands theorizing attuned to human variety and versatility. In the hands of multicultural theorists, for instance, human agency remains tied to social structure, but the tie-ins diversify. We begin to see that evidence of agency often gets conceptually buried by labels such as "victim" or "underdog"; that expressions of agency reflect people's positions in multiple, intersecting hierarchies; that the visible agency of hyperprivileged members depends on the invisible labors of less privileged members.

What this all means is that the days of narrowly construed feminist theory or sociological theory or any other kind of social theory lie in our past. In the 1990s Betty Friedan could no more credibly write *The Feminine Mystique* than Eldridge Cleaver could write *Soul on Ice*. The mostly white, largely middle-class homemakers whose alienation Friedan dramatized have flown the nest, been yanked into the labor force, reentered school, become single parents, or divorced and remarried and blended families while holding down a full-time job outside the home. The social facts have indeed changed, and so has our awareness. Today's "feminine mystique" would have to be writ large in terms allowing for lesbians' and bisexual women's experiences, old women's stories, Chicana and Asian American and American Indian as well as Euro-American women's prospects and outcomes, cancer-ridden and HIV-positive and crack-addicted women, and all those other big groupings of women whose experiences used to be missing or distorted in the works of social theorists and culture critics. Similarly, Cleaver's narrative has no clear-cut place in today's multicultural drama. It ignores, even celebrates, gender inequities; it says virtually nothing about racial oppression beyond the black/white dichotomy historically institutionalized as the "race problem" in our society. Like Friedan, Cleaver would have to enlarge his theoretical scope before claiming a place at the multicultural table.

Coming to that table means seeing the overlapping pains, dilemmas, deprivations, and fears wrought within interlocking systems of domination in our society. It means seeing that intragroup diversity is as worthy of notice as intergroup differences and that both varieties of differentiation have cultural roots. Coming to the multicultural table means, then, forswearing feminist theory rooted mostly in white, middle-class women's experiences; it means forswearing sociological theory that is out of touch with the hum and buzz of cultural diversity buried beneath the grand narratives of much systems theory, psychoanalytic theory, and rational-choice theory. It means taking seriously the theoretical efforts of thinkers like those found in *Multicultural Experiences, Multicultural Theories*. Finally, it means thinking about the social construction of knowledge, the multiple functions of social theory, and the costs of either/or thinking.

Multicultural awareness assumes many forms, as the readings in this volume show. It helps us see how "difference" routinely takes hold of consciousness without raising the question, "Different from whom or what?" Once we raise this multicultural question, our theoretical consciousness gains force. "Different from whom or what?" opens the floor for questions about how "difference" rather than "similarity" comes to the fore when people think about women and men, gays and straights, the poor and the rich, the old and the young; the black, the white, the brown, the yellow, the red. It raises questions about whose standards, preferences, and priorities hold sway; about how such standards come to prevail; about how the beliefs and perceptions of oppressed people often give expression to standards that malign them; about how collective action can shift people's perceptions and expectations while transforming social structure. Fundamentally, multicultural awareness sensitizes us to the pervasively social character of what we know. It alerts us to how people construct knowledge in the light of their past experiences, current social locations, and perceived prospects. Multicultural awareness thus promotes a process-centered approach to social realities, especially those that have gotten constructed as "natural" and "normal"—that is, especially those that have been naturalized and normalized through institutionalization.

A multicultural standpoint advances our understanding of the social construction of theory, too. It helps us see that the concepts centralized in a given theory, its key propositions, its grounding in these rather than those empirical data, and its applicability to the real world of diverse groups all take shape from the choices and activities of flesh-and-blood people with careers to advance, bills to pay, reputations to cultivate, and deadlines to meet. Typically positioned in academic bureaucracies inhabited mostly by white upper-middle-class male professionals and overseen by white male administrators, social theorists have often refracted the social and material circumstances of their work in their theories. By and large, they have theorized safe, clean, fairly stable worlds. They have theorized actors whose masculine prerogatives, white privilege, able bodies, heterosexuality, and affluence are taken for granted.

Over the past several decades many social theorists have widened their theoretical scope, at least superficially. One can now turn to the index of book-length treatises and find such terms as "Women," "Hispanic Americans," and "Lesbians (see Homosexuality)." Commonly, one comes across "men and women" and "his or her," if only in response to widespread requirements of gender-inclusive language. One seldom sees, however, social theorists positioned high in the academic hierarchy—at Ivy League universities, for instance, or in the internationally known circle of renowned social theorists—advancing a culturally inclusive theory or theorizing the experiences of people "different" from themselves. Such undertakings are mostly left to those of us who are "different" and those few who are exceptions to the rule of homosocial reproduction.

Since all theory is socially constructed, we are certain to develop richer social theory from the work of theorists who come from cultural backgrounds other than those of white, middle-class males. Looking at the social world from the standpoint of a lesbian feminist, for instance, is likely to foreground heterosexuality as a social institution; looking at that same world from the standpoint of American Indians is likely to foreground the connections between art and community more than those between art and individuality; looking at it from the standpoint of a working-class or working-poor person is likely to foreground the pathos of mass advertising and the American Dream. As previously excluded people enter academic life, however marginalized they remain there, they change not only its demographics but also, though inconsistently, its culture and its products. In social theory they have broken through the institutionalized limits on subject matter and have introduced perspectives heretofore absent or minimized. Although multiculturalism comes in many varieties, its proponents share at root a commitment to using the perspectives historically lodged in *many cultures,* not just falling back on the values, beliefs, and normative leanings of the dominant groupings in society.

As multiple cultural perspectives are adopted by social theorists, the face of social theory begins to change. It starts to look more human and feel more alive; its voice varies more in pitch and volume, and its rhythms ebb and flow much as our daily experiences do. So, too, theory's functions broaden. Meant now to illuminate diverse people's lived experiences and to transform culture and social structure, social theory begins making noise where once silence prevailed. Multicultural social theory demystifies; it challenges and defamiliarizes mundane realities once seen mostly from hyperprivileged perspectives. It confronts the sad, hard questions of social life having to do with brutality, exploitation, abuse, trauma, cruelty, snobbery, and greed. Yet multicultural social theory also exposes resistance, resourcefulness, stamina, courage, and resilience where once theorists saw mostly the passivity, resignation, and fatalism of victims. Multicultural social theory diversifies the standpoints, concerns, and purposes of social theory. To that extent it enlarges the theoretical realm, making room for those tales of daily living and struggling that ultimately anchor all telling, theoretical and otherwise.

Ultimately, multiculturalism underscores our capacity to see cultural groups as *both* similar to *and* different from one another, not the same as or the opposite of one another. Each of us has different lessons to learn from multiculturalism, depending on our past experiences and current situations. Some of us, for example, exaggerate the differences between people of color and "white" people so we habitually overlook the similarities between African American and white parents or between Latina/o and Anglo upper-middle-class professionals. All of us reap rewards from multicultural exposure, but what we reap differs from one to the other of us.

We all, though, reap insights into the complexities each of us embodies. Multiculturalism illuminates our diverse "subject positions" as gendered, raced, aged, classed, embodied, sexual, ethnic individuals. To that extent it illuminates the grounds of our dignity. Human dignity affirms the differences between this individual and that individual, between this grouping and that grouping. As Peter Berger notes, dignity concerns "intrinsic humanity"; it "pertains to the self as such, to the individual regardless of . . . position in society." Like honor, dignity involves "moral enterprise."[5] The concept thus puts us in touch with the ethical dimension of multiculturalism.

Dignity, which historically supported a politics of human rights, gets little attention in social theory today. By contrast, its close cousin "identity" gets a great deal of attention. Over the past several decades identity has evoked a politics of difference, emphasizing various groups' historical and cultural distinctiveness. The philosopher Charles Taylor is scarcely alone in calling for some middle ground between a politics based on an "homogenizing demand for recognition of equal worth" and a politics based on various "ethnocentric standards."[6]

The "middle" ground is a multiculturalism anchored in our public schools but fanning out to other institutions including businesses, religions, and governments. Most multicultural perspectives emphasize the cultural diversity among those entitled to equality of rights and opportunities. The *politics of dignity* is an apt term for the dynamics of such a multiculturalism. As Berger emphasizes, dignity concerns individuals apart from their social positions and roles. No individuals exist apart from the enabling and constraining values, beliefs, norms, and lifeways of their cultures, however. Above and beyond and beneath our roles, then, stands a self whose dignity rests on culturally shaped distinctiveness. Ultimately, dignity derives neither from our species nor our roles but from the cultural affiliations specifying the boundaries of our individuality. As Susan Sontag has noted, a group's culture is its claim to members' dignity.[7] It is how a group provides for the selfhood of its members. Differently put, social structure and human dignity are historically intertwined projects. That lesson ties together the readings at hand.

Also tying these readings together are the social identities of their authors who, by and large, belong to marginalized groupings.[8] They represent gay, American Indian, Latina/o, lesbian, African American, Chicano/a, feminist, Asian American, Hispanic American, and other comakers of our society who dare not take their dignity or even their human rights for granted. That circumstance often finds expression in their work and thus differentiates them on average from "mainstream theorists," those whose social identities generally go unremarked in discussions of their work. One rarely hears, for example, "the white male sociologist Randall Collins," but one often hears "the African American feminist sociologist Patricia Hill Collins." The former individual gets cast as a full-fledged, unadulterated sociologist; the latter, as a "kind" of sociologist.[9] "Mainstream theory" generally centers on matters other than power, dignity, and social exclusion or marginalization. Its legitimacy is relatively uncontested, even though its rigor may be fiercely debated. Mainstream theory is discernibly rooted in influential, respectable traditions; it is canonized or likely to be canonized, that is, institutionally endorsed and transmitted.

Unlike mainstream theorists, multicultural theorists often cite their own experiences as partial grounds for their insights; they routinely inveigh against the hierarchical status quo and demand attention to what is fair; they make efforts to overcome the essentializing tendencies in mainstream theory. As we will soon see, multicultural theorists also favor broadly postmodernist stances emphasizing the fluid, localized nature of sociocultural realities. Typically, then, they concern themselves with contextualizing whatever generalizations tempt them. Doing so means habitually asking, Which members? Under what circumstances?

Another characteristic difference between multicultural and mainstream theorists revolves around the distinction between theory and metatheory.[10] Mainstream theorists produce a lot of metatheory, that is, theorizing about the ins and outs of theorizing. Metatheoretical concerns include such matters as the structure of scientific explanation, the nature of scholarly rhetoric, and the limits of rational models of human action. Open any theory textbook or journal, and metatheory is much in evidence. At hand, I have the March, 1994 issue of *Sociological Theory,* a journal of the American Sociological Association. Among its six papers is Sharon Hays's examination of the "conceptual prism in which structure, agency, and culture are all poorly understood"[11] because of social theorists' inadequate definitions and misguided presuppositions. Multicultural social theorists write relatively few such papers. They do challenge extant conceptions and models and thus stimulate metatheoretical undertakings. Yet they routinely subordinate such challenges to the project of presenting innovative descriptions and other accounts of the social realities that concern them. Above all, those realities comprise the actualities that flesh-and-blood individuals face in their everyday lives. Afrocentrist scholars spend relatively little time, then, criticizing racist models of social mobility or "vanilla" portrayals of the class structure. In the face of gaping holes in our knowledge about African American culture and the various subcultures of African Americans, they focus mostly on substantive questions such as why African American preadolescence and adolescence pose severe hazards for males and how we might eliminate those hazards.

Multicultural social theory exhibits a bold, eclectic shape. It comprises "idea systems" that "have a *wide range* of application" and "deal with *centrally important social issues.*"[12] Grounded not only in real people's real lives but also in pressing social issues of the day, multicultural social theory tends to be unpretentious and down to earth. By and large, it illustrates that "theory doesn't have to be grand to be good."[13] It often shows us that theory need not be linguistically contorted, unduly abstract, and purportedly universalist in its claims before it can advance our knowledge of people's circumstances and experiences.

Because they favor both/and thinking, multicultural social theorists invite attention to the continuities between themselves and their mainstream colleagues. Jargon—more kindly, a technical vocabulary—is one obvious continuity, as is scholarly writing that entails footnotes or endnotes, bibliographies, and little apparent interest in the mass distribution of the author's ideas. Another continuity is the academic affiliations most theorists enjoy. Also, multicultural and mainstream social theorists today identify themselves as transdisciplinary thinkers able to leap across the institutionalized boundaries dividing the social sciences and, for the more daring, the boundaries dividing the humanities and the social sciences. Finally, mainstream and multicultural social theorists join hands around questions about the future of social theory, its place in educational curricula, and its connections with practices ranging from empirical research to community organizing.

Thus, no either/or divides multicultural from mainstream theorists. In fact, a number of mainstream theorists offer concepts and principles highly resonant with multicultural social theory. I try to show this in the brief essays introducing each section of *Multicultural Experiences, Multicultural Theories*. There I draw on theorists well established within the "malestream" of social theory. By weaving their ideas into the multicultural tapestry, I hope to demonstrate some overlap of outlook between the two groupings. Such points of connection are as theoretically instructive as the divergences between the two broad groupings.

One aim of this book, then, is to give you grounds for seeing how similar to and different from mainstream social theory these multicultural works are. Another aim is to offer you multicultural substance sufficient for building up a sense of the topics of inquiry that multicultural theorists deem important. Thus, I have grouped the readings by broad themes rather than by their authors' social identities. Another reason for organizing the readings thematically is to dispel any sense that members (or seeming members) of a given cultural grouping belong together regardless of their own preferences and projects.

Above all, this volume aims to enliven your thinking about social theory while furthering your understanding of our multicultural society. Social theory engages one's consciousness with the very stuff of social life—its triumphs and pitfalls, its dominant structures and subversive processes, its pathos and profundity. Since nearly all the theorists speaking in this volume belong to groups of people facing an uphill struggle in our society, the pictures they draw of social life and how they frame their pictures not only portray multicultural experiences but also stretch social theory as a humanistic enterprise. At the same time these theorists' contributions, like those of other theorists, illustrate how social location, biography, and cultural heritage shape one's standpoint, including the very terms one favors when talking about society and culture. Significantly, to read these theorists is to hear voices attesting to the essential dignity of the individual, to the promise each of us holds of balancing absolute singularity with meaningful memberships.

To read these theorists is also to gain some irreplaceable tools for assessing mainstream theory. I teach both classical and contemporary social theory. Over the past twenty years I have experienced great satisfaction in furthering students' acquaintanceship with Karl Marx, Emile Durkheim, Max Weber, Georg Simmel, and Sigmund Freud; with C. Wright Mills, Peter Berger and Thomas Luckmann, Erving Goffman, Pierre Bourdieu, Anthony Giddens, Michel Foucault, and others. I have no doubt that reading these theorists is essential to cultivating sociological consciousness and theoretical prowess. By now, though, I believe that we gain in theoretical wisdom as well as multicultural awareness by reading mainstream theoretical texts, both classical and contemporary, in a far-reaching context that helps us see their vacancies and holes, their faulty presuppositions and overextended generalizations, and their privileged underpinnings alongside their pathbreaking analyses of social realities such as industrial capitalism, the Protestant ethic, power and discipline, or impression management. To extend and refine the heritage we claim as students and scholars, we need the context multicultural social theorists are creating. Within that context we learn, much as C. Wright Mills observed in "The Decline of the Left," that we must "release the human imagination" and "explore all the alternatives now open to the human community."[14]

The criteria whereby I chose these readings emerged over many months. In the end I devoted considerable space to lesser known voices in hopes of forestalling elitism on the theoretical landscape now taking multicultural shape. Also, integrating established and emergent voices reflects multiculturalism's inclusionary spirit and both/and thinking. For the most part, I cast my net over works published within the past five years. Because Chicana feminist theory and other varieties of multicultural theory are growing as if to make up for lost time, they exhibit dizzying dynamism. Fresh concepts come into play with great frequency, and debates ebb and flow with high-level energy. Besides, these theorists' citations offer signposts into the past of multicultural theorizing. In the respects they pay to their predecessors you can trace the emergence of this or that strand of multicultural theory.

Another criterion was to limit myself largely to American theorists. Even though multiculturalism has emerged as a public-policy issue in Australia, the Netherlands, England, Canada, and other countries, its center lies in the United States. Feminists, self-identified queers, people of color, and other marginalized groups have staked a big theoretical claim that no scholar in the social sciences, education, or the humanities can credibly ignore. The size of that claim means that the pages of this volume filled up before I could include much work from international multiculturalists.

The final criterion I used was theoretical diversity. I wanted you to taste the divergences among multicultural theorists as well as their convergences. I wanted you to be able to imagine them debating such matters as essentialism and intragroup diversity. I wanted you to see that the adjective "multicultural" applies to anyone whose work addresses issues of dominance, exploitation, social justice, and dignity in strongly anti-elitist fashion.

I close with questions we all might beneficially ponder. Might we appreciate given theories in proportion to our needs? What might those needs involve beyond the need to understand? Might ethical, affiliative, civic, and other needs make us receptive to some theories but not others? Finally, what about our fears? Might we, for instance, fear that an African American lesbian poet and culture critic such as Audre Lorde has as much to show us as a straight white male theorist? Might such fears turn into intellectual exhilaration when we see, as never before, that she and you and I are alike as well as different, that we have lots to learn from one another, and that that learning can help us change the circumstances that evoke our most stubborn fears? In our society one such circumstance is "that the purchase of guns has become an overwhelming civilian response to perceived fractures in the social compact."[15] Multicultural social theory shows us what a reasonable, decent compact might ask of and give to each of us regardless of the specific culture(s) anchoring our dignity.

NOTES

1 George F. Will, "Literary Politics," *Newsweek* (April 22, 1991), p. 72.

2 John Murray Cuddihy, *The Ordeal of Civility: Freud, Marx, Levi-Strauss, and the Jewish Struggle with Modernity,* New York, Dell Publishing Company, 1976, p. 13.

3 Johnnella Butler and Betty Schmitz, "Ethnic Studies, Women's Studies, and Multiculturalism," *Change* (January/February, 1992), p. 38.

4 Patrice DiQuinzio, "Exclusion and Essentialism in Feminist Theory: The Problem of Mothering," *Hypatia* 8 (Summer, 1993), p. 6.

5 Peter Berger, "Excursus: On the Obsolescence of the Concept of Honor," in Peter Berger, Brigitte Berger, and Hansfried Kellner, *The Homeless Mind: Modernization and Consciousness,* New York, Vintage Books, 1974, pp. 89, 90.

6 Charles Taylor, "The Politics of Recognition," in Amy Gutmann (ed.), *Multiculturalism and "The Politics of Recognition": An Essay by Charles Taylor,* Princeton, NJ, Princeton University Press, 1992, p. 72.

7 Susan Sontag, "Waiting for Godot in Sarajevo," a lecture at the Philadelphia Free Library, May 23, 1994.

8 Many other Americans dwell at the margins of our institutions. Of particular concern to me are imprisoned people and poor people. I did look at "prison literature" while choosing readings for this volume. There I found mostly fiction, poetry, and autobiographical statements. Unwilling to widen my field of sources that dramatically, I left that literature for later examination. As for the impoverished people among us, the illiteracy and semiliteracy common among them join with their structural marginalization to make published works a rare achievement. Refugees, sexual workers, illegal aliens, seasonal and migrant workers, working-class people, immigrants, and the physically challenged represent still other groupings whose published works are either scant or less "theoretical" than the readings included here.

9 Cf. Elizabeth Kamarck Minnich, *Transforming Knowledge,* Philadelphia, Temple University Press, 1990, pp. 40–43.

10 I owe this insight to George Ritzer; personal communication, August 8, 1994.

11 Sharon Hays, "Structure and Agency and the Sticky Problem of Culture," *Sociological Theory* 12, 1 (March, 1994), 57.

12 George Ritzer, *Sociological Theory,* New York, McGraw-Hill, Inc., 1992, 3rd Ed., p. 4.

13 Kenneth R. Hoover, *The Elements of Social Scientific Thinking,* New York, St. Martin's Press, 1992, 5th Ed., p. 59.

14 C. Wright Mills, "The Decline of the Left," in Irving Louis Horowitz (ed.), *Power, Politics, and People: The Collected Essays of C. Wright Mills,* New York, Oxford University Press, 1967, p. 235.

15 Adrienne Rich, "The Hermit's Scream," *PMLA: Publications of the Modern Language Association of America,* 108, 5 (October, 1993), p. 1161.

THEORY—WHAT? WHY? HOW?

To theorize is to engage in abstraction for the sake of understanding. Theory gives us a place to stand beyond the boundaries of our thoughts and feelings, beyond the limits of our observations, beyond the interactions constituting our connections with other people. No matter where we stand, though, we remain agents embodied in social space and historical time. Theory thus offers no escape from the situated, material character of our lives. Rather, it gives us tools for strengthening our grasp of whatever facets of social life press upon our consciousness as consequential or interesting. To that extent theory empowers us, but it does so within cultural limits. While exploring those limits, the readings in this first section raise questions about what social theory is, the purposes it properly serves, and how it best gets created.

When I was a graduate student during the 1960s, defining social theory was less a challenge than it is in the 1990s. Yesterday's claims about universal generalizations, scientific explanation, and general theories of this or that are now suspect. For most multicultural social theorists, such claims are at best naive and retrogressive; at worst, indefensible and oppressive. As Jane Flax (p. 18) points out, much theory expresses "an entrepreneurial interest, a territorial mentality," such as the "white male insiderism" Robert K. Merton wrote about in 1972 (see Collins, p. 50). Theory's claims may sometimes be universalistic, but its authors can find no "universal" place to stand. The theorist's interests and social position routinely shape the contours and content of his/her work. Worse yet, as Maria C. Lugones and Elizabeth Spelman indicate, theorists' work often justifies the privilege and domination of the groups theorists belong to or identify with. Social theory often augments the "relations of ruling," then.[1] It promotes some groups' hegemony—that is, cultural dominance and political clout—in taken-for-granted ways that multiculturalists aim to expose. At the same time mainstream social theory

11

erases and excludes the experiences of some groups of people and thus renders them invisible, as each of the readings in this section illustrates in one way or other.

For multicultural social theorists, theory is meant not to dominate or control those who might challenge social hierarchies. Instead, it should inspire and empower such individuals. It should also be inclusive. Multicultural scholars promote on-behalf-of theory. Feminist theory, for instance, is—as these first readings show—on behalf of women from any and every social grouping insofar as their sex limits their opportunities and cheats them of their just rewards. Yet feminist theorists face the hard challenge of respecting women's diversity while speaking on their collective behalf as a sociosexual grouping.

The first four readings speak to that challenge which all multicultural theorists face with reference to one grouping or other. At root, the challenge is to balance one's acknowledgment of intragroup diversity with one's attention to group members' common oppression. Flax (p. 19) implies that we might begin by giving up the "pretense that theory can be neutral." Ridding ourselves of that pretense heightens our consciousness of the rhetorical and logical limits intragroup diversity imposes. In Lugones and Spelman's (pp. 25, 26) view we need also to understand that since members of a diverse grouping such as women or African Americans speak "different languages," a "non-imperialist feminism" must be multilingual. Multicultural theorizing thus requires multiple vocabularies deriving from diverse cultural traditions and social locations (see Asante). At its best it comprises *internal translations* whereby a text moves forward using the languages of or the terms associated with diverse groupings of women, much as Collins several times translates "mule" into "dog" as she addresses the convergences and divergences in African American and Euro-American women's experiences.

For her part Collins urges that we forego either/or thinking, or what she calls "dichotomous oppositional thinking," that backs us into corners where we overgeneralize and thus advance a culturally imperialist theory. Collins (p. 44) illustrates a multipolar, both/and stance when she cites "socially constructed Black women's cultures," on the one hand, "that collectively form Black women's culture," on the other hand. She achieves the same effect when she says that African American women may arrive at "certain commonalities of outlook" but that the diversity among them gives rise to "different expressions of these common themes" (p. 37). Hooks's is the most complex commentary on the challenge at hand. She emphasizes that abjuring elitism is ultimately our only hope for balancing diversity with commonality.

Understandably, multicultural social theorists commonly conjoin the roles of scholar, advocate, cultural worker, and activist. Put differently, they are well aware of their multiple subject positions as investigators committed to illuminating and affirming the diversity of the social world. "Subject positions," as we saw, concern the multiple vantage points each of us can meaningfully occupy to make sense of our experiences. No human individual has only one vantage point, in other words. No one of us can see the world solely as an Asian American, a heterosexual, a Roman Catholic, or a quadriplegic. Each of us occupies a number of socially consequential statuses. Any of these subject positions can provide us a place to stand while making sense.

Multicultural theorists disclose their own multiple subject positions and thus illustrate the diverse subject positions we all have at hand. One way they explicitly claim their multiple subject positions is by invoking the first-person pronouns. Flax opens her essay, "I begin . . ." and as her narrative moves forward, so does our sense of who "I" is. We learn, for instance, that she has worked as a feminist therapist, and we learn about the needs and goals that have prompted her theoretical work. In the next reading the "Hispana voice," in particular, claims multiple and conflicting subject positions when discussing problems with pronouns. Her first statement launches that discussion, and later (p. 24) "we" gets explored as a painful challenge for some speakers trying to tell their stories. Still later (p. 26) comes the question, "Where do *we* begin?" In Collins's and Asante's papers "I" does make an appearance, but its presence presses less on our consciousness than Flax's "I" or Lugones's "we," which makes for a virtual and gentle debate among these theorists about methods of narrating. While they all seem to favor diversity and eclecticism—hallmarks of multicultural social theory—each favors a distinctive blend of pronominal usages, experiential grounding, and autobiographical content. In hooks's paper who are "we"? What subject positions does hooks claim? By now you can probably see that the answers to such questions are important to multicultural theorists, not only because "we" and other commonplace words have imperialist and non-imperialist usages but also because selves routinely assert their presence or get washed away in such commonplaces.

"I" announces a biographical creature whose experiences grow out of and beyond an array of social roles and subject positions. Its presence presses against the traditional boundaries of social theory and raises awareness of the multiple sites of consciousness where theory originates and takes shape. "I" reminds us that theory reflects more than the conventions institutionalized among theorists. It also expresses something of its originator's culturally anchored selfhood. In their invocations of "I" and "we" multicultural social theorists invite us to reject the idea of objectivity unadulterated by the dynamics of history, culture, social structure, and individuals' life stories.

In any event theorists' subject positions show up in their texts even when they say virtually nothing about their personal experiences. Even when an author cites no patently personal experiences—for example, that she graduated from Our Lady of the Elms College before pursuing her Ph.D. at Temple University—readers imagine what types of experiences she has had. They tend to build up a sense of what *type* of individual she is. The literary critic Wayne C. Booth calls this diffuse sense of an author's self the "implied author" of the text.[2] Usually, readers take from their texts some sense of the author as a participant in or affiliate of this or that sociocultural grouping. Most scholarly journals, for instance, indicate their authors' affiliations with academic institutions and professional associations as well as identify them with specific disciplines and intellectual traditions. Less obvious, though now coming into view thanks to multicultural theorists, are the informal, taken-for-granted affiliations shaping authors' texts.

Historically, "the majority of humankind was excluded from education and the making of what has been called knowledge"; historically, *the dominant few not only defined themselves as the inclusive kind of human being but also as the norm and the ideal.*"[3] Unmarked and unqualified, knowledge made under academic or other prestigious auspices passed as objective and applicable to all of humankind even though an unrepresentative, privileged few had produced it. By contrast, knowledge made under less auspicious circumstances by members of disprivileged groups got tagged as feminist theology, African American literature, or American Indian art (likelier, "crafts"). Seen as some "particular kind" or variant of "the thing-itself," such contributions are widely ignored by those few individuals culturally authorized to produce the "real," full-fledged, generic thing. At best, the contributions made by those beyond the privileged few get ghettoized as deviations from or variations of "the real, the significant, the best." Consequently, "privileged white men's theory" sounds strange to most people while "black feminist thought" makes obvious sense. Elizabeth Kamarck Minnich concludes that one can easily find "key instances of false universalization in the dominant meaning system. One need only note where prefixes, or markers, are not used and *would be startling:* 'the white male philosopher Kant.' "[4] Stated differently, knowledge gets made "by people situated in various ways in various institutions, with various loyalties, values, responsibilities, privileges, and identifications."[5]

By laying bare the biases characteristic of mainstream social theory, multiculturalists disclose it as a thoroughly human product with multiple functions in society and culture. In its place they aim to put theory that deviates dramatically from today's standard fare. For multicultural social theorists, theory is distinct from but not entirely discontinuous with other forms of narration such as fiction and confessional writing (cf. Collins; hooks; Asante). What multicultural theorists seek is an experientially rooted, action-oriented expression of critical consciousness. Such theory often involves what Flax (p. 18) describes as "a *systematic, analytic* approach to everyday experience," or doing consciously and carefully what we already do without much thought in our everyday lives. Such theorizing means "not divorcing life from the telling of it or talking about it," and the measure of its success is that we "recognize ourselves in" it (Lugones and Spelman, pp. 22, 26). Theory and experience thus constitute a two-way relationship with one another whereby "experienced reality is used as a valid source of knowledge" and theory "offers new ways of seeing . . . experienced reality" (Collins, p. 53).

Multiculturalists also emphasize the critical dimension of theory. Critical consciousness perhaps begins with "defining and valuing one's consciousness" in resistance to taken-for-granted understandings, especially those tied in with "systems of domination" (Collins, p. 39). Such consciousness turns timid in the face of sweeping generalizations and grandiose visions. It recognizes that "we can clobber people to destruction with our visions, our versions, of what is better" (Lugones and Spelman, p. 30). Critical consciousness is confident and disciplined but humble; it is eager to understand but bent toward circumspection, if only because of its respect for lived experiences. That respect most expresses itself in accessibility, a feature of multicultural social theory these first readings emphasize. Like all theory, the multicultural variety is abstract, but you will see that its abstractions are mild-mannered compared with the linguistic contortions commonplace among mainstream theorists.

As these observations about theory imply, most multiculturalists think that one purpose of theory is to make us aware of our limited capacity to transcend historical time, social location, and cultural codes as we make knowledge. Multicultural social theorists aim to keep themselves and us in our cultural places, that is, knowing full well "that we all speak from a particular social and historical standpoint without being contained by that position."[6] By explicitly taking such circumstances into account, theory gains in rigor and applicability as it loses in pretense and misguidedness. Such multicultural social theory resonates with the sociology of knowledge, especially as Peter L. Berger and Thomas Luckmann delineate it.[7]

For multiculturalists, another purpose of theorizing is to transform knowledge—"to disrupt chains of signification and . . . unsettle dominant meaning structures."[8] Such transformations entail transgressing conventions without making such transgression "the latest convention."[9] Above all, transforming knowledge requires a "multicentric perspective"[10] that opens up theoretical space for diverse groups' cultures and experiences. Such a perspective is not merely multidimensional; such a perspective has no one center. Instead, it has multiple, fluctuating centers that a theorist draws on for an analytical choreography capable of giving all cultural groupings center stage. Social theory thus has among its multicultural purposes the democratization of knowledge, or the disprivileging of its grossly unrepresentative concepts and ideas. Thus, demystification—of power and respectability, of normality and "the natural," of the party line and the official stance—is a central aim of multicultural theory.

The transformations multiculturalists seek scarcely end there, however. By their theorizing, multiculturalists mean to change social structure and culture as well as individuals' prospects. Most broadly, multicultural social theory aims at "overcom[ing] oppression" and elitism (Flax, p. 19; hooks, p. 57). It aims not "to exchange one set of controlling images for another" but to subvert "the dehumanization essential to systems of domination" (Collins, p. 39). Such theory offers individuals grounds for self-affirmation and liberation. It tells them that they have "the freedom to both be different and to be part of the solidarity of humanity" (Collins, p. 54).

These and closely related purposes necessitate a distinctive way of theorizing centered on the theorist's extremely critical consciousness not only of others' theorizing but also of his or her own. Incessantly vigilant for signs of social exclusion, cultural bias, and intellectual presumptuousness, such theorists consistently ask, "In whose interests?"[11] Such theorizing is a daring, painstaking project. To illustrate its extreme challenges, let us look briefly at the insider/outsider rhetoric that appears not only in several of these first readings but in much multicultural theorizing.

Like most dualities in use, insider/outsider often implies a clear-cut divide where none exists. Its characteristic uses, even in social theory, involve no explicit attention to the irony that in order to specify what lies "*outside* the norm, one needs first to place oneself *inside* dominant definitions." Put differently, "We cannot assert ourselves to be entirely outside . . . , not entirely inside, because each of these terms achieves its meaning in relation to the other." We thus confront "the social construction of [the] inside/outside opposition."[12] At the same time we get alerted to the likelihood that that opposition serves purposes other than registering the exclusion of "outsiders" from the centers of power and privilege. Like other dualistic oppositions, insider/outsider washes away the complexities and gradations associated with exclusionary patterns in societies like ours. It erases the "compound identities" (Lugones and Spelman, p. 23) that make virtually all of us insiders and outsiders depending on which axis of domination is at issue. Thus, insider/outsider may be an effective rhetorical device, but it disallows the complex, intersecting systems making most of us oppressed in some spheres and oppressing in other spheres. We will return to these either/or modes of thinking at the beginning of the next section in connection with postmodernism. In the interim consider the singular promise of Collins's "outsider within" for analytically breaking into the intersecting systems of domination that assign many of us to social positions that pull us in diverse directions.

Finally, consider Molefi Kete Asante's (p. 65) point that "perspective is not a biological issue." However culture constitutes our "biological" statuses as females or males, young or old, people of color or "white" people, ablebodied or not, it cannot thereby constitute our perspective. Each of us has some say over whose perspective(s) we adopt. Like most multicultural theorists, Asante (p. 72) invites us to consider any "traditional discipline suicide." He thus invites us to leap the disciplinary boundaries that are no less divisive than the other us/them boundaries culturally mapped onto our consciousness. In the process he anticipates the second set of readings, for his boundary-defying stance is at once a pro-theoretical, anti-universalist, resistance-oriented affirmation energized by a "critique of domination" (p. 66). His paper thus bridges the first and second sets of readings.

NOTES

1 See Dorothy E. Smith, *Texts, Facts, and Femininity: Exploring the Relations of Ruling,* Boston, New York, Routledge, 1990, especially Chapter One.

2 Wayne C. Booth, *Critical Understanding: The Powers and Limits of Pluralism,* Chicago, University of Chicago Press, 1979.

3 Elizabeth Kamarck Minnich, *Transforming Knowledge,* Philadelphia, Temple University Press, 1990, pp. 37–38.

4 Ibid., pp. 42, 43.

5 Naomi Scheman, *Engenderings: Constructions of Knowledge, Authority, and Privilege,* New York, Routledge, 1993, p. 218.

6 Janice M. Irvine, "A Place in the Rainbow: Theorizing Lesbian and Gay Culture," *Sociological Theory* 12, 2 (July, 1994), p. 243.

7 Peter L. Berger and Thomas Luckmann, *The Social Construction of Reality: A Treatise on the Sociology of Knowledge,* New York, Anchor Books, 1967.

8 Peter McLaren, "Moral Panic, Schooling, and Gay Identity: Critical Pedagogy and the Politics of Resistance," *The High School Journal* (October/November, 1993; December/January, 1994), p. 163.

9 Susan David Bernstein, "Confessing Feminist Theory: What's 'I' Got to Do with It?" *Hypatia* 7 (Spring, 1992), p. 121.

10 Henry A. Giroux, "Border Pedagogy and the Politics of Postmodernism," *Education and Society* 9, No. 1 (1991), p. 34.

11 McLaren, "Moral Panic . . . ," p. 159.

12 Ki Namaste, "The Politics of Inside/Out: Queer Theory, Poststructuralism, and a Sociological Approach to Sexuality," *Sociological Theory* 12, 2 (July, 1994), pp. 224, 225.

Women Do Theory

Jane Flax

I begin with an overview of feminist theory and a discussion of the activity of theorizing. I then present a theoretical framework that I've developed after trying various theories and finding none of them sufficient to explain the range of things I think a feminist theorist needs to explain.

Let me say a little about how I ended up doing feminist theory. I have been interested in philosophy and political theory for a long time. I am also interested in psychoanalysis, and have practiced as a feminist therapist. So, partly, I've been trying to put together more traditional ideas of theory with those I've learned as a therapist, especially from psychoanalysis.

Very early I began to connect theory with political activity. I chose political science because I thought there I would learn about politics—which was a mistake. Some political scientists seem to consider theory to be something done 3,000 years ago by Aristotle and Plato, unrelated to the present world. And yet, one of my attractions to theory was that through it, I could learn to systematize my experience. Political science was not much help.

Over time, however, I have found traditional theory to be very helpful in recognizing other people's mental processes as they try to understand the structure of the world systematically. That is, much traditional theory is a kind of internal discourse among thinkers—like a 3,000-year conversation in which people take up each others' ideas and reapply them. I'm interested in many parts of that discourse: what can politics do; what is the ideal political system; what are just relationships; what does "equality" mean?

These issues have been dealt with in the women's movement, but not always in the context of theory. For instance what it would mean to have a really liberated society is a question of equality and justice that has been debated since the first political theory was attempted. But feminists don't often think of our questions as part of that ongoing political discourse.

In traditional political theory, however, the relationships between men and women, and the status of women are rarely discussed. They are certainly not generally seen as problems. Some traditional political theorists talk about the family and the role it plays for the state of course; and some have argued for the liberation of women. Plato, for instance, argued that women *could* be philosopher kings since these should be chosen on merit and no inherent proof existed that women were any less intellectually capable than men.* Other political theorists, however, have argued that woman cannot think abstractly and has a less developed moral sense. Thus, part of the problem feminist theorists face is taking the general "grammar" and concepts of traditional theory and applying them to women and the issues that affect us.

---

*An interesting sidelight is that the hero of Plato's academy was a woman who was stoned by the Christians—one of the first of the Christians' many acts against women playing an intellectual, active role.

This brings me to the questions, "what is feminist theory?" and, more generally, "what is theory?" The most important characteristic of theory is that it is a *systematic, analytic* approach to everyday experience. This everybody does unconsciously. To theorize, then, is to bring this unconscious process to a conscious level so it can be developed and refined. All of us operate on theories, though most of them are implicit. We screen out certain things; we allow others to affect us; we make choices and we don't always understand why. Theory, in other words, makes those choices conscious, and enables us to use them more efficiently.

For example, implicit in my choices about the work I could do is an understanding of where power lies, what I'm likely to be able to do, where I'm likely to meet the most frustration, and when I'm likely to be most effective. I might not think through those things consciously, but I make choices on these bases. If you push that explanation, you'll find a series of assumptions about the way the world works, what's available (to me), and what isn't. That's implicit theory-making. The problem is to make it explicit.

BLOCKS TO EXPLICIT THEORY

One of the problems with theory is that women aren't supposed to be able to do it; women aren't supposed to be able to think abstractly. So when you say to a woman, "Okay, now let's read theory," she's likely to panic.

In addition, theoretical writing is often so full of jargon that it seems divorced from ordinary experience. Unfortunately, many theorists have an entrepreneurial interest, a territorial mentality, and they encourage everyone else to believe that their work is impossibly complex. This discourages women—and men—from engaging in theory because it seems hostile and unintelligible. I don't think that the issues *are* inherently so difficult or so far removed from ordinary understanding. I think theorists build turfs and *make* it difficult for others to understand that turf—just like any other professional.

FEMINIST THEORY

Feminist theory is based on a series of assumptions. First, it assumes that men and women have different experiences; that the world is not the same for men and women. Some women think the experiences of women should be identical to the experiences of men. Others would like to transform the world so that there are no such dichotomous experiences. Proponents of both views, however, assume that women's experiences differ from men's, and that one task of feminist theory is to explain that difference.

Secondly, feminist theory assumes that women's oppression is not a subset of some other social relationship. Some argue that if the class system were destroyed, then women would not be oppressed—I don't classify that as feminist theory. Feminist theory assumes that women's oppression is a unique constellation of social problems and has to be understood in itself, and not as a subset of class or any other structure.

It also assumes that women's oppression is not merely a case of what the Chinese call "bad attitudes." I have problems with the word "sexism," because the term implies that women's oppression will disappear when men become more enlightened. On the contrary, I think feminist theory assumes that the oppression of women is part of the way the structure of the world is organized, and that one task of feminist theory is to explain how and why this structure evolved.

Feminist theory names this structure "patriarchy," and assumes that it is an historical force that has a material and psychological base. What we mean by "patriarchy" is the system in which men have more power than women, and have more access to whatever society esteems. What society esteems obviously varies from culture to culture; but if you look at the spheres of power, you'll find that all who have it are male. This is a long-term historical fact rooted in real things. It's not a question of bad attitudes; it's not an historical accident—there are real advantages to men in retaining control over women. Feminist theorists want to explain why that's so.

Patriarchy works backwards as well. It affects the way men and women feel about themselves, and is so deeply internalized that we can't imagine a world without gender. As much as we talk about androgyny, or some situation in which gender isn't so significant, I don't think any of us could imagine a world in which gender would not bring with it many special meanings. *We* may still want to attach special meanings to gender, but a feminist theory would argue that the power attached to gender should disappear; it should not determine whether a person is excluded or included in whatever is esteemed by society.

GOALS OF FEMINIST THEORY

Feminist theory has several purposes. The first is to understand the power differential between men and women. How did it come into being? Why does it exist now? What maintains it? How do the power relations between men and women affect other power relations—for instance, race and class—and how does patriarchy reinforce other oppressive power structures?

Secondly, the purpose is to understand women's oppression—how it evolved, how it changes over time, how it's related to other forms of oppression, and finally, how to change our oppression.

In feminist theory, one issue that emerges consistently is the necessity to understand the family, because it is one of the central mediating structures between all other structures of oppression. The family is where we're internally formed, where we learn about gender, where we experience class and race systems in personal and intimate ways. Therefore, understanding the functions of the family should be one of the crucial goals of feminist theory; yet it remains an area that is particularly undeveloped.

A third purpose of feminist theory is to overcome oppression. Feminist theory is the foundation of action and there is no pretense that theory can be neutral. Within feminist theory is a commitment to change oppressive structures and to connect abstract ideas with concrete problems for political action. It is senseless to study the situation of women without a concomitant commitment to do something about it. The theorist has to draw out the consequences of the theory and use life experience as a part of her basis for understanding, for feeding into the development of theory.

Traditional political theory has always been attached to action. Plato wrote *The Republic* partly because he thought that Athenian democracy was degenerating and he wanted to understand why, and how. It's only contemporary social science theory that claims to be objective, neutral, value-free. I don't think any form of knowledge is neutral, but certainly feminist theory cannot claim neutrality. I think that's one of the problems of women's studies programs. They are too often developed as though they are mere intellectual exercises; some may be, but the study of women is not.

THE EVOLVING THEORETICAL FRAMEWORK

I assume that feminist theory must point to a clear and real base for the oppression of women—feminist theory has to be rooted in human experience. I also assume that there are three basic realms of human activity.

The first is production—we need to produce food, clothing and shelter for our survival. (Obviously, different cultures will produce in different ways. Even people who live on tropical islands have to organize the gathering and preparation of coconuts.) Marx called this the material substructure of human life, and I call it the realm of production.

People also need to reproduce. Not only must we produce the next generation biologically, but we also need to reproduce good citizens for the society. We need to inculcate the values, attitudes, and beliefs appropriate to that culture. A good American citizen will have ideas and expectations very different from a good Mesopotamian citizen living 3,000 years ago. But no matter which society, somehow the unformed person must be trained in its values. In our society, acculturation is conducted by a variety of organizations, including the family and later the school, and the state is involved in setting out certain policies which translate into procedures for acculturating individuals.

The third realm of human activity is the individual's internal life. This is what Freud called "the unconscious," and what I call "psychodynamics." The psychodynamic sphere is where our biological and our mental lives meet, and must be organized. One of the most important aspects of this sphere is sexuality. One of the questions feminists must ask is how a basically "polymorphous species"* ends up, in most cultures, a genitally oriented, heterosexual and monogamous species. Though all cultures allow varying degrees and varieties of sexual pleasure, every civilization channels its citizens' eroticism into practices acceptable to the society.

When we talk about the situation of women, we must examine how all three spheres cooperate to produce our oppression. The elimination of an oppressive structure in one sphere only is inadequate because the other spheres will re-emerge as even more oppressive.

. . .

---

*Polymorphous means that we can derive erotic pleasure from a wide variety of experiences; not only from experiences between ourselves and other persons, but also between ourselves and all sorts of physical objects.

Have We Got a Theory for You! Feminist Theory, Cultural Imperialism and the Demand for 'The Woman's Voice'

María C. Lugones and Elizabeth V. Spelman

Prologue

(In an Hispana voice)

A veces quisiera mezclar en una voz el sonido canyenge, tristón y urbano del porteñismo que llevo adentro con la cadencia apacible, serrana y llena de corage de la hispana nuevo mejicana. Contrastar y unir

el piolín y la cuerda
el traé y el pepéname
el camión y la troca
la lluvia y el llanto

Pero este querer se me va cuando veo que he confundido la solidaridad con la falta de diferencia. La solidaridad requiere el reconocer, comprender, respetar y amar lo que nos lleva a llorar en distintas cadencias. El imperialismo cultural desea lo contrario, por eso necesitamos muchas voces. Porque una sola voz nos mata a las dos.

No quiero hablar por ti sino contigo. Pero si no aprendo tus modos y tu los mios la conversación es sólo aparente. Y la apariencia se levanta como una barrera sin sentido entre las dos. Sin sentido y sin sentimiento. Por eso no me debes dejar que te dicte tu ser y no me dictes el mio. Porque entonces ya no dialogamos. El diálogo entre nosotras requiere dos voces y no una.

Tal vez un día jugaremos juntas y nos hablaremos no en una lengua universal sino que vos me hablarás mi voz y yo la tuya.

Preface

This paper is the result of our dialogue, of our thinking together about differences among women and how these differences are silenced. (Think, for example, of all the silences there are connected with the fact that this paper is in English—for that is a borrowed tongue for one of us.) In the process of our talking and writing together, we saw that the differences between us did not permit our speaking in one voice. For example, when we agreed we expressed the thought differently; there were some things that both of us thought were true but could not express as true of each of us; sometimes we could not say 'we'; and sometimes one of us could not express the thought in the first person singular, and to express it in the third person would be to present an outsider's and not an insider's perspective. Thus the use of two voices is central both to the process of constructing this paper and to the substance of it. We are both the authors of this paper and not just sections of it but we write together without presupposing unity of expression or of experience. So when we speak in unison it means just that—there are two voices and not just one.

I. INTRODUCTION

(In the voice of a white/Anglo woman who has been teaching and writing about feminist theory)

Feminism is, among other things, a response to the fact that women either have been left out of, or included in demeaning and disfiguring ways in what has been an almost exclusively male account of the world. And so while part of what feminists want and demand for women is the right to move and to act in accordance with our own wills and not against them, another part is the desire and insistence that we give our *own* accounts of these movements and actions. For it matters to us what is said about us, who says it, and to whom it is said: having the opportunity to talk about one's life, to give an account of it, to interpret it, is integral to leading that life rather than being led through it; hence our distrust of the male monopoly over accounts of women's lives. To put the same point slightly differently, part of human life, human living, is talking about it, and we can be sure that being silenced in one's own account of one's life is a kind of amputation that signals oppression. Another reason for not divorcing life from the telling of it or talking about it is that as humans our experiences are deeply influenced by what is said about them, by ourselves or powerful (as opposed to significant) others. Indeed, the phenomenon of internalized oppression is only possible because this is so: one experiences her life in terms of the impoverished and degrading concepts others have found it convenient to use to describe her. We can't separate lives from the accounts given of them; the articulation of our experience is part of our experience.

Sometimes feminists have made even stronger claims about the importance of speaking about our own lives and the destructiveness of others presuming to speak about us or for us. First of all, the claim has been made that on the whole men's accounts of women's lives have been at best false, a function of ignorance; and at worst malicious lies, a function of a knowledgeable desire to exploit and oppress. Since it matters to us that falsehood and lies not be told about us, we demand, of those who have been responsible for those falsehoods and lies, or those who continue to transmit them, not just that we speak but that they learn to be able to hear us. It has also been claimed that talking about one's life, telling one's story, in the company of those doing the same (as in consciousness-raising sessions), is constitutive of feminist method.[1]

And so the demand that the woman's voice be heard and attended to has been made for a variety of reasons: not just so as to greatly increase the chances that true accounts of women's lives will be given, but also because the articulation of experience (in myriad ways) is among the hallmarks of a self-determining individual or community. There are not just epistemological, but moral and political reasons for demanding that the woman's voice be heard, after centuries of androcentric din.

But what more exactly is the feminist demand that the woman's voice be heard? There are several crucial notes to make about it. First of all, the demand grows out of a

---

[1]For a recent example, see Mackinnon (1982).

complaint, and in order to understand the scope and focus of the demand we have to look at the scope and focus of the complaint. The complaint does not specify *which* women have been silenced, and in one way this is appropriate to the conditions it is a complaint about: virtually no women have had a voice, whatever their race, class, ethnicity, religion, sexual alliance, whatever place and period in history they lived. And if it is as women that women have been silenced, then of course the demand must be that women as women have a voice. But in another way the complaint is very misleading, insofar as it suggests that it is women as women who have been silenced, and that whether a woman is rich or poor, Black, brown or white, etc. is irrelevant to what it means for her to be a woman. For the demand thus simply made ignores at least two related points: (1) it is only possible for a woman who does not feel highly vulnerable with respect to other parts of her identity, e.g. race, class, ethnicity, religion, sexual alliance, etc., to conceive of her voice simply or essentially as a 'woman's voice'; (2) just because not all women are equally vulnerable with respect to race, class, etc., some women's voices are more likely to be heard than others by those who have heretofore been giving—or silencing—the accounts of women's lives. For all these reasons, the women's voices most likely to come forth and the women's voices most likely to be heard are, in the US anyway, those of white, middle-class, heterosexual Christian (or anyway not self-identified non-Christian) women. Indeed, many Hispanas, Black women, Jewish women—to name a few groups—have felt it an invitation to silence rather than speech to be requested—if they are requested at all—to speak about being 'women' (with the plain wrapper—as if there were one) in distinction from speaking about being Hispana, Black, Jewish, working-class, etc., women.

The demand that the 'woman's voice' be heard, and the search for the 'woman's voice' as central to feminist methodology, reflects nascent feminist theory. It reflects nascent empirical theory insofar as it presupposes that the silencing of women is systematic, shows up in regular, patterned ways, and that there are discoverable causes of this widespread observable phenomenon: the demand reflects nascent political theory insofar as it presupposes that the silencing of women reveals a systematic pattern of power and authority; and it reflects nascent moral theory insofar as it presupposes that the silencing is unjust and that there are particular ways of remedying this injustice. Indeed, whatever else we know feminism to include—e.g. concrete direct political action—theorizing is integral to it: theories about the nature of oppression, the causes of it, the relation of the oppression of women to other forms of oppression. And certainly the concept of the woman's voice is itself a theoretical concept, in the sense that it presupposes a theory according to which our identities as human beings are actually compound identities, a kind of fusion or confusion of our otherwise separate identities as women or men, as Black or brown or white, etc. That is no less a theoretical stance than Plato's division of the person into soul and body or Aristotle's parcelling of the soul into various functions.

The demand that the 'woman's voice' be heard also invites some further directions in the exploration of women's lives and discourages or excludes others. For reasons mentioned above, systematic, sustained reflection on being a woman—the kind of contemplation that 'doing theory' requires—is most likely to be done by women who vis-à-vis other women enjoy a certain amount of political, social and economic privilege because of their skin color, class membership, ethnic identity. There is a relationship between the content of our contemplation and the fact that we have the time to engage in it at some length—otherwise we shall have to say that it is a mere accident of history that white middle-class women in the United States have in the main developed 'feminist theory' (as opposed to 'Black feminist theory', 'Chicana feminist theory', etc.) and that so much of the theory has failed to be relevant to the lives of women who are not white or middle class. Feminist theory—of all kinds—is to be based on, or anyway touch base with, the variety of real life stories women provide about themselves. But in fact, because, among other things, of the structural political and social and economic inequalities among women, the tail has been wagging the dog: feminist theory has not for the most part arisen out of a medley or women's voices; instead, the theory has arisen out of the voices, the experiences, of a fairly small handful of women, and if other women's voices do not sing in harmony with the theory, they aren't counted as women's voices—rather, they are the voices of the woman as Hispana, Black, Jew, etc. There is another sense in which the tail is wagging the dog, too: it is presumed to be the case that those who do the theory know more about those who are theorized than vice versa: hence it ought to be the case that if it is white/Anglo women who write for and about all other women, then white/Anglo women must know more about all other women than other women know about them. But in fact just in order to survive, brown and Black women have to know a lot more about white/Anglo women—not through the sustained contemplation theory requires, but through the sharp observation stark exigency demands.

(In an Hispana voice)

I think it necessary to explain why in so many cases when women of color appear in front of white/Anglo women to talk about feminism and women of color, we mainly raise a complaint: the complaint of exclusion, of silencing, of being included in a universe we have not chosen. We usually raise the complaint with a certain amount of disguised or undisguised anger. I can only attempt to explain this phenomenon from a Hispanic viewpoint and a fairly narrow one at that: the viewpoint of an Argentinian woman who has lived in the US for 16 yr, who has attempted to come to terms with the devaluation of things Hispanic and Hispanic people in 'America' and who is most familiar with Hispano life in the Southwest of the US. I am quite unfamiliar with daily Hispano life in the urban centers, though not with some of the themes and some of the salient experiences of urban Hispano life.

When I say 'we',[2] I am referring to Hispanas. I am accustomed to use the 'we' in this way. I am also pained by the tenuousness of this 'we' given that I am not a native of the US. Through the years I have come to be recognized and I have come to recognize myself more and more firmly as part of this 'we'. I also have a profound yearning for

---

[2] I must note that when I think this 'we', I think it in Spanish—and in Spanish this 'we' is gendered, 'nosotras'. I also use 'nosotros' lovingly and with ease and in it I include all members of 'La raza cosmica' (Spanish-speaking people of the Americas, la gente de colores: people of many colors). In the US, I use 'we' contextually with varying degrees of discomfort: 'we' in the house, 'we' in the department, 'we' in the classroom, 'we' in the meeting. The discomfort springs from the sense of community in the 'we' and the varying degrees of lack of community in the context in which the 'we' is used.

this firmness since I am a displaced person and I am conscious of not being of and I am unwilling to make myself of—even if this were possible—the white/Anglo community.

When I say 'you' I mean not the non-Hispanic but the white/Anglo women that I address. 'We' and 'you' do not capture my relation to other non-white women. The complexity of that relation is not addressed here, but it is vivid to me as I write down my thoughts on the subject at hand.

I see two related reasons for our complaint-full discourse with white/Anglo women. Both of these reasons plague our world, they contaminate it through and through. It takes some hardening of oneself, some self-acceptance of our own anger to face them, for to face them is to decide that maybe we can change our situation in self-constructive ways and we know fully well that the possibilities are minimal. We know that we cannot rest from facing these reasons, that the tenderness towards others in us undermines our possibilities, that we have to fight our own niceness because it clouds our minds and hearts. Yet we know that a thoroughgoing hardening would dehumanize us. So, we have to walk through our days in a peculiarly fragile psychic state, one that we have to struggle to maintain, one that we do not often succeed in maintaining.

We and you do not talk the same language. When we talk to you we use your language: the language of your experience and of your theories. We try to use it to communicate our world of experience. But since your language and your theories are inadequate in expressing our experiences, we only succeed in communicating our experience of exclusion. We cannot talk to you in our language because you do not understand it. So the brute facts that we understand your language and that the place where most theorizing about women is taking place is your place, both combine to require that we either use your language and distort our experience not just in the speaking about it, but in the living of it, or that we remain silent. Complaining about exclusion is a way of remaining silent.

You are ill at ease in our world. You are ill at ease in our world in a very different way that we are ill at ease in yours. You are not of our world and again, you are not of our world in a very different way that we are not of yours. In the intimacy of a personal relationship we appear to you many times to be wholly there, to have broken through or to have dissipated the barriers that separate us because you are Anglo and we are raza. When we let go of the psychic state that I referred to above in the direction of sympathy, we appear to ourselves equally whole in your presence but our intimacy is thoroughly incomplete. When we are in your world many times you remake us in your own image, although sometimes you clearly and explicitly acknowledge that we are not wholly there in our being with you. When we are in your world we ourselves feel the discomfort of having our own being Hispanas disfigured or not understood. And yet, we have had to be in your world and learn its ways. We have to participate in it, make a living in it, live in it, be mistreated in it, be ignored in it, and rarely, be appreciated in it. In learning to do these things or in learning to suffer them or in learning to enjoy what is to be enjoyed or in learning to understand your conception of us, we have had to learn your culture and thus your language and self-conceptions. But there is nothing that necessitates that you understand our world: understand, that is, not as an observer understands things, but as a participant, as someone who has a stake in them understands them. So your being ill at ease in our world lacks the features of our being ill at ease in yours precisely because you can leave and you can always tell yourselves that you will be soon out of there and because the wholeness of your selves is never touched by us, we have no tendency to remake you in our image.

But you theorize about women and we are women, so you understand yourselves to be theorizing about us and we understand you to be theorizing about us. Yet none of the feminist theories developed so far seem to me to help Hispanas in the articulation of our experience. We have a sense that in using them we are distorting our experiences. Most Hispanas cannot even understand the language used in these theories—and only in some cases the reason is that the Hispana cannot understand English. We do not recognize ourselves in these theories. They create in us a schizophrenic split between our concern for ourselves as women and ourselves as Hispanas, one that we do not feel otherwise. Thus they seem to us to force us to assimilate to some version of Anglo culture, however revised that version may be. They seem to ask that we leave our communities or that we become alienated so completely in them that we feel hollow. When we see that you feel alienated in your own communities, this confuses us because we think that maybe every feminist has to suffer this alienation. But we see that recognition of your alienation leads many of you to be empowered into the remaking of your culture, while we are paralyzed into a state of displacement with no place to go.

So I think that we need to think carefully about the relation between the articulation of our own experience, the interpretation of our own experience, and theory making by us and other non-Hispanic women about themselves and other 'women'.

The only motive that makes sense to me for your joining us in this investigation is the motive of friendship, out of friendship. A non–imperialist feminism requires that you make a real space for our articulating, interpreting, theorizing and reflecting about the connections among them—a real space must be a non-coerced space—and/or that you follow us into our world out of friendship. I see the 'out of friendship' as the only sensical motivation for this following because the task at hand for you is one of extraordinary difficulty. It requires that you be willing to devote a great part of your life to it and that you be willing to suffer alienation and self-disruption. Self-interest has been proposed as a possible motive for entering this task. But self-interest does not seem to me to be a realistic motive, since whatever the benefits you may accrue from such a journey, they cannot be concrete enough for you at this time and they not be worth your while. I do not think that you have any obligation to understand us. You do have an obligation to abandon your imperialism, your universal claims, your reduction of us to your selves simply because they seriously harm us.

I think that the fact that we are so ill at ease with your theorizing in the ways indicated above does indicate that there is something wrong with these theories. But what is it that is wrong? Is it simply that the theories are flawed if meant to be universal but accurate so long as they are confined to your particular group(s)? Is it that the theories are not really flawed but need to be translated? Can they be translated? Is it something about the process of theorizing that is flawed? How do the two reasons for our complaint-full discourse affect the validity of your theories? Where do *we* begin? To what extent are our experience and its articulation affected by our being a colonized people, and thus by your culture, theories and conceptions? Should we theorize in community and thus as part of community life and outside the academy and other intellectual circles? What is the point of making theory? Is theory making a good thing for us to do at this time? When are we making theory and when are we just articulating and/or interpreting our experiences?

II. SOME QUESTIONABLE ASSUMPTIONS ABOUT FEMINIST THEORIZING

(Unproblematically in Vicky's & Maria's voice)

Feminist theories aren't just about what happens to the female population in any given society or across all societies; they are about the meaning of those experiences in the lives of women. They are about beings who give their own accounts of what is happening to them or of what they are doing, who have culturally constructed ways of reflecting on their lives. But how can the theorizer get at the meaning of those experiences? What should the relation be between a woman's own account of her experiences and the theorizer's account of it?

Let us describe two different ways of arriving at an account of another woman's experience. It is one thing for both me and you to observe you and come up with our different accounts of what you are doing; it is quite another for me to observe myself and others much like me culturally and in other ways and to develop an account of myself and then use that account to give an account of you. In the first case you are the 'insider' and I am the 'outsider'. When the outsider makes clear that she is an outsider and that this is an outsider's account of your behavior, there is a touch of honesty about what she is doing. Most of the time the 'interpretation by an outsider' is left understood and most of the time the distance of outsidedness is understood to mark objectivity in the interpretation. But why is the outsider as an outsider interpreting your behavior? Is she doing it so that you can understand how she sees you? Is she doing it so that other outsiders will understand how you *are?* Is she doing it so that *you* will understand how you are? It would seem that if the outsider wants you to understand how she sees you and you have given your account of how you see yourself to her, there is a possibility of genuine dialogue between the two. It also seems that the lack of reciprocity could bar genuine dialogue. For why should you engage in such a one-sided dialogue? As soon as we ask this question, a host of other conditions for the possibility of a genuine dialogue between us arise: conditions having to do with your position relative to me in the various social, political and economic structures in which we might come across each other or in which you may run face to face with my account of you and my use of your account of yourself. Is this kind of dialogue necessary for me to get at the meaning of your experiences? That is, is this kind of dialogue necessary for feminist theorizing that is not seriously flawed?

Obviously the most dangerous of the understanding of what I—an outsider—am doing in giving an account of your experience is the one that describes what I'm doing as giving an account of who and how you are whether it be given to you or to other outsiders. Why should you or anyone else believe me; that is why should you or anyone else believe that you are as I say you are? Could I be right? What conditions would have to obtain for my being right? That many women are put in the position of not knowing whether or not to believe outsiders' accounts of their experiences is clear. The pressures to believe these accounts are enormous even when the woman in question does not see herself in the account. She is thus led to doubt her own judgment and to doubt all interpretation of her experience. This leads her to experience her life differently. Since the consequences of outsiders' accounts can be so significant, it is crucial that we reflect on whether or not this type of account can ever be right and if so, under what conditions.

The last point leads us to the second way of arriving at an account of another woman's experience, viz. the case in which I observe myself and others like me culturally and in other ways and use that account to give an account of you. In doing this, I remake you in my own image. Feminist theorizing approaches this remaking insofar as it depends on the concept of women as women. For it has not arrived at this concept as a consequence of dialogue with many women who are culturally different, or by any other kind of investigation of cultural differences which may include different conceptions of what it is to be a woman; it has simply presupposed this concept.

Our suggestion in this paper, and at this time it is no more than a suggestion, is that only when genuine and reciprocal dialogue takes place between 'outsiders' and 'insiders' can we trust the outsider's account. At first sight it may appear that the insider/outsider distinction disappears in the dialogue, but it is important to notice that all that happens is that we are now both outsider and insider with respect to each other. The dialogue puts us both in position to give a better account of each other's and our own experience. Here we should again note that white/Anglo women are much less prepared for this dialogue with women of color than women of color are for dialogue with them in that women of color have had to learn white/Anglo ways, self–conceptions, and conceptions of them.

But both the possibility and the desirability of this dialogue are very much in question. We need to think about the possible motivations for engaging in this dialogue, whether doing theory jointly would be a good thing, in what ways and for whom, and whether doing theory is in itself a good thing at this time for women of color or white/Anglo women. In motivating the last question let us remember the hierarchical distinctions between theorizers and those theorized about and between theorizers and doers. These distinctions are endorsed by the same views and institutions which endorse and support hierarchical distinctions between men/women, master race/inferior race, intellectuals/manual workers. Of what use is the activity of theorizing to those of us who are women of color engaged day in and day out in the task of empowering women and men of color face to face with them? Should we be articulating and interpreting their experience for them with the aid of theories? Whose theories?

III. WAYS OF TALKING OR BEING TALKED ABOUT THAT ARE HELPFUL, ILLUMINATING, EMPOWERING, RESPECTFUL

(Unproblematically in Maria's & Vicky's voice)

Feminists have been quite diligent about pointing out the ways in which empirical, philosophical and moral theories have been androcentric. They have thought it crucial to ask, with respect to such theories: who makes them? for whom do they make them?

about what or whom are the theories? why? how are theories tested? what are the criteria for such tests and where did the criteria come from? Without posing such questions and trying to answer them, we'd never have been able to begin to mount evidence for our claims that particular theories are androcentric, sexist, biased, paternalistic, etc. Certain philosophers have become fond of—indeed, have made their careers on—pointing out that characterizing a statement as true or false is only one of many ways possible of characterizing it; it might also be, oh, rude, funny, disarming, etc.; it may be intended to soothe or to hurt; or it may have the effect, intended or not, of soothing or hurting. Similarly, theories appear to be the kinds of things that are true or false; but they also are the kinds of things that can be, e.g. useless, arrogant, disrespectful, ignorant, ethnocentric, imperialistic. The immediate point is that feminist theory is no less immune to such characterizations than, say, Plato's political theory, or Freud's theory of female psychosexual development. Of course this is not to say that if feminist theory manages to be respectful or helpful it will follow that it must be true. But if, say, an empirical theory is purported to be about 'women' and in fact is only about certain women, it is certainly false, probably ethnocentric, and of dubious usefulness except to those whose position in the world it strengthens (and theories, as we know, don't have to be true in order to be used to strengthen people's positions in the world).

Many reasons can be and have been given for the production of accounts of people's lives that plainly have nothing to do with illuminating those lives for the benefit of those living them. It is likely that both the method of investigation and the content of many accounts would be different if illuminating the lives of the people the accounts are about were the aim of the studies. Though we cannot say ahead of time how feminist theory-making would be different if all (or many more) of those people it is meant to be about were more intimately part of the theory–making process, we do suggest some specific ways being talked about can be helpful:

(1) The theory or account can be helpful if it enables one to see how parts of one's life fit together, for example, to see connections among parts of one's life one hasn't seen before. No account can do this if it doesn't get the parts right to begin with, and this cannot happen if the concepts used to describe a life are utterly foreign.

(2) A useful theory will help one locate oneself concretely in the world, rather than add to the mystification of the world and one's location in it. New concepts may be of significance here, but they will not be useful if there is no way they can be translated into already existing concepts. Suppose a theory locates you in the home, because you are a woman, but you know full well that is not where you spend most of your time? Or suppose you can't locate yourself easily in any particular class as defined by some version of marxist theory?

(3) A theory or account not only ought to accurately locate one in the world but also enable one to think about the extent to which one is responsible or not for being in that location. Otherwise, for those whose location is as oppressed peoples, it usually occurs that the oppressed have no way to see themselves as in any way self-determining, as having any sense of being worthwhile or having grounds for pride, and paradoxically at the same time feeling at fault for the position they are in. A useful theory will help people sort out just what is and is not due to themselves and their own activities as opposed to those who have power over them.

It may seem odd to make these criteria criteria of a useful theory, if the usefulness is not to be at odds with the issue of the truth of the theory: for the focus on feeling worthwhile or having pride seems to rule out the possibility that the truth might just be that such-and-such a group of people has been under the control of others for centuries and that the only explanation of that is that they are worthless and weak people, and will never be able to change that. Feminist theorizing seems implicitly if not explicitly committed to the moral view that women *are* worthwhile beings, and the metaphysical theory that we are beings capable of bringing about a change in our situations. Does this mean feminist theory is 'biased'? Not any more than any other theory, e.g. psychoanalytic theory. What is odd here is not the feminist presupposition that women are worthwhile but rather that feminist theory (and other theory) often has the effect of empowering one group and demoralizing another.

Aspects of feminist theory are as unabashedly value–laden as other political and moral theories. It is not just an examination of women's positions, for it includes, indeed begins with, moral and political judgments about the injustice (or, where relevant, justice) of them. This means that there are implicit or explicit judgments also about what kind of changes constitute a better or worse situation for women.

(4) In this connection a theory that is useful will provide criteria for change and make suggestions for modes of resistance that don't merely reflect the situation and values of the theorizer. A theory that is respectful of those about whom it is a theory will not assume that changes that are perceived as making life better for some women are changes that will make, and will be perceived as making, life better for other women. This is NOT to say that if some women do not find a situation oppressive, other women ought never to suggest to the contrary that there might be very good reasons to think that the situation nevertheless *is* oppressive. But it is to say that, e.g., the prescription that life for women will be better when we're in the workforce rather than at home, when we are completely free of religious beliefs with patriarchal origins, when we live in complete separation from men, etc., are seen as slaps in the face to women whose life would be better if they could spend more time at home, whose identity is inseparable from their religious beliefs and cultural practices (which is not to say those beliefs and practices are to remain completely uncriticized and unchanged), who have ties to men—whether erotic or not—such that to have them severed in the name of some vision of what is 'better' is, at that time and for those women, absurd. Our visions of what is better are always informed by our perception of what is bad about our present situation. Surely we've learned enough from the history of clumsy missionaries, and the white suffragists of the 19th century (who couldn't imagine why Black women 'couldn't see' how crucial getting the vote for 'women' was) to know that we can clobber people to destruction with our visions, our versions, of what is better. BUT: this does not mean women are not to offer supportive and tentative criticism of one another. But there is a very important difference between (a) developing ideas together, in a 'pre-theoretical' stage, engaged as equals in joint enquiry, and (b) one group developing, on the basis of their own experience, a set of criteria for good change for women—and then reluctantly making revisions in the criteria at the insistence of women to whom such criteria seem ethnocentric and arrogant. The deck is stacked when one group takes it upon itself to develop the theory and then have others criticize it. Categories are quick to congeal, and the experi-

ences of women whose lives do not fit the categories will appear as anomalous when in fact the theory should have grown out of them as much as others from the beginning. This, of course, is why any organization or conference having to do with 'women'—with no qualification—that seriously does not want to be 'solipsistic' will from the beginning be multi-cultural or state the appropriate qualifications. How we think and what we think about does depend in large part on who is there—not to mention who is expected or encouraged to speak. (Recall the boys in the *Symposium* sending the flute girls out.) Conversations and criticism take place in particular circumstances. Turf matters. So does the fact of who if anyone already has set up the terms of the conversations.

(5) Theory cannot be useful to anyone interested in resistance and change unless there is reason to believe that knowing what a theory means and believing it to be true have some connection to resistance and change. As we make theory and offer it up to others, what do we assume is the connection between theory and consciousness? Do we expect others to read theory, understand it, believe it, and have their consciousness and lives thereby transformed? If we really want theory to make a difference to people's lives, how ought we to present it? Do we think people come to consciousness by reading? only by reading? Speaking to people through theory (orally or in writing) is a *very* specific context-dependent activity. That is, theory-makers and their methods and concepts constitute a community of people and of shared meanings. Their language can be just as opaque and foreign to those not in the community as a foreign tongue or dialect.[3] Why do we engage in *this* activity and what effect do we think it ought to have? As Helen Longino has asked: 'Is "doing theory" just a bonding ritual for academic or educationally privileged feminists/women?' Again, whom does our theory-making serve?

IV. SOME SUGGESTIONS ABOUT HOW TO DO THEORY THAT IS NOT IMPERIALISTIC, ETHNOCENTRIC, DISRESPECTFUL

(Problematically in the voice of a woman of color)

What are the things we need to know about others, and about ourselves, in order to speak intelligently, intelligibly, sensitively, and helpfully about their lives? We can show respect, or lack of it, in writing theoretically about others no less than in talking directly with them. This is not to say that here we have a well-worked out concept of respect, but only to suggest that together all of us consider what it would mean to theorize in a respectful way.

When we speak, write, and publish our theories, to whom do we think we are accountable? Are the concerns we have in being accountable to 'the profession' at odds with the concerns we have in being accountable to those about whom we theorize? Do commitments to 'the profession', method, getting something published, getting tenure, lead us to talk and act in ways at odds with what we ourselves (let alone others) would regard as ordinary, decent behavior? To what extent do we presuppose that really under-

---

[3]See Bernstein (1972). Bernstein would probably, and we think wrongly, insist that theoretical terms and statements have meanings *not* 'tied to a local relationship and to a local social structure', unlike the vocabulary of, e.g., working-class children.

standing another person or culture requires our behaving in ways that are disrespectful, even violent? That is, to what extent do we presuppose that getting and/or publishing the requisite information requires or may require disregarding the wishes of others, lying to them, wresting information from them against their wills? Why and how do we think theorizing about others provides *understanding* of them? Is there any sense in which theorizing about others is a short-cut to understanding them?

Finally, if we think doing theory is an important activity, and we think that some conditions lead to better theorizing than others, what are we going to do about creating those conditions? If we think it not just desirable but necessary for women of different racial and ethnic identities to create feminist theory jointly, how shall that be arranged for? It may be the case that at this particular point we ought not even try to do that—that feminist theory by and and [sic] for Hispanas needs to be done separately from feminist theory by and for Black women, white women, etc. But it must be recognized that white/Anglo women have more power and privilege than Hispanas, Black women, etc., and at the very least they can use such advantage to provide space and time for other women to speak (with the above caveats about implicit restrictions on what counts as 'the woman's voice'). And once again it is important to remember that the power of white/Anglo women vis-à-vis Hispanas and Black women is in inverse proportion to their working knowledge of each other.

This asymmetry is a crucial fact about the background of possible relationships between white women and women of color, whether as political co-workers, professional colleagues, or friends.

If white/Anglo women and women of color are to do theory jointly, in helpful, respectful, illuminating and empowering ways, the task ahead of white/Anglo women because of this asymmetry, is a very hard task. The task is a very complex one. In part, to make an analogy, the task can be compared to learning a text without the aid of teachers. We all know the lack of contact felt when we want to discuss a particular issue that requires knowledge of a text with someone who does not know the text at all. Or the discomfort and impatience that arise in us when we are discussing an issue that presupposes a text and someone walks into the conversation who does not know the text. That person is either left out or will impose herself on us and either try to engage in the discussion or try to change the subject. Women of color are put in these situations by white/Anglo women and men constantly. Now imagine yourself simply left out but wanting to do theory with us. The first thing to recognize and accept is that you disturb our own dialogues by putting yourself in the left-out position and not leaving us in some meaningful sense to ourselves.

You must also recognize and accept that you must learn the text. But the text is an extraordinarily complex one: viz. our many different cultures. You are asking us to make ourselves more vulnerable to you than we already are before we have any reason to trust that you will not take advantage of this vulnerability. So you need to learn to become unintrusive, unimportant, patient to the point of tears, while at the same time open to learning any possible lessons. You will also have to come to terms with the sense of alienation, of not belonging, of having your world thoroughly disrupted, having it criticized and scrutinized from the point of view of those who have been harmed by it, having important concepts central to it dismissed, being viewed with mistrust, being seen as of no consequence except as an object of mistrust.

Why would any white/Anglo woman engage in this task? Out of self-interest? What in engaging in this task would be, not just in her interest, but perceived as such by her before the task is completed or well underway? Why should we want you to come into our world out of self-interest? Two points need to be made here. The task as described could be entered into with the intention of finding out as much as possible about us so as to better dominate us. The person engaged in this task would act as a spy. The motivation is not unfamiliar to us. We have heard it said that now that Third World countries are more powerful as a bloc, westerners need to learn more about them, that it is in their self–interest to do so. Obviously there is no reason why people of color should welcome white/Anglo women into their world for the carrying out of this intention. It is also obvious that white/Anglo feminists should not engage in this task under this description since the task under this description would not lead to joint theorizing of the desired sort: respectful, illuminating, helpful and empowering. It would be helpful and empowering only in a one-sided way.

Self-interest is also mentioned as a possible motive in another way. White/Anglo women sometimes say that the task of understanding women of color would entail self-growth or self-expansion. If the task is conceived as described here, then one should doubt that growth or expansion will be the result. The severe self-disruption that the task entails should place a doubt in anyone who takes the task seriously about her possibilities of coming out of the task whole, with a self that is not as fragile as the selves of those who have been the victims of racism. But also, why should women of color embrace white/Anglo women's self-betterment without reciprocity? At this time women of color cannot afford this generous affirmation of white/Anglo women.

Another possible motive for engaging in this task is the motive of duty, 'out of obligation', because white/Anglos have done people of color wrong. Here again two considerations: coming into Hispano, Black, Native American worlds out of obligation puts white/Anglos in a morally self-righteous position that is inappropriate. You are active, we are passive. We become the vehicles of your own redemption. Secondly, we couldn't want you to come into our worlds 'out of obligation'. That is like wanting someone to make love to you out of obligation. So, whether or not you have an obligation to do this (and we would deny that you do), or whether this task could even be done out of obligation, this is an inappropriate motive.

Out of obligation you should stay out of our way, respect us and our distance, and forego the use of whatever power you have over us—for example, the power to use your language in our meetings, the power to overwhelm us with your education, the power to intrude in our communities in order to research us and to record the supposed dying of our cultures, the power to engrain in us a sense that we are members of dying cultures and are doomed to assimilate, the power to keep us in a defensive posture with respect to our own cultures.

So the motive of friendship remains as both the only appropriate and understandable motive for white/Anglo feminists engaging in the task as described above. If you enter the task out of friendship with us, then you will be moved to attain the appropriate reciprocity of care for your and our wellbeing as whole beings, you will have a stake in us and in our world, you will be moved to satisfy the need for reciprocity of understanding that will enable you to follow us in our experiences as we are able to follow you in yours.

We are not suggesting that if the learning of the text is to be done out of friendship, you must enter into a friendship with a whole community and for the purpose of making theory. In order to understand what it is that we are suggesting, it is important to remember that during the description of her experience of exclusion, the Hispana voice said that Hispanas experience the intimacy of friendship with white/Anglo women friends as thoroughly incomplete. It is not until this fact is acknowledged by our white/Anglo women friends and felt as a profound lack in our experience of each other that white/Anglo women can begin to see us. Seeing us in our communities will make clear and concrete to you how incomplete we really are in our relationships with you. It is this beginning that forms the proper background for the yearning to understand the text of our cultures that can lead to joint theory-making.

Thus, the suggestion made here is that if white/Anglo women are to understand our voices, they must understand our communities and us in them. Again, this is not to suggest that you set out to make friends with our communities, though you may become friends with some of the members, nor is it to suggest that you should try to befriend us for the purpose of making theory with us. The latter would be a perversion of friendship. Rather, from within friendship you may be moved by friendship to undergo the very difficult task of understanding the text of our cultures by understanding our lives in our communities. This learning calls for circumspection, for questioning of yourselves and your roles in your own culture. It necessitates a striving to understand while in the comfortable position of not having an official calling card (as 'scientific' observers of our communities have); it demands recognition that you do not have the authority of knowledge; it requires coming to the task without ready-made theories to frame our lives. This learning is then extremely hard because it requires openness (including openness to severe criticism of the white/Anglo world), sensitivity, concentration, self-questioning, circumspection. It should be clear that it does not consist in a passive immersion in our cultures, but in a striving to understand what it is that our voices are saying. Only then can we engage in a mutual dialogue that does not reduce each one of us to instances of the abstraction called 'woman'.

REFERENCES

Bernstein, Basil, 1972. Social class, language and socialization." In Giglioli, Pier Paolo, ed., *Language and Social Context,* pp. 157–178. Penguin, Harmondsworth, Middlesex.

Mackinnon, Catherine. 1982. Feminism, marxism, method, and the State: an agenda for theory." *Signs* 7(3):515–544.

Learning from the Outsider Within: The Sociological Significance of Black Feminist Thought

Patricia Hill Collins

Afro-American women have long been privy to some of the most intimate secrets of white society. Countless numbers of Black women have ridden buses to their white "families," where they not only cooked, cleaned, and executed other domestic duties, but where they also nurtured their "other" children, shrewdly offered guidance to their employers, and frequently, became honorary members of their white "families." These women have seen white elites, both actual and aspiring, from perspectives largely obscured from their Black spouses and from these groups themselves.[1]

On one level, this "insider" relationship has been satisfying to all involved. The memoirs of affluent whites often mention their love for their Black "mothers," while accounts of Black domestic workers stress the sense of self-affirmation they experienced at seeing white power demystified—of knowing that it was not the intellect, talent, or humanity of their employers that supported their superior status, but largely just the advantages of racism.[2] But on another level, these same Black women knew they could never belong to their white "families." In spite of their involvement, they remained "outsiders."[3]

This "outsider within" status has provided a special standpoint on self, family, and society for Afro-American women.[4] A careful review of the emerging Black feminist literature reveals that many Black intellectuals, especially those in touch with their marginality in academic settings, tap this standpoint in producing distinctive analyses of race, class, and gender. For example, Zora Neal Hurston's 1937 novel, *Their Eyes Were Watching God,* most certainly reflects her skill at using the strengths and transcending

SOCIAL PROBLEMS, Vol. 33, No. 6, December 1986

    Editor's note: I wish to thank Lynn Weber Cannon, Bonnie Thornton Dill, Alison M. Jaggar, Joan Hartman, Ellen Messer-Davidow, and several anonymous reviewers for their helpful comments about earlier drafts of this paper. Correspondence to: Department of Afro-American Studies, University of Cincinnati, ML 370, Cincinnati, OH 45221.

    [1]In 1940, almost 60 percent of employed Afro-American women were domestics. The 1970 census was the first time this category of work did not contain the largest segment of the Black female labor force. See Rollins (1985) for a discussion of Black domestic work.

    [2]For example, in *Of Women Born: Motherhood as Experience and Institution,* Adrienne Rich has fond memories of her Black "mother," a young, unstereotypically slim Black woman she loved. Similarly, Dill's (1980) study of Black domestic workers reveals Black women's sense of affirmation at knowing that they were better mothers than their employers, and that they frequently had to teach their employers the basics about children and interaction in general. Even though the Black domestic workers were officially subordinates, they gained a sense of self-worth at knowing they were good at things that they felt mattered.

    [3]For example, in spite of Rich's warm memories of her Black "mother," she had all but forgotten her until beginning research for her book. Similarly, the Black domestic workers in both Dill's (1980) and Rollins' (1985) studies discussed the limitations that their subordinate roles placed on them.

    [4]For a discussion of the notion of a special standpoint or point of view of oppressed groups, see Hartsock (1983). See Merton's (1972) analysis of the potential contributions of insider and outsider perspectives to sociology. For a related discussion of outsider within status, see his section "Insiders as 'Outsiders' " (1972:29–30).

the limitations both of her academic training and of her background in traditional Afro-American community life.[5] Black feminist historian E. Frances White (1984) suggests that Black women's ideas have been honed at the juncture between movements for racial and sexual equality, and contends that Afro-American women have been pushed by "their marginalization in both arenas" to create Black feminism. Finally, Black feminist critic Bell Hooks captures the unique standpoint that the outsider within status can generate. In describing her small-town, Kentucky childhood, she notes, "living as we did—on the edge—we developed a particular way of seeing reality. We looked both from the outside and in from the inside out . . . we understood both" (1984:vii).

In spite of the obstacles that can confront outsiders within, such individuals can benefit from this status. Simmel's (1921) essay on the sociological significance of what he called the "stranger" offers a helpful starting point for understanding the largely unexplored area of Black female outsider within status and the usefulness of the standpoint it might produce. Some of the potential benefits of outsider within status include: (1) Simmel's definition of "objectivity" as "a peculiar composition of nearness and remoteness, concern and indifference"; (2) the tendency for people to confide in a "stranger" in ways they never would with each other; and (3) the ability of the "stranger" to see patterns that may be more difficult for those immersed in the situation to see. Mannheim (1936) labels the "strangers" in academia "marginal intellectuals" and argues that the critical posture such individuals bring to academic endeavors may be essential to the creative development of academic disciplines themselves. Finally, in assessing the potentially positive qualities of social difference, specifically marginality, Lee notes, "for a time this marginality can be a most stimulating, albeit often a painful, experience. For some, it is debilitating . . . for others, it is an excitement to creativity" (1973:64).[6]

Sociologists might benefit greatly from serious consideration of the emerging, cross-disciplinary literature that I label Black feminist thought, precisely because, for many Afro-American female intellectuals, "marginality" has been an excitement to creativity. As outsiders within, Black feminist scholars may be one of many distinct groups of marginal intellectuals whose standpoints promise to enrich contemporary sociological discourse. Bringing this group—as well as others who share an outsider within status vis-a-vis sociology—into the center of analysis may reveal aspects of reality obscured by more orthodox approaches.

In the remainder of this essay, I examine the sociological significance of the Black feminist thought stimulated by Black women's outsider within status. First, I outline three key themes that characterize the emerging cross-disciplinary literature that I label

[5]Hurston has been widely discussed in Black feminist literary criticism. For example, see selected essays in Walker's (1979) edited volume on Hurston.

[6]By stressing the potentially positive features of outsider within status, I in no way want to deny the very real problem this social status has for large numbers of Black women. American sociology has long identified marginal status as problematic. However, my sense of the "problems" diverge from those espoused by traditional sociologists. For example, Robert Park states, "the marginal man . . . is one whom fate has condemned to live in two societies and in two, not merely different but antagonistic cultures (1950:373)." From Park's perspective, marginality and difference themselves were problems. This perspective quite rationally led to the social policy solution of assimilation, one aimed at eliminating difference, or if that didn't work, pretending it was not important. In contrast, I argue that it is the meaning attached to difference that is the problem. See Lorde (1984:114–23 and passim) for a Black feminist perspective on difference.

Black feminist thought.[7] For each theme, I summarize its content, supply examples from Black feminist and other works that illustrate its nature, and discuss its importance. Second, I explain the significance these key themes in Black feminist thought may have for sociologists by describing why Black women's outsider within status might generate a distinctive standpoint vis-a-vis existing sociological paradigms. Finally, I discuss one general implication of this essay for social scientists: namely, the potential usefulness of identifying and using one's own standpoint in conducting research.

THREE KEY THEMES IN BLACK FEMINIST THOUGHT

Black feminist thought consists of ideas produced by Black women that clarify a standpoint of and for Black women. Several assumptions underlie this working definition. First, the definition suggests that it is impossible to separate the structure and thematic content of thought from the historical and material conditions shaping the lives of its producers (Berger and Luckmann 1966; Mannheim 1936). Therefore, while Black feminist thought may be recorded by others, it is produced by Black women. Second, the definition assumes that Black women possess a unique standpoint on, or perspective of, their experiences and that there will be certain commonalities of perception shared by Black women as a group. Third, while living life as Black women may produce certain commonalities of outlook, the diversity of class, region, age, and sexual orientation shaping individual Black women's lives has resulted in different expressions of these common themes. Thus, universal themes included in the Black women's standpoint may be experienced and expressed differently by distinct groups of Afro-American women. Finally, the definition assumes that, while a Black women's standpoint exists, its contours may not be clear to Black women themselves. Therefore, one role for Black female intellectuals is to produce facts and theories about the Black female experience that will clarify a Black woman's standpoint for Black women. In other words, Black feminist thought contains observations and interpretations about Afro-American womanhood that describe and explain different expressions of common themes.

No one Black feminist platform exists from which one can measure the "correctness" of a particular thinker; nor should there be one. Rather, as I defined it above, there is a long and rich tradition of Black feminist thought. Much of it has been oral and has been produced by ordinary Black women in their roles as mothers, teachers, musicians, and preachers.[8] Since the civil rights and women's movements, Black women's ideas have been increasingly documented and are reaching wider audiences. The following discus-

---

[7]In addition to familiarizing readers with the contours of Black feminist thought, I place Black women's ideas in the center of my analysis for another reason. Black women's ideas have long been viewed as peripheral to serious intellectual endeavors. By treating Black feminist thought as central, I hope to avoid the tendency of starting with the body of thought needing the critique—in this case sociology—fitting in the dissenting ideas, and thus, in the process, reifying the very systems of thought one hopes to transform.

[8]On this point, I diverge somewhat from Berger and Luckmann's (1966) definition of specialized thought. They suggest that only a limited group of individuals engages in theorizing and that "pure theory" emerges with the development of specialized legitimating theories and their administration by full-time legitimators. Using this approach, groups denied the material resources to support pure theorists cannot be capable of developing specialized theoretical knowledge. In contrast, I argue that "traditional wisdom" is a system of thought and that it reflects the material positions of its practitioners.

sion of three key themes in Black feminist thought is itself part of this emerging process of documentation and interpretation. The three themes I have chosen are not exhaustive but, in my assessment, they do represent the thrust of much of the existing dialogue.

The Meaning of Self-Definition and Self-Valuation

An affirmation of the importance of Black women's self-definition and self-valuation is the first key theme that pervades historical and contemporary statements of Black feminist thought. Self-definition involves challenging the political knowledge-validation process that has resulted in externally-defined, stereotypical images of Afro-American womanhood. In contrast, self-valuation stresses the content of Black women's self-definitions—namely, replacing externally-derived images with authentic Black female images.

Both Mae King's (1973) and Cheryl Gilkes' (1981) analyses of the importance of stereotypes offer useful insights for grasping the importance of Black women's self-definition. King suggests that stereotypes represent externally-defined, controlling images of Afro-American womanhood that have been central to the dehumanization of Black women and the exploitation of Black women's labor. Gilkes points out that Black women's assertiveness in resisting the multifaceted oppression they experience has been a consistent threat to the status quo. As punishment, Black women have been assaulted with a variety of externally-defined negative images designed to control assertive Black female behavior.

The value of King's and Gilkes' analyses lies in their emphasis on the function of stereotypes in controlling dominated groups. Both point out that replacing negative stereotypes with ostensibly positive ones can be equally problematic if the function of stereotypes as controlling images remains unrecognized. John Gwaltney's (1980) interview with Nancy White, a 73-year-old Black woman, suggests that ordinary Black women may also be aware of the power of these controlling images in their everyday experiences. In the following passage, Ms. White assesses the difference between the controlling images applied to Afro-American and white women as being those of degree, and not of kind:

> My mother used to say that the black woman is the white man's mule and the white woman is his dog. Now, she said that to say this: we do the heavy work and get beat whether we do it well or not. But the white woman is closer to the master and he pats them on the head and lets them sleep in the house, but he ain't gon' treat neither one like he was dealing with a person (1980:148).

This passage suggests that while both groups are stereotyped, albeit in different ways, the function of the images is to dehumanize and control both groups. Seen in this light, it makes little sense, in the long run, for Black women to exchange one set of controlling images for another even if, in the short run, positive stereotypes bring better treatment.

The insistence on Black female self-definition reframes the entire dialogue from one of determining the technical accuracy of an image, to one stressing the power dynamics underlying the very process of definition itself. Black feminists have questioned not only what has been said about Black women, but the credibility and the intentions of those possessing the power to define. When Black women define themselves, they clearly reject the taken-for-granted assumption that those in positions granting them the authority to describe and analyze reality are entitled to do so. Regardless of the actual content of Black women's self-definitions, the act of insisting on Black female self-definition validates Black women's power as human subjects.

The related theme of Black female self-valuation pushes this entire process one step further. While Black female self-definition speaks to the power dynamics involved in the act of defining images of self and community, the theme of Black female self-valuation addresses the actual content of these self-definitions. Many of the attributes extant in Black female stereotypes are actually distorted renderings of those aspects of Black female behavior seen as most threatening to white patriarchy (Gilkes, 1981; White, 1985). For example, aggressive Afro-American women are threatening because they challenge white patriarchal definitions of femininity. To ridicule assertive women by labeling them Sapphires reflects an effort to put all women in their place. In their roles as central figures in socializing the next generation of Black adults, strong mothers are similarly threatening, because they contradict patriarchal views of family power relations. To ridicule strong Black mothers by labelling them matriarchs (Higginbotham, 1982) reflects a similar effort to control another aspect of Black female behavior that is especially threatening to the status quo.

When Black females choose to value those aspects of Afro-American womanhood that are stereotyped, ridiculed, and maligned in academic scholarship and the popular media, they are actually questioning some of the basic ideas used to control dominated groups in general. It is one thing to counsel Afro-American women to resist the Sapphire stereotype by altering their behavior to become meek, docile, and stereotypically "feminine." It is quite another to advise Black women to embrace their assertiveness, to value their sassiness, and to continue to use these qualities to survive in and transcend the harsh environments that circumscribe so many Black women's lives. By defining and valuing assertiveness and other "unfeminine" qualities as necessary and functional attributes for Afro-American womanhood, Black women's self-valuation challenges the content of externally-defined controlling images.

This Black feminist concern—that Black women create their own standards for evaluating Afro-American womanhood and value their creations—pervades a wide range of literary and social science works. For example, Alice Walker's 1982 novel, *The Color Purple,* and Ntozake Shang's 1978 choreopoem, *For Colored Girls Who Have Considered Suicide,* are both bold statements of the necessity for Black female self-definition and self-valuation. Lena Wright Myers' (1980) work shows that Black women judge their behavior by comparing themselves to Black women facing similar situations and thus demonstrates the presence of Black female definitions of Afro-American womanhood. The recent spate of Black female historiography suggests that self-defined, self-valuating Black women have long populated the ranks of Afro-American female leaders (Giddings, 1984; Loewenberg and Bogin, 1976).

Black women's insistence on self-definition, self-valuation, and the necessity for a Black female-centered analysis is significant for two reasons. First, defining and valuing one's consciousness of one's own self-defined standpoint in the face of images that foster a self-definition as the objectified "other" is an important way of resisting the dehumanization essential to systems of domination. The status of being the "other" implies being "other than" or different from the assumed norm of white male behavior. In this model, powerful white males define themselves as subjects, the true actors, and classify people of color and women in terms of their position vis-a-vis this white male hub. Since Black women have been denied the authority to challenge these definitions, this model consists of images that define Black women as a negative other, the virtual antithesis of positive white male images. Moreover, as Brittan and Maynard (1984:199) point out, "domination always involves the objectification of the dominated; all forms of oppression imply the devaluation of the subjectivity of the oppressed."

One of the best examples of this process is described by Judith Rollins (1985). As part of her fieldwork on Black domestics, Rollins worked as a domestic for six months. She describes several incidents where her employers treated her as if she were not really present. On one occasion while she sat in the kitchen having lunch, her employers had a conversation as if she were not there. Her sense of invisibility became so great that she took out a pad of paper and began writing field notes. Even though Rollins wrote for 10 minutes, finished lunch, and returned to work, her employers showed no evidence of having seen her at all. Rollins notes,

> It was this aspect of servitude I found to be one of the strongest affronts to my dignity as a human being. . . . These gestures of ignoring my presence were not, I think, intended as insults; they were expressions of the employers' ability to annihilate the humanness and even, at times, the very existence of me, a servant and a black woman (1985:209).

Racist and sexist ideologies both share the common feature of treating dominated groups—the "others"—as objects lacking full human subjectivity. For example, seeing Black women as obstinate mules and viewing white women as obedient dogs objectifies both groups, but in different ways. Neither is seen as fully human, and therefore both become eligible for race/gender specific modes of domination. But if Black women refuse to accept their assigned status as the quintessential "other," then the entire rationale for such domination is challenged. In brief, abusing a mule or a dog may be easier than abusing a person who is a reflection of one's own humanness.

A second reason that Black female self-definition and self-valuation are significant concerns their value in allowing Afro-American women to reject internalized, psychological oppression (Baldwin, 1980). The potential damage of internalized control to Afro-American women's self-esteem can be great, even to the prepared. Enduring the frequent assaults of controlling images requires considerable inner strength. Nancy White, cited earlier, also points out how debilitating being treated as less than human can be if Black women are not self-defined. She notes, "Now, you know that no woman is a dog or a mule, but if folks keep making you feel that way, if you don't have a mind of your own, you can start letting them tell you what you are" (Gwaltney, 1980:152). Seen in this light, self-definition and self-valuation are not luxuries—they are necessary for Black female survival.

The Interlocking Nature of Oppression

Attention to the interlocking nature of race, gender, and class oppression is a second recurring theme in the works of Black feminists (Beale, 1970; Davis, 1981; Dill, 1983;

Hooks, 1981; Lewis, 1977; Murray, 1970; Steady, 1981).[9] While different socio-historical periods may have increased the saliency of one or another type of oppression, the thesis of the linked nature of oppression has long pervaded Black feminist thought. For example, Ida Wells Barnett and Frances Ellen Watkins Harper, two prominent Black feminists of the late 1800s, both spoke out against the growing violence directed against Black men. They realized that civil rights held little meaning for Black men and women if the right to life itself went unprotected (Loewenberg and Bogin, 1976:26). Black women's absence from organized feminist movements has mistakenly been attributed to a lack of feminist consciousness. In actuality, Black feminists have possessed an ideological commitment to addressing interlocking oppression yet have been excluded from arenas that would have allowed them to do so (Davis, 1981).

As Barbara Smith points out, "the concept of the simultaneity of oppression is still the crux of a Black feminist understanding of political reality and . . . is one of the most significant ideological contributions of Black feminist thought" (1983:xxxii). This should come as no surprise since Black women should be among the first to realize that minimizing one form of oppression, while essential, may still leave them oppressed in other equally dehumanizing ways. Sojourner Truth knew this when she stated, "there is a great stir about colored men getting their rights, and not colored women theirs, you see the colored men will be masters over the women, and it will be just as bad as before" (Loewenberg and Bogin, 1976:238). To use Nancy White's metaphors, the Black woman as "mule" knows that she is perceived to be an animal. In contrast, the white woman as "dog" may be similarly dehumanized, and may think that she is an equal part of the family when, in actuality, she is a well-cared-for pet. The significant factor shaping Truth's and White's clearer view of their own subordination than that of Black men or white women is their experience at the intersection of multiple structures of domination.[10] Both Truth and White are Black, female, and poor. They therefore have a clearer view of oppression than other groups who occupy more contradictory positions vis-a-vis white male power—unlike white women, they have no illusions that their whiteness will negate female subordination, and unlike Black men, they cannot use a questionable appeal to manhood to neutralize the stigma of being Black.

The Black feminist attention to the interlocking nature of oppression is significant for two reasons. First, this viewpoint shifts the entire focus of investigation from one aimed at explicating elements of race or gender or class oppression to one whose goal is

---

[9]Emerging Black feminist research is demonstrating a growing awareness of the importance of including the simultaneity of oppression in studies of Black women. For example, Paula Giddings' (1984) history of Afro-American women emphasizes the role of class in shaping relations between Afro-American and white women, and among Black women themselves. Elizabeth Higginbotham's (1985) study of Black college women examines race and class barriers to Black women's college attendance. Especially noteworthy is the growing attention to Black women's labor market experiences. Studies such as those by Dill (1980), Rollins (1985), Higginbotham (1983), and Mullings (1986b) indicate a new sensitivity to the interactive nature of race, gender, and class. By studying Black women, such studies capture the interaction of race and gender. Moreover, by examining Black women's roles in capitalist development, such work taps the key variable of class.

[10]The thesis that those affected by multiple systems of domination will develop a sharper view of the interlocking nature of oppression is illustrated by the prominence of Black lesbian feminists among Black feminist thinkers. For more on this, see Smith (1983), Lorde (1984), and White (1984:22–24).

to determine what the links are among these systems. The first approach typically prioritizes one form of oppression as being primary, then handles remaining types of oppression as variables within what is seen as the most important system. For example, the efforts to insert race and gender into Marxist theory exemplify this effort. In contrast, the more holistic approach implied in Black feminist thought treats the interaction among multiple systems as the object of study. Rather than adding to existing theories by inserting previously excluded variables, Black feminists aim to develop new theoretical interpretations of the interaction itself.

Black male scholars, white female scholars, and more recently, Black feminists like Bell Hooks, may have identified one critical link among interlocking systems of oppression. These groups have pointed out that certain basic ideas crosscut multiple systems of domination. One such idea is either/or dualistic thinking, claimed by Hooks to be "the central ideological component of all systems of domination in Western society" (1984:29).

While Hooks' claim may be somewhat premature, there is growing scholarly support for her viewpoint.[11] Either/or dualistic thinking, or what I will refer to as the construct of dichotomous oppositional difference, may be a philosophical lynchpin in systems of race, class, and gender oppression. One fundamental characteristic of this construct is the categorization of people, things, and ideas in terms of their difference from one another. For example, the terms in dichotomies such as black/white, male/female, reason/emotion, fact/opinion, and subject/object gain their meaning only in *relation* to their difference from their oppositional counterparts. Another fundamental characteristic of this construct is that difference is not complementary in that the halves of the dichotomy do not enhance each other. Rather, the dichotomous halves are different and inherently opposed to one another. A third and more important characteristic is that these oppositional relationships are intrinsically unstable. Since such dualities rarely represent different but equal relationships, the inherently unstable relationship is resolved by subordinating one half of each pair to the other. Thus, whites rule Blacks, males dominate females, reason is touted as superior to emotion in ascertaining truth, facts supercede opinion in evaluating knowledge, and subjects rule objects. Dichotomous oppositional differences invariably imply relationships of superiority and inferiority, hierarchical relationships that mesh with political economies of domination and subordination.

---

[11]For example, African and Afro-American scholars point to the role dualistic thinking has played in domestic racism (Asante, 1980; Baldwin, 1980; Richards 1980). Feminist scholars note the linkage of duality with conceptualizations of gender in Western cultures (Chodorow, 1978; Keller, 1983; Rosaldo, 1983). Recently, Brittan and Maynard, two British scholars, have suggested that dualistic thinking plays a major role in linking systems of racial oppression with those of sexual oppression. They note that

there is an implicit belief in the duality of culture and nature. Men are the creators and mediators of culture—women are the manifestations of nature. The implication is that men develop culture in order to understand and control the natural world, while women being the embodiment of forces of nature, must be brought under the civilizing control of men . . . This duality of culture and nature . . . is also used to distinguish between so-called higher nations or civilizations, and those deemed to be culturally backward. . . . Non-European peoples are conceived of as being nearer to nature than Europeans. Hence, the justification . . . for slavery and colonialism . . . (1984:193–94).

The oppression experienced by most Black women is shaped by their subordinate status in an array of either/or dualities. Afro-American women have been assigned the inferior half of several dualities, and this placement has been central to their continued domination. For example, the allegedly emotional, passionate nature of Afro-American women has long been used as a rationale for their sexual exploitation. Similarly, denying Black women literacy—then claiming that they lack the facts for sound judgment—illustrates another case of assigning a group inferior status, then using that inferior status as proof of the group's inferiority. Finally, denying Black women agency as subjects and treating them as objectified "others" represents yet another dimension of the power that dichotomous oppositional constructs have in maintaining systems of domination.

While Afro-American women may have a vested interest in recognizing the connections among these dualities that together comprise the construct of dichotomous oppositional difference, that more women have not done so is not surprising. Either/or dualistic thinking is so pervasive that it suppresses other alternatives. As Dill points out, "the choice between identifying as black or female is a product of the patriarchal strategy of divide-and-conquer and the continued importance of class, patriarchal, and racial divisions, perpetuate such choices both within our consciousness and within the concrete realities of our daily lives" (1983:136). In spite of this difficulty, Black women experience oppression in a personal, holistic fashion and emerging Black feminist perspectives appear to be embracing an equally holistic analysis of oppression.

Second, Black feminist attention to the interlocking nature of oppression is significant in that, implicit in this view, is an alternative humanist vision of societal organization. This alternative world view is cogently expressed in the following passage from an 1893 speech delivered by the Black feminist educator, Anna Julia Cooper:

> We take our stand on the solidarity of humanity, the oneness of life, and the unnaturalness and injustice of all special favoritisms, whether of sex, race, country, or condition. . . . The colored woman feels that woman's cause is one and universal; and that . . . not till race, color, sex, and condition are seen as accidents, and not the substance of life; not till the universal title of humanity to life, liberty, and the pursuit of happiness is conceded to be inalienable to all; not till then is woman's lesson taught and woman's cause won—not the white woman's nor the black woman's, nor the red woman's, but the cause of every man and of every woman who has writhed silently under a mighty wrong (Loewenberg and Bogin, 1976:330–31).

I cite the above passage at length because it represents one of the clearest statements of the humanist vision extant in Black feminist thought.[12] Black feminists who see the simultaneity of oppression affecting Black women appear to be more sensitive to how these same oppressive systems affect Afro-American men, people of color, women, and the dominant group itself. Thus, while Black feminist activists may work on behalf of Black women, they rarely project separatist solutions to Black female

---

[12]This humanist vision takes both religious and secular forms. For religious statements, see Andrews' (1986) collection of the autobiographies of three nineteenth-century, Black female evangelical preachers. For a discussion of the humanist tradition in Afro-American religion that has contributed to this dimension of Black feminist thought, see Paris (1985). Much of contemporary Black feminist writing draws on this religious tradition, but reframes the basic vision in secular terms.

oppression. Rather, the vision is one that, like Cooper's, takes its "stand on the solidarity of humanity."

The Importance of Afro-American Women's Culture

A third key theme characterizing Black feminist thought involves efforts to redefine and explain the importance of Black women's culture. In doing so, Black feminists have not only uncovered previously unexplored areas of the Black female experience, but they have also identified concrete areas of social relations where Afro-American women create and pass on self-definitions and self-valuations essential to coping with the simultaneity of oppression they experience.

In contrast to views of culture stressing the unique, ahistorical values of a particular group, Black feminist approaches have placed greater emphasis on the role of historically specific political economies in explaining the endurance of certain cultural themes. The following definition of culture typifies the approach taken by many Black feminists. According to Mullings, culture is composed of

> the symbols and values that create the ideological frame of reference through which people attempt to deal with the circumstances in which they find themselves. Culture . . . is not composed of static, discrete traits moved from one locale to another. It is constantly changing and transformed, as new forms are created out of old ones. Thus culture . . . does not arise out of nothing: it is created and modified by material conditions (1986a:13).

Seen in this light, Black women's culture may help provide the ideological frame of reference—namely, the symbols and values of self-definition and self-valuation—that assist Black women in seeing the circumstances shaping race, class, and gender oppression. Moreover, Mullings' definition of culture suggests that the values which accompany self-definition and self-valuation will have concrete, material expression: they will be present in social institutions like church and family, in creative expression of art, music, and dance, and, if unsuppressed, in patterns of economic and political activity. Finally, this approach to culture stresses its historically concrete nature. While common themes may link Black women's lives, these themes will be experienced differently by Black women of different classes, ages, regions, and sexual preferences as well as by Black women in different historical settings. Thus, there is no monolithic Black women's culture—rather, there are socially-constructed Black women's cultures that collectively form Black women's culture.

The interest in redefining Black women's culture has directed attention to several unexplored areas of the Black female experience. One such area concerns the interpersonal relationships that Black women share with each other. It appears that the notion of sisterhood—generally understood to mean a supportive feeling of loyalty and attachment to other women stemming from a shared feeling of oppression—has been an important part of Black women's culture (Dill, 1983: 132). Two representative works in the emerging tradition of Black feminist research illustrate how this concept of sisterhood, while expressed differently in response to different material conditions, has been a significant feature of Black women's culture. For example, Debra Gray White (1985) documents the ways Black slave women assisted each other in childbirth, cared for each other's children, worked together in sex-segregated work units when pregnant or nursing children, and depended on one another when married to males living on distant farms. White paints a convincing portrait of Black female slave communities where sisterhood was necessary and assumed. Similarly, Gilkes' (1985) work on Black women's traditions in the Sanctified Church suggests that the sisterhood Black women found had tangible psychological and political benefits.[13]

The attention to Black women's culture has stimulated interest in a second type of inter-personal relationship: that shared by Black women with their biological children, the children in their extended families, and with the Black community's children. In reassessing Afro-American motherhood, Black feminist researchers have emphasized the connections between (1) choices available to Black mothers resulting from their placement in historically specific political economies, (2) Black mothers' perceptions of their children's choices as compared to what mothers thought those choices should be, and (3) actual strategies employed by Black mothers both in raising their children and in dealing with institutions that affected their children's lives. For example, Janice Hale (1980) suggests that effective Black mothers are sophisticated mediators between the competing offerings of an oppressive dominant culture and a nurturing Black value-structure. Dill's (1980) study of the childrearing goals of Black domestics stresses the goals the women in her sample had for their children and the strategies these women pursued to help their children go further than they themselves had gone. Gilkes (1980) offers yet another perspective on the power of Black motherhood by observing that many of the Black female political activists in her study became involved in community work through their role as mothers. What typically began as work on behalf of their own children evolved into work on behalf of the community's children.

Another dimension of Black women's culture that has generated considerable interest among Black feminists is the role of creative expression in shaping and sustaining Black women's self-definitions and self-valuations. In addition to documenting Black women's achievements as writers, dancers, musicians, artists, and actresses, the emerging literature also investigates why creative expression has been such an important element of Black women's culture.[14] Alice Walker's (1974) classic essay, "In Search of Our Mothers' Gardens," explains the necessity of Black women's creativity, even if in very limited spheres, in resisting objectification and asserting Black women's subjectivity as fully human beings. Illustrating Walker's thesis, Willie Mae Ford Smith, a prominent gospel singer featured in the 1984 documentary, "Say Amen Somebody," describes what singing means to her. She notes, "it's just a feeling within. You can't

---

[13]During a period when Black women were widely devalued by the dominant culture, Sanctified Church members addressed each other as "Saints." During the early 1900s, when basic literacy was an illusive goal for many Blacks, Black women in the Church not only stressed education as a key component of a sanctified life, but supported each other's efforts at educational excellence. In addition to these psychological supports, the Church provided Afro-American women with genuine opportunities for influence, leadership, and political clout. The important thing to remember here is that the Church was not an abstract, bureaucratic structure that ministered to Black women. Rather, the Church was a predominantly female community of individuals in which women had prominent spheres of influence.

[14]Since much Black feminist thought is contained in the works of Black women writers, literary criticism by Black feminist critics provides an especially fertile source of Black women's ideas. See Tate (1983) and Christian (1985).

help yourself. . . . I feel like I can fly away. I forget I'm in the world sometimes. I just want to take off." For Mother Smith, her creativity is a sphere of freedom, one that helps her cope with and transcend daily life.

This third key theme in Black feminist thought—the focus on Black women's culture—is significant for three reasons. First, the data from Black women's culture suggest that the relationship between oppressed people's consciousness of oppression and the actions they take in dealing with oppressive structures may be far more complex than that suggested by existing social theory. Conventional social science continues to assume a fit between consciousness and activity; hence, accurate measures of human behavior are thought to produce accurate portraits of human consciousness of self and social structure (Westkott, 1979). In contrast, Black women's experiences suggest that Black women may overtly conform to the societal roles laid out for them, yet covertly oppose these roles in numerous spheres, an opposition shaped by the consciousness of being on the bottom. Black women's activities in families, churches, community institutions, and creative expression may represent more than an effort to mitigate pressures stemming from oppression. Rather, the Black female ideological frame of reference that Black women acquire through sisterhood, motherhood, and creative expression may serve the added purpose of shaping a Black female consciousness about the workings of oppression. Moreover, this consciousness is shaped not only through abstract, rational reflection, but also is developed through concrete rational action. For example, while Black mothers may develop consciousness through talking with and listening to their children, they may also shape consciousness by how they live their lives, the actions they take on behalf of their children. That these activities have been obscured from traditional social scientists should come as no surprise. Oppressed peoples may maintain hidden consciousness and may not reveal their true selves for reasons of self-protection.[15]

A second reason that the focus on Black women's culture is significant is that it points to the problematic nature of existing conceptualizations of the term "activism." While Black women's reality cannot be understood without attention to the interlocking structures of oppression that limit Black women's lives, Afro-American women's experiences suggest that possibilities for activism exist even within such multiple structures of domination. Such activism can take several forms. For Black women under extremely harsh conditions, the private decision to reject external definitions of Afro-American womanhood may itself be a form of activism. If Black women find themselves in settings where total conformity is expected, and where traditional forms of activism such as voting, participating in collective movements, and officeholding are impossible, then the individual women who in their consciousness choose to be self-defined and self-evaluating are, in fact, activists. They are retaining a grip over their definition as subjects, as full humans, and rejecting definitions of themselves as the objectified "other." For example, while Black slave women were forced to conform to the specific oppression facing them, they may have had very different assessments of themselves and slavery than did the slave-

---

[15]Audre Lorde (1984:114) describes this conscious hiding of one's self as follows: "in order to survive, those of us for whom oppression is as American as apple pie have always had to be watchers, to become familiar with the language and manners of the oppressor, even sometimes adopting them for some illusion of protection."

owners. In this sense, consciousness can be viewed as one potential sphere of freedom, one that may exist simultaneously with unfree, allegedly conforming behavior (Westkott, 1979). Moreover, if Black women simultaneously use all resources available to them—their roles as mothers, their participation in churches, their support of one another in Black female networks, their creative expression—to be self-defined and self-valuating and to encourage others to reject objectification, then Black women's everyday behavior itself is a form of activism. People who view themselves as fully human, as subjects, become activists, no matter how limited the sphere of their activism may be. By returning subjectivity to Black women, Black feminists return activism as well.

A third reason that the focus on Black women's culture is significant is that an analytical model exploring the relationship between oppression, consciousness, and activism is implicit in the way Black feminists have studied Black women's culture. With the exception of Dill (1983), few scholars have deliberately set out to develop such a model. However, the type of work done suggests that an implicit model paralleling that proposed by Mullings (1986a) has influenced Black feminist research.

Several features pervade emerging Black feminist approaches. First, researchers stress the interdependent relationship between the interlocking oppression that has shaped Black women's choices and Black women's actions in the context of those choices. Black feminist researchers rarely describe Black women's behavior without attention to the opportunity structures shaping their subjects' lives (Higginbotham, 1985; Ladner, 1971; Myers, 1980). Second, the question of whether oppressive structures and limited choices stimulate Black women's behavior characterized by apathy and alienation, or behavior demonstrating subjectivity and activism is seen as ultimately dependent on Black women's perceptions of their choices. In other words, Black women's consciousness—their analytical, emotional, and ethical perspective of themselves and their place in society—becomes a critical part of the relationship between the working of oppression and Black women's actions. Finally, this relationship between oppression, consciousness, and action can be seen as a dialectical one. In this model, oppressive structures create patterns of choices which are perceived in varying ways by Black women. Depending on their consciousness of themselves and their relationship to these choices, Black women may or may not develop Black-female spheres of influence where they develop and validate what will be appropriate, Black-female sanctioned responses to oppression. Black women's activism in constructing Black-female spheres of influence may, in turn, affect their perceptions of the political and economic choices offered to them by oppressive structures, influence actions actually taken, and ultimately, alter the nature of oppression they experience.

THE SOCIOLOGICAL SIGNIFICANCE OF BLACK FEMINIST THOUGHT

Taken together, the three key themes in Black feminist thought—the meaning of self-definition and self-valuation, the interlocking nature of oppression, and the importance of redefining culture—have made significant contributions to the task of clarifying a Black women's standpoint of and for Black women. While this accomplishment is important in and of itself, Black feminist thought has potential contributions to make to the diverse disciplines housing its practitioners.

The sociological significance of Black feminist thought lies in two areas. First, the content of Black women's ideas has been influenced by and contributes to on-going dialogues in a variety of sociological specialties. While this area merits attention, it is not my primary concern in this section. Instead, I investigate a second area of sociological significance: the process by which these specific ideas were produced by this specific group of individuals. In other words, I examine the influence of Black women's outsider within status in academia on the actual thought produced. Thus far, I have proceeded on the assumption that it is impossible to separate the structure and thematic content of thought. In this section, I spell out exactly what form the relationship between the three key themes in Black feminist thought and Black women's outsider within status might take for women scholars generally, with special attention to Black female sociologists.

First, I briefly summarize the role sociological paradigms play in shaping the facts and theories used by sociologists. Second, I explain how Black women's outsider within status might encourage Black women to have a distinctive standpoint vis-a-vis sociology's paradigmatic facts and theories. I argue that the thematic content of Black feminist thought described above represents elements of just such a standpoint and give examples of how the combination of sociology's paradigms and Black women's outsider within status as sociologists directed their attention to specific areas of sociological inquiry.

Two Elements of Sociological Paradigms

Kuhn defines a paradigm as the "entire constellation of beliefs, values, techniques, and so on shared by the members of a given community" (1962:175). As such, a paradigm consists of two fundamental elements: the thought itself and its producers and practitioners.[16] In this sense, the discipline of sociology is itself a paradigm—it consists of a system of knowledge shared by sociologists—and simultaneously consists of a plurality of paradigms (e.g., functionalism, Marxist sociology, feminist sociology, existential sociology), each produced by its own practitioners.

Two dimensions of thought itself are of special interest to this discussion. First, systems of knowledge are never complete. Rather, they represent guidelines for "thinking as usual." Kuhn (1962) refers to these guidelines as "maps," while Schutz (1944) describes them as "recipes." As Schutz points out, while "thinking as usual" is actually only partially organized and partially clear, and may contain contradictions, to its practitioners it provides sufficient coherence, clarity, and consistency. Second, while thought itself contains diverse elements, I will focus mainly on the important fact/theory relationship. As Kuhn (1962) suggests, facts or observations become meaningful in the context of theories or interpretations of those observations. Conversely, theories "fit the facts" by transforming previously accessible observations into facts. According to Mulkay, "observation is not separate from interpretation; rather these are two facets of a single process" (1979:49).

---

[16]In this sense, sociology is a special case of the more generalized process discussed by Mannheim (1936). Also, see Berman (1981) for a discussion of Western thought as a paradigm, Mulkay (1979) for a sociology of knowledge analysis of the natural sciences, and Berger and Luckmann (1966) for a generalized discussion of how everyday knowledge is socially constructed.

Several dimensions of the second element of sociological paradigms—the community formed by a paradigm's practitioners—are of special interest to this discussion. First, group insiders have similar worldviews, acquired through similar educational and professional training, that separate them from everyone else. Insider worldviews may be especially alike if group members have similar social class, gender, and racial backgrounds. Schutz describes the insider worldview as the "cultural pattern of group life"—namely, all the values and behaviors which characterize the social group at a given moment in its history. In brief, insiders have undergone similar experiences, possess a common history, and share taken-for-granted knowledge that characterizes "thinking as usual."

A second dimension of the community of practitioners involves the process of becoming an insider. How does one know when an individual is really an insider and not an outsider in disguise? Merton suggests that socialization into the life of a group is a lengthy process of being immersed in group life, because only then can "one understand the fine-grained meanings of behavior, feeling, and values . . . and decipher the unwritten grammar of conduct and nuances of cultural idiom" (1972:15). The process is analogous to immersion in a foreign culture in order to learn its ways and its language (Merton, 1972; Schutz, 1944). One becomes an insider by translating a theory or worldview into one's own language until, one day, the individual converts to thinking and acting according to that worldview.

A final dimension of the community of practitioners concerns the process of remaining an insider. A sociologist typically does this by furthering the discipline in ways described as appropriate by sociology generally, and by areas of specialization particularly. Normal foci for scientific sociological investigation include: (1) determining significant facts; (2) matching facts with existing theoretical interpretations to "test" the paradigm's ability to predict facts; and (3) resolving ambiguities in the paradigm itself by articulating and clarifying theory (Kuhn, 1962).

Black Women and the Outsider Within Status

Black women may encounter much less of a fit between their personal and cultural experiences and both elements of sociological paradigms than that facing other sociologists. On the one hand, Black women who undergo sociology's lengthy socialization process, who immerse themselves in the cultural pattern of sociology's group life, certainly wish to acquire the insider skills of thinking in and acting according to a sociological worldview. But on the other hand, Black women's experienced realities, both prior to contact and after initiation, may provide them with "special perspectives and insights . . . available to that category of outsiders who have been systematically frustrated by the social system" (Merton, 1972:29). In brief, their outsider allegiances may militate against their choosing full insider status, and they may be more apt to remain outsiders within.[17]

---

[17]Jackson (1974) reports that 21 of the 145 Black sociologists receiving doctoral degrees between 1945 and 1972 were women. Kulis et al. (1986) report that Blacks comprised 5.7 percent of all sociology faculties in 1984. These data suggest that historically, Black females have not been sociological insiders, and currently, Black women as a group comprise a small portion of sociologists in the United States.

In essence, to become sociological insiders, Black women must assimilate a standpoint that is quite different than their own. White males have long been the dominant group in sociology, and the sociological worldview understandably reflects the concerns of this group of practitioners. As Merton observes, "white male insiderism in American sociology during the past generations has largely been of the tacit or de facto . . . variety. It has simply taken the form of patterned expectations about the appropriate . . . problems for investigation" (1972:12). In contrast, a good deal of the Black female experience has been spent coping with, avoiding, subverting, and challenging the workings of this same white male insiderism. It should come as no surprise that Black women's efforts in dealing with the effects of interlocking systems of oppression might produce a standpoint quite distinct from, and in many ways opposed to, that of white male insiders.

Seen from this perspective, Black women's socialization into sociology represents a more intense case of the normal challenges facing sociology graduate students and junior professionals in the discipline. Black women become, to use Simmel's (1921) and Schutz's terminology, penultimate "strangers."

> The stranger . . . does not share the basic assumptions of the group. He becomes essentially the man who has to place in question nearly everything that seems to be unquestionable to the members of the approached group. . . . To him the cultural patterns of the approached group do not have the authority of a tested system of recipes . . . because he does not partake in the vivid historical tradition by which it has been formed (Schutz, 1944:502).

Like everyone else, Black women may see sociological "thinking as usual" as partially organized, partially clear, and contradictory, and may question these existing recipes. However, for them, this questioning process may be more acute, for the material that they encounter—white male insider-influenced observations and interpretations about human society—places white male subjectivity at the center of analysis and assigns Afro-American womanhood a position on the margins.

In spite of a lengthy socialization process, it may also be more difficult for Afro-American women to experience conversion and begin totally to think in and act according to a sociological worldview. Indeed, since past generations of white male insiderism has shaped a sociological worldview reflecting this group's concerns, it may be self-destructive for Black women to embrace that worldview. For example, Black women would have to accept certain fundamental and self-devaluing assumptions: (1) white males are more worthy of study because they are more fully human than everyone else; and (2) dichotomous oppositional thinking is natural and normal. More importantly, Black women would have to act in accordance with their place in a white male worldview. This involves accepting one's own subordination or regretting the accident of not being born white and male. In short, it may be extremely difficult for Black women to accept a worldview predicated upon Black female inferiority.

Remaining in sociology by doing normal scientific investigation may also be less complicated for traditional sociologists than for Afro-American women. Unlike Black women, learners from backgrounds where the insider information and experiences of sociology are more familiar may be less likely to see the taken-for-granted assumptions of sociology and may be more prone to apply their creativity to "normal science." In other words, the transition from student status to that of a practitioner engaged in finding significant facts that sociological paradigms deem important, matching facts with existing theories, and furthering paradigmatic development itself may proceed more smoothly for white middle-class males than for working-class Black females. The latter group is much more inclined to be struck by the mismatch of its own experiences and the paradigms of sociology itself. Moreover, those Black women with a strong foundation in Black women's culture (e.g., those that recognize the value of self-definition and self-valuation, and that have a concrete understanding of sisterhood and motherhood) may be more apt to take a critical posture toward the entire sociological enterprise. In brief, where traditional sociologists may see sociology as "normal" and define their role as furthering knowledge about a normal world with taken-for-granted assumptions, outsiders within are liable to see anomalies.

The types of anomalies typically seen by Black female academicians grow directly from Black women's outsider within status and appear central in shaping the direction Black feminist thought has taken thus far. Two types of anomalies are characteristically noted by Black female scholars. First, Black female sociologists typically report the omission of facts or observations about Afro-American women in the sociological paradigms they encounter. As Scott points out, "from reading the literature, one might easily develop the impression that Black women have never played any role in this society" (1982:85). Where white males may take it as perfectly normal to generalize findings from studies of white males to other groups, Black women are more likely to see such a practice as problematic, as an anomaly. Similarly, when white feminists produce generalizations about "women," Black feminists routinely ask "which women do you mean?" In the same way that Rollins (1985) felt invisible in her employer's kitchen, Afro-American female scholars are repeatedly struck by their own invisibility, both as full human subjects included in sociological facts and observations, and as practitioners in the discipline itself. It should come as no surprise that much of Black feminist thought aims to counter this invisibility by presenting sociological analyses of Black women as fully human subjects. For example, the growing research describing Black women's historical and contemporary behavior as mothers, community workers, church leaders, teachers, and employed workers, and Black women's ideas about themselves and their opportunities, reflects an effort to respond to the omission of facts about Afro-American women.

A second type of anomaly typically noted by Black female scholars concerns distortions of facts and observations about Black women. Afro-American women in academia are frequently struck by the difference between their own experiences and sociological descriptions of the same phenomena. For example, while Black women have and are themselves mothers, they encounter distorted versions of themselves and their mothers under the mantle of the Black matriarchy thesis. Similarly, for those Black women who confront racial and sexual discrimination and know that their mothers and grandmothers certainly did, explanations of Black women's poverty that stress low achievement motivation and the lack of Black female "human capital" are less likely to ring true. The response to these perceived distortions has been one of redefining distorted images—for example, debunking the Sapphire and Mammy myths.

Since facts or observations become meaningful in the context of a theory, this emphasis on producing accurate descriptions of Black women's lives has also refocused attention on major omissions and distortions in sociological theories themselves. By drawing on the strengths of sociology's plurality of subdisciplines, yet taking a critical posture toward them, the work of Black feminist scholars taps some fundamental questions facing all sociologists. One such question concerns the fundamental elements of society that should be studied. Black feminist researchers' response has been to move Black women's voices to the center of the analysis, to study people, and by doing so, to reaffirm human subjectivity and intentionality. They point to the dangers of omission and distortion that can occur if sociological concepts are studied at the expense of human subjectivity. For example, there is a distinct difference between conducting a statistical analysis of Black women's work, where Afro-American women are studied as a reconstituted amalgam of researcher-defined variables (e.g., race, sex, years of education, and father's occupation), and examining Black women's self-definitions and self-valuations of themselves as workers in oppressive jobs. While both approaches can further sociological knowledge about the concept of work, the former runs the risk of objectifying Black women, of reproducing constructs of dichotomous oppositional difference, and of producing distorted findings about the nature of work itself.

A second question facing sociologists concerns the adequacy of current interpretations of key sociological concepts. For example, few sociologists would question that work and family are two fundamental concepts for sociology. However, bringing Black feminist thought into the center of conceptual analysis raises issues of how comprehensive current sociological interpretations of these two concepts really are. For example, labor theories that relegate Afro-American women's work experiences to the fringe of analysis miss the critical theme of the interlocking nature of Black women as female workers (e.g., Black women's unpaid domestic labor) and Black women as racially-oppressed workers (e.g., Black women's unpaid slave labor and exploited wage labor). Examining the extreme case offered by Afro-American women's unpaid and paid work experiences raises questions about the adequacy of generalizations about work itself. For example, Black feminists' emphasis on the simultaneity of oppression redefines the economic system itself as problematic. From this perspective, all generalizations about the normal workings of labor markets, organizational structure, occupational mobility, and income differences that do not explicitly see oppression as problematic become suspect. In short, Black feminists suggest that all generalizations about groups of employed and unemployed workers (e.g., managers, welfare mothers, union members, secretaries, Black teenagers) that do not account for interlocking structures of group placement and oppression in an economy as simply less complete than those that do.

Similarly, sociological generalizations about families that do not account for Black women's experience will fail to see how the public/private split shaping household composition varies across social and class groupings, how racial/ethnic family members are differentially integrated into wage labor, and how families alter their household structure in response to changing political economies (e.g., adding more people and becoming extended, fragmenting and becoming female-headed, and migrating to locate better opportunities). Black women's family experiences represent a clear case of the workings of race, gender, and class oppression in shaping family life. Bringing undistorted observations of Afro-American women's family experiences into the center of analysis again raises the question of how other families are affected by these same forces.

While Black women who stand outside academia may be familiar with omissions and distortions of the Black female experience, as outsiders to sociology, they lack legitimated professional authority to challenge the sociological anomalies. Similarly, traditional sociological insiders, whether white males or their nonwhite and/or female disciples, are certainly in no position to notice the specific anomalies apparent to Afro-American women, because these same sociological insiders produced them. In contrast, those Black women who remain rooted in their own experiences as Black women—and who master sociological paradigms yet retain a critical posture toward them—are in a better position to bring a special perspective not only to the study of Black women, but to some of the fundamental issues facing sociology itself.

TOWARD SYNTHESIS: OUTSIDERS WITHIN SOCIOLOGY

Black women are not the only outsiders within sociology. As an extreme case of outsiders moving into a community that historically excluded them, Black women's experiences highlight the tension experienced by any group of less powerful outsiders encountering the paradigmatic thought of a more powerful insider community. In this sense, a variety of individuals can learn from Black women's experiences as outsiders within: Black men, working-class individuals, white women, other people of color, religious and sexual minorities, and all individuals who, while from social strata that provided them with the benefits of white male insiderism, have never felt comfortable with its taken-for-granted assumptions.

Outsider within status is bound to generate tension, for people who become outsiders within are forever changed by their new status. Learning the subject matter of sociology stimulates a reexamination of one's own personal and cultural experiences; and, yet, these same experiences paradoxically help to illuminate sociology's anomalies. Outsiders within occupy a special place—they become different people, and their difference sensitizes them to patterns that may be more difficult for established sociological insiders to see. Some outsiders within try to resolve the tension generated by their new status by leaving sociology and remaining sociological outsiders. Others choose to suppress their difference by striving to become bonafide, "thinking as usual" sociological insiders. Both choices rob sociology of diversity and ultimately weaken the discipline.

A third alternative is to conserve the creative tension of outsider within status by encouraging and institutionalizing outsider within ways of seeing. This alternative has merit not only for actual outsiders within, but also for other sociologists as well. The approach suggested by the experiences of outsiders within is one where intellectuals learn to trust their own personal and cultural biographies as significant sources of knowledge. In contrast to approaches that require submerging these dimensions of self in the process of becoming an allegedly unbiased, objective social scientist, outsiders within bring these ways of knowing back into the research process. At its best, outsider within status seems to offer its occupants a powerful balance between the strengths of their sociological training and the offerings of their personal and cultural experiences. Neither is subordinated to the other. Rather, experienced reality is used as a valid source of knowledge for critiquing sociological facts and theories, while sociological thought offers new ways of seeing that experienced reality.

What many Black feminists appear to be doing is embracing the creative potential of their outsider within status and using it wisely. In doing so, they move themselves and their disciplines closer to the humanist vision implicit in their work—namely, the freedom both to be different and part of the solidarity of humanity.

REFERENCES

Andrews, William L. (ed.), 1986 Sisters of the Spirit. Bloomington, IN: Indiana University Press.

Asante, Molefi Kete, 1980 "International/intercultural relations." Pp. 43–58 in Molefi Kete Asante and Abdulai S. Vandi (eds.), Contemporary Black Thought, Beverly Hills, CA: Sage.

Baldwin, Joseph A., 1980 "The psychology of oppression." Pp. 95–110 in Molefi Kete Asante and Abdulai S. Vandi (eds.), Contemporary Black Thought. Beverly Hills, CA: Sage.

Beale, Frances, 1970 "Double jeopardy: to be Black and female." Pp. 90–110 in Toni Cade (ed.), The Black Woman. New York: Signet.

Berger, Peter L. and Thomas Luckmann, 1966 The Social Construction of Reality. New York: Doubleday.

Berman, Morris, 1981 The Reenchantment of the World, Bantam.

Brittan, Arthur and Mary Maynard, 1984 Sexism, Racism and Oppression. Basil Blackwell.

Chodorow, Nancy, 1978 The Reproduction of Mothering. Berkeley, CA: University of California Press.

Christian, Barbara, 1985 Black Feminist Criticism: Perspectives on Black Women Writers. New York: Pergamon.

Davis, Angela, 1981 Women, Race and Class. New York: Random House.

Dill, Bonnie Thornton, 1980 " 'The means to put my children through': child-rearing goals and strategies among Black female domestic servants." Pp. 107–23 in LaFrances Rodgers-Rose (ed.), The Black Woman, Beverly Hills, CA: Sage, 1983 "Race, class, and gender: prospects for an all-inclusive sisterhood." Feminist Studies 9:131–50.

Giddings, Paula, 1984 When and Where I Enter . . . The Impact of Black Women on Race and Sex in America. New York: William Morrow.

Gilkes, Cheryl Townsend, 1980 " 'Holding back the ocean with a broom': Black women and community work." Pp. 217–31 in LaFrances Rodgers-Rose (ed.), The Black Woman. Beverly Hills, CA: Sage. 1981 "From slavery to social welfare: racism and the control of Black women." Pp. 288–300 in Amy Smerdlow and Helen Lessinger (eds.), Class, Race, and Sex: The Dynamics of Control. Boston: G.K. Hall. 1985 " 'Together and in harness': women's traditions in the sanctified church." Signs 10:678–99.

Gwaltney, John Langston, 1980 Drylongso, a Self-portrait of Black America. New York: Vintage.

Hale, Janice, 1980 "The Black woman and child rearing." Pp. 79–88 in LaFrances Rodgers-Rose (ed.), The Black Woman. Beverly Hills, CA: Sage.

Hartsock, Nancy M., 1983 "The feminist standpoint: developing the ground for a specifically feminist historical materialism," Pp. 283–310 in Sandra Harding and Merrill Hintikka (eds.), Discovering Reality. Boston: D. Reidel.

Higginbotham, Elizabeth, 1982 "Two representative issues in contemporary sociological work on Black women." Pp. 93–98 in Gloria T. Hull, Patricia Bell Scott, and Barbara Smith (eds.), But Some of Us Are Brave. Old Westbury, NY: Feminist Press. 1983 "Laid bare by the system: work and survival for Black and Hispanic women." Pp. 200–15 in Amy Smerdlow and Helen Lessinger (eds.), Class, Race, and Sex: The Dynamics of Control. Boston: G.K. Hall. 1985 "Race and class barriers to Black women's college attendance." Journal of Ethnic Studies 13:89–107.

Hooks, Bell, 1981 Ain't I a Woman: Black Women and Feminism. Boston: South End Press. 1984 From Margin to Center. Boston: South End Press.

Jackson, Jacquelyn, 1974 "Black female sociologists." Pp. 267–98 in James E. Blackwell and Morris Janowitz (eds.), Black Sociologists. Chicago: University of Chicago Press.

Keller, Evelyn Fox, 1983 "Gender and science." Pp. 187–206 in Sandra Harding and Merrill Hintikka (eds.), Discovering Reality. Boston: D. Reidel.

King, Mae, 1973 "The politics of sexual stereotypes." Black Scholar 4:12–23.

Kuhn, Thomas S, 1970 The Structure of Scientific Revolutions. 2d Edition. Chicago: [1962] University of Chicago Press.

Kulis, Stephen, Karen A. Miller, Morris Axelrod, and Leonard Gordon, 1986 "Minority representation of U.S. departments," ASA Footnotes 14:3.

Ladner, Joyce, 1971 Tomorrow's Tomorrow: The Black Woman. Garden City, NY: Anchor.

Lee, Alfred McClung, 1973 Toward Humanist Sociology. Englewood Cliffs, NJ: Prentice-Hall.

Lewis, Diane, 1977 "A response to inequality: Black women, racism and sexism." Signs 3:339–61.

Loewenberg, Bert James and Ruth Bogin (eds.) 1976 Black Women in Nineteenth-century Life. University Park, PA: Pennsylvania State University.

Lorde, Audre, 1984 Sister Outsider. Trumansburg, NY: The Crossing Press.

Mannheim, Karl, 1954 Ideology and Utopia: An Introduction to the Sociology of [1936] Knowledge. New York: Harcourt, Brace & Co.

Merton, Robert K., 1972 "Insiders and outsiders: a chapter in the sociology of knowledge." American Journal of Sociology 78:9–47.

Mulkay, Michael, 1979 Science and the Sociology of Knowledge. Boston: George Allen & Unwin.

Mullings, Leith, 1986a "Anthropological perspectives on the Afro-American family." American Journal of Social Psychiatry 6:11–16. 1986b "Uneven development: class, race and gender in the United States before 1900." Pp. 41–57 in Eleanor Leacock and Helen Safa (eds.), Women's Work, Development and the Division of Labor by Gender. South Hadley, MA: Bergin & Garvey.

Murray, Pauli, 1970 "The liberation of Black women." Pp. 87–102 in Mary Lou Thompson (ed.), Voices of the New Feminism. Boston: Beacon Press.

Myers, Lena Wright, 1980 Black Women: Do They Cope Better? Englewood Cliffs, NJ: Prentice-Hall.

Paris, Peter J., 1985 The Social Teaching of the Black Churches. Philadelphia: Fortress Press.

Park, Robert E., 1950 Race and Culture. Glencoe, IL: Free Press.

Rich, Adrienne, 1976 Of Woman Born: Motherhood as Experience and Institution. New York: Norton.

Richards, Dona, 1980 "European mythology; the ideology of 'progress'." Pp. 59–79 in Molefi Kete Asante and Abdulai S. Vandi (eds.), Contemporary Black Thought. Beverly Hills, CA: Sage.

Rollins, Judith, 1985 Between Women, Domestics and Their Employers. Philadelphia: Temple University Press.

Rosaldo, Michelle Z, 1983 "Moral/analytic dilemmas posed by the intersection of feminism and social science," Pp. 76–96 in Norma Hann, Robert N. Bellah, Paul Rabinow, and

William Sullivan (eds.), Social Science as Moral Inquiry. New York: Columbia University Press.

Schutz, Alfred, 1944 "The stranger: an essay in social psychology." American Journal of Sociology 49:499–507.

Scott, Patricia Bell, 1982 "Debunking sapphire: toward a non-racist and non-sexist social science." Pp. 85–92 in Gloria T. Hull, Patricia Bell Scott, and Barbara Smith (eds.), But Some of Us Are Brave. Old Westbury, NY: Feminist Press.

Simmel, Georg, 1921 "The sociological significance of the 'stranger'." Pp. 322–27 in Robert E. Park and Ernest W. Burgess (eds.), Introduction to the Science of Sociology. Chicago: University of Chicago Press.

Smith, Barbara (ed.), 1983 Home Girls: A Black Feminist Anthology. New York: Kitchen Table, Women of Color Press.

Steady, Filomina Chioma, 1981 "The Black woman cross-culturally: an overview." Pp. 7–42 in Filomina Chioma Steady (ed.), The Black Woman Cross-culturally. Cambridge, MA: Schenkman.

Tate, Claudia, 1983 Black Women Writers at Work. New York: Continuum.

Walker, Alice, 1974 "In search of our mothers' gardens." Pp. 231–43 in, In Search of Our Mothers' Gardens. New York: Harcourt Brace Javanovich.

Walker, Alice (ed.), 1979 I Love Myself When I Am Laughing . . . A Zora Neal Hurston Reader. Westbury, NY: Feminist Press.

Westkott, Marcia, 1979 "Feminist criticism of the social sciences." Harvard Educational Review 49:422–30.

White, Deborah Gray, 1985 Art'n't I a Woman? Female Slaves in the Plantation South. New York: W.W. Norton.

White, E. Frances, 1984 "Listening to the voices of Black feminism." Radical America 18:7–25.

Feminist Theory: A Radical Agenda

bell hooks

Any constructive examination of feminist scholarship and its political implication must necessarily focus on feminist theory. In these times of grave political and economic crisis, as we are subjected to more overt attacks by anti-feminists who either deny the validity of feminist liberation struggle or simplify the nature of that struggle, we must be actively engaged in ongoing critical dialogue about the future of feminist movement, about the direction and shape of feminist theory.

Without liberatory feminist theory, there can be no effective feminist movement. To fulfill this purpose, feminist theory must provide a structure of analysis and thought that synthesizes that which is most visionary in feminist thinking, talk, and discourse—those models of change that emerge from our understanding of sexism and sexist oppression in everyday life, coupled with strategies of resistance that effectively eradicate domination and engage us fully in a liberatory praxis.

Given this framework, feminist theory should necessarily be directed to masses of women and men in our society, educating us collectively for critical consciousness so that we can explore and understand better the workings of sexism and sexist oppression, the political basis of feminist critique, and be better able to work out strategies for resistance. Currently in the United States, the primary site for the production of feminist theory is the corporate university, and workers in this arena are primarily university educated scholars, usually from privileged race and class backgrounds with a few exceptions. Since the work of feminist theorists necessitates fundamental questioning and critiquing of the ideological structures of the prevailing white-supremacist, patriarchal hegemony, it is fitting that the university be identified as a useful site for radical political work, for feminist movement. It must be remembered that it is not and should not be the only site of such work. Academic women and men engaged in the production of feminist theory must be responsible for setting up ways to disseminate feminist thought that not only transcend the boundaries of the university setting, but that of the printed page as well. It is also our responsibility to promote and encourage the development of feminist theory by folks who are not academics. As long as the university remains "the" central site for the development of feminist scholarship, it will be necessary for us to examine the ways in which our work can be and is undermined.

Major problems with the production and dissemination of feminist theory are rooted in the various contradictions we confront within university settings. Increasingly, only one type of theory is seen as valuable—that which is Euro-centric, linguistically convoluted, and rooted in Western white male sexist and racially biased philosophical frameworks. Here I want to be clear that my criticism is not that feminist theorists focus on such work but that such work is increasingly seen as the only theory that has meaning and significance. This is problematic. Rather than expanding our notions of theory to include types of theory that can be produced in many different writing styles (hopefully we will even produce theory that begins with the experiential before it enters the printed stage), the vision of what theory is becomes a narrow, constricting concept. Rather than breaking down structures of domination, such theory is often employed to promote an academic elitism which embraces traditional structures of domination. Academics who produce theory along these lines often see themselves as superior to those who do not. Oppressive hierarchy is thus reinforced and maintained. Feminist theory is rapidly becoming another sphere of academic elitism, wherein work that is linguistically convoluted, which draws on other such works, is deemed more intellectually sophisticated, in fact is deemed more theoretical (since the stereotype of theory is that it is synonymous with that which is difficult to comprehend, linguistically convoluted) than work which is more accessible. Each time this happens, the radical, subversive potential of feminist scholarship and feminist theory in particular is undermined.

When Audre Lorde made that much quoted yet often misunderstood cautionary statement warning us that "the master's tools will never dismantle the master's house," she was urging us to remember that we must engage in a process of visionary thinking that transcends the ways of knowing privileged by the oppressive powerful if we are to truly make revolutionary change. She was, in the deep structure of this statement, reminding us that it is easy for women and any exploited or oppressed group to become complicit in structures of domination, using power in ways that reinforce rather than challenge or change. As institutional structures impose values, modes of thought, ways of being on our consciousness, those of us who work in academic settings often unwittingly become engaged in the production of a feminist theory that aims to create a new sphere of theoretical elitism. Feminist scholars who do work that is not considered theoretical or intellectually rigorous are excluded from this arena of privileged bonding. This seriously undermines feminist movement. It means that we not only lose sight of the need to produce feminist theory that is directly related to the concrete lives of women and men who are most affected by sexist oppression, but that we become engaged in an unproductive and unnecessary power struggle which deflects our critical energies and defeats our purpose.

Production and dissemination of feminist theory in forms that alienate, that cannot be understood, has promoted the continued growth of feminist anti-intellectualism and intensified the antagonism toward theory that has been pervasive throughout contemporary feminist movement. Early on, feminist educators like Charlotte Bunch emphasized the need for feminist education that would seek to alter the anti-theoretical impulse many women have learned from patriarchal conditioning. When that feminist theory deemed most valuable is articulated in a form that does not allow effective communication of ideas, it reinforces the fear, especially on the part of the exploited and oppressed, that the intent of theorizing is not to liberate but to mystify. Anti-theoretical backlash tends to privilege concrete actions and experiential resistance to sexism, however narrowly focussed their impact.

As long as university settings are the central site for the production of theory and academics are simultaneously engaged in a competitive work arena that supports and perpetuates all forms of domination, feminist theorists will need to be conscientious about not supporting monolithic notions of theory. We will need to continually assert the need for multiple theories emerging from diverse perspectives in a variety of styles. Often we simply passively accept this false dichotomy between the so-called "theoretical" and that writing which appears to be more directly related to the experiential.

In many feminist theory classes, this problem is addressed by including work that is taken to represent "real life" experience or fictional portrayals of concrete reality along with work that is deemed highly theoretical. Often such attempts reinforce racism and elitism by identifying writing by working-class women and women of color as "experiential" while the writing of white women represents "theory." This past year, I saw a Women's Studies feminist theory course syllabus in which the only work by a woman of color and the only non-theoretical work was Alice Walker's novel, *The Color Purple*. Another course had a required list that included material by white women Nancy Hartsock, Zillah Eisenstein, Julia Kristeva, Alice Jardine, and then *The Color Purple*. Often novels or confessional autobiographical writings are used to mediate the tension between academic writing, theory, and the experiential. This seems to be especially the case when the issue is inclusion of works by women of color in feminist theory courses. Much of the little theoretical work done by women of color is not readily accessible—yet it can be found.

Anti-intellectual biases within feminist movement directly effect the extent to which women of color feel compelled to produce feminist theory. Many of us come from class backgrounds where intellectual activity and writing are seen as non-valuable work so we are already working to overcome this obstacle. It is profoundly disturbing to see how little feminist theory is being written by black women and other women of color. The paucity of material is not simply linked to absence of motivation; it is related to the privileging of material within feminist circles by women of color that is not only not theoretical but in some cases anti-theoretical. Why should women of color work to produce feminist theory that is likely to be ignored or devalued? How many women of color teach courses in feminist theory? Though I have done theoretical writing, I am much more likely to be asked to teach a course focussing on women and race than on theory. In those university settings where I have talked with white women who have higher rank about my desire to teach a course on feminist theory, the response is always that it is an area which is being covered already. Women of color who are theorists are devalued because of racial biases. Often our work is appropriated.

In my teaching and in my writing, I have tried, in the spirit of Charlotte Bunch (whose early writings on women and education were important precisely because they sought to encourage women not to be wary of theory), to encourage women—and particularly black women—to recognize the value and importance of theory, to acknowledge that we all use it in daily life. Theory is not an alien sphere. Even though there is much theoretical writing that may be difficult to understand, I think it useful for us not to simply dismiss or downgrade it but to talk about why it is intimidating, what possible uses it may have, and how it can be interpreted, translated, etc. so that it can be understood.

It is a disservice to black women writers and all women writers when feminist readers demand that our imaginative works serve purposes that should be addressed by feminist theory. Novels and confessional writing can and do enhance our understanding of the way individuals critically reflect about gender, the way we develop strategies to resist sexism, to change lives, but they cannot and do not take the place of theory. More importantly, it does not serve the interests of feminist movement for feminist scholars to support this unnecessary and dangerous separation of "theoretical" work and that work which focusses more on the experiential. It was disturbing to me recently to read Barbara Christian's essay, "The Race for Theory," in which she suggested again and again that black women and "people of color have always theorized—but in forms quite different from the Western form of abstract logic." This statement is simply inaccurate. Had it been made by a white person, I think many more people would be disturbed by its message. When I read it, I immediately thought about different groups of African people, like the Dogon, who have very abstract logical schemas to support rituals that focus on creating gendered subjects. I constantly tell students who use the word "abstract" to dismiss work that in everyday life we use both language and concepts that are very abstract. This point is made quite wonderfully in the collective work, *Female Sexualization*, edited by Frigga Haug who writes: "Contrary to reputation, our everyday language is more than a little abstract: it suppresses the concreteness of feelings, thoughts, and experiences, speaking of them only from a distance." Recently walking by a black male street person, I greeted him by saying, "Hi Ya' doing." And he responded, "Halfway, I'm just halfway." In my African-American literature course that day I used his comment to talk about abstraction, language, and interpretation; and the problem of assuming that "basic black people" or everyday folks do not use abstract theory. At one point, Barbara Christian writes, "I and many of my sisters do not see the world as being so simple. And perhaps that is why we have not rushed to create abstract theories."

Yes! We are not rushing to create feminist theory and I for one think that is tragic. We may not be doing so precisely because of our fears of articulating that which is abstract. All theory as I see it emerges in the realm of abstraction, even that which emerges from the most concrete of everyday experiences. My goal as a feminist thinker and theorist is to take that abstraction and articulate it in a language that renders it accessible—not less complex or rigorous—but simply more accessible.

While I agree with Barbara Christian's critique of the way in which certain types of feminist theory are not seen as an "authoritative discourse," and pointing to the dangers of that is one concern of this essay, it is important that we do not resist this hierarchical tendency by devaluing theory in general. There is a place for theory that uses convoluted language, metalanguage, yet such theory cannot become the groundwork for feminist movement unless it is more accessible. It is not uncommon for women who write theory to discount its importance when questioned about how it relates to "real life," to woman's day-to-day experience. Such dismissals reinforce the misguided assumption that all theory is and has to be inaccessible. In more recent years, focus on the experiential in some feminist circles as part of attempts to deflect attention away from theoretical work has obscured critical gaps in feminist thought and blocked awareness of the pressing need for the production of visionary feminist theory. Such theory emerges only from a context in which there is either an integration of critical thinking and concrete experience or a recognition of the way in which critical ideas, abstractly formulated, will impact on everyday life experience. Visionary feminist theory must be articulated in a manner that is accessible if it is to have meaningful impact. This is not to suggest that everyone will be able to read such work. Inability to read or write makes it impossible for masses of people to learn about written feminist theory. Literacy must become a strategic priority for feminists. Yet what cannot be read can be talked about, and talking, both in lectures and in everyday conversation, is as effective a way to share information about feminist theory as is published material. Even though the groundwork of theory may be laid in a written discourse, it need not end there.

Works of feminist scholarship and feminist theory do exist which are accessible to large numbers of readers and which can be easily discussed. To name a few: *Class and Feminism* edited by Charlotte Bunch and Nancy Myron (1974); *Women and the New World,* an anonymous pamphlet published in 1976; *Top Ranking: Essays on Racism and Classism in Lesbian Communities* edited by Joan Gibbs and Sara Bennett (1979); *Building Feminist Theory* (1981); and *The Politics of Reality: Essays in Feminist Theory* by Marilyn Frye. Most of these works would not appear on the syllabi of feminist theory courses today. In fact, with one or two exceptions, this material is out of print, hard to find, or not well known. Significantly, work within feminist theory that is difficult to comprehend is more likely to be read in theory courses, especially on the graduate level. The recent rise to prominence of a particular style of French feminist theory which is linguistically convoluted is an example of this trend. While such work enriches our understanding of gender politics, it is important to remember that this is not a universal discourse, that it is politically and culturally specific, and emerges from specific relationships particular French feminist scholars have to their political and social reality. Two thinkers whose work immediately comes to mind are Luce Irigaray *(Speculum of the Other Women)* and Julia Kristeva *(Desire in Language).* Although this work honors the relationship between feminist discourse and political practice, it is often used within university settings to establish a select intellectual elite and to reinforce and perpetuate systems of domination, most obviously white Western cultural imperialism. When any feminist theory is employed in this way, feminist movement to end sexist domination is undermined.

At this particular stage of feminist movement in the United States, feminist scholars must pause to reconsider the approach we take to our work within the university. We must be willing to critically examine anew the tensions that arise when we simultaneously try to educate in such a way as to ensure the progression of a liberatory feminist movement and work to create a respected place for feminist scholarship within academic institutions. We must also reexamine the tensions that arise when we try to subvert while working to keep jobs, to be promoted, etc. These practical concerns are factors that influence and/or determine the type of scholarship deemed important. Often, attempts to mediate or reconcile these tensions lead to frustration, despair, cooptation, complicity, or shifts in allegiance. To reaffirm the primacy of feminist struggle, feminist scholars must renew our collective commitment to a radical theoretical agenda, to a feminist education that is the practice of freedom. We begin this task by acknowledging that feminist theory is losing its vital connection to feminist struggle and that connection must be firmly reestablished and understood if our work is to have significant political impact.

The Afrocentric Metatheory and Disciplinary Implications

Molefi Kete Asante

It is my intention to discuss the Afrocentric metatheory, research methodologies and the Africological discipline with an eye toward the development of an ongoing discourse about the future of this relatively new field of inquiry. As we know, methods refer to processes and procedures which govern how we approach a subject. Methodology, on the other hand, is the study of methods or the science of methods. A discipline manifests itself in its attachment to certain theoretical directions, philosophical assumptions, and methods of engaging phenomena.

In examining these topics I will begin, of course, with a discussion of Afrocentricity as a theoretical instrument for the examination of phenomena. Afrocentricity is a simple idea. At its base, it is concerned with African people being the subjects of historical and social experiences rather than objects in the margins of European experiences. I recall seeing the book by Charles Wesley and Carter Woodson entitled *The Negro In Our History* and feeling that they were truly speaking from and to a Eurocentric perspective if they felt that such a title captured the essence of our experience. These were two of the most successful African American historians and yet they could not totally disengage their critical thinking from the traditional framework of Eurocentric scholarship. Viewing phenomena from the perspective of Africans as central, rather than peripheral, means that you secure a better vantage point on the facts.

Afrocentricity is a metatheoretical framework, a philosophical position. Therefore, one cannot speak logically of several types of Afrocentricity, since it is, as I have explained in my own works, a metatheory. There may be various theories within the metatheory but the metatheory itself is decided, it is not debated. One either operates from an Afrocentric perspective or one does not. Of course, one can take the *khephra* position and push the ball in many directions; you can be Afrocentric on some things and not on others. The definition of what constitutes an Afrocentric perspective has been expounded in several places, again, including my own articles and books on the subject. There should not be or there does not have to be any confusion about the meaning of Afrocentricity.

This does not means that a *cartouche* of positions is impossible; it simply means that you must choose your positions carefully. Neither is this an attempt to concentrate solely on the question of identity, though in most cases, for the scholar of African descent especially, it is useful; the past few hundred years of domination have often dislocated us. However, what is more important is to say that such concentration on making something alien does not necessarily make them or you hostile. E.T. was definitely portrayed as an alien, but not unfriendly. To concentrate on my family and find the origin of my own roots may make others strangers, but not hostile strangers.

Dislocation, location and *relocation* are the principal calling cards of the Afrocentric theoretical position. My attempt is always to locate a situation, an event, an author. Location tells you where someone is, that is, where they are standing. It may not tell you where they are headed, but you do know where they are given certain markers of identity. Thus, the person who uses terms like minority, third world, primitives, natives, mainstream is definitely in a particular intellectual space. As I would know a political conservative, a Marxist, a deconstructionist, or a racist by language and behavior, I can also know a Eurocentrist. Of course, one can frequently use language to signify, that is, as an instrument to conceal or point to a direction away from representation. Sometimes that space may not be of the person's choosing; one could be pushed into a space by circumstances. Of course, in such instances we will say that the person is a servant of forces beyond his or her immediate control. Not controlling one's space seems to reflect more of the slave than a human agent acting with authority. More will be said on this throughout the presentation.

I have identified through historical and literary analysis two fallacies of position: the *locational* fallacy and the *linguistic* fallacy. The first occurs when a person is de-centered, misoriented, or disoriented and cannot possibly be looking from the proper angle. This is a problem Malcolm X recognized when he spoke of some enslaved Africans thinking they had come to America with the Mayflower or when he told us that there were some who took the slavemaster's perspective when it came to the plantation. Such people are not only dislocated but disoriented. The second fallacy occurs when a person is located in the proper place but does not have the experience or the ability to explain or describe what is being seen. The second fallacy leads to a sort of naive nationalism because the viewer has only a vantage point but no adequate discipline or skill for analysis. Both types of persons abound in the academy.

THEORY AND RESEARCH

Research which is most instrumental to the development of Africology as a discipline will have to be conducted within the context of theory development. I have recently read Perry A. Hall's "Historical Transformation in African American Musical Culture" published in the Spring 1991 issue of *WORD: A BLACK CULTURE JOURNAL.* The work is an example of good scholarship about African people that is neither Afrocentric nor Africological. That is, it does not deal with a particular vantage point or perspective on the facts and phenomena which places it uniquely within the discipline of Africology. I have no intention of saying that Hall's research is not useful or should not have been done. My point is that such work adds little to the development of the discipline. Anyone from psychology could have taken Erving Goffman's work and done the same kind of "Goffmanian" analysis. Yet the author had available to him a number of Africological instruments that would have assisted him in his research if he had been interested. The question most scholars ask is, what are the elements of theory and method most useful in the advancement of our intellectual discipline?

I believe that a high priority should be assigned to research in Africology that makes a contribution to theory for several reasons. In the first place, any field of study prospers or languishes according to the power of its theory. Secondly, theory sets the tone for the research methods, allows the scholars to find ways to discover new truths. Theory, for me, does not refer only to formal propositions that characterize the hard sciences, but more generally to a coherent set of concepts that serve as a central focus of a field of study. We have begun to develop such concepts, gaining some of them from traditional fields, and adding others that have emerged out of our own research. Africology, as an area of inquiry, aspires to reach mature disciplinary status. As such, it must address a portion of what it does to the generating of conceptual focus. This is the most valuable contribution scholars can now make to the future bank of Africology. Unlike the field of physics, the Africologist is not seeking to find verification or prediction but explanation and clarification. Our research should help us to clarify theory by subjecting our key concepts, e.g., location, dislocation, Africa-centeredness, etc., to intense critical tests. With regard to this point it should be noted that conceptual clarification and consequent development of theory will probably add a bias in favor of the social/behavioral area rather than the more humanities oriented cultural/aesthetic area. This will happen simply because observation rather than textual or historical analyses are the central elements of empiricism. This does not mean that we must throw away concepts that are irrelevant to observations but rather that we must be aware of the dual possibilities of our particular discipline.

SPECIFICATION OF RELATIONS

The problem of specification of relations is tied to methods because it deals with how symbols and signs, concepts and values, contexts and contents are related to each other. From a methodological point of view one must ask questions about relationships of concepts and contents in order to understand the material or physical interaction in any given case of Africological research. I have worked with my students on developing an approach to what has been called ethnography, a term I abhor because it is a Eurocentric word that sees us as objects. We have developed the concept of introspection, which means what you as the researcher feel about the topic before you undertake to study it. Thus, in any ethnography we ask the scholar to put down his or her introspection first. We are working on these issues because theory is intimately related to research method, and theory is the principal power behind the creation of disciplinary maturity. Theory-oriented research should be encouraged in all departments with the aim of clarification and explanation.

THE LACK OF CLARITY

To object to Afrocentricity, a fundamental stepping stone to any multicultural project, as an effort to marginalize African Americans, is to criticize amiss. The aim, that is, the purpose of centered positions which contribute to the multicultural discussion is to bring about harmony within society. Otherwise what one gets is an off-white contribution to the pale white stream. A better option is always to contribute the richness of the African American, the Latino, the Asian, the Native American, and the European to the common purpose. But there is no mainstream; this is a misnomer. Those who speak of a mainstream are often speaking about a white stream with African eddies bubbling on the side. Whatever the word "mainstream" means it has rarely included Africans. And those who use the term do not think of African American poetry or people as being mainstream. Those who speak of "mainstream" and "universals" are most often speaking of whites. And therefore when someone says "universal man" it is not simply a reflection of women but of the Mandinka, the Zulu, the Hmong, the Yaqui, the African American. Yet there really are only tributaries and our cultural flow is a part of the grand delta of ideas.

The opposition to racism is not abstract, it is concrete. In our present social, economic, and intellectual condition the resistance to white supremacy is not black supremacy but pluralism without hierarchy, a frightening concept in the context of prolonged white domination of ideas. Manning Marable has developed a similar thesis in his book, ***How Capitalism Underdeveloped Black America.*** Afrocentricity is not a black version of Eurocentricity, which is an arrogant imposition of a particular view as if it is a universal view. Such a position is ethnocentric and leads to racism when it is enforced by custom, law, or physical force. It degrades other views and valorizes the European viewpoint.

THE AFRICAN AMERICAN STUDIES IDEA

My thesis is simply stated. During the past twenty or so years since the establishment of African American Studies, two major changes have occurred in the American Academy which have altered the academic landscape for years to come. The first was the institutionalization of African American Studies, Africology, as a discipline alongside other disciplines within the Academy. The second was the creation and mounting of the first doctoral program in African American Studies in the nation at Temple University. The first transformed the student movement of the 60s into a concrete reality in academic units as well as in theories and methods. The second transcended the parochial and provincial role which had been assigned to the field by keepers of the Academy. What were the characteristics that manifested themselves in this flowering of new intellectual activity?

I am a child of the Black Studies Movement, having been born to it in the late night and early morning labors of love and emotion that saw young men and women at UCLA, members of the Harambee Club, and later SNCC-UCLA (of which I was chair) totally absorbed in the creation of the new, the novel, and the radical. The processes by which the curricula documents were produced by African American students in the late 1960s and early 70s were unknown in the history of the creation of academic fields and very few of us at that time had any real idea what the future would bring. Curricula were inseparable from the concept of the university, just as lungs and breathing could not be separated from the inhaling and exhaling of oxygen. With the curricula changes there would have to be fundamental changes in the institution. We knew this, it now seems, instinctively because the few African American professors who were on those campuses often had not been there long or could not give us advice. As the first permanent director of the UCLA Center for Afro American Studies I wrote the interdisciplinary M.A. program and in 1968 started, along with Robert Singleton, who had been an interim director at the Center, the *Journal of Black Studies.* We knew then, as most of you knew, that Black Studies was not the mere aggregation of courses about our experiences but had to be courses taught from what we called at the time "the black perspective." In our rush to establish the perspective, we even demanded that only black teachers teach the programs until we discovered that perspective is not a biological issue. Some of the black professors taught from a white perspective. It is from this reality that I shall attempt to answer the question posed above regarding the nature of disciplinary transformations, their characteristics, and future.

THE CONTEXT OF METHODS

African American Studies is a discrete discipline with certain critical perspectives, theories, and methods which are necessary for its role in discovery and understanding. The attendant propositions suggest creativity, innovation, genius, and authority in disciplines. Assaults on Africology as a discipline, as we shall see, are nothing more than attacks on the idea that African Americans can neither create theories nor disciplines, and is ultimately the same tune played in previous discussions of African intelligence. A number of books, such as George Mosse's *A History of Racism in Europe*, Michael Bradley's *The Ice Man Inheritance*, and Stephen J. Gould's *The Mismeasure of Man*, exist on this subject. When this tune is played by Africans themselves it is often the result of dislocation, that is, the assumption of the place where Africans have been pushed by white racial hegemony within the Academy. In such situations the African feels that he or she must act much more "correct" in the white sense than the whites themselves. There is a felt pressure to be hard, as it were, on any African who raises the possibility of escape from the mental plantation. What I am saying is that it becomes necessary to suspend judgement or to kill one's traditional sensibilities so to speak in order to understand the language of the new reality, that is, Africans as subjects instead of objects in the European project. This is difficult to discern from the same tired portals of traditions which are rooted in the conquest of Africans by Europeans. Africology becomes a discipline whose mission is, inter alia, the critique of domination.

ISSUES IN INQUIRY

I am not sure whether it is necessary any longer to debate the question of perspective in terms of the Africological discipline, as has been the case during the past twenty years; at least, in the circle of scholars with whom I am associated, it is fairly well agreed that the fundamental basis for Africology as a separate discipline is a unique perspective. Nevertheless, the ground is clearly established in the works of several scholars with whom you are familiar. Their arguments are expertly placed within the on-going creative project of African liberation, now more than ever, an intellectual liberation.

Let me digress a bit here and discuss the issue of Kemet, that is, the primacy of Kemet in the thinking of Afrocentrists. First of all, it is not a desire to go back to Africa because African Americans are African, just as white Australians are Europeans. Moreover, it is not a desire for gloriana, for self esteem, any more than factual historical information in any context about any culture is gloriana. Furthermore, it is not an attempt to replace the European information we have learned with African information. Rather, for the discipline of Africology, it is the endeavor to see in the most monumental civilization of antiquity patterns, concepts, connections, and relationships which will assist us in the process of explanation and clarification. Cheikh Anta Diop said it, "Egypt is to Africa and African people everywhere as Greece is to Europe and European people." What he meant was that until we were able to examine the classical Nile Valley civilizations we would not know how to handle our contemporary cultural manifestations, either on the continent or in the Diaspora. I do not believe, as E. Franklin Frazier believed, that Africa disappeared in the African American during the Enslavement.

Therefore, the Afrocentric enterprise is framed by cosmological, epistemological, axiological, and aesthetic issues. In this regard the Afrocentric method pursues a world voice distinctly Africa-centered in relationship to external phenomena. I did not say distinctly African, which is another issue, but Africa-centered, a theoretical perspective. The work of Robert Farris Thompson, Basil Davidson, and Sidney Wilhelm should be cited in connection with their research that has shown Africans as subjects rather than objects.

COSMOLOGICAL ISSUE

The place of African culture in the philosophy, myths and legends, literatures, and oratories of African people constitutes, at the mythological level, the cosmological issue within the Afrocentric enterprise, which is an enterprise entirely within the Africalogical discipline. What role does the African culture play in the African's interface with the cosmos? The debate over "African cultures or culture" is answered definitionally within the context of the Afrocentric perspective so I will not discuss it at this juncture, no more than to say that it has been dealt with in the writings of Afrocentric scholars. One might see particularly the book of *African Culture: The Rhythms of Unity* edited by Kariamu Asante and myself for a discussion of the issue.

Among the questions that might be dealt with under the cosmological umbrella are: What dramas of life and death, in the African tradition, are reflected in the metaphysical metaphors? How are those dramas translated by lunar, solar, or stellar figures? The fundamental assumptions of Africological inquiry are based on the African orientation of the cosmos. By "African" I clearly mean a "composite African", not a specific, discrete African ethnicity, which would rather mean, African American, Yoruba, Ibo, Fulani, Zulu, Mandingo, Kikongo, etc. C.T. Keto has taken this up in his book *Afrocentricity and History* by writing that "African American thinkers were among the first to feel the need to create the concept 'composite' African and, in so doing, their reference was the whole of the African continent which included, historically, ancient Kemet." [Keto (1991, p.5)]. He continues that "denied a precise ethnic linkage, they created a holistic African vision that . . . influenced Africans on the continent."

There are several concerns which might be considered cosmological in that they are fundamental frames for research initiatives in this discipline. I shall only make reference to them here and refer you to my recent book, *Kemet, Afrocentricity, and Knowledge*, for additional commentary. The concerns are: Racial Formation, Culture, Gender, and Class. Race as a social factor remains prevalent in heterogeneous, but hegemonically Eurocentric, societies. In the United States, the most developed example of such a society, the question of race is the most dominant aspect of intersocial relations. Cultural questions are usefully viewed in the context of shared perceptions, attitudes, and predispositions that allow communities of people to organize responses in similar ways. Gender also must be seen as a substantial research area in questions of social, political, economic, and cultural dimensions. Since the liberation of women is not an act of charity but a basic premise of the Afrocentric project, the researcher must be cognizant of sexist language, terminology, and perspectives. Class becomes, for the Afrocentrist aware of our history, much more complicated than capitalists and workers, or bourgeoisie and proletariat. Finding the relevant class positions and places in given situations will assist the Africalogical scholar with analysis. Indeed, Eurocentrism with all its potential for asserting its particular self as universal becomes the repository for race, class, and gender conflict. Rather than an isolated or isolatable discussion of race, or class, or gender one begins to view the dominant Eurocentric mythos as containing all of these elements.

EPISTEMOLOGICAL ISSUE

What constitutes the search for truth in the Afrocentric enterprise? In Africology, language, myth, ancestral memory, dance-music-art, and science provide the sources of knowledge, the canons of proof, and the structure of truth.

Discussions of language from an Afrocentric perspective or research into African language, diasporan or continental, may lead to understanding about the nature of truth. Ebonics, the African American language, serves as the archetype of African American language in the United States. A variety of languages in Brazil, Ecuador, Colombia, Panama and Belize. One of our students, for example, is centering her research on the Garifuna people of Belize. However, while her work will include much that is historical and linguistic, she is principally concerned with an epistemological question rooted in the inquiry on methods of retention as expressed in the declarative culture, as opposed to the cognitive, of the people.

The strong, expressive, and inescapable myth of the African presence in America, indeed in the world, has value for the discovery of truth in many dimensions of human life. Thus, behind and in front of our banquet of possibilities are the refracting elements of myths which appropriately mediate our relationships. Knowing these myths, making a habit of investigating them in a serious manner, allows the researcher to form new metaphors about our experiences. In dance-music-art, performing and representational art forms are central to interpretation of cultural and social reality. Our analysis is informed by the way dance is seen in the African culture, even in the way we view the Africanization of the walkman.

AXIOLOGICAL ISSUE

The question of value is at the core of the Afrocentric quest for truth because ethical issues have always been connected to the advancement of the discipline. One cannot speak of Africology apart from its origin in the drive to humanize education, to democratize the curriculum, to advance the understanding of humanity. This is the birthright of the discipline more than any other disciplines in the social sciences or the humanities. What constitutes the good is a matter of historical conditions and cultural developments within a particular society. A common expression among us relates to the good and beautiful in this way, "Beauty is what beauty does." We are also sure that a person "is beautiful because he or she is good." When a sister says, "that's a beautiful brother," she is usually meaning something more than his physical looks. Doing good is equivalent to being beautiful. The Afrocentric method isolates conduct and action in social or literary analysis. The aim is to see what conduct has been sanctioned, and if sanctioned, carried out.

AESTHETIC ISSUE

Kariamu Welsh Asante has identified seven aspects of the African aesthetic which she calls "senses". Based upon her field research into Zimbabwe dance she isolated *polyrhythm, polycentrism, dimensionality, repetition, curvilinearity, epic memory,* and *wholism* as investigative categories for African aesthetics. Each aspect might be examined from the disciplinary perspective by any researcher using the idea of African centrality. Particularly useful in the context of drama, dance, the plastic arts, and literature, the aesthetic senses represent an Afrocentric approach to the subject of African art.

Our motifs should be reflective of our historical experiences and where we have found them, the people have responded. The best of our music, the best of our art, and the best of our literature use the motifs of the people's path. This is culture. What is it to be a cultured person if you are an African American? Does this mean that you master only the European historical experiences? Are those the ones that we have been reinforced in and therefore believe are superior to our own? How should a scholar study the person who seeks to write or paint as an African? Does it not depend upon what the person claims to be doing?

THE SHAPE OF THE DISCIPLINE

The groundedness of observations and behavior in the historical experiences of Africans becomes the main base for operation in the field of African American Studies. Centrism, the operation of the African as subject or the Latino as subject, or the European as subject, and so forth, allows Africology to take its place alongside other disciplines without hierarchy and without hegemony. As a discipline, Africology is sustained by a commitment to centering the study of African phenomena, events, and persons in the particular cultural voice of the composite African people. But it does not promote such a view as universal. Furthermore, it opens the door for interpretations of reality based upon evidence and data secured by reference to that world voice.

The anteriority of the classical African civilizations must be entertained by any Africological inquiry, simply because without that perspective, our work hangs in the air, detached, and isolated or becomes nothing more than a sub-set of the Eurocentric disciplines. As I have often said, without employing Afrocentricity in this manner, our research becomes disconnected, lacks historical continuity, and is incidental and nonorganic.

The Eurocentric dogma creates an intellectual structure that locks the African in a conceptual prison. One key to this dogma is that philosophy is the highest discipline, and that philosophy is Greek. Thus, Greece becomes the model for the structure of knowledge in the West. According to this dogma, everything starts with the Greeks: philosophy, politics, art, drama, literature, and mathematics. There is no philosophy in Africa, Asia, or the Americas, only the Europeans have philosophy. However, since the first Greek philosophers, Thales and Isocrates studied philosophy in Kemet (Ancient Egypt), philosophy could not have started with the Greeks. Cheikh Anta Diop, perhaps the greatest African intellect of the 20th century, argued that there could be no understanding of things African without linkage to ancient Kemet. Thus, Egypt is to the rest of the African world as Greece is to the rest of the European world. Europe constitutes itself around several principals including its connection, however mythical or distant, to ancient Greece, to certain ideas that are traced to the Greeks and to the Romans, and to Christianity as a unifying theme from the 10th Century A.D. onward.

SUBJECT FIELDS

To say that Africology is a discipline does not mean that it is without subject fields or interest areas. There are seven general subject fields which I have identified following the work of Maulana Karenga in *Introduction to Black Studies*: communicative, social, historical, cultural, political, economic, and psychological. Most of the people who are working in the field are approaching their work from one of the above subject fields. A student of Africology chooses a research issue which falls within one or more of those subject fields. In any endeavor to uncover, analyze, criticize, or anticipate an issue, the Africologist works to use the appropriate methods for the subject. To examine cultural nationalism, for example, within the historical or political subject field would require a constant method for research.

There are three paradigmatic approaches to research in Africology: *functional, categorical,* and *etymological*. The first represents needs, policy, and action orientations.

Categorical refers to schemes, gender, class, and themes. The etymological paradigm deals with language, literatures, and oratories. Studies of either sort might be conducted in the context of African society, either on the continent or in the Americas. The aim is to provide research results that are ultimately verifiable in human experience.

A student of Africology might choose to study in the general field of history but use the functional paradigm. Of course, many combinations are possible and the student is limited only by her or his ability to properly conceptualize the topic for study in an Afrocentric manner. Since Africology is not history, political science, communication, literary analysis, or sociology, the student must be well-grounded in the assumptions of the Afrocentric approach to human knowledge. Scholars in our field have often been handicapped in their quest for clear and authoritative statements by a lack of methodological direction for collection and analyzing data, choosing and interpreting research themes, approaching and appreciating cultural artifacts, and isolating and evaluating facts. This has been the case although works by Larry Neal and Paul Carter Harrison in the literary theory field introduced us to the possibilities inherent in our own centered positions as early as the Sixties. However, as an increasingly self-conscious field, African American studies, Africology, has begun to produce a variety of philosophical approaches to Afrocentric inquiry. These studies have served to underscore the need for a solid, methodological approach at the level of basic premises of the field and have become, in effect, pioneer works in a new perspective on phenomena.

The Afrocentric psychologists have led the reconceptualization of the field of African personality theories. Certainly, I count the work of Daudi Azibo, Joseph Baldwin, Linda Myers, and Wade Nobles in this vein. They have explored areas of human psychology which impinge on the African experience. Political Scientists qua political scientists such as Ronald Walter, Leonard Jeffries, Mack Jones, Manning Marable, and James Turner have argued positions that may be called Afrocentric. Maulana Karenga, Patrick Bellegarde-Smith, and Jacob Carruthers, from their original base in political science, have become Afrocentrists. The work of Houston Baker in the area of vernacular theory might be considered Afrocentric inasmuch as the source of his images are culturally centered. In addition, the works of several writers, such as Henry Louis Gates, Abu Abarry, Joyce Joyce, and Eleanor Taylor have elements of centered locations. The field of sociology, since the early days of the first departments in 1882 and 1884 at Chicago and Columbia respectively, has remained bogged down in social problems and paradigms that do not permit adequate assessment of African cultural data. A number of African American sociologists are attempting to break out of those quagmires. Robert Staples had been an early pioneer in this field and now the work of Bruce Hare at Syracuse is significant in this respect. Vivian Gordon has long been a major force in the Africana Womanist project in which sex and race are joined rather than separated as in the work of the Afrofemcentrists of the Black Feminists. Indeed, Gordon's work is joined with that of Clenora Hudson Weems and Brenda Verner to make the most Afrocentric statement on the women question we have seen in Africology. They have found their models, like Donna Marimba Richards, in the ancient models of Auset-Ausar and Mawu-Lisa. In design and architecture, scholars such as Bill Harris at the University of Virginia are exploring Afrocentric designs in housing. What would we have done without the African porch as a daycare platform?

Africology is defined as the Afrocentric study of phenomena, events, ideas, and personalities related to Africa. The mere study of African phenomena is not Africology but some other intellectual enterprise. I make no judgment on those enterprises, I simply say that they are not Africalogical. Like other disciplines, more or less severe, our discipline is based on certain assumptions, objectives, and constructions of language. Thus, the Temple Circle of Afrocentric scholars has tried to exorcise terms such as sub-Saharan, Hottentot, Bushmen, pygmy, and minority. Such a massive project of redressing the de-centering of Africans will surely take us well into the 21st century. The scholar who generates research questions based upon the centrality of Africa is engaged in a very different research inquiry than the one who imposes Western criteria on the phenomena. "Afrocentric" is the most important word in the definition, otherwise one might think that any study of African phenomena or peoples constitutes Africology. It is the commitment to perspective and method that distinguishes the discipline from others.

GEOGRAPHICAL SCOPE

The geographical scope of the African world, and hence, the Africological enterprise, includes Africa, the Americas, the Caribbean, various regions in Asia, and the Pacific. Wherever people declare themselves as African, despite the distance from the continent or the recency of their out-migration, they are accepted as part of the African world. Thus, the indigenous people of Australia and New Guinea are considered African and in a larger context subject for Africalogists who maintain a full analytical and theoretical discussion of African phenomena.

Although the major regions of African culture are Africa, the Caribbean, and the Americas, even within those regions there are varying degrees of cultural and technological affinity to an African world voice. Africology is concerned with Africans in any particular as well as all regions. Thus, Abdias do Nascimento, our visiting professor from Brazil at Temple this year, can remind us that Brazil is significant for understanding the African presence in the Americas. In Brazil, Zumbi (the greatest king of the Palmares Republic), Luisa Mahin, and Luiz Gama are principal figures in the making of history; in the Dominican Republic, Diego de Campo and Lemba provide the same historical and intellectual energy one finds in Venezuela with Oyocta, King Miguel, and King Bayano; in Columbia there is Benkos Bioho; and in Mexico, the great African American, Yanga.

Africology rejects the Africanist idea of the separation of African people on the continent from African people in the Diaspora as being intellectually short-sighted, analytically vapid, and philosophically unsound. One cannot study Africans in the United States or Brazil or Jamaica without some appreciation for the historical and cultural significance of Africa as source and origin. The reactionary position which sees African American Studies as African Slave Studies, or a branch of European Studies of the Slave (that is, the making and the unmaking of the slave) is categorically rejected. Thus, if one studies Africans in a Northeast city of the United States, one must do it with the idea that one is studying African people, not made-in-America Negroes without historical depth. By being conscious of this history one does not have to record it every time, only understand its connection to the project at hand. This has a direct bearing on data gathered for any analysis or study of African people. The researcher must examine everything possible to be able to make an adequate case. Actually, the gathering of data must proceed on the basis that everything that can be used must be used. Therefore, it is impossible for a person to become an Africalogist simply by using the historical method, or the critical method, or the experimental method, and so forth. In order to become the best type of Africalogist one must use all the elements of data gathering, in any particular area, for an adequate assessment. This means that I might have to use literary analysis and historical analysis in examining one theme or issue. Video records and oral records are as important as written records and must be seen as part of the portfolio of documentation that is available to the Africologist.

THE TEMPLE PROJECT

A final statement ought to be made about the classificatory aspects of Africology. These ideas are given within the framework of the creation of the doctoral program at Temple. Two fields, cultural aesthetics and social behavioral, exist in our department. They are the results of debate, discussion, and consensus within the faculty. With twelve faculty members, we have established a reputation for intellectual debate and dialogue that opens the discourse on discipline questions. Africology is a severe discipline. It became necessary for us to commit traditional discipline suicide in order to advance Africology within the structure of the university. The students we are training will not have that particular problem. They will start out being Africalogists who have read everything in their concentration, as well as the theoretical works in the discipline. Already we have seen our students expand the discourse in almost every field. Thus, we have proposed the following two area of research and responsibility:

Creative, Inventive, Artistic, and Literary:

Epistemic issues, ethics, politics, psychology, and *modes of behavior;*
Scientific issues, history, linguistics, economics, and *methods of investigation;*
Artistic issues, iconography, art, motifs, symbols, and *types of presentation.*

Social, Behavioral, Action, and Historical:

Relationships, the living, the dead, the unborn;
Cosmos, culture, race, class, gender;
Mythoforms, origins, struggles, victories; and
Recognitions, conduct, designs, and signs.

These principal areas, cultural/aesthetic and socio/behavioral, constitute the grounds upon which we must stand as we continue to build this discipline. I am certain that scholars who replace us will advance the relocating process in theory and practice the generalship of the field improved in the give-and-take of critical debate. As it has been necessary in every aspect of the African's existence for the past five hundred years, it is also necessary in the area of human knowledge for us to struggle to enhance an Afrocentric perspective, recovering from it the distorted junk heap of European hegemony. As in the past, there will be those scholars of whatever cultural and racial and academic background who will understand our abiding interest in free and full inquiry from our own centered perspective and who will become the new Melville Herskovits and Robert Farris Thompsons. A field of study must be open to all who share its perspective and methodology; ours is no different.

The future of Africology will depend upon those who are committed to the principles of academic excellence and social responsibility and who, through their research methods, demonstrate the vision of harmony. Those principles must be interpreted within the framework of an Afrocentric vision in order to maintain a space and location for Africology within the Academy. I have no doubt that this will be done by the scholars and students who are coming after us. They will find in their own time the energy and will to carry out their intellectual mission, as we are trying to carry out ours, in order to create new spaces for human discussion.

REFERENCES

Asante, Molefi K. and K.W. Asante. **African Culture: The Rhythms of Unity.** Trenton: Africa World Press, 1988.

Asante, Molefi K. **Afrocentricity.** Trenton: Africa World Press, 1987.

Asante, Molefi K. **Kemet, Afrocentricity and Knowledge.** Trenton: Africa World Press, 1990.

Asante, Molefi K. **The Afrocentric Idea.** Philadelphia: Temple University Press, 1987.

Bellegarde-Smith, Patrick. Haiti: The Breached Citadel. Boulder: Westview Press, 1990.

Bradley, Michael. **The Ice Man Inheritance.** Toronto: Dorset, 1980.

Diop, C.A. **The African Origin of Civilization.** New York: Lawrence Hill, 1991.

Diop, C.A. **The Cultural Unity of Black Africa.** Chicago: Third World Books, 1976.

Gould, Stephen J. **The Mismeasure of Man.** New York: Norton, 1981.

Karenga, M. **Introduction to Black Studies.** Los Angeles: University of Sankore Press, 1987, (edition).

Keto, C.T. **The Africa-centered Perspective of History.** Blackwood, N.J.: K & A Publishers, 1988.

Marable, Manning **How Capitalism Underdeveloped Black America.** Boston: South End Press, 1983.

Mosse, George. **A History of Racism in Europe: Toward the Final Solution.** Madison: University of Wisconsin Press, 1985.

Nascimento, Elisa. **Pan Africanism and South America.** Buffalo: Afrodiaspora, 1979.

Obenga, Theophile. **The African Origin of Philosophy.** Paris: Presence Africaine, 1990.

Richards, Dona. **Let the Circle Be Unbroken.** Trenton: Africa World Press, 1991.

Rodney, Walter. **How Europe Underdeveloped Africa.** Washington: Howard University Press, 1980.

Thompson, Robert Farris. **The Flash of the Spirit.** Berkeley: University of California, 1986.

LANGUAGE, KNOWLEDGE, AND IDEOLOGY

The term "scientist" originated in an 1834 book review as a label for "practitioners in the various fields of natural philosophy." The reviewer's term stuck, but the book and its author disappeared from the history of science. A "self-taught master of mathematics and natural science" and "premier scientific lady of the ages," Mary Somerville (1780–1872) the author was abandoned by historians.[1] Her sex denied her a place in the annals of science just as it elicited—and still would to some extent—phrases like "female scientist" or "scientific lady."

Language is a key to understanding Somerville's experiences and outcomes. Phenomenologically, *language* is a vast array of types whereby we name the objects of our experiences. Not only do we name those objects but simultaneously we typify them, that is, we experience them as similar to other objects of the same type. Language is central to our experiencing. As the resource letting us sort out, store, and anticipate our experiences, it pervasively shapes our personal and collective lives. What we name, how we name it, and how we connect the names in our linguistic repertoire are matters of utmost importance theoretically and politically. Words such as "pervert," "troublemaker," "security risk," "nymphomaniac," and "patriot" are illustrative. What does each term valorize or trivialize? Whose interests does each term reflect? How might each term justify discriminatory treatment? Who is authorized to say what counts as an instance of each category?

Terms such as these more or less clearly lack neutrality. Less obviously but just as surely, the types constitutive of language can never be entirely neutral. They emerge out of some group's interests and stay in use by benefiting some members. Needless to say, not all members of society have an equal chance to shape the language(s) most in use. In societies like ours people controlling the mass media disproportionately shape our vocabulary. They originate or give credence to neologisms like "cocooning," "mommy track," "pro-life movement," and "feminazi." Officeholders, scholars, religious leaders, celebrities, and social-movement leaders (among others) have their say, but most rely heavily on the mass media for getting the word out.

Trinh T. Minh-ha says language is both "the locus of power and unconscious servility," and Dorothy E. Smith says that "our work begins and ends in language."[2] We might fruitfully extend their generalizations to everything passing for "knowledge" in society. For multicultural theorists the very term "knowledge" requires interrogation. What, for example, differentiates it from common sense, insight, wisdom, opinions, hunches, and all else that might guide our choices and actions? By what processes and whose authority do those distinctions get institutionalized so that people commonly treat them as obvious?

Trinh observes that "the *minor*-ity's voice is always personal; that of the *major*-ity, always impersonal."[3] In other terms, some knowledge takes on the aura of *objectivity,* that is, it seems transpersonally valid. Objective knowledge seems universal, while subjective knowledge smacks of the local or parochial. It is no accident that dominant groups' favored vocabulary and knowledge get experienced as impersonal and neutral, while subordinated groups' parallel resources get experienced as personal and biased. The institutional forces behind those outcomes are systematic and sweeping. They extend from formal schooling to formal worshipping, from mass advertising to mass media. The sociology of knowledge concerns itself with such processes as *objectivation,* the transformation of subjectively based and historically contingent knowledge into knowledge that seems unbiased and universal.[4] It also concerns itself with how objectivation furthers the relations of ruling that divide us into dominant and subordinate members.

In this latter connection Smith's sociology of knowledge stands out. She insists that "objectified knowledges . . . are essential constituents of the relations of ruling of contemporary capitalism."[5] By *relations of ruling* she means "the complex of extra-local relations that provide in contemporary societies a specialization of organization, control, and initiative." Included in such relations are "bureaucracy, administration, management, professional organizations, and the media." Also included are the "discourses, scientific, technical, and cultural, that intersect, interpenetrate, and coordinate the multiple sites of ruling." In Smith's view scholarly knowledge augments the social relations of ruling. Sociology, for example, "created and creates a construct of society that is specifically discontinuous with the world known, lived, experienced, and acted in."[6] That discontinuity is no sign of sociologists' naiveté or malevolence. Rather it reflects academe's linkages with those social and cultural forms that justify the status quo by updating the vocabulary of ruling and reinforcing the knowledge claims of those who rule.

By excluding the messiness and ambiguities of lived experience from its models, social sciences like sociology help construct subordinated members as "different," as "Others." Those of us who are the "wrong" color, those of us unable to consign the dreary part of our work to staff people, those of us who mop our own floors and pump our own gas, those of us who bathe the children and turn the bedridden, those of us whose teeth are falling out for lack of medical insurance, those of us whose sexual orientations make us familial pariahs are mostly left out of the sociological picture. When we do make an appearance, we are usually paraded about under the rubric of social dis-organization, social problems, deviance, social movements, and other specializations that put us beyond the "normalities" universalized in models of rationality and such. We become "Others" counted as exceptions to the rules that, when followed, presumably stabilize society. For the most part, mainstream social theory universalizes the experiences of the materially privileged straight white male minority and leaves the rest of us seeming in need of a makeover of one sort or other.

Besides normalizing the numerical minority's experiences as universal, theoretical portrayals of a world discontinuous with the life-world we actually inhabit mystifies the procedures of scientists, scholars, and other experts. Even though "There is no such thing as non-participant observation,"[7] social scientists typically make it seem as if there is. Their research reports erase the sloppiness and arbitrariness of their procedures just as surely as they erase lived experiences in the flesh-and-blood world. Thereby they mask a key methodological principle: "We can only know society as insiders, regardless of the sociological artifices constructing social systems and structures as external to the knowing subject."[8] In its stead social scientists promote the principle of the dispassionate observer who by virtue of rigorous training will come up with the same findings that any similarly trained observer would arrive at using the same procedures under the same circumstances. Smith rejects that principle as one more element of mystified professionalism. She urges that we "take up methods of inquiry in which the method itself is explicated as an integral aspect of the inquiry."[9] Trinh makes a resonant point about social theory. She says that "theory no longer is theoretical when it loses sight of its own conditional nature, takes no risk in speculation, and circulates as a form of administrative inquisition."[10] Both theorists thus call for extreme self-scrutinizing when we do our work and extremely critical consciousness when we lay hold of a word, a method, a topic of inquiry, or a finding.

Multiculturalists, especially those influenced by Karl Marx, Friedrich Nietzsche, and Louis Althusser, commonly respond to such calls. Giving critique priority in their work, they aim for demystification. They want to show how "dominant or ruling class ideologies are authorized and inscribed in subjectivities, institutional arrangements, texts of ruling, various cultural narratives, and . . . sociological theories. . . ."[11] Postmodernism often orients their critiques of such elements of domination.

Postmodernists reject the idea of theory that treats humankind, human societies, or human history in universal, transcendental terms. They look askance at so-called master narratives peddling some version or other of essentialism, that is, some account of what "essentially" motivates human beings or what "necessarily" fulfills them or why they "inevitably" establish some variant of a given social institution. Postmodernists favor theoretical multipolarity. They believe that what is "normal," "natural," or "inevitable" is little more than the localized, contingent outcomes continuously emanating from people's plans, projects, impulses, habits, and fantasies. That people routinely act in concert with or reaction to one another only adds further color to the postmodernist spectrum.

The range of that spectrum derives from its systematic rejection of either/or thinking. The modernist vision is bifocal—female/male, nature/culture, body/mind, humanities/sciences, sacred/secular, rural/urban, black/white, damned/saved, insider/outsider.

Its dualisms support hierarchy and promote divisiveness. Few, if any, thinkers seriously believe in moral or cultural equality between the categories paired in modernist outlooks. Instead, one category takes precedence over the other. Postmodernists dismantle those dualistic, opposed categories by disclosing the diversity each category masks and the similarities between the one category and the other. Postmodernists thus favor both/and perspectives.

As the first two readings imply, "discourse" and "deconstruction" make frequent appearances in postmodernist writings. Used mostly in the manner of the French philosopher Michel Foucault, *discourse* is any widely applicable set of assumptions and assertions that facilitate people's sense making and problem solving. One can speak, for instance, of a sociobiological, sociological, or religious discourse, each of which can presumably help one make sense of AIDS, inner-city poverty, divorce rates, social mobility, crime rates, and the heteropatriarchal family. One can also speak of a multicultural discourse, and one of the fruits of reading this volume is to gain grounds for saying what that discourse comprises. Before you begin the last set of readings, we will return to this question of multicultural discourse.

Alongside discourse as a common topic of inquiry stands deconstruction as a common method of inquiry among postmodernist thinkers.[12] Developed by the French philosopher Jacques Derrida, *deconstruction* involves systematically sorting through the layers, nuances, and gaps in a text such as the one you are now reading. It posits meaning as a contingent achievement based not only on a text's signifiers (words, punctuation, capitalization) and significations (denotations, connotations, logical implications), but also on its readers' needs, desires, and social locations as well as the context of its appearance or use. Deconstruction posits a radically unfinished text perpetually under construction. Deconstructing a text means disclosing the terms and ramifications of its construction by audiences reading under various historical and cultural conditions. Often, then, deconstruction is a semiotic (that is, sign-centered) as well as historicized, cross-cultural project. Its most ambitious undertakings focus on the cross-textual continuities that reflect significant discourses in society or master narratives in social theory. Heterosexist discourse that treats heterosexuals as the norm and sexual minorities as "Others" is one such discourse in our society today; the story of Western societies sloughing off premodern shackles by developing industrial-capitalist systems represents a master narrative in social theory. Like other social discourses and master narratives, these represent "regimes of signification."[13]

Such regimes face challenges from many sides today, not the least of which come from multicultural theorists such as those whose papers appear in this section. Alan Banks, Dwight Billings, and Karen Tice introduce us to the "kaleidoscopic" character of postmodernism. After laying out some postmodernist tenets, they apply them to Appalachian Studies. Banks, Billings, and Tice not only illustrate the "postmodernist style" but also acquaint us with a field of study tied in with multicultural education and politics. They also show how region can serve as a basis of identity and, therefore, of "difference."

Sexual orientation also anchors people's identities while functioning as a site of "difference." Queer theory brings together those multiculturalists who theorize the politics of sexual identity. Like Appalachian Studies, queer theory is a recent development in academic life. Only now is it being institutionalized, an intellectually and politically hazardous process in Donald Morton's judgment.

Like Banks, Billings, and Tice, Morton writes as an insider, a contributor to and participant in the area of study he discusses. Also like them, he is familiar with postmodernist perspectives. Morton parts company with Banks, Billings, and Tice, however, with his concern about maintaining the radical, oppositional character of queer theory. Morton also diverges from them with his reservations about "the dominant form of (post)modern theory and its mode of cultural investigation, which privilege politically unproductive understandings. . . ."

Morton differentiates critique from criticism. The latter aims at undermining or destroying what the critic dislikes. Critique, on the other hand, is "undertaken in solidarity." It involves identification with and involvement in the matter at hand; its purpose is to preserve the vital character and transformative potential of what has won one's loyalty. Morton offers a critique of queer theory that interrogates its political and cultural ramifications as an academic, postmodernist development. His overriding concern is that the radical promise of queer theory may get compromised as it gains academic acceptance.

The excerpt you will be reading from Morton's paper focuses more on the intellectual context he establishes for his critique than on the critique itself. Noting that queer theorists are "following the path" of feminists and Afrocentrists (among others), Morton frames his critique by noting the current struggle about "how culture itself is to be theorized" (pp. 92–93). That struggle pits textual studies against cultural studies. The latter area of endeavor, itself divided into "experiential" and "critical" varieties, provides the context wherein Morton explores theory's capacity for furthering either oppression or resistance. He urges queer theorists to treat homophobia not as a "prejudice" or "attitude," which leaves oppressive structures unchallenged, but as "a structure of exploitation linked—not eccentrically, locally, or contingently, but systemically—to other social practices" (p. 91–92).

Those other practices include the heteropatriarchal family currently valorized under the rubic "family values" as well as less obvious institutions such as the heterosexualized school.[14] Those other practices also include the pervasive gendering that stigmatizes members of the "transgender community . . . made up of transsexuals (pre-, post-, and nonoperative), transvestites, drag queens, passing women, hermaphrodites, stone butches, and gender outlaws who defy regulatory sex/gender taxonomies."[15] Queer theory exposes those regulatory practices and the social fictions they advance about our sexual identities. Queer theorists treat sexual identities as "less a function of knowledge than performance, or in Foucauldian terms, less a matter of final discovery than perpetual reinvention."[16] Then, too, they "view heterosexuality and homosexuality . . . as categories of knowledge, a language that frames what we know as bodies, desires, sexualities, identities. . . ."[17] Queer theory, which emerged in the late 1980s, thus implodes "lesbian and gay studies." According to Arlene Stein and Ken Plummer, the latter rubric

did not seem inclusive enough; it did not encapsulate the ambivalence many lesbian/gay scholars felt, and the difficulties they faced in fitting sexuality into the "ethnicity" model which provided the template for such fields as African-American and women's studies, and indeed for identity politics in general.[18]

Morton's paper thus offers a critique aimed at keeping queer theory implosive and radical. By implication, it cautions multicultural theorists in general to keep their work transgressive even as it gains recognition from and credibility among mainstream theorists.

Following Morton's paper is Wendy Rose's on whiteshamanism, which offers a critique not only of culturally imperialist artists but also of such linguists and social scientists. She inveighs against the latter's universalism and essentialism that obscure the cultural specificity of values such as freedom and practices such as art. Rose asks us to think long and hard about the circumstances making "All of us . . . ethnocentric at our deepest levels." She points out that ethnocentrism makes "Ethnicity, for the mainstream . . . specifically the domain of Others" and accounts for Euroamericans' wanting everyone to be "a different shade of the same thing" and "a member of the same cultural 'reality' except for things which are 'safely' different. . . ." such as food. (p. 105)

The remaining two papers on language, knowledge, and ideology focus on the imperialistic character of specific academic disciplines. Michelle Fine offers a poignant critique of psychologists' models of "coping." She argues that coping strategies necessarily have culture-specific shapes that may or may not involve "taking control" in the white, middle-class, masculine—that is, extremely individualistic—ways valorized in psychological models. Critical of psychology's "therapeutic hegemony," Fine argues for contextualizing our standpoints by looking at social, cultural, and political circumstances "through the eyes of those . . . affected," that is, by putting their meanings at the center of our outlook.

Finally, Alan J. Bishop (p. 123) challenges those who believe "theirs is the only system of counting and recording numbers," the only mathematics. He shows that all cultures advance conceptions of space and forms and that mathematics is pan-cultural. Given its status as a supposed exemplar of neutrality, mathematics is a particularly powerful vehicle of cultural imperialism. Bishop shows that the mathematics now internationalized as a hegemonic practice comprises four sets of values that likely affected indigenous people schooled to adopt it. Bishop then brings this section to a close by delineating the responses, including resistance, that might be fruitfully made to cultural imperialism built into academic disciplines, including those like mathematics that pass as insipidly neutral.

NOTES

1 David F. Noble, *A World Without Women: The Christian Clerical Culture of Western Science,* New York, Alfred A. Knopf, 1992, p. 279.
2 Trinh T. Minh-ha, *Woman, Native, Other: Writing Postcoloniality and Feminism,* Bloomington, Indiana University Press, 1989, p. 52; Dorothy E. Smith, *Texts, Facts, and Femininity: Exploring the Relations of Ruling,* New York, Routledge, 1990, p. 91.
3 Trinh, *op. cit.,* p. 28.
4 Cf. Peter L. Berger and Thomas Luckmann, *The Social Construction of Reality: A Treatise on the Sociology of Knowledge,* New York, Anchor Books, 1967, pp. 34ff.

5 Smith, *op. cit.,* p. 1.

6 *Ibid.,* pp. 6, 1.

7 *Ibid.,* p. 87.

8 *Ibid.,* p. 164.

9 *Ibid.,* p. 91.

10 Trinh, *op. cit.,* p. 42.

11 Chrys Ingraham, "The Heterosexual Imaginary: Feminist Sociology and Theories of Gender," *Sociological Theory* 12, 2 (July, 1994), p. 207.

12 I am not distinguishing between poststructuralist and postmodernist perspectives, even though that distinction is important for purposes lying beyond our purview here.

13 Peter McLaren, "Moral Panic, Schooling, and Gay Identity: Critical Pedagogy and the Politics of Resistance," *The High School Journal* (October/November, 1993; December/January, 1994), p. 164.

14 On the heterosexualized school, see Barrie Thorne, *Gender Play: Girls and Boys in School,* New Brunswick, NJ, Rutgers University Press, 1993; also see Linda Christian-Smith.

15 Ki Namaste, "The Politics of Inside/Out: Queer Theory, Poststructuralism, and a Sociological Approach to Sexuality," *Sociological Theory* 12, 2 (July, 1994), p. 228.

16 Diana Fuss, "Inside/Out" in Diana Fuss (ed.), *Inside/Out: Lesbian Theories, Gay Theories,* New York, Routledge, 1991, pp. 6–7.

17 Steven Seidman, "Queer Theory/Sociology: A Dialogue," *Sociological Theory* 12, 2 (July, 1994), p. 174.

18 Arlene Stein and Ken Plummer, " 'I Can't Even Think Straight': 'Queer' Theory and the Missing Sexual Revolution in Sociology," *Sociological Theory* 12, 2 (July, 1994), p. 181.

Appalachian Studies and Postmodernism

Alan Banks, Dwight Billings, and Karen Tice

WHAT IS POSTMODERNISM?

The meaning of "postmodernism" is hotly debated in the arts, literature, philosophy, and social sciences. Some writers view postmodernism as an entirely new era of history and a new form of society.[1] They picture a society marked by fragmentation and heterogeneity, where Star Wars and Disney World replace social reality and substitute for meaning. Others interpret postmodernism less grandly as the ideological expression of the "cultural logic" of mass-consumer capitalism.[2] Still others view postmodernism even more narrowly as simply an artistic or narrative style. We choose to think about postmodernism as a new sensibility that involves a heightened and healthy skepticism about truth claims. "Postmodernism," as the feminist scholar Michelle Barret puts it, "is a cultural climate as well as an intellectual position, a political reality as well as an academic fashion."[3] This way of understanding postmodernism has important implications for how people think and write about the world, including Appalachia.

The postmodern sensibility calls into question common-sense notions about thinking (reason) and how thoughts are expressed (representation). With Clifford Geertz, we take postmodernism to be a new "way of thinking about the way we think." This new sensibility entails "not just another redrawing of the cultural map . . . but an alteration of the principles of mapping."[4] In Appalachian Studies, such new mapping principles have important political implications for how we think about and represent Appalachian regional identities as well as for the relationship between scholars and grassroots activism.

The modern understanding of thinking—which postmodernism leaves behind—came into being most fully during the eighteenth-century Enlightenment. It took the objectivity of reason as an article of faith. Enlightenment philosophers assumed that human reason was the vehicle that would lead to progressive social change, the means through which people could throw off their chains. For example, when Thomas Jefferson and the other signers of the Declaration of Independence justified the American colonies' secession from Great Britain in terms of "truths" they held "to be self evident," they expressed the belief that reason's truths were readily apparent to all who could think for themselves—all those, that is, freed from the blinders of dogma and tradition.[5]

What we are calling "postmodernism" signals an end to this faith in reason and its effects. As the authors of *Brave New World* and *1984* depict, and as Hiroshima and Auschwitz symbolize, rationality has deeply penetrated most aspects of life in modern society, yet it has failed to secure life, liberty, and happiness. We are left in a position where rationality without reason permeates all aspects of social life, where schooling is informative but not enlightening, where work is sustaining but not humanizing, and agriculture is efficient but not sustainable.[6]

As early as the late nineteenth century, Friedrich Nietzsche, whose ideas were a precursor to postmodernism, challenged the "god's eye" view of truth that was taken for granted by the Enlightenment in general and science in particular, noting that it presupposes "an eye such as no living creature can imagine, an eye required to have no direction, to abrogate its active and interpretive powers—precisely those powers alone that make seeing, seeing something." Thus, according to Nietzsche, "all seeing is essentially perspective, and so is all knowing."[7] Since Nietzsche, the idea that truth is always and inevitably relative to one's cultural standpoint has been widely advanced.

We have come to understand, for instance, that the natural sciences do not operate with an objective god's eye. Scientific "facts" are not independently existing realities waiting "out there" to be discovered but rather are produced through the application of theories, assumptions, conventions, methods, procedures, and beliefs held by the scientific community.[8] In this view, science, no less than any other art or discipline, is understood to be a culturally conditioned way of acting upon the world, of seeing as well as not seeing. In large measure, "what we call postmodern philosophy today is precisely about questioning the fundamental authority of science."[9] Consequently, as science loses the aura of absolute certainty that once seemed to privilege it among other ways of knowing, the demarcations between science, the humanities, the arts, and other cultural belief systems become unsure. These fields, as Geertz notes, become "blurred genres."[10]

Besides making explicit the cultural givens and practices that make thinking possible, postmodernism also refutes the naive idea that meaning precedes representation. Rather than being transparent vessels that convey truths without influencing their content, representations help to shape what can be seen and thus accepted as true. As Hayden White observes, "in any account of reality"—whether its genre is science, history, or fiction—"narrativity is present." He adds that "every narrative, however seemingly full, is constructed on the basis of a set of events which might have been included but were left out."[11]

One example of the importance of narrativity is a recent representation of Appalachia by David Cattell-Gordon as "a [regionwide] culturally transmitted traumatic stress syndrome."[12] Heavily indebted to the views of Appalachia espoused by Caudill and Weller,[13] this account of "the effects of [Appalachian] history" as social trauma "bred in the bones of the people of the region" is flawed because it constitutes Appalachians solely as "victims" and obscures the potentiality of diverse subjects' making history. In particular, oppositional movements and actions are excluded from the narrative, thereby minimizing the possibilities for agency and empowerment. Such an account leaves unquestioned paradigmatic views of Appalachia that have the effect of either marginalizing and excluding Appalachians as fully human beings or else treating them as a monolithic category. In contrast to Cattell-Gordon's clinical portrait, a postmodern sensibility would suggest that a more kaleidoscopic view of culture and history is essential for capturing the complexity of Appalachia's past and potential.

Many writers are troubled by postmodernism's abandonment of the unitary vision of objective truth in favor of unapologetically partial viewpoints. Some interpret postmodernism as "cultural helplessness," claiming that "postmodernism is above all post-1960s. . . . It is post–Viet Nam, post–New Left, post-hippie, post-Watergate . . . [where] belief has become difficult."[14] Others are even more critical, claiming that the "corrosive skepticism and nihilism" of most postmodernist thinking "disables both theoretical inquiry and political practice."[15] We reject such harshly critical views of postmodernism. Like

Geertz, we discern "a distinctly democratic temper" in postmodernism's "fluid, plural, uncentered, and ineradicably untidy" approach.[16] Thus, we see postmodernism as having the potential to point Appalachian Studies in some important new directions. In particular, we believe that a cautious use of postmodern insights can guide our efforts in making sure that Appalachian Studies continues to be one of the region's voices of dissent.

THE POSTMODERN CHALLENGE: AVOIDING UNIVERSALISM AND ESSENTIALISM

Appalachian Studies and Women's Studies both emerged as prominent features of university life in the 1970s in response to democratic impulses at the grassroots level in the late 1960s. Both have struggled with how to critique widespread stereotypes, accommodate the plurality of experiences and perspectives among participants, and further the common goals of academics and activists in struggles for social justice. We believe that the feminists' extensive wrestling with postmodernism, its political implications for feminist practice, and its place in the academy has much to contribute to Appalachian Studies. Applications include not only how to incorporate an understanding of gender into our work on Appalachia, but also how to think about regional identities in new and less restrictive ways.

Increasingly, many feminists are beginning to represent the social world in a postmodern manner in order to avoid explanations that are universalistic. These feminists question the validity of any unitary ways of knowing that claim to understand and describe the complexity of social relations in a totalistic fashion. Such universalistic knowledge claims and truth assertions—"metanarratives"—are rejected as reductionistic and ahistorical. As Nancy Fraser and Linda Nicholson note, feminists are calling into question "the dominant [modernist] philosophical project of seeking objectivity in the guise of a god's eye view which transcends any situation or perspective."[17]

As power conversations or privileged discourses, metanarratives are the ideological manifestations of inequitable social relations. In the case of gender, they falsely universalize white male expressions and experiences and, at the same time, peripheralize the diverse experiences of women. Instead, many feminist scholars are taking a more kaleidoscopic point of view that does not collapse the multiplicity of women's experiences, preoccupations, and expressions into the universal woman. They debunk descriptions that lump women into a monolithic category by exploring not only commonalities but differences among women.[18]

Thus, as postmodernists, feminist scholars have grown deeply suspicious of any descriptions of women and men, minorities, or humanity in general—and here we should add regions and regional populations—that rely on a universal image, model, norm, or method. They challenge as ideological assertions that repress multiplicity and diversity. Feminists also advocate a "deconstructive strategy" that takes apart falsely unified conceptions such as "women"—or, in our case, "Appalachians"—in order to reveal the internal diversity and plurality that such representations mask.

These feminist scholars are calling for approaches that are non-universalistic, self-conscious about perspective and values, and open to the multiplicity and diversity of experiences. If applied to Appalachian Studies, this approach would challenge us to replace unitary notions of Appalachians and Appalachian identity with plural and complexly constructed conceptions of social identity. The paradigmatic Appalachian would thus be replaced by a conception that represents Appalachian regional identities—these being decidedly plural—as "one strand among others, attending also to class, race, ethnicity, age, and sexual orientation . . . in short . . . more like a tapestry composed of many threads of many hues than one woven in a single color."[19]

In addition to a critique of universalistic thinking that represses the diversity of experiences among Appalachian peoples, postmodern feminist scholars can also teach us to challenge essentialistic thinking about Appalachia. "Essentialism" is the tendency to treat historical and social constructions as "fixed, natural, and absolute."[20] Essentialistic thinking further tends to reduce complex relations to fixed, and often binary, oppositions that are hierarchically ordered. In Appalachian Studies, we are accustomed to thinking in terms of such oppositions as Appalachian/non-Appalachian, insider/outsider, scholars/activists, culture folk/action folk. In such cases, interrelatedness is reduced to sets of either/ors. Postmodernism challenges us to rethink these taken-for-granted categories and to ask instead how they are constituted in historically situated social relations.

Taken together, opposition to universalistic and essentialistic thinking provides Appalachian Studies with avenues to transform our knowledge base and inform our practice of regional politics. In the remainder of this paper we wish to highlight steps in this direction already evident in Appalachian Studies.

POSTMODERN DIRECTIONS IN APPALACHIAN STUDIES

Several recent contributions to the Appalachian literature advance a postmodern sensibility. Herbert Reid, for instance, challenges the either/or of class versus culture in Appalachian Studies by suggesting how a "critical and viable concept of [Appalachian] regionalism" can be developed that does not obscure the continuities between regional and national cultural life as well as cultural and class differences within the region. Ron Lewis and Sally Maggard discount, respectively, the either/ors of class versus race and class versus gender in studies of the interplay of the lived experiences of gender, race, and class stratification in the Appalachian coalfields. John Gaventa, Barbara Smith, and Alex Willingham connect struggles for economic justice and alternative forms of economic development in Appalachia to similar grassroots struggles in other parts of the South and to national patterns of deindustrialization.[21]

Perhaps the earliest and, in many ways, still the most radically postmodern study of Appalachia is Henry Shapiro's *Appalachia on Our Mind*. Shapiro's intellectual history of the "idea of Appalachia" does much to deconstruct the "mythic system" that interprets Appalachia as "a coherent region with a uniform culture and homogenous population." Shapiro shows that the representation of the Appalachian population as "a distinct people with distinct and describable characteristics" owes much to a stereotyped tradition of writing about life in the southern mountains that originated in late nineteenth-century local color fiction as well as in missionaries' accounts depicting Appalachia as "a strange land and a peculiar people."[22]

The radical implications of Shapiro's work for Appalachian Studies are overlooked when his text is read simply as providing empirical support for an essentialistic and reductionistic understanding of Appalachia as a "colony." In such accounts, an essentialistic understanding of Appalachia as a traditional or poverty subculture is replaced by an equally essentialistic understanding of Appalachia as an exploited colony. But Shapiro does much more than simply document the imperialistic practices of missionaries and social workers in the region's past. By remaining skeptical about the existence of any essential Appalachian experience or unitary Appalachian identity, Shapiro calls attention to how mythical versions of Appalachia are produced every day in discursive representations of the region. Thus he highlights the fact that activists and scholars produce partial versions of reality every time they write about or act in the name of Appalachia. The obvious shortcoming of Shapiro's work, however, is that there is more to Appalachia than simply language about the region.[23] Thus, his work overlooks the nondiscursive realities in the region: real-life events such as death and injury in the mines; black lung and brown lung; economic exploitation, poverty, and unemployment; gender and racial oppression. The problem that Shapiro's study of representation raises is how to deconstruct universalizing and essentializing myths of Appalachia while sustaining viable forms of regional politics.

A partially successful effort in this direction combines Shapiro's stress on how Appalachia is represented in discourses with large narratives about changes in social organization. Rodger Cunningham's *Apples on the Flood* is a sophisticated and deeply probing application of the colonial model of Appalachia and an extended essay on the cultural and psychological consequences of peripheralization.[24] Its thesis is that the internalization of pejorative discourses and opinions about Appalachia by Appalachians results in their infantilization and the development of damaged selves. Such a "psychological heredity" would undoubtedly have important negative implications for contemporary Appalachians' ability to make their own history and organize themselves collectively to resist exploitation and oppression. Floating like apples on the tide of historical circumstances, today's Appalachians are tragically portrayed by Cunningham as damaged souls—in the final analysis, victims of the pernicious effects of modernity itself—who are overidentified with their oppressors and closed off from an authentic and self-centered existence.

In style—but not in substance—Cunningham's work partakes of the new postmodern sensibility we have been describing. The author deliberately blurs the genres of anthropology, history, psychology, folklore, sociology, and comparative literature to produce an ambiguous and challenging text that defies categorization as factual social history, social science, fiction, or autobiography. He calls attention to the power of representations by showing how they operate through internalization in the social psychology of colonialism, and he directs attention toward their operation in his own text by pointing out his own narrative strategies and the effects he hopes them to have upon his readers. But in marked contrast with postmodern writers who deliberately produce ambiguous, contradictory, and open-ended texts in order to "destabilize stable ways of looking at the world" and to include the reader as an active participant in constructing the various meanings a text may come to have,[25] Cunningham supplies fixed and final answers in his portrayal of a paradigmatic Appalachia. In doing so, he subverts his own wish for Appalachian peoples to be the authors of their own identities by succumbing to the temptation of writing a metanarrative from a god's eye perspective no less Olympian than that of Caudill and Weller, of whom he is critical.

Whereas Shapiro critically examines the pejorative discourses that constitute the "myth of Appalachia," Cunningham's exploration of the psychological consequences of the internalization of such discourses has the effect of universalizing and essentializing his understanding of the Scotch-Irish experience in a manner that reduces the complexity and open-endedness of Appalachian experiences to a static and bleakly pessimistic caricature: Li'l Abner with a severely neurotic personality.[26]

Just as women, blacks, and the Eastern European miners of West Virginia and eastern Kentucky are erased from Cunningham's narrative of Appalachian history, so too is the likelihood of resistance and dissent. And having presented a deterministic account of "the present mainly as a product of past forces" and admittedly told "only half the story," Cunningham's only way out lies in "the liberating power of true myth." Thus an author "repelled . . . by [Appalachian] social activists' tendency to dismiss, ignore, or pigeon-hole cultural questions" in the early seventies dispatches activism to the "realm of imagination."[27]

We believe that the solution to Cunningham's dilemma—how to convey the interrelationship of politics and culture in Appalachia—lies in adopting a postmodern view of culture. In contrast to Cunningham's essentialistic understanding of culture as a singular "structure of meanings," we suggest the value of Jerome Bruner's conceptualization of culture as "a forum for negotiating and re-negotiating meaning." According to Bruner, "it is the forum aspect of culture that gives its participants a role in constantly making and remaking the culture—an active role as participants rather than as performing spectators who play out their canonical roles according to rule when the appropriate cues occur."[28] This non-essentialistic view of culture allows for multiplicity and diversity at the same time that it recognizes culture as providing ample resources for its participants to engage in the sort of "identity politics" modeled above by contemporary feminists.

Stephen Foster's recent study, *The Past Is Another Country,*[29] makes exemplary use of such a model of culture in an investigation of grassroots resistance in Appalachia that is premised on an appreciation of Appalachia's cultural diversity. Rather than presenting a fixed image of local culture as a set of collective traits, Foster documents the "politics of culture" in Ashe County, North Carolina—that is, the changing and strategic discourses of self- and community representation. From this perspective Foster remarks that the local culture "appears in this context as extraordinarily fluid and changeable; it operates as a placeholder, a representation that shifts, deviates, and often wobbles in an unstable and quixotic fashion, depending on the desires, options, constraints, and interventions operating at the crossroads of the present."[30]

In his analysis of the successful efforts of local citizens in 1975 to prevent the Appalachian Power Company from damming a portion of the New River to create a reservoir that would have displaced 287 families, Foster examines local resistance as a "politics of representation." In stark contrast to Cunningham's interpretation that the "mountaineer's notorious 'present-orientation' " is evidence of his "being cut off from the past," Foster highlights the practices whereby Ashe County citizens objectified a version of their culture and their past to planners and outside policy-makers as a way of life worth preserving. Here, the "domination of imposed discourses of economic necessity and economic interest" by elites were countered by local folk festivals that served both to mobilize support to "save the river" and to objectify local culture. Ironically, however, by choosing to represent their threatened way of life in terms of stereotyped images, folk-culture artifacts, and music, grassroots activists opened the door to the commodification of a partial version of their culture and thus potentially to further elite domination. Foster returned to Ashe County nearly ten years later to find that the embrace of mythic forms of ethnic identity that had served to stop the dam project had also begun to change the rhetorical forms through which local people understood themselves, their history, and their community.

Foster's image of culture as a discursive forum rather than a configuration of traits or a unitary structure of meaning should alert us in Appalachian Studies to the variety of discourses that constitute social identity as well as to the diversity of subjects actively involved in making history in Appalachia. Further, his refusal to describe local culture the way it "really" is, in any fixed or final way—that is, his refusal to write a "metanarrative"—exemplifies the postmodern ethnographic ideal of "apprehend[ing] and inscrib[ing] 'others' in such a way as not to deny or diffuse their claims to subjecthood."[31] As such, his study provides not only important insights into problematic aspects of grassroots activism but also a model for how Appalachian scholars can learn to write about the region without succumbing to the temptation of speaking like the invisible, know-it-all "over-voice" that is a commonplace in television advertising and mass media broadcasting.

CONCLUSION

In challenging the notion that writers can attain a god's eye view of truth and represent reality in its totality, postmodernism has the potential to make all of us, activists and scholars, more humble and reflective about what we claim and assert. From the recognition that "truths" are always "truths for some particular person or group," it follows that our common-sense notions of what "Appalachia" is, or who "Appalachians" are, can always be opened up to include more diversity or, as postmodernists like to say, more "difference." Yet, as many feminists have been forced to admit, the recognition of difference and diversity is a political challenge. As Teresa Ebert notes, the recognition of differences among women "opens up the multiplicity of differences among (within) women, but in doing so it undermines the unity or collectivity of women and gender as categories on which an oppositional politics can be based."[32] The achievement of diversity and unity can only result from political effort.

The recognition of difference—indeed, the positive valorization of difference—that postmodern thinking encourages should help us to appreciate that what we have been doing in the Appalachian Studies movement and in the Appalachian Studies Association has been a positive yet fragile accomplishment. Still, if the Appalachian Studies movement is to fulfill its promise of "help[ing] to reconstruct a public sphere through which people can participate in democratizing the structures of political economy and everyday life,"[33] difference and diversity must be further embraced and accommodated. Mythical images of a homogeneous Appalachia must not be allowed to suppress the important class, race, ethnic, and gender differences that figure in the life of the region. Likewise, the organizational structures and processes of the ASA must be revised in ways that support such diversity.

Ours, as we have seen, is not the only scholarly association to face new organizational tensions that result from growth and success and raise concerns about how to remain connected to founding ideals—the grass-roots basis of our common identity and purpose. Many current tensions in the ASA mirror those in other movement-based organizations that are likewise committed to supporting democratic struggles. For instance, Lisa Hall has observed that the linkages between community- and academically based participants in women's studies and ethnic studies have weakened. "Academic feminism and ethnic studies as a whole," she says, "have not maintained the direct connections with the communities that helped to create them."[34]

Organizational reforms within the ASA itself may help to combat the trend toward academicization and contribute to the preservation and strengthening of ties between the Appalachian Studies movement and the grassroots. If ASA conferences are becoming too large and its sessions too specialized, then noncompetitive plenary sessions, arranged to include scholarly activists and activist scholars, can be used to front-stage important conversations that have regionwide implications. Ideally, annual conferences—now typically coordinated by local colleges—could be co-sponsored by local grassroots organizations that would conduct off-site sessions highlighting local issues and struggles and thus challenging the ASA to reaffirm its original goal of relating scholarship to regional needs and the concerns of Appalachian people. The steering committee that governs the association, increasingly peopled by academicians, can change its membership criteria to create formal slots for individuals representing grassroots organizations, while caucuses can be organized to reflect and encourage diversity within the general membership. We hope that such small but self-conscious efforts can help to keep alive an important form of cooperation in the region that has great potential to contribute further to Appalachian and American public life.

NOTES

1 Jean Baudrillard, *Selected Writings,* ed. Mark Poster (Stanford, Calif: Stanford University Press, 1988); Jean-Francois Lyotard, *The Postmodern Condition* (Minneapolis: University of Minneapolis Press, [1979] 1984).

2 For example, Fredric Jameson, "Postmodernism or the Cultural Logic of Late Capitalism," *New Left Review,* no. 146 (July–August 1984): 53–92.

3 Quoted in Ebert, "Postmodernism's Infinite Variety," 24–25.

4 Clifford Geertz, *Local Knowledge* (New York: Basic Books, 1983), 20.

5 The model for such freethinking was empirical science. Simply observing the world as it really was—rather than passively accepting the way it was described by religious or political authorities—promised liberation from ignorance, superstition, and fear. And, until the past few decades, many people have shared the Enlightenment faith that when the eye of reason judged social institutions, it would guarantee a critical vision that would lead the march to Progress.

6 Along with the loss of faith in reason's ability to perfect society, we have also become increasingly skeptical about reason's ability even to understand and represent social life.

In particular, the simple, unmediated, unitary vision of reason has been called into question.

7 Quoted in W. T. Jones, *Kant and the Nineteenth Century* (New York: Harcourt Brace Jovanovich, 1975), 237.

8 Thomas S. Kuhn, *The Structure of Scientific Revolutions* (Chicago: University of Chicago Press, 1970).

9 Cornel West, "Interview," in Andrew Ross, ed., *Universal Abandon?* (Minneapolis: University of Minnesota Press, 1988), 272.

10 See Geertz, *Local Knowledge,* 19.

11 Hayden White, *The Content of the Form* (Baltimore: Johns Hopkins University Press, 1987), 14.

12 David Cattell-Gordon, "The Appalachian Inheritance: A Culturally Transmitted Traumatic Stress Syndrome?" *Journal of Progressive Human Services* 1 (1990): 41–57. Also see Karen W. Tice and Dwight B. Billings, "Appalachian Culture and Resistance," *Journal of Progressive Human Services* 2 (1991): 1–18.

13 See Jack Weller, *Yesterday's People* (Lexington: University Press of Kentucky, 1965) and Harry M. Caudill, *Night Comes to the Cumberlands: A Biography of a Depressed Area* (Boston: Little, Brown/Atlantic Monthly, 1962)—Ed. note.

14 See Todd Gitlin, "Hip Deep in Post-Modernism," *New York Times Book Review,* November 6, 1988, 35–36.

15 For example, Douglas Kellner, "Critical Theory and the Crisis of Social Theory," *Sociological Perspectives* 33 (Spring 1990): 11–17.

16 Geertz, *Local Knowledge,* 21.

17 Nancy Fraser and Linda Nicholson, "Social Criticism Without Philosophy: An Encounter Between Feminism and Postmodernism," *Theory, Culture & Society* 5 (1988): 391.

18 For example, the work of Carol Gilligan on women's moral development and Nancy Chodorow on mothering has been criticized for their failure to consider important differences between white women and women of color and the accommodations that slavery and domestic work have demanded of African-American women. See Fraser and Nicholson, "Social Criticism"; Sandra Morgan, *To See Ourselves, To See Our Sisters* (Memphis, Tenn.: Memphis State University Press/Center for Research on Women, 1986); and Carol Stack, "The Culture of Gender: Women and Men of Color," *Signs* 11(1986): 321–24.

19 Fraser and Nicholson, "Social Criticism," 391.

20 Joan Scott, "Deconstructing Equality-Versus-Difference: Or, The Uses of Poststructuralist Theory for Feminism," *Feminist Studies* 14 (1988):33–50.

21 Herbert Reid, "Appalachian Studies: Class, Culture and Politics—II," *Appalachian Journal* 9 (1982):144; Ronald L. Lewis, *Black Coal Miners in America: Race, Class, and Community Conflict, 1780–1980* (Lexington: University Press of Kentucky, 1987); Sally Maggard, "Eastern Kentucky Women on Strike: A Study of Gender, Class and Political Action in the 1970s" (Ph.D. diss., University of Kentucky, 1988); and John Gaventa, Barbara E. Smith, and Alex Willingham, eds., *Communities in Economic Crisis: Appalachia and the South* (Philadelphia: Temple University Press, 1990). Also note that many of these points are raised in a special issue of *Appalachian Journal* 9, entitled "Assessing Appalachian Studies" (Winter/Spring 1982).

22 Henry D. Shapiro, *Appalachia on Our Mind: The Southern Mountains and Mountaineers in the American Consciousness, 1870–1920* (Chapel Hill: University of North Carolina Press, 1978), 265.

23 See Herbert Reid, "Appalachian Policy, the Corporate State and American Values," *Policy Studies Journal* 9 (Special Issue no. 2, 1980–81):622–33.

24 Rodger Cunningham, *Apples on the Flood: The Southern Mountain Experience* (Knoxville: University of Tennessee Press, 1987).

25 Gurney Norman and Lance Olsen, "Frankenstein in Palestine or: Postmodernism in Appalachia," in *Pine Mountain Sand and Gravel,* ed. Jim Webb et al. (Whitesburg, Ky.: Appalshop Productions, 1988), 83.

26 By taking the Scotch-Irish as the predominant ethnic group to settle and influence the region, Cunningham suppresses much of the diversity that can be found throughout Appalachia, essentializing it as a Scotch-Irish enclave. For a different look at early settlement patterns, see John Solomon Otto, "The Migration of the Southern Plain Folk: An Interdisciplinary Synthesis," *Journal of Southern History* 51 (1985):183–200. For a look at the ethnic and racial diversity that came to characterize coal camp living, see Lewis, *Black Coal Miners in America.*

27 Cunningham, *Apples on the Flood,* xvii, 160, 162.

28 Jerome Bruner, *Actual Minds, Possible Worlds* (Cambridge: Harvard University Press, 1986), 94, 123.

29 Stephen William Foster, *The Past Is Another Country: Representation, Historical Consciousness, and Resistance in the Blue Ridge* (Berkeley, Los Angeles and London: University of California Press, 1988).

30 Ibid., 203.

31 Frances Mascia-Lees et al., "The Postmodernist Turn in Anthropology: Cautions from a Feminist Perspective," *Signs* 15 (1989):12.

32 Ebert, "Postmodernism's Infinite Variety," 24.

33 Reid, "Appalachian Studies," 141.

34 Lisa Hall, "Trapped in the Ivory Tower?" *Women's Review of Books* 11 (May 1991):25.

The Politics of Queer Theory in the (Post)Modern Moment

Donald Morton

It is by now a cliché of contemporary thought that (post)modernism has ushered in knowledge/power breaks of vast significance: Foucault's genealogical analyses marked some previous ones and forecast that we are approaching another, and commentators as "different" as (post)structuralist feminist Alice Jardine, on the one hand, and former State Department official Francis Fukuyama, on the other, seem to agree in proposing that we are nearing another radical "end," the end of history itself.[1] Few if any spots on the cultural map have escaped the discourse of rupture and innovation: having thoroughly permeated the politically dominant cultural spaces, it is now sweeping through the politically marginal ones, a sequencing which should tell us something about the politics of the relations involved.[2] Thus a narrative of momentous change, if not of out-

GENDERS Number 17, Fall 1993

right triumph, is circulating today in American academic and intellectual circles regarding the status of Queer Theory.

For instance, in October 1990, the *Chronicle of Higher Education* announced that "the gay-studies movement is gaining acceptance in academe . . . with a surge in sophisticated scholarship."[3] The *Chronicle* supported its announcement with two articles: one is concerned with the movement at large and cites such evidence as the Lesbian, Bisexual, and Gay Studies Conference held at Harvard in the fall of 1990 (the fourth such annual meeting), the establishment of a Center for Lesbian and Gay Studies at CUNY, and the initiation of a gay studies series by Columbia University Press; the other article is concerned with the "sophisticated scholarship," taking as its focus an "influential yet controversial . . . Duke University Professor" (that is, Eve Sedgwick) who has become a "lightning rod for [those] working in gay studies."[4] Reinforcing this narrative of break and break-through, as if from within, Ed Cohen has recently observed that he is "confounded by how quickly things have changed so much—for me as a gay man, for the profession of literary studies in America, for me as a professional academic, for gay professors, and especially for academics professing 'gayness.' "[5] "During the last twelve months," he continues, "I have turned thirty; moved from San Francisco to New York City; completed a highly enjoyable first year as a tenure-track assistant professor; managed to write a number of talks and articles, all well received if not (yet) published; been solicited to write this [present essay] as well as several other new 'gay studies' pieces; and garnered not one but three contracts for my first book."[6] Although he goes on to admit that at times it all seems like a "dream,"[7] he is nevertheless highly enthusiastic about queer studies, which he understands as the project of making "heretofore 'eccentric' experiences not only visible but intelligible."[8] Enthusiasm aside, such confident formulations raise a number of urgent questions: What has in fact produced this "incredible good fortune"? Should Queer Theory really take as its goal rendering queer "experience" visible? What is the relation between "visibility" and "intelligibility"? Does the phrase "make intelligible" mean finally "make intelligible" in terms of dominant discourses or in opposition to them?

The moment seems right for looking into this narrative of the new-found "success" of Queer Theory by inquiring into the politics that underlies the manner in which cultural studies at large is currently taking shape in the American academy. The mode of my inquiry here will be critique, which must be distinguished from criticism.[9] The criticism of queer studies being launched today from the political right is aimed at undermining its legitimacy and at erasing it from all cultural sites. The critique of queer studies, which is undertaken in solidarity, recognizes the importance and necessity of such studies but questions whether their present location in academic and intellectual spaces is productive for the radical change needed to combat exploitation and oppression in all forms. Queer Theory, I will argue, cannot limit itself to the local politics of fighting homophobia only; it must recognize that without a dialectical historical knowledge of the social totality it will become merely a reformist politics. The emancipation of the "queer" cannot be achieved without a radical transformation of the regimes of labor, family, . . . and other social structures that produce homophobia in the first place. In other words, it is my argument that homophobia is not a "prejudice," not an "attitude" that can be overcome by the strategies of consciousness-raising and education: it is, on the contrary, a *structure* of exploitation linked—not eccentrically, locally, or contingently, but systemically—to other social practices.

. . . My argument is that the "dreamlike" success of Queer Theory today is enabled precisely by its tendency to endorse and celebrate the dominant academy's narrative of progressive change.[10] In other words, in its eagerness to become "visible and intelligible," Queer Theory is rapidly following the path taken by most other marginal groups (feminists, African-Americanists, and so on) and is joining with the dominant form of (post)modern theory and its mode of cultural investigation, which privilege politically unproductive understandings of such categories as "desire," "discourse," and the "material."

It must be said at the outset that in spite of claims to the contrary, the kind of critique-al practice undertaken here is quite uncommon in academic and intellectual circles. Indeed, inquiries such as the present one will inevitably appear, to the common sense (the consensus) of culture, to operate entirely as "negation" and thus encounter the demand for the elaboration of a "positive alternative." Along the "personal" axis, the demand for the affirmative appears as a call to "give due credit" to those critiqued. Of course, inasmuch as critique is directed at the "dominant," the critiqued discourses have "all the credit" that counts under the present regime already. They are already credited! It is the very self-evidentness of this "credit-worthiness" to which critique addresses itself: indeed credit could be "given" only by a self-defeating "stepping outside" the critique-al domain to reaffirm the existing space of present social arrangements. Such a gesture would end in complicity with the "pragmatic" and the "realistic" (that is, with the status quo). The demand for the positive is thus an ideological alibi: a "legitimate"-seeming way to contain and exclude the critique-al discourse.

Along the "impersonal" axis, the demand for the affirmative appears as a call to "describe the alternative," which amounts to an invitation to the utopian gesture—which radical political materialism must reject—of outlining the ideal society. As Marcuse has put it, from the Marxian perspective the ideological aim of such calls for the "affirmative" is to distract attention from the "factual world of the daily struggle for existence."[11] In any case, Marxian critique is a mode of negation within which the affirmative is already inscribed as what might be called an "immanent utopia."[12] This is both an "old" and "new" question, traceable in urgent terms from Marx to Marcuse to the recent (spring 1992) special issue of the socialist journal *Science and Society,* which in the wake of historic changes in the Soviet Union and Eastern Europe first planned a special issue on the topic "Socialism: Alternative Visions and Models" and then ran into dissent within its own editorial board over the problem of the "affirmative." It posed the issue in the following question (to which, it should be clear by now, my answer is "yes"): "Is presentation of models—abstract representations—of socialist institutions essentially a utopian exercise, of the sort deliberately eschewed by Marx and Engels in favor of scientific analysis and critique of existing conditions?"[13]

Before entering on the critique of Queer Theory, however, it is necessary first to outline some broader developments in the study of culture at large.

At the present historical juncture, an urgent contestation is now under way in America over how culture itself is to be theorized: this struggle is being fought out between proponents of textual studies, on the one hand, and cultural studies, on the other.[14] Although these two forms of cultural understanding have both been shaped by the impact of (post)modern thought, they nevertheless have distinct presuppositions and point in significantly different political directions.[15] Textual studies, which relies on (post)structuralist theory and its privileging of the concept of "textuality," is concerned with the mechanics of signification, the "playful" relation of signifier to signified (hence the term *ludic*), and therefore stresses the supposedly decisive rupture produced by Saussurean linguistics. It basically defines "politics" as those reading activities that "delay" the connection of the signifier to the signified and disrupt the easy trafficking of meaning in culture.[16] This disruption is understood as the continual subversion of the denotative or literal meanings of the texts of culture by their ever-shifting and unstable connotative or figural undersides. Furthermore, this interminable sliding along the chain of signifiers is driven by unsatisfiable "desire." This slide cannot stop, in Derrida's terms, because the signifier can no longer acquire representational authority by anchoring itself in the "transcendental signified."[17] From such a perspective the term *culture* in cultural studies is itself the effect of logocentric metaphysics: a transcendental signified which aims at a coercive stopping of the "free play" of the signifier. For textual studies, culture is merely another signifier. On the textualist view, the "material" is the material part of the sign, that is, the signifier. And inasmuch as the sign is conceived of as being deployed specifically in textualist thought by the *speaking subject,* the material is also associated by ludic textualism with the domain of the body; for, as Barthes—a Queer Theorist before the letter—has proposed, the body contributes to moments of signification through the phatic dimension of speech which folds an opacity (a meaninglessness) into the process of meaning-production.[18] This move of delaying the easy trafficking of meaning in culture, far from being a trivial philosophical game (as some seem to think), is actually aimed ultimately at rendering knowledge itself unreliable. Thus, for textual studies, there really can be no "knowable" "public sphere" understood as the site of a collective political project; in fact, as post-Marxist textualists like Ernest Laclau avow, society—being itself a text operating as the "infinite play of differences"—is "impossible."[19] Thus, textual studies puts in question the very validity of cultural studies in general; for since it regards culture itself to be textual (and thus subject to the effects of *différance*), culture is not really available for investigation in any reliable manner.

As developed in Britain, particularly through the Birmingham School, cultural studies by contrast depends on the continuing possibilities of speaking "knowledgeably" and "effectively" about entities called "culture" and "society." Although it takes signification into account (seeing language as a form of social praxis), cultural studies is suspicious of textual studies's overtextualization of all cultural phenomena and is primarily concerned with the reproduction and maintenance of subjectivities. More specifically, it is concerned with the reproduction and maintenance of subjectivities *in ideology and in the accompanying social/economic/cultural/political . . . structures that produce social inequalities.* Thus, for cultural studies, the "material" means (not as in textual studies, the signifier or the body, but) these structures as well as the supposedly "abstract" ideas which support and legitimate them. Thus, although cultural studies is concerned with "subjects," its analytics moves away from the narrowly "personal" and toward the "transpersonal."

The story of recent developments does not end here, however, for under the impact of current cultural politics, cultural studies has itself split into two opposing modes, a "critical" and "experiential" mode. The dominant form of cultural studies today, which is exemplified in the theoretically updated work of writers such as John Fiske, Constance Penley, and Andrew Ross,[20] must be called "experiential cultural studies." It "describes" various emerging, suppressed cultural groups and its goal is to give voice to their previously un- or little-known "experience," to let them "speak for themselves." Over against this dominant form stands "critical cultural studies" (a reaffirmation of the concerns of classic cultural studies) which, even in the wake of (post)modern thought, still privileges conceptuality (while accounting for textuality), takes as its radical political project the transformation of the very social/political/economic . . . structures which have suppressed those groups in the first place and prevented them from speaking. Unlike experiential cultural studies, whose mode is "descriptive" and whose effect is to give the (native) bourgeois student of culture the pleasure of encounter with the exotic "other," the mode of critical cultural studies is "explanatory" and its effect is to alter the settled and exploitative relations between the bourgeois reader and her/his "other." The point of critical cultural studies is not simply to "witness" cultural events but to intervene in them, that is, to produce socially transformative cultural understandings. It does so by refusing to take "experience" (either the sensations of empirical traditionalism or the signs of a supposedly anti-empirical textualism)[21] as a given, for to do so is to accept a highly restricted and restricting understanding of the "materiality" of culture, that is, as what a given subject "experiences": her thoughts, feelings, opinions, physical and bodily states . . . Of course, under the impact of "textualism" (which has presumably torn the philosophical ground out from under what traditionalists understand as "experience"), there is today a greatly increased sophistication about the notion of "experience": "experience" itself has been reunderstood, not in traditional terms as the direct contact of an "essentialized" subject with her own self-expressive and self-defining thoughts and sensations but rather in ludic (post)modern terms as the recognition of one's textual and linguistic construction. In other words, "experience" today is also understood by many theorists as the experience of the "slide along the chain of signifiers" that produces one as a subject. In this way, something called "experience" has today become the space in which, for the sake of a politically "safe" eclectic approach to the study of culture, the very distinctions between the theories underlying textual studies and cultural studies are being blurred: many of the dominant academy's most "sophisticated" critics swing uncertainly today between the two. This new elision of textual and cultural studies allows one to begin to understand why the essentialism/constructionism debate has dwindling force today, since each approach still enables the privileging of "experience."[22] Rather than focusing on experience, critical cultural studies "moves beyond" experience (as given) and understands the "materiality" of culture as the historical conditions and the social and economic structures which in fact produce that "experience." While for its part experiential cultural studies tends to restrict the understanding of the "material" at the level of micro-practices, critical cultural studies understands the "material" at the level of macro-practices in relation to the level of micro-practices.

It is important to add that no matter how theoretically sophisticated it may be, experiential cultural studies (whether it thinks of "experience" in traditionalist or ludic "textualist" terms) is, in the last analysis, hostile to "theory" (that is, to "conceptuality"), seeing it ultimately as a potentially "oppressive" (Enlightenment) structure of abstract and "totalizing" (even "totalitarian") ideas, threatening to disrupt the individual subject's "security" by breaking his grip on "his experience." For its part, critical cultural studies sees theory not as something to be resisted in general but as itself—as Mas'ud Zavarzadeh has strongly argued—a form of resistance.[23]

In its focus on the production and maintenance of subjectivities in ideology, critical cultural studies understands "politics" ultimately as a struggle over access to the material base of power/knowledge/resources. Rather than being any form of opacity (of the signifier, the body . . .), the material is understood in this perspective as the overdetermination and effectivity of all cultural phenomena as they are grasped "socially," which is to say, rendered intelligible through the mediation of the concept. On this view, theory itself, as Marx has argued, is a "material force."[24] Desire here is not the localized and privatized entity it is in textual studies (not "my" desire attached to "my" body driving me along "my" chain of signifiers) but is reunderstood in relation to the collective requirements of social justice. Marx is again relevant here: "Men make their own history, but they do not make it just as they please; they do not make it under circumstances chosen by themselves, but under circumstances directly found, given and transmitted from the past."[25] Among these circumstances, as critical cultural studies proposes, is the construction of those desires, under presently prevailing relations of power, which we call "our" desires.

The struggle over cultural theory just outlined constitutes the historical context for what a British commentator has called the current "blossoming" of queer studies.[26] This narrative of a queer studies "break" and "break-through" deserves careful attention; and toward this goal it is helpful to situate within the current contestations several recently published exemplary texts: Greenberg's *The Construction of Homosexuality* (1988), Sedgwick's *Epistemology of the Closet* (1990), Sinfield's *Literature, Politics, and Culture in Postwar Britain* (1989), and de Lauretis's "Sexual Indifference and Lesbian Representation" (1988; reprinted 1990).[27] In broad terms, it may be said that Greenberg's text generally attempts to evade ludic theory, de Lauretis's draws most fully on it, while Sedgwick's and Sinfield's texts use it—to varying degrees—to update traditional humanist understandings of culture. In spite of their differences, however, all of these projects are ideologically symptomatic of the situation at the end of the 1980s, a time when the crisis in the academy could no longer be plausibly framed as the contestation between traditionalism and deconstruction and the battle lines had been redrawn between ludic textualism grafted onto traditionalism (textual studies and experiential cultural studies), on the one hand, and political radicalism (critical cultural studies), on the other.

. . .

NOTES

1 Of course, what Jardine proposes is that, in the wake of the kind of "feminocentric" understanding that (post)structuralism represents to her, it is phallocentric history that is coming to an end; see Jardine, *Gynesis: Configurations of Woman and Modernity* (Ithaca, 1985). For his part, Fukuyama argues that what is coming to an end is all opposition to individualistic Western liberal democracy and capitalism as mode of production; see Fukuyama, "The End of History," *National Interest* (Summer 1989): 3–18.

2 For a critique of the supposedly radical break produced by the dominant ludic theory, see Mas'ud Zavarzadeh and Donald Morton, *Theory (Post)Modernity Opposition: An "Other" Introduction to Literary and Cultural Theory* (Washington, D.C., 1991), chap. 5.

3 Scott Heller, "Gay- and Lesbian-Studies Movement Gains Acceptance in Many Areas of Scholarship and Teaching," *Chronicle of Higher Education,* October 24, 1990, A-4.

4 Scott Heller, "Individual yet Controversial among Literary Scholars, Duke U. Professor Uses Sexuality in Analyzing Culture," *Chronicle of Higher Education,* October 24, 1990, A-4.

5 Ed Cohen, "Are We (Not) What We Are Becoming? 'Gay' 'Identity,' 'Gay Studies,' and the Disciplining of Knowledge," in *Engendering Men: The Question of Male Feminist Criticism,* ed. Joseph A. Boone and Michael Cadden (New York and London, 1990), 161.

6 Ibid.

7 Ibid.

8 Ibid.

9 For a further inquiry into the differences between criticism and critique and of the forms of (post)modern critique, see Zavarzadeh and Morton, *Theory,* 13 ff.

10 This essay undertakes a critique of contemporary Queer Theory (and inquires into its celebration) which involves attention to the politics of argument and the cultural logic deployed by some well-known theorists, theorists who have achieved celebrity in the existing U.S. academy. To quote another celebrity, Gayatri Spivak, in a discussion with a noncelebrity lesbian over what kind of subjectivity is the most "commodifiable" (see *The Post-Colonial Critic* [New York: Routledge, 1989], 86), celebrities are "highly commodified" subjects who are therefore sites of academic "investment." Any transgression against the writings of these celebrities is seen by the custodians of the academy as nothing less than an act that damages such investments and reduces their exchange value. The production of celebrity academics by the culture industry goes on apace in 1993, the current "justification" being the "need" for "public intellectuals" who can speak to and write for larger audiences; see, for instance, Scott Heller, "Humanists Renew Public Intellectual Tradition, Answer Criticism," *Chronicle of Higher Education,* April 7, 1993, A-6 ff., which features such writers as Michael Warner, cited elsewhere in this text, as an instance of a "transacademic" intellectual. The extent of this interest in preserving celebrities became increasingly clear to me while I was seeking a publisher for this essay. The essay was turned down by several journal editors on the grounds that it "personalizes," becomes "polemical" rather than scholarly. The scholarly/polemical binary itself is of course maintained by the very people who are maintaining the dominant academic power relations; they need the term "polemic" to get rid of that scholarship that is not in their class interests.

To be precise: when I sent the prefinal text of this essay to *Critical Inquiry,* two editors, W. J. T. Mitchell and Lauren Berlant, initially received it enthusiastically, stating that "we've read your essay on Gay and Lesbian cultural/academic politics with pleasure and admiration" and asking for revision. I spent a lot of time working on the essay to strengthen its argument, which drew for support on nontraditional sources such as the *Chronicle of Higher Education . . . ,* so that—although it had all along been "polemical"—the argument of the final version was a more inclusive and sustained critique. Having read the second version, Mitchell rejected the essay on the grounds that "the kind of energy and (even) rage that made your piece attractive in the first place seem, in this version, to have lost their charm." The final version was no longer "charming" in the sense that it didn't leave as much room for that compromise and accommodation which pass in the dominant academy as scholarship. It is very interesting that a supposedly "nonscholarly" essay can be acceptable if it remains "charming" but is unacceptable if it is "polemical." Of course the shift from "charming" (acceptable) to "polemical" (unacceptable) has everything to do with the moment when the reader senses that her/his own practices, not just the practices of "those other people," have been critiqued. Mitchell went on to explain his rejection of my essay by remarking that it "seems to say that anyone who has a successful academic career must be automatically complicit with 'the system' of social dominance."

My point in referring to this case is that I do not think the editor of *Critical Inquiry* (or indeed anyone else) speaks in a vacuum: to a very large extent, editors are able to say what they say because what they say is the obvious common sense of the academy. They know that the readers of my essay will agree with them because even though the majority of readers, while they are not themselves celebrities, nevertheless aspire to "celebrity," are therefore "celebrities-in-waiting," stand-ins for that signified of which they hope—through career success—to become finally the signifier. Hence, common sense dictates that one should not critique celebrities because such a critique will be read as nothing more than the expression of resentment at their success. Such an argument seems quite reasonable until one realizes that it is a strategy for preserving the system of celebrities and for policing the domain of acceptable knowledges. The reading of this essay as a resentment-text allows the reader to remain comfortable in her/his institutional complacency and simply to dismiss texts such as mine. Such a reading is an ideological alibi for marginalizing contesting voices as irrational, angry, and therefore not "properly" belonging to the academy. While my immediate subject is Queer Theory, in writing about that issue I am at the same time addressing the forms of surveillance in the academy I have marked more directly here.

11 Herbert Marcuse, *Negations,* trans. J. J. Shapiro (Boston, 1969), 95.

12 Seyla Benhabib, *Critique, Norm, and Utopia: A Study of the Foundations of Critical Theory* (New York, 1986), 35.

13 "Editorial Perspectives," *Science & Society* 56, no. 1 (Spring 1992):3.

14 For recent discussions of cultural studies, see Patrick Brantlinger, *Crusoe's Footprints: Cultural Studies in Britain and America* (New York, London, 1990); Graeme Turner, *British Cultural Studies: An Introduction* (Boston: Unwin, Hyman, 1990); L. Grossberg et al., *Cultural Studies* (New York, 1991): Donald Morton and Mas'ud Zavarzadeh, *Theory/Pedagogy/Politics: Texts for Change* (Chicago and London, 1991), 22 ff.

15 For a theorization of the differences between ludic (post)modernism and resistance (post)modernism, see Teresa Ebert, "Rewriting the (Post)Modern: Resistance (Post)Modernism," *Legal Studies Forum* 15, no. 4 (1991): 291–303, Teresa Ebert, "Political Semiosis in/of American Cultural Studies," *American Journal of Semiotics* 8, no. ½ (1991): 113–136, and Teresa Ebert, "Ludic Feminism, the Body, Performance, and Labor: Bringing *Materialism* Back into Feminist Cultural Studies," *Cultural Critique* 23 (Winter 1992–93): 5–50.

16 For an extended theorization of these points, see Mas'ud Zavarzadeh, "Theory as Resistance," *Rethinking Marxism* 2, no. 1 (1989): 50–70.

17 Jacques Derrida, *Of Grammatology,* trans. Gayatri Spivak (Baltimore, 1976), 20.

18 For an articulation of these questions, see Donald Morton, "The Body and/In the Text: The Politics of Clitoral Theoretics," *American Journal of Semiotics* 6, no. ⅔ (1989): 299–305.

19 Ernesto Laclau, "The Impossibility of Society," *Canadian Journal of Political and Social Theory* 15, no. 1–3 (1991): 25.

20 See, for example, John Fiske, *Reading the Popular* (Boston, 1989); John Fiske, *Understanding Popular Culture* (Boston, 1989); Constance Penley, Elizabeth Lyon, Lynn Spiegel, and Janet Bergstrom, eds., *Close Encounters: Film, Feminism, and Science Fiction* (Minneapolis, 1991); Andrew Ross, *Strange Weather* (New York, 1991); and Andrew Ross, *No Respect* (New York, 1989).

21 On the question of ludic theory's supposed "break" with empiricism, see Zavarzadeh and Morton, *Theory,* chap. 5.

22 Compare Michael Warner, "Fear of a Queer Planet," *Social Text* 22 (1991): "The major theoretical debate over constructionism seems exhausted" (5). Recent discussions of aspects of constructionism are available in such texts as David F. Greenberg, *The Construction of Homosexuality* (Chicago, 1988); Diana Fuss, *Essentially Speaking: Feminism, Nature, and Difference* (New York, London, 1989); Judith Butler, *Gender Trouble: Feminism and the Subversion of Identity* (New York, London, 1990); Edward Stein, *Forms of Desire: Sexual Orientation and the Social Constructionist Controversy* (New York and London, 1992); and Anja van Koofen Niekerek and Theo van der Meer, eds., *Homosexuality? Which Homosexuality? Essays from the International Scientific Conference on Lesbian and Gay Studies* (London, 1989).

A recent interview with John Boswell (see Lawrence Mass, "Sexual Categories, Sexual Universals: An Interview with John Boswell," *Christopher Street* 151 [1990]: 23ff.) makes it clear that what is far more important than the constructionist/essentialist debate today is the question of the "empirical" or "experience" as the ground of knowledge, a premise which unites both arch-conservatives like Boswell and ludic (post)modernists. Indeed the desire of the Reagan/Bush era culture industry to "secure" and "stabilize" thinking about sexuality is indicated by the fact that Boswell's attack on constructionism, in the guise of a review of Greenberg's book, was published not in a journal for historians but in the popular *Atlantic*. Although Boswell represents himself as the "objective" historian whose "authority" rests on the "accuracy" (ideology-free-ness) of his handling of "facts," his review is nothing more than a tissue of reassertions of empiricist and historicist clichés of traditional humanist ideology. See John Boswell, "Gay History," rev. of David F. Greenberg, *The Construction of Homosexuality, Atlantic* 163, no. 2 (February 1989): 74–78.

23 Again, see Zavarzadeh, "Theory as Resistance."

24 Karl Marx, *Early Writings,* trans. R. Livingston and G. Benton (New York, 1975), 251.

25 Karl Marx and Frederick Engels, *Collected Works* (New York, 1978), 11: 103.

26 Ken Plummer, rev. of D. Greenberg, *The Construction of Homosexuality, Theory, Culture & Society* 8 (1991): 174. While praising Greenberg's book (see next note), Plummer expresses some reservations concerning its theoretical dimensions, but his "quibbles" do not amount to a critique.

27 David F. Greenberg, *The Construction of Homosexuality* (Chicago, 1988); Eve Kosofsky Sedgwick, *Epistemology of the Closet* (Berkeley, 1990); Alan Sinfield, *Literature, Politics, and Culture in Postwar Britain* (Berkeley and Los Angeles, 1989); and Teresa de Lauretis, "Sexual Indifference and Lesbian Representation," in *Performing Feminisms: Feminist Critical Theory and Theatre,* ed. Sue-Ellen Case (Baltimore, 1990), 17–39.

The Great Pretenders
Further Reflections on Whiteshamanism

Wendy Rose

They came for our land, for what grew or could be grown on it, for the resources in it, and for our clean air and pure water. They stole these things from us, and in the taking they also stole our free ways and the best of our leaders, killed in battle or assassinated. And now, after all that, they've come for the very last of our possessions; now they want our pride, our history, our spiritual traditions. They want to rewrite and remake these things, to claim them for themselves. The lies and thefts just never end.

Margo Thunderbird, 1988

I am that most schizophrenic of creatures, an American Indian who is both poet and anthropologist. I have, in fact, a little row of buttons up and down my ribs that I can press for the appropriate response: *click,* I'm an Indian; *click,* I'm an anthropologist; *click,* I'll just forget the whole thing and write a poem. I have also been a critic of the "whiteshaman movement," to use an expression coined by Geary Hobson, Cherokee critic. The term "whiteshaman," he says, rightly belongs to "the apparently growing number of small-press poets of generally white, Euro-Christian American background, who in their poems assume the persona of the shaman, usually in the guise of an American Indian medicine man. To be a poet is simply not enough; they must claim a power from higher sources."[1] Actually, the presses involved are not always small, as is witnessed by the persona adopted by Gary Snyder in his Pulitzer Prize-winning book of verse, *Turtle Island.*[2] In any event, Hobson is referring to a group of writers, including Louis Simpson, Charles Olson, Jim Cody, John Brandi, Gene Fowler, Norman Moser, Michael McClure, Barry Gifford, Paul Steinmetz, and David Cloutier, all of whom subscribe to—and go decisively beyond the original intent of—Jerome Rothenburg's 1976 assertion that:

> The poet, like the shaman, withdraws to solitude to find his poem or vision, then returns to sound it, give it life. He performs alone—because his presence is considered crucial and no one else has arisen to act in his place. He is also like the shaman in being at once an outsider, and yet a person needed for the validation of a certain type of experience important to the group . . . like the shaman, he will not only be allowed to act mad in public, but he will often be expected to do so. The act of the poet—& his poetry—is like a public act of madness. It is like what the Senecas, in their great dream ceremony, now obsolete, called "turning the mind upside down" . . . It is the primal exercise of human freedom against/& for the tribe.[3]

I would expand upon Hobson's definition by observing that not all whiteshamans are Americans, poets, nor even white. A perfect example is that of Carlos Castaneda, author of the best-selling series of "Don Juan" epics purporting to accurately reveal the "innermost secrets" of a purely invented "Yaqui sorcerer."[4] I would further add that whiteshamans pretending to higher sources may or may not refer to themselves as shamanic. Some of those within the movement have professed more secular intimacies with Native

American cultures and traditions. This is well illustrated by Ruth Beebe Hill, who pretended in her book *Hanta Yo* to have utilized her association with a single American Indian man—"Chunksa Yuha," otherwise known as Alonzo Blacksmith—to uncover not only 19th-century social, sexual, and spiritual forms, but an "archaic dialect" of the Lakota language unknown to the Lakota themselves.[5]

Such claims, whether sacred or secular, are uniformly made with none of the community acknowledgment and training essential to the positions in question. Would it not be absurd to aver to be a Rabbi if one were neither Jewish nor even possessed an elementary knowledge of Judaism? Or that one were a jet aircraft pilot without having been inside an airplane? Yet, preposterous as whiteshaman assertions may be on the face of it, there seems to be an unending desire on the part of the American public to absorb such "knowledge" as the charlatans care to produce. Further, the proliferation of such "information" typically occurs to the exclusion of far more accurate and/or genuinely native material, a matter solidly reinforcing the profound ignorance of things Indian afflicting most of society. As the Lakota scholar Vine Deloria, Jr. has put it:

> The realities of Indian belief and existence have become so misunderstood and distorted at this point that when a real Indian stands up and speaks the truth at any given moment, he or she is not only unlikely to be believed, but will probably be contradicted and "corrected" by the citation of some non-Indian and totally inaccurate "expert." More, young Indians in universities are now being trained to see themselves and their cultures in terms prescribed by such experts rather than in the traditional terms of the tribal elders . . . In this way, the experts are perfecting a system of self-validation in which all semblance of honesty and accuracy is lost. This is not only a travesty of scholarship, but it is absolutely devastating to Indian societies.[6]

Hobson and others have suggested that the assumption of shaman status or its secular counterparts by non-native writers is part of a process of "cultural imperialism" directly related to other claims on Native American land and lives.[7] By appropriating indigenous cultures and distorting them for its own purposes, their reasoning goes, the dominant society can neatly eclipse every aspect of contemporary native reality, from land rights to issues of religious freedom. Pam Colorado, an Oneida scholar working at the University of Calgary in Canada, frames the matter:

> The process is ultimately intended to supplant Indians, even in areas of their own customs and spirituality. In the end, non-Indians will have complete power to define what is and is not Indian, even for Indians. We are talking here about an absolute ideological/conceptual subordination of Indian people in addition to the total physical subordination [we] already experience. When this happens, the last vestiges of real Indian society and Indian rights will disappear. Non-Indians will then "own" our heritage and ideas as thoroughly as they now claim to own our land and resources."[8]

Whiteshamans and their defenders, assuming a rather amazing gullibility on the part of American Indians, usually contend they are "totally apolitical." Some have pointed out that the word "shaman" is itself of Tungus (Siberian) origin[9] and insist that their use of it thus implies nothing specifically Native American, either in literal content or by impression.[10] They often add the insulting caveat that American Indian writers know less of their ancestral traditions and culture than non-native anthropologists.[11] Finally, most argue that "artistic license" or "freedom of speech" inherently empowers them to do what they do, no matter whether Indians like it (and, ultimately, no matter the cost to native societies).[12] Native American scholars, writers, and activists have heard these polemics over and over again. It is time to separate fact from fantasy in this regard.

ANATOMY OF WHITESHAMANISM

First, it must be noted that the term "shaman" is merely one of convenience, as are the terms "Indian," "American Indian," "Native American," and so on. The Siberian origin of the word is in this sense irrelevant at best and, more often, polemically obfuscatory. Moreover, whiteshamans do not construct their writings or antics after the Siberian model, even when they use the term "shaman" to describe themselves and the processes of their craft. Their works, whether poetic, novelistic, or theoretical, are uniformly designed and intended to convey conceptions of "Indian-ness" to their readers. This remains true regardless of the literal content of the material at issue, as is readily evident in "Blackfoot/Cherokee" author Jamake Highwater's (aka: Jay Marks, a non-Indian) extended repackaging of Greek mythology and pop psychology in the garb of supposed "primal Native American legends."[13]

Further, during performances, whiteshamans typically don a bastardized composite of pseudo-Indian "style" buckskins, beadwork, headbands, moccasins, and sometimes paper masks intended to portray native spiritual beings such as Coyote or Raven. They often appear carrying gourd rattles, eagle feathers, "peace pipes," medicine bags, and other items reflective of native ceremonial life. Their readings are frequently accompanied by the burning of sage, "pipe ceremonies," the conducting of chants and beating of drums of vaguely native type, and the like. One may be hard-pressed to identify a particular indigenous culture being portrayed, but the obviously intended effect is American Indian. The point is that the whiteshaman reader/performer aspires to "embody the Indian," in effect "becoming" *the* "real" Indian even when actual native people are present. Native reality is thereby subsumed and negated by imposition of a "greater" or "more universal" contrivance.

This leads to a second major point. Whiteshamanism functions as a subset of a much broader assumption within the matrix of contemporary Eurocentric domination holding that non-Indians always (inherently) know more about Indians than do Indians themselves. It is from this larger whole that whiteshamanism draws its emotional and theoretical sustenance and finds the sense of empowerment from which it presumes to extend itself as "spokesperson" for Indians, and ultimately to substitute itself for Indians altogether. Illustrations of this abound, especially within anthropology, linguistics, and the various social sciences.

. . .

THE "PIONEER SPIRIT"

What are the implications of this? Consider that a working (if often sublimated) definition of "universality" is very much involved. It is reflected perfectly in the presumed structure of knowledge and in the real structure of "universities" through which this knowledge is imparted in contemporary society. The "core" of information constituting the essential canon of every discipline in academe—from philosophy to literature, from history to physical science, from art to mathematics—is explicitly derived from thought embodied in the European tradition. This is construed as encapsulating all that is fundamentally meaningful within the "universal attainment of human intellect." The achievements and contributions of all other cultures are considered, when they are considered at all, only in terms of appendage (filtered through the lens of Eurocentric interpretation), adornment (to prove the superiority of the Euro-derived tradition), esoteric specialization (to prove that other traditions, unlike those derived from Europe, are narrow and provincial rather than broad and universal).[14]

Always and everywhere, the inclusion of non-European intellectual content in the academy is absolutely predicated upon its conformity to sets of "standards" conceived and administered by those adhering to the basic precepts of Euro-derivation. The basic "qualification" demanded by academe of those who would teach non-European content is that they first receive "advanced training" and "socialization" in doctoral programs steeped in the supposed universality of Euro-derivation. Non-European subject matters are thus intrinsically subordinated to the demands of Eurocentrism at every level within U.S. institutions of higher learning. There are no exceptions: the intended function of such inclusion is to fit non-European traditions into positions assigned them by those of the Eurocentric persuasion. The purpose is to occupy and consume other cultures just as surely as their land and resources have been occupied and consumed.[15]

Such circumstances are quite informative in terms of the more generalized socio-cultural situation. In the construction at hand, those who embrace the Euro-derivation of "universal knowledge" are considered by definition to be the normative expression of intellectual advancement among all humanity. They are "citizens of the world," holders of "the big picture," having inherent rights to impose themselves and their "insights" everywhere and at all times, with military force if need be. The rest of us are consigned by the same definition to our "parochialism" and "provinciality," perceived as "barriers to progress" in many instances, "helped" by our intellectual "betters" to overcome our "conceptual deficiencies" in others.[16] The phenomenon is integral to Euroamerican culture, transcending all ideological boundaries demarcating conservatism and progressivism; a poster popular among science fiction readers of both political persuasions shows a 15th-century European ship sailing a star-map and asks: "What would have happened if Ferdinand and Isabella had said no?"

If, as the academics would have it, Indians "no longer really know" or at least lack access to their traditions and spirituality (not to mention land tenure), then it follows that they are no longer "truly" Indian. If culture, tradition, spirituality, oral literature, and land are not theirs to protect, then such things are free for the taking. An anthropologist or folklorist hears a story or a song and electronically reproduces it, eventually catalogues it and perhaps publishes it. According to the culture of the scholar, it is then *owned* by "science" in exactly the same fashion as native land, once "settled" by colonizers, is said to be owned by them.[17] Stories, songs, ceremonies, and other cultural ingredients can be—and often are—stolen as surely as if they were tangible objects removed by force. There is a stereotype about the "savage" who is afraid a camera will steal his soul. It will indeed, and much more, as will the tape recorder, the typewriter, and the video cassette. The process is as capable, and as purposeful, in first displacing and then replacing native people within their own cultural contexts as were earlier processes of "discovery" and "settlement" in displacing us from and replacing us upon our land. What is at issue is the extension across intellectual terrain of the more physically oriented 19th-century premise of "Manifest Destiny."

Anthropologists often contend they do not have any appreciable effect upon their own societies, but the fact is that the public does swallow and regurgitate anthropological concepts, usually after about twenty years. At that point, one generally finds efforts undertaken to put to popular use the cultural territory that anthropology has discovered, claimed, and tentatively expropriated in behalf of the dominant society. The subsequent popular endeavors serve to settle and "put to good use" this new cultural territory. This is the role of the whiteshamans. Theirs is a fully sanctioned, even socially mandated activity within the overall imperial process of Eurocentrism. It should thus come as no surprise to serious students of American culture that editors, publishers, reviewers, and most readers greatly prefer the nonsense of whiteshamanism to the genuine literature of American Indians. The situation is simply a continuation of the "Pioneer Spirit" in American life.

APPROPRIATION AND DENIAL

The anthropologist of me is always a little embarrassed. When I am called upon to speak anthropologically, I find myself apologizing or stammering that I'm not *that* kind of anthropologist. I feel like the housewife-prostitute who must go home to clean house for her unknowing husband. She must lie or she must admit her guilt. Native Americans expect me to reflect the behavior they have come to anticipate from non-native anthropologists. If I live in *their* camp, the native reasoning goes, it follows that I must have joined ranks with them; it is therefore expected that I will attempt to insinuate myself into tribal politics where I have no business. Non-native anthropologists expect me either to be what Delmos Jones has called a "superinformant" or a spy for the American Indian Movement, watching their every action with the intent of "causing trouble."[18]

The irony of all this is that I'm really NOT that kind of anthropologist. My dissertation involves a cultural-historical perspective on published literature by American Indians. Such a degree should be, perhaps, granted by the English or literature departments, but such is not the case. At the university where I worked toward my doctorate in anthropology, the English department refused to acknowledge two qualified American Indian applicants for a position during the '80s, with the statement—made to the Coordinator of Native American Studies—that "Native American literature is not part of American Literature." In the same English department, a non-Indian graduate student was also awarded a degree on the basis of a dissertation on "Native American Literature." The student focused upon the work of four authors, *none* of whom was an Indian. The four writers are all known whiteshamans.

Native American literature is considered (by Euroamericans) to be "owned" by anthropology, as American Indians themselves are seen as "owned" by anthropologists.

Our literature is merely ethnographic, along with our material culture and kinship systems. This is not, of course, restricted to Native American societies; Fourth World peoples everywhere are considered copyrightable in the same way. Maori, Native Hawaiian, Papuan, Cuna, Thai, and other people around the globe have been literarily colonized just as they have been economically, politically, and militarily colonized.[19] Not so the literature of the Euro-derived (with certain exceptions, such as homosexuals, prisoners, etc.—all groups not "normal"). My position is that all literature must be viewed ethnographically. All literatures provide information about the culture of both writer and subject. All literatures are potential tools for the anthropologist—but not one "type" of literature more than any other. What literature is not ethnic? What person has no ethnicity? American Indians are not "more ethnic" than Polish-Americans or Anglo-Americans; they are simply called upon more frequently and intensively to deal with their ethnicity.

I do not believe the work of N. Scott Momaday, Leslie Marmon Silko, and Simon J. Ortiz is "ethnic" more so than the work of Robert Creeley, Studs Terkel, or Charles Bukowski. But you will not usually find Momaday, Silko, and Ortiz in bookstores or libraries according to their genre (fiction or poetry). Their work will most often be shelved as "anthropology," "Native Americana," "Indians," "Western," or even "Juvenile" (Indians being "kid stuff"). One plays Indian, one dresses up and pretends. Bookstore managers have told me that neither Leslie Silko's novel *Ceremony* nor her later volume of prose and poems, *Storyteller,* could be classified or sold as "regular fiction" because no one would buy them unless they were specifically interested in Indians. Hence, the work is shelved under "Indian." Period. A book by Silko thereby becomes a mere artifact, a curio. It is presumed to be unimportant that hers also happens to be some of the finest prose and poetry available from any author, of either gender or any ethnic background. The same can be said of the writing of others—Maurice Kenny, Joy Harjo, James Welch, Linda Hogan, Barnie Bush, and Mary TallMountain among them—forced into the same "quaint" pigeonhole of classification.

But, if a Native American writer happens to gain international prominence, as in the case of Scott Momaday—his novel *A House Made of Dawn* won the 1969 Pulitzer Prize for Literature—the critics and ethnographers exclaim that the author and his or her work is "not really Indian."[20] Rather, it suddenly falls within the "mainstream of American letters."[21] On the other hand, the stereotypical and grossly distortive work of Hyemeyohsts Storm, a man only marginally Indian, and whose material earned him the wrath of the Northern Cheyenne people with whom he claimed affiliation,[22] was considered by a specialist in "minority American literature" to be more "genuinely Indian" than the writing of Momaday, whose genetic and cultural heritage cannot be questioned (his father is a well-known Kiowa artist, his mother an equally well-known Cherokee educator).[23] A great many comparable examples of this phenomenon might be cited.

FREEDOM (WITH RESERVATIONS)

While the Indian of me is continually bent double from the force of being hit by the literary-colonial canon, the anthropologist of me is always looking for cultural explanations for whiteshamanism and its emotional impact. Feelings run deep on both sides and people tend to take sides on the issue, even if they are not otherwise interested in literary matters. I have found that much of the controversy over whiteshamanism involves fundamental, cherished concepts held by Europeans and Euroamericans involving art, freedom, and what it means to be an artist. These ideas do not, as is often claimed by their advocates, deviate from—much less transcend—the more directly and overtly imperialist manifestations discussed above. To the contrary, they dovetail quite nicely with the rest of the Pioneer Spirit.

All of us, native and non-native, are ethnocentric at our deepest levels. No amount of anthropological training or insight can abolish ethnocentrism, although we can become aware of it and learn to take it into consideration on a day-to-day basis. The problem is that the notion of intrinsic universalism lodged within Euro-derived tradition usually precludes those of that tradition from acknowledging either the fact or the meaning of their own ethnicity. I've encountered literally scores of white students over the years who have professed in various ways to have "no culture." Sometimes they bemoan this circumstance, sometimes they appear to take a certain pleasure in it. Either way, they purport to inhabit "reality," while culture is a habitat reserved exclusively for those whose heritage deviates from their own. Ethnicity, for the mainstream, is thus specifically the domain of Others. The attitude is absolutely pervasive: A short time ago, I even saw a section in a variety store advertising its products for "ethnic hair."

Rather than taking pride in their own deeply rooted ethnicity, most Euroamericans feel duty-bound to sublimate it. Instead of being proud of who they are, they run about making liberal statements about "loving everybody," believing everyone to be "the same under the skin" and so on. The fact is that even the most avowedly progressive Euroamericans seem to want a Disney-ish world in which everyone is a different shade of the same thing, everyone a member of the same cultural "reality" except for things which are "safely" different: food, dress, dancing, and crafts; sometimes language. Beyond these distinctions, they hold that we should *all* be "entitled" to "share equally" in what they hold to be the loftiest and "most natural" aspiration of humanity: Freedom, the more total the better. In noting this to be the case, Edmund Carpenter observed, "The message is clear: we should love them because they are like us. But the statement has its questioning brother: what if they *aren't* like us?"[24]

What Euroamerican, other than those of fascistic persuasion, can be comfortable with the notion that total freedom is a pathological concept? Yet my father's Hopi people see it that way. In the Hopi view, no one would want to be that completely alone and uncontrolled unless there was something seriously wrong with them. In the Hopi Way, and in most other native traditions, to want to be away from people is seen as a form of madness. The very worst punishment indigenous societies can inflict, much worse than death or imprisonment, is exile or to be stigmatized by your people. Conversely, to be allowed to participate in society represents the essence of fulfillment: To be assigned responsibility and acknowledged by the group as having made a useful contribution is the highest accolade. Acceptance by and inclusion among the people are the highest principles governing native life.

By contrast, the typical Euro-derived pattern, in an ideal state, would be for people to live absolutely "free" or "unbound." Euroamericans define freedom in a certain way, primarily politically, and no longer think to question whether it's bad or good. The pursuit of freedom is supposedly why their ancestors left Europe. Freedom is why their ancestors fought for independence from Europe. Freedom is why they continuously penetrated "the frontier." Freedom is why they came in the California and Yukon gold rushes; if you have enough money, you can "live free." Freedom is why they save up (or compulsively spend) that money today. Freedom is why they went to college, send their kids to college. Freedom is why they retire at a certain age. And yet "freedom" as they envision it is an extremely culture-specific value.

Likewise, "art" and being "an artist" are culture-specific ideas that relate to freedom; the "freest" individuals in society are supposed to be artists. Artists can be eccentric, they act however they wish, only to be forgiven because they are artists and therefore free. It is freedom and not creativity that arouses jealousy among Euroamerican non-artists. When a Euroamerican hears that I give poetry readings all over the country, she or he invariably turns wistful and remarks, "You're so lucky. You have all that freedom to travel. I sure wish I could." (Could what? Write poetry? No, freely travel). Native people, on the other hand, often extend genuine condolences that my work forces me to spend so much time so far from home, away from the obligations and responsibilities which lend a central meaning to life. The dichotomy in values couldn't be clearer. These ideas about art and freedom are at the center of the conflict about whiteshamanism.

In Euro-derived society, art is separated from everyday life. For instance, an artist typically works at night rather than when other people work. Art is special, elite (much of it requiring specialized training in "appreciation"), non-utilitarian, self-expressive, solitary, ego-identified, self-validating, innovative (to make it perpetually "new"), unique, and—in its "highest" forms—"without rules." It is a hallmark of the greatest artists, those who "change history," that they break rules, discarding everything "old." Scholars and critics refer to favored artists as "breaking the mold" or "flying in the face of tradition." The whiteshaman says to the American Indian critic, "You can't tell me what to write. I have the right to do whatever I want. This is art; there are no rules." Within the context of whiteshaman culture, truth and freedom are at stake. He or she honestly views the Indian critic as abusing artistic freedom (or "poetic license"), as trying to restrict the unrestrictable, as *trespassing*. The pioneer cannot allow the native to say "go home."[25]

Native American views are different regarding freedom and art. We are not a uniform people, of course, from arctic to tropic and coast to coast, and so my statements must be generalizations, more or less true for most American Indian societies. In life and art, there are rules, and this is good. These rules were given to us, they belong to us, and we must not only follow them, but guard them. Rules exist governing form, content, context, and personnel. Of these, context may be the most important, and yet for the Euro-derived artist it seems to be of negligible significance. A white male art teacher once said to me, "Art is everywhere." Even the many movements which call themselves "countercultural" or "revolutionary" have bought into the European system enough to revolt against it and use its structure to fuel the revolt. Their "alternatives" are merely extensions of the European tradition. They are not, and have never been, "a whole new thing."

American Indian views on art tend to be trans-tribal, especially now when so many diverse native cultures are united by a single colonial language and electronic media.

Art must be community-oriented (it may be sacred, but not supernatural; *nothing* is supernatural), it must be useful, it must be beautiful and functional at the same time (the ideas are inseparable, for functioning is part of beauty, and vice versa), it is good if more than one person has a hand in its production, and its completion is always an excellent excuse for a party. There are occasions when the party (or feast, or ceremony) is part of the art form. The artist is not above or otherwise separated from the rest of society; she or he feels no particular desire to be recognized alone or considered different from other people. The artist contributes a particular skill to the welfare and survival, not to mention happiness, of the community.

Native American art is fitted into a continuum where it may or may not change, but certainly will not be pressured to be innovative. Innovation is a consideration that is more often than not rejected by the group, but successful, acceptable, useful innovation is always welcome. The point is that the artist does not innovate just for the sake of innovating; by itself, innovation is not part of the criteria for "good art." The artist is not expected to be eccentric or any way noticeably different from anyone else. Quite the contrary. These ideas—the Euroamerican and American Indian—are obviously in fundamental conflict. It is equally obvious that people on both sides will not normally think about them as I have presented them; people just don't sit down and analyze their behavior in a cultural context. So the conflicts go unrecognized, the whiteshaman and the Native American writer occupying the same turf, but running according to different sets of rules.

. . .

CULTS OF THE CULTURE VULTURES

One thing Indians are spectacularly ill-equipped to do that whiteshamans appear to do quite effortlessly is build a cult around themselves. The whiteshamans become self-proclaimed "gurus," dispensing not only poetry but "healing" and "medicine," "blessing" people. In this area, they have no competition at all. I do not know of a single Native American poet who would make such a claim, although you will find a scattering of non-poets, such as the notorious "Sun Bear" (Vincent LaDuke) involved in these goings on.[26] You will find whiteshamans at bogus "medicine wheel" gatherings, ersatz sweat-lodge ceremonies, and other fad events using vaguely Indian motifs. You will not usually find them around Indians at genuine Indian events. Even Sun Bear, who is a Chippewa by "blood," admitted to members of Colorado AIM that he never participated in or attended bona fide native activities.[27] Given the nature of his own transgressions against the cultural integrity of his people, he felt—undoubtedly accurately—that he'd be "unwelcome."

When you deal with cultists, you are in deep waters. A while ago, in Alaska, I spoke to a university audience and made some mention that I believed the information in books by Carlos Castaneda to be fabricated. A non-Indian woman stood up and angrily shouted that I was anti-semitic and probably didn't believe in the Holocaust either.[28] At a more recent event at a small university in upstate New York, I was confronted by a non-native man who took it upon himself to "explain" to me how Jamake Highwater's transparently bogus ramblings had "done more for Indians than the work of any other writer." When I and several Indian colleagues sharply disagreed, the man informed us we were "hopelessly deluded."[29] I know of no legitimate Indian writer with such a fanatical following, for Indians are taught, above all, to value truth. The sanctity of language must not, within our traditions, be used to abuse this value. The last thing a Don Juan cultist wants is to meet a *real* Yaqui holy person.

This is standard fare in whiteshaman circles, and it knows no ideological boundaries. A truly amazing example involves a sector of Euroamerican feminism devoted to "rediscovering the lost power of women through the ages." Not unnaturally, native women—who have traditionally experienced a full measure of social, economic, political, and spiritual empowerment within their own cultures—have become the focus of considerable attention from this quarter. But, given their interest in Indian women, have these feminists turned to their native sisters for insight, inspiration, and guidance? No. Instead, they flock to the books and lectures of Lynn Andrews, a white woman from Beverly Hills who has grown rich claiming to have been taught by two traditional Cree women (with Lakota names) in Canada about the eternal struggle between the righteousness of native women's "spirit power" against malignantly evil male spirits.[30]

Andrews, of course, maintains she has been "sent back as a spiritual messenger" by her invented teachers to spread the word of these utterly un-Indian "revelations." And, inevitably, any time a native woman—even a Cree such as Sharon Venne—attempts to refute the author's false assertions, she is shouted down by her white "sisters," often for not knowing the "inner meaning" of native culture as well as Andrews, and usually for having internalized the "sexism" by which "Indian men prevent the truth from being known" by women.[31] Typically, subscribers to the Andrews cult describe the *Indian* women who confront their guru as being "arrogant and insensitive," a truly incredible projection of their own psychological and behavioral characteristics upon the primary victims of their actions. Small wonder, under the circumstances, that Native American women have always been conspicuously absent from "the women's movement."

When I discussed my view of Andrews' *Medicine Woman* with a well-known white male scholar of Indian literature, I was startled when he stated his belief that such ludicrous fiction could be true—as it was and is promoted to be true—because if a person *were* to serve as a "bridge" between Indians and whites, it would *have* to be a white person. He could never really articulate why he thought this to be so necessarily true. Such unidirectional presumption lies at the very core of all Eurocentric cultural imperialism and offers lucid illustration as to the crux of what has served to impair intercultural understanding and communication in this society for so long. In the end, he is as much a part of the Andrews cult as any of the near-giggling groupies lining up to obtain autographed copies of her "literary works."

FEAR AND LOATHING AMONG THE LITERATI

Before closing, I would like to talk about certain misunderstandings regarding criticism by Native Americans of the whiteshamans and their followers. The fear exists among non-native writers that we are somehow trying to bar them from writing about Indians at all, that Indian people might be "staking a claim" as the sole interpreters of Indian cultures, most especially of that which is sacred, and asserting that only Indians can make valid observations on themselves. Such fears are not based in fact; I know of no Indian who has ever said this. Nor do I know of any who secretly think it. We accept as given that whites have as much prerogative to write and speak about us and our cultures as we have to write and speak about them and theirs. The question is how this is done and, to some extent, why it is done.

The problem with whiteshamans is one of integrity and intent, not topic, style, interest, or experimentation. Many non-Indian people have—from the stated perspective of the non-native viewing things native—written honestly and eloquently about any number of Indian topics, including those we hold sacred. We readily acknowledge the beauty of some poetry by non-natives dealing with Indian people, values, legends, or the relationship between human beings and the American environment. A non-native poet is obviously as capable of writing about Coyote and Hawk as an Indian poet. The difference is in the promotion, so to speak. A non-native poet cannot produce an *Indian* perspective on Coyote or Hawk, cannot see Coyote or Hawk in an Indian way, and cannot produce a poem expressing Indian spirituality. What can be produced is another perspective, another view, another spiritual expression. The issue, as I said, is one of integrity and intent.

The principle works in both directions. As an Indian person who was deeply impressed with the oral literature of the Catholic Church during my childhood, I might compose verse based in this poetic form. I might go on to publish the poems. I might also perform them, with proper intonation, as in Mass. All of this is appropriate and permissible. But I would not and *could* not claim to be a priest. I could not tell the audience they were actually experiencing the transmutation that occurs during Mass. At the point I did endeavor to do such things, a discernable line of integrity—both personal and artistic—would have been crossed. Artistic freedom and emotional identification would not make me a priest, nor would the "uplifting" of my audience—no matter how gratifying to them, and to me—make them participants in Mass. To evoke my impression of the feel of the Mass and its liturgy does not necessitate my lying about it.

There is a world of difference between a non-Indian man like Frank Waters writing about Indians and a non-Indian man like Jamake Highwater claiming through his writing that he has in fact *become* "an Indian." Similar differences exist between a non-Indian woman like Marla N. Powers who expresses her feelings about native spirituality honestly, stating that they are her perceptions, and white women like Lynn Andrews and "Mary Summer Rain" perpetrating the fraud of having been appointed "mediums" of Indian culture.[32] And, of course, the differences between non-Indians like John Neihardt who rely for their information upon actual native sources, and those like Andrews and Castaneda who simply invent them, should speak for themselves. As an Indian, as a poet, and as an anthropologist, I can wholeheartedly and without inconsistency accept the prerogatives claimed by the former in each case while rejecting the latter without hesitancy or equivocation. And I know of no American Indian aligned with his or her own heritage and traditions who would react otherwise.

CONCLUSION

So what is to be done about all this? For starters, readers of this essay should take the point that whiteshamanism is neither "okay," "harmless," nor "irrelevant," no more than any other form of racist, colonialist behavior. Correspondingly, they must understand that there is nothing "unreasonable" or "unfair" about the Indian position on the matter. As concerns the literary arena, we demand only informational and artistic integrity and mutual respect. It is incumbent upon Euroamerica, first and foremost, to make the whiteshamans and their followers understand that their "right" to use material from other cultures stems from those cultures, not from themselves. It must be impressed on them in no uncertain terms that there is nothing innately superior separating them from the rest of humanity, entitling them to trample upon the rights of others, or enabling them to absorb and "perfect" unfamiliar material better than the originators of that material. The only *right* they have when dealing with native-derived subject matters is to present them honestly, accurately, and—if the material is sensitive or belongs to another group or specific person—with permission. If their response to what they've seen, heard, or otherwise experienced is subjective and interpretive, we insist only that they make this known from the outset, so as not to confuse their impressions with the real article.

Application of a bit of common sense by the public would prove helpful. Those who have a genuine desire to learn about American Indians should go out of their way to avoid being *misled* into thinking they are reading, seeing, or hearing a native work. Most whiteshamans have demonstrated a profound ignorance of the very traditions they are trying to imitate or subsume, and so they have mostly imitated each other. Many of them claim to deploy an authentically Native American model, but speak rhetoric about "inventing their own myths," a literal impossibility within *real* indigenous traditions. Any mythology stemming from experiences in a university or along city streets is unlikely to include any recognizable coyotes, and confusion in this area precludes genuine intercultural communication faster and more thoroughly than any other single factor. Until such communication is realized, we are all going to remain very much mired in the same mess in which we now collectively find ourselves, interculturally speaking.

Adoption of a pro-active attitude in this regard on the part of avowed progressives would likely prove effective. If they are truly progressive, they will demand—loudly and clearly—that not only authors, but publishers and organizers of events make it plain when "the facts" are being interpreted by a representative of a non-native culture. The extension of misinformation along these lines should be treated as seriously as any other sort of propaganda, and transgressors discredited—branded as liars, or perhaps sued for fraud—when revealed. It follows that bookstores—especially alleged "alternative" outlets—need to hear, with emphasis, that their progressive clientele objects to both their stocking of whiteshaman trash *and* to the absence of real Native American material on their shelves. Those who queue up to participate in, defend, or apologize for whiteshamanism must at last be viewed and treated as what they are. An unequivocally negative response to this sort of cultural imperialism on the part of large numbers of non-Indians would undoubtedly go far toward ending at least the worst of the practices at issue.

Native people, on the other hand, must come to understand that whiteshamans did not just pop up out of the blue and decide to offend Indians. They are responding, at least to some extent, to a genuinely felt emotional need within the dominant society. The fact that they are concomitantly exploiting other people for profit according to the sanctions and procedures of their own culture does not alter this circumstance. In spite of itself, whiteshamanism has touched upon something very real. An entire population is crying out for help, for alternatives to the spiritual barrenness they experience, for a way out of the painful trap in which their own worldview and way of life have ensnared them. They know, perhaps intuitively, that the answers—or part of the answers—to the questions producing their agony may be found within the codes of knowledge belonging to the native peoples of this land. Despite what they have done to us during the past 500 years, it would be far less than Indian of us were we not to endeavor to help them. Such are our Ways, and have always been our Ways.

Perhaps we can treaty now. Perhaps we can regain a balance that once was here, but now seems lost. If poets and artists are the prophets and expressers of history—as thinkers of both the American Indian and Euro-derived traditions have suggested in different ways—then it may well be that our task is simply to take back our heritage from the whiteshamans, shake it clean and bring it home. In doing so, we not only save ourselves from much that is happening to us, but empower ourselves to aid those who have stolen and would continue to steal so much from us, to help them locate their *own* power, their *own* traditions as human beings among human beings, as relatives among relatives not only of the human kind. Perhaps then they can come into themselves as they might be, rather than as they have been, or as they are. Perhaps then we can at last clasp hands, not as people on this land, but of this land, and go forward together. As Seattle, leader of the Suquamish people, once put it, "Perhaps we will be brothers after all . . . We shall see."

NOTES

1 Hobson, Geary, "The Rise of the White Shaman as a New Version of Cultural Imperialism," in Geary Hobson, ed., *The Remembered Earth,* Red Earth Press, Albuquerque, NM, 1978, pp. 100–8. An interesting, if unintended, history of the evolution of whiteshamanism in American letters may be found in Castro, Michael, *Interpreting the Indian: Twentieth Century Poets and the Native American,* University of New Mexico Press, Albuquerque, 1983.

2 Snyder, Gary, *Turtle Island,* New Directions Publishers, New York, 1974. It should be noted that Snyder may have set the entire whiteshaman phenomenon in motion with his "shaman songs" included in his *Myths and Texts,* Totem Press, New York, 1960.

3 Rothenberg, Jerome, "Pre-Face to a Symposium on Ethnopoetics," *Alcheringa: Ethnopoetics,* n.s. 2, No. 4, p. 4. Rothenberg is, like Gary Snyder, in some ways the prototype of the contemporary whiteshaman: see his *Poems, 1964–67,* Black Sparrow Press, Los Angeles, 1968; *A Book of Testimony,* Tree Books, San Francisco, 1971; *Poems for the Game of Silence, 1960–1970,* Dial Press, New York, 1971; *The Notebooks,* Membrane Press, Milwaukee, 1976; and *A Seneca Journal,* New Directions Publishers, New York, 1978. His essays are also of interest: see "Total Translation," in Abraham Chapman, ed.,

Literature of the American Indians: Views and Interpretations, New American Library, New York, 1978, pp. 292–307; and "Changing the Present, Changing the Past: A New Poetics," in *Talking Poetics from Naropa Institute,* Vol. 2, Shambala Publications, Boulder, CO, 1978. His "expertise" on shamanism is also "confirmed" in certain of the collections he's edited: see *Technicians of the Sacred: A Range of Poetries from Africa, America, Asia and Oceania,* Doubleday Publishers, Garden City, NY, 1969; *Shaking the Pumpkin: Traditional Poetry of the Indian North Americas,* Doubleday Publishers, Garden City, NY, 1972; and, with George Quasha, *America, a Prophecy: A New Reading of American Poetry from Pre-Columbian Times to the Present,* Random House Publishers, New York, 1974.

4 The Castaneda books in question are *The Teachings of Don Juan: A Yaqui Way of Knowledge,* University of California Press, Los Angeles, 1968; *A Separate Reality: Further Conversations with Don Juan,* Simon and Schuster, New York, 1971; *Journey to Ixtlan: The Lessons of Don Juan,* Simon and Schuster, New York, 1972; *Tales of Power,* Simon and Schuster, New York, 1974; and *The Second Ring of Power,* Simon and Schuster, New York, 1977. All of Castaneda's assertions were "academically validated" through his publication of a "scholarly paper" entitled "The didactic uses of hallucinogenic plants: An examination of a system of teaching," in *Abstracts of the 67th Annual Meeting of the American Anthropological Association* in 1968 and UCLA's 1973 award of a Ph.D. in anthropology to Castaneda on the basis of a dissertation entitled *Sorcery: A Description of the World* (actually a retitled manuscript of *Journey to Ixtlan*).

5 Hill, Ruth Beebe, *Hanta Yo: An American Saga,* Doubleday Publishers, Garden City, NY, 1977. For detailed American Indian criticism, see Deloria, Vine Jr., "Hanta Yo: Super Hype" *Co-Evolution Quarterly,* Fall 1979 and "The Twisted World of Hanta Yo," *Minority Notes,* Vol. 1, No. 1, Spring 1979. Also see Medicine, Beatrice, "Hanta Yo: A New Phenomenon," *The Indian Historian,* Vol. 12, No. 2, Spring 1979 and Taylor, Allan R., "The Literary Offenses of Ruth Beebe Hill," *American Indian Culture and Research Journal,* Vol. 4, No. 3, Summer 1980.

6 Deloria, Vine Jr., lecture presented during American Indian Awareness Week, University of Colorado at Boulder, as quoted by Ward Churchill in "A Little Matter of Genocide: Native American Spirituality and New Age Hucksterism," *Bloomsbury Review,* Vol. 8, No. 5, September/October 1988, pp. 23–4.

7 Marmon Silko, Leslie, "An Old-time Indian Attack Conducted in Two Parts: Part One, Imitation 'Indian' Poems; Part Two, Gary Snyder's *Turtle Island,*" in Hobson, ed., op. cit., pp. 211–6; Young Bear, Ray, "in disgust and in response to indian-type poetry written by whites published in a mag which keeps rejectin' me," in *Winter of the Salamander: The Keeper of Importance,* Harper and Row Publishers, New York, 1979, pp. 118–20; Rose, Wendy, "For the White Poets Who Would be Indian" and "The Anthropology Convention," in *Lost Copper,* Malki Museum Press, Morongo Indian Reservation, Banning, CA, 1980; Sainte-Marie, Buffy, "This Country Tis of Thy People Your Dying," in *The Buffy Sainte-Marie Songbook,* Grosset and Dunlap Publishers, New York, 1971, pp. 164–6.

8 Pam Colorado, as quoted in Churchill, op. cit.

9 As Hobson (op. cit., p. 108) puts it: "[I]n *Webster's New Collegiate Dictionary* (1968) Shaman is shown to have evolved from Russian, and from Tungusic saman, and perhaps, even ultimately from the Sanskrit s'ramana—meaning beggar monk. Its current meaning seems to be 'a priest or conjurer of shamanism; loosely, a medicine man.' Shamanism, in the same dictionary, is defined as 'primarily, the primitive religion of the Ural-Altic peo-

ples of northern Asia and Europe, in which the unseen world of gods, demons, and ancestral spirits is conceived as being responsive only to the shamans.' Funk & Wagnall's *Standard College Dictionary* (1963) confirms these definitions, adding only the word 'wizard' in regard to the shaman."

10 This is not always the case, however. See Mary Douglas, "The Authenticity of Castaneda"—a rabid defense of his whiteshamanism and its validity in terms of "understanding" Native Americans ("a great advance in anthropology")—in Richard B. de Mille, ed., *The Don Juan Papers: Further Castaneda Controversies,* Ross-Erikson Publishers, Santa Barbara, CA, 1980, pp. 25–31.

11 For an exemplary display of this sort of argument and attitude, see Clifton, James E., *The Invented Indian: Cultural Fictions and Government Policies,* Transaction Books, New York, 1990.

12 A near-perfect example of this argument appears in a letter by Judith Abel of McKlouth, Kansas appearing in the February 1991 issue of *Z Magazine.* Abel's letter addresses Ward Churchill's article, "Advent of the Plastic Medicine Men"—in which he contends "spiritual hucksters" are complicit in the cultural genocide of American Indians—appearing in the December 1990 issue of the same magazine. Churchill's analysis appears correct, Able holds, but is marred by his missing the "fact" that such activities are legitimate insofar as they fall under "free speech."

13 The books in question are Highwater's *Ritual of the Wind,* Viking Press, New York, 1977; *Anpao: An American Indian Odyssey,* J.J. Lippincott Publishers, Philadelphia, 1977; *The Sweetgrass Lives On: Fifty Contemporary Indian Artists,* Lippincott and Crowell Publishers, New York, 1980; *The Sun, He Dies: The End of the Aztec World,* Harper and Row Publishers, New York, 1980; and especially *The Primal Mind: Vision and Reality in Indian America,* Harper and Row Publishers, New York, 1981. The Grecian content of Highwater's "interpretations" of American Indian mythos has been exhaustively demonstrated by Assiniboin-Sioux scholar Hank Adams in a manuscript entitled *Cannibal Green.* Adams' material has, of course, gone unpublished, other than an extract printed in the native rights journal *Akwesasne Notes* in early 1985. All the better to allow promoters such as David Jackson to pen pieces such as "Jamake Highwater's Native Intelligence," *Village Voice,* May 3, 1983, pp. 37–9.

14 For an in-depth examination of these assumptions, see Carnoy, Martin, *Education as Cultural Imperialism,* David McKay Publishers, New York, 1974.

15 Analysis of these problems is offered in Jaimes, M. Annette, "American Indian Studies: Toward an Indigenous Model," *American Indian Culture and Research Journal,* Vol. 11, No. 3, 1987, pp. 1–16. Also see Deloria, Vine Jr., "Education and Imperialism," *Integrateducation,* Vol. 19, Nos. 1–2, 1982.

16 This way of thinking is discussed brilliantly in Amin, Samir, *Eurocentrism,* Monthly Review Press, New York, 1989.

17 This is precisely the tradition whiteshamans have picked up on. Its literary origins may probably be found in Mary Hunter Austin's appropriative *Path of the Rainbow: An Anthology of Songs and Chants from the Indians of North America,* Liveright Publishers, New York, 1918 and *The American Rhythm: Studies and Re-Expressions of Amerindian Songs,* Houghton-Mifflin Co., Boston, 1923. Oliver LaFarge pioneered contemporary Euroamerica's ethnographic appropriation of "Indian-ness" in literature, writing as a Navajo in his Pulitzer Prize-winning 1927 novel, *Laughing Boy,* Pocket Books Edition, New York, 1969. Vachel Lindsay was perhaps the first modern Euroamerican poet to cash in, adopting an Indian "persona" in "Our Mother Pocahontas" (see his *Collected Poems,* Macmillan Publishers, New York, 1946.

18 Jones, Delmos J., "Towards a Native Anthropology," *Human Organization,* Vol. 29, No. 4, 1970, pp. 251–9.

19 For an exposition on this topic, see Graburn, Nelson H.H., ed., *Ethnic and Tourist Arts: Cultural Expressions from the Fourth World,* University of California Press, Berkeley, 1976, pp. 1–2 of the introduction.

20 Momaday, N. Scott, *A House Made of Dawn,* Harper and Row Publishers, New York, 1968.

21 This argument is advanced most formally in Sollors, Werner, *Beyond Ethnicity: Descent and Consent in American Culture,* Oxford University Publishers, New York/London, 1986.

22 Storm, Hyemeyohsts, *Seven Arrows,* Ballantine Books, New York, 1972. For the Northern Cheyenne response, see *Wassaja,* Vol. 2, No. 7, April–May, 1974 and Vol. 2, No. 7, August 1974. Also see Costo, Rupert, "Seven Arrows Desecrates Cheyennes," *The Indian Historian,* Vol. 4, No. 2, Summer 1972, p. 41. Despite such protests from the people allegedly depicted, Storm's subsequent book, *Song of the Heyoehkah,* Harper and Row Publishers, San Francisco, 1981, is in precisely the same vein . . . and produced with equal lavishness by the publisher.

23 Larson, Charles R., *American Indian Fiction,* University of New Mexico Press, Albuquerque, 1978, pp. 1–2.

24 Carpenter, Edmund, *Oh, What a Blow that Phantom Gave Me!* Holt, Rinehart, and Winston Publishers, New York, 1972, p. 97.

25 All of this is epitomized in the vernacular of the poetic trade. See Sutton, Walter, *American Free Verse: The Modern Revolution in Poetry,* New Directions Press, New York, 1973.

26 Sun Bear's books, many of them written in collaboration with a bona fide whiteshaman "Wabun" (Marlise James), include *At Home in the Wilderness,* Naturegraph Publications, 1973; *Buffalo Hearts,* Bear Tribe Publications, Spokane, WA, 1976; *The Bear Tribe's Self-Reliance Book,* Bear Tribe Publications, Spokane, WA, 1977 (reprinted by Prentice-Hall Press, New York, 1988); *Sun Bear: The Path of Power,* Bear Tribe Publications, Spokane, WA, 1983 (reprinted by Prentice-Hall Press, New York, 1987); *The Roaring of the Sacred River,* Prentice-Hall Press, New York, 1986; *The Book of the Vision Quest,* Prentice-Hall Press, New York, 1987; *Walk in Balance: The Path to Healthy, Happy, Harmonious Living,* Prentice-Hall Press, New York, 1989; and *Black Dawn/Bright Day,* Bear Tribe Publications, Spokane, WA, 1990. Other "Indians" involved in this sort of thing include Doug Boyd, a supposed Cherokee who has authored *Rolling Thunder,* Dell Books, New York, 1976 and Tony Shearer, allegedly of non-specific "tribal" heritage, whose *The Lord of the Dawn: Quetzalcoatl,* Naturegraph Publications, 1971 and *The Praying Flute,* Naturegraph Publications, 1988, are rather worse than Castaneda's.

27 Churchill, "Plastic Medicine Men," op. cit.

28 Such a reaction is hardly extraordinary. For published versions of the same thing, see Staniford, Philip, "I Come to Praise Carlos, Not to Bury Don Juan," in de Mille, op. cit., pp. 151–3. This behavior is quite in line with the sort of validation Castaneda has received from "scholarly" sources (e.g.: Littleton, C. Scott, "An emic account of sorcery: Carlos Castaneda and the rise of a new anthropology," *Journal of Latin American Lore,* Vol. 2, No. 2, 1976; McDermott, Richard, "Reason, Rules and the Ring of Experience: Reading our World into Carlos Castaneda's Works," *Human Studies,* Vol. 2, No. 1, 1979, pp. 31–46) even after the dimensions of the hoax he'd perpetrated were becoming apparent to anyone who cared to look.

29 This exchange occurred during the "Voices from Native North America" conference series at Alfred University, Alfred, New York, February 9, 1991.

30 The book at issue here is Andrews, Lynn, *Medicine Woman,* Harper and Row Publishers, New York, 1982. Andrews' other volumes, all of them in kind, include *Flight of the Seventh Moon: The Teaching of the Shields,* Harper and Row Publishers, New York, 1985; *Jaguar Woman,* Harper and Row Publishers, New York, 1986; *Star Woman,* Harper and Row Publishers, New York, 1987; *Teachings Around the Sacred Wheel,* Harper and Row Publishers, New York, 1989; and *Crystal Woman,* Warner Books, New York, 1990. In 1988, Harper and Row also packaged *Medicine Woman, Jaguar Woman,* and *Star Woman* as a boxed set under the title *Medicine Woman Trilogy.*

31 Venne brought this up during her presentation at the "Voices from Native North America" conference series at Alfred University, Alfred, NY, November 10, 1990.

32 The Mary Summer Rain books include *Spirit Song* (1986), *Phoenix Rising: No-Eyes Vision of Things to Come* (1987), *Dreamwalker: The Path of Sacred Power* (1988), and *Phantoms Afoot: Journies Into the Night* (1989), all published by Whitford Press, West Chester, PA.

Coping with Rape: Critical Perspectives on Consciousness

Michelle Fine

Prosecute? No, I just want to get home. While I'm pickin' some guy out of some line, who knows who's messin' around with my momma and my baby.

Altamese Thomas,
24-year-old rape survivor
October 1981, Hospital Emergency Room

At 2:00 a.m. one October morning, Altamese Thomas was led out of a police car, entered the hospital in pain, smelling of alcohol. Altamese had been drinking with some women friends in a poor, high crime, largely Black neighborhood in Philadelphia. She found herself in an alley, intoxicated, with pants down. She reports being gang-raped. The story unfolds, from intake nurse, the police and from Altamese herself.

I was awakened, in the small office for volunteer rape counselors, when the emergency room nurse telephoned me: "A Code-R just arrived." "Code-R" is the euphemism used to describe a woman who has been raped. I spent the remainder of the evening and some of the morning with Altamese. A twenty-four-year-old Black mother of three, two of her children have been placed by the state in foster care. From 2:00 a.m. until 7:00 a.m. we held hands as she smarted through two painful injections to ward off infection; traveled through the hospital in search of X-rays for a leg that felt (but wasn't) broken; waited for the Sex Offender Officers to arrive; watched Altamese refuse to speak with them; and returned to the X-ray room for a repeat performance—and we talked.

I introduced myself and explained my role. Interested primarily and impatiently in washing "the dirt off" and receiving necessary medical care, Altamese was unambivalent about her priorities. She did not want to prosecute, nor talk with social workers or counselors. She couldn't call upon her social supports. She just wanted to get home. For five hours, we talked. Our conversation systematically disrupted my belief that I understood anything much about the psychology of taking control in the face of injustice. . . .

THE PSYCHOLOGY OF TAKING CONTROL

When confronting life crises, injustices or tragedies, psychologists argue, people fare best by assuming control over their circumstances. . . . This article examines the assumptions which underlie present formulations of Taking-Control-Yields-Coping. Weaving relevant theory and research . . . it will be argued that the prevailing coping-through-control ideologies are often limited by class, race and gender biases. Further, these models are disproportionately effective for only a small and privileged sector of society.

. . .

The current Taking-Control arguments often assume that people *can* control the forces which victimize them, *should* utilize available social programs, and *will* benefit if they rely on social supports. What is not explicit is that these prescribed means of coping are likely to be ineffectual for most people.[1] Persons of relatively low ascribed social power—by virtue of social class position, ethnicity, race, gender, disability or sexual preference—cannot control those forces which limit their opportunities. But while it has been proposed that many then learn to be helpless,[2] I maintain instead that they do assert control in ways ignored by psychologists. For many, taking control involves ignoring advice to solve one's problems individually and recognizing instead the need for collective, structural change.[3] Taking control may mean rejecting available social programs as inappropriate to one's needs, or recognizing that one's social supports are too vulnerable to be relied upon.[4] Such acts of taking control have long been misclassified by psychologists as acts of relinquishing control.

ACCESS TO MEANS OF TAKING CONTROL: A FUNCTION OF SOCIAL POWER

The control-yields-well-being proposition is empirically robust and admittedly compelling. As a psychologist interested in the social psychology of injustice, I study and support efforts which encourage people to take control of their lives. A review of this literature reveals, however, *individualistic* coping strategies, effective for persons of relatively high social power, promoted *as if* they were optimal and universal ways to cope. By establishing a hierarchy of appropriate ways to take control, this literature often 1) denies the complex circumstances many people confront, 2) *de facto* delegitimates those strategies for taking control employed by persons of relatively low social power, 3) encourages psychological and individualistic responses to injustice, which often reinforce existing power inequities,[5] and 4) justifies prevailing social structures.

Advancing the position that people need to exert individual control over their lives presumes that all people are able to do so, that all people want to do so, and that to improve their life circumstances, people need to change themselves rather than social structures. Three fundamental problems with this formulation emerge.

First, if asserting individual control promotes psychological health it may be because individualism is socially reinforced in our society.[6] Positive reinforcement follows individualistic acts (e.g., "Pulling oneself up by the boot-straps")[7] with social disapproval displayed for collective acts (e.g., in school these collective acts may be considered cheating; at work trouble making). The health that is associated with acts of individualistic control may therefore derive from social and ideological supports in our culture, not because individual control is inherently healthy.

Given that psychological well being stems in part from social rewards for individualism and internality, a second problem emerges with this model of coping. If unfair treatment occurs and control of that treatment is unlikely, a presumption of internality may be delusional! Externality may benefit persons whose life conditions are indeed beyond their control.[8] To nurture the much-encouraged illusion of internality in many circumstances would be unreasonable. In situations of low probability of success for redressing an injustice, attempts to redress injustice personally can breed helplessness.

It may be true that when persons of relatively high social power assert a single act of "taking control" (e.g., voice a grievance or file a complaint) they are likely to succeed. In contrast, the undocumented worker who is sexually harassed by her factory foreman might be foolish to file a grievance. "Bearing it" does not mean she has given up, but rather that she determined a solution by which she can be in control and employed. Establishing strategies to survive, when change is unlikely, needs to be recognized as acts of control.

A third problem with current control formulations is that they often decontextualize coping[9]. . . . The strategies popular in the literature and undoubtedly effective in many cases, may benefit persons of relatively high social power (e.g., by attributing successes to stable internal factors and failures to unstable factors; taking responsibility for solutions; relying on social supports, or utilizing available social programs). As psychologists, however, we lack an understanding of how people who are systematically discriminated against and restricted to low power positions take control. We fail to understand how they determine what is controllable and what is not. We dismiss control strategies that look like "giving up" but are in fact ways to survive. Even more serious, we avoid the study of those ways of taking control which systematically disrupt traditional power relations. Our literature legitimates existing power asymmetries.

There are two major consequences to these theoretical problems. First, control efforts enacted by low power persons are often misdiagnosed as giving up. Such attempts to take control tend to be misread as counter productive ("Why don't they do something about their work conditions if they are dissatisfied, rather than slowing down on productivity?"); distorted as self-effacing ("Even she blames herself for the rape."); diagnosed as masochistic ("She must enjoy the abuse, why else would she stay?"); classified as learned helplessness ("She always says—'I can't do anything about it.' "); or denigrated as psychological resistance ("I tried to offer help but he won't listen!") by laypersons and psychologists alike. These behaviors may indeed function as strategies of asserting control; if not resistance.

Second, the existing body of research on allegedly healthy ways of coping reproduces existing power inequities by prescribing *as optimal* those ways of coping which are effective for high power persons. Social programs designed for low power persons are often organized toward coping strategies (such as individualism and reliance on social institutions) effective for high power persons. The models are deceptive for persons of low social power who depend on higher power persons, economically, socially, and/or psychologically, and have other low power persons (e.g., kin) highly dependent upon them. This precarious web of interdependencies creates conditions in which social institutions are likely to be unresponsive and individualism to be inappropriate. Many low power persons will not improve their own circumstances at expense to others, and most are unlikely to have access to standard tools of control (e.g., grievance procedures, money, or leverage with Congressional representatives). If they do, these tools are unlikely to promote the kinds of changes they need.[10] Consequently, when low power persons decide *not* to use the resources or programs offered them (e.g., "Because my mother is sick, and I have to take care of my children.") their disadvantaged circumstances may come to be viewed as deserved. The perception that they are *unwilling* to act on their own behalf provides evidence of helplessness, if not laziness. Their need to rely on high power persons is then confirmed. The power asymmetries built into these relationships are systematically justified.[11]

. . .

ASSERTING RELATIONAL CONTROL

At first glance, one might say that Altamese abdicated control: She "gave up." Unwilling to prosecute, uninterested in utilizing her social supports, she relied on God for justice. Resistant to mental health, social service, educational and criminal justice assistance, she rejected available options. Her coping mechanisms might be said to include denial, repression, and paranoia. She doesn't trust her friends to testify, her family to listen, her social worker to be supportive, her teachers to understand or the police to assist. She has refused available mechanisms of control.

And yet through our dialogue it was obvious that each of her decisions embodies a significant assertion of control. Likely to be misclassified as helpless or paranoid, she asserted strategies for taking control which insure both her well-being and that of her kin. Altamese organized coping around relational concerns. Worried about her mother, child and siblings, she rejected options offered to help her cope. She viewed my trust in the justice system as somewhat absurd; my commitment to talking about the rape to friends, social workers, teachers or family somewhat impulsive; my expectations of witnesss coming forth almost naive, and even my role as volunteer counselor somewhat unusual.

. . .

Most people are denied the means to assume control over fundamentally changing their lives. Although prevailing ideology argues otherwise, Altamese and the millions of women who are unemployed, poor, minority and/or disabled and responsible for a network of kin, have limited options.[12] Although pursuing college, she may perhaps qualify for a low pay job some day. Given unemployment statistics, her personal style, life circumstances and lack of qualifications, her chances are slim.

The standard means of taking control promoted by counselors, policy makers and researchers, tend to be individualistic and most effective for a privileged slice of society. Trusting social institutions, maximizing interpersonal supports, and engaging in self disclosure are strategies most appropriate for middle class and affluent individuals whose interests are served by those institutions, whose social supports can multiply available resources and contacts and for whom self-disclosure may in fact lead not only to personal change, but to structural change.

Unable to trust existing institutions, for Altamese self-disclosure would have exposed wounds unlikely to be healed. Responsible for a network of kin, Altamese could not rely on but had to protect her social supports. Resisting social institutions, withholding information and preserving emotional invulnerability emerged as her strategies for maintaining control. Expecting God to prosecute, loss of memory to insure coping and fantasy to anesthetize reality, Altamese is by no means helpless.

While her social and economic circumstances are such that Altamese cannot change the basic oppressive structures which affect her, the social and psychological strategies she employs are mechanisms of control—protection for self and others.[13] An abstract pursuit of justice was not possible given her social context, commitments and concerns. She organized the realities of her life so as to manage effectively the multiple forces which *are* out to get her and her kin. . . . Altamese exhibited what may be considered relational coping.

With little attention paid to relational concerns and a systematic neglect of power relations, psychologists have prescribed ways to cope as if a consensus about their utility had been established; as if there were no alternatives; as if universals could be applied across contexts, and as if these strategies were uninfluenced by our position in social and economic hierarchies. . . . [They] have an obligation to expose the dialectics of psychological control and structural control, as experienced by women and men across lines of social class, ethnicity and race, levels of physical ability and disability and sexual preferences. In the absence of such knowledge psychologists impose, as healthy and universal, what may be narrow and elitist strategies for taking control.

One particular strategy, examined below, involves the prescription that persons treated unjustly or confronted by tragedy utilize available social programs. If Altamese is any indication such social programs are likely to be severely underutilized so long as they are designed top-down *for* (and not by) the persons supposedly served.

COPING WITH OPTIONS

One way to take control over adversity, supported by much psychological research (including my own), is to do something to improve one's own life circumstances; to use available options. To battered women, it may be suggested that they leave their abusive homes; to the unemployed, that they enroll for skills retraining; to the underpaid, that they learn to be assertive; to rape victims, that they "ventilate" and prosecute. Social programs have proliferated to offer individuals these services. These programs are generally designed by relatively high power individuals for persons who have what are considered personal problems. Offered as *opportunities* to improve the quality of life experienced by low power persons, these programs generally aim to correct presumed deficits.[14] Some disabled persons have the *opportunity* to work in sheltered workshops, often earning less than minimum wages, trained for non-marketable skills. Some battered women have the *opportunity* to be sheltered in facilities which exclude women with drug or alcohol addictions, are located in unsafe neighborhoods, and limit a maximum stay to two weeks, promising an alternative to violent homes. Some Black high school dropouts have the *opportunity* to earn their Graduate Equivalency Diplomas, promising greater vocational mobility, despite the fact that Black adolescent unemployment figures range from 39 percent to 44 percent for high school graduates and dropouts, respectively.[15]

Efforts to fix people and not change structures, many of these options reinforce the recipient's low power position. It is therefore most interesting that when such persons dismiss these options as inappropriate, ineffective or as decoys for the "real issues," these persons are often derogated. Individuals who reject available options, such as disabled adults who picket the Jerry Lewis Telethon claiming it to be condescending and reinforcing of the worst stereotypes, are viewed as ungrateful, unappreciative and sometimes even deserving of their circumstances. The same option that appears valuable to a high power person may be critiqued as a charade by low power persons.

. . .

As social scientists generate master strategies for taking control and promote them as universally applicable, the paradox of "therapeutic hegemony" emerges. Those individuals with the least control over the causes of their problems, much less the means for structural resolution, are prescribed psychological models for individual efficacy. As long as individual victims (or survivors) act alone to improve their circumstances, oppressive economic and social arrangements will persist. The effects of such acts of psychological control may ultimately be indistinguishable from the effects of surrender. Even acts of resistance, if initiated individualistically, ultimately buttress power differentials. Altamese's unwillingness to use the justice system, her non-reliance on kin, and her trust that God will provide or punish, do nothing for the women that these rapist(s) will attack next. Nor do they stem the wave of violence against women. What these behaviors accomplish is that they give Altamese a control strategy by which she can survive, with her remaining child, her mother, and her brothers, in a community where she can get some support. Unfortunately these behaviors also allow psychologists to continue to weave the fantasy that Altamese needs to be educated about options available to her and taught to be assertive about her needs. Psychologists can remain ever convinced that if *only* Altamese would learn to use it, the system would work to her advantage. . . . [ellipsis in original]

EPILOGUE

And so as psychologists we are faced with a conceptual dilemma. Should we expand the definition of "taking control" to incorporate the lived experiences of women and men across class, race, and ethnic lines? Or, do we dispense with the concept of "taking control" totally, rejected as too narrow to be salvaged? I would argue the former. Taking control is undoubtedly a significant psychological experience; knowing that one can effect change in one's environment makes a difference. How individuals accomplish this, however, does vary by economic and social circumstance, gender and perhaps personal style. The phenomenology of individuals like Altamese need be integrated into our conceptions of taking control in order for the concept to have meaning for those persons most likely to confront injustice, tragedy or other life crises. A feminist psychology needs to value relational coping and to contextualize, through the eyes of those women affected, the meaning of victimization and taking control. The continued assessment of "women's coping" as helplessness need be reframed.

NOTES

1 R. Silver and C. Wortman, Coping with Undesirable Life Events, in *Human Helplessness,* J. Garber and M. Seligman (eds.), Academic Press, New York, 1980; R. Unger, Controlling Out the Obvious: Power, Status and Social Psychology, paper presented at American Psychological Association, Washington, D.C., 1982.

2 M. Seligman, *Helplessness: On Depression, Development and Death,* W. H. Freeman, San Francisco, 1975.

3 W. Ryan, *Equality,* Pantheon Books, New York, 1981.

4 M. Fine, Perspectives on Inequity: Voices from Urban Schools, in *Applied Social Psychology Annual,* L. Brickman (ed.), *4,* Sage, Beverly Hills, 1983(b); C. Gilligan, *In a Different Voice,* Harvard University Press, Cambridge, 1982.

5 E. Sampson, Cognitive Psychology as Ideology, *American Psychologist,* 36:7, pp. 730–743, 1981.

6 E. Cagan, Individualism, Collectivism and Radical Educational Reform, *Harvard Educational Review,* 48, pp. 227–266, 1978.

7 J. Anyon, Intersections of Gender and Class: Accommodation and Resistance by Working Class and Affluent Females in Contradictory Sex-Role Ideologies, in *Gender, Class and Education,* L. Barton and S. Walker (eds.), Fatiner Press, England, 1982.

8 L. Furby, Individualist Bias in Studies of Locus of Control, in *Psychology in Social Context,* A. Buss (ed.), Irvington Publishers, New York, pp. 169–190, 1979.

9 A. Buss (ed.), *Psychology in Social Context,* Irvington Publishers, New York, 1979.

10 P. Gurin, G. Gurin, R. Lao, and M. Beattie, Internal-External Control in the Motivational Dynamics of Negro Youth, *Journal of Social Issues,* 25, pp. 29–53, 1969.

11 L. Kidder and M. Fine, The Justice of Rights versus Needs, paper presented at the meeting of the International Society for Political Psychology, Washington, D.C., 1982.

12 E. Apfelbaum, Relations of Domination and Movements for Liberation: An Analysis of Power Between Groups, in *The Social Psychology of Intergroup Relations,* W. Austin and S. Worchel (eds.), Brooks/Cole, Monterey, 1979; b. hooks, *Ain't I a Woman?,* South End Press, Boston, 1981.

13 E. Genovese, *Roll, Jordan, Roll: The World the Slaves Made,* Vintage, New York, 1972.

14 W. Gaylin, I. Glasser, S. Marcus, and D. Rothman, *Doing Good: The Limits of Benevolence,* Pantheon Books, New York, 1978.

15 A. Young, School and Work Among Youths During the 1970s, *Monthly Labor Review,* 9, pp. 44–47.

Western Mathematics: The Secret Weapon of Cultural Imperialism

Alan J. Bishop

Of all the school subjects which were imposed on indigenous pupils in the colonial schools, arguably the one which could have been considered the least culturally-loaded was mathematics. Even today, that belief prevails. Whereas educational arguments have taken place over which language(s) should be taught, what history or religion, and whether, for example, 'French civilisation' is an appropriate school subject for pupils living thousands of kilometres from France, mathematics has somehow always been felt to be universal and, therefore, culture-free. It had in colonial times, and for most people it continues to have today, the status of a culturally neutral phenomenon in the otherwise turbulent waters of education and imperialism.

This article challenges that myth, and places what many now call 'western mathematics' in its rightful position in the arguments—namely, as one of the most powerful weapons in the imposition of western culture.

Up to fifteen years or so ago, the conventional wisdom was that mathematics was culture-free knowledge. After all, the popular argument went, two twos are four, a negative number times a negative number gives a positive number, and all triangles have angles which add up to 180 degrees. These are true statements the world over. They have universal validity. Surely, therefore, it follows that mathematics must be free from the influence of any culture?

There is no doubt that mathematical truths like those are universal. They are valid everywhere, because of their intentionally abstract and general nature. So, it doesn't matter where you are, if you draw a flat triangle, measure all the angles with a protractor, and add the degrees together, the total will always be approximately 180 degrees. (The 'approximate' nature is only due to the imperfections of drawing and measuring—if you were able to draw the ideal and perfect triangle, then the total would be exactly 180 degrees!) Because mathematical truths like these are abstractions from the real world, they are necessarily context-free and universal.

But where do 'degrees' come from? Why is the total 180? Why not 200, or 100? Indeed, why are we interested in triangles and their properties at all? The answer to all these questions is, essentially, 'because some people determined that it should be that way'. Mathematical ideas, like any other ideas, are humanly constructed. They have a cultural history.

The anthropological literature demonstrates for all who wish to see it that the mathematics which most people learn in contemporary schools is not the only mathematics that exists. For example, we are now aware of the fact that many different counting systems exist in the world. In Papua New Guinea, Lean has documented nearly 600 (there are more than 750 languages there) containing various cycles of numbers, not all base ten.[1] As well as finger counting, there is documented use of body counting, where one points to a part of the body and uses the name of that part as the number. Numbers are also recorded in knotted strings, carved on wooden tablets or on rocks, and beads are used, as well as many different written systems of numerals.[2] The richness is both fascinating and provocative for anyone imagining initially that theirs is the only system of counting and recording numbers.

Nor only is it in number that we find interesting differences. The conception of space which underlies Euclidean geometry is also only one conception—it relies particularly on the 'atomistic' and object-oriented ideas of points, lines, planes and solids. Other conceptions exist, such as that of the Navajos where space is neither subdivided nor objectified, and where everything is in motion.[3] Perhaps even more fundamentally, we are more aware of the forms of classification which are different from western hierarchical systems—Lancy, again in Papua New Guinea, identified what he referred to as 'edge-classification', which is more linear than hierarchical.[4] The language and logic of the Indo-European group have developed layers of abstract terms within the hierarchical classification matrix, but this has not happened in all language groups, resulting in different logics and in different ways of relating phenomena.

Facts like these challenge fundamental assumptions and long-held beliefs about mathematics. Recognising symbolisations of alternative arithmetics, geometries and logics implies that we should, therefore, raise the question of whether alternative mathematical systems exist. Some would argue[5] that facts like those above already demonstrate the existence of what they call 'ethno-mathematics', a more localised and specific set of mathematical ideas which may not aim to be as general nor as systematised as 'mainstream' mathematics. Clearly, it is now possible to put forward the thesis that all cultures have generated mathematical ideas, just as all cultures have generated language, religion, morals, customs and kinship systems. Mathematics is now starting to be understood as a pan-cultural phenomenon.[6]

We must, therefore, henceforth take much more care with our labels. We cannot now talk about 'mathematics' without being more specific, unless we are referring to the generic form (like language, religion, etc.). The particular kind of mathematics which is now the internationalised subject most of us recognise is a product of a cultural history, and in the last three centuries of that history, it was developing as part of western European culture (if that is a well-defined term). That is why the title of this article refers to 'western mathematics'. In a sense, that term is also inappropriate, since many cultures have contributed to this knowledge and there are many practising mathematicians all over the world who would object to being thought of as western cultural researchers developing a part of western culture. Indeed, the history of western mathematics is itself being rewritten at present as more evidence comes to light, but more of that later. Nevertheless, in my view it is thoroughly appropriate to identify 'western mathematics', since it was western culture, and more specifically western European culture, which played such a powerful role in achieving the goals of imperialism.[7]

There seem to have been three major mediating agents in the process of cultural invasion in colonised countries by western mathematics: trade, administration and education.[8] Regarding trade and the commercial field generally, this is clearly the area where measures, units, numbers, currency and some geometric notions were employed. More specifically, it would have been western ideas of length, area, volume, weight, time and money which would have been imposed on the indigenous societies.

If there was any knowledge of indigenous measure systems at all, or even currency units, there is little reference made to them in the literature. Researchers have only fairly recently begun to document this area and it is perfectly clear that many indigenous systems did (and do) exist.[9] Nevertheless, the units used in trade were (and still are) almost entirely western, and those local units which have survived are either becoming more and more westernised or are in the process of dying out. In some cases, there were simply no local units for measuring the kinds of quantities needed to be used by the western traders—as Jones' informant showed in Papua New Guinea in a recent investigation: 'It could be said [that two gardens are equal in area] but it would always be debated' and 'There is no way of comparing the volume of rock with the volume of water, there being no reason for it'.[10]

The second way in which western mathematics would have impinged on other cultures is through the mechanisms of administration and government. In particular, the numbers and computations necessary for keeping track of large numbers of people and commodities would have necessitated western numerical procedures being used in most cases. According to the research evidence, the vast majority of counting systems in the world are and were finite and limited in nature, and with a variety of different numerical bases. There is certainly evidence of some systems being able to handle large numbers in sophisticated ways if the societal needs are there (e.g., by the Igbo people and the Incas),[11] but though these, and presumably others, did exist, there was little evidence that they were even known by the colonial administrators, let alone encouraged or used. The one exception would have been the use by the Chinese, and by other people, of the abacus in certain colonies, which clearly was felt to be a sufficiently sophisticated system for administrative purposes.[12]

The other aspect to be imposed through administration would have been the language of hierarchy, through structuring people and their functions. It may seem a relatively insignificant example to choose, but it is very difficult for anyone used to the western obsession with naming and classification to imagine that there exist other ways of conceptualising and using language. The research of Lancy and of Philp have made us aware of this. As Lancy, for example, says:

> In Britain, parents teach their children that the most important function of language is reference. They prepare their children for a society that places a premium on knowing the names and classes of things. The Kaluli of the Southern Highlands of PNG invest—if anything—more time in teaching language to their children than do the British, but their aim is very different. The Kaluli child learns that the most important language functions are expressive; specifically, that the competent language user is one who can use speech to manipulate and control the behavior of others.

Any enforced use of other language structures is thus likely to cause difficulties and confusion,[13] but, more than that, any western European colonial governmental and administrative activity which concerned system, structure and the role of personnel would inevitably, and perhaps unwittingly, have imposed a western European mode of linguistic and logical classification.

The third and major medium for cultural invasion was education, which played such a critical role in promoting western mathematical ideas and, thereby, western culture. In most colonial societies, the imposed education functioned at two levels, mirroring what existed in the European country concerned. The first level, that of elementary education, developed hardly at all in the early colonial period. In India, for example, the 'filtering down' principle, whereby it was assumed that it was only necessary to educate the elite few and the knowledge would somehow 'filter down to the masses', was paramount. In some of the mission schools and in the latter years of colonialism when elementary schooling began to be taken more seriously, it was, of course, the European content which dominated. The need was felt to educate the indigenous people only in order to enable them to function adequately in the European-dominated trade, commercial and administrative structures which had been established. Mathematically, the only content of any significance was arithmetic with its related applications.[14]

Of much more interest to the theme of this essay is the secondary education given to the elite few in the colonised countries. In India and Africa, schools and colleges were established which, in their education, mirrored once again their comparable institutions in the 'home' country.[15] The fact that the education differed in French-controlled institutions from their English counterparts merely reflected the differences existing in the current philosophies of French and English education.

At best, the mathematics curriculum of some of the schools was just laughably and pathetically inappropriate. Mmari quotes some typical problems from Tanzanian colonial textbooks (recommended for use in schools by British colonial education officers):[16]

If a cricketer scores altogether r runs in x innings, n times not out, his average is $\frac{r}{x-n}$ runs. Find his average if he scores 204 runs in 15 innings, 3 times not out.

Reduce 207,042 farthings; 89,761 half-pence; 5,708 ½ shillings to £.s.d.

The escalator at the Holborn tube station is 156 feet long and makes the ascent in 65 seconds. Find the speed in miles per hour.

But then, 'appropriateness' was entirely judged in terms of cultural transmission.

At worst, the mathematics curriculum was abstract, irrelevant, selective and elitist—as indeed it was in Europe—governed by structures like the Cambridge Overseas Certificate, and culturally laden to a very high degree.[17] It was part of a deliberate strategy of acculturation—intentional in its efforts to instruct in 'the best of the West', and convinced of its superiority to any indigenous mathematical systems and culture. As it was essentially a university-preparatory education, the aspirations of the students were towards attending western universities. They were educated away from their culture and away from their society. For example, Watson quotes Wilkinson, criticising Malayan education at the turn of the century in these terms: 'unpractical, to make the people litigious, to inspire a distaste for manual and technical work and to create a class of literary malcontents, useless to their communities and a source of trouble to the Empire'.[18] Mathematics and science—subjects which, in fact, could so easily have made connections with the indigenous culture and environment, and which could have been made relevant to the needs of the indigenous society—were just not thought of in those terms, despite many of the teachers' good intentions. They were seen merely as two of the pillars of western culture, significant as part of a cultured person's education in the nineteenth and early twentieth centuries.[19]

So, it is clear that through the three media of trade, administration and education, the symbolisations and structures of western mathematics would have been imposed on the indigenous cultures just as significantly as were those linguistic symbolisations and structures of English, French, Dutch or whichever was the European language of the particular dominant colonial power in the country.

However, also like a language, the particular symbolisations used were, in a way, the least significant aspect of mathematics. Of far more importance, particularly in cultural terms, were the values which the symbolisations carried with them. Of course, it goes without saying that it was also conventional wisdom that mathematics was value free. How could it have values if it was universal and culture free? We now know better, and an analysis of the historical, anthropological and cross-cultural literatures suggests that there are four clusters of values which are associated with western European mathematics, and which must have had a tremendous impact on the indigenous cultures.

First, there is the area of rationalism, which is at the very heart of western mathematics. If one had to choose a single value and attribute which has guaranteed the power and authority of mathematics within western culture, it is rationalism. As Kline says: 'In its broadest aspect mathematics is a spirit, the spirit of rationality. It is this spirit that challenges, stimulates, invigorates, and drives human minds to exercise themselves to the fullest.'[20] With its focus on deductive reasoning and logic, it poured scorn on mere trial and error practices, traditional wisdom and witchcraft. So, consider this quotation, from Gay and Cole in Liberia:

> A Kpelle college student accepted *all* the following statements: (1) the Bible is literally true, thus all living things were created in the six days described in Genesis; (2) the Bible is a book like other books, written by relatively primitive peoples over a long period of time and contains contradiction and error; (3) all living things have gradually evolved over millions of years from primitive matter; (4) a 'spirit' tree in a nearby village had been cut down, had put itself back together, and had grown to full size again in one day. He had learned these statements from his Fundamentalist pastor, his college bible course, his zoology course, and the still-pervasive animist culture. He accepted all, because all were sanctioned by authorities to which he feels he must pay respect.[21]

One can understand Gay and Cole's discomfort at this revelation, but one can also understand how much more confusing it must have been to the student to learn that anything which was not 'rational' in the western sense was not to be trusted.

Second, a complementary set of values associated with western mathematics can be termed objectism, a way of perceiving the world as if it were composed of discrete objects, able to be removed and abstracted, so to speak, from their context. To decontextualise, in order to be able to generalise, is at the heart of western mathematics and science; but if your culture encourages you to believe, instead, that everything belongs and exists in its relationship with everything else, then removing it from its context makes it literally meaningless. In early Greek civilisation, there was also a deep controversy over 'object' or 'process' as the fundamental core of being. Heraclitos, in 600–500BC, argued that the essential feature of phenomena is that they are always in flux, always moving and always changing. Democritus, and the Pythagoreans, preferred the world-view of 'atoms', which eventually was to prevail and develop within western mathematics and science.[22]

Horton sees objectism in another light. He compares this view with what he sees as the preferred African use of personal idiom as explanation. He argues that this has developed for the traditional African the sense that the personal and social 'world' is knowable, whereas the impersonal and the 'world of things' is essentially unknowable. The opposite tendency holds for the westerner. Horton's argument proceeds as follows:

> In complex, rapidly changing industrial societies the human scene is in flux. Order, regularity, predictability, simplicity, all these seem lamentably absent. It is in the world of inanimate things that such qualities are most readily seen. This is why many people can find themselves less at home with their fellow men than with things. And this too, I suggest, is why the mind in quest of explanatory analogies turns most readily to the inanimate. In the traditional societies of Africa, we find the situation reversed. The human scene is the locus *par excellence* of order, predictability, regularity. In the world of the inanimate [by which he means 'natural' rather than man-made], these qualities are far less evident. Here being less at home with people than with things is unimaginable. And here, the mind in quest of explanatory analogies turns naturally to people and their relation.[23]

We can see, therefore, that with both rationalism and objectism as core values, western mathematics presents a dehumanised, objectified, ideological world-view which will emerge necessarily through mathematics teaching of the traditional colonial kind.

A third set of values concerns the power and control aspect of western mathematics. Mathematical ideas are used either as directly applicable concepts and techniques, or indirectly through science and technology, as ways to control the physical and social environment. As Schaaf says in relation to the history of mathematics: 'The spirit of the nineteenth and twentieth centuries, is typified by man's increasing mastery over his physical environment.'[24] So, using numbers and measurements in trade, industry, commerce and administration would all have emphasised the power and control values of mathematics. It was (and still is) so clearly useful knowledge, powerful knowledge, and it seduced the majority of peoples who came into contact with it.

However, a complementary set of values, which is concerned with progress and change, has also grown and developed in order to gain yet more control over one's environment. An awareness of the values of control allied to the rational analysis of problems feeds a complementary value of rational progress, and so there is a concern to question, to doubt and to enquire into alternatives. Horton again points to this value when he contrasts western scientific ideas with traditional African values: 'In traditional cultures there is no developed awareness of alternatives to the established body of theoretical tenets; whereas in scientifically oriented cultures such an awareness is highly developed'.[25] Whether that conclusion has validity or not, there can be no doubting the unsettling effect of an elitist education which was preaching 'control' and 'progress' in traditional societies, nor could one imagine that these values were what was needed by the indigenous population in the countries concerned.

Certainly, even if progress were sought by the indigenous population, which itself is not necessarily obvious, what was offered was a westernised, industrialised and product-oriented version of progress, which seemed only to reinforce the disparity between progressive, dynamic and aggressive western European imperialists and traditional, stable and non-proselytising colonised peoples. Mathematically inspired progress through technology and science was clearly one of the reasons why the colonial powers had progressed as far as they had, and that is why mathematics was such a significant tool in the cultural kitbag of the imperialists.

In total, then, these values amount to a mathematico-technological cultural force, which is what indeed the imperialist powers generally represented. Mathematics with its clear rationalism, and cold logic, its precision, its so-called 'objective' facts (seemingly culture and value free), its lack of human frailty, its power to predict and to control, its encouragement to challenge and to question, and its thrust towards yet more secure knowledge, was a most powerful weapon indeed. When allied to the use of technology, to the development of industry and commerce through scientific applications and to the increasing utility of tangible, commercial products, its status was felt to be indisputable.

From those colonial times through to today, the power of this mathematico-technological culture has grown apace—so much so that western mathematics is taught nowadays in every country in the world. Once again, it is mainly taught with the assumptions of universality and cultural neutrality. From colonialism through to neo-colonialism, the cultural imperialism of western mathematics has yet to be fully realised and understood. Gradually, greater understanding of its impact is being acquired, but one must wonder whether its all-pervading influence is now out of control.

As awareness of the cultural nature and influence of western mathematics is spreading and developing, so various levels of responses can also be seen. At the first level, there is an increasing interest in the study of ethno-mathematics, through both analyses of the anthropological literature and investigations in real-life situations. Whilst recognising that many now-important ideas may well not have seemed to be so by earlier generations of anthropologists, there is, nevertheless, still a great deal of information to be gleaned from the existing literature.

This kind of literature analysis is, of course, aided by theoretical structures which help us conceptualise just what mathematics, as the pan-cultural phenomenon, might be. It is reiterated that mathematics is a cultural product—a symbolic technology, developed through engaging in various environmental activities.[26] Six universal activities may be identified, by which I mean that no cultural group has been documented which does not appear to carry out these activities in some form.[27] They are:

• Counting: the use of a systematic way to compare and order discrete objects. It may involve body or finger counting, tallying, or using objects or string to record, or special number names. Calculation can also be done with the numbers, with magical and predictive properties associated with some of them.

- Locating: exploring one's spatial environment, and conceptualising and symbolising that environment, with models, maps, drawings and other devices. This is the aspect of geometry where orientation, navigation, astronomy and geography play a strong role.
- Measuring: quantifying qualities like length and weight, for the purposes of comparing and ordering objects. Measuring is usually used where phenomena cannot be counted (e.g., water, rice), but money is also a unit of measure of economic worth.
- Designing: creating a shape or a design for an object or for any part of one's spatial environment. It may involve making the object as a copyable 'template', or drawing it in some conventionalised way. The object can be designed for technological or spiritual uses and 'shape' is a fundamental geometrical concept.
- Playing: devising, and engaging in, games and pastimes with more or less formalised rules that all players must abide by. Games frequently model a significant aspect of social reality, and often involve hypothetical reasoning.
- Explaining: finding ways to represent the relationships between phenomena. In particular, exploring the 'patterns' of number, location, measure and design, which create an 'inner world' of mathematical relationships which model, and thereby explain, the outer world of reality.[28]

We now have extensive documentary evidence from many different cultures confirming the existence of all of these activities, and this structure is one which is enabling more detailed searches to be undertaken in the research literature. Ethno-mathematics is, however, still not a well-defined term,[29] and, indeed, in view of the ideas and data we now have, perhaps it would be better not to use that term but rather to be more precise about which, and whose, mathematics one is referring to in any context. Moreover, the search should also focus on the values aspect as well. In considering the problems and issues of culture-conflict in education, it is all too easy to remain at the level of symbolisations and language, whereas of much more significance educationally are the differences in cultural values which may exist. They need serious attention in future research.

At the second level, there is a response in many developing countries and former colonies which is aimed at creating a greater awareness of one's own culture. Cultural rebirth or reawakening is a recognised goal of the educational process in several countries. Gerdes, in Mozambique, is a mathematics educator who has done a great deal of work in this area. He seeks not only to demonstrate important mathematical aspects of Mozambican society, but also to develop the process of 'defreezing' the 'frozen' mathematics which he uncovers. For example, with the plaiting methods used by fishermen to make their fish traps, he demonstrates significant geometric ideas which could easily be assimilated into the mathematics curriculum in order to create what he considers to be a genuine Mozambican mathematics education for the young people there.[30]

Clearly, the ideas of the first level will inform and stimulate work at this second level—another reason why ethno-mathematical research needs to be updated. This activity is not restricted to developing countries either. In Australia with the Aborigines, in North America with the Navajos and other Amerindian groups and in other countries where there exist cultural and ethnic minorities, there is a great deal of interest in discovering and developing local, folk or indigenous mathematics which may have been lying dormant for many centuries.[31] These ideas may then help to shape a more relevant, and culturally meaningful, curriculum in the local schools.

One of the greatest ironies in this whole field is that several different cultures and societies have contributed to the development of what is called western mathematics: the Egyptians, the Chinese, the Indians, the Arabs, the Greeks, as well as the western Europeans. Yet when western cultural imperialism imposed its version of mathematics on the colonised societies, it was scarcely recognisable as anything to which these societies might have contributed. In Iran, in the early 1970s, for example, there appeared to be little awareness amongst the local mathematics educators of the massive contribution which the Muslim empire had made to the development of the mathematics which they were struggling to teach to their young people. Nowadays, with the rise of fundamentalism, there is growing an increasing awareness of both this contribution and also of an essential Islamic philosophy of education, which will shape the mathematical and scientific curricula in the fundamentalist schools.[32] We are, therefore, beginning to see the assimilation, in place of the imposition, of western mathematics into other cultures. This is a world-wide development and can only help to stimulate cultural regrowth.

The third level of response to the cultural imperialism of western mathematics is, paradoxically, to re-examine the whole history of western mathematics itself. It is no accident that this history has been written predominantly by white, male, western European or American researchers, and there is a concern that, for example, the contribution of Black Africa has been undervalued. Van Sertima's book *Blacks in Science* is a deliberate attack on this prejudiced view of mathematical development.[33] Various contributors to this book point to the scientific, technological and mathematical ideas and inventions developed in Africa centuries ago, yet rarely referred to. Other contributors argue that the contribution of the Greeks to mathematics has been over-emphasized; that they only consolidated and structured what had been thoroughly developed by the Babylonians and the Egyptians earlier; that Euclid worked in Alexandria and is more likely to have been African rather than Greek; that the archaeological evidence has either been ignored or misrepresented.[34]

Joseph[35] emphasises the strong role played by the Muslim empire in bringing mathematical ideas from the East to the notice of a wider people, not just in Europe. Needham's work[36] demonstrates very well the contributions which began in China and grew through India where the Muslims made contact with them. There is certainly no reason to claim that what we know as western mathematics was entirely the product of western European culture.

In my view, however, the significance of cultural values has been underestimated in much of this historical analysis so far, and that when that dimension is fully recognised, there will be a great deal more re-analysing to do. The separation of symbolisations from cultural values is difficult to achieve, but we know how even the language of English carries different messages on both sides of the Atlantic because of the different cultural values existing there. The same symbolisations of mathematics may well have carried with them different kinds of values in different cultures in the past. Perhaps the best example of this is with India. Indian mathematics, along with that of other eastern cultural groups, had strong religious and spiritual values associated with it. Western mathematics on the other hand, was identified strongly with western science, with dehumanised, so-called 'objective' knowledge, and with empirical and rational interpretations of natural phenomena. Yet, in most Indian schools today, it is western mathematics which is taught and it is the western values that are thereby fostered. Of course, many of the symbolisations (numbers, etc.) are the bases for our own symbolisations and many of the ideas of arithmetic were developed by the Hindus. The values, though, are markedly different. Some Indian mathematics educators[37] are now arguing for developments to redress the balance, although a further irony is that there may well be more interest in this kind of educational development among the Indian community in, for example, England than in India, where the educational conflicts are apparently felt less deeply. Nevertheless, the relationship between values and symbolisations is likely to be a promising area for further research.

I began by describing the myth of western mathematics' cultural neutrality. Increasingly, modern evidence serves to destroy this naive belief. Nevertheless, the belief in that myth has had, and continues to have, powerful implications. Those implications relate to education, to national developments and to a continuation of cultural imperialism. Indeed, it is not too sweeping to state that most of the modern world has accepted western mathematics, values included, as a fundamental part of its education. In Hungary in 1988 the Sixth International Congress on Mathematics Education (which is held every four years) was attended by around 3,000 mathematics educators. They came from every country in the world that was able to support participation, and those that were not there will now be purchasing copies of the proceedings and the reports. Such is the magnet of western mathematics and its principal acolyte, western mathematics education. Clearly, many societies have recognised the benefits to their peoples of adopting western mathematics, science and technology.

However, taking a broader view, one must ask: should there not be more resistance to this cultural hegemony? Indeed, there is some awareness to build on. In addition to the three major responses mentioned earlier, in recent years, as the kinds of evidence and issues referred to in this article have become more widely disseminated and more seriously discussed, so there has grown a recognition of the need to reflect these concerns at such congresses. At the Hungary conference, one whole day was given over to the theme of 'Mathematics, education and society' on which many papers were presented, discussion stimulated and awareness kindled. Included in that day's programme were topics central to the issues discussed here.[38]

Resistance is growing, critical debate is informing theoretical development, and research is increasing, particularly in educational situations where culture-conflict is recognised. The secret weapon is secret no longer.

NOTES

1 G.A. Lean, *Counting Systems of Papua New Guinea* (Papua New Guinea, 1986); C. Zaslavsky, *Africa Counts* (Boston, 1973); M.P. Closs, *Native American Mathematics* (Austin, Texas, 1986).

2 K. Menninger, *Number Words and Number Symbols: a cultural history of numbers* (Cambridge, Mass, 1969).

3 R. Pinxten, I. van Dooren and F. Harvey, *The Anthropology of Space* (University of Pennsylvania Press, 1983).

4 D.F. Lancy, *Cross-cultural Studies in Cognition and Mathematics* (New York, 1983); H. Philp, 'Mathematical education in developing countries' in A.G. Howson (ed.), *Developments in Mathematical Education* (Cambridge, 1973).

5 See, for example, U. d'Ambrosio 'Ethnomathematics and its place in the history and pedagogy of mathematics', *For the Learning of Mathematics* (1985), and P. Gerdes, 'How to recognise hidden geometrical thinking: a contribution to the development of anthropological mathematics', *For the Learning of Mathematics* (1986).

6 'Pan-cultural' is used to convey the sense that all cultures engage in mathematical activities.

7 In the late nineteenth century and early twentieth century, one can also recognise the increasing contribution of American and Australian influences, which nevertheless stem from the western European cultural tradition.

8 A fourth candidate would be 'technology'. Its influence is clear: see, for example, D.R. Headrick's *The Tools of Empire* (Oxford, 1981); but what is rather less clear is the mathematical relationship with technology. As science and mathematics developed in their power and control, they undoubtedly influenced technology, particularly later in the imperialist era.

9 See Zaslavsky, op. cit. and Menninger, op. cit.

10 J. Jones, *Cognitive Studies with Students in Papua New Guinea* (Papua New Guinea, 1974).

11 See Ascher, op. cit.

12 Even today, the abacus has survived the calculator invasion and is still in prolific use in the countries of Asia.

13 See P.W. Bridgman, 'Quo Vadis', *Daedalus* (No. 87, 1958), and L.C.S. Dawe, 'The influence of a bilingual child's first language competence on reasoning in mathematics' (unpublished PhD thesis, University of Cambridge, 1982). As Awoniyi points out: 'A foreign language is more than a different set of words for the same ideas; it is a new and strange way of looking at things, an unfamiliar grouping of ideas', T.A. Awoniyi, 'Yoruba language and the schools system; a study in colonial language policy in Nigeria 1882–1952', *The International Journal of African Historical Studies* (Vol. VIII, 1975).

14 In the main, of course, there was felt to be little need for anything beyond reading, in order to understand either the bible translated into a local language, or simple work instructions. In India, after the orientalist phase, English was the language used predominantly in the schools and the acquisition of English became *the* goal of education to the exclusion of anything else.

15 For example, Budo College, Uganda, the Alliance High School, Kenya, Elphinstone College, India. See M. Carnoy, *Education as Cultural Imperialism* (Longman, 1974) and R.J. Njoroge and G.A. Bennaars, *Philosophy and Education in Africa* (Nairobi, 1986).

16 G.R.V. Mmari, 'The United Republic of Tanzania: mathematics for social transformation' in F.J. Swetz (ed.) *Socialist Mathematics Education* (Southampton, PA 1978). He also says: 'Textbooks of the period in question indicate the use of foreign units of measure of length, weight, capacity, volume, and currency which support this theory of direct interaction between business practices and the cultural background of the then dominant existing business community'.

17 P. Damerow says 'The transfer of the European mathematics curriculum to developing countries was closely associated with the establishment of schools for the elite by colonial administrations. Under these circumstances it seemed natural to simply copy European patterns', 'Individual development and cultural evolution of arithmetical thinking' in S. Strauss (ed.), *Ontogeny and Historical Development* (Pennsylvania, 1986).

18 J.K.P. Watson *Education in the Third World* (London, 1982).

19 Indeed, there was no great attempt in the 'home' countries themselves to make science and mathematics relevant either.

20 M. Kline, *Mathematics in Western Culture* (London, 1972).

21 J. Gay and M. Cole, *The New Mathematics in an Old Culture* (New York, 1967).

22 See C.A. Ronan, *The Cambridge Illustrated History of the World's Science* (Cambridge Press, 1983), and C.H. Waddington, *Tools for Thought* (St Albans, 1977), for a recent analysis.

23 R. Horton, 'African traditional thought and Western science' *Africa,* (Vol XXXVII, 1967), also in M.F.F. Young (ed.), *Knowledge and Control* (London, 1971).

24 W.L. Schaaf, *Our Mathematical Heritage* (New York, 1963).

25 Horton, op. cit.

26 For a fuller examination of these ideas, see A.J. Bishop, *Mathematical Enculturation: a cultural perspective on mathematics education* (Dordrecht, Holland, 1988).

27 The caveat may perhaps seem unnecessary, but to a mathematician the word 'universal' does cause certain problems. For further discussion of this general issue, see G.P. Murdoch, 'The common denominator of cultures' in R. Linton (ed.), *The Science of Man in the World Crisis* (New York, 1945).

28 In order for mathematical knowledge to develop, it is necessary for these activities to integrate and to interact. Without this integration, the set of activities could be argued to be pre-mathematical.

29 See d'Ambrosio op. cit. and M. Ascher and R. Ascher, 'Ethnomathematics', *History of Science* (Vol. XXIV, 1986) for different perspectives. The Aschers argue specifically for ethnomathematics to be the province of 'non-literate peoples', while d'Ambrosio's view encompasses all mathematical ideas not exposed by 'mainstream' mathematics.

30 See Gerdes (1986) op. cit. and P. Gerdes, 'On possible uses of traditional Angolan sand drawings in the mathematics classroom', *Educational Studies in Mathematics* (No. 19, 1988).

31 See P. Harris *Measurement in Tribal Aboriginal Communities* (Northern Territory Department of Education, Australia, 1980), and Closs, op. cit.

32 See S.H. Nasr, *Islamic Science: an illustrated study* (Essex, UK, 1976) and I.R. Al-Faruqi and A.D. Naseef, *Social and Natural Science: the Islamic perspective* (London, 1981).

33 I. van Sertima, *Blacks in Science* (New Brunswick, 1986).

34 For example, B. Lumpkin, 'Africa in the mainstream of mathematics history', in van Sertima, op. cit.

35 G.G. Joseph, 'Foundations of Eurocentrism in Mathematics', *Race and Class* (Vol. XXVIII, 1987).

36 See C.A. Ronan, *The Shorter Science and Civilization in China,* Vol. 2 (Cambridge, 1981).

37 See, for example, D.S. Kothari's keynote address in the *Proceedings of the Asian Regional Seminar of the Commonwealth Association of Science and Mathematics Educators* (London, 1978).

38 See A.J. Bishop, P. Damerow, P. Gerdes and C. Keitel, 'Mathematics, Education and Society' in A. Hirst and K. Hirst, *Proceedings of the Sixth International Congress on Mathematical Education* (University of Southampton, 1988); also, there is a special UNESCO publication of the whole day's papers and proceedings (C. Keitel, A.J. Bishop, P. Damerow and P. Gerdes *Mathematics, Education and Society* (Document Series 35, Paris, 1989)).

SOCIAL STRUCTURE, SUBORDINATION, AND RESISTANCE

Social subordination is sometimes extreme enough to necessitate conscious attention, sporadically or continually, to the challenge of surviving. Survival concerns the cultural as well as physical integrity essential to the individual's continuing experience of self-sameness. Audre Lorde reminds us that it entails not only "learning how to stand alone" but also "how to make common cause with those others identified as outside the structures in order to define and seek a world in which we can all flourish."[1]

Thus, subordinated individuals commonly find that their meaningful survival mandates resistance to the systems of domination denying or assaulting their dignity. Indeed, such resistance is an assertion of dignity. Regardless of whether subordinated individuals have secured their survival, they frequently—perhaps typically—go about the business of resisting those bent on dominating, controlling, and oppressing them. Full-time or part-time, long-term or short-term, they step out of the line where people like them are supposed to queue up for their paltry share of society's opportunities and rewards. They become agents of social change by asserting their wills against the status quo inferiorizing them.

Domination is the ongoing process of systematically subordinating an individual or a group. Under extreme but scarcely rare circumstances it involves brute force and unspeakable horrors. More routinely, domination "operates by seducing, pressuring, or forcing . . . members of subordinate groups to replace individual and cultural ways of knowing with the dominant group's specialized thought."[2] Thereby systems of domination—the hierarchies of society, the weighted dice of history—come to seem natural, fixed, and unassailable for all practical purposes. What Ellen Swartz (p. 164) calls " 'standard' knowledge" is thus a telling measure of our collective progress toward or rejection of inclusionary, multivocal ideas.

The social stock of knowledge, which includes subjugated as well as standard knowledges, is partioned by class, race, gender, and the other "axes of oppression" constituting what Patricia Hill Collins calls the *matrix of domination* in our society. In that stock of knowledge lie the recipes for resistance and the tools of transformation. As Collins puts it, consciousness can serve as "a sphere of freedom" within "community structures [that] provide a primary line of resistance against . . . oppression."[3] In community with one another subordinate individuals can use what Collins calls their "power of self-definition" to reclaim their dignity while changing the circumstances that assault or deny it.

Unlike subordinate members of society, dominators need not generally concern themselves with survival as such. Overall, their focus is on self-aggrandizement and, to the extent that it advances one's own fortunes, group-aggrandizement. Under some historical circumstances they do concern themselves with resistance, namely, resistance to the actual or perceived advances of their social "inferiors." Their resistance is called *backlash,* which "succeeds to the degree that it appears *not* to be political, that it appears not to be a struggle at all."[4] Although backlash is extremely consequential, our focus here is subordinate members' strategies of surviving and resisting.

Physical survival is the focus of the first reading. Barry Adam's paper illustrates that a matrix of domination derives support from all the major institutions of a society. He shows that the "Nazi machine" was a matrix of domination involving a "three-fold coalition" among industry, church, and the military. Adam's portrayal dramatizes the monolithic force a matrix of domination can unleash against those human beings socially constructed as society's outcasts, misfits, and troublemakers.

Adam's paper also shows us that with its hierarchy of triangles, the Holocaust materialized the dense connections among ethnocentrism, racism, homophobia, misogyny, and other group hatreds. Whatever else the Nazis showed us—and we are yet learning their horrific lessons—they demonstrated once and for all that few of us have hateful, intolerant attitudes toward only one or two groups of human beings. The matrix of domination more or less ensures that people get *pervasively* infected with such attitudes so that loathing for people of color or physically challenged people readily translates into dis-ease in the presence of lesbians and gay men (when we recognize them as such) or old, old people. *Elitism* is the overarching ideology whereby heterosexual white males of high status and material privilege serve as the standard against which the rest of us lose power, status, and material resources in varying degrees. Those losses represent the standing costs of subordination to the straight white hyperprivileged male minority whose members are the primary beneficiaries of our lower salaries, restricted rights, and limited opportunities.

In the preceding sentences I have used the first-person plural as a reminder that most people, whether on the planet or in our society, are not straight, white, hyperprivileged males. Indeed, most of us falling outside those boundaries do so in multiple ways. We are working-class, bisexual, and Chicano; we are lower-middle class and confined to a wheelchair; we are lesbian professionals of color; we are African American men trapped in the urban underclass; we are American Indian women; we are the less visible, less heard, less privileged, and less protected members of society. Therein lies a major paradox of group subordination. Often said to need "looking after for their own good," subordinated members get less protection than dominant members of society. There is no sociological surprise in that circumstance, but there is a good bit of social irony that takes such cruel forms as unenforced child-support orders, a law enforcement system unequipped to ensure battered women's safety, and a judicial system disproportionately meting out the death penalty to men of color.

Most of us belong, then, to at least one subordinate grouping in society, and many of us belong to two or more such groupings. Those circumstances mean that for the most part we belong at one and the same time to oppressed groups and oppressing groups. Thus, unless we commit to the role of activist or advocate, we inescapably enact the divide-and-conquer realities bound up with the matrix of domination. Lorde recommended the activist pathway:

> Each of us is blessed in some particular way, whether we recognize our blessings or not. And each one of us, somewhere in our lives, must clear a space within that blessing where she can call upon whatever resources are available to her in the name of something that must be done.[5]

What must be done covers two big territories—critique and resistance.[6] We have already seen that multicultural social theory comprises critique. At the macro level, social movements, such as the gay and lesbian rights movement or the reproductive rights movement, represent resistance to the status quo injurious to certain groups; at the micro level, "talking back" expresses resistance. As bell hooks describes it, *talking back* revolves around "speaking as an equal to an authority figure" or dominant-group member; it entails making a statement "that compels listeners, one that is heard"; it aims at dialogue—"the sharing of speech *and* recognition." (my emphasis) Thus, talking back "is an act of resistance, a political gesture that challenges the politics of domination that would render [subordinate members] nameless and voiceless."[7]

Talking back is but one form of what Carole Anne Taylor calls "assertive subjectivity."[8] Such subjectivity is a resisting consciousness bent on negating to one degree or other the putdowns and slights as well as the more extreme unfairnesses definitive of subordination. Taylor indicates that "some forms of dominance" invite assertive subjectivity; other forms invite "problematized subjectivity." Before looking at problematized consciousness, we need to note how domination typically eventuates not only in the withholding of opportunities and rewards but also in the colonizing of consciousness. As Peter L. Berger notes, socialization routinely entails internalization whereby "The structures of society become the structures of our own consciousness."[9] When those hierarchical structures leave us on the lower, losing end of multiple pecking orders, internalization results in a self-inferiorizing consciousness or a colonized consciousness. Earlier Lugones and Spelman (p. 22) as well as Collins (p. 40) referred to such phenomena as "internalized oppression." Under these circumstances resistance to the status quo necessitates problematizing one's own consciousness so as to curtail its service to the existing order. Such resistance builds up subjugated knowledges, in large measure by displacing hegemonic definitions with counterhegemonic definitions.

Resistance based on problematizing one's own consciousness presupposes some practical knowledge of the matrix of domination, knowledge commonly in hand among subordinated individuals needing it to survive. The first lesson of that knowledge is, as Adam's paper illustrates, that the matrix of domination rests on multiple, interlocking institutions as well as the dominant language (mass-media English). In practical terms that lesson means that subordinated people need, usually in community with one another, to look critically at the full sweep of social structure. Every institution tied in with the hegemony of hyperprivileged, straight, white males is a candidate for critique, as the remaining readings in this section illustrate with reference to four institutions—literature, government, religion, and education.

Carroll Smith-Rosenberg shows how popular literature can promote or subvert the hegemony of Euro-Americans. Her first focus is American Indian captivity narratives written by Euro-American women that historically helped to construct members of their ethnic group as "true Americans" by portraying indigenous Americans as "savages." Then Smith-Rosenberg turns to the popular romance that ultimately "raises more questions than it can answer" (p. 152) and thus has subversive potential. Her analysis, not included in detail here, shows how popular texts can either draw readers into elitist consciousness or problematize such consciousness. In the process she also shows how Euro-American women from the literate classes, themselves racially and materially privileged, variously reinforced and challenged that axis of oppression casting American Indians as expendable Others.

In the next paper W. Roger Buffalohead broadly surveys the long-term aftermath of socially constructing Native Americans as Others. His paper reports on the federal government's historically variable policies on American Indians' cultural rights and resources. Concerned with cultural equity in our society and the cultural sovereignty of American Indians, Buffalohead recognizes cultural self-determination as a necessary condition of overcoming subordination.

Next Clovis E. Semmes looks at Eurocentric religions from an Afrocentric perspective. Thus, his paper treats the same axis of oppression as Smith-Rosenberg's and Buffalohead's, namely, the one pitting Euro-Americans against Americans of color. Semmes argues that religion can spawn as much cultural imperialism based on "universalist claims" as any institution and thus necessitate a reclamation of consciousness. Overcoming what Semmes calls "conditioned dislogic," a variety of colonized consciousness, is central to such reclamation. Invoking W. E. B. Du Bois, Semmes also emphasizes the "double consciousness" whereby oppressed individuals "hav[e] to view the world through the eyes of their oppressor" (p. 159) as well as through the truths of their own lived experiences. Semmes implies that problematizing consciousness is an integral part of movement toward "a formal religious structure that is empowering, status enhancing, and liberating" (p. 162).

Ellen Swartz implies the same thing about educational structures. She looks at how public school textbooks decontextualize slavery, the abolition movement, and the Reconstruction and thus marginalize and disempower African Americans (and women to an extent) by misrepresenting them. Her concern lies with schools as the promulgators of "hegemonic scholarship." Much to her credit, Swartz shows how "compensatory" gestures such as portraying a few African Americans in sidebars to the main—that is, hegemonic—text reproduces "standard" knowledge wherein such individuals exist only in the margins of society. Such gestures also promote *exceptionalism,* the treatment of one or a few individuals as rare, atypical members of an inferior grouping. Besides deconstructing so-called compensatory approaches, Swartz illustrates how point of view routinely reinforces hegemonic understandings. Depicting slave revolts from white people's (men's?) point of view, for example, renders them "violent and threatening" rather than "daring" and "revolutionary" (p. 169). Similarly, portraying oppressed people as "voiceless victims" (p. 172) reinforces hegemonic denials of their agency. Such portrayals point to a circumstance necessitating both problematized subjectivity and assertive subjectivity.

That circumstance is the profusion of social stereotypes wherein "no behavior *counts* as resistance. . . ."[10] Talking back, as hooks herself points out, can be written off as an expression of madness, and each of us can write off our problematized subjectivity as no more than a phase or a temporary aberration of consciousness. Generally, every subordinate group is the target of stereotypes that serve in part to misname resistance by translating it into something else, especially something that in turn legitimates that group's continuing subordination. For example, stereotypes of women write off their "uppity"—that is, resistant—behavior as an expression of their hormones. Women are commonly stereotyped as emotionally overexpressive or unstable so that their resistance gets taken as a commentary on their moods rather than on their situation. They are also stereotyped as instinctually destined for motherhood so that those resisting or foregoing that option are not "real" women and those giving up custody of their child(ren) are beyond the gendered pale. One subtle, painful cost of subordination, then, is that one's rejection of it is hard to register effectively. Doing so requires risking one's safety and sanity, says hooks. She is quick, though, to "bear witness . . . to the strength and power that emerge from sustained resistance and the profound conviction that these forces can be healing, can protect us from dehumanization and despair."[11]

The readings in this section, like the others in this volume, are best seen as expressions of critical consciousness aimed at effective resistance. For the most part they imply that in our actual lives critique and resistance intertwine. One sharpens the focus of the other; one tests the other. Multicultural social theory has among its distinguishing features a theory/practice conjunction where theorists craft their texts with practice in mind and craft their practice—in the classroom, on the streets, in governmental chambers—with an eye on its theoretical import. Better put, multicultural social theorists generally see theorizing as one among many transformative practices.

NOTES

1 Audre Lorde, *Sister Outsider: Essays and Speeches,* Freedom, CA, The Crossing Press, 1984, p. 112.

2 Patricia Hill Collins, *Black Feminist Thought: Knowledge, Consciousness, and the Politics of Empowerment,* New York, Routledge, 1991, p. 229.

3 *Ibid.,* pp. 226, 228.

4 Susan Faludi, *Backlash: The Undeclared War Against American Women,* New York, Anchor Books, 1992, p. xxii.

5 Audre Lorde, "Two Excerpts from *A Burst of Light: Living with Cancer"* in Barbara Sang, Joyce Warshow, and Adrienne J. Smith (eds.), *Lesbians at Midlife: The Creative Transition,* San Francisco, Spinsters Book Company, 1991, p. 265.

6 Cf. Sandra Lee Bartky, "Reply to Commentators on *Femininity and Domination,"* *Hypatia* 8 (Winter, 1993), 193.

7 bell hooks, *Talking Back: Thinking Feminist, Thinking Black,* Boston, South End Press, 1989, pp. 5–9.

8 Carole Anne Taylor, "Positioning Subjects and Objects: Agency, Narration, Relationality," *Hypatia* (Winter, 1993), 70.

9 Peter L. Berger, *Invitation to Sociology: A Humanistic Perspective,* New York, Anchor Books, 1963, p. 121.

10 Sarah Lucia Hoagland, *Lesbian Ethics: Toward New Value,* Palo Alto, CA, Institute of Lesbian Studies, 1988, p. 40.

11 hooks, *op. cit.,* p. 7.

The Holocaust

Barry D. Adam

[Gay people] had their golden age a half century ago, a lost continent obliterated by the totalitarian bloodbath.

—Guy Hocquenghem, *Race d'Ep.*

NEW SOURCES FOR OLD FEARS

The breaking up of feudal society organized around kin and hierarchy created a world with new possibilities, especially for traditionally oppressed classes: peasants and serfs, women, national minorities, and Jews. In this new world, "comrade attachment" between men and between women found new avenues for expression and new voices. But capitalism is no unitary phenomenon and its development through the particular political makeup of different nations resulted in divergent conditions for the emergence of a gay people. Increasingly evident from the historical record is the fact that "homogenic love" faced difficulties that were not merely a question of overcoming older holdovers but hindrances stemming from modern sources (Adam 1985).

Though the rise of capitalism opened new channels for homosexual expression, it also laid the groundwork for the reorganization and rejuvenation of older doctrines proscribing it. This unstable mix of ambivalent and contradictory trends presented little security to lesbians and gay men whose social niches remained vulnerable to larger events beyond their control. In countries where feudal remnants, still smarting from recent defeats, combined with big business, particularly murderous coalitions came about to crush the gains of traditionally disenfranchised peoples. In countries where the state itself became the sole capitalist, there was no countervailing force to the imposition of particularly virulent forms of the productivist/reproductivist ideology.

To understand the changing prospects of the gay and lesbian movement, we cannot neglect the larger social milieu that provided both the resources for the emergence of a homosexual people and an impetus for other social classes to seek the destruction of the gay world. Nor can the postwar movement ignore the lessons of the Holocaust, where the early gay movement came to such a bitter end.

STALINISM

When the Russian Revolution succeeded in abolishing Europe's last absolute monarchy, all eyes turned toward the new social experiment in the East. In a single blow, an ancient autocracy had apparently given way to a popular democracy of workers' councils and peasant communes accompanied by sweeping reforms in family and sexual life. The new constitution mandated the legal equality of women, voluntary marriage and divorce, legalized contraception and abortion, state-supported day care, employment rights for women, and maternity leave provisions (Millett 1969, 168). Criminal penalties for adultery and homosexuality were dropped in favor of an official policy of withdrawing the state from the private realm. Soviet delegates to the World League for Sexual Reform reiterated the official position throughout the 1920s. In the words of Dr. Baktis's *The Sexual Revolution in Russia:* "As for homosexuality, sodomy, and whatever other forms of sexuality that are considered as moral violations by European legal codes, Soviet law treats them just the same as so-called natural intercourse. All forms of intercourse are private matters." (22, my translation).

This clear-cut policy helped influence the leftward drift of the gay movement in Germany as the German Communist party assured gays in the 1928 election campaign that "there is no need to emphasize that we will continue to wage the most resolute struggle for the repeal of these laws [Paragraph 175] in the future" (Steakley 1975, 85). Wilhelm Reich's Sexpol movement became active within the party in 1930–31 and Communist deputies supported repeal in parliamentary committees at this time.

The dream of a land with the freedom to love recurs frequently in gay writing. Whether in Melville's voyages to Polynesia, the flight of so many American writers to Paris, Isherwood in Berlin, or Gide in Algeria, many sought (and some found) countries where they could escape the antisexual suffocation of their homeland. The socialist critique of bourgeois morality promised as well to overcome the contemporary system that claimed liberty and equality for itself but instead appropriated them for the monied classes. That the Soviet Union raised such hopes in the 1920s cannot be surprising, and Gide among others became increasingly involved in the Communist movement (Mann 1948, 151). With high expectations, Gide went to Moscow in 1936 where he found not freedom but a new bureaucratic class upholding the Stalin personality cult and enforcing a rigid ideological conformity in the press, in art and music, and in family and sexual life (see Gide 1937).

What went wrong? The debates over the "betrayal" of the Russian Revolution continue unabated today, though few efforts have been made to explain the dramatic reversals of Soviet policy on the family and sexuality. What we do know is that grass-roots organizations gave way to a new dictatorial state that exerted unprecedented control over all of Russian life. As early as 1921, workers' councils were replaced by a central administration for directing economic production and distribution. By 1929, unions had lost "rights to participate in enterprise management and to bargain over wages and working conditions on behalf of their worker members" (Skocpol 1979, 219, 228); moreover, the nonparty press was choked off (Medvedev 1977, 205). The Communist state under Stalin's leadership embarked on a crash program to industrialize an essentially peasant society and to seize direct control of agricultural production from its peasant holders. The result, in Alvin Gouldner's words, was "a regime of terror aiming at the collectivization of property" conducted by an "urban-centered power elite that had set out to dominate a largely rural society to which they related as an alien colonial power" (1980, 214, 226). This war against the peasantry consolidated a centralized state that suppressed all opposition through a massive police and prison apparatus that knew no bounds in imagining enemies.

From 1933 to 1938 the terror encompassed the Communist party itself. Half of the party membership was arrested, and as Nikita Khrushchev later revealed, 70 percent of the party's Central Committee was "arrested and shot": "Stalin killed and tortured more

Communists than any other dictator in the 20th century" (233, 256). Thus, Stalin and the Soviet state bureaucracy succeeded through the 1930s in eliminating most of the original revolutionaries and much of the socialist program. "Persons were jailed, shot or exiled not because of what they had done but because of their supposed readiness to do injury to Soviet society inferred on the basis of their social category: social origin, nationality or group membership" (234). Ironically, Stalin restored many of the characteristics of absolute monarchy in his personal dictatorship and persecution of traditional outgroups of Russian society: Jews, intellectuals, national minorities—and gay people.

John Lauritsen and David Thorstad state:

> In January 1934, mass arrests of gays were carried out in Moscow, Leningrad, Kharkov, and Odessa. Among those arrested were a great many actors, musicians, and other artists. They were accused of engaging in "homosexual orgies," and were sentenced to several years of imprisonment or exile in Siberia. (1974, 68; see also Hauer 1984)

Homosexuality was recriminalized in 1934, punishable by a five-year prison sentence, and other social legislation was rolled back: abortion of first pregnancies was outlawed in 1936, and all abortions in 1944. Divorce became subject to fines and common-law marriage lost legal recognition (Millett 1969, 172).

Because the subject of homosexuality remain[ed] under ban in the Soviet Union . . . , little is known about early gay life in the country. . . . Herbert Marcuse's analysis of Soviet Marxism suggests one explanation for the reactionary morality of Stalinism (1961). As the Soviet state pressed for rapid industrialization, it installed the productivist/reproductivist ethic favored by Victorian capitalists, which similarly aimed to create an expanding labor supply and disciplined work force. The anti-homosexual laws of the Stalinist period remain on the books to this day, and the state monopoly of the communications media assures an almost unbroken silence on the subject. The full story of the Stalinist terror and gay people has yet to be told (but see Jong 1985).

NAZISM

In 1933 the early gay movement came to an abrupt end. With the Nazi party in power, the German state made every effort to wipe away the restive, subordinated groups who agitated for their rightful places in German society. The Nazi machine crushed workers' and women's movements, Communists and socialists, peace activists and dissidents. With a racial ideology glorifying the "Aryan," it developed a network of concentration camps to contain and destroy "inferior" peoples: Jews, Slavs, Gypsies, criminals, the disabled, Jehovah's Witnesses—and gay people. The Nazis wanted to roll back history to an earlier, supposedly more harmonious era of German greatness. To do so required the removal of the "abrasive" groups of the modern period. Ernst Röhm, leader of the Nazi party militia (the *Sturmabteilung*), characterized the ascendance of Nazism in these words: "National Socialism signifies a spiritual rupture with the thinking of the French Revolution of 1789" (Gallo 1972, 36). Not only would the peoples released by the collapse of feudalism be driven out; even the memory of them would be extinguished. And, with the gay movement, they almost succeeded. Even after World War II, the early gay movement shrank to no more than a rumor and a hope for the mass of lesbians and gay men. A new generation grew up isolated from a cultural heritage that had embodied its experiences and possibilities.

Extreme conservative forces had always been forthright in their hatred of gay people. They had assaulted Hirschfeld in 1920, and in 1921 he was so badly beaten that some newspapers printed an obituary. With shifting government coalitions in the 1920s, censorship returned and gay and lesbian journals were banned in 1926 and 1928. Anti-vice crusaders, some with roots in the established Protestant church, called more stridently for the suppression of homosexuality.[1] The Nazi party had been unambiguous in its reply to Adolf Brand's survey of candidates for the 1928 election: "Anyone who even thinks of homosexual love is our enemy. We reject anything which emasculates our people and makes it a plaything for our enemies, for we know that life is a fight and it's madness to think that men will ever embrace fraternally" (Steakley 1975, 84).

Still, it seems that many in the gay movement—like so many others—did not take the Nazi threat seriously in the early days. Was not Ernst Röhm himself homosexual and a member of the Bund für Menschenrecht? Still even the Social Democrats, in a replay of 1907, could not resist baiting the Nazis with the charge of homosexuality in high places, thereby adopting the Nazi's own rhetoric by claiming that the "moral and physical health of German youth stands at risk" because of it (Stümke and Finkler 1981, 124). As the Gestapo closed the gay press in the first months of the Nazi regime, the final issues of gay journals were announcing upcoming dances and meetings, showing few signs of their impending fate.[2] Christopher Isherwood remarked, "Boy bars of every sort were being raided, now, and many were shut down" (1976, 124). (Isherwood subsequently fled Berlin for England.) On 27 February 1933, Max Hodann and Felix Halle of the Institute for Sex Research were arrested, and on 23 March Kurt Hiller, the leading organizer of the sex law reform coalition of the 1920s, was seized and imprisoned in the Oranienburg concentration camp. (Hiller was released after nine months and escaped to Prague and later London with Walter Schultz, a man he met in the Oranienburg camp who was to become his lover of thirty years.)

On the morning of 6 May 1933, a hundred Nazi students from a nearby school for physical education appeared at the doors of the Institute for Sex Research.

> They smashed the doors down and rushed into the building. They spent the morning pouring ink over carpets and manuscripts and loading their trucks with books from the Institute's library, including many which had nothing to do with sex: historical works, art journals, etc. . . . A few days after the raid, the seized books and papers were publicly burned along with a bust of Hirschfeld, on the square in front of the Opera House. (Isherwood 1976, 129).

Like the sacking of the ancient library at Alexandria, which blotted out a good deal of ancient culture from human history, the Nazis destroyed twelve thousand books and thirty-five thousand pictures (Steakley 1975, 105), burning much of the heritage of those who dared to love others of their own sex. Hirschfeld was already outside Germany and tried to start again in Paris, but he died in Nice on 15 May 1935. His lover, Kurt Giese, once a secretary at the institute, moved on to Prague, where he committed suicide in 1936 (Isherwood 1976, 129).

Switzerland became a sanctuary for other refugees from Nazism. Helene Stöcker, Anita Augspurg, and Lida Heymann, all veterans of Mutterschutz and the struggle to define a progressive women's movement, fled to Switzerland. Stöcker continued on to the United States. All three died in 1943 (Evans 1976, 264). Stefan George, the homo-erotic poet, also took refuge in Switzerland, and *Der Kreis,* a publication founded in 1932, became the only gay journal to survive the war by moving to Zurich (Hoc-quenghem 1979, 93; Bullough 1976, 664).

Just what elements of German society propelled the Nazi party to power remains a subject of scholarly debate. Most evidence points to a three-fold coalition. Among the early adherents of Nazism were followers of the old conservative political parties: the agrarian aristocracy (the Junkers), the military, the bureaucracy, and the church—in short, the old imperial establishment deposed at the end of World War I. The second major bloc of support came from major industrialists, who still remembered the 1918 revolution and saw Nazism as a bulwark against the popularity of socialism among Ger-man workers. When the Nazis did come to power, they assured a passive work force for the capitalist elite by abolishing or taking over trade unions and imprisoning the political Left. Third and more difficult to assess is the mass base of the Nazi movement. Strong suspicion has also been cast upon those elements of the German population who had lost status during the preceding decades because their jobs had disappeared owing to the advance of technology, competition from big business, or the inflation crisis of 1923–24. It was "the small peasant farmers, the independent artisans and the rest of the multifarious mass of individual tradesmen, petty entrepreneurs, salesmen and shop-keepers" (Sohn-Rethel 1978, 131) who were most attracted to the Nazi promise to restore a lost, more orderly and comfortable world.[3]

This powerful reactionary coalition lashed out at all the symbols of the modern era that provoked in them such insecurity and resentment. Nazism revived much of the ultraconservative ideology propagated by the prewar imperial court. Adolf Stöcker, the court preacher attached to the kaiser, had consistently denounced Jews, feminists, liber-als, and gay people for creating the ills of German society throughout the imperial regime (Steakley 1975, 37). Now Himmler believed women's organizations to be "a catastrophe," which masculinized women, destroyed their charm, and led the way to gender-mixing and homosexuality (Vismar 1977, 314, my translation). Ironically, the Bund Deutsches Frauenverein, the major women's organization, was already on record as "combating sexual libertarianism, pornography, abortion, venereal diseases, adver-tisements for contraceptives and the double standard" and could only vainly protest its solidarity with Nazism when it was dissolved in 1933 in favor of the Nazis' own *Frauenfront* (Evans 1976, 237, 254ff.). In the 1930s, women were removed from gov-ernment and the professions in accord with Nazi policy, which prescribed women's place as being among "children, church, and kitchen" *(Kinder, Kirche, Küche),* but women quietly resumed wage labor during the war years, as they did in the United States, in order to fill the labor shortage created as male workers went to battle (Evans 1976, 262; Millett 1969, 159–66).

For those who nourished illusions about Nazi intentions toward gay people, the Night of Long Knives was a grim awakening. On the weekend of 30 June through 1 July 1934, Hitler, Himmler, and Göring had several hundred political rivals murdered. Among them were the Strasser brothers, who had taken too seriously the "Socialist" claim of "National Socialism" by calling for implementation of such early elements of the Nazi program as abolition of incomes unearned through work, nationalization of trusts, and a ban on land speculation. Also executed where the holdouts from the old imperial regime who balked at the Nazi line. But the best-known victim was Ernst Röhm, who led a "vicious and quite popular struggle against the old order in general" and had dared to call for a "Second Revolution" against "reactionaries [and] bourgeois conformists" in April of 1934 (Gallo 1972, 37; Geyer 1984, 204).

When Adolf Hitler stood before the Reichstag two weeks after the Night of Long Knives, he denounced supposed international Communist and Jewish "conspiracies," Röhm's "plot" against the regime, and his "vice," claiming that some of Röhm's associates had been caught in bed with male lovers on that fateful weekend. Meanwhile the Nazi press defamed Röhm's militia for its "homosexual cliques."

Nazi doctrine constructed homosexuality as an urban corruption and a disease alien to "healthy" village life, but easily spread through seduction and propaganda. With a single-minded pronatalist policy aimed toward producing "Aryan" Germans, sterilization and extermination were reserved for subordinated peoples, including homosexuals. In 1934, Paragraph 175 was extended to include "a kiss, an embrace, even homosexual fantasies," and in 1936, Himmler reorganized the Gestapo to create a division responsible for ferreting out political and religious dissidents, Freemasons, and homosexuals. In 1940, Himmler ordered that everyone completing a prison term under Paragraph 175 was to be sent to a concentration camp if they had had "more than one partner."[4]

Just how many gay people died at the hands of the Nazis will never be known. Concentration camp officials destroyed many of the records as the Allied armies marched into Germany, and other records held in East Germany remain closed. From his examination of extant camp records, Rüdiger Lautmann offers a conservative estimate of five thousand to fifteen thousand camp inmates designated as homosexuals by a pink triangle (1980–81). The Gestapo had a number of ready-made resources for locating gay people when Hitler became chancellor of Germany. One police district alone in Berlin had an accumulated list of thirty thousand names of suspected homosexuals in its files. Some fifty thousand people were convicted under Paragraph 175 during the Nazi period, and judicial files existed on many more convicted before 1933 (Steakley 1975, 110, 113; Herzer 1985; Stümke and Finkler 1981, 263–67). And certainly the many collaborators and sympathizers with Nazism were no more loath to turn in their homosexual neighbors than they were to hand over Jews and the many other victims of Nazi terror.

As Germany invaded other European countries, it cast its deadly net wider. The Nederlandsch Wetenschappelijk-Humanitair Kommittee, which had existed from 1911, fell in 1940, and bar raids took many more, a move welcomed by the Dutch Roman Catholic church, which had been campaigning for the suppression of gay people throughout the 1920s (Tielman 1979; Rogier 1969). Heinz Heger, a twenty-two-year-old Austrian student, was arrested in 1939 on the basis of an intercepted postcard he had addressed to his lover (1980, 19, 39). Those caught by the police network included "unskilled workers and shop assistants, skilled tradesmen and independent craftsmen, musicians and artists, professors and clergy, even aristocratic landowners" (Heger 1980, 9; see Lenz 1979, 29).

Camp prisoners were classified by a set of colored triangles: green for criminals, red for Communists, blue for emigrants, black for "asocials," purple for Jehovah's Witnesses, brown for Gypsies, yellow for Jews, and pink for homosexuals (Lautmann 1980–81). Most camp observers agree that, despite the desperate conditions afflicting all prisoners, an internal hierarchy could be discerned. Greens and reds more often achieved easier jobs, supervisory positions, and thus better diets, while brown, yellow, and pink triangles were subjected to disproportionate violence, hard labor, and starvation (Heger 1980, 32; Kogon 1976, 44). Heger recounts the relentless beatings and pointless labor experienced by pink-triangle inmates, being forced to stand naked in subzero weather, and dawn-to-dusk work moving snow with their bare hands from one side of a road to the other and then back again (Heger 1980, 35).[5] In Sachsenhausen, most homosexuals were included among laborers sent to the clay pits (for brick manufacture) in order to load and push rail carts. Supplied with a diet that fell below the daily minimum necessary for survival and subjected to Gestapo violence, homosexuals suffered an extremely high death rate. Lautmann, Grikschat, and Schmidt quote a survivor who observed: "The SS were glad if several 175ers were left on the road by evening. When in January 1943, the number of dead homosexuals at Klinker [clay pits] reached a total of 24 in a single day, commanding headquarters became somewhat disquieted. There followed a pause." (1977, 349, my translation). Comparison of the camp records of red-, purple-, and pink-triangle prisoners shows that the death rate for homosexuals was half again as high as for the other two categories (350).

Late in the war, Himmler toyed with the idea of "curing" homosexuals by forcing them to visit brothels. (Heger asked stand-ins to take his place.) Once, he ordered that homosexuals willing to be castrated would be released to fight at the Russian front (Heger 1980, 98; Lenz 1979, 31). Tiring of this, the Gestapo subjected homosexuals and other prisoners to the notorious "medical experiments" conducted by physicians who mutilated, injected, burned, and froze prisoners to death in the name of science.

. . .

Perhaps most ironic of all is what little effect the genocide of gay people had upon homosexuality as a whole. Eugen Kogon observed that "homosexual practices were actually very widespread in the camps. The prisoners, however, ostracized only those whom the SS marked with the pink triangle" (1976, 43; see Heger 1980, 61). Heger could never quite understand why his persecutors would beat him for being homosexual and then force him to commit homosexual acts with them (29)! It was as if a great enough sacrifice to the altar of morality released them from its obligations (see Adam 1978, 69–77, 54–58). Whatever gods the Nazis served, the genocide of a generation of homosexuals, the extermination of gay thought, and the intense supervision of those who might be tempted to homosexuality were not enough to contain the human potential for same-sex love.

The Holocaust then effectively wiped away most of the early gay culture and its movement through systematic extermination and ideological control. Its legacy was a willful forgetting by both capitalist and communist elites who tacitly confirmed the Nazis' work by denying lesbians and gay men any public existence. The doctors, the bishops, and the police could now fully occupy the gay domain. A new generation awoke to homosexual feelings reviled as "sick," "sinful," and "criminal"; they could find one another and their tradition only at great personal cost. But unlike the third- and fourth-world peoples decimated or annihilated by European colonialism, lesbians and gay men emerged in undiminished numbers in new generations. Not reliant on biological reproduction, a gay and lesbian nation grew up again in the very heart of its enemies. No matter how fervent the hatred of judges or psychiatrists, politicians or business people, preachers or patriarchs, same-sex love appeared again among their own sons and daughters as it did in the rest of society.

NOTES

1 Steakley 1975, 88; Isherwood 1976, 18; Kokula 1984; Bleuel 1974, 5; for the most complete history of this period see Stümke and Finkler 1981.
2 Personal communication from James Steakley.
3 See Abraham 1981; Blackbourn and Eley 1984; Dobkowski and Walliman 1983; Moore 1966; Hamilton 1982.
4 On Nazi ideologies of homosexuality, see Schilling 1983; Herzer 1985; Stümke and Finkler 1981; Bock 1983; Mosse 1982; Steakley 1975.
5 Much of this was dramatized in Martin Sherman's 1980 play *Bent*.

REFERENCES

Abraham, David. 1981. *The Collapse of the Weimar Republic*. Princeton, N.J.: Princeton University Press.
Adam, Barry D. 1978. *The Survival of Domination*. New York: Elsevier/Greenwood.
——1985. "Structural Foundations of the Gay World." *Comparative Studies in Society and History* 27 (4):658.
Blackbourn, David, and Geoff Eley. 1984. *The Peculiarities of German History*. Oxford: Oxford University Press.
Bleuel, Hans Peter. 1974. *Sex and Society in Nazi Germany*. Philadelphia: Lippincott.
Bock, Gisela. 1983. "Racism and Sexism in Nazi Germany." *Signs* 8 (3):400.
Bullough, Vern. 1976. *Sexual Variance in Society and History*. New York: Wiley.
Dobkowski, Michael, and Isidor Wallimann. 1983. *Towards the Holocaust*. Westport, Conn.: Greenwood.
Evans, Richard. 1976. *The Feminist Movement in Germany, 1894–1933*. London: Sage.
Gallo, Max. 1972. *The Night of Long Knives*. New York: Harper & Row.
Geyer, Michael. 1984. "The State in National Socialist Germany." In *Statemaking and Social Movements,* edited by Charles Bright and Susan Harding. Ann Arbor: University of Michigan Press.
Gide, André. 1937. *Return from the USSR*. New York: Knopf.
Gouldner, Alvin. 1980. "Stalinism." In *Political Power and Social Theory*. Vol. 1, edited by Maurice Zeitlin. Greenwich, Conn.: JAI.
Hamilton, Richard. 1982. *Who Voted for Hitler?* Princeton, N.J.: Princeton University Press.
Hauer, Gudrun, et al. 1984. *Rosa Liebe unterm roten Stern*. Hamburg: Frühlings Erwachen.
Heger, Heinz. 1980. *The Men with the Pink Triangle*. Boston: Alyson.
Herzer, Manfred. 1985. "Nazis, Psychiatrists, and Gays." *Cabirion* 12 (Spring-Summer):1.

Hocquenghem, Guy. 1979. *Race d'Ep!*. Paris: Editions Libres/Hallier.

Isherwood, Christopher. 1976. *Christopher and His Kind, 1929–1939*. New York: Farrar, Straus & Giroux.

Jong, Ben De. 1985. "An Intolerable Kind of Moral Degeneration." In *IGA Pink Book 1985*, edited by the International Gay Association. Amsterdam: COC-magazijn.

Karlinsky, Simon. 1979. "Death and Resurrection of Mikhail Kuzmin." *Slavic Review* 38:92.

Kogon, Eugen. 1976. *The Theory and Practice of Hell*. New York: Octagon.

Kokula, Ilse [Ina Kuckuc, pseud.]. 1984. "Lesbisch leben von Weimar bis zur Nachkriegszeit." In *Eldorado*, edited by the Berlin Museum. Berlin: Frölich & Kaufmann.

Lauritsen, John, and David Thorstad. 1974. *The Early Homosexual Rights Movement (1864–1935)*. New York: Times Change Press.

Lautmann, Rüdiger. 1980–81. "The Pink Triangle." *Journal of Homosexuality* 6 (1–2):146.

Lautmann, Rüdiger, Winifred Grikschat, and Egbert Schmidt. 1977. "Der rosa Winkel in den nationalsozialistischen Konzentrationslagern." In *Seminar: Gesellschaft und Homosexualität*, edited by Rüdiger Lautmann. Frankfurt: Suhrkamp.

Lenz, Reimar. 1979. *The Wholesale Murder of Homosexuals in the Third Reich*. Los Angeles: Urania Manuscripts.

Mann, Klaus. 1948. *André Gide and the Crisis of Modern Thought*. London: Dennis Dobson.

Marcuse, Herbert. 1961. *Soviet Marxism*. New York: Vintage.

Medvedev, Roy. 1977. "New Pages from the Political Biography of Stalin." In *Stalinism*, edited by Robert Tucker. New York: Norton.

Millett, Kate. 1969. *Sexual Politics*. New York: Avon.

Moore, Barrington. 1966. *The Social Origins of Dictatorship and Democracy*. Boston: Beacon.

Mosse, George. 1982. "Nationalism and Respectability." *Journal of Contemporary History* 77:221.

Rogier, Jan. 1969. "75 Jahre Emanzipation in den Niederlanden." In *Weder Krankheit noch Verbrechen*, edited by Rolf Italiaander. Hamburg: Gala Verlag.

Schilling, Heinz-Dieter. 1983. *Schwule und Faschismus*. Berlin: Elefanten.

Skocpol, Theda. 1979. *States and Social Revolutions*. New York: Cambridge University Press.

Sohn-Rethel, Alfred. 1978. *Economy and Class Structure of German Fascism*. London: CSE Books.

Steakley, James. 1975. *The Homosexual Emancipation Movement in Germany*. New York: Arno.

Stümke, Hans-George, and Rudi Finkler. 1981. *Rosa Winkel, Rosa Listen*. Hamburg: Rowohlt.

Tielman, Rob. 1979. *The Persecution of Homosexuals in the Netherlands during the Second World War*. Los Angeles: Urania Manuscripts.

Vismar, Erhard. 1977. "Perversion and Verfolgung unter dem deutschen Faschismus." In *Seminar: Gesellschaft und Homosexualität*, edited by Rüdiger Lautmann. Frankfurt: Suhrkamp.

Captured Subjects / Savage Others: Violently Engendering the New American

Carroll Smith-Rosenberg

Centuries ago Shakespeare's Juliet posed what is probably the best known challenge to post-structuralism's privileging of language and refusal of material reality. 'What's in a name?' she asks us across time. 'That which we call a rose by any other word would smell as sweet.'[1] Whatever the truth may be about roses and Romeo, Juliet's observation fails to represent accurately the processes by which Euro-Americans established a sense of national identity. For Euro-Americans, the *name* has been the game, as much as, or more than, the seizure of land or the exercise of military power. This is not to say that land seizures and power were not terribly important—simply that they were not enough. In creating a national identity, British and other European settlers and their descendants had not only to seize America's land, they had to legitimate that seizure by seizing the name American as well. Put another way, they had to imagine themselves Americans and, in the imagining, constitute a radical new imperial category—white Americans. What is particularly fascinating about the Euro-American imagination is not only that it imagined white Americans, but that, in the face of reason and historical evidence, it imagined white Americans the true Americans. Only if white Americans were true Americans could they legitimate their physical possession of America's land and their exercise of political suzerainty.[2]

This essay addresses three questions. First, how did white Americans imagine themselves the true Americans, and imagine all other Americans—American Indians, African Americans, and Hispanic Americans (all of whom have resided in America far longer than most white Americans, who are, for the most part, descendants of *nineteenth* and *twentieth*-century European immigrants)—as peculiar, marginal types of Americans? Second, how did the Euro-American imagination and rhetoric differ from contemporary European images and rhetoric? How, that is, did creole rhetoric differ from cosmopolitan rhetoric? Third, what role did white women play in constituting the Euro-American imagination? Indeed, how, by participating in that process, did white women constitute a political subjectivity for themselves, authorize themselves as writers and engender the American female?

To claim the name American, eighteenth-century British settlers in North America had to defy common sense. From a European perspective, at least, the real Americans were, of course, the first inhabitants of this continent. Indeed, until the late eighteenth century the English used the word American to refer to American Indians, not to Englishmen resident in America. They also had to break with a European iconic tradition that went back to the Renaissance, one that made a naked American Indian woman the icon, the graphic representation of the new continent and its peoples.[3] To make the white American the true American, British and other European settlers in America had to refute that traditional image as a misconception. They did so in two ways. By naming the original inhabitants 'Indians', they displaced those inhabitants from America to an alien hemisphere (from America to India), referenced another dark people and another site of British imperialism.[4] Even more insistently, they represented these original inhabitants as wild and inhuman savages, positioned half way between the beasts with whom they shared the American continent and the cultured Europeans who described them.

British-American settlers in North America writing about the peoples *native* to North America thus began the long and complex process by which the politically neutral meaning of the word *native* (as in the sentences 'The marmot is a *native* of the Alps', or 'certain plants are *native* to Cornwall') was transformed into the racial and imperialist meaning of *native* as an inferior person of color. (The *Unabridged Oxford English Dictionary* does not reference this latter meaning until 1848, but the origins of the process can be discovered in seventeenth and eighteenth-century British writings in and about America.[5]) Once *native* Americans had become savage *natives* the way was clear to make the True Americans Europeans who, having renounced the political and religious corruptions of Europe, took up land and identity in America. The true 'American' was the child of the figurative marriage of European culture and American land. Literal marriages between Europeans and *native* Americans, on the other hand, produced only degenerate and untrustworthy half-*breeds,* a name more appropriate to animals than humans.

To accomplish the transmogrification of indigenous Americans into marginal natives, British settlers in North America had to refute the positive representations of indigenous Americans found within the British imperial discourses—in Walter Raleigh's pledge to honor and respect the peoples of Guiana and his condemnation of Spanish savagery in the New World, in John Smith's praise of Powhatan's imperial power and military skills, in early settlers' recognition of their dependence on indigenous Americans' agricultural resources and generosity.[6] Most troubling of all was the recurrent European representation of American Indians as noble savages, as prelapsarian man residing in a golden land. We find this noble savage graphically represented in de Bry's sixteenth-century engravings of explorations and discoveries, regenerated a century later by Locke, and later still by Rousseau and other popular Enlightenment writers.[7] English settlers on the American continent sought to counter these valorizing representations with tales of tribal atrocities, of savage attacks upon innocent, productive farming families and, especially, upon their women and children. By the end of the seventeenth century, a distinctly imperial and uniquely American discourse had developed among British settlers in North America, a discourse that, originating in Puritan New England, took as its quintessential form the captivity narrative.

What has this to do with women's political and national identities as Americans? Euro-American women played a complex role in the construction of the American Indian as savage and inhuman and hence of European residents in America as True Americans. In so doing, British-American women both constructed a national and political identity for themselves and participated in the process by which the women in a number of critical tribes (Creek, Cherokee, Iroquois) lost their right to land ownership, their control of agricultural production, their right to a significant political and religious voice in tribal affairs. The process that Gayatri Spivak referred to in her reading of *Jane*

Eyre as a colonialist text—that to contest with white men for a liberal humanist subjectivity, nineteenth-century white women joined with white men in espousing Europe's imperial venture and, in so doing, denied subjectivity to women of color—began years before Charlotte Bronte put pen to paper.[8] It began in the seventeenth century, in British North America.

British-American women helped construct white Americans as true Americans and native Americans as savages in three distinct moves: by assuming the role of innocent victims of barbarous savagery, by assuming the role of authoritative writers, and by authorizing themselves as an alternative white icon for America. In appropriating the right to write and to represent a white America, Euro-American women assumed the dominant male discourses of imperialism and social order. But since language works in complex ways and ideology is never simple, by the late eighteenth century Euro-American women writers had also acquired the agency to resist and subvert the very discourses they helped to construct.

To trace these complex processes, I will examine two distinct types of sources, the American Indian captivity narrative and the popular novel or romance. I chose the American Indian captivity narrative first because its great popularity extended from the late seventeenth far into the nineteenth century, and second because the American Indian captivity narrative more than any other genre asserts the Euro-Americans' American and civil identity, denying both to the American Indian. While frequently incorporating themes from the captivity narrative, the novel differs from the narrative in one highly significant manner. Where the captivity narrative seeks to speak with polemic certainty, the novel, by its very nature, problematizes, interrogates itself and its readers, raises more questions than it can answer. The diversity of characters and the novel's reliance on conflict and change for the development of plot and character encourage both the overt and covert expression of ambiguities and contradictions. Its evocative nature intensifies its ability to enact discursive inconsistencies and social conflict. While the prescriptive genres of a culture—sermons, advice books, political rhetoric, and captivity narratives—seek to repress ambiguity, the novel plays upon dangerous desires. Ultimately affirming the permissible, it makes its readers familiar with the forbidden and the transgressive.

. . .

NOTES

1   *Romeo and Juliet*, II.ii, 43–44.
2   American nationalism may thus involve a more complex series of identifications than those involved in the construction of at least certain European national identities. Not only did Euro-Americans constitute themselves citizens of a new nation and a new republic, they racialized their citizenship, using a series of racial and ethnic negative others in constituting themselves 'Americans'. This argument presumes that at least certain European identities are based on a concept of political citizenship rather than that of ethnic identity. I wonder if that argument does not obscure deep-rooted European racism directed towards a number of negative others, not least of whom would include Jews and Muslims. It might

also fail to appreciate the important role colonial ventures dating back to the Renaissance played in the development of nationalisms in both southern and northern Europe.

3 On the origins and development of this tradition, see: Bernadette Bucher, *Icon and Conquest. A Structural Analysis of the Illustrations of de Bry's Great Voyages,* tr. Basia Miller Gulati (University of Chicago Press, Chicago, 1981); Hugh Honour, *The New Golden Land. European Images of America from the Discoveries to the Present Time* (Pantheon Books, New York, 1975); Peter Hulme, 'Polytropic Man: Tropes of Sexuality and Mobility in Early Colonial Discourse', In *Europe and Its Others: Proceedings of the Essex Conference on the Sociology of Literature,* July 1984, ed. Francis Barker, et al., 2 vols (University of Essex, Colchester, 1985); E. McClung Fleming, 'The American Image as Indian Princess, 1765–1783', *Winterthur Portfolio,* 2 (1965), pp. 65–81; Clare Le Corbeiller, 'Miss America and Her Sisters: Personifications of the Four Parts of the World', *Metropolitan Museum Bulletin,* n.s. 19/20 (1960), pp. 209–23; Gary E. Nash, 'The Image of the Indian in the Southern Colonial Mind', *William and Mary Quarterly,* 29 (April 1972), pp. 197–230.

4 I am particularly grateful to Phyllis Rackin for pointing out the significance of the word 'India' in constituting American *Indians* sub-human other to the white Euro-*American.* The meanings associated with the word 'Indian' have been anything but static. When originally applied by Columbus to residents of the West Indies, it referenced not the subcontinent of India but the East Indies and possibly the entire Eastern hemisphere. Certainly in sixteenth-century England, the term referenced the 'Orient', which stretched from the Middle East through Asia. By the eighteenth century, however, the word had begun to refer more specifically to the subcontinent of 'India' and the British Indian Empire. See 'India', *The Compact Edition of the Oxford English Dictionary* (London, 1979).

5 'Native', O.E.D.

6 See Walter Raleigh's *The Discoverie of the large, rich and beautifull Empire of Guiana, with a relation of the great and golden citie of Manoa (which the Spaniards call El Dorado . . . Performed in the yeere 1595 by Sir Walter Raleigh,* reprinted in Richard Hakluyt's *The principal navigations, voyages traffiques & discoveries of the English nation,* 3 vols (London, 1598–1600). John Smith, *A Map of Virginia. With a Description of the Countrey, the Commodities, People, Government and Religion* (Oxford, 1612) and *The Proceedings of the English Colonie in Virginia since Their First Beginning from England in the Yeare of Our Lord 1606* (Oxford, 1612).

7 Of course, European attitudes towards the inhabitants of the Americas were extremely complex. Different European writers and the same European writers at different times represented 'American Indians' as savage and cannibalistic devil worshippers, descendants of the lost tribes of Israel, heathens awaiting the word of God, man before the fall. English residents in North America drew upon these negative visions of American Indians as well as upon their own immediate experiences and interests in framing their captivity narratives. For discussions of these varied and ambivalent European attitudes, see: Anthony Pagden, *The Fall of Natural Man: The American Indian and the Origins of Comparative Ethnology,* rev. ed. (Cambridge University Press, Cambridge, 1986); Honour, *The New Golden Land;* Bucher, *Icon and Conquest;* Louis Montrose, 'The Work of Gender in the Discourse of Discovery', *Representations,* 33 (Winter 1991), pp. 1–41; Peter Hulme, *Colonial Encounters: Europe and the Native Caribbean, 1492–1797* (Methuen, London, 1986); P. J. Marshall and Glyndwr Williams, *The Great Map of Mankind, Perceptions of New Worlds in the Age of Enlightenment* (Harvard University Press, Cambridge, 1982); Benjamin Bissell, *The American Indian in English Literature of the 18th Century* (Yale

University Press, New Haven, 1925); Frank E. Manuel, *The Eighteenth Century Confronts the Gods* (Harvard University Press, Cambridge, 1959).

8 Gayatri Chakravorty Spivak, 'Three Women's Texts and a Critique of Imperialism', *Critical Inquiry,* 12 (Autumn 1985). For a suggestive theoretical analysis of women's positioning inside and outside of ideology and of women's power to resist hegemonic discourses see Teresa de Lauretis, *Technologies of Gender* (Indiana University Press, Bloomington, 1987), pp. 1–30.

Reflections on Native American Cultural Rights and Resources

W. Roger Buffalohead

The carriers of cultural tradition have been the unsung heroes and heroines of Native American history. Seldom in the historical spotlight, these ordinary community members somehow managed to pass cultural traditions to the next generation, despite the political and cultural oppression surrounding their lives. We rarely read about their extraordinary accomplishments, and we know little about their motivation except that they were powerfully moved by their cultural experience to keep what they could of it alive. What survives of native heritage we owe to them—the "cultural sovereignty activists"—who believed that the death of the culture also meant the death of the people. Without their efforts, much of what is happening today to preserve and develop native culture and win respect for and protection of native cultural rights and resources would not be possible.

In the past, United States policies with respect to Indian cultural rights and resources reflected the interests and assumptions of the larger society. These policies fluctuated between deliberate attempts to destroy Indian culture and efforts to use Indian language and culture as a foundation for eventual assimilation into American life. Accepting the widespread belief in the nineteenth and early twentieth centuries that Indian culture was destined to disappear from the American scene, museum professionals, academics, government officials, and many Americans assumed that Indians possessed few, if any, cultural rights that needed to be recognized or respected. Similarly, Indian cultural resources were viewed as part of the public domain, for scientific study and educational purposes. As a result, collections of Indian human remains, funerary objects, sacred materials, and other cultural items came into the possession of cultural, educational, and governmental institutions, often without the knowledge or consent of native communities. However much these practices resulted in the preservation of Indian culture that might otherwise have been lost, another reality intervened—that Indian cultures changed over time rather than disappearing, and Indian tribes survived into the present century as legal and political entities with a legitimate interest in native cultural rights and resources.

In the last twenty-five years or so, Native Americans have made significant progress at the national and local level in reasserting their cultural rights and winning protection for their cultural resources. The Indian repatriation movement deserves much of the credit for bringing about long-overdue changes in national attitudes and policies towards native heritage. In place now are the National Museum of the American Indian Act of 1989 and the Native American Graves Protection and Repatriation Act of 1990, as well as a host of state laws extending various kinds of protection to Indian graves.

The establishment of the National Museum of the American Indian on the mall in Washington, D. C., along with a satellite museum in New York City, means that Indian heritage has finally joined the family of world cultures as an equal member. Although still in the planning and development stage, the museum will showcase native ideas, contributions, and cultural diversity. It also will provide educational and cultural programs designed to share the native heritage with the public, both nationally and worldwide.

In a similar manner, the recent federal repatriation legislation is an acknowledgment that Indian nations and tribes possess political and cultural rights that the larger society must respect and consider in order to reconcile the past and safeguard the present and future. The Native American Graves Protection and Repatriation Act, along with the repatriation agreement with the Smithsonian Institution, establishes policies and procedures to govern the return of Indian human remains, funerary objects, and sacred materials and to strengthen and broaden the scope of existing laws protecting Indian cultural resources. Again, although the outcomes of these initiatives are yet to be realized, the promise of cultural equity for American Indians has never been greater. Equally important, the notion that Indian culture eventually will disappear seems to be fading gradually from American thought.

The Native American struggle for cultural equity in the United States, however, now faces an even greater challenge. Although most Americans believe that Indians have the same religious freedoms as other Americans, this is not always the case. As a result of previous land policies and the seeming inability of the larger society to comprehend the nature of Indian religions, there are several major constraints surrounding Indian religious freedom that still need to be resolved.

Among the most important of these Indian religious freedom issues are the return of sacred land and sites essential to the functioning of Indian religious beliefs and practices; Indian access to and use of flora and fauna protected by federal law and international agreements; and, because of a recent Supreme Court decision that threatens Indian religious freedom, equal protection for the religious beliefs and practices of the Native American Church. These issues are too complex to be discussed here, but, until they are resolved, the promise of cultural equity for American Indians will remain only a promise. Currently, legislative remedies for these problems are being pursued by native groups and other Americans who support their quest for religious freedom.

If cultural equity for Indians poses a challenge for the nation, cultural integrity is an equally difficult challenge facing Indian communities. Because of growing public interest in Native American culture and because of changes over time in Indian societies, cultural issues have become controversial throughout Indian Country. These issues range from "ethnic fraud"—Indian impostors in all walks of life—to the hucksterism of native culture for profit, to growing tensions between traditional and contemporary-oriented community members over the direction of Indian political, economic, and social life. In the resolution of these issues, Indian nations and tribes should be the final arbiters of cultural authenticity and, according to their own needs, should determine cultural directions for the growth and development of their communities. Anything short of self-determination cannot be described as cultural integrity or cultural sovereignty.

A combination of factors accounts for the astonishing success of Native Americans in changing national policies towards their cultural rights and resources. After nearly five hundred years of cultural misunderstanding, Indians are saying enough is enough. In the larger society, there is a growing awareness and acceptance of cultural diversity and its significance in American political, economic, and social life. Perhaps American Indians and American society can achieve cultural coexistence and transcend the past with mutual respect, understanding, and enrichment.

Religion and the Challenge of Afrocentric Thought

Clovis E. Semmes

Afrocentric or African-centered thought elevates the African experience, on a global scale, to an equitable footing with other scholarly examinations of the human experience. Beyond this, it applies correctives to the hegemonic and deformed aspects of Eurocentric discourse and imagery. The roots of a distorted Eurocentric epistemology reside in the social construction of White supremacy, that is, the ideological elevation of one race above another.[1] European expansion and domination, which involved chattel slavery, colonialism, and the establishment of numerous settler colonies (these colonies resulted in the extermination and subjugation of millions of people), accelerated extant ethnocentric and racialist thinking to produce a full-blown system of White supremacy.[2] This system achieved normative status in Western thought and consciousness.[3] Currently, as layers of social, cultural, economic, and political oppression are challenged and transformed, the normative dimensions of White supremacy must come under greater scrutiny and, in fact, constitute a major impetus for African American studies as an evolving body of knowledge.[4] The challenge to transform normative White supremacy parallels the challenge to transform the gross structured inequality created by massive Western oppression and exploitation.

As the historical process of liberation unfolds, the scrutinization of religion and its role as an imperial force must gain ascendancy. An important consideration for American Africans is that they have been denied religious freedom in a way that is different from most other groups in American society. The "Bill of Rights" of the Constitution reads, "Congress shall make no law respecting an establishment of religion, or prohibiting the free exercise thereof. . . ." The protection of religious freedoms preserved the ability of European ethnic groups to nourish and retain their cultural heritage. Their previous national and ethnic identities and cultural unity were sustained through their religious institutions, which included religious-based educational institutions, voluntary organizations, fraternal orders, and the like.[5] Of course, ethnic pluralism through religious freedom, as guaranteed by the Constitution, only applied to Europeans (White Americans) and Western Christian traditions.

African religions, including the practice of Islam, were systematically suppressed as this nation was formed. European groups were not attacked in this way. Furthermore, Eurocentric religious doctrines provided the justification and ideological glue for chattel slavery and the inferiorization of Africans. They became the principal vehicles for social control, acculturation (de-Africanization), and White supremacy.[6] Western religious imperialism, with its normative White supremacy, obscured the process of African cultural effacement through universalist claims and has avoided confronting its inherent and underlying religious intolerance. As a consequence, religious imperialism has helped to spawn among African Americans the perennial problems of religious fragmentation and cultural disunity, intragroup religious intolerance, self alienation, psychological dependency on White approval, and weakened institutional development. Two metaphors provide some illustration.

The results of European contact and the subsequent sojourn of Africans American in this hemisphere have been like a volcanic eruption. When such devastation occurs, all vegetation is destroyed. There is no greenery anywhere, only gray volcanic ash. It almost seems as if life, nature, is no longer possible. For American Africans, this type of devastation symbolizes a kind of submerged consciousness, as E. Franklin Frazier would call it, "forgotten memories." Nevertheless, as time passes, a few green sprouts emerge, nature reasserts itself, and the gray volcanic environment is transformed into a lush and life sustaining ambiance. This process symbolizes the rebirth of an African consciousness, the reassembling of culture, the reconstruction of critical vehicles for survival, human growth, and human advancement. This is Afrocentric transformation and human liberation at its best, a projection of African humanity seeking regeneration, salvation, and elevation. Afrocentric analysis becomes the 180 degree reclamation of mental processes that have been systematically expropriated by others; it is the struggle against cultural hegemony.[7]

Religious thinking, this writer argues, is at the root of this process of reclamation. Such thinking provides existential harmony; it defines a natural or normative order that functions in a precognitive way, that is, it stands behind how one perceives one's self and others. Religious thinking places deep within the subconscious mind a sense of the natural order of things; it sets boundaries, establishes order and hierarchies, and encapsulates one's vision of self. For example, in many instances religious thinking provides anthropomorphic notions about the gender, race, and personality characteristics of God, and who, in the scale of human relationships, has the most influence with God. Fundamentally, the destruction, oppression, and control of any group requires the manipulation of religious thinking.

Drawing upon another metaphor, the manipulation of African American religious thinking, in the context of White supremacy, has contributed to the dilemma of the "Robocop" mentality. The story line of the movie *Robocop* was that a police officer who had been mortally wounded was brought back to life as a human robot. This humanoid was constructed as an efficient killing machine and law enforcement officer by a large corporation. Ultimately, the idea was to remove the human element from the process of "law enforcement." However, Robocop still had some human qualities and represented a transition to a more efficient system of social control, using machines. As things turned out, an evil element had helped to create Robocop, but Robocop was programmed to never act against that which had created him. As a consequence, Robocop could not resolve a critical dilemma of his existence. He was programmed to root out evil doers, but he could not turn against the evil element that had created him. In short, Robocop was stopped by his programming or, as one might argue, his mode of religious thinking.

Afrocentric analysis has potential for giving direction to reconstructing a liberating mode of religious thinking, but it is impeded by an added dimension to the Robocop metaphor. The problem is that Blacks are able to maintain contradictory ideas simultaneously without any apparent recognition of the need to resolve these contradictions. Thus, new knowledge does not automatically alter behavior or belief, even when we seemingly give legitimacy to that new knowledge. It seems that recognition of the political and humanly shaped aspects of religious beliefs, particularly as these beliefs were shaped and utilized to oppress others, is easily ignored. As a result, African Americans have difficulty separating spiritual truths from the institutional forms of religious life acquired through enslavement.

The writer calls this self-enslaving behavior *conditioned dislogic*. Conditioned dislogic is the continuation of beliefs and behaviors that are culturally negating, oppressive, and logically untenable. These beliefs and behaviors cannot be confronted by those who hold and engage in them because the result is too traumatic. The trauma, of course, arises from the possibility of having to reject a familiar social reality, one that is supported by tradition, and linked to a complexity of reinforcing institutional forms. One problem is that there does not seem to be a compelling alternative to the old or "dislogical" way of living and thinking.

There is a fundamental difference between religion and spirituality. Spirituality involves the deep feeling that reality and existence is an extension of God or some greater creative force. As a consequence, life is governed by a desire to understand, respect, and be in harmony with that creative force. Recognition of this relationship frequently spawns universalistic laws for relating to others and one's environment that promote mutual well-being. Religion may embody spirituality, but it is defined more by organizational, bureaucratic, and institutional requirements; specific doctrines, rituals, and traditions; and the need to perpetuate itself. A given religion may be tolerant and respectful of other religions or it may not. Also a religion may focus less on the universalistic spiritual qualities that it shares with other religions and more on the particularistic characteristics which it may deem superior to other religions. Further, a religion may feel that it must replace other religions as the "true" religion and use its doctrinal configurations to justify the subjugation of others. Such imperial religions, for example, suffer from the tendency to subvert and obscure their own stated spiritual truths.

An important Afrocentric analysis that can inform the way of seeing and understanding the unchanging river of African spirituality in the face of oppressive, religious institutional forms is the study by historian Sterling Stuckey entitled *Slave Culture: Nationalist Theory and Foundations of Black America.* Stuckey describes the critical process of the emergence of a pan-African consciousness from disparate African ethnic groups. He analyzed the basis for cultural unity among Africans in the Americas. A common impetus for cultural unity was the experience of enslavement, but, more than this, there was the unifying experience of a common spiritual ethic which was embodied in the practice of the ring shout.[8] The ring shout was a circular, counter-clockwise form of devotional dancing that was practiced everywhere by New World Africans. This mode of spiritual devotion expressed common African spiritual beliefs that eventually became submerged within European Christian religious forms. The ring shout reified the African concern for the condition of the soul. This concern was so critical that hell was the equivalent of a soul that wandered for eternity and could not achieve the peace of returning to God.[9]

The African belief in a transcendent God or creative spirit that was discernible and approachable through the mediations of lessor gods, along with the earthly interventions of the ancestors, was a cornerstone of African religious cosmology. For many, the sun was the symbol for the transcendent God, and the movement of the sun symbolized the cycle of life, death, and rebirth. Some West Africans utilized the symbolism of the cross to denote the four moments of the sun as it ascended to its heavenly apex and descended below the horizon. The vertical line stood for the highest and lowest points of the sun, and the horizontal line marked the division between the earthly world and the other world of spiritual and unseen existence. The symbolism of immersion into water stood for movement into and out of the spiritual other world. Through water, rebirth and purification were possible.

Thus, a complex African spiritual ethic, which included the cross as a symbol, already existed prior to European contact. Therefore, baptism in European Christian forms was easily incorporated by many New World Africans. The image of Jesus replaced the role of the lesser gods as a mediator between humans and the transcendent God. In African culture, dance (which included music) was a principle method of spiritual devotion and the meditative tool to achieve oneness with God. The ring shout symbolized the counterclockwise movement of the sun from east to west as Africans expressed their understanding of spiritual reality. Europeans, of course, attempted to stamp out all forms of devotional dancing. They also attempted to destroy African religious expression, when they could recognize it.[10]

Europeans, however, were not always aware of African spirituality and religious practices, and Africans actively hid their rituals and beliefs while conforming to European Christian forms. Secret societies among New World Africans were further testimony to African efforts to hide their African religious rituals and beliefs from Europeans.[11] Over time, however, an African spiritual consciousness succumbed to European expression. African Americans continued African-based, devotional forms in their sacred and secular expressions, but lost consciousness of their African meanings. The result was the double-consciousness observed by Du Bois, that is, the problem of an oppressed people having to view the world through the eyes of their oppressor. However, one must recognize that before double-consciousness, there was double-meaning. This meant that New World Africans were initially aware of the African meanings they attached to their religious rituals, even while practicing European religious forms. Thus, while double-meaning describes African self-consciousness and the African struggle to be free, double-consciousness describes the movement toward historical amnesia and religious and cultural fragmentation.

Afrocentric scholars have attempted to dislodge American Africans from the conditioned dislogic attached to the internalization of Eurocentric religious forms by revealing two fundamental facts. First, Western Christianity attempted to preserve White supremacy by hiding African influences in Judeo-Christian tradition. This included obscuring the African roots of many biblical personalities. Second, Western Christianity attempted to hide its political and syncretic dimensions which showed that it has borrowed from previous religious myths and has altered these myths to accomplish political ends. Indeed, many of the pagan symbols and practices that remained under Romanized Christianity persisted because it was impossible to completely destroy the attachment of the masses to their previous religious practices.

No religion springs forth anew; it pays some debt to other religions. Europeans typically ignored the similarities between more ancient African religions and European Christian religious forms in order to advance the idea that Africans had no religion or had defective religions. Western Christianity also ignored the fact that numerous other religions around the world have similar but prior myths regarding creation, a great flood, the fall of man, and savior-gods. Some scholars have also argued that much of the Bible can be traced back to the sacred writings of ancient Egypt.[12] John Jackson has argued that the African father of the Christian church, St. Augustine, acknowledged that the Christian religion existed among the ancients. Jackson said that according to Augustine, there was not a time when Christianity did not exist.[13] He suggests that the fundamental ethical components of the religion were of much earlier origin. Recent scholarship supports the fundamental conclusion that African religious ontology formed the basis of Western Christianity.[14]

Jackson points to the existence of savior-god religions before Christianity. He elaborates upon the possible origins of the Christ myth as theoretical food for thought. Jackson argued that the Christ myth was based on the allegorical veneration of nature, that is, the material universe and the forces, spiritual or otherwise, that are at work in the cosmos. Underlying the veneration of these forces was the practical ability to harmoniously live with nature through an understanding of cyclical relationships. The ancient savior-gods were personifications of the sun, and the Christ myth represented the movement, allegorically, of the sun through the twelve signs of the zodiac. Lunar, vegetation, and astral elements were also included. Jackson explained that in ancient Egypt the birth date of the sun-god was the 25th of December, a period which reflected the first noticeable lengthening of the day following the winter solstice (the shortest day of the year). During this ancient period the sun was in the zodiacal sign of Capricorn and was then known as the Stable of Augeas. Thus, the newly born sun emerged from a stable. On the meridian was Sirius (the Eastern star). Virgo the virgin was rising from the east. To the right of Sirius was the constellation Orion, the Great Hunter, who had three stars in his belt. These stars were in a straight line and pointed at Sirius. They were known in ancient times as the Three Kings.[15]

Another scholar of comparative religions described the diffusion of the African image of Isis and Horus (mother and child) into European Christendom as the image of the Black Madonna and Child. This image was later whitened. The cult of the African goddess Isis had widespread appeal in Europe. However, the fifth century saw the elevation of the Madonna and Child image to compete with Isis and Horus. The worship of Isis was suppressed.[16]

Yosef ben-Jochannan contends that the idea of Western religions is a misnomer since these religions came from Asia Minor, Arabia, North Africa, West Africa, and East Africa.[17] For example, he observed that the "Negative Confession," a much larger body of ethical statements, included what have been called the ten commandments over 1,300 years before the time of Moses.[18] Further, the Proverbs ascribed to King Solomon appear to be similar to a collection of poetry and songs by an indigenous African King, Amen-em-ope, hundreds of years before Solomon's reign.[19] Also, ben-Jochannan suggests that the significance of the antiquity and presence of Ethiopian or Falasha Jews is obscured and ignored in the interpretations of Eurocentrically dominated religious history and theology.[20]

Other scholars pointed to indigenous Africans who made significant contributions to early Western Christianity. They contend that three Popes have been indigenous Africans. Years later their images were painted by Europeans as Europeans. These artists, they argue, simply used their own ethnocentric imaginations. Augustine, Cyprian, and Tertullian (a contemporary of the indigenous African Roman emperor, Septimus Severus) are other examples of indigenous Africans who had important roles in the early formation of Western Christian traditions. African-centered scholars clarify that because Rome occupied North Africa, this does not mean that the indigenous people ceased being African.[21] Thus, a more expansive view of history shows that Judeo-Christian traditions are indebted to Africa and to Africans, but White supremacy has obscured and distorted this reality. In addition, traditional Eurocentric scholarship overlooks African influences in Islam, Buddhism, and Hinduism.[22] A systematic assessment of the existence, historical evolution, and dispersion of African peoples in the ancient world makes their involvement in the formation of world religions easily plausible.

Explorations into comparative religious history and an Afrocentric focus serves to reveal the human constructions of religion. They reveal the machinations of imperial religions and White supremacy, and raise fundamental questions concerning how one should interpret religious doctrine. An underlying message is that religious doctrine as metaphor embodies spiritual truths, but religious doctrine as literal truth embodies particularistic elements that may fuel human oppression. One may see this in the racial hypocrisy emerging from the way the Western world has characterized its religious traditions. White elites removed the African presence from their religious history, and they altered the meaning and structure of the ancient (African) religious traditions they embraced.

American, continental, and other diasporic Africans have questioned and reacted to the contradictions of Eurocentric religious traditions imposed upon them. Some have attempted to Blacken or Africanize the tradition by noting its African roots. One strategy is to utilize Black images and/or African-like rituals, dress, and music in their (Christian) religious services. Others have claimed that Christian theology refers specifically to African people and that Jesus is the Black messiah. Still others have tried to reform Western Christianity and link it to Black struggle by emphasizing its alleged theology of liberation. They argue that African Americans have practiced the "true" meaning of Western Christianity and, in some sense, have tried to shame Whites by pointing to the hypocrisy of Western racism in the light of Western religious doctrine. Within this context, others have tried to combine Marxism with Christianity to promote its legitimacy as a liberating rather than as an oppressive doctrine. Some have included Black nationalist and Black power rhetoric in their interpretations of Western Christian theology and embraced Malcolm X as a symbol of this radical metamorphosis. The irony here, of course, is that the doctrinal contradiction is never discussed. For Black-liberation-theology advocates, can Malcolm X, a Muslim, join them in heaven? Still, many African Americans turn to Islam, Buddhism, and other non-Western religions, or more tolerant Western ones. Others remain outside of formal religion but seek continued attachment to a spiritual ethic.[23]

The above behavior and the fact that African Americans have always shifted to diverse religions and to diverse denominations, sects, and cults within a single religion, point to the continuing search by African Americans for an appropriate way to embody an uninterrupted African-based spirituality in a formal religious structure that is empowering, status enhancing, and liberating. This searching is quite different from the religious behavior of most Whites, who have unbroken historical, ethnic, and nationalistic ties to specific variants of Western religions. These ties determine how Whites define themselves in relationship to other Whites and, at times, become the source of intense internecine struggle. Black scholars, ministers, and theologians, for the most part, remain tied to Eurocentric religious doctrines and reward structures. There is little open and sustained dialogue over the religious/spiritual question, as a basis for cultural (which includes political and economic) unity. Afrocentric, comparative religious inquiry demands open and honest discussion over the literal interpretations of Western sacred mythology and its role in White supremacy, imperialism, and human oppression.[24] The African American religious experience indicates that a more insightful and unifying religious vehicle must be found if African Americans are to develop and advance in American society and the world.

NOTES

1 See for example, Cheikh Anta Diop, *The African Origins of Civilization: Myth or Reality,* translated and edited by Mercer Cook (Westport, Conn.: Lawrence Hill, 1974). Diop, in his chapter, "The Falsification of History," makes an interesting exploration into the ideological construction of White supremacy.

2 For a discussion of the development of European settler colonies see E. Franklin Frazier, *Race and Culture Contacts in the Modern World* (Boston: Beacon, 1957); Vincent Bakpetu Thompson, *The Making of the African Diaspora in the Americas 1441–1900* (New York: Longman, 1987). Also see St. Clair Drake, *Black Folk Here and There: An Essay in History and Anthropology,* 2 vols. (Los Angeles: University of California, Center for Afro-American Studies, 1987–1990) for a detailed discussion of the origins of racism and racial slavery.

3 See Diop, *The African Origins of Civilization;* Chuk-wuemeka Onwubu, "The Intellectual Foundations of Racism," in Talmadge Anderson, ed., *Black Studies: Theory, Method, and Cultural Perspective* (Pullman, Wash.: Washington State University Press, 1990), pp. 77–88.

4 Clovis E. Semmes (Jabulani K. Makalani), *Cultural Hegemony and African American Development* (Westport, Conn.: Praeger, 1992).

5 See Charles H. Anderson, *White Protestant Americans: From National Origins to Religious Group* (Englewood Cliffs, N.J.: Prentice Hall, 1970); G. William Domhoff, *Who Rules America Now?* (New York: Simon & Schuster, Touchstone Edition, 1986).

6 See Sterling Stuckey, *Slave Culture: Nationalist Theory and the Foundations of Black America* (New York: Oxford University Press, 1987); Albert J. Raboteau, *Slave Religion* (New York: Oxford University Press, 1978); John W. Blassingame, *The Slave Community,* rev. edn. (New York: Oxford University Press, 1979); Frances Cress Welsing, *The Isis Papers: The Keys to the Colors* (Chicago: Third World Press, 1991); Alan Davies, *Infected Christianity: A Study of Modern Racism* (Kingston and Montreal: McGill-Queen's University Press, 1988).

7 Semmes, *Cultural Hegemony.*

8 Stuckey, *Slave Culture,* pp. 3–17, 34–36.

9 Ibid.

10 Ibid.

11 Ibid.

12 For a discussion by scholars in the Afrocentric tradition see John G. Jackson, *Man, God and Civilization* (New Hyde Park, N.Y.: University Books, 1972) and *Christianity Before Christ* (Austin, Texas: American Atheist Press, 1985); Diop, *The African Origins of Civilization;* ben-Jochannan, *African Origins of the Major "Western Religions."* For a recent and detailed discussion of ancient Egyptian (Kemitic) influences on the development of Western Christianity by a scholar whose work supports many Afrocentric assertions but who is not in that tradition see Karl W. Luckert, *Egyptian Light and Hebrew Fire: Theological and Philosophical Roots of Christendom in Evolutionary Perspective* (Albany, N.Y.: State University of New York Press, 1991). Also see John S. Mbiti, *African Religions and Philosophy,* second edn. (Oxford: Heineman, 1989) for a discussion of various traditional African religious myths that are similar to "Western" biblical myths.

13 See Jackson, *Christianity Before Christ,* p. 1.

14 Luckert, *Egyptian Light.*

15 Ibid., pp. 126–127 and *Man, God and Civilization,* pp. 133–134.

16 Danita Redd, "Black Madonnas of Europe: Diffusion of the African Isis" in Ivan Van Sertima, ed., *African Presence in Early Europe* (New Brunswick, N.J.: Transaction Publishers, 1985), pp. 108–133.

17 ben-Jochannan, *African Origins of the Major "Western Religions."*

18 Ibid., p. 70; also see Maulana Karenga, "Black Religion" in Gayraud S. Wilmore, ed., *African American Religious Studies: An Interdisciplinary Anthology* (Durham, N.C.: Duke University Press, 1989), pp. 171–300.

19 ben-Jochannan, *African Origins of the Major "Western Religions,"* p. 164.

20 Ibid.

21 See Edward Scobie, "African Popes" in Ivan Van Sertima, ed., *African Presence in Early Europe,* pp. 96–107.

22 John G. Jackson, "Krishna and Buddha of India: Black Gods of Asia" in Ivan Van Sertima and Runoko Rashidi, eds., *African Presence in Early Asia,* rev. ed. (New Brunswick, N.J.: Transaction Books, 1988), pp. 106–111; J. C. deGraft-Johnson, *African Glory: The Story of Vanished Negro Civilizations* (Baltimore: Black Classic Press, 1986); ben-Jochannan, *African Origins of the Major "Western Religions."*

23 The fluidity and diversity of Black religious expression are exemplified by such works as James Cone, *For My People: Black Theology and the Black Church* (Maryknoll, N.Y.: Orbis Books, 1984) and *A Black Theology of Liberation* (Maryknoll, N.Y.: Orbis, 1986; Albert B. Cleage, Jr., *The Black Messiah* (Trenton, N.J.: African World Press, 1989);

Cornell West, *Prophesy Deliverance!: An Afro-American Revolutionary Christianity* (Philadelphia: Westminster Press, 1982); Leonard E. Barrett, *Soul Force: African Heritage in Afro-American Religion* (Garden City, N.Y.: Anchor Press/Doubleday, 1974); Joseph Washington, *Black Sects and Cults* (Garden City, N.Y.: Anchor Books/Doubleday, 1973); St. Clair Drake, *The Redemption of Africa and Black Religion* (Chicago: Third World Press, 1970); Arthur Huff Fauset, *Black Gods of the Metropolis: Negro Religious Cults in the Urban North* (Philadelphia: University of Pennsylvania Press, 1944); C. Eric Lincoln, *The Black Muslims in the United States* (Boston: Beacon, 1964); C. Eric Lincoln and Lawrence H. Mamiya, *The Black Church in the American Experience* (Durham, N.C.: Duke University Press, 1990).

24 See the discussion by Semmes, *Cultural Hegemony,* pp. 163–64.

Emancipatory Narratives: Rewriting the Master Script in the School Curriculum

Ellen Swartz

INTRODUCTION

The current debate in public schools over curricular knowledge pits the constructed supremacy of Western cultural knowledge against the inherent primacy of the multiple and collective origins of knowledge. Fundamentally, this debate over the centrality or marginality of race, class, and gender groups in the production of knowledge (hooks, 1991; Wallace, 1989; West, 1989; Wynter, 1990a) is not over the relative importance of historical figures and events, nor is it over the potential impact of the curricular experience on self-esteem or the modeling of race, gender, and class heroes and heroines. Rather, it is a debate over emancipatory versus hegemonic scholarship and the maintenance or disruption of the Eurocentrically bound "master script" that public schools currently impart to their students.

In education, the master script refers to classroom practices, pedagogy, and instructional materials—as well as to the theoretical paradigms from which these aspects are constructed—that are grounded in Eurocentric and White supremacist ideologies. Master scripting silences multiple voices and perspectives, primarily by legitimizing dominant, White, upper-class, male voicings as the "standard" knowledge students need to know. All other accounts and perspectives are omitted from the master script unless they can be disempowered through misrepresentation. Thus, content that does not reflect the dominant voice must be brought under control, *mastered,* and then reshaped before it can become part of the master script.

Master scripts exist in all disciplines. For example, through the denigration and later appropriation of Kemetic history and culture by Europeans, disciplines such as science, mathematics, and medicine as well as literature, history, the arts, and philosophy have been and are denied their African origins (Bernal, 1987, 1989, 1991; Diop, 1974, 1987; James, 1954/1988). This denial results in the excision of African-informed epistemology from historical thought and current practices of these disciplines. Since master scripts are monovocal expressions, the few inclusions of African content are usually misrepresentations. This appropriation and distortion violates basic standards of academic scholarship; yet, before public schools complete their legal obligation to their respective states, the basic tenets of Eurocentric ideology are inscribed upon the minds of students through repetition of a monological, exclusionary knowledge base that legitimates and replicates inequitable power relations from one generation to the next (Aronowitz & Giroux, 1985; Bowles & Gintis, 1976; Giroux, 1986; Wynter, 1990b).

The term "Eurocentric" refers to an ideology or body of myths, symbols, ideas, and practices that exclusively or predominantly values the worldview and cultural manifestations (e.g., history, politics, art, language, music, literature, technology, economics, etc.) of people of European origin, and that denigrates and subordinates the cultural manifestations of people from all other lands of origin. Critical assessments of materials and practices as Eurocentric include a critique of race, class, and gender supremacies. Such critiques are not attacks upon, nor attempts to remove or marginalize, the history and culture of White, upper/middle-class males of European origin. Rather, such critiques seek to transform the centrism reflected by a dominating European, patrician, and patriarchal orientation so as to place it in a context that requires the inclusion and accurate representation of all cultures and groups.

The struggle for inclusion and representation of historically omitted race, class, and gender groups in school knowledge has been ongoing for decades (Banks, 1990; FitzGerald, 1979; Sleeter & Grant, 1988, 1991; Woodson, 1933/1977). This search for equity has been fueled by the contradiction between our national democratic ideology and the pervasive inequities in social justice that have plagued this nation (Banks, 1988). These inequities have been clearly demonstrated by the repeated failure of educational systems to equitably educate children across race, class, and gender (Wynter, 1990a). Early forms of what we now call multicultural education were developed to address these inequities but largely served as compensatory vehicles that sought to make up for educational inequities through curricular fairness and inclusion (Sleeter & Grant, 1988; Swartz, 1992) rather than to rethink and rewrite the master script (or what Wynter [1990b] refers to as "system-conserving mainstream perspectives" [pp. 2–3]).

COUNTING AND DISCOUNTING VOICE AND PRESENCE

Recent textbook and curricular responses to demands for diversity are being carried out largely through the mentioning of the previously unmentioned, and without a reconceptualization of content (e.g., Apple & Christian-Smith, 1991; Armento, Mash, Salter, & Wixson, 1991; Beyer, Craven, McFarland, & Parker, 1990). This approach continues to reproduce a textuality in which hierarchical relationships of power are affirmed, and in which Western, patrician, and patriarchal culture remains the master. Emancipatory narratives, on the other hand, reflect the multiple and collective origins of knowledge, and correct sanitized, repressive, and monovocal textbook portrayals of historically marginalized cultures and groups. These narratives are reformative curricular interventions that strive to reflect the indigeneity of those involved. As such, they require the collective representation of diverse cultures and groups as significant to the production of knowledge. They also require a liberative student-teacher relationship that opens up written and oral text to analysis, reconceptualization, and reconstruction. Such critical, "problem-posing" interactions (Freire, 1970) stimulate both students and teachers to be producers of knowledge rather than passive receptors of the preformulated and privileged knowledge of others. In this way students and teachers "make" (not make up) history rather than merely memorize and restate it.

Compensatory approaches such as the benign inclusion of a few famous "ethnic" or female contributors in textbooks or curricula remain comfortable approaches for most publishers and educators, who primarily acknowledge diversity only because of pressure from so-called special interest groups and changing demographics. These approaches, however, actually lend support to the master script by facilitating the marginalization of Indigenous peoples of North America and people of African, Asian, and Latin American ancestry. For example, curricula, instructional materials, and pedagogy that attempt to provide an African American presence through largely biographical and decontextualized inclusion actually obstruct more than facilitate that presence. For example, this is seen in textbooks that compensate African Americans for the previous inattention to indigenous interpretations of the system of slavery by including heroizing, yet decontextualized lessons about Frederick Douglass, Sojourner Truth, and Harriet Tubman, rather than by presenting comprehensive, accurate portrayals of African Americans' collective struggle against the holocaustal atrocities committed by slavery's perpetrators.

The individualistic, biographical approach obscures or omits the sociopolitical contexts in which the lives and work of famous people unfolded. Moreover, it labels and presents them as famous at the expense of showing their connection to the social world of which they were a part. The result of this absence of context is that now-included famous "others" become marginalized and disconnected from their time and place, and their contributions are severed from the eras or movements that constructed them and which they, in turn, collectively constructed. If historically excluded "others" are presently included in standard classroom texts, albeit in very limited and constricted ways, their presence fails to address underlying issues such as the purpose, cause, and consequence of events and systems such as slavery. Though slightly increased numbers of men and women of color now sit as silenced sentinels on scattered textbook pages to meet the ethnic and gender counts of publishers, they are effectively robbed of their indigenous analyses and oppositional voices and perspectives. Their biographical presence, usually presented as textual vignettes or side-bars, becomes side-barred in classroom practice because of the lack of contextualized information that would centralize their voices in the broader historical discourse to which they are individually and representatively central. Lacking contextualization, the voice and presence of African Americans and other people of color remains controlled and marginalized—set to the edge of the "standard" knowledge base.

Marginalization can also be seen in what widely adopted school textbooks present about those individuals they decide to canonize within the text. For example, in many of these books, information on Crispus Attucks is included only to tell students that he was a former slave who died in the Boston Massacre, rather than tell them that he was a symbol of both colonial independence and African American leadership and liberation. Marginalization is also at work when instructional materials portray civil rights leader Martin Luther King, Jr., as preaching and dreaming about democratic values, brotherhood, and overcoming injustice, while the social conditions and inequitable power relations that were the motivations for his actions are obfuscated and submerged. This compensatory approach only strengthens the grip of Eurocentrism on the construction of knowledge. In no way does it ensure that the voices and perspectives of men and women from diverse cultures and groups will be included (Swartz & Goodwin, in press). Such externally conceived inclusions—which are literally counted and percentaged by publishers to validate their claims of an increased focus on diversity—remain characteristic of the most current textbooks, even though they discount and deny the very voices and perspectives they represent.

For example, although historical evidence reveals that Crispus Attucks was neither passive nor voiceless, one recently published fifth-grade history textbook, *America Will Be* (Armento et al., 1991), simplistically presents him as such:

> Crispus Attucks was a runaway slave who worked on the docks in Boston. He was about 50 years old when he was killed in the Boston Massacre. (p. 250)

Apparently, even in his freedom Attucks must be defined foremost as a slave—and a runaway slave at that—although he liberated himself from slavery in 1750, 20 years before the Boston Massacre. This (pre)dominant image of Attucks as "slave" raises the question of how long one must be free to be free in the land of textbook history. The prior enslavement of Attucks and its significance could be alternatively stated in a way that would draw a stronger connection between his personal experiences of achieving freedom from chattel slavery and his efforts as the leader of the colonial rebels who charged up King Street to confront British soldiers in 1770. Notice the different perspective presented in the following suggested revision:

> Crispus Attucks was a dock worker in Boston who believed deeply in freedom. In 1750 he took his freedom by escaping from the system of slavery. In 1770, at the age of almost 50 years, he showed how much he still believed in freedom when he led colonial patriots in a demonstration against British soldiers in Boston. Attucks was one of five men to be killed in what was later called the Boston Massacre. (Swartz & Goodwin, in press)

This revision of the master script pulls Attucks away from the margins of the patriotic struggle. Students can experience his presence through his beliefs and hear his voice through his actions. Attucks is no longer only circumstantially present. His inclusion in the historical record compensates for nothing. He is not included because it is "fair" to do so, but because more accurate, nonhegemonic, and nonracist scholarship demands his role in the patriotic struggle be centralized. Such ventilated formulations are grist for the mill of multiculturality, which is a framework of knowledge that has the capacity to produce emancipatory narratives.

INTERROGATING AND RETHINKING THE MASTER SCRIPT

Slavery Revisited

The slavery discourse in most American history textbooks, inappropriately the first and most extensive inclusion of Africans and African Americans, generally serves to justify and normalize the system of slavery. As one textbook, *The United States and Its Neigh-*

bors (Beyer et al., 1990), states, "Most cotton planters in the South believed their way of life depended on slave labor" (p. 393). Is this statement false? No, but in addition to (and as a way of) normalizing slavery, nowhere does this text present the perspectives or beliefs of those who were enslaved. This type of presentation blocks conscious and critical student analysis of the system of slavery by framing it solely in terms of the benefits it brought to planters; omitted is discussion of the disbenefits of the slavery system to its victims. The use of slave labor was a choice, not a necessity; yet the textbook's use of a term such as "depended on" implies that slavery was natural, inevitable, and unalterable. Indeed, it is appalling that contemporary textbooks continue to include sympathetic, apologetic accounts of slaveowners, a tendency that reflects the racist denial of slavery as a totalizing (though not monolithic) experience for enslaved people. Notice the difference in perspective that can be achieved with the following suggested revision:

> Most cotton planters in the South prospered from the forced and free labor of millions of African American men, women, children. Even though the white planter's way of life created misery for so many people, they were not willing to give up profits made from slavery.

The following passage from an eighth-grade social studies text, *Spirit of Liberty, An American History* (Hart & Baker, 1987), while it attempts to present variation, is clearly a sympathetic reading of slavery:

> Conditions varied from master to master. Some saw their slaves as part of their plantation family, both white and black. Others showed no concern for their slaves' well-being. Although most slaves probably lived better than very poor people in the city slums of the North, they lacked what even the poorest Northerners had—freedom. (p. 354)

As Goodwin (1992) points out, and as this text neglects to mention, the condition of bondage did not vary "from master to master." Moreover, viewing one's slaves as part of one's "plantation family" does not demonstrate "concern"; the only way for a slaveowner to have shown true concern would have been to manumit his (or her) slaves. This option, however, is ignored in the textbook cited above. By accepting and justifying slavery as a social construction, White slaveowners, and the White textbook authors who currently reconstitute them, affirm(ed) their "rightness," even to the extent of promoting their beliefs that at least some people who were enslaved benefited. Additionally, the juxtaposition of northern poverty and freedom in the above textbook passage suggests that material well-being and freedom can be weighed on the same scale, and that to live "better than very poor people in the city slums of the North" was in some sense a trade-off for enslavement. Further, this text's regular and implicit references to Northerners as White people, as seen in the above reference, renders northern poor Black people invisible.[1] As racism and the threat of kidnap and enslavement were lived contra-

---

[1]This invisibility is solidified and protected by what seems to be textbook policy to label people "Black" when they can be counted or used to meet some arbitrary diversity quota. Generally, textbooks never label persons as "White" unless the discourse is racial; thus, "people" are assumed to be White unless students are told otherwise. In this way, the collective, universalistic (yet exclusionary) "we" stands for White people and is repeatedly instantiated in textbooks. Racism is further promoted when textbooks take a separatist approach to inclusion with sections entitled, for example, "Blacks in the War" and "Civil Rights for Blacks." Ironically, these segregated sections rarely contain much information relevant to their title.

dictions to the legal freedom of Black Northerners of all classes, the silencing of these contradictions disallows a reading that would include Black people in the text's reference to "very poor people in the city slums of the North." Again, this (and most existing) textual discourse only allows students to see, hear, and know about the presence of Black people in very limited ways.

Textbooks commonly render slavery and White supremacy normative by promoting a general sympathy for the "problems" of slaveowners and by excluding the accounts of the very people around which the content is centered. Standard textbooks generally advance only the perspectives of slaveowners or of the White leaders who struggled against each other for power, as shown in the following two examples from *America Will Be:*

> The map on p. 446 shows how Congress solved the problem of slavery in the territories. This compromise [the Missouri Compromise of 1820] ended the crisis, but tensions between North and South remained. (p. 447)

> Escaping slaves had always been a problem for slave-owners, but in the 1840s, the problem grew even worse. Northerners had begun to help slaves escape. This made it almost impossible for planters to capture slaves that [should be "who"] had run away. (p. 449)

I know of no textbook account of the struggle over the balance of power between the so-called free and slave states that includes discussion of the impact of this power struggle on those who were victimized by it; nor, to my knowledge, does any existing textbook account describe the strategies and counteractions of free and enslaved Black Americans who worked to oppose the expansion of slavery in newly forming states. If mentioned at all, African American resistance and revolts against slavery are presented not only as violent and threatening to White people but also ultimately as failures rather than as daring revolutionary acts or blows for freedom. Most texts present accounts of slave revolts through the eyes of White people, as shown in the following text from *The United States and Its Neighbors:*

> [Nat] Turner's slave rebellion began with six men armed with axes. In 24 hours there were 70 rebel slaves, and some 60 whites lay dead. Only then was the violence stopped.
> In the South, Nat Turner's rebellion seemed like a nightmare come true. But in the North, some people saw Turner as a hero. They decided it was time to speak out against slavery. (p. 393)

Omitted in the above passage are the voices of those Black people who died under Turner's charge and those others (estimates range from scores to hundreds) who, despite having no connection to Turner, were murdered by vengeful White mobs following the revolt. Instead, standard textbook accounts tell students only of the White people who lost their lives during the revolt. Omitted also is discussion of the fact that both Black and White people had been writing, petitioning, organizing, and speaking out against slavery well before the 1831 revolt.

Turner's rebellion is called a "nightmare," but slavery in the Americas was a nightmare for people of African descent for over 300 years. The text does not include mention of this. Thus, we see that, as late as 1990, American history textbooks still attempt to elicit sympathy for White slaveowners while condemning the acts of those who rose up to end the inhuman system of slavery (which, to my knowledge, has never been referred to as "violent" in standard textbooks).

Such an uncritical, monovocal account reveals an orientation that King (1991) calls "dysconscious racism," or "a form of racism that tacitly accepts dominant White norms and privileges" (p. 135). According to King, this dysconscious racism "is not an *absence* of consciousness (that is, not unconsciousness) but *impaired* consciousness or a distorted way of thinking about race" (p. 135). Textbook content about slavery and abolition is a clear example of this dysconscious internalization, in which ideological justifications of White privilege and supremacy are sanctioned through normative and uncontested portrayals of these practices. Textbook authors' perceptions and attitudes about the "rightness" of White supremacy as the existing order, one that should not be challenged, is a clear subtextual message in the master script.

The Abolition Movement Revisited

Standard monovocal portrayals omit collective and emancipatory efforts where they have occurred. Thus, for example, the common struggle for a legal framework of freedom, by African Americans (free, manumitted, and enslaved) and women (enslaved, manumitted, and free; yet dominated and "civilly dead" [Aptheker, 1982]) during the pre- and post-Civil War periods are rendered invisible in standard textbooks and instruction. By contrast, a multivoiced presentation reveals the success of the abolitionists' and suffragists' liberatory struggles as central to the revolutionary vision of a democratic society circumscribed by unacknowledged double standards. Unfortunately, these double standards are still at work today, disallowing the conceptualization of these struggles as revolutionary movements toward a more democratic society.

During the pre- and post-Civil War period, simultaneous efforts were waged by civil and human rights activists and revolutionaries to expose, challenge, and remove inequities representing diverse yet collective strands of race, class, and gender oppression. These efforts were grounded in the ideology of abolition and the far-from-achieved national ideology of democracy, freedom, and equality. Many of these activists conceptualized a truly revolutionary and emancipatory movement that would not only overthrow the ruling class of slaveholders who dominated the country politically, militarily, and economically, but also challenge the patriarchal dominance of women, who were still viewed as the property of men (Aptheker, 1982).

The refusal of textbook authors to connect the abolition movement's Black and (later) White architects to improvements in the practice of democracy is first seen in the standard textbook appropriation of abolition as the province of White Northerners. The following excerpt comes from *America Will Be:*

> Slavery also was being attacked by some people in the northern states. These people were called *abolitionists* because they believed that slavery was wrong and should be abolished, or ended. (pp. 405–406)

This text passage is placed between a description of Nat Turner's revolt, which does not make explicit Turner's connection to the abolition movement; and a description of

William Lloyd Garrison, who textually embodies White northern abolitionists in this and all other public school social studies texts. African American efforts to end slavery are not presented as central or essential to abolition efforts in *America Will Be* (or in any other texts reviewed by this author). Thirty pages later, Frederick Douglass is only briefly mentioned as an abolitionist among other reformers of the 19th century (pp. 436–437). As well, Douglass is effectively disconnected from other African American efforts to end slavery. Instead, Garrison is given the central position. The text highlights Garrison's efforts to publish the abolitionist newspaper, *The Liberator,* and the physical mistreatment he suffered as an advocate of abolition. Not only are African Americans denied their central role in efforts to abolish the system that enslaved them—efforts that predated the White-identified abolition involvement of the 1830s by hundreds of years— but the connection between the abolitionists' efforts and the democratization of American society is never made. This modern-day unwillingness to portray abolition as a democratizing influence and as a movement that attempted to bring integrity to this country's revolutionary vision reinforces and replicates the same unacknowledged double standards that framed that era.

Moreover, traditional and contemporary school textbooks typically present abolition as the invention of White men, designed by them, with a few well-known African Americans as their "assistants." Thus, figures such as Frederick Douglass, Sojourner Truth, and Harriet Tubman are presented as special cases whose individual determination enabled them to come to the aid of the White abolitionist movement. The renowned suffragist Susan B. Anthony, a White woman, was also against slavery, but standard texts effectively separate her advocacy for women's rights from her involvement in the abolition movement. Indeed, such texts further omit that 18th-century White women such as Anthony, Lucretia Mott, and Elizabeth Cady Stanton were actually "schooled" in the anti-slavery movement. Black women such as Sojourner Truth, Sarah Paraker Remond, Charlotte Forten, and Lucretia Still were abolitionists who acknowledged and acted upon the natural relationship between abolition and the emancipation of women. Their double (actually triple, by adding class in most cases) oppression widened their conceptual framework of emancipation and defined the common edge of both movements. Together, Black and White women pressed for their right to organize, speak, and petition; and abolition was the common ground on which they first stood (Aptheker, 1982).[2]

Contemporary textbook writers, editors, and curriculum developers continue to reflect racist and separatist intent in their inability and/or unwillingness to conceptualize and present African American men and women as intellectual leaders and decision makers in

---

[2]The collective and emancipatory work of women across race and class lines did not conceal, however, the entrenched racism that was present among White suffragists. For example, one account of the 1852 Women's Rights convention in Akron, Ohio, describes the racist response of White women when Sojourner Truth arrived (Fauset, 1938/1971). White women's rights advocates did not want her to speak. Their fear that her identification as an abolitionist would become mixed with *their* cause of women's rights, and thus compromise *their* efforts, was only a thin veil for their racially separatist intent. Yet, when Truth approached the platform to speak, no one dared to stop her. Truth's short presentation, known as the "Ain't I a Woman?" speech, irrefutably linked race, class, and gender oppression, and delegitimized the separatist preferences of those White women present (and not present) who unabashedly expressed their White privilege, even from the repressive (by law and by custom) social, economic, and political location that White men imposed upon them.

the abolition movement. To be consistent with this unscholarly denial (through omission) that Black men and women were active and organized in their own liberation struggle prior to the activities of White abolitionists, these authors must ignore and sidestep quite a lot of information. For example, mention and analysis of slave revolts dating back to the 16th century and pre-Revolutionary War legislative petitions and court cases presented by persons of African descent must be omitted, as must acknowledgment of historical evidence confirming that the first antislavery organizations were formed and led by African Americans. In this light, the appearance in 1827 of the first African American newspaper, *Freedom's Journal,* edited by Samuel E. Cornish and John B. Russwurm, becomes too hard to explain. This newspaper and others that shortly followed, articulated to the masses the assertion of African American civil and political rights, equal education, and economic development.

The fact that David Walker's *Appeal,* an uncompromising abolitionist pamphlet was published in 1829, two years prior to William Lloyd Garrison's first issue of *The Liberator,* must also be omitted to keep intact Garrison's image as the period's foremost abolitionist and socially conscious "radical" author on abolition. It thus cannot be mentioned that Walker's pamphlet, published in Boston, was banned in most southern states. Nor can it be stated that Garrison opposed its circulation, yet reprinted most of Walker's work two years later when he began publishing *The Liberator* in that same city (Wiltse, 1965/1985). It must further be denied, by omission, that successful Black businessmen such as James Forten and Robert Purvis were large financial contributors to the Garrisonian abolition movement. Admitting that Garrison financially depended upon Black abolitionists would suggest a Black agency and empowerment that does not mesh with the master script's account of slavery and abolition.

These vast gaps in the content of American history, as it has been and is presently related to American schoolchildren, result in the fictive portrayal of African Americans as voiceless victims of slavery who, at best, merely assisted the "noble" efforts of White abolitionists on their behalf. This silencing through omission is accompanied by the strategic and consistent placement and scripting of African Americans in ways that accentuate passivity. Even when opportunities exist to portray the social agency of empowered individual and collective actions, these opportunities are ignored. For example, *America Will Be* blatantly restricts information about successful middle-class or wealthy African Americans of the era, and when such mention is included, the successes and social agency of those persons are obscured. The following is a caption that appears under a picture of William Whipper:

> Throughout this time, more and more Americans opposed slavery. William Whipper (above), a free black, spoke out against slavery and helped runaway slaves from his home in Pennsylvania. (p. 442, caption)

The inclusion of William Whipper could have been used to demonstrate and symbolize Black economic, political, and social voice and agency during the Civil War period. Instead, the text omits vital information about Whipper that could bring his empowered voice and presence to students. Whipper was part of the northern Black intellectual class of the mid-1800s who spoke in favor of nonviolent resistance more than a decade before Henry David Thoreau wrote on civil disobedience. He owned a successful lumberyard, financed the passage of self-liberated Black people to Canada, contributed $5,000 to the Union cause during the Civil War, and worked toward improved conditions of northern freedmen. The omission of this type of content further demonstrates that inclusion is no assurance of indigenous voice or accurate representation.

The range and depth of accomplishments that could establish African Americans as the conceptual designers and initial purveyors and participants in the abolition movement are constricted and censored from the so-called standard knowledge (master script) of school textbooks. Thus, Frederick Douglass is in, but the wide breadth of his accomplishments is out. Douglass was renowned as an organizer and station master of the Underground Railroad, as an author, publisher, politician, women's rights advocate, and statesman as well as great orator. Notwithstanding, the following truncated characterization of Douglass, found in the fifth grade social studies text, *Exploring America's Heritage* (Ver Steeg & Skinner, 1991), is typical of most textbooks:

> Douglass was a powerful speaker. Because he could move an audience, Douglass joined Garrison and others around New England, speaking out against slavery. (p. 336)

Emancipatory text knowledge is not as unattainable as textbook publishers would lead us to believe. For example, inclusion of Douglass's own words would help to clarify his moral and intellectual contribution to the abolition movement and emancipate the limited text portrayal of him found in most school books. A suggested revision for an intermediate-level textbook might include the following reference to Douglass:

> Douglass was a great thinker, writer, and politician as well as a powerful speaker. As a young man he worked with Garrison, speaking out against the inhumanity of slavery at abolition rallies around New England. Douglass made it very clear that slavery was as harmful to the country as it was immoral. He said that the country was "cursed with the infernal [hated, disgusting] spirit of slavery, robbery, and wrong" [cited in Douglass, 1881/1983].

The above rethinking and reformulating of textual accounts reveals, demystifies, and discredits the master script regarding slavery and abolition by demonstrating the centrality of African American men and women in the 19th-century revolutionary vision of a more humane and democratic society. Such textual reconceptualizations are needed to correct for the monovocality that has become epistemologically embedded in the multiple knowledge bases that inform the content of public schooling.

If textbooks were to change their monovocal and exclusionary approach, what would happen to the role of, for example, White people in the abolition movement? To begin with, they would no longer falsely dominate textbook accounts of the movement, as in the case of Garrison mentioned above. Nor would their roles be characterized as separatist and limited to ones of moderation and compromise, as in the case of northern White abolitionists satisfied with incremental, individualistic steps toward ending slavery. The revolutionary abolitionist efforts of John Brown, and the uncompromising congressional activities of other White men such as Thaddeus Stevens and Charles Sumner—each of whom enacted significantly different strategies to end the system of slavery—would no longer be misrepresented and marginalized in standard textbooks and curricula. These men are also denigrated or omitted from the master script. For example, *Exploring America's Heritage* altogether neglects to mention Sumner and Stevens, and it presents the radical abolitionist John Brown as a "crazed" individual who "claimed he could stare at a dog or cat and make it slink out of his sight" (p. 354, caption). This delegitimizing process begins with a stern-looking 1856 photograph of Brown, followed by text that states:

> After leaving Kansas, John Brown set up his own crazed plan to destroy slavery and disrupt the Southern way of life. He would stir up slave revolts in Virginia and Maryland and set up a government of free blacks. . . . Brown himself was convicted of treason and murder as well as of encouraging slave rebellion. He was hanged for his crimes. (p. 354)

First, the text presents a photo and caption of John Brown that portray him as a frightening-looking man who seemed to enjoy intimidating cats and dogs. Then students are implicitly told that planning "to destroy slavery and disrupt the Southern way of life" is insane, even though the text's authors would probably argue that they merely judge Brown's plan as "crazed." Further, the use of the phrase "stir up slave revolts" suggests to children that Brown was a troublemaker; and (as if that is not enough to discredit Brown) students are told that his actions were "criminal." While this text (nor any other text ever seen by this author) never states that American slavery itself was criminal, a revolutionary act aimed at ending it is so labeled. Such biased accounts and omissions of White abolition advocates such as Brown, Stevens, and Sumner suggest that their emancipatory efforts are viewed as attempts to challenge the ruling class and change the dominant social order. Their work was, and apparently still is, seen as a threat that must be discredited or written out of the dominant master script of history.

When nonhegemonic, nonracist scholarship is used to present the contributions of men and women such as Douglass, Walker, Truth, Stevens, Remond, Anthony, Forten, and Brown, their efforts bear witness to the merged interests, collective strategies, and raised consciousness that grew out of the common struggle to oppose White, male, ruling-class dominance. When these efforts are ideologically portrayed through their confluence and intersection rather than through their division and separation (which is not to suggest that conflicts and divisions did not exist), students can see more clearly the multiple layers of the revolutionary and emancipatory movement toward an egalitarian society in the pre- and post-Civil War period.

Reconstruction Revisited

Also characteristic of the monovocal master script is the minimal treatment of Reconstruction offered in most textbooks. Omitted is mention of the reign of terror waged against Black people in many southern states following the Civil War. Omitted are explorations of the communal and collective efforts of African Americans to fund and build new schools in the South and to provide for the political and social welfare of their own communities. Even though the South lost the war, textbooks such as *The United States and Its Neighbors* continue to present antebellum entrepreneurs from the upper-class White southern planter's perspective, that is, as "carpetbaggers" and "scalawags":

> So these Northerners were called carpetbaggers. Most white Southerners believed carpetbaggers had come only to make money at the South's expense.

Other new leaders were Southerners who stayed loyal to the Union. Many were poor whites who had never owned slaves. These white Southerners were called scalawags. A scalawag, said one Southern observer, was no better than a "mangy dog." (p. 421)

What did African American Southerners and poor White Southerners think about Northerners who came to the South during Reconstruction? In the usual uncritical manner of standard textbooks, the accounts and perspectives of those who were oppressed are omitted, inferring their insignificance. Moreover, the description of scalawags not only omits the perspective of poor White Southerners but it demeans them as well.

The United States and Its Neighbors devotes an eight-paragraph section entitled "Blacks in the South." The first two paragraphs discuss the unhappiness and anger of White people regarding Reconstruction; the next five paragraphs inform readers about the use of violence, fraud, intimidation, and unjust laws to stop African Americans from voting and running for public office; and the last paragraph introduces and describes the concept of Jim Crow segregation (pp. 421–422). Although this section presents information about how White people victimized African American people after the abolition of slavery, it offers nothing about the gains, achievements, lifestyles, or political and economic experiences of African American men and women in the South during Reconstruction. Again, students are told what White people thought and felt, but they learn nothing about what African Americans thought, felt, or accomplished.

LIBERATORY PEDAGOGY AND PRACTICE

The implicit racism, classism, and sexism of current textbook authors can perhaps best be understood through King's (1991) concept of "dysconsciousness," which she defines as "an uncritical habit of mind (including perceptions, attitudes, assumptions, and beliefs) that justifies inequity and exploitation by accepting the existing order of things as given" (p. 135). Resultantly, most textbooks consistently omit, marginalize, and distort the ontological experience and knowledge bases of women from all cultures, and peoples of both sexes of Indigenous (Native) American, African, Asian, and Latin American origin (who each comprise internal and overlapping multiplicities such as nationality and class). However, the primary goal of multiculturality as an approach to curriculum development and instruction is to help students bridge the gap between so called "standard" knowledge and what they need to know. To do this, students must be shown the mechanisms by which this gap is maintained, so that ultimately they learn to read, write, and talk between, over, under, and through the lines of the master script.

One way to help students perceive the mechanisms of omission, distortion, and marginalization in any monological presentation is for instructors to ask questions and assign tasks that trigger an awareness in students that only some of the people who were historically present and involved are being discussed or considered (Crichlow, Goodwin, Shakes, & Swartz, 1990). Dialogue and tasks that facilitate this process guide students toward recognizing the consistent omission of the voices, experiences, and perspectives of oppressed peoples. Such a liberatory pedagogy is transformative. It empowers students to become more conscious and connected to the particularistic narratives which they themselves embody, and helps them to value their own and other knowledge bases as significant to their learning. As students think critically and interrogate knowledge,

they come to understand more fully whose interests are served by the gaps and insuffi-
ciencies in Eurocentric presentations; further, they begin to understand in what ways
their own (past and present) voices have been and are significant in the production of
knowledge.

As students are assisted to contest knowledge and "read" their own (ancestral and
current) lives against the standard, monovocal text, canonical knowledge, and school
practices, they begin to deconstruct or take apart the mechanisms that have been used to
build and sustain Eurocentric constructions. They begin to find and use their own voices
and come to experience the power in their own discourses. They learn how to develop
and use mechanisms (e.g, inclusion, accurate representation, centrality of indigenous
voices, multiple-voiced accounts and perspectives) to legitimate their own (present and
past) narratives. This critical practice or reworking of the mechanisms of dominant
knowledge construction helps students to name and define their world (Freire, 1970),
and to experience schools as "sites of possibility" (Giroux, 1986). By constructing such
sites, Giroux suggests that an emancipated discourse of schooling can educate students
toward positions of empowerment as opposed to positions of subordination. This process
of critically reworking dominant knowledge formulations models empowerment
by assisting students to identify, rethink, re-image, and rewrite the master script that
has been used to reify the relationship between school knowledge and their own social
positionality.

Student-teacher production of written, verbal, and visual narratives that are inclusive
and representational results from the merger of critical scholarship and lived experiences. This dialogic and emancipatory interaction between students and teachers
unchains knowledge by making it more accessible to student analysis and expansion.
The inclusionary and representational framework proposed herein can effectively portray
the collective efforts of diverse groups as well as interrogate and reject the typical master narratives found throughout public school curricula and instructional materials. Such
a pedagogical framework hopes to end the current control of knowledge, surveyed as
the narrative property of those who represent White, patrician, and patriarchal privilege.

REFERENCES

Apple, M. W., & Christian-Smith, L. K. (1991). The politics of the textbook. In M. W. Apple
& L. K. Christian-Smith (Eds.), *The politics of the textbook* (pp. 1–21). New York: Routledge.

Aptheker, B. (1982). *Women's legacy.* Amherst, MA: University of Massachusetts Press.

Armento, B. J., Mash, G. B., Slater, C. L, & Wixson, K. K. (1991). *America will be.* Boston:
Houghton Mifflin.

Aronowitz, S., & Giroux, H. A. (1985). *Education under siege: The conservative, liberal
and radical debate over schooling.* London: Routledge & Kegan Paul.

Banks, J. A. (1988). *Multiethnic education, theory and practice.* Newton, MA: Allyn &
Bacon.

Banks, J. A. (1990). Multicultural education: Its effects on students' racial and gender role
attitudes. In J. P. Shaver (Ed.), *Handbook of research on social studies, teaching, and
learning* (pp. 459–469). New York: Macmillan.

Bernal, M. (1987, 1991). *Black Athena* (Volumes 1 & 2). New Brunswick, NJ: Rutgers University Press.

Bernal, M. (1989, October 29). The roots of ancient Greece. *Newsday,* p. 5.

Beyer, B. K., Craven, J., McFarland, M. A., & Parker, W. C. (1990). *The United States and its neighbors.* New York: Macmillan.

Bowles, S., & Gintis, H. (1976). *Schooling in capitalist America.* New York: Basic Books.

Crichlow, W., Goodwin, S., Shakes, G., & Swartz, E. (1990). Multicultural ways of knowing: Implications for practice. *Boston Journal of Education,* 172(2), 101–117.

Diop, C. A. (M. Cook, trans.). (1974). *The African origins of civilization: Myth or reality?* Westport, CT: Lawrence Hill.

Diop, C. A. (1987). *Pre-colonial Black Africa.* Westport, CT: Lawrence Hill.

Douglass, F. (1983). *Life and times of Frederick Douglass.* Secaucus, NJ: Citadel Press. (Original work published 1881)

Fauset, A. H. (1971). *Sojourner Truth, God's faithful pilgrim.* New York: Russell & Russell. (Original work published 1938)

Fine, M. (1991). *Framing dropouts: Notes on the politics of an urban public high school.* Albany, NY: State University of New York Press.

FitzGerald, F. (1979). *America revised.* New York: Vintage Books.

Freire, P. (1970). *Pedagogy of the oppressed.* New York: The Seabury Press.

Giroux, H. A. (1986). Radical pedagogy and the politics of student voice. *Interchange,* 17(1), 48–67.

Goodwin, S. (1992, March 14). *Rethinking the content of instruction.* A paper presented at a meeting of the Syracuse University Stay in School Partnership Project.

Hart, D., & Baker, D. (1987). *Spirit of liberty, an American history.* Menlo Park, CA: Addison-Wesley.

hooks, b. (1991). *Yearning: Race, gender, and cultural politics.* Boston: South End Press.

James, G. G. M. (1988). *Stolen legacy.* San Francisco: Julian Richardson Associates. (Original work published 1954)

King, J. E. (1991). Dysconscious racism: Ideology, identity, and the miseducation of teachers. *Journal of Negro Education,* 60,(2), 133–146.

Sleeter, C. E., & Grant, C. A. (1988). *Making choices for multicultural education.* New York: Merrill.

Sleeter, C. E., & Grant, C. A. (1991). Race, class, gender, and disability in current textbooks. In M. W. Apple & L. K. Christian-Smith (Eds.), *Politics of the textbook* (pp. 78–110). New York: Routledge.

Swartz, E. (1992). Multicultural education: From a compensatory to a scholarly foundation. In C. A. Grant (Ed.), *Research and multicultural education: From the margins to the mainstream* (pp. 32–43). London: Falmer Press.

Swartz, E., & Goodwin, S. (in press). Multiculturality: Liberating classroom pedagogy and practice. *Social Science Record.*

Ver Steeg, C. L., & Skinner, C. A. (1991). *Exploring America's heritage.* Lexington, MA: D. C. Heath.

Wallace, M. (1989). Reading 1968 and the great American whitewash. In B. Druger & P. Mariani (Eds.), *Remaking history* (Dia Art Foundation Discussions in Contemporary Culture No. 4) (pp. 97–109). Seattle, WA: Bay Press.

West, C. (1989). Black culture and postmodernism. In B. Druger & P. Mariani (Eds.), *Remaking history* (Dia Art Foundation Discussions in Contemporary Culture No. 4) (pp. 87–96). Seattle, WA: Bay Press.

Wiltse, C. M. (Ed.). (1985). (Ed.). *David Walker's appeal to the coloured citizens of the world, but in particular, and very expressly, to those of the United States of America.* New York: Hill & Wang. (Original work published 1829; reprinted 1965)

Woodson, C. G. (1977). *The mis-education of the Negro.* New York: AMS Press. (Original work published 1933)

Wynter, S. (1990a, September 9). *America as a world: A Black studies perspective and "cultural model" framework.* Unpublished manuscript submitted to the California State Board of Education.

Wynter, S. (1990b, September 25). A cultural model critique of the textbook, *America will be.* Unpublished manuscript submitted to the California State Board of Education.

CONTESTED BODIES

Our bodies force attention to a suspect, retrogressive feature of social theory. We often theorize "human being," "consciousness," "agency," and other key terms as if people were narrowly cognitive and radically disembodied. We set aside people's bodies as if they were excess baggage impeding our swift passage to theoretical insights. For all practical purposes, the body functions as an "absent presence" in social theory.[1] The body has thus faced the same theoretical erasure that people of color, lesbians and gay men, and other excluded and marginalized groups have faced.

In fact, the erasure of the body and the erasure of such groups correlate with one another. As Naomi Scheman points out,

> All the oppressed—the obviously exploited and the others—share in the minds of the privileged a defining connection to the body, whether it is seen primarily as the laboring body, the sexual body, the body insufficiently under the control of the rational will, or some combination of these. The privileged are precisely those who are defined not by the meanings and uses of their bodies for others but by their ability either to control their bodies for their own ends or to seem to exist virtually bodilessly. They are those who have conquered the sexual, dependent, mortal, and messy parts of themselves—in part by projecting all those qualities onto others, whom they thereby earn the right to dominate and, if the occasion arises, to exploit.[2]

In multiple ways, then, the bodies of dominated groups serve as a central site of their oppression—a site as central, to be sure, as their consciousness. That "the body" (as if it existed preculturally) gets erased from social theory dovetails, then, with their subordination and with elite males' historical monopoly over theory and other privileged knowledge.

Over the past ten years or so "body studies" has emerged as a transdisciplinary arena for taking the body into scholarly account. An outgrowth of postmodernist theorizing—

whether by feminists or queers, the heirs apparent of Freud or Foucault, philosophers or anthropologists—body studies puts our bodies at the center of any theorizing about the who, what, and how of human being. Often enough, such centering discloses the body as a site of contestation.

For centuries that insight has informed social and political theory. Whatever their political persuasions and theoretical propensities, scholars of power have long regarded violence or coercion as its ultimate foundation. Push often comes to shove, and such escalation eventuates in physically controlling the subordinate(s) in a situation. Members of subordinate groups have little, if any, difficulty seeing connections between oppression and their bodies. Often they have experienced their own bodies as sites of humiliation, degradation, brutalization and torture; they know or can readily imagine the feel of shackles, hunger, spit in their faces, and people's eagerness to do them bodily harm for no reason other than their sexual orientation, skin color, gender, race, or ethnicity. Not surprisingly, then, multicultural social theorists are major contributors to body studies. Their own identities and experiences prime them for seeing through the disembodied creatures populating most mainstream theories.

As Erving Goffman emphasized, social life comprises a "design of vulnerability" wherein a "central factor [is] the vulnerability of a subject's body."[3] Like other socially conditioned circumstances, this one involves unequal opportunities and outcomes among society's members. Broadly, some members' bodies are more vulnerable than others. The institution of slavery drove that lesson home most palpably, as does the institution of the patriarchal family for its abused wives, daughters, sons, and infirm elders. To understand social subordination one must understand such extreme but not uncommon realities. One must understand hate crimes, rape and the threat of rape, prisoner abuse, abortion-clinic violence, hazardous working conditions, AIDS, anorexia nervosa and other eating disorders, unsafe housing, and much else.

For our multicultural purposes one must also understand how such bodily violations and hazards raise issues of dignity at the most fundamental level. Here Goffman's insights are invaluable. He distinguishes pride, honor, and dignity at the micro level in ways resonant with Berger's (see p. 5) attention to honor and dignity as cultural values. Goffman says that in social situations agency involves having a face to maintain, and bearing some responsibility for the quality of the situation. Under such conditions bodies and selves get implicated in the *"expressive order . . . that regulates the flow of events, large or small, so that anything that appears to be expressed by them will be consistent with [one's] face."*[4] When we do what we can to maintain the expressive order out of duty to ourselves, pride is at work; when our efforts derive from duty to others, honor is operative. But, says Goffman,

> with expressive events derived from the way in which the person handles his [or her] body, . . . emotions, and the things with which he [or she] has physical contact, one speaks of *dignity,* this being an aspect of expressive control that is always praised and never studied.[5]

At the most fundamental level, then, dignity concerns how we handle our bodies and our feelings. When we cannot do our expected part to sustain the expressive order of a situation, our dignity is in jeopardy; when we are held back from or denied the opportunity to do what a credible participant is expected to do to sustain the expressive order, our dignity is under attack; when our very presence suspends the expressive order culturally associated with civility, our dignity is denied and violated. The control others allow us over our bodies and emotions is thus their basic testament to our dignity. The less control they discernibly allow us, the more uncertain is their recognition of and respect for our dignity. In the extreme, others can annihilate our dignity, at least momentarily, by seizing control of our bodies and trying to commandeer our emotions. In somewhat less extreme situations like the ones Goffman studied in total institutions—high-surveillance, custodial organizations—one can be mortified by routinized varieties of "abasements, degradations, humiliations, and profanations of self." Goffman wanted to show that what happens in total institutions "can help us see the arrangements that ordinary establishments must guarantee if members are to preserve their civilian selves."[6] In other terms, he wanted to provide grounds for inferring the social-structural, interactional, and cultural bases of dignity.

Goffman delineated, for example, the "indignities of speech and action" imposed on inmates of total institutions. Sometimes they are required to use deferential forms of address to staff members, or they are required to ask or even beg for small things like a pencil, a match, or extra dessert. Alongside those indignities are "the indignities of treatment others accord" the inmates. These include "verbal or gestural profanations" such as being taunted, cursed, or called obscene names. Goffman goes on to observe that

> Whatever the form or the source of these various indignities, the individual has to engage in activity whose symbolic implications are incompatible with his [or her] conception of self. A more diffuse example of this kind of mortification occurs when the individual is required to undertake a daily round of life that he [or she] considers alien . . .—to take on a disidentifying role.[7]

Indignities thus involve violating the "territories of the self" so that "the boundary . . . between [one's] being and the environment is invaded and the embodiments of self profaned." Such "contaminative exposure" is one thing; "forced interpersonal contact and, in consequence, a forced social relationship" are another thing along the same self-mortifying continuum. Rape, Goffman suggests, is the "model for [such] interpersonal contamination in our society. . . ."[8]

To understand social subordination one must also understand the less immediately harsh but no less effective ways some members' bodies become significant sites of social regulation. One must be attuned to the practical ramifications of culturally evoked body loathing, expensive and time-consuming body regimens, females' large-scale exclusion from competitive team sports, and even "menopause discourse." As Margaret Morganroth Gullette indicates, such discourse "flourishes . . . when women are seen to be getting powerful, independent, and increasingly self-assured."[9] In that discourse, promulgated by pharmaceutical and other companies as well as "self-help" books and talk shows, menopause "has become a code word for aging. Thus, in a society that fears old age and despises its signs, *only women age.*" To that extent even after menarche, pregnancy, parturition, breastfeeding, and menstruation are behind them, women get reminded that their bodies are *still* a handicap and a problem—something "different" about them that requires special efforts or attention. Seen as problematically embodied, women thus get seen as "different." As Sherry Ortner observes, they get associated with nature the way men get associated with culture.[10]

"Difference," then, is often lodged in the socially constructed, culturally inscribed bodies of oppressed groups, as Judith Lorber indicates in the first reading of this section. Their brains, hormones, and sexual drives are "different"; their body makeup— amount of body fat and upper-body strength, for instance—is "different"; their height, weight, and bodily talents are "different." In those culturally constituted differences lie ideological grounds for group-specific forms of oppression. In those same differences lie the grounds implicitly making the privileged white male's body the standard whereby other groups fail to measure up. Thus, theorizing "the" body first necessitates pluralizing it. As Lorber (p. 194) points out, "Deconstructing sex, sexuality, and gender reveals many possible categories embedded in . . . social experiences and social practices. . . ." Theorizing bodies requires disclosing those hidden, erased, or unrecognized categories.

Thereafter such theorizing necessitates attention to the contestations whereby some members' bodies are more subject(ed) to social control than others' bodies are. That social circumstance bears on people's human rights, well-being, and identities; it infiltrates their everyday lives and thus shapes their biographies; it also points to a likely focus of backlash against their advancement in society. To be oppressed, to be exploited, to be subordinated or excluded or marginalized means, at root, to bear a contested body, a body that cannot be taken for granted. A contested body is a problem, an impediment, or a challenge demanding one's anxious attention.

Focusing on women's bodies, the remaining readings in this section drive those far-reaching lessons home. We first look at the history of wife battering in our society. Linda Gordon shows that over the decades various rhetorics have been used to combat that violence. Gordon makes many substantial points revolving around the principle that "systems of domination . . . are systems of conflict." Thus, resistance and counterviolence coexist with wife battering, but their forms vary with social conditions. Gordon shows, for instance, that whether the victims of battering invoke their needs as mothers or their rights as women depends heavily on their practical, socially conditioned possibilities. Gordon also suggests that first-wave feminism, spanning the nineteenth and early twentieth centuries, may have undercut battered wives' willingness to counter violence with violence. Doing so meant violating hegemonic conceptions, shared by feminists and nonfeminists alike, of respectable white femininity. Finally, Gordon explores the social construction of resistance while broadly defining its practical limits under given sociohistorical conditions. In the end she portrays severely contested bodies among wives engaged in contests of dignity with the very people who are supposed to love them. Gordon's is thus a study of what Goffman called "forced social relationships," but these have the woeful distinction of taking their toll in one's own home.

Nicole Gavey also focuses on how women's bodies often get contested in their intimate encounters or relationships with men. Gavey's focus is coerced sexual intercourse. Her paper deals not with acquaintance or marital rape as such but with how discourse helps to institutionalize heterosexuality along lines promoting sexually coercive behavior by men and sexually compliant responses from women. An example on many campuses today, perhaps your own, involves fraternity "little sisters" who "participate enthusiastically in their own sexual objectification and sexual exploitation," sometimes including unwanted sex.[11] Gavey (p. 212) mentions various "discursive fields," including popular culture, wherein such heterosexuality gets normalized. Think, for instance, of one circumstance replayed *ad infinitum* in popular culture and in everyday life: The male partner is supposed to be bigger, never mind older or more educated or higher earning, that is, higher status. Heterosexuality gets institutionalized in male-dominant/female-subordinate ways that also include such commonplaces as males covering the expenses of dates with females.

Gavey's paper ties in with an emergent literature theorizing the absence of women's desires from discourses about sexuality. Gavey alludes to a substantial dimension of that literature when she refers to women's "lack of *obvious* resistance" (p. 209; emphasis added). By problematizing the notion of "consent," as her paper repeatedly does, Gavey points to the multiple ways hegemonic femininity facilitates coercive heterosexuality. Taught to be nice, to please, to think of others' needs, women are scarcely well positioned to register their vehement rejection of unwanted sex. Besides, like the wives in Gordon's study, the women in Gavey's study sometimes find that the conditions of their actual lives make such sex "seem like the best of all possible options. . . ." (p. 213) Gavey indicates that like heterosexuality itself or like wife battering from Gordon's standpoint, desire is a socially constructed constellation. That claim does not imply that in the absence of social conditioning desire would not emerge. It means that without language, discourse, and social structure, desire would be inchoate and inarticulable. It means, then, that those enabling and constraining realities give desire its palpable shape, its lived meanings, and its odds of being acted upon in this or that fashion. The central principle serving as a theoretical hub of Gavey's paper has less to do with desire, however, than with the gendered character of institutionalized heterosexuality. Ultimately, the focus of her theoretical work is the discursive erasure of contested bodies that results from "the gender-specific deployment of sexuality enabl[ing] . . . heterosexual practice which contains much invisible coercion." (p. 212) Yet, as Gavey's closing paragraph indicates, heterosexual women's talk about their sexual experiences can constitute a counterdiscourse signalling resistance to hegemonic definitions of who they can be as heterosexual partners.

Like Gordon and Gavey, Wendi Hadd theorizes the (female) body in terms of the discourses shaping its contestation. Hadd's primary focus is the body as a prospectively reproductive entity that cannot be separated from the rest of the individual. Rejecting the mind/body dualism that pervades debates about reproductive rights, Hadd shows how feminist, medical, scientific, and legal discourses perpetuate that dualism to women's—and ultimately men's—disadvantage. Like heterosexuality, then, reproduction involves a gender-specific deployment centering on the issue of whether or not women have the right to "control their own bodies." We *are* our bodies, Hadd asserts. In her judgment any discourse asserting otherwise reflects a patriarchal, capitalist perspective that commodifies and reifies our bodies. Hadd thus argues against stances that treat the body as a means. Pointing to abortion decisions, surrogate reproduction, genetic engineering, and ultrasound technology, she sketches a social world where the mind/body dualism prevails more often than not.

Hadd's own paper illustrates the difficulties of discursively constructing the body so as to make it other than a container of consciousness, a home for the mind, or a lodging for the brain. Yet she succeeds in alerting us to the retrogressive baggage built into the discourses we mean to constitute as resistant and progressive. Beyond that, she does us the great service of implicitly asking how our dignity as human beings is compromised by the mind/body dualism widely used to keep women in their place and men in ultimate control of that place. As Hadd indicates, ultrasound illustrates a technological incursion into pregnant women's experiences. In line with Gavey's and Gordon's papers one might also add that it provides men "access to a female world from which they have been excluded because of their limited biological role in reproduction."[12] In any case, Hadd treats the very realms where we expect dignity to find ready, not contested, expression. Yet neither pregnancy nor parturition is any longer constructed as such a realm. In that circumstance, Hadd implies, lies a tale of discourse run amok along the same tracks as socially unregulated technologies. Under those circumstances, the integrity of women's experiences is likely to come up against further contestation. In the end, Hadd implies that this section of the book might best be entitled "contested experiences" or "contested integrity" so as not to reproduce the mind/body dualism making the "mother of flesh" a meaningful counterpart of the "father of Reason." (p. 217)

Finally, we come to a form of physical contestation atypical yet instructive, namely, prisoners' contested bodies. Karlene Faith's paper returns us to Goffman's notion of total institutions, and we would do well to recall that his interest in such organizations was to illuminate what ordinary social arrangements must do to protect dignity. Faith's is the only paper in *Multicultural Experiences, Multicultural Theories* that deals with prisoners' situation. In it she links dignity with power and privacy. Noting that prisons employ some "over-institutionalized" staff members, Faith dramatizes "the indignities of extraordinary powerlessness within already-disempowering circumstances." (pp. 224, 225) She implicitly raises questions about the employment of male guards in women's prisons and, more generally, theorizes "control over one's body" in ways that Hadd rejects. Yet one must ask, as Tania Modleski has about anti-essentialist stances, whether rejecting that idiom might be "a luxury open only to the most privileged women."[13] Whether or not that is the case is less important than our continuing awareness that some forms of resistance presuppose social privileges along one or more axes. We must interrogate the typical preconditions of specific sorts of resistance in the interest of showing that not all members are positioned so as to resist in ways you and I might consider the most effective or meaningful.

In any case Faith's attention to self-injurious behavior merits mention inasmuch as it points to a widespread consequence of oppression. Those who are oppressed develop an inferiorized consciousness that typically finds expression in the choices they make, the practices they undertake, and the dreams they entertain about their prospects. Such colonized consciousness is capable of making the oppressed individual an agent of her or his own subordination, and in the extreme that self-denying agency can involve physically damaging or destroying oneself. Internalized oppression involves a great deal more, then, than self-inferiorizing consciousness. It often involves a consciousness disposed toward choices that continue one's subordination, harm one's self, or promote one's destruction. Problematizing such consciousness is thus a *desideratum* for everyone who affirms life and growth over their alternatives. It is also a *desideratum* for theorists intent on disclosing how the matrix of domination shapes consciousness so as to make its victims agents helping to perpetuate that matrix.

NOTES

1 Chris Shilling, *The Body and Social Theory,* Sage Publications, London and Newbury Park, 1993, p. 19.

2 Naomi Scheman, *Engenderings: Constructions of Authority, Knowledge, and Privilege,* Routledge, New York, 1993, p. 88.

3 Erving Goffman, *Relations in Public: Microstudies of the Public Order,* Harper Colophon Books, New York, 1971, pp. 283, 284.

4 Erving Goffman, *Interaction Ritual: Essays on Face-to-Face Behavior,* Anchor Books, New York, 1967, p. 9.

5 *Ibid.,* p. 10; emphasis added.

6 Erving Goffman, *Asylums: Essays on the Social Situation of Mental Patients and Other Inmates,* Anchor Books, New York, 1961, p. 14.

7 *Ibid.,* p. 23.

8 *Ibid.,* pp. 23, 28.

9 Margaret Morganroth Gullette, "What, Menopause Again? A Guide to Cultural Combat," *MS.,* (July/August, 1993), 34, 36.

10 Sherry Ortner, "Is Female to Male as Nature Is to Culture?" in M. Evans (ed.), *The Woman Question,* Fontana Books, London, 1982.

11 See Mindy Stombler, " 'Buddies' or 'Slutties': The Collective Sexual Reputation of Fraternity Little Sisters," *Gender & Society* 8, 3 (September, 1994), 317.

12 Margarete Sandelowski, "Separate, But Less Unequal: Fetal Ultrasonography and the Transformation of Expectant Mother/Fatherhood," *Gender & Society* 8, 2 (June 1994), 230.

13 Tania Modleski, *Feminism Without Women: Culture and Criticism in a "Postfeminist" Age,* Routledge, New York, 1991, p. 22.

Believing Is Seeing: Biology as Ideology

Judith Lorber

Until the eighteenth century, Western philosophers and scientists thought that there was one sex and that women's internal genitalia were the inverse of men's external genitalia: the womb and vagina were the penis and scrotum turned inside out (Lacquer 1990). Current Western thinking sees women and men as so different physically as to sometimes seem two species. The bodies, which have been mapped inside and out for hundreds of years, have not changed. What has changed are the justifications for gender inequality. When the social position of all human beings was believed to be set by natural law or was considered God-given, biology was irrelevant; women and men of different classes all had their assigned places. When scientists began to question the divine basis of social order and replaced faith with empirical knowledge, what they saw was that women were very different from men in that they had wombs and menstruated. Such anatomical differences destined them for an entirely different social life from men.

In actuality, the basic bodily material *is* the same for females and males, and except for procreative hormones and organs, female and male human beings have similar bodies (Naftolin and Butz 1981). Furthermore, as has been known since the middle of the nineteenth century, male and female genitalia develop from the same fetal tissue, and so infants can be born with ambiguous genitalia (Money and Ehrhardt 1972). When they are, biology is used quite arbitrarily in sex assignment. Suzanne Kessler (1990) interviewed six medical specialists in pediatric intersexuality and found that whether an infant with XY chromosomes and anomalous genitalia was categorized as a boy or a girl depended on the size of the penis—if a penis was very small, the child was categorized as a girl, and sex-change surgery was used to make an artificial vagina. In the late nineteenth century, the presence or absence of ovaries was the determining criterion of gender assignment for hermaphrodites because a woman who could not procreate was not a complete woman (Kessler 1990, 20).

Yet in Western societies, we see two discrete sexes and two distinguishable genders because our society is built on two classes of people, "women" and "men." Once the gender category is given, the attributes of the person are also gendered: Whatever a "woman" is has to be "female"; whatever a "man" is has to be "male." Analyzing the social processes that construct the categories we call "female and male," "women and men," and "homosexual and heterosexual" uncovers the ideology and power differentials congealed in these categories (Foucault 1978). This article will use two familiar areas of social life—sports and technological competence—to show how myriad physiological differences are transformed into similar-appearing, gendered social bodies. My perspective goes beyond accepted feminist views that gender is a cultural overlay that modifies physiological sex differences. That perspective assumes either that there are two fairly similar sexes distorted by social practices into two genders with purposefully different characteristics or that there are two sexes whose essential differences are rendered unequal by social practices. I am arguing that bodies differ in many ways physiologically, but they are completely transformed by social practices to fit into the salient categories of a society, the most pervasive of which are "female" and "male" and "women" and "men."

Neither sex nor gender are pure categories. Combinations of incongruous genes, genitalia, and hormonal input are ignored in sex categorization, just as combinations of incongruous physiology, identity, sexuality, appearance, and behavior are ignored in the social construction of gender statuses. Menstruation, lactation, and gestation do not demarcate women from men. Only some women are pregnant and then only some of the time; some women do not have a uterus or ovaries. Some women have stopped menstruating temporarily, others have reached menopause, and some have had hysterectomies. Some women breastfeed some of the time, but some men lactate (Jaggar 1983, 165fn). Menstruation, lactation, and gestation are individual experiences of womanhood (Levesque-Lopman 1988), but not determinants of the social category "woman," or even "female." Similarly, "men are not always sperm-producers, and in fact, not all sperm producers are men. A male-to-female transsexual, prior to surgery, can be socially a woman, though still potentially (or actually) capable of spermatogenesis" (Kessler and Mckenna [1978] 1985, 2).

When gender assignment is contested in sports, where the categories of competitors are rigidly divided into women and men, chromosomes are now used to determine in which category the athlete is to compete. However, an anomaly common enough to be found in several women at every major international sports competition are XY chromosomes that have not produced male anatomy or physiology because of a genetic defect. Because these women are women in every way significant for sports competition, the prestigious International Amateur Athletic Federation has urged that sex be determined by simple genital inspection (Kolata 1992). Transsexuals would pass this test, but it took a lawsuit for Renée Richards, a male-to-female transsexual, to be able to play tournament tennis as a woman, despite his male sex chromosomes (Richards 1983). Oddly, neither basis for gender categorization—chromosomes nor genitalia—has anything to do with sports prowess (Birrell and Cole 1990).

In the Olympics, in cases of chromosomal ambiguity, women must undergo "a battery of gynecological and physical exams to see if she is 'female enough' to compete. Men are not tested" (Carlson 1991, 26). The purpose is not to categorize women and men accurately, but to make sure men don't enter women's competitions, where, it is felt, they will have the advantage of size and strength. This practice sounds fair only because it is assumed that all men are similar in size and strength and different from all women. Yet in Olympics boxing and wrestling matches, men are matched within weight classes. Some women might similarly successfully compete with some men in many sports. Women did not run in marathons until about twenty years ago. In twenty years of marathon competition, women have reduced their finish times by more than one-and-one-half hours; they are expected to run as fast as men in that race by 1998 and might catch up with men's running times in races of other lengths within the next 50 years because they are increasing their fastest speeds more rapidly than are men (Fausto-Sterling 1985, 213–18).

The reliance on only two sex and gender categories in the biological and social sciences is as epistemologically spurious as the reliance on chromosomal or genital tests to group athletes. Most research designs do not investigate whether physical skills or physical abilities are really more or less common in women and men (Epstein 1988). They start out with two social categories ("women," "men"), assume they are biologically different ("female," "male"), look for similarities among them and differences between them, and attribute what they have found for the social categories to sex differences (Gelman, Collman, and Maccoby 1986). These designs rarely question the categorization of their subjects into two and only two groups, even though they often find more significant within-group differences than between-group differences (Hyde 1990). The social construction perspective on sex and gender suggests that instead of starting with the two presumed dichotomies in each category—female, male; woman, man—it might be more useful in gender studies to group patterns of behavior and only then look for identifying markers of the people likely to enact such behaviors.

WHAT SPORTS ILLUSTRATE

Competitive sports have become, for boys and men, as players and as spectators, a way of constructing a masculine identity, a legitimated outlet for violence and aggression, and an avenue for upward mobility (Dunning 1986; Kemper 1990, 167–206; Messner 1992). For men in Western societies, physical competence is an important marker of masculinity (Fine 1987; Glassner 1992; Majors 1990). In professional and collegiate sports, physiological differences are invoked to justify women's secondary status, despite the clear evidence that gender status overrides physiological capabilities. Assumptions about women's physiology have influenced rules of competition; subsequent sports performances then validate how women and men are treated in sports competitions.

Gymnastic equipment is geared to slim, wiry, prepubescent girls and not to mature women; conversely, men's gymnastic equipment is tailored for muscular, mature men, not slim, wiry prepubescent boys. Boys could compete with girls, but are not allowed to; women gymnasts are left out entirely. Girl gymnasts are just that—little girls who will be disqualified as soon as they grow up (Vecsey 1990). Men gymnasts have men's status. In women's basketball, the size of the ball and rules for handling the ball change the style of play to "a slower, less intense, and less exciting modification of the 'regular' or men's game" (Watson 1987, 441). In the 1992 Winter Olympics, men figure skaters were required to complete three triple jumps in their required program; women figure skaters were forbidden to do more than *one*. These rules penalized artistic men skaters and athletic women skaters (Janofsky 1992). For the most part, Western sports are built on physically trained men's bodies:

> Speed, size, and strength seem to be the essence of sports. Women *are* naturally inferior at "sports" so conceived.
> But if women had been the historically dominant sex, our concept of sport would no doubt have evolved differently. Competitions emphasizing flexibility, balance, strength, timing, and small size might dominate Sunday afternoon television and offer salaries in six figures. (English 1982, 266, emphasis in original)

Organized sports are big businesses and, thus, who has access and at what level is a distributive or equity issue. The overall status of women and men athletes is an economic, political, and ideological issue that has less to do with individual physiological capabilities than with their cultural and social meaning and who defines and profits from them (Messner and Sabo 1990; Slatton and Birrell 1984). Twenty years after the passage of Title IX of the U.S. Civil Rights Act, which forbade gender inequality in any school receiving federal funds, the *goal* for collegiate sports in the next five years is 60 percent men, 40 percent women in sports participation, scholarships, and funding (Moran 1992).

How access and distribution of rewards (prestigious and financial) are justified is an ideological, even moral, issue (Birrell 1988, 473–76; Hargreaves 1982). One way is that men athletes are glorified and women athletes ignored in the mass media. Messner and his colleagues found that in 1989, in TV sports news in the United States, men's sports got 92 percent of the coverage and women's sports 5 percent, with the rest mixed or gender-neutral (Messner, Duncan, and Jensen 1993). In 1990, in four of the top-selling newspapers in the United States, stories on men's sports outnumbered those on women's sports 23 to 1. Messner and his colleagues also found an implicit hierarchy in naming, with women athletes most likely to be called by first names, followed by Black men athletes, and only white men athletes routinely referred to by their last names. Similarly, women's collegiate sports teams are named or marked in ways that symbolically feminize and trivialize them—the men's team is called Tigers, the women's Kittens (Eitzen and Baca Zinn 1989).

Assumptions about men's and women's bodies and their capacities are crafted in ways that make unequal access and distribution of rewards acceptable (Hudson 1978; Messner 1988). Media images of modern men athletes glorify their strength and power, even their violence (Hargreaves 1986). Media images of modern women athletes tend to focus on feminine beauty and grace (so they are not really athletes) or on their thin, small, wiry androgynous bodies (so they are not really women). In coverage of the Olympics,

> loving and detailed attention is paid to pixie-like gymnasts; special and extended coverage is given to graceful and dazzling figure skaters; the camera painstakingly records the fluid movements of swimmers and divers. And then, in a blinding flash of fragmented images, viewers see a few minutes of volleyball, basketball, speed skating, track and field, and alpine skiing, as television gives its nod to the mere existence of these events. (Boutilier and SanGiovanni 1983, 190)

Extraordinary feats by women athletes who were presented as mature adults might force sports organizers and audiences to rethink their stereotypes of women's capabilities, the way elves, mermaids, and ice queens do not. Sports, therefore, construct men's bodies to be powerful; women's bodies to be sexual. As Connell says,

> The meanings in the bodily sense of masculinity concern, above all else, the superiority of men to women, and the exaltation of hegemonic masculinity over other groups of men which is essential for the domination of women. (1987, 85)

In the late 1970s, as women entered more and more athletic competitions, supposedly good scientific studies showed that women who exercised intensely would cease menstruating because they would not have enough body fat to sustain ovulation (Brozan 1978). When one set of researchers did a yearlong study that compared 66 women—21 who were training for a marathon, 22 who ran more than an hour a week, and 23 who did less than an hour of aerobic exercise a week—they discovered that only 20 percent of the women in any of these groups had "normal" menstrual cycles every month (Prior et al. 1990). The dangers of intensive training for women's fertility therefore were exaggerated as women began to compete successfully in arenas formerly closed to them.

Given the association of sports with masculinity in the United States, women athletes have to manage a contradictory status. One study of women college basketball players found that although they "did athlete" on the court—"pushing, shoving, fouling, hard running, fast breaks, defense, obscenities and sweat" (Watson 1987, 441), they "did woman" off the court, using the locker room as their staging area:

> While it typically took fifteen minutes to prepare for the game, it took approximately fifteen minutes after the game to shower and remove the sweat of an athlete, *and* it took another thirty minutes to dress, apply make-up and style hair. It did not seem to matter whether the players were going out into the public or getting on a van for a long ride home. Average dressing time and rituals did not change. (Watson 1987, 443)

Another way women manage these status dilemmas is to redefine the activity or its result as feminine or womanly (Mangan and Park 1987). Thus women bodybuilders claim that "flex appeal is sex appeal" (Duff and Hong 1984, 378).

Such a redefinition of women's physicality affirms the ideological subtext of sports that physical strength is men's prerogative and justifies men's physical and sexual domination of women (Hargreaves 1986; Messner 1992, 164–72; Olson 1990; Theberge 1987; Willis 1982). When women demonstrate physical strength, they are labeled unfeminine:

> It's threatening to one's takeability, one's rapeability, one's femininity, to be strong and physically self-possessed. To be able to resist rape, not to communicate rapeability with one's body, to hold one's body for uses and meanings other than that can transform what *being a woman means.* (MacKinnon 1987, 122, emphasis in original)

Resistance to that transformation, ironically, was evident in the policies of American women physical education professionals throughout most of the twentieth century. They minimized exertion, maximized a feminine appearance and manner, and left organized sports competition to men (Birrell 1988, 461–62; Mangan and Park 1987).

DIRTY LITTLE SECRETS

As sports construct gendered bodies, technology constructs gendered skills. Meta-analysis of studies of gender differences in spatial and mathematical ability have found that men have a large advantage in ability to mentally rotate an image, a moderate advantage in a visual perception of horizontality and verticality and in mathematical performance, and a small advantage in ability to pick a figure out of a field (Hyde 1990). It could be argued that these advantages explain why, within the short space of time that computers have become ubiquitous in offices, schools, and homes, work on them and with them has become gendered: Men create, program, and market computers, make war and produce science and art with them; women microwire them in computer factories and enter data in computerized offices; boys play games, socialize, and commit crimes with computers; girls are rarely seen in computer clubs, camps, and classrooms. But women were hired as computer programmers in the 1940s because

> the work seemed to resemble simple clerical tasks. In fact, however, programming demanded complex skills in abstract logic, mathematics, electrical circuitry, and machinery, all of which . . . women used to perform in their work. Once programming was recognized as "intellectually demanding," it became attractive to men. (Donato 1990, 170)

A woman mathematician and pioneer in data processing, Grace M. Hopper, was famous for her work on programming language (Perry and Greber 1990, 86). By the 1960s, programming was split into more and less skilled specialties, and the entry of women into the computer field in the 1970s and 1980s was confined to the lower-paid specialties. At each stage, employers invoked women's and men's purportedly natural capabilities for the jobs for which they were hired (Cockburn 1983, 1985; Donato 1990; Hartmann 1987; Hartmann, Kraut, and Tilly 1986; Kramer and Lehman 1990; Wright et al. 1987; Zimmerman 1983).

It is the taken-for-grantedness of such everyday gendered behavior that gives credence to the belief that the widespread differences in what women and men do must come from biology. To take one ordinarily unremarked scenario: In modern societies, if a man and woman who are a couple are in a car together, he is much more likely to take the wheel than she is, even if she is the more competent driver. Molly Haskell calls this taken-for-granted phenomenon "the dirty little secret of marriage: the husband-lousy-driver syndrome" (1989, 26). Men drive cars whether they are good drivers or not because men and machines are a "natural" combination (Scharff 1991). But the ability to drive gives one mobility; it is a form of social power.

In the early days of the automobile, feminists co-opted the symbolism of mobility as emancipation: "Donning goggles and dusters, wielding tire irons and tool kits, taking the wheel, they announced their intention to move beyond the bounds of women's place" (Scharff 1991, 68). Driving enabled them to campaign for women's suffrage in parts of the United States not served by public transportation, and they effectively used motorcades and speaking from cars as campaign tactics (Scharff 1991, 67–88). Sandra Gilbert also notes that during World War I, women's ability to drive was physically, mentally, and even sensually liberating:

> For nurses and ambulance drivers, women doctors and women messengers, the phenomenon of modern battle was very different from that experienced by entrenched combatants. Finally given a chance to take the wheel, these post-Victorian girls raced motorcars along foreign roads like adventurers exploring new lands, while their brothers dug deeper into the mud of France. . . . Retrieving the wounded and the dead from deadly positions, these once-decorous daughters had at last been allowed to prove their valor, and they swooped over the wastelands of the war with the energetic love of Wagnerian Valkyries,

their mobility alone transporting countless immobilized heroes to safe havens. (1983, 438–39)

Not incidentally, women in the United States and England got the vote for their war efforts in World War I.

SOCIAL BODIES AND THE BATHROOM PROBLEM

People of the same racial ethnic group and social class are roughly the same size and shape—but there are many varieties of bodies. People have different genitalia, different secondary sex characteristics, different contributions to procreation, different orgasmic experiences, different patterns of illness and aging. Each of us experiences our bodies differently, and these experiences change as we grow, age, sicken, and die. The bodies of pregnant and nonpregnant women, short and tall people, those with intact and functioning limbs and those whose bodies are physically challenged are all different. But the salient categories of a society group these attributes in ways that ride roughshod over individual experiences and more meaningful clusters of people.

I am not saying that physical differences between male and female bodies don't exist, but that these differences are socially meaningless until social practices transform them into social facts. West Point Military Academy's curriculum is designed to produce leaders, and physical competence is used as a significant measure of leadership ability (Yoder 1989). When women were accepted as West Point cadets, it became clear that the tests of physical competence, such as rapidly scaling an eight-foot wall, had been constructed for male physiques—pulling oneself up and over using upper-body strength. Rather than devise tests of physical competence for women, West Point provided boosters that mostly women used—but that lost them test points—in the case of the wall, a platform. Finally, the women themselves figured out how to use their bodies successfully. Janice Yoder describes this situation:

> I was observing this obstacle one day, when a woman approached the wall in the old prescribed way, got her fingertips grip, and did an unusual thing: she walked her dangling legs up the wall until she was in a position where both her hands and feet were atop the wall. She then simply pulled up her sagging bottom and went over. She solved the problem by capitalizing on one of women's physical assets: lower-body strength. (1989, 530)

In short, if West Point is going to measure leadership capability by physical strength, women's pelvises will do just as well as men's shoulders.

The social transformation of female and male physiology into a condition of inequality is well illustrated by the bathroom problem. Most buildings that have gender-segregated bathrooms have an equal number for women and for men. Where there are crowds, there are always long lines in front of women's bathrooms but rarely in front of men's bathrooms. The cultural, physiological, and demographic combinations of clothing, frequency of urination, menstruation, and child care add up to generally greater bathroom use by women than men. Thus, although an equal number of bathrooms seems fair, equity would mean more women's bathrooms or allowing women to use men's bathrooms for a certain amount of time (Molotch 1988).

The bathroom problem is the outcome of the way gendered bodies are differentially evaluated in Western cultures: Men's social bodies are the measure of what is "human." Gray's *Anatomy,* in use for 100 years, well into the twentieth century, presented the human body as male. The female body was shown only where it differed from the male (Laqueur 1990, 166–67). Denise Riley says that if we envisage women's bodies, men's bodies, and human bodies "as a triangle of identifications, then it is rarely an equilateral triangle in which both sexes are pitched at matching distances from the apex of the human" (1988, 197). Catharine MacKinnon also contends that in Western society, universal "humanness" is male because

> virtually every quality that distinguishes men from women is already affirmatively compensated in this society. Men's physiology defines most sports, their needs define auto and health insurance coverage, their socially defined biographies define workplace expectations and successful career patterns, their perspectives and concerns define quality in scholarship, their experiences and obsessions define merit, their objectification of life defines art, their military service defines citizenship, their presence defines family, their inability to get along with each other—their wars and rulerships—define history, their image defines god, and their genitals define sex. For each of their differences from women, what amounts to an affirmative action plan is in effect, otherwise known as the structure and values of American society. (1987, 36)

THE PARADOX OF HUMAN NATURE

Gendered people do not emerge from physiology or hormones but from the exigencies of the social order, mostly, from the need for a reliable division of the work of food production and the social (not physical) reproduction of new members. The moral imperatives of religion and cultural representations reinforce the boundary lines among genders and ensure that what is demanded, what is permitted, and what is tabooed for the people in each gender is well-known and followed by most. Political power, control of scarce resources, and, if necessary, violence uphold the gendered social order in the face of resistance and rebellion. Most people, however, voluntarily go along with their society's prescriptions for those of their gender status because the norms and expectations get built into their sense of worth and identity as a certain kind of human being and because they believe their society's way is the natural way. These beliefs emerge from the imagery that pervades the way we think, the way we see and hear and speak, the way we fantasize, and the way we feel. There is no core or bedrock human nature below these endlessly looping processes of the social production of sex and gender, self and other, identity and psyche, each of which is a "complex cultural construction" (Butler 1990, 36). The paradox of "human nature" is that it is *always* a manifestation of cultural meanings, social relationships, and power politics—"not biology, but culture, becomes destiny" (Butler 1990, 8).

Feminist inquiry has long questioned the conventional categories of social science, but much of the current work in feminist sociology has not gone beyond adding the universal category "women" to the universal category "men." Our current debates over the global assumptions of only two categories and the insistence that they must be nuanced to include race and class are steps in the direction I would like to see feminist research go, but race and class are *also* global categories (Collins 1990; Spelman 1988). Deconstructing sex, sexuality, and gender reveals many possible categories embedded in the social experiences and social practices of what Dorothy Smith calls the "everyday/everynight world" (1990, 31–57). These emergent categories group some people together for comparison with other people without prior assumptions about who is like whom. Categories can be broken up and people regrouped differently into new categories for comparison. This process of discovering categories from similarities and differences in people's behavior or responses can be more meaningful for feminist research than discovering similarities and differences between "females" and "males" or "women" and "men" because the social construction of the conventional sex and gender categories already assumes differences between them and similarities among them. When we rely only on the conventional categories of sex and gender, we end up finding what we looked for—we see what we believe, whether it is that "females" and "males" are essentially different or that "women" and "men" are essentially the same.

REFERENCES

Birrell, Susan J. 1988. Discourses on the gender/sport relationship: From women in sport to gender relations. In *Exercise and sport science reviews.* Vol. 16, edited by Kent Pandolf. New York: Macmillan.

Birrell, Susan J., and Sheryl L. Cole. 1990. Double fault: Renée Richards and the construction and naturalization of difference. *Sociology of Sport Journal* 7:1–21.

Boutilier, Mary A., and Lucinda SanGiovanni. 1983. *The sporting woman.* Champaign, IL: Human Kinetics.

Brozan, Nadine. 1978. Training linked to disruption of female reproductive cycle. *New York Times,* 17 April.

Butler, Judith. 1990. *Gender trouble: Feminism and the subversion of identity.* New York and London: Routledge & Kegan Paul.

Carlson, Alison. 1991. When is a woman not a woman? *Women's Sport and Fitness* March:24–29.

Cockburn, Cynthia. 1983. *Brothers: Male dominance and technological change.* London: Pluto.

———. 1985. *Machinery of dominance: Women, men and technical know-how.* London: Pluto.

Collins, Patricia Hill. 1990. *Black feminist thought: Knowledge, consciousness, and the politics of empowerment.* Boston: Unwin Hyman.

Connell, R. W. 1987. *Gender and power.* Stanford, CA: Stanford University Press.

Donato, Katharine M. 1990. Programming for change? The growing demand for women systems analysts. In *Job queues, gender queues: Explaining women's inroads into male occupations,* written and edited by Barbara F. Reskin and Patricia A. Roos. Philadelphia: Temple University Press.

Duff, Robert W., and Lawrence K. Hong, 1984. Self-images of women bodybuilders. *Sociology of Sport Journal* 2:374–80.

Dunning, Eric. 1986. Sport as a male preserve: Notes on the social sources of masculine identity and its transformations. *Theory, Culture and Society* 3:79–90.

Eitzen, D. Stanley, and Maxine Baca Zinn. 1989. The deathleticization of women: The naming and gender marking of collegiate sport teams. *Sociology of Sport Journal* 6:362–70.

English, Jane. 1982. Sex equality in sports. In *Femininity, masculinity, and androgyny,* edited by Mary Vetterling-Braggin. Boston: Littlefield, Adams.

Epstein, Cynthia Fuchs. 1988. *Deceptive distinctions: Sex, gender and the social order.* New Haven, CT: Yale University Press.

Fausto-Sterling, Anne. 1985. *Myths of gender: Biological theories about women and men.* New York: Basic Books.

Fine, Gary Alan. 1987. *With the boys: Little League baseball and preadolescent culture.* Chicago: University of Chicago Press.

Foucault, Michel. 1978. *The history of sexuality: An introduction.* Translated by Robert Hurley. New York: Pantheon.

Gelman, Susan A., Pamela Collman, and Eleanor E. Maccoby. 1986. Inferring properties from categories versus inferring categories from properties: The case of gender. *Child Development* 57:396–404.

Gilbert, Sandra M. 1983. Soldier's heart: Literary men, literary women, and the Great War. *Signs: Journal of Women in Culture and Society* 8:422–50.

Glassner, Barry. 1992. Men and muscles. In *Men's lives,* edited by Michael S. Kimmel and Michael A. Messner. New York: Macmillan.

Hargreaves, Jennifer A., ed. 1982. *Sport, culture, and ideology.* London: Routledge & Kegan Paul.

———. 1986. Where's the virtue? Where's the grace? A discussion of the social production of gender relations in and through sport. *Theory, Culture, and Society* 3:109–21.

Hartmann, Heidi I., ed. 1987. *Computer chips and paper clips: Technology and women's employment.* Vol. 2. Washington, DC: National Academy Press.

Hartmann, Heidi I., Robert E. Kraut, and Louise A. Tilly, eds. 1986. *Computer chips and paper clips: Technology and women's employment.* Vol. 1. Washington, DC: National Academy Press.

Haskell, Molly. 1989. Hers: He drives me crazy. *New York Times Magazine,* 24 September, 26, 28.

Hudson, Jackie. 1978. Physical parameters used for female exclusion from law enforcement and athletics. In *Women and sport: From myth to reality,* edited by Carole A. Oglesby. Philadelphia: Lea and Febiger.

Hyde, Janet Shibley. 1990. Meta-analysis and the psychology of gender differences. *Signs: Journal of Women in Culture and Society* 16:55–73.

Jaggar, Alison M. 1983. *Feminist politics and human nature.* Totowa, NJ: Rowman & Allanheld.

Janofsky, Michael. 1992. Yamaguchi has the delicate and golden touch. *New York Times,* 22 February.

Kemper, Theodore D. 1990. *Social structure and testosterone: Explorations of the socio-bio-social chain.* Brunswick, NJ: Rutgers University Press.

Kessler, Suzanne J. 1990. The medical construction of gender: Case management of intersexed infants. *Signs: Journal of Women in Culture and Society* 16:3–26.

Kessler, Suzanne J., and Wendy McKenna. [1978] 1985. *Gender: An ethnomethodological approach.* Chicago: University of Chicago Press.

Kolata, Gina. 1992. Track federation urges end to gene test for femaleness. *New York Times,* 12 February.

Kramer, Pamela E., and Sheila Lehman. 1990. Mismeasuring women: A critique of research on computer ability and avoidance. *Signs: Journal of Women in Culture and Society* 16:158–72.

Laqueur, Thomas. 1990. *Making sex: Body and gender from the Greeks to Freud.* Cambridge, MA: Harvard University Press.

Levesque-Lopman, Louise. 1988. *Claiming reality: Phenomenology and women's experience.* Totowa, NJ: Rowman & Littlefield.

MacKinnon, Catharine. 1987. *Feminism unmodified.* Cambridge, MA: Harvard University Press.

Majors, Richard. 1990. Cool pose: Black masculinity in sports. In *Sport, men, and the gender order: Critical feminist perspectives,* edited by Michael A. Messner and Donald F. Sabo. Champaign, IL: Human Kinetics.

Mangan, J. A., and Roberta J. Park. 1987. *From fair sex to feminism: Sport and the socialization of women in the industrial and post-industrial eras.* London: Frank Cass.

Messner, Michael A. 1988. Sports and male domination: The female athlete as contested ideological terrain. *Sociology of Sport Journal* 5:197–211.

———. 1992. *Power at play: Sports and the problem of masculinity.* Boston: Beacon Press.

Messner, Michael A., Margaret Carlisle Duncan, and Kerry Jensen. 1993. Separating the men from the girls: The gendered language of televised sports. *Gender & Society* 7:121–37.

Messner, Michael A., and Donald F. Sabo, eds. 1990. *Sport, men, and the gender order: Critical feminist perspectives.* Champaign, IL: Human Kinetics.

Molotch, Harvey. 1988. The restroom and equal opportunity. *Sociological Forum* 3:128–32.

Money, John, and Anke A. Ehrhardt. 1972. *Man & woman, boy & girl.* Baltimore, MD: Johns Hopkins University Press.

Moran, Malcolm. 1992. Title IX: A 20-year search for equity. *New York Times* Sports Section, 21, 22, 23 June.

Naftolin, F., and E. Butz, eds. 1981. Sexual dimorphism. *Science* 211:1263–1324.

Olson, Wendy. 1990. Beyond Title IX: Toward an agenda for women and sports in the 1990s. *Yale Journal of Law and Feminism* 3:105–51.

Perry, Ruth, and Lisa Greber. 1990. Women and computers: An introduction. *Signs: Journal of Women in Culture and Society* 16:74–101.

Prior, Jerilynn C., Yvette M. Yigna, Martin T. Shechter, and Arthur E. Burgess. 1990. Spinal bone loss and ovulatory disturbances. *New England Journal of Medicine* 323:1221–27.

Richards, Renée, with Jack Ames. 1983. *Second serve.* New York: Stein and Day.

Riley, Denise. 1988. *Am I that name? Feminism and the category of women in history.* Minneapolis: University of Minnesota Press.

Scharff, Virginia. 1991. *Taking the wheel: Women and the coming of the motor age.* New York: Free Press.

Slatton, Bonnie, and Susan Birrell. 1984. The politics of women's sport. *Arena Review* 8.

Smith, Dorothy E. 1990. *The conceptual practices of power: A feminist sociology of knowledge.* Toronto: University of Toronto Press.

Spelman, Elizabeth. 1988. *Inessential woman: Problems of exclusion in feminist thought.* Boston: Beacon Press.

Theberge, Nancy. 1987. Sport and women's empowerment. *Women's Studies International Forum* 10:387–93.

Vecsey, George. 1990. Cathy Rigby, unlike Peter, did grow up. *New York Times* Sports Section, 19 December.

Watson, Tracey. 1987. Women athletes and athletic women: The dilemmas and contradictions of managing incongruent identities. *Sociological Inquiry* 57:431–46.

Willis, Paul. 1982. Women in sport in ideology. In *Sport, culture, and ideology,* edited by Jennifer A. Hargreaves. London: Routledge & Kegan Paul.

Wright, Barbara Drygulski et al., eds. 1987. *Women, work, and technology: Transforma-tions.* Ann Arbor: University of Michigan Press.

Yoder, Janice D. 1989. Women at West Point: Lessons for token women in male-dominated occupations. In *Women: A feminist perspective,* edited by Jo Freeman. 4th ed. Palo Alto, CA: Mayfield.

Zimmerman, Jan, ed. 1983. *The technological woman: Interfacing with tomorrow.* New York: Praeger.

Women's Agency, Social Control, and "Rights" Among Battered Women

Linda Gordon

The very "discovery" or invention of family violence in the 1870s was conditioned by the women's rights movement. The identification of child abuse as a problem was a part of a discourse that condemned corporal punishment and opened the family and "home" to scrutiny. This women's movement contained a substantial campaign against wife beating, a campaign that has been underestimated because it produced no separate organizations and operated largely from within a discourse about temperance, voluntary motherhood, and social purity (Pleck 1983). The image of the beaten wife, the indirect victim of drink, was prominent in temperance rhetoric from the 1830s. In the later half of the century, particularly in the work of the Women's Christian Temperance Union, drinking was a veritable code word for male violence (Nadelhaft n.d.; Bordin 1981:162; Epstein 1981:114). The child protectors were usually temperance advocates who considered family violence the inevitable result of drink. Putting a temperance frame around criticisms of male behavior allowed feminists to score points obliquely, without attacking marriage or men in general. Male brutality, not male tyranny, was the target. The problem came from exceptional, "depraved" men, not from the male sex in general. Nevertheless, temperance agitation made drunkenness a gendered voice—male—and its victims quintessentially female. Considered as a veil thrown over challenges to male supremacy, temperance was a thin cloth indeed.

Another frame in which shocking narratives about wife beating were told was the feminist campaign for divorce. Feminist divorce advocates actually harped more on marital rape (although they did not use this term but rather discussed brutality and "excessive demands") than they did on wife beating, probably because they believed the latter had remedies in criminal law, while the former had none. Women's rights leaders publicized particular cases, usually those whose victims were of high social standing or popular appeal. Feminists sheltered runaway wives, agitated in divorce and child-custody cases, and held a few public meetings about egregious cases (DuBois 1981:95; Pleck 1983).

Women's rights advocates also agitated against wife beating in the context of child-raising discourse. Elizabeth Cady Stanton (DuBois 1981:95) summed up a common view when she said that "the condition of the child always follows that of the mother."

Mothers of any properly operating families were not conceived to have interests separate from, let alone antithetical to, those of their children. Damage to one was damage to both.

The very feminists who talked of women's right to vote, the right of married women to own property, and women's right to an education spoke less often and less militantly of women's rights vis-à-vis their husbands. The voluntary motherhood slogan called for women to be able to refuse their husbands sexually because involuntary sex was immoral, unnatural, and produced inferior babies, yet there was little talk resembling what we would today call reproductive rights. When feminists condemned wife beating, they did so in a chivalric mode, positioning women as vulnerable and men who would abuse their wives as monstrous and depraved, lacking in true manhood. Some spoke of a woman's "ownership" of her body but not of her right to freedom from violence (Gordon 1990).

By the end of the nineteenth century the public discourse surrounding wife abuse showed significant feminist effect, although that influence cannot be accurately measured by suffrage or other legal reforms. Contrary to some common misconceptions, wife beating became radically delegitimated in the middle classes during the century; it was not generally accepted as a husband's prerogative but regarded as a disreputable, seamy practice (Pleck 1979). And despite the fact that reformers avoided the language of women's rights, by the 1870s courts commonly denied men the right to physically chastise wives (Gordon 1988b:255, 364n.).

VICTIM'S DISCOURSE

If wife beating was not widely considered legitimate, neither was public discussion of it. Most feminists as well as more conservative moralists preferred that it remain a hidden, euphemistic, or at least whispered subject, and this preference characterized the child protectors as well. At times they may not have "heard" women's complaints of abuse, which in turn forced clients who sought help from them to find a language they would hear. At other times, however, case records show female clients reluctant to see themselves as abused when the social workers offered that construction of their family life. This reluctance is common still today, as women who are stuck with abusive men may understand that their lives only become harder if they name themselves victims, so many may prefer to deny the abuse. Perhaps more important, or at least more evident in the case records, many of these clients rejected a view of themselves as victims and preferred to present themselves as strong.

The class and cultural differences between poor immigrant clients and social workers may have affected their differing views of marital abuse. Most preindustrial communities had tolerated a male privilege to hit ("punish") wives. This does not mean that prior to modern feminism women never objected to or resisted beating. Perhaps the best way for us to understand this traditional "tolerance" of wife beating is as a tense compromise between male supremacy and female resistance in a system which rested to a great extent on mutual interest in cooperation between men and women. Communities had standards as to what constituted excessive violence. Recently, such notions as the "rule of thumb"—that a man might not use a stick thicker than his thumb to beat his wife—

have been cited as evidence of women's total humiliation and powerlessness. On the contrary, such regulation was evidence of a degree of women's power, albeit enforceable mainly through the willingness of others to defend it. But women often had allies within a patriarchal community. If that much abused word *patriarchy* is to have any usefulness, it must be employed to describe a system larger than any individual family, a system that requires regulation even of its privileged members. While patriarchal fathers could control their households, they in turn were subject to sanctions—social control—by the community, whose power brokers included not only fellow patriarchs but women, particularly senior women. The agency clients were accustomed to appealing to fathers as well as mothers, brothers as well as sisters and friends, for support against abusive husbands.

Nevertheless, in the nineteenth and early twentieth centuries, many women clients did not seem to believe they were entitled to freedom from physical violence. When social workers expressed disgust at the way they were treated, the clients sometimes considered that reaction naïve. They spoke of the inevitability of male violence. Their refusal to condemn marital violence in moral terms must be interpreted carefully; it did not mean that they were fatalistic about beatings. They often resisted assault by fighting back, running away, attempting to embarrass the men in front of others, and calling the police or other authorities. And they expressed moral outrage if the men crossed some border of tolerability. There is no contradiction here. Traditional societies tended to have few absolute individual entitlements but many overlapping, even competing social rights. The exact measure of any individual's or group's exercise of traditional prerogatives was determined by conflict and bargaining. Because the client women did not conduct a head-on challenge to their husbands' right to hit them does not mean they liked being hit or believed that their virtue required accepting it. Failure to make this distinction is the result of flat and ahistorical conceptions of what patriarchy and female subordination have been like. There was no society in which women so "internalized" their inferiority, to use a modern explanation, that they did not try to improve their situation. All systems of domination—gender, class, race, wage labor, slave—are systems of conflict.

In the last thirty years of the study, after about 1930, a new tactic was discernable [sic] in women's struggles against abusive men and women's complaints to social workers. This new discourse claimed an entitlement to *absolute* freedom from physical molestation and was grounded in terms of a "right." In the context of this particular study—dealings with social work agencies—this new discourse means that clients felt entitled to ask for help in leaving their abusive marriages. This was a claim women began making only when they had some reasonable expectation that they could win; until then, strategies other than head-on confrontation with a husband's prerogatives were more effective. Furthermore, this rights claim expressed the erosion of certain other forms of protections that had been characteristic of more patriarchal societies.

Women's invention of a right not to be beaten came from a dialectic between changing social possibilities and aspirations. When women's best hope was their husbands' kindness, because they were economically dependent on marriage, they did not protest violations of their individual rights but rested their case on their importance as mothers. One might categorize this earlier discourse about marital abuse as a kind of social "needs" talk (Fraser 1990). Women appealed to social necessity, for example, women's importance in raising healthy, disciplined children, as the reason wife beating was bad. As women's possibilities expanded to include wage earning, remarriage after divorce, some control of child-bearing, and aid to single mothers, women's best hopes escalated to focus on their own, individual aspirations, including escape from marital violence altogether.

For example, in the earlier decades of this study, several women clients complained bitterly about their husbands' obscene language and its effect on children. A 1916 wife who had left her husband agreed that she would "keep his house if he would treat her respectfully and use decent language before the chn" (case 3,646).[1] A 1920 mother thought her husband's "dirty mouth" was "the hardest thing we have to bear in this house, harder even than [his] not working" (case 3,240).

By far the most striking and consistent women's complaint, however, until the 1930s, focused on husbands' nonsupport rather than abuse. Nonsupport cases involved married women whose husbands did not adequately provide for them, for reasons that might include unemployment, illness, drunkenness, hostility, or negligence. In 1910 a mother who was permanently crippled by her husband's beatings, who had appeared to the police and her priest so badly bruised that they advised her to have him arrested, complained to the MSPCC only about his failure to provide (case 2,027). In 1901 a young mother complained only about nonsupport; yet the abuse discovered was so severe that an MSPCC agent began making secret plans to sneak the mother and two children out of the house after the father had gone off to work (case 3,363).

The emphasis so many women placed on nonsupport does not necessarily mean that they considered it more unbearable than beating. Rather, they had strategic reasons for their claims. First, in approaching child-saving agencies, they knew they had to present evidence of mistreatment of children, not just of themselves. Some women apparently calculated that foul language and nonsupport were violations of norms of child raising that social control agents could be expected to defend. Second, they may have believed, and with a great deal of evidence, that nonsupport was more criminal and actionable to social workers and courts than wife beating. They themselves likely felt more entitled to support than to bodily integrity. They believed that they had a claim on the community, as represented by the social work agencies, for their support by husbands, but not to protection from physical violence in marriage. (Although court precedents against wife beating had been established, these precedents did not necessarily prevail in the lower courts; also, likelihood of conviction was high only in egregious cases or ones that included nonsupport or intemperance.)

Without directly challenging male authority, women tried to get social control agencies to support their bids for autonomy. An 1893 wife complained she had left her husband "with his permission," but that later he broke his word (case 1,040). In 1917 a wife and children were beaten for not fulfilling the father's work demands, but the woman complained only about his demands, not about the beatings. She asked the case workers to persuade him to take in fewer boarders, as the work was too much for her. Her logic differed from that of the agency, which was willing to investigate the violence but told her that the "agency was not in [the] business" of regulating his labor demands (case 2,523).

Surprisingly, women's direct complaints to agencies about wife beating grew in number just as feminism was at its nadir. In this study the 1930s form a divide after which the majority of women clients complained directly rather than indirectly about wife beating, and after which the records increasingly show formulations about rights and willingness to press criminal charges. In 1934, for example, a young mother of three, married through a matchmaker at age sixteen to an Italian-born man, repeatedly made assault and battery complaints against him. He too was also a nonsupporter, but her logic differed from that of earlier clients, and it was the beatings that appeared to her actionable. This American-born woman was much younger than her immigrant husband, and she may have had less patriarchal expectations than average among the largely immigrant family-violence clients. Her husband's probation officer described her as a "high-type Italian," and the case worker thought she expected "people to do things for her" (case 4,007A). Women continued to allege child abuse in order to get agency help, but in the ensuing investigations they protected about their own abuse more strongly than previously. One MSPCC agent complained in 1940 that the mother was not really very interested in her son's problems but only wanted to talk about herself (case 4,584).

In other cases that year women rationalized their battering in new ways—not as an inevitable part of the female condition or the male nature, but as something they individually deserved. One woman said, "This is my punishment for marrying against my mo.'s wishes" (case 4,284). Thus even in their self-blaming they expressed a new sensibility that wife beating should not be the inevitable lot of women.

Wife-beating accusations stand out still more because of the virtual disappearance of nonsupport complaints, even in the midst of the Great Depression. This striking inverse correlation between nonsupport and wife-beating complaints stimulates an economistic hypothesis: economic dependence prevented women's formulation of a sense of entitlement to protection against marital violence, but it also gave them a sense of entitlement to support; by contrast, the growth of a wage labor economy, bringing unemployment, transience, and dispersal of kinfolk, deprived women of a certainty that they could get support from their husbands, but allowed them to insist on their physical integrity. It is a reasonable hypothesis that the Depression, by the leveling impact of its widespread unemployment, actually encouraged women regarding the possibility of independence and therefore of individual rights claims. (That a distinct increase in wife-beating complaints to social workers appeared in the 1930s does not, of course, constitute evidence against the influence of organized feminism. Organized feminism was and remains a complex influence, continuing to work even as feminist organizational forms diminish, and always combining, as I have argued, with a sense of the possible largely determined by economic and social opportunities for independence.)

Progress is rarely homogeneous, and a change is noticeable here: the increase in battered women's claims to a right not to be beaten coincided with a decline in complaints about marital sexual abuse. I noted earlier that nineteenth-century feminists spoke a great deal about marital rape, condemning men's "unnatural" and "excessive" demands. There were many complaints in the case records, too, about husbands' sexual abuse. These complaints were less visible in more recent decades. Social workers brought to family cases a new sense of "normal" marital sex which was vigilant against female frigidity and tolerant of a wide range of male-initiated heterosexual activity. But clients too had lost a basis from which to condemn any particular amount or range of sexual demands from husbands: few things were immoral, and there was no longer a feminist discourse about the appropriateness of wives' refusal. From a contemporary feminist perspective, this appears as a contradiction, since we are inclined to consider sexual pressure a form of violence, and because we know that many women are beaten over sexual disagreements. The formulation of a "right" was delimited within particular boundary lines.

THE CONSTRUCTION OF RESISTANCE

There is no evidence that these battered women were taught this application of rights language by organized feminists. We have seen that nineteenth-century feminists did not discuss family violence in terms of rights, and the rights talk appeared among the battered women at a low ebb in feminist discourse. But the appearance of rights talk among battered women in the 1930s did not escalate their overall resistance. On the contrary, we see continuous and relatively steady levels of resistance from the beginning to the end of this study. Moreover, a second continuity across the eighty years is that the wife-beating complaints to social work agencies produced little help for most women. Most were unable either to change the man's behavior or to leave the relationship.

The difficulties these women experienced were essentially those faced by single mothers. The biggest obstacle for most women living with abusive men was that they did not wish to lose their children; indeed, their motherhood was for most of them (including many who were categorized as abusive or neglectful parents) their greatest source of pleasure, self-esteem, and social status. In escaping they had to find a way simultaneously to earn money and raise children in an economy of limited jobs for women, little child care, and almost no reliable aid to single mothers. They had to do this with the often low confidence characteristic of women trying to take unconventional action. Moreover, these women had the added burden of defying a social norm condemning marital separation and encouraging submission as a womanly virtue.

Consider one woman's dilemma. Mrs. O'Brien (not her real name), whose story began in Charlestown in 1910, changed her mind repeatedly about how she wanted to deal with her husband's abuse. One might imagine her inconsistent behavior was interpreted by social workers as a sign that she was masochistic or at least passive, not really wanting to escape her victimization. Scrutinized more closely, her seeming ambivalence reflects the lack of options she and so many others had. Both she and Mr. O'Brien were born in Ireland; he worked as a freight handler for the B&M Railroad. They had three surviving children in 1910, and four more were born as the case continued, with three of them surviving. The beatings she suffered were so apparent that several outside authorities—the police, her priest, the MSPCC—all took her side. The police advised her to have him arrested; but she responded, speaking for thousands, "She does not want to lose her chn. however and the little money which she does receive from fa. enables her to keep her home together." Instead, she tried to get the MSPCC agent to "scare" him into treating her and her children "right," even though previous jail terms had not "reformed" him. She agreed to another prosecution at one peak of rage—"would rather starve than endure the treatment"—then changed her mind and agreed to let him return to live with her if he would give her all his wages. The MSPCC got her to agree that it would collect $10 per week from him and give it to her. When he agreed to this, she raised her demand to $11, evidently dreading taking him back. But he agreed to this too. Three months later he was sentenced to six months for assaulting her; she was pregnant and soon began campaigning to get him out of jail. This pattern continued for years. In 1914 and again in 1920 she was threatening to murder him, describing herself as in a "desperate state of mind" (case 2,027).

Mrs. O'Brien's ambivalence was a rational response to her situation. Her children, numbering six by 1920, literally forced her to submit to her husband. Her problems illustrate the limited usefulness of prosecution as a remedy in the absence of economic provisions for single mothers. (It also suggests why prosecution might have different meanings today, when greater employment opportunities, ADC, and shelters offer women somewhat more chance of survival alone with their children.) But Mrs. O'Brien, like many victims, believed in the potential benefit of prosecution as a deterrent; this was not an option forced on her by social control agents.

And her contradictory behavior was typical. Many women who successfully prosecuted their husbands for abuse then quickly petitioned for their pardon, and the numbers who withdrew their complaints before trial or whose husbands were not convicted must have been even greater but were untraceable. To cite but one of scores of examples: Arnold W., a second offender whose wife had testified that she was afraid for her life, was sentenced to five months in 1870 by a judge who considered him "incorrigible." But Mrs. W. returned within two months to say she had testified against him "while angry" but now needed his release on grounds of poverty; the district attorney, supporting her petition, wrote that "certainly she is right, if the starved appearance of her children is any indication" (Executive Council Records 1969–1970).

Batterers often realized that women could not prosecute for fear of losing economic support. One husband threatened that "if she ever sues for divorce or separation or if she ever has him brought into court . . . he will throw up his job and then she will be without support" (case 6,040). Others derided their wives' chance for independence: "if you want to come back, all right, if not all right, we will see who wins out in this deal. . . . I work for W. C. Hill, when you want me arrested," one wife beater wrote in 1911 to his wife who had left (case 2,024).

Short of and more common than prosecution, women sought to use the police to threaten prosecution, hoping to frighten the men. Police were called in 49 percent of these wife-beating cases (with very little change over time in the rate of police involvement). Women had no other agency to call for emergency help, but what they got was almost always unsatisfactory. Their stories sound familiar: The police implicitly (and sometimes explicitly) identified with the husband, and while urging him to moderate his violence and to sober up, sympathized with his frustration and trivialized his assaults. They often removed the angry man from his home for a while and calmed him down, and this service was of some limited value to women. Sometimes the police threatened men with arrest and jail. Often, too, the police knew that little they could do would be useful to the women, who could not survive without these men. At times the police were worse than useless: in one 1910 case a woman who went to the station to complain about her husband was arrested herself for drunkenness (case 3,040). Often the police simply refused to respond to domestic disturbance calls. In 1930 one officer told a social worker, "she is always calling on the Police for the slightest things and the Police will no longer go to the home when [she] requests them to" (case 3,560A). Or as another woman reported in 1960, the police pacified her husband in another room and did not talk with her at all (case 6,041).

Mrs. O'Brien's ultimate desire was for a "separation and maintenance" agreement, as such provisions were then known: she wanted the state to guarantee her the right to a separate household and require her husband to pay support. Such plans were the most common desire of the beaten wives in this study. As another woman explained, "She did not wish him to be put away as he is a steady worker but wd. like the case arranged so that he wd. live apart and support her and the chn." (case 3,040). Mrs. O'Brien managed to get aid from the new Massachusetts mother's pension program in 1920, but only after she had been struggling against her husband's abuse for at least ten years, he having built up a record of convictions and jail terms for assault and nonsupport.

Failing to get separation-and-maintenance agreements and unable to collect support even when it was promised, the remaining option—called desertion—was taken only by the most depressed, disheartened, and desperate women. A moralistic nomenclature no longer common, desertion meant a woman leaving a husband *and* children. Female desertion was extremely uncommon in these cases, especially in contrast to the prevalence of male desertion. The low female desertion rate revealed the strength of women's attachments to their children. Moreover, the guilt and stigma attached to such action usually meant that women "deserters" simultaneously cut themselves off from friends or kin. All in all, it was unlikely that ridding themselves of the burdens of children would lead to better futures for wife-beating victims.

Another response to beatings was fighting. The incidence of mutual combat and female aggression in marital violence has been obscured by the legacy of victim blaming in the interpretation of the problem. For differing reasons, both feminists and sexists have been reluctant to recognize or acknowledge women's physical aggression. Moreover, poor women of the past may have been more comfortable with fighting than "respectable" women and contemporary women. Of the marital violence cases I studied, 16 percent contained some female violence—8 percent mutual violence and 8 percent husband beating.

Most of women's violence was responsive or reactive, as distinguished from men's violence, which grew out of mutual conflict, to be sure, but was more often a regular tactic in an ongoing power struggle. In these records I found three patterns in women's violence toward their husbands. The most common pattern comprises women's active, ongoing participation in mutual violence. Consider the 1934 case of an Irish Catholic woman married to a Danish fisherman. He was at sea all but thirty days a year, and there was violence whenever he returned. One particular target of his rage was Catholicism: he beat his sons, she claimed, to prevent them from going to church with her and loudly cursed the Irish and the Catholics—he was an atheist. The neighbors took her side and would hide her three sons when their father was in a rage. The downstairs tenant took his side. They reported that she swore, yelled, hit him, and chased him with a butcher knife, that she threw herself down some stairs to make it look like he had beaten her. Amid these conflicting charges it was certain, however, that she wanted to leave her husband, but he refused to let her have custody of the children; after a year of attempted mediation, the MSPCC ultimately lent its support for a separation (case 4,060; see also, e.g., cases 2,008, 2,561, 3,541, 3,546, 5,085). In this case the woman responded with violence to a situation she was eager to leave, while he used violence to hold her in the marriage. Her violence, as well as her maintenance of neighborhood support, worked relatively effectively to give her some leverage and ultimately to get her out of the situation. An analogous pattern with the sexes reversed could not be found—indeed probably could not occur. Women's violence in these situations was a matter of holding their own or hurting a hated partner whom they were not free to leave. The case records contain many plaintive letters from wife beaters begging for their wives' return: "the suspense is awful at times especially at night, when I arrive Home, I call it Home yet, when I do not hear those gentle voices and innocent souls whisper and speak my name" (case 2,024).

The second pattern consists of extremely frightened, usually fatalistic wives who occasionally defended themselves with a weapon. In 1960, for example, the MSPCC took on a case of such a woman; she was underweight, malnourished, and very frightened of her husband, who had a record for drunkenness as well as a diagnosis of mental illness. Profane and abusive, he was hospitalized as a result of a powerful blow she had given him on the head (case 6,042; see also cases 3,363, 5,543). This is the pattern that most commonly led, and leads, to murder.

In a third pattern, the least common, women are the primary aggressors. In one 1932 case a mother, an obese, unhealthy woman described as slovenly, kicked and slammed her six children around, locked them out of the house, knocked them down the stairs, and scratched them as well as beating her husband and forcing him and an oldest daughter to do all the housework. His employer described him as "weak and spineless, but very good-hearted." Ultimately this woman was committed to a state mental hospital, at her own request, as a psychotic (case 3,024; see also cases 4,261, 4,501, 6,086). I cannot resist the only partly humorous observation that if there is a pattern of "masochism" in violent marriages, it describes male better than female behavior since it is mainly the men who appear to want to continue the violent relationships.

Of the three patterns of female violence, the latter two usually involved extremely distressed, depressed, even disoriented women. The fighting women in mutual violence cases were not depressed and may have been better off then the more peaceful ones. They were often struggling, albeit sometimes ambivalently, for separation, defending rights their husbands were challenging (for example, an outside job), or battling over resources and labor.

Over the period of this study there appears to have been a decline in mutual violence and women's aggression (Straus 1980; Pleck et al. 1978). Particularly noticeable is the disappearance of cases of women attacking other women. In the first decades of this study there were several cases like that in 1910 of an Irish-American woman who had "drinking parties" with other women which not infrequently ended in name-calling and fights; she and her daughter fought physically in front of an MSPCC agent; and her daughter was arrested for a fight with another girl (case 2,047). This decline was offset by an increase in women leaving marriages. A likely hypothesis is that a trade-off occurred between women's physical violence and their ability to get separations or divorces.

Although women usually lost in physical fights with men, the decline in women's violence was not a clear gain for women and their families. Condemnation of female violence went along with romanticization of female passivity, which contributed to women's participation in their own victimization. Historian Nancy Tomes found that a decline in women's violence in England between 1850 and 1890 correspond to an increase in women's sense of shame about wife beating and their reluctance to report or discuss it (Tomes 1978). In this area, feminism's impact on women in violent families was mixed. The delegitimization of wife beating increased battered women's guilt about their inability to escape; they increasingly thought themselves exceptional, adding to their shame. First-wave feminism, expressing its relatively elite class base, helped construct a femininity that was oppressive to battered women: by emphasizing the superiority of women's peacefulness, feminist influence made women loathe and attempt to suppress their own aggressiveness and anger.

Few battered women attempted to resolve their problems privately with their husbands, whether violently or otherwise. That neighbors, kinfolk, and friends were of limited help was not because the victims failed to ask. Beaten women often asked for places to stay, the minimum condition for escape. One 1910 incest and wife-beating case developed in part *because* of a woman's lack of a place to live. She had previously left her abusive husband to stay with her mother but was left homeless when her mother died; she returned to her husband in 1911; in 1914 he was convicted of assault and battery on her and in 1916 of incest with their oldest daughter (case 2,054A).

Or women might ask for money to help maintain their own households. Close neighbors, landladies, and relatives might be asked for child care, for credit, or for food. One very young wife, at age twenty-one already a four-year veteran of extreme abuse, had at first displayed the typical ambivalent pattern, leaving several times to stay with her relatives and always returning. Taking a firm decision when she discovered that he had infected her and her young daughter with venereal disease, she left for good, able to return to a household that still contained a mother, sister, and brother who supplied child care as well as a home. This support was her ticket to success: four years later, in 1914, she was managing on her own, her daughter cared for by her sister while she worked as a stenographer (case 2,058A). But kinship support was no guarantee of safety. In Charlestown in 1917 a beaten wife stayed with her parents and took a job, but whenever her payday came, the estranged husband would arrive to demand her money. When her father refused to let him in, the wife would meet him secretly and give him money (case 2,520). In a 1940 case, a battered wife had already left her husband and gone to live with her mother, but he threatened and attacked his mother-in-law too until she became frightened to have her daughter with her; he also terrorized the welfare workers who were, in his view, supporting his wife's defiance (case 4,502).

Occasionally I found cases in which there was more direct intervention by relatives; these were more frequent in the first forty years of this study. In 1910 one extremely patriarchal Italian father tried to stop his son from assaulting his wife (case 2,042). In 1893 a woman's brother traveled to another part of Boston each night to protect her from her husband, "who would lie in wait for her with a club" (case 1,040). But relatives also set clear limits on their involvement. In 1917 an Italian-born husband who had battered his wife for years ended their relationship by committing her to a mental hospital (despite the attempts of a thirteen-year-old daughter to convince an MSPCC agent that abuse was her mother's main mental problem). The wife's parents lived close by, and the wife had fled to them on several occasions. They vociferously condemned her husband in speaking to a social worker, and when the wife's mother died they blamed it on her anguish at her daughter's abuse. But when the husband demanded the wife's return, her parents were unwilling to interfere with his authority so far as to shelter her. Moreover, after committing his wife, the husband retained his right to be accepted by her relatives as a member of the family (case 2,800A).

More important than the material help offered by neighbors, friends, and relatives was their influence on how victims defined the standards of treatment they would tolerate. The reactions of confidants, or even of neighbors who heard the fights, affected the responses of victims and assailants. Some counseled resignation and passivity, while others, by their outrage of partisanship, suggested that battering need not be accepted. Parents like those above who expressed their commitment by their willingness to take their daughter in, but nevertheless deferred to her abusive husband's ultimate authority, were telling their daughter that beatings should be tolerated. By contrast, in another Italian-American family, the mother and sister of a battered woman not only took her in with her six children but brought her to complain to the MSPCC (case 6,300).

Battered women sometimes turned to child welfare agencies because their informal networks could not protect them, but often they added these agencies in to a reservoir of resistance strategies, just as they had added rights claims to others. Sometimes they benefited from the agencies, mainly when they were able to obtain legitimation and financial support for leaving their marriages. Such benefits were owing sometimes to the skill and insight of social workers, but more to the ingenuity of the victims. Indeed, sometimes the victims taught the social workers the best helping techniques, chipping away at their hostility to separation, divorce, and female-headed households, just as the victims learned from social workers what aspirations might be within their reach (Gordon 1988a).

I do not mean to suggest that clients were equals in their contacts with the child protectors; on the contrary, cumulatively the agencies were more successful in imposing their standards, just as men could not usually be brought to change their behavior. We must be clear that concepts like agency and resistance do not mean victory; nor should they work to soften the ugly and painful history of victimization. Indeed, many forms of resistance were probably poor choices, although one might argue that the impulse to do *something,* however ineffective, was usually preferable to resignation. The problem so evident in women's history—and in much other scholarship from the standpoint of subordinated groups—of romanticizing either victimization or resistance is closely associated with moralism. Historical accounts need to avoid moral categories whenever possible. Oppression may be evil, but victims are not therefore "good" or "nice" or "wise."

What can we learn from this enumeration of forms of resistance to wife beating? First, we see that resistance is itself an interpretation, a construction, one participated in by the historian and reader, certainly, as by the wife-beating victim herself. To resist is to experience autonomy, to experience oneself as planning against one's assailant, and to interpret the assault as something avoidable or controllable. One expert on contemporary wife beating has explained how a victim may appear to be provoking an assault—as, for example, by belittling a violent and insecure husband—when her (experienced) intention is to control when, where, and how severe it will be (Walker 1979). The same actions might have quite a different meaning in a different context—if, for example, she does not expect to be beaten, or if she wants to be beaten (a hypothetical for which I found no evidence). At the very least, the range and stubbornness of some of these modes of resistance are too great to be constructions exclusively of social workers.

Second, we see that rights claims seemed to emerge under certain specifiable conditions. Feminists and battered women alike seemed to avoid rights talk about wife beating while social and economic conditions made it difficult and disrespectable for married women to become independent of their husbands. Moreover, rights talk seems to fit best with absolute claims—no physical coercion at all should be tolerated. This position simply did not fit the life conditions of many women, for whom putting up with a husband's fists might not be worse than the poverty and loss of one's children attendant to separation. This reading of the evidence suggests that battered women's claim to rights, a claim upon the state to protect them from violence, arose precisely because of the weakening of patriarchy, while other forms of resistance had been an essential part of patriarchal systems.

NOTES

1 The author's data are from the case records of Boston child welfare agencies (1880–1960), most prominently the Massachusetts Society for the Prevention of Cruelty to Children (MSPCC).—Ed. note

REFERENCES

Bordin, R. 1981. *Women and Temperance: The Quest for Power and Liberty, 1873–1900.* Philadelphia: Temple University Press.

DuBois, E. C., ed. 1981. *Elizabeth Cady Stanton, Susan B. Anthony: Correspondence, Writings, Speeches.* New York: Schocken.

Epstein, B. L. 1981. *The Politics of Domesticity: Women, Evangelism, and Temperance in Nineteenth-Century America.* Middletown, Conn.: Wesleyan University Press.

Executive Council Records, Commonwealth of Massachusetts. 1969–1970. Pardon, Communication, and Parole files, unnumbered box, Massachusetts State Archives, Boston.

Fraser, N. 1990. "Struggle over Needs: Outline of a Socialist-Feminist Critical Theory of Late-Capitalist Political Culture." In *Women, the State, and Welfare,* ed. Linda Gordon, 199–225. Madison: University of Wisconsin Press.

Gordon, L. 1988a. "The Frustrations of Family Violence Social Work: An Historical Critique." *Journal of Sociology and Social Welfare* 15:139–160.

———. 1988b. *Heroes of Their Own Lives: The Politics and History of Family Violence, Boston, 1880–1960.* New York: Viking.

———. 1990. *Woman's Body, Woman's Right: A Social History of Birth Control in America.* 2d ed. New York: Penguin.

Nadelhaft, J. N.d. "Domestic Violence in the Literature of the Temperance Movement." Manuscript quoted in Elizabeth Pleck, *Domestic Tyranny: The Making of American Social Policy against Family Violence from Colonial Times to the Present,* 98–101. New York: Oxford University Press, 1987.

Pleck, E. 1979. "Wife Beating in Nineteenth-Century America." *Victimology* 4:60–74.

———. 1983. "Feminist Responses to Crimes against Women, 1868–1896." *Signs* 8:451–470.

Pleck, E., J. H. Pleck, M. Grossman, and P. B. Bart. 1978. "The Battered Data Syndrome: A Comment on Steinmetz' Article." *Victimology* 2:680–683.

Straus, M. 1980. "Victims and Aggressors in Marital Violence." *American Behavioral Scientist* 23 (May–June): 681–704.

Tomes, N. 1978. "A 'Torrent of Abuse': Crimes of Violence between Working Class Men and Women in London, 1840–1875." *Journal of Social History* 11:328–345.

Walker, L. 1979. *The Battered Woman.* New York: Harper and Row.

Technologies and Effects of Heterosexual Coercion

Nicola Gavey

To say that women often engage in unwanted sex with men is paradoxically both to state the obvious and to speak the unspeakable. While this assertion will not come as a surprise to many women, it embodies a subjugated knowledge which usually remains private and hidden. Unwanted and coerced sex are thus an aspect of some women's experiences of oppression which have remained to a large extent unrecognized, yet implicitly condoned, and even encouraged.

In this study I want to show how language and discourses on sexuality have the power to effect the material practice of heterosexuality in ways that subordinate women. Dominant discourses on sexuality provide subject positions for women which are relatively passive, and which prescribe compliance with or submission to male initiatives or demands. This compliance can be seen to be an effect of 'technologies of heterosexual coercion', which reproduce relations of power and dominance in the domain of heterosexual sex such that men's interests take precedence. My specific focus in this study is an exploration of women's experiences of unwanted and coerced sex within heterosexual relationships. It has been shown that rape and sexual aggression are relatively prevalent within heterosexual relationships (e.g. Gavey, 1991a, 1991b; Russell, 1982). Feminists have suggested, however, that recognized forms of sexual violence are only the extreme manifestation of a more pervasive coercive heterosexuality (see Gavey, 1990, for a fuller discussion). Women can be coerced into having sex with men in many more subtle ways than through physical force, or violence, or the threat of violence (e.g. Finkelhor and Yllo, 1983, 1985; Gavey, 1989, 1990; Muehlenhard and Schrag, 1991). In this study, I was particularly interested in how to account for those operations of power that do not involve direct force or violence, and/or which appear to involve the woman's consent or, at least, lack of obvious resistance. . . . Some of the instances I discuss involved subtle coercion, while others involved quite obvious coercion or force but were somehow unable to be conceptualized as 'rape' or sometimes even as 'forced', by the woman at the time. The sorts of dynamics that I look at relate primarily to heterosexual women, but some of the less subtle mechanisms of male sexual coercion will apply more generally to all women. I do not address the possibility of how some forms of sexual coercion may also operate in similar ways within lesbian sexual relations.

DISCOURSE AND SUBJECT POSITIONS FOR WOMEN

At this point, I very briefly outline a general theory of discourse that provides a framework for the analyses in this study. From a poststructuralist perspective, language is always located in discourse. Discourse refers to an interrelated 'system of statements which cohere around common meanings and values . . . [that] are a product of social factors, of powers and practices, rather than an individual's set of ideas' (Hollway, 1983: 231). It is a broad concept referring to ways of constituting meaning which are specific to particular groups, cultures and historical periods. Discourse both constitutes, and is reproduced in, social institutions, modes of thought and individual subjectivities. Within any discourse subject positions are available to the individual, but these are not coterminous with the individual (Henriques et al., 1984). Subject positions offer us ways of being and behaving, and of understanding ourselves and events in our world. Because of the relationship between discourse, power and subjectivity, most women are likely to be positioned within dominant, prevailing discourses—although these positionings will always be to some extent partial, as they are contested and interrupted by other discursive possibilities. Indeed, subjectivity is fragmentary and any individual's subjectivity would never be entirely consistent with a unitary subject position from any one discourse. Rather, subjectivity is a process which is likely to be the transient, always changing, product of a discursive battle (Weedon, 1987)—hence the contradictions and ambiguities in women's experiences.

SEXUALITY AS SOCIALLY CONSTRUCTED

It is by now widely accepted that what we think of as 'sexuality' is not a natural and pre-existent entity, but rather a social construction. Thus, sex is not a seething mass of natural drives and urges that our society has repressed, but rather, sexual practices, desires, subjectivities, forms of identity and so on, have been produced and continue to be produced through the 'deployment of sexuality' (Foucault, 1981). According to Foucault (1980, 1981), sexuality has been 'deployed' in relatively recent times as a domain of regulation and social control. This theorization of sexuality allows an understanding of how the positions available to women (and men) in dominant discourses on sexuality are not natural and fixed, and nor are they neutral—sexuality is deployed in ways that are directly related to relations of power.

DISCIPLINARY POWER

The analyses presented in this study also rely on some of Michel Foucault's ideas about power. Central to a Foucauldian analysis of power is the recognition that power is not a unitary force that is independent of us and operates only from the top down, through repression and denial. Rather, Foucault has argued that over time traditional sovereign forms of power have been intersected with (but not replaced by) what he has called 'disciplinary power' (Diamond and Quinby, 1988). 'Discipline' regulates human life, imposing particular forms of behaviour and 'assuring the ordering of human multiplicities' (Foucault, 1979: 218). It 'produces subjected and practised bodies, "docile" bodies' (Foucault, 1979: 138). In this sense, power is 'positive'. That is, it is *productive* and *constitutive*—it produces meanings, desires, behaviours, practices and so on. Discipline is infused in multiple and diffuse ways throughout the whole 'social body', and disciplinary power is exercised through its invisibility (Foucault, 1979). Disciplinary power thus works through 'subtle coercion' (Foucault, 1979: 209), making the exercise of power more effective.

The concept of disciplinary power promises fruitful openings for exploring sexual coercion (particularly subtle forms) within heterosexual relationships. However, the differential, gendered, operations of power through the deployment of sex for men and women must be highlighted (e.g. de Lauretis, 1987; Bartky, 1988). Disciplinary power may produce 'docile bodies', but there are profound gender differences in the forms this takes with regard to heterosexuality.

Apparent Complicity in Heterosexual Coercion

The concept of disciplinary power allows an understanding of how women may be persuaded into apparent complicity in the process of our own subjugation, through the regulation and normalization of our subjectivities and behaviours. The panoptic schema, which Foucault (1979) referred to for illustrating how disciplinary power functions, provides an interesting model for understanding how subjects are enlisted into the service of regulating their own behaviour, thus becoming their own jailors (Bartky, 1988). The Panopticon is an architectural model (designed by Jeremy Bentham) for a prison, which consists of a central watchtower surrounded by a circular building divided into cells. Each cell extends the width of the building and has a window on both the outside and inside walls, thus creating an effect of backlighting which makes the cell occupant visible from the central tower. Furthermore, the central tower is designed so that the observer is not visible to the prisoners in their cells. This arrangement ensures 'that the surveillance is permanent in its effects' (Foucault, 1979: 201), without needing to be continuous in its action (that is, the supervisor need not always be present). In this model, power is both visible and unverifiable. That is, the inmates are constantly aware of the central tower from which they are observed, but they never know if they are being looked at at any one particular time. Thus, the Panopticon induces 'a state of conscious and permanent visibility that assures the automatic functioning of power' (Foucault, 1979: 201). This model illustrates how subjects can be regulated and normalized through the operation of disciplinary power.

Sandra Lee Bartky (1988: 81), in a feminist Foucauldian analysis of 'femininity', has argued the following:

> The woman who checks her makeup half a dozen times a day to see if her foundation has caked or her mascara has run, who worries that the wind or the rain may spoil her hairdo,

who looks frequently to see if her stockings have bagged at the ankle or who, feeling fat, monitors everything she eats, has become, just as surely as the inmate of the Panopticon, a self-policing subject, a self committed to a relentless self-surveillance. This self-surveillance is a form of obedience to patriarchy. It is also the reflection in the woman's consciousness of the fact that *she* is under surveillance in ways that *he* is not, that whatever else she may become, she is importantly a body designed to please or excite. There has been induced in many women, then, in Foucault's words, a 'state of conscious and permanent visibility that assures the automatic functioning of power'.

'In contemporary patriarchal culture', Bartky suggested, 'a panoptical male connoisseur resides within the consciousness of most women' (Bartky, 1988: 72). Many parallels can be drawn between Bartky's incisive analysis of the vigilance of some women over their feminine appearance and the 'obedience' of some women in our sexual relations with men. Women involved in heterosexual encounters are also engaged in self-surveillance, and are encouraged to become self-policing subjects who comply with the normative heterosexual narrative scripts which demand our consent and participation irrespective of our sexual desire. Thus, while women may not engage in conscious and deliberate submission, disciplinary power nevertheless produces what can be seen as a form of obedience. While the individual male's behaviour in the interaction is not insignificant, the operations of power involved may transcend his particular actions.

TECHNOLOGIES OF HETEROSEXUAL COERCION

In Foucault's use of the metaphor 'technologies of power', it is suggested that just as we understand technology as a set of applied knowledges and practices that develop and construct material objects in our physical world, which structure that world and mediate our relationship to it and its meaning, so too do *social* 'technologies' construct and reproduce practices in, and experiences and meanings of, our personal and social worlds. Teresa de Lauretis (1987: 28) uses the technology metaphor to discuss 'the techniques and discursive strategies by which gender is constructed'. Thus, gender 'is the product of various social technologies, such as cinema, and of institutionalized discourses, epistemologies, and critical practices, as well as practices of daily life' (de Lauretis, 1987: 2). Similarly, this metaphor can be extended to understand the ways in which the gender-specific deployment of sexuality enables, if not actually encourages, heterosexual practice which contains much invisible coercion. That is, the normalizing social technologies of sex produce a material practice of heterosexuality in which women are produced as subjects who are encouraged to regulate our own behaviour in ways which comply with androcentric versions of sexuality (see Jackson, 1984, for a discussion of androcentric and heterosexist sexuality). In these versions of sexuality, heterosexuality is assumed as a given and is 'compulsory' (Rich, 1980), women's sexual desire is relatively neglected and, concomitantly, women often lack power to determine our involvement in heterosexual relations—both in general, and in specific forms of sex. The practices, knowledges and strategies that reproduce this state of affairs can be thought of as 'technologies of heterosexual coercion'.

The discursive fields in which these power relations are prescribed, enacted and reproduced as social technologies are many and varied. They would include women's and men's accounts and representations of their heterosexual sexuality and relationships; representations of sexuality and heterosexual relations in popular women's magazines, film, television, romance and other fiction, pornography and sex manuals; sexology and the practice of sex therapy; practices of contraception; sexual humour; church prescriptions on sexuality; sex education in schools; legislation on sexuality and sexual violence; sociobiological explanations for sexual violence, and so on. Exploration of the representations of sexuality and heterosexual relations and practice in any one of these areas would also lead to some understanding of the technologies and effects of heterosexual coercion. In this study, I focus on women's accounts of their sexual experiences with men as one discursive field through which technologies of heterosexual coercion operate. Women's personal accounts provide direct access to the discourses available to these women, the subject positions offered by these discourses and the ways in which power operates through these discourses, and in relation to specific discursive positionings.

To say that there exist technologies of heterosexual coercion is not to say that it is not possible for women to be positioned in ways in which we do have power and agency in sexual relations with men, and in which our desire is articulated and acted upon (e.g. Hollway, 1984; and see Gavey, 1991c, for a discussion of the missing discourse of desire as it relates to understandings of sexual violence). There are certainly discourses (e.g. feminisms) that impinge on heterosexuality which do allow such power and desire, although such discourses are not available as yet to all women. Furthermore, it would be naive to believe that an individual woman will achieve 'liberation' by positioning herself in a feminist discourse on sexuality in an otherwise misogynist material context. It is important to remember that the continued existence of more brutal forms of male (sexual and non-sexual) violence against women acts as an important signification and reminder of the lack of *ultimate* control and power that many women have in our sexual and/or other relations with men. To forget this material condition of women's lives is, perhaps, to move onto the slippery slope of victim-blaming. There are also other conditions of women's lives, such as economic and social disadvantages, which contribute to what may be seen as women's complicity in our sexual coercion. These conditions can frame or contextualize the prospect of engaging in unwanted sex in a way that makes it seem like the best of all possible options to the woman involved.

. . .

CONCLUSIONS

In this study I have discussed some of the ways in which the deployment of sex through technologies of heterosexual coercion constitutes possibilities for the domination of women through heterosexual practice, even in the absence of overt physical force or violence. By examining discourses on heterosexuality through women's accounts of their experiences (which, of course, do not exist in isolation from other discursive fields and material practices), we can see how 'language functions to create us as subjects' (Diamond and Quinby, 1988: 201), who are sometimes solicited into the processes of our own subjugation. In sampling from the data of six women's accounts of some of their experiences of coercive heterosexuality, including unwanted and forced sex with men, I have highlighted some of the ways in which this happens.

One way heterosexual coercion occurs is through the discursive framing of heterosexual encounters within a narrative in which (past a certain point in the encounter and/or relationship) certain forms of sex are prescribed, and sexual intercourse is required. Anything else is not easily accommodated. It may just seem 'silly', or it may lead to a woman being positioned as 'uptight', or it may, from her perspective, be regarded as an alternative to rape. Being positioned as 'uptight', as in Ann's case, may even occur when a woman is not gracious about having been raped by a man she knows. Or, as in Rosemary's case, a woman may be regarded as 'psychologically undone' because she cannot physically tolerate repeated violent sexual intercourse (rape), carried out on her by her husband.

Another important factor in this constitution of women as passive, compliant heterosexual subjects, seems to be the relative silence in articulating positions for women as active, desiring subjects (Gavey, 1991c). When, as Catharine MacKinnon (1983: 650) has observed, 'sex is normally something men do to women', consent can be a very passive action. Women are thus sometimes not aware of consent and non-consent as distinct choices (given certain, acceptable, parameters of the relationship). This is not surprising given the power of normative prescriptions for heterosexual practice—*and* given that women's sexual desire is often invisible, unspoken. When desire is absent in discourses on female sexuality, 'this constriction of what is called sexuality allows girls [and women] one primary decision—to say yes or no—to a question not necessarily their own' (Fine, 1988: 34). This silence allows the unwitting perpetuation of a form of (compulsory) heterosexuality in which women's agency and resistance exist only to the degree to which we can *limit* and *control* male sexual access (women's traditional imperative within heterosexuality). (We must remember, however, that sexual desire itself is not essential or unproblematic, but that it, too, is constructed and produced through the deployment of sexuality, and is itself inscribed by gender/power relations.)

I have also discussed actions arising from nurturance and pragmatism as examples of how the mechanisms of disciplinary power function in ways which conceal the operation of such power. By appealing to these nurturant or pragmatic reasons for having sex, women are 'disciplined'—our behaviour is regulated in ways in which the gender-specific operation of power is disguised. This invisible operation of power is extremely efficient because it obviates the need for overt force and violence.

The political implications of this analysis differ from some traditional analyses. Traditional feminist analyses have often relied on the notion of a simple top-down domination of women by patriarchal power, which is exercised by individual men and from which (all) men directly or indirectly benefit. This traditional understanding of domination, and its expression in the language of control, 'presumes a centering of power that may no longer exist in contemporary society: we are asked to seize power when power is no longer held by a clearly identifiable and coherent group' (Diamond and Quinby 1988: 195). An analysis which focuses on the regulating and normalizing functions of disciplinary power, however, does not rely on the presumption of unitary and centralized sources of power. It is, therefore, particularly useful for explaining women's compliance with unwanted sex and those forms of heterosexual coercion which do not involve overt force or violence.

One of the aims of this research was to interrogate, contest and disturb dominant conceptualizations of heterosexual sex. The deconstructive impulse of this research is not neutral, however. Women I have talked with about heterosexual coercion have sometimes told me that they have come to see their experiences in a different light as a result of talking or thinking about such experiences in the context of this research. To the extent that these new ways of making sense of their experiences create space for new discursive positionings which are more positive and open up possibilities for both resistance to coercion and the active pursuit of pleasure, then this is a positive, political implication of the research. We cannot avoid technologies of sex but, by understanding some of the ways in which they work, we can hopefully resist, challenge and contest technologies of heterosexual coercion.

REFERENCES

Bartky, Sandra Lee (1988) 'Foucault, Femininity, and the Modernization of Patriarchal Power', in Irene Diamond and Lee Quinby (eds) *Feminism and Foucault: Reflections on Resistance,* pp. 61–86. Boston, MA: Northeastern University Press.

de Lauretis, Teresa (1987) *Technologies of Gender: Essays on Theory, Film, and Fiction.* Bloomington, IL and Indianapolis, IN: Indiana University Press.

Diamond, Irene and Quinby, Lee (1988) 'American Feminism and the Language of Control', in Irene Diamond and Lee Quinby (eds) *Feminism and Foucault: Reflections on Resistance,* pp. 193–206. Boston, MA: Northeastern University Press.

Fine, Michelle (1988) 'Sexuality, Schooling, and Adolescent Females: The Missing Discourse of Desire', *Harvard Educational Review* 58: 29–53.

Finkelhor, David and Yllo, Kersti (1983) 'Rape in Marriage: A Sociological View', in David Finkelhor, Richard J. Gelles, Gerald T. Hotaling and Murray A. Straus (eds) *The Dark Side of Families: Current Family Violence Research,* pp. 119–30. Newbury Park, CA: Sage.

Finkelhor, David and Yllo, Kersti (1985) *License to Rape: Sexual Abuse of Wives.* New York: The Free Press.

Foucault, Michel (1979) *Discipline and Punish: The Birth of the Prison.* Trans by Alan Sheridan. London: Penguin (Original work published in 1975).

Foucault, Michel (1980) in Colin Gordon (ed.) *Power/Knowledge: Selected Interviews and Other Writings 1972–1977, by Michel Foucault.* Trans by Colin Gordon, Leo Marshall, John Mepham and Kate Soper. New York: Pantheon.

Foucault, Michel (1981) *The History of Sexuality (Volume 1: An Introduction).* Trans by Robert Hurley. Harmondsworth, Middlesex: Penguin (Original work published in 1976).

Gavey, Nicola (1989) 'Feminist Poststructuralism and Discourse Analysis: Contributions to Feminist Psychology', *Psychology of Women Quarterly* 13: 459–75.

Gavey, Nicola (1990) 'Rape and Sexual Coercion within Heterosexual Relationships: An Intersection of Psychological, Feminist, and Postmodern Inquiries', unpublished doctoral thesis, University of Auckland.

Gavey, Nicola J. (1991a) 'Sexual Victimization Prevalence among Auckland University Students: How Much and Who Does It?', *New Zealand Journal of Psychology* 20: 63–70.

Gavey, Nicola (1991b) 'Sexual Victimization Prevalence among New Zealand University Students', *Journal of Consulting and Clinical Psychology* 59: 464–6.

Gavey, Nicola J. (1991c) 'Women's Desire in Sexual Violence Discourse', Paper presented at the Fourth International Conference on Language and Social Psychology, August, Santa Barbara, CA.

Henriques, Julian, Hollway, Wendy, Urwin, Cathy, Venn, Couze and Walkerdine, Valerie (1984) *Changing the Subject: Psychology, Social Regulation and Subjectivity.* London: Methuen.

Hollway, Wendy (1983) 'Heterosexual Sex: Power and Desire for the Other', in Sue Cartledge and Joanna Ryan (eds) *Sex and Love: New Thoughts on Old Contradictions,* pp. 124–40. London: The Women's Press.

Hollway, Wendy (1984) 'Women's Power in Heterosexual Sex', *Women's Studies International Forum* 7: 63–8.

Jackson, Margaret (1984) 'Sex Research and the Construction of Sexuality: A Tool of Male Supremacy?', *Women's Studies International Forum* 7: 43–51.

MacKinnon, Catharine (1983) 'Feminism, Marxism, Method, and the State: Toward Feminist Jurisprudence', *Signs: Journal of Women in Culture and Society* 8: 635–58.

Muehlenhard, Charlene, L. and Schrag, Jennifer, L. (1991) 'Nonviolent Sexual Coercion', in Andrea Parrot and Laurie Bechhofer (eds) *Acquaintance Rape: The Hidden Crime,* pp. 115–28. New York: Wiley.

Rich, Adrienne (1980) 'Compulsory Heterosexuality and Lesbian Existence', *Signs: Journal of Women in Culture and Society* 5: 631–60.

Russell, Diana, E.H. (1982) *Rape in Marriage.* New York: Macmillan.

Weedon, Chris (1987) *Feminist Practice and Poststructuralist Theory.* Oxford: Basil Blackwell.

A Womb With A View: Women as Mothers and the Discourse of the Body

Wendi Hadd

New reproductive technologies are a melange of medical procedures used to produce healthy babies. The procedures themselves, while medical in nature, are created within a particular cultural and social framework. Feminist analyses of reproductive technologies have documented that the medical community cannot be considered as having the best interests of women at heart when they develop, test, and market new technologies aimed at "helping" women to conceive and to bear healthy babies. The predominant discourse within feminist literature has been one which supports self-determination for women, stressing that women must have freedom of choice in regards to technologies and that women must be the ones to control how the technology is used on their bodies. Taking its cue from the discourse on abortion and abortion-rights, the call has been for a recognition of women's right to "control" their own bodies.

As a feminist I agree with this dialogue in general and I actively support the vocal and vociferous defense of women and their rights. However, I would like to address the idea of controlling one's own body and to suggest why it is inappropriate and how it justifies many of the techniques being made available to women in the field of reproductive technologies.

CONCEPTS OF MIND AND BODY

The notion of being entitled to control one's body is formulated from within a discourse which accepts as a given the concept of mind/body dualism. It is possible to trace the discourse on the body from the Greeks and Romans to Judeo-Christian thought, through to the rise of science (Synnott, 1988). The principle point of debate is whether the mind (or soul) and the body are one, or if the mind and body are separate, ranked hierarchically and subsequently under the control of one or the other. The discourse on the body throughout history has swung on a pendulum between the acceptance and the subsequent rejection of dualism.

The rise of science brought with it a renewed belief in dualism. Cynthia Russett pinpointed the origins of modern scientific thought on the mind and body in Victorian era scientific exploration. The superiority of the mind over the body was established and explained through the use of a metaphor linking the functioning of the human body to the superior machinery of the day and the belief in the superiority of the laws of natural science. The prevailing metaphor used to explain this concept was that of the human body as a machine; more specifically the human body as an engine within which the mind acts as the engineer; "the engineer at the controls of the engine—it was an attractive metaphor that suggested an intellectual mastery over the material flesh" (1989:108). For women, the metaphor and the paradigm of mind over body were seen as inverse in proportion to the opposition of male and female. Whereas males were great minds in control of bodies, the uterus was the controlling organ in the female body (Ehrenreich & English, 1978:120–121). There is no biological differences that make one gender more tied to the body than the other but Sara Ruddick (1989) traces the philosophical association of the male with the mind and the female with the body to women's intimate knowledge of the body that arises from birthing labor, nursing, and menstruation. In Ruddick's view, reproduction acts against the control of reason. In early, woman-centered religion, female reproduction was a positive facet of life. In modern history, we see that the concept of the female body changes from the life-affirming, warm, giving, generous, secret, paradoxical yet inviting source of life to an image of the female body as known, negative, cold, selfish, the source of disease. Both images are ideals—from the positive ideal to the negative ideal—from Mother Madonna/Goddess to Mother Whore/Witch; from Mother Earth to Mother of Flesh and therefore of disease and unnatural. The mother of flesh is juxtaposed with the father of Reason. The idea of control, then, is paramount to the concept of dualism. From the Victorian era we have inherited the firm understanding that the body is something that can, and must, be controlled. The continued view of the body as machine and, by extension, of the body as a collection of parts increasingly open to manipulation justifies the perception of the body as object. Not only are the body and the mind distinct in an abstract sense but the body can be treated as though it is physically detached from the mind.

"When science treats the person as a machine and assumes the body can be fixed by mechanical manipulations, it ignores, and it encourages us to ignore, other aspects of ourselves, such as our emotions or our relations with other people" (Martin, 1987:19–20). The body becomes an object, a container which stores and is controlled by the mind, rather than an integral part of the whole and an essential component of what constitutes a human being.

CONTROLLING THE BODY

The battle that feminists have fought and continue to fight, has been to eradicate the perception of women as objects defined by their sexual and/or reproductive capacities. Yet the general liberal discourse within which their fight is waged does not negate the concept of mind/body dualism. The arguments continue to be articulated within a particular social/cultural framework that does not counter the entrenched attitudes toward control. Rather, feminism argues for a shift in control. While it is apparent that if anyone is going to control a body the "owner" of that body should be in control, arguing for a shift in control is, in essence, reaffirming the belief in the body as object. Rather than seeking change from within this discourse, we must approach the issue from the standpoint that the body, male and female, is not an object, and therefore to talk of owning one's body and controlling one's body is to obfuscate the real issues at hand.

Taking the abortion issue as an example, we can see an entire coalition fighting for women's right to *control* their bodies. The real truth is that women should be entitled to abortion on demand not because they have the right to "do" with their bodies what they will but because women *are* their bodies and any policy that seeks to control women's bodies seeks to control women. Saying 'I have the right to do with my own body' is placing the argument and the fight for rights in a false framework. It bears repeating: We do not "do" with our bodies—we *are* our bodies. This necessary shift in thinking will place emphasis back where it belongs—onto the entire human being. A woman carries a fetus in her womb, but a pregnancy courses through her entire being; it is not a purely tangible experience. The demands that my son makes on me are very often of a physical nature but as he grows and changes so too do his demands; they increasingly involve a more rational type of care as he reaches out to the world. My task is to meet his demands; his demands of reason and rationality as well as his physical demands. Any woman contemplating a pregnancy knows that the demands placed upon her will not be solely physical. She will be asked, or forced, to involve all of her being in raising a child. Whether she decides that she welcomes this experience or not, she makes her decision on many levels. Abortion on demand should be a woman's right, not because she has the right to control her body, but because she has the right to choose what experiences she will and will not live. Deciding to abort or to bear a child is not only about the physical but is also about the emotional and the mental.

As a feminist I do wish to avoid the argument of biological determinism but I also wish to avoid the argument of pure social constructionism as the main theoretical basis of women's mothering. "We cannot abandon our corporeal identity and simply drift away in a cloud of disembodied social constructionism" (Rose, 1987:157–158). Rose goes on to say that "epistemology must take on both the material reality of social relations and the material reality of nature, including our bodily selves." The prerequisite for this is to understand that the bodily self is an integral part of the mental self and that it has an influence in the same way as do social relations. Epistemology then must reject the science that incorporates the belief in dualism. "We can dismiss as unnecessary the question whether the soul and body are one: it is as though we were to ask whether the wax and its shape are one" (Aristotle: quoted in Synnott, 1988). When we speak of the body as a machine and as separate from the mind we deny our humanity, deny our personality, deny that we possess what may well be a soul but at the very least is the intricate and delicate essence of our humanity. Technology threatens this belief and threatens to treat all human beings as though they are but interchangeable parts.

With prenatal diagnostics, genetic counselling, and genetic engineering we are coming face to face with questions about what it means to be human. Feminist theory should take the lead in arguing that an epistemology that accepts as a given the idea of dualism is inadequate. The question of dualism will continue to be an essential part of reproductive issues. If bodies can and must be controlled, who will control a woman's body when she houses the body of a fetus or a baby? We must stop insisting that women have the right to control; instead we should be insisting on the right to define our "selves" and our collective right and need to define what it means to be a thinking person in a physical body. We must come to terms with the abstract and the concrete as one.

If we insist on reformulating our beliefs within the discourse of dualism, then we must understand that our perception of the body as an object to be controlled has as one result the increasing commodification of the body and its parts. When the body is experienced as a commodity it is not perceived as having an intrinsic value but rather as having exchange value; which is to say, if the body or its parts can be modified in some way it will acquire added value. The body therefore is not an end but instead a means to an end (Shannon, 1988). If my body is an object which I am entitled to control, then I can do with it what I will; including modifying it in some way as to profit from it. Using Kant's argument against prostitution, Thomas Shannon makes an articulate and compelling case against the state sanctioned objectification and commodification of the body.

> The underlying moral principle is that man is not his own property and cannot do with his body what he will. The body is part of the self; in its togetherness with the self it constitutes a person; a man cannot make of his person a thing (Kant: quoted in Shannon, 1988:70).

While Shannon's main focus is the issue of surrogate mothers, his treatment of the ethical issues involved in reproductive technologies demonstrate the ways in which our perception of the body is reified by the medical community. This reification of the body as object and commodity alienates women from their bodies and from the "product" of their bodies—their children.

Shannon makes the point that human beings do not have the right or the freedom to do what they will with their bodies; while the United States allows the selling of blood and sperm, in other countries, including Canada, Australia, England and Japan, selling blood and sperm is illegal. These laws do not exist to prevent poor people from using their bodies to make a living but rather to prevent society as a whole from sliding into large-scale buying and selling of human bodies and body parts; to protect the integrity of the human body as an integral part of our personhood. With this in mind, the underlying assumptions that occur when we defend the rights of the business of surrogate mothers speak volumes about the way in which society views women's bodies.

When a woman reproduces a child in her body for the purposes of selling that child to its father, she might feel that she is selling a service rather than a product. Regardless of her personal beliefs and/or rationalizations, her body loses some of its intrinsic value in the transaction. Do we then say she has the freedom to do what she chooses with her body? She is using her body in a way which defiles her personhood, not as an end in itself but as a means to an end. This is, in essence, the underlying freedom that advocates of surrogacy speak of when they speak of a woman's freedom to choose to create a child to sell. A society that permits this, and worse yet, creates a situation for women where they have an economic need to use themselves in this way is a society that desecrates the inherent intrinsic value of humanity. When we mask the reality of these actions in terms of giving women the freedom to control their own reproductive lives, and in terms of equality in that men are also able to use their bodies to their own ends we violate the meaning of freedom and equality. Andrea Dworkin points out:

> the bitter fact that the only time that equality is considered a value is in a situation like this where some extremely degrading transaction is being rationalized. And the only time that freedom is considered important to women as such is when we're talking about the freedom to prostitute oneself in one way or another (Quoted in Corea, 1985:227).

The freedom of a woman, then, is reduced to the freedom to sell her body or parts of her body; eggs, the space in her womb, a child that she bears. Our bodies are objectified and our acceptance of the commodification of bodies, especially female bodies, results in the view of fetuses and children as products that can be bought and sold.

While we can see the commodification of the body most clearly when using surrogacy as an example, its scope is not limited to this one "technology." Genetic engineering furthers the concept with its emphasis on quality control of the product. Testing ensures the fetus is a quality product; it is free of defects. If not, it can be terminated and another created to take its place. The appeal of genetic engineering is that it can be combined with other technologies, including IVF and AID. The very near future will bring us routine screening of all fetuses for defects. Doctors already advocate intervention in every pregnancy regardless of its classification in terms of high or low risk. Dr. Edwards, one of the doctors involved in the conception of Louise Brown, known as the world's first "test-tube baby", says that "some sort of intervention is essential in conception to ensure that children are born as normal as we can possibly ensure" (Edwards, 1983). The term "normal" is so vague as to be nonsensical and Dr. Edwards' statement belies the fact that most babies born with disabilities and/or disease do so as the result of poverty and extreme youth or age of the mothers (Baruch, et al, 1988:233). Basic medical care and proper nutrition will help these babies, not genetic screening and high technology.

Our concepts of what is human, of what it means to be a "normal" human are too underdeveloped to keep pace with scientific advancements. Do we want to believe in the engineered perfection of the human body? In the medical model the body is a product that can be manufactured artificially; science controls the quality of the product, the consumer is spared the sorrow of receiving damaged goods. Knowing in advance that this attitude characterizes the scientific and medical perception of the human body, we cannot expect our scientists to also be our moral philosophers and our ethicists, we cannot give them the liberty to be our collective conscience and to define for society according to their own limited world view. So when we say that doctors can screen for defects, it must be society as a whole that determines what is a legitimate defect, what type of defects, if any, all of society accepts as warranting elimination. As a society we must learn to distinguish between defects that have a medical criteria and those which have only social criteria. We are a society that is often intolerant of handicaps and differences and we cannot allow our intolerance to guide us in our quest for the definition of what it means to be a person.

The arena of disability rights is where the intolerances of our society come to light. The body as object, the child as product gives way to the assessment of the body in terms of quality control and it is only one step away to the belief that it would be better not to have these bodies about at all. Margery Shaw argues that "parents might incur a legal duty to obtain an abortion" if a fetus has a birth defect and that "From the viewpoint of the child, a rational argument can be made that non-existence is preferable to existence filled with incapacities and suffering" (Quoted in Holtzman, 1989:220). We are setting ourselves up for a time when bodies that cannot or will not produce perfect bodies will have to cease production altogether and women will be denied the opportunity to give birth to an affected child (Holtzman, 1989:225). To prevent this scenario from becoming a reality, we must formulate an analysis in which reproductive rights are not pitted against disability rights (Baruch et al, 1988). At the same time we must guard against the tendency to dismiss real medical breakthroughs out of hand simply because they present a technological solution. Medical techniques in and of themselves are neither good nor bad; they can be used for positive or negative ends. Technology is a means to an end. The definition of what ends merit research, the allocation of research funds, and the personal goals of scientists and researchers however, create and transform technology and in doing so recreate and transform society. It is the socio-legal forces that control technology that must be critically appraised. Even the techniques of abortion, a relatively simple procedure, can be used to particular socio-legal ends by either being withheld from or forced upon women.

CONTROLLING THE REPRODUCTIVE BODY

In the field of reproduction the discourse of the medical community is such that the objectification of the body is taken as a given and any seemingly natural phenomena are reconstructed in such a way as to show how they are potentially dangerous and less desirable than artificial means. "The organic unity of mother and fetus can no longer be assumed" (Martin, 1987:20). The fetus is seen, not as an integral part of a woman's emotional and physical body, but rather as a separate person who has needs that conflict with that of the mother. "Mother/fetus are seen in the medical model as a conflicting dyad rather than as an integral unit" (Rothman, 1982:48). The development of the medical specialty of "Fetologist" reinforces the construct of the fetus as an autonomous person in need of and entitled to, medical care. Lawyer George Annas writes: "After birth the fetus becomes a child and can thereafter be treated in its own right. Before birth, we can obtain access to the fetus only through its mother, and in the absence of her informed consent, can only do so by treating her as a fetal container, a nonperson without rights to bodily integrity" (Quoted in Holtzman, 1989:228).

Ultrasound has become a routine procedure for many women and one effect of that has been to present the fetus to the mother, to legitimize its existence in such a way as to denigrate her own bodily experiences of it. "Photographs [of fetuses] have represented the fetus as primary and autonomous, the woman as absent or peripheral" (Petchesky, 1987:62). The fetus is taken from her body through the use of visual images, given a form and a legitimacy of its own by the doctor and then given back to the woman as though it were the doctor, not the woman, who created the fetus. Information concerning the fetus given by the woman is discounted in favor of information garnered by technology; technology that is controlled by the doctor. The fetus is treated as if it were a separate person, outside of the woman's body because it can be viewed (Petchesky, 1987:65). The woman's experiences within her body are ignored. While Petchesky makes the point that "to suggest that feeling is somehow more natural than seeing contradicts women's changing historical experience," the emphasis placed on seeing reinforces our belief in the body as object, the fetus as object; as apart from the woman in whose body it grows. Thus the woman who believes in her fetus' existence more firmly when she sees it, and discounts her own sensations of feeling it, reinforces our societal perceptions of the body as "other" and forces the question of bodily integrity. She is alienated from her own body, perceives herself as object, the glass womb through which, if we use enough technology, we can see the fetus, thus verifying its existence.

Increasingly, the law has taken the view that pregnant women have a diminished capacity for decision making and they are not entitled to all the rights and privileges of other individuals (Rodgers, 1989a:174). This trend, combined with the view of the fetus as a child in need of protection, has resulted in various cases before the courts that effectively limit the choices a pregnant woman has in regards to her own personhood. "She is the passive recipient of [decisions] made by others. . . . Can there be anything that comports less with human dignity and self-respect? How can a woman in this position have any sense of security with respect to her person?" (Madame Justice Wilson quoted in Rodgers, 1989b:200). The truth is that in these times a woman cannot have a strong sense of security with respect to her person if her person is pregnant. In Canada, women have had their fetuses made wards of the court under provisions of the Child and Family Services Act and the Mental Health Act. Women have been charged with criminal injury allegedly done to their fetuses. The definition of criminal injury changes according to medical and legal interpretation so that there exists the possibility of prosecution of pregnant women for lifestyle offenses; smoking, social drinking, strenuous physical activity, having sexual relations during a high risk pregnancy against the advice of her doctor (Rodgers, 1989a:180).

These examples of how and when it is possible to justify removing "control" of a woman's body from the woman and transferring it to the legal system, under the impetus of the powerful medical system, show how the discourse of the dualism of the body is an inadequate framework within which to argue for women's autonomy. Controlling women from within a medicolegal framework is only justifiable if we accept the concept of the body as object, apart from the self. If we reject this, then dismissing a pregnant woman's right to self-determination is indefensible. The body is not only a physical manifestation of the self but an integral component of the self; it is not just where we live but an element of our living.

A discourse that insists upon the concepts of ownership and control is one formulated and articulated from a patriarchal, capitalist perspective. Regardless of whether the discourse is formulated by feminists or not, it can only extend so far and cannot breach the boundaries of the system within which it is derived. If we, as feminists, continue to insist upon women's right to control, we risk losing that control to medicolegal forces and we deny our undeniable link to humanity through our bodily selves and our mental, spiritual selves. The body as object, as commodity, is perceived as sharing qualities of other objects, other commodities; houses, land, cars. If we extend the analogy, our fight for control and our unwavering belief in ownership of the body must then, adhere to the laws of ownership that govern other objects. We must reject this thesis as it desecrates what it is to be human and reduces humanity to laws of contract and property.

Mary Beth Whitehead lost custody of her daughter by a ruling pertaining to *contract* law, not family law, and that ruling, in essence, validated the perception of women as fetal containers (Chesler, 1988). The state has the power to sanction specific rules and regulations designed to limit the ways in which we can control that which we own; zoning laws, drunk driving laws, and increasingly, laws which govern the behavior of pregnant women. If a fruit tree on one's property drops leaves and fruit onto the neighbors' lawn, the neighbor must rake the leaves but is also entitled to the fruit; if a woman carries a fetus that will share social space with all of society, that may incur state spending due to any handicaps it may have, then the state is entitled to a say in the fetus' future. These are the arguments that we must expect when we justify the concept of control and ownership. These are the arguments that compel me to say that feminists must reject the liberal discourse of the body and begin the restructuring of a discourse that validates the social and the biological construction of the body; that confirms the integrity of the body; and that believes in the integration of the body and the mind. As feminists, we must continue to fight for the rights of women. The fight within the field of reproductive technologies necessitates a reevaluation of what it means to be human and what we need and desire for our own sense of humanity.

REFERENCES

Baruch, Elaine Hoffman, Amadeo D'Adamo and Joni Seager (eds), 1988, *Embryos, Ethics, and Women's Right. Exploring the New Reproductive Technologies*. New York: Haworth Press.

Chesler, Phyllis, 1988, *The Sacred Bond*. New York: Vintage Books.

Corea, Gena, 1985, *The Mother Machine. Reproductive Technologies from Artificial Insemination to Artificial Wombs*. New York: Harper & Row.

Edwards, R.G., 1983, "The Galton Lecture, 1982: The Current Clinical and Ethical Situation of Human Conception In Vitro," in C.O. Carter ed., *Developments in Human Reproduction and their Eugenic, Ethical Implications*. London: Academic Press.

Ehrenreich, Barbara and Deirdre English, 1978, *For Her Own Good. 150 Years of the Experts' Advice to Women*. New York: Doubleday.

Holtzman, Neil A., 1989, *Proceed With Caution. Predicting Genetic Risks in the Recombinant DNA Era.* Maryland: Johns Hopkins University Press.

Martin, Emily, 1987, *The Woman in the Body. A Cultural Analysis of Reproduction.* Boston: Beacon Press.

Petchesky, Rosalind Pollack, 1987, "Foetal Images: The Power of Visual Culture in the Politics of Reproduction," in Michelle Stanworth ed., *Reproductive Technologies. Gender, Motherhood and Medicine.* Minneapolis: University of Minnesota Press.

Rodgers, Sandra, 1989a, "Pregnancy as Justification for Loss of Juridical Autonomy," in Christine Overall ed., *The Future of Human Reproduction.* Toronto: The Women's Press. 1989b, "The Future of Abortion in Canada," in Christine Overall ed., *The Future of Human Reproduction.* Toronto: The Women's Press.

Rose, Hilary, 1987, "Victorian Values in the Test-Tube: The Politics of Reproductive Science and Technology," in Michelle Stanworth ed., *Reproductive Technologies. Gender, Motherhood and Medicine.* Minneapolis: University of Minnesota Press.

Ruddick, Sara, 1989, *Maternal Thinking. Towards a Politics of Peace.* New York: Ballantine Books.

Russett, Cynthia Eagle, 1989, *Sexual Science. The Victorian Construction of Womanhood.* Cambridge: Harvard University Press.

Shannon, Thomas A., 1988, *Surrogate Motherhood. The Ethics of Using Human Beings.* New York: Crossroads.

Synnott, Anthony, 1988, *The Body Social.* Montreal: Concordia University.

Institutionalized Violence

Karlene Faith

IN THE NAME OF SECURITY

When I speak of "institutionalized violence" I am concerned with institutional dangers presented to prisoners by the unchecked "authority" of abusive employees who are themselves over-institutionalized. Exceptionally abusive people are a distinct minority among "correctional officers" but those who are guilty can cause incalculable harm. Examples abound of systematic abuse against people confined to institutions, and in prisons the most frequent and insidious of these harms are those justified in the name of security and punishment for institutional infractions. In a major understatement, a member of an investigative committee said of strip-searching in the California prison, "the undressing of women in the 'quiet room' by male guards is demeaning" (ASCC, 1977: 191).

In male prisons, convicted child molesters and rapists are the pariahs among the more respectable lawbreakers. Among female prisoners, those convicted of any form of sexual assault are a tiny minority, if they are present at all. The rare, anomalous women who are convicted of killing, molesting or otherwise harming children and young people are not commonly physically attacked, but they may be ostracized by other prisoners or placed in "protective" custody, which usually means solitary confinement.

Ordinarily there's no relationship between the nature of one's crime and the punishment of super-maximum security segregation units, the prison within the prison (a.k.a. "dissociation unit," "protective-" or "administrative-custody," "adjustment cell," "quiet room" or "isolation," or, in prisoner vernacular, "seg," "hole," "digger," "dungeon" or "rack"). Women who have harmed children may be "protected" by isolation, as may women who have "ratted" to the staff on other prisoners' institutional infractions. But any disorderly or uncooperative prisoner might gain direct knowledge of the inhumanity of foul segregation units in which prisoners are strip-searched; kept in virtual cages under bright lights and camera surveillance; have food pushed through a slot at the bottom of the bars; are denied privacy for toilet activity; are harassed, ridiculed and humiliated by uncaring guards; are denied visits with their children and other family members; and are otherwise subjected to the indignities of extraordinary powerlessness within already-disempowering circumstances.

In their experience of the pains and degradations of segregation, and in other features of incarceration, women share almost everything in common with men in prison. During the 1970s male prisoners in North America took the first initiatives in filing one court case after another to protest the inhumane conditions of the institutions in which they were incarcerated. Paradoxically, in this same era, female prisoners began to file gender discrimination appeals in the courts, pleading for reforms on the grounds that they lacked equal rights with incarcerated men relative to, for example, classification; vocational, educational and recreational programs; condition and diversity of facilities; visitation rights; and health care (see, for example, Muraskin, 1993). Given that women cannot be seen as "similarly situated" with men in the larger society, given their special needs as an historically oppressed group and, especially, as primary caretakers of children, there has been considerable merit to the spirit of these legal challenges. However, if we view prisons in their concrete totality and recognize the sustained conditions of dehumanization in men's institutions, one can only conclude that imprisonment is one arena in which it is foolhardy to plead for gender equality. Equal misery cannot be perceived as a social advance for women or anyone.

Elie Wiesel, the renowned author and survivor of the mid-20th century Holocaust (in which an estimated 6 million Jews and uncounted homosexuals, gypsies, mentally ill and physically disabled people were tortured, burned, slaughtered and starved to death), speaks of how, in order to detach themselves from the horror, people learned to hold their spirit separate from their body. . . . Therapists working with survivors of childhood sexual abuse also attest to the pervasiveness of this ability to "dissociate" as a psychic survival strategy. Indeed, it is a familiar adage in prison communities that "they can take my body but they can't take my mind [or soul]." But this is often more a battle cry than a statement of fact. Despite the prevalence of such testimony, for many women the body/mind/soul can't be separated, and for such women one of the most devastating aspects of imprisonment is indeed losing control over one's own body. A woman in California in the first year of a five-years-to-life sentence for selling marijuana, for whom incarceration was intolerable, was unsuccessful in a suicide attempt. The response of the authorities was to teach her just how complete was her loss. As she recounted to me in an interview:

As soon as the hospital released me, I was sent before the Disciplinary Board. It's against the rules to attempt to kill yourself, and the Board sentenced me to 30 days in solitary detention—a very long, lonely thirty days. The only human being I saw in that time was the matron who brought the food around. By the time I was released from the "quiet room" I was so withdrawn I couldn't communicate with other people, so my closed custody status, where I could only leave my cell to go to work and to the Central Feeding Unit, was extended by six months.

The claiming of the prisoner's body begins with admission and is unremitting for the duration of imprisonment. As Jose-Kampfner noted from interviews with women serving life sentences in the United States, "cavity searches" cause a "humiliation that they never get used to" (1990: 112). Russell Dobash, Rebecca Dobash and Sue Gutteridge similarly note that women imprisoned in the United Kingdom "found body searches increasingly hard to bear" (1986: 204). For the women who experience it, a forced vaginal exam is tantamount to state-authorized rape, and torturing and shaming women in this way seems clearly intended to reinforce their dehumanized, prisoner status. The following excerpted text, by Lyn MacDonald, accompanied "a collaborative sculptural installation" by Vancouver artist Persimmon Blackbridge:

When I was transferred from one jail to another, they gave me a vaginal "exam"—whole hand style. . . . The full exam went like this—vaginal (speculum and bi-manually) and checks through all your body hair; nose; mouth; ears; between toes; bottoms of feet. We had lice shampoo squirted into our hands and had to rub it into our pubic hair and shampoo with it while one or two guards watched. We stood naked and spread-eagled while these guards circled us with clipboards noting our various scars, birthmarks and tattoos. I flipped out when the nurse stuck her hand in me and stated, "You've been pregnant." I COULDN'T STAND her having that knowledge without me telling her. I felt like they could start peeling me in layers, down to my raw nerves. . . . I started screaming at her/them, backing into the wall, hugging myself, threatening them. Fortunately, another nurse quickly covered me with a robe and led me to a chair. I got myself together . . . these outbursts are usually punished with isolation or worse. (Blackbridge et al., 1992: 23)

SELF-INJURY

. . . In most women's prisons in this century, women who "slash" or "carve" themselves (a.k.a. "letting"), or otherwise demonstrate that they've reached their limit of endurance, including those who attempt suicide, have been most commonly sent to "dissociation" (a.k.a. segregation units). The rationale is to observe them for potential suicide attempts. But the women perceive the policy as punishment for tampering with state property, namely their own bodies, and paradoxically women are more apt to slash while in segregation than within the general population (Heney, 1990: 15).

Slashing has been an aggravation to . . . prison administration for at least three reasons: (1) if the injury is serious enough to require ambulance transportation to a hospital it can cost the institution hundreds of dollars; (2) when one woman slashes herself, other women who are on the edge follow suit in a domino reaction which is burdensome to staff; and (3) more generally, a slashing "disrupts the discipline and order of the institution," in the words of a senior guard supervisor (recounted in Kershaw and Lasovich,

1991: 98). In other words, administrative expense and inconvenience is at issue, not the profound pain, or the reasons for it, which induce and follow from a woman's self-injurious actions.

It is not only women who slash themselves; men in prison are also vulnerable to this practice (Jackson, 1983: 80). But the greater reported frequency with which it occurs among women is consistent with theories that men are conditioned to turn anger, blame or frustration against others, whereas women turn such feelings against themselves. Estimates of women who slash vary from one institution to another, and according to time periods. A 1979 study of Ontario female provincial prisoners found that 86 percent had engaged in self-mutilation (Ross and McKay, 1979). From interviews with forty-four federal female prisoners in Canada a decade later, Jan Heney found that 59 percent had engaged in self-injurious behaviour, primarily slashing (92 percent) but also headbanging (8 percent) or "head-banging, starvation, burning and/or tattooing in addition to slashing" (Heney, 1990: 8). It is Heney's view that "self-injurious behavior is a *coping strategy* that manifests itself as a result of childhood abuse (usually sexual)" (Ibid.: 4).

> The woman may cope with feelings of powerlessness by dissociating, or psychologically separating herself from her body, a tactic often used to survive the actual abuse during childhood. Self-injury may be a desire to reconnect with one's own body—a desire to ensure that one can feel. In this sense it is a life-preserving measure. (Pollack, 1993: 59)

Whereas the prison experience is not usually the underlying cause of slashing, a lack of support systems for incarcerated women and a sense of absolute powerlessness exacerbate the impulse. An apparent increase in slashing over the past decade could be related to an increase in suicides. Although slashing and attempted suicide are not at all synonymous, the suicide of a prisoner triggers a slashing response from other women, and slashing itself has a domino effect. Overall, "prison tension" is cited as the impetus for slashing by over half the women interviewed by Heney. As a prisoner says

> Friendships are intensified in the prison. When someone you care about slashes, it upsets you because you are already upset about the same shit she is. When your friend slashes it tilts you because of her distress. (Heney, 1990: 10)

Heney emphasizes that "self-injurious behaviour is a mental health issue as opposed to a security issue," citing the women's repeated insistence that they slash when they lack someone to talk with about their problems. Almost half indicated the need for more counselors but others suggested that a friend, including another prisoner, would be just as useful. Heney emphasizes that treating slashing as a security issue compounds the problem, and she encourages greater attention to mental health services which would include giving prisoners more opportunities to develop structured peer support systems. She also emphasizes the need to take seriously the pervasiveness of childhood sexual abuse among women who self-injure, which is experienced as "loss of control [and] determination over the fundamental right to their bodies" (Ibid.: 24–29, 38).

REFERENCES

Assembly Special Committee on Corrections (ASCC) (1977). *Report on Incarcerated Women.* Sacramento: California State Legislature.

Blackbridge, Persimmon with Geri Ferguson, Michelle Kanashiro-Christensen, Lyn Mac-Donald and Bea Walkus (1992). "A Collaborative Sculptural Installation: Doing Time." *Matriart: A Canadian Feminist Art Journal* 3(1): 23–25.

Dobash, Russell P., R. Emerson Dobash and Sue Gutteridge (1986). *The Imprisonment of Women.* London: Basil Blackwell.

Heney, Jan (1990). "Report on Self-Injurious Behaviour in the Kingston Prison for Women." Ottawa: Ministry of the Solicitor General, Corrections Branch.

Jackson, Michael (1983). *Prisoners of Isolation: Solitary Confinement in Canada.* Toronto: University of Toronto Press.

Jose-Kampfner, Christina (1990). "Coming to Terms with Existential Death: An Analysis of Women's Adaptation to Life in Prison." *Social Justice* 17(2): 110–25.

Kershaw, Anne and Mary Lasovich (1991). *Rock-a-Bye Baby: A Death Behind Bars.* Toronto: McClelland & Stewart.

Muraskin, Roslyn (1993). "Disparate Treatment in Correctional Facilities," in R. Muraskin and T. Alleman (Eds.), *It's a Crime: Women and Justice.* Englewood Cliffs: Prentice Hall, 211–25.

Pollack, Shoshana (1993). "Opening the Window on a Very Dark Day: A Program Evaluation of the Peer Support Team at the Kingston Prison for Women." Unpublished Master's Thesis. Ottawa: Carleton University.

Ross, R. and H. McKay (1979). *Self-Mutilation.* Toronto: Lexington Books.

IDENTITY, EMOTIONS, AND THE SOCIAL CONSTRUCTION OF DIFFERENCE(S)

"Identity" is a concept much beloved by sociologists and social psychologists as well as by officialdom and bureaucracies of all types. The term is also a key to understanding those contemporary social movements galvanized around "identity politics." Such politics mobilizes people around the stigmatized identity they have in common.

Erving Goffman brought stigmatization to the sociological fore in the early 1960s with *Stigma: Notes on the Management of Spoiled Identity*. Stigmatization spoils an individual's identity by problematizing it in one of two ways. When an individual's stigma is visible or widely known about, the person is *discredited;* when it is neither readily visible nor widely known about, the person is *discreditable.* The first type of spoiled identity necessitates managing one's presentation of self to nonstigmatized others if one wants to fit in and gain acceptance; the second type necessitates controlling information about oneself so as not to be discredited in nonstigmatized circles. Commonly, a social stigma rests on an individual's physical "failings" such as a badly scarred face or a hearing impairment, an individual's characterological failings such as spouse abuse or a DUI conviction, or an individual's tribal affiliations such as race, sex, or ethnicity.[1]

Typically, stigmatization comprises dualisms distinguishing between "normal" and stigmatized individuals. As Elizabeth Martinez emphasizes in the first reading, a racial dualism undergirds racism and racist oppression in American society. That black-white dualism erases many people of color or vaguely situates them in "that after-thought construction, 'Blacks and other minorities' " (p. 238). Similarly, the straight-gay dualism renders bisexual, asexual, and other non-gay queer people invisible, which is one reason "queer" may have considerable appeal across the diverse terrain uncharted by institutionalized heterosexuality. The dualisms commonly applied to diverse human populations, then, tend to erase many individuals and groups. In the process, such dualisms ironically, though only virtually, normalize one kind of Otherness while ignoring and dismissing other departures from what is hegemonic and institutionally normalized.

By now, a number of social movements aim to advance the rights and interests of stigmatized individuals. Such movements—the gay and lesbian rights movement and the more embryonic sexual workers' movement, for example—mobilize participants by invoking the spoiled identity they share. Participants in such movements not only aim to secure their rights but also to redefine the social identity they have in common. Such redefinition can be substantive or axiological. *Substantive redefinitions* occur when group members deny that the social identity outsiders impute to them is valid and meaningful. Members might, for example, go to great lengths to deny that they are sexually promiscuous or condone pedophilia. *Axiological redefinitions* occur when group members express pride in the very identity that is socially spoiled in mainstream society. They might, for instance, devote considerable energy to reclaiming the name "queer" by making it a term expressive of group pride and anti-assimilationist values. In women's movements substantive redefinitions revolve around emphasizing how similar women and men are, while axiological redefinitions entail valorizing women's ethic of caring and their fluid ego boundaries.

Whatever the redefinitions under way, identity politics emphasizes commonality of identity, not a commonality of class or other daily circumstances. Unlike homeless people or prisoners whose everyday lives are starkly similar, for example, lesbians and gay men differ dramatically in their everyday circumstances. Some are closeted and move with relative ease in straight society; others are "out" and some are "in your face" about their sexual orientation. Some lesbians and gay men worry like other parents about the cost of their kids' braces or their safety coming and going to school; others are proud to be "child-free" and enjoy a measure of affluence that makes them an attractive market niche. Like women or ethnic minorities, lesbians and gay men share a spoiled identity much more consequentially than they share a lifestyle or a set of material circumstances, as Larry Gross's selection indicates. Needless to say, such individuals do have a lot of experiences in common, namely, those deriving from stigmatization and thus crossing class, gender, and other lines of their lives. Nevertheless their in-group differences are substantial enough to matter politically and culturally.

Yet, as Shane Phelan emphasizes, identity politics seeks an "unmediated unity, a unity that carries as its twin an excessive fear of difference."[2] In the lesbian and gay rights movement, for instance, bisexual individuals have no comfortable, clear-cut place if they are "out" as such.[3] Often seen as "in transition" between heterosexuality and homosexuality and unduly benefiting from—indeed, taking advantage of—heterosexual privilege, as Mariana Valverde's selection indicates, bisexuals have an ambiguous identity in relation to the hetero/homo dichotomy. Identity politics transforms one's spoiled identity into a badge of honor; it reverses the cruelties and injustices of the mainstream world. As Valverde shows, people such as bisexuals whose identities introduce ambiguities into that process thus pose problems, particularly if their "different" identities appear to introduce some of the mainstream trappings participants are trying to escape or overcome.

Ironically but understandably, then, identity politics sometimes means fending off or even putting down those whose identities are not spoiled in quite the "right" ways. As Phelan indicates, such individuals are often written off as "neurotic or unaware of [their] oppression or in other ways defective";[4] therein lies supposed justification for "ignor[ing] or denigrat[ing] their] self-understandings and desires." The charge might, for instance, be that if the individual faced up to her *real* feelings and had the courage of her convictions, she would have nothing further to do with men as prospective sexual partners. Wendy Chapkis gives the example of a " 'less feminist than thou' guilt" that kept her from sharing with her feminist friends.[5] Of necessity perhaps, identity politics eventuates in such assessments. Rather than acknowledging diversity of circumstances and opinions among movement participants, identity politics draws fairly hard and fast boundaries between those who are "one of us" and those who are not. Such politics thus constructs its own version of the insider/outsider dichotomy. It involves "a pretense to a homogeneity of experience . . . that does not in fact exist."[6] Ed Cohen reports that "no matter how sensitively we go about it, 'identity politics' has great difficulty in affirming difference(s)."[7] As Phelan puts it, such politics is "totalizing." It "traps its practitioners by commanding that every facet of life be measured by one yardstick that, in turn, is seemingly clear and authentic."[8] Alternatively, as Valverde suggests, one can say that marginalized subject positions such as homosexuality often get institutionalized themselves.

The matter of identity politics centers most of Larry Gross's selection, which focuses on broad theoretical and political questions about the social construction of lesbian and gay identities and communities based on members' sexual identities. Gross begins by looking at a strategy distinctive to some lesbian/gay identity politics, namely, outing. He (p. 249) defines it as a "selective 'lavendering' of individuals who are already visible to mainstream society and therefore are known and often respected and even loved by millions who do not believe that they know any homosexuals." Gross goes on to look at the essentialist/constructionist debate, if only because "important . . . political differences flow from these two positions" (p. 253), which he treats less dichotomously than most theorists. Thereafter Gross portrays the identity challenges lesbians and gay men face whether they opt for a closeted life, a double life, or the lifelong processes of coming out and going public. In his portrayal of poignant identity issues Gross underscores how central community is to managing a relatively uncloseted identity, much as Goffman emphasized the preciousness of "one's own" and "the wise" among discredited and discreditable individuals of all ilks.[9] Thereby Gross not only anticipates themes in the next section but also, and more significantly, problematizes the notion of a "community" based on "largely the commonality of [members'] difference from, and oppression by, the dominant culture." (p. 256) He thus resists the totalizing perspective often tied in with formulations such as "the gay community."

Like Gross, Phelan recommends "resist[ing] the impulse for total separatism and for purity in our allies in favor of workable coalitions and porous but meaningful communities." She wants an identity politics "based, not only on identity, but on an appreciation for politics as the art of living together. Politics that ignores our identities . . . is useless; but nonnegotiable identities will enslave us whether they are imposed from within or without."[10] Audre Lorde lands on the same side of the issue:

I am a lesbian woman of Color whose children eat regularly because I work in a university. If their full bellies make me fail to recognize my commonality with a woman of Color whose children do not eat because she cannot find work, or who has no children because her insides are rotted from home abortions and sterilization; if I fail to recognize the lesbian who chooses not to have children, the woman who remains closeted because her homophobic community is her only life support, the woman who chooses silence instead of another death, the woman who is terrified lest my anger trigger an explosion of hers; if I fail to recognize them as other faces of myself, then I am contributing not only to each of their oppressions but also to my own. . . .[11]

These observations about identity politics illustrate a problematic associated with "identity" and its politics. Identity can be a means of social control as powerful as any other means rooted in human consciousness and sustained by social interaction. Identity can be a means of self-inhibition, a social-psychological rut wherein we dodge choices and avoid wearisome complexities. Undermining those constrictive eventualities requires seeing identity as "a set of repeated acts within a highly rigid regulatory frame that congeal over time to produce the appearance of substance, of a natural sort of being." Seen for what it is in mainstream society, identity is a "regulatory practice."

Thus does Judith Butler argue that identity is best seen as a practice. Yet she says that that practice need not be regulatory. Instead, we can conceive of our identities as "signifying" practices whereby we render ourselves "culturally intelligible subjects." From that perspective our agency is "located within the possibility of a variation on that repetition" of significations we call our identity. Agency thus presupposes the *possibility* of deviance. In those terms Butler sees "political possibilities" in "a radical critique of the categories of identity."[12] On that ground she meets Phelan who says,

> The truths of our lives are not to be found exclusively in our self-representations. By this I mean that not only do we not understand the consequences of our generalized statements, but we do not, in fact, live the lives that our theoretic representations would suggest. Far from being a weakness, this is . . . the strength of human life exceeding verbalization.[13]

A great deal of the human life exceeding verbalization and representations implicates our emotions which, like our bodies, are largely absent from theorists' models of agency, consciousness, and even community. Gross's selection, especially in its attention to coming out and going public, implies the emotional demands a lesbian or gay identity entails in a society where homophobia runs rampant. The next reading, Sandra Lee Bartky's "Feeding Egos and Tending Wounds," traces the emotional and moral contours of hegemonic femininity played out in a gendered division of labor that casts heterosexual women as the caretakers of men and children.

Bartky's is a skeptical stance toward those who blithely affirm women's nurturing activities in the heteropatriarchal family or in a conventional heterosexual relationship. She argues that "a complex and contradictory female subjectivity is constructed within the relations of caregiving." (p. 269) On the one side, heterosexual women can and do feel empowered through their lived experiences of nurturing their husbands, lovers, or boyfriends. Such expressions of "conventional femininity" are "profoundly seductive" for many such women. (p. 270) On the other side, however, stand the epistemic, ethical, and status costs of such caregiving. In the interstices of everyday life women's caregiving serves as "an affirmation of male importance that is unreciprocated" (p. 265), and in that circumstance lies a host of hazards most heterosexual women are hard pressed to bypass. At one point Bartky (p. 265) notes that "few things are as disempowering as having to beg." There she harkens back to Goffman's exposition of the indignities associated with total institutions where the need to ask for small things attests to inmates' violated dignity.

The unreciprocated caregiving widely expected of heterosexual women casts them in precisely that sort of situation. More often than not, their partners "receive [their] attention as a kind of entitlement," while they often have to ask to be appreciated, to go out for the evening with their friends, or to be understood on their own terms. In her delineation of hegemonic femininity Bartky thus traces the tangle of identity, emotions, and power constitutive of domestic politics often experienced as little more than "the innocent pleasures of everyday life" (p. 272).

Yet sometimes anger does infiltrate such situations more than momentarily. In the preceding section Linda Gordon's piece on battered wives illustrates that circumstance in the extreme. The next reading in this section deals with long-term anger more diffuse in nature. Audre Lorde (p. 275) advises, "We cannot allow our fear of anger to deflect us nor seduce us into settling for anything less than the hard work of excavating honesty. . . ." In that broad principle she would seem to join hands with Bartky and other multicultural theorists advocating intellectual honesty as an antidote to the dishonesty institutionalized, both by design and by default, in mainstream social theory.

Lorde's focuses are anger about oppression, especially racial oppression, and anger among women. The way she tackles these matters puts her in the position of further deconstructing the hegemonic femininity Bartky sketches. Moreover, Lorde's approach lets her construct a counterhegemonic femininity centered on strength and courage as well as honesty. Lorde (p. 275) knows well the "virulent hatred leveled . . . against all of us who are seeking to examine the particulars of our lives as we resist our oppressions, moving toward coalition and effective action." Also from her experiences she knows that anger is central to resistance, coalition, and effective action. Lorde (p. 275) juxtaposes it with hatred:

> Hatred is the fury of those who do not share our goals, and its object is death and destruction. Anger is a grief of distortions between peers, and its object is change.

Lorde (p. 276) says that even in their anger toward (racialized) one another, women can come together "upon a common basis to examine difference, and to alter those distortions which history has created around [their] difference." They can come together to defeat elitism. To some extent, Lorde implies, such possibilities hinge on deconstructing guilt and moving beyond its constraining grasp.

In the final reading of this section Christine Sypnowich traces our Western, historical trajectory toward preoccupation with "difference" from the Enlightenment to the postmodernist present. Then she briefly looks at several theorists' efforts to show how "difference" and "justice" can together inform a viable politics. Sypnowich remains unconvinced. She fears that "Difference is . . . bound to defeat the political theories which seek to emphasize and resolve it." Thereafter she expresses high-powered reservations about current strategies of invoking difference in order to change institutions of domination through a democratic politics. Sypnowich (p. 286) concludes, "If we are to tackle injustice, which is after all the preoccupation of difference theorists, then we need a broader inquiry than that of difference itself." Without totalizing or universalizing, Sypnowich ends up favoring "discourses of rights and impartiality" as "the means for struggling for that ever-elusive but nonetheless inspiring universalist ideal." In the process she emphasizes that "Questions of human needs, the constituents of human dignity, the prerequisites for self-respect, these are the universal ideals to which rights refer" (p. 287). She urges less attention to identities and differences with a concomitant renewal of attention to "the interests that accrue from different identities and the extent to which they figure as claims for justice" (p. 289).

To a substantial extent *Multicultural Experiences, Multicultural Theories* resonates with Sypnowich's position. Rather than emphasizing differences as such, it underscores the inequalities of power and the infringements on dignity that largely define our social structure. By exploring those matters in and through yet beyond and beneath the concept of difference(s), it steers a theoretical course capable of challenging elitism in our theories and practices without furthering the social constructions of the very "differences" used to demean, hurt, and oppress most of us.

This section of the book suggests that the notion of identity, a cultural correlate of "difference(s)," involves a problematic with consequences for selfhood, community, and social movements. As individuals, we need to understand that "every label we use to identify ourselves carries with it its own limitations for our behavior. . . ."[14] As makers of community, we need to challenge any "unity" built up around "exclusionary norm[s] of solidarity at the level of identity. . . ."[15] We need, then, to interrogate our experiences of and others' claims about "difference" as a source of "tension, fear, dominance, submission, conquest, feelings of being powerful or powerless, feelings of being in control or out of control."[16] (Paradoxically, only community with one another gives us stable grounds for such interrogations.) Finally, as participants in or analysts of social movements we need to see that shibboleths about "unity" may preclude "disrupt[ing] the very borders of identity concepts . . ." that inhibit freedom and precipitate oppression. We need to ask "what sort of politics demands that kind of advance purchase on unity?"[17] What sort of social-justice politics would further the either/or thinking that has kept this tired old oppressive world going? Has the time not come to challenge any movement, any model, or any stance insistent that a practice is either this *or* that with no other typifications allowed and all ambiguities prohibited? Butler thinks so, if only because such posturing foreshortens "the flexibility in our lives that is so needed"[18]—the flexibility needed to shape our own life stories as well as our collective story.

We might look, then, to multicultural social theorists to liberate the concept of identity from the stranglehold that mainstream theorists have put on it. We might look to them to unfold the possibility that

> The opposite of oppression . . . is, not truth or respect, but humor or lightheartedness—the humor that comes from seeing all categories, all explanations, all identities as provisional. Such a sense is rooted in the appreciation of ambiguity. . . .[19]

Such a sense is also rooted in a taste for improvisation. It has roots, too, in a propensity for what Georg Simmel called *flirtation* where "the possibility of the Perhaps" holds sway, where one "oscillat[es] . . . between interest and indifference," where one "ensures that in definitive not-having, there is still a sense in which we can have."[20] No rhetoric of differences prepares us for such zesty prospects, and no eyes focused on "Others" can see the appeal in such a playful, deadly serious engagement with life.

NOTES

1 Erving Goffman, *Stigma: Notes on the Management of Spoiled Identity,* Harper Colophon, New York, 1963.
2 Shane Phelan, *Identity Politics: Lesbian Feminism and the Limits of Community,* Temple University Press, Philadelphia, 1989, p. 57.
3 Lillian Faderman, *Surpassing the Love of Men: Romantic Friendship and Love Between Women from the Renaissance to the Present,* William Morrow And Company, New York, 1981, p. 415.
4 Phelan, *op. cit.,* pp. 155–56.
5 Wendy Chapkis, *Beauty Secrets,* South End Press, Boston, 1986, p. 2.
6 Audre Lorde, *Sister Outsider: Essays and Speeches,* The Crossing Press, Freedom, CA, 1984, p. 116.
7 Ed Cohen, "Who Are 'We'? Gay 'Identity As Political (E)motion: A Theoretical Rumination" in Diana Fuss (ed.), *Inside/Out: Lesbian Theories, Gay Theories,* Routledge, New York, 1991, p. 76.
8 Phelan, *op. cit.,* p. 138.
9 Goffman, *op. cit.*
10 Phelan, *op. cit.,* pp. 166, 170.
11 Lorde, *op. cit.,* p. 132.
12 Judith Butler, *Gender Trouble: Feminism and the Subversion of Identity,* Routledge, New York, 1990, pp. ix, 32, 33, 145.
13 Phelan, *op. cit.,* p. 157.
14 Julia Penelope, *Call Me Lesbian: Lesbian Lives, Lesbian Theory,* The Crossing Press, Freedom, CA, 1992, p. 4.
15 Butler, *op. cit.,* p. 15.
16 Penelope, *op. cit.,* p. 106.
17 Butler, *op. cit.,* pp. 14, 15.
18 *Ibid.,* p. 139.
19 Phelan, *op. cit.,* pp. 156–57.
20 Georg Simmel, "Flirtation" in Guy Oakes (ed. and tr.), *Georg Simmel on Women, Sexuality, and Love,* Yale University Press, New Haven, 1984 [orig. 1911], pp. 143, 146, 150.

Beyond Black/White: The Racisms of Our Time

Elizabeth Martínez

BY WAY OF INTRODUCTION

Let me begin by admitting that I have [an] axe to grind. A bell to toll, a *grito* to shout, a banner to wave. The banner was fashioned during 10 years in the Black civil rights-human rights movement followed by 10 years in the Chicano *movimiento*. Those years taught that liberation has similar meanings in both histories: an end to racist oppression, the birth of collective self-respect, and a dream of social justice. Those years taught that alliances among progressive people of color can and must help realize the dream.

Such alliances require a knowledge and wisdom that we have yet to attain. For the present, it remains painful to see how divide-and-conquer strategies succeed among our peoples. It is painful to see how prejudice, resentment, petty competitiveness, and sheer ignorance fester. It is positively pitiful to see how often we echo Anglo stereotypes about one another.

All this suggests that we urgently need some fresh and fearless thinking about racism at this moment in history. Fresh thinking might begin with analyzing the strong tendency among Americans to frame real issues in strictly Black-white terms. Do such terms make sense when changing demographics point to a U.S. population that will be 32% Latino, Asian/Pacific American, and Native American—that is, neither Black nor white—by the year 2050? Not to mention the increasing numbers of mixed people who incorporate two, three, or more "races" or nationalities? Don't we need to imagine multiple forms of racism rather than a single, Black-white model?

Practical questions related to the fight against racism also arise. Doesn't the exclusively Black-white framework discourage perception of common interests among people of color—primarily in the working class—and thus sustain White Supremacy? Doesn't the view of institutionalized racism as a problem experienced only by Black people isolate them from potential allies? Doesn't the Black-white definition encourage a tendency often found among people of color to spend too much energy understanding our lives in relation to Whiteness, obsessing about what the White will think? That tendency is inevitable in some ways: the locus of power over our lives has long been white (although big shifts have recently taken place in the color of capital) and the oppressed have always survived by becoming experts on the oppressor's ways. But that can become a prison of sorts, a trap of compulsive vigilance. Let us liberate ourselves, then, from the tunnel vision of Whiteness and behold the colors around us!

To criticize the Black-white framework is not simply a resentful demand from other people of color for equal sympathy, equal funding, equal clout, equal patronage. It is not simply us-too resentment at being ignored or minimized. It is not just another round of mindless competition in the victimhood tournament. Too often we make the categories of race, class, gender, sexuality, age, physical condition, etc., contend for the title of "most oppressed." Within "race," various population groups then compete for that top spot. Instead, we need to understand that various forms and histories of oppression exist. We need to recognize that they include differences in extent and intensity. Yet pursuing some hierarchy of competing oppressions leads us down dead-end streets where we will never find the linkage between oppressions or how to overcome them.

The goal in reexamining the Black-white definition is to find an effective strategy for vanquishing an evil that has expanded rather than diminished in recent years. Three recent developments come to mind. First is the worldwide economic recession in which the increasingly grim struggle for sheer survival encourages the scapegoating of working-class people—especially immigrants, especially those of color—by other working-class people. This has become so widespread in the West that a Klan cross-burning in London's Trafalgar Square or on Paris' Champs Élysée doesn't seem hard to imagine. The globalization of racism is mounting rapidly.

Second, and relatedly, the reorganization of the international division of labor continues, with changing demands for workers that are affecting demographics everywhere. History tells us of the close relationship between capital's need for labor and racism. If that relationship changes, so may the nature of racism.

Finally, in the U.S., we have passed through a dozen years of powerful reaction against the civil-rights agenda set in the 1960s. This has combined with the recession's effects and other socioeconomic developments to make people go into a defensive, hunkering-down mode, each community on its own, at a time when we need more rather than less solidarity. Acts of racist violence now occur in communities that never saw them before (although they always could have happened). An intensification of racism is upon us.

We see it in the anti-immigrant emotions being whipped up and new divisions based on racism and nativism. We see escalating white fears of becoming the minority population, the minority power, after centuries of domination. As U.S. demographics change rapidly, as the "Latinization" of major regions and cities escalates, a cross fire of fears begins to crackle. In that climate the mass media breed both cynical hopelessness and fear. Look only at that October 1992 *Atlantic* magazine cover proclaiming "BLACKS VS. BROWNS: Immigration and the New American Dilemma" for one chilling symptom of an assumed, inevitable hostility.

Today the task of building solidarity among people of color promises to be more necessary and difficult than ever. An exclusively Black-white definition of racism makes our task all the harder. That's the banner that will be raised here: an urgent need for 21st-century thinking, which can move us beyond the Black/white framework without negating its central, historical role in the construction of U.S. racism. We do need much more understanding of how racism and its effects developed, not only similarly, but also differently for different peoples according to whether they were victimized by genocide, enslavement, or colonization in various forms.

Greater solidarity among peoples of color must be hammered out, painstakingly. With solidarity a prize could be won even bigger than demolishing racism. The prize could be a U.S. society whose national identity not only ceases to be white, but also advances beyond "equality"—beyond a multiculturalism that gives people of color a respect equal to whites. Toni Morrison has written eloquently in *Playing in the Dark* of this goal from an Africanist perspective: "American means white, and Africanist people struggle to make the term applicable to themselves with ethnicity and hyphen after hyphen after hyphen. . . . In the scholarship on the formation of an American character [a] . . . major item to be added to the list must be an Africanist presence—decidedly not American, decidedly other" (Morrison, 1992: 47).

We need to dream of replacing the white national identity with an identity grounded in cultures oriented to respect for all forms of life and balance rather than domination as their guiding star. Such cultures, whose roots rest in indigenous, precolonial societies of the Americas and Africa, can help define a new U.S. identity unshackled from the capitalist worldview. Still alive today, they color my banner bright.

. . .

Let us begin that dialogue about the exclusively Black-white model of racism and its effects with the question: does that definition prevail and, if so, why?

Alas, it does prevail. Major studies of "minorities" up to 1970 rarely contain more than a paragraph on our second largest "minority," Mexican-Americans (Blauner, 1972: 165). In two dozen books of 1960s movement history, I found inadequate treatment of the Black Civil Rights Movement, but almost total silence about the Chicano, Native American, and Asian American movements of those years (Martínez, 1989). Today, not a week goes by without a major media discussion of race and race relations that totally ignores the presence in U.S. society of Native Americans, Latinos, Asian/Pacific Americans, and Arab-Americans.

East Coast-based media and publishers are the worst offenders. Even a progressive magazine like *The Nation* can somehow publish a special issue entitled "The Assault on Equality: Race, Rights, and the New Orthodoxy" (December 9, 1991) containing only two brief phrases relating to people of color other than African-Americans in 27 pages. Outbreaks of Latino unrest or social uprising, such as we saw in the Mt. Pleasant section of Washington, D.C., make little if any dent. New York, that center of ideological influence, somehow remains indifferent to the fact that in 1991, Latinos totaled 24.4% of its population while Asians formed 6.9%.

Even in California, this most multinational of the states, where Latinos have always been the most numerous population of color, it is not rare for major reports on contemporary racial issues to stay strictly inside the Black-white framework. Journalists in San Francisco, a city almost half Latino or Asian/Pacific-American, can see no need to acknowledge "This article will be about African-Americans only"—which would be quite acceptable—in articles on racial issues. At best we may hear that after-thought construction, "Blacks and other minorities."

Again, momentous events that speak to Latino experience of racist oppression fail to shake the prevailing view. Millions of Americans saw massive Latino participation in the April 1992 Los Angeles uprising on their TV screens. Studies show that, taken as a whole, the most heavily damaged areas of L.A. were 49% Latino, and the majority of people arrested were Latino (Pastor, 1993). Yet the mass media and most people have continued to view that event as "a Black riot."

Predominantly Anglo left forces have not been much better than the mainstream and liberals. The most consistently myopic view could be heard from the Communist Party

U.S.A., which has seen the African-American experience as the only model of racism. Left groups that adopted the Black Nation thesis rarely analyzed the validity of Chicano nationalism in the Southwest, or advocated giving lands back to the Native Americans, or questioned the "model minority" myth about Asian/Pacific Americans.

A semi-contemptuous indifference toward Latinos—to focus on this one group—has emanated from institutions in the dominant society for decades. Echoing this attitude are many individual Anglos. To cite a handful of personal experiences: Anglos will admit to having made a racist remark or gesture toward an African-American much more quickly than toward a Latino. Or if you bring up some Anglo's racist action toward a Latino, they will change the subject almost instantly to racism toward a Black person. Or they may respond to an account of police brutality toward Latinos with some remark of elusive relevance about Spanish crimes against indigenous people in the Americas.

A stunning ignorance also prevails. Race-relations scholar Robert (Bob) Blauner has rightly noted that:

> Even informed Anglos know almost nothing about La Raza, its historical experience, its present situation. . . . And the average citizen doesn't have the foggiest notion that Chicanos have been lynched in the Southwest and continue to be abused by the police, that an entire population has been exploited economically, dominated politically, and raped culturally (Blauner, 1972: 166).

Above all, there seems to be little comprehension of what it means to suffer total disenfranchisement in the most literal sense. Millions of Latinos, like many Asian/Pacific Americans, lack basic political rights. They are often extremely vulnerable to oppression and the most intense oppression occurs when people have problems of legal status. This means the borderlands, where vulnerability rests on having formal admission documents or not. Aside from South Africa's pass system, it is hard to imagine any mechanism in modern times so well designed to control, humiliate, and disempower vast numbers of workers than the border and its requirements.

WHY THE BLACK-WHITE FRAMEWORK?

Three of the reasons for the Black-white framework of racial issues seem obvious: numbers, geography, and history. African-Americans have long been the largest population of color in the U.S.; only recently has this begun to change. Also, African-Americans have long been found in sizable numbers in most of the United States, including major cities. On the other hand, Latinos—to focus on this group—are found primarily in the Southwest plus parts of the Northwest and Midwest and they have been (wrongly) perceived as a primarily rural people—therefore of less note.

Historically, it has been only 150 years since the U.S. seized half of Mexico and incorporated those lands and their peoples into this nation. The Black/white relationship, on the other hand, has long been entrenched in the nation's collective memory. White enslavement of Black people together with white genocide against Native Americans provided the original models for racism as it developed here. Slavery and the struggle against it form a central theme in this country's only civil war—a prolonged, momentous conflict—and continuing Black rebellion. Enslaved Africans in the U.S. and

African-Americans have created an unmatched history of massive, persistent, dramatic, and infinitely courageous resistance, with individual leaders of worldwide note. They cracked the structure of racism in this country during the first Reconstruction and again during the second, the 1960s Civil Rights Movement, as no other people of color have done.

Interwoven with these historical factors are possible psychological explanations of the Black/white definition. In the eyes of Jefferson and other leaders, Native Americans did not arouse white sexual anxieties or seem a threat to racial purity, as did Blacks. In any case, White Supremacy's fear of Indian resistance had greatly diminished by the late 1800s as a result of relentless genocide accompanied by colonization. Black rebelliousness, on the other hand, remains an inescapable nightmare to the dominant white society. There is also the fact that contemporary Black rebellion has been urban: right in the Man's face, scary.

A relative indifference toward Mexican people developed in Occupied America in the late 1800s. Like the massacre of Indians and enslavement of Africans, the successful colonization of Mexicans in what became the Southwest was key to U.S. economic growth. One would expect to see racist institutions and ideology emerge, and so they did in certain areas. Yet even in places like the Texas borderlands, where whites have historically reviled and abused Latinos, the Mexican presence didn't arouse a high level of white sexual anxiety and other irrational fears. Today Latinos often say Anglo attitudes make them feel they are less hated than dismissed as inconsequential. "There's no Mau-Mau factor," observed a Black friend half humorously about Latino invisibility.

Of course there may be an emergent Mau-Mau factor, called demographics. Anglo indifference to Latinos may be yielding to a new fear. The white response to anticipation of becoming a minority during one's own lifetime is often panic as well as hatred and those "hordes" at the gate are of colors other than Black. But the new frenzy has yet to show the same fear-stricken face toward Latinos—or Asian/Pacific Americans—as toward African-Americans.

Robert Blauner, an Anglo and one of the few authors on racism to have examined the Black/white framework, looks at these psychological factors as revealed in literature:

> . . . We buy black writer not only because they can write and have something to say, but because the white racial mind is obsessed with blackness. . . . Mexican-Americans, on the other hand, have been unseen as individuals and as a people. . . . James Baldwin has pointed to the deep mutual involvement of black and white in America. The profound ambivalence, the love-hate relationship, which Baldwin's own work expresses and dissects, does not exist in the racism that comes down on La Raza. . . . Even the racial stereotypes that plague Mexican-Americans tend to lack those positive attributes that mark antiblack fantasies—supersexuality, inborn athletic and musical power, natural rhythm. Mexicans are dirty, lazy, treacherous, thieving bandits—and revolutionaries (Blauner, 1972:11–164).

(Not that I would want to choose between having Rhythm or Roaches.)

A final reason for the Black/white framework may be found in the general U.S. political culture, which is not only white-dominated, but also embraces an extremely stubborn form of national self-centeredness. This U.S.-centrism has meant that the political culture lacks any global vision other than relations of domination. In particular, the U.S.

has consistently demonstrated contempt for Latin America, its people, their languages, and their issues. The U.S. refuses to see itself as one nation sitting on a continent with 20 others whose dominant languages are Spanish and Portuguese. That myopia has surely nurtured the Black/white framework for racism.

THE CULTURE OF COLOR

Color is crucial to understanding the Black/white framework of racial issues. Early in this nation's history, Benjamin Franklin perceived a tri-racial society based on skin color—"the lovely white," black, and "tawny," as Ron Takaki tells us in *Iron Cages*. Echoing this triad, we still have the saying "If you're white, you're all right; if you're Black, get back; if you're brown, stick around." As that old saying indicates, racism is experienced differently by Native Americans, African-Americans, Latinos, and Asian/Pacific Americans. In the case of Latinos, we find them somewhat more likely to be invisibilized—rendered "unseen"—than problematized (with thanks to writer/activist Linda Burnham for that concept). Color explains much of this.

The relatively light skin and "Caucasian" features of many Latinos mean they are less threatening in the eyes of white racism and can even can "pass"—unnoticed, invisible—much more often than African-Americans. Obviously this carries certain advantages in a racist society. Many Latinos would like to pass, work hard to assimilate, and succeed.

Until 1990 the U.S. Census categorized Latinos as "White," and even in that year it generated mass confusion on this issue; today the common term "Non-Hispanic Whites" certainly suggests a view of Latinos as white. At the same time, a 1992 poll of Latinos has shown an unexpectedly strong lack of self-identification as such. More than 90%, for example, said they did not belong to any ethnic organizations and less than 13% participated in any political activities organized around their national groups.

The term Hispanic (Her Panic, His Panic), whose emergence accompanied the rise of a Latino middle-class in the late 1970s to 1980s, encourages the wannabe whites/don't wannabe Indians. Always the unspoken goal has been to sidestep racist treatment, and who can be criticized for that? But we must also recognize the difference between those whom racism's obsession with color allows to try, and those with no such choice. "Passing" is an option for very few African-Americans. If it is possible for some Latinos to assimilate, one cannot say that of most African-Americans; they can only accommodate.

Latinos themselves buy into the hierarchy of color. Too often we fail to recognize the ways in which we sustain racism ideologically. We do it when we express prejudice against those among us who look *indio,* mulatto, or just Black. We do it when we favor being lighter. Such prejudice dehumanizes fellow human beings, it divides our forces in the struggle for social justice, and must be confronted.

THE DEVILS OF DUALISM

The issue of color, and the entire Black/white definition, feed on a dualism that shaped the U.S. value system as it developed from the time of this nation's birth. Dualism sees reality as consisting of two irreducible elements, usually oppositional, like: good and evil, mind and body, civilized and savage. A Western, Protestant version of dualism was used by the invaders, colonizers, and enslavers of today's United States to rationalize their actions by stratifying supposed opposites along race and gender lines (e.g., mind is European and male, body is Colored and female). The uses of dualism in relation to racism, along with the Enlightenment impulse to classify for the sake of social "order," have been studied by various scholars of racial theory. One simple example tells a great deal: the U.S. insistence on classifying as Black a child with a single Black ancestor, no matter how "white" that child might otherwise be. If the child is not white, it has to be Black. If not good, then evil. And so forth.

The dread of "race-mixing" as a threat to White Supremacy enshrined dualism. Today we see that ". . . a disdain for mixture haunts and inhibits U.S. culture. Because it does not recognize hybridism, this country's racial framework emphasizes separateness and offers no ground for mutual inclusion," as David Hayes-Bautista and Gregory Rodriguez put it (1993). I, for one, remember growing up haunted by that crushing word "half-breed," meaning me. It was years before *mestizaje*—mixing—began to suggest to me a cultural wealth rather than a polluted bloodline. U.S. society, the Dean of Denial, still has no use for that idea, still scorns the hybrid as mysteriously "un-American."

Such disdain helps explain why the nature of Latino identity seems to baffle and frustrate so many folk in this country. The dominant culture doesn't sit happy with complex ideas or people, or dialectics of any sort. And the Latino/a must be among the most complex creatures walking this earth, biologically as well as culturally. They originated as a 16th-century continentwide mix of at least three "racial" groupings, which led philosopher José Vasconcelos to apply the phrase *la raza cósmica*—the cosmic people, La Raza.

In the 16th century they moved north, and a new *mestizaje* took place with Native Americans. The Raza took on still more dimensions with the 1846 U.S. occupation of Mexico and some intermarriage with Anglos. Then, in the early 20th century, newly arrived Mexicans began to join those descendants of Mexicans already here. The mix continues today, ever more complex, with notable differences between first, second, third, and 20th-generation people of Mexican descent.

All this means Latinos are *not* an immigrant population and yet they are. On the one hand, they are a colonized people displaced from their ancestral homeland, with roots here that go back centuries. On the other hand, many have come to the U.S. more recently as economic refugees seeking work or as political refugees fleeing war and repression. Politically, the reality is even more dialectical: today's Chicanos were born from a process of colonization in Mexico by whites, then became colonizers themselves in what is today's Southwest, only to be colonized again by other whites!

Such complexity is too much for most Anglos and, let's face it, for some Latinos, too. Noted writer Cherríe Moraga articulates the sense of paradox:

> *"Los Estados Unidos es mi país, pero no es mi patria."* (It is my land, but not my country.) I cannot flee the United States, my land resides beneath its borders. . . . Chicanos with memory banks like our Indian counterparts recognize that we are a nation within a nation (Moraga, 1993: 18).

We must also remember that the very word "Latino" is a monumental simplification. Chicanos/as, already multifaceted, are only one Latino people. In the U.S., we also have

Puerto Ricans, Dominicans, Cubans, Central Americans, Panamanians, South Americans, and so forth. We have a broad range in terms of class status and color (a light-skinned Argentine psychiatrist, for example, has little in common with a dark Mexican tomato picker or a Black Dominican taxi driver).

The eye-opening variety and ambiguity of Latino people and experience led poet Bernice Zamora to write:

> *You insult me*
> *When you say I'm*
> *Schizophrenic.*
> *My divisions are*
> *Infinite.*

Yet dualism prefers a Black/white view in all matters, leaving no room for an in-between color like brown—much less a wildly multicolored, multilingual presence called "Latino." And so, along with being invisibilized by the dominant society, Latinos are homogenized.

THE COLOR OF CULTURE

If there is a culture of color in these racist United States, is it possible we also have a color of culture?

In trying to understand the Black/white construct, one might distinguish between racial oppression (derived from physical appearance, especially skin color), and national minority oppression (derived from cultural differences or nationality). According to these criteria Latinos—like Asian/Pacific Americans—would be victims of national minority rather than racial oppression. Racism itself, then, would indeed be strictly white on Black.

Does the distinction hold? Do Latinos suffer for reasons of culture and nationality, but not for their "race"?

On one hand, cultural difference (especially language) and nationality are indeed used in oppressing a colonized people like Mexicans or those of Mexican descent in the U.S. The right to speak Spanish on the job or in a school playground has been historically denied. A Spanish accent (though not a British or French accent) is a liability in many professional situations. Children are ridiculed at school for bringing Mexican lunches, their names are Anglicized by white teachers, humiliation is daily fare. Later in life, they will be treated as foreigners; citizens will be denied citizen rights and noncitizens will be denied human rights.

Culturally, Latinos are seen as *exotica,* outside the mainstream, alien. They speak a funny language, some say (the most beautiful in the world, others say), and nobody outside the *barrio* can understand their best jokes, their beloved play-on-words, or self-mocking style. This isolation largely results from tactics of self-defense: culture has provided a longstanding survival mechanism for many people of Latino origin in a hostile world. It is a mechanism whose strength has continued to flow, given the proximity of Mexico, Central America, and the Caribbean to the United States. Latino efforts to move from outside to inside have intensified in the last 25 years and will continue, but the sense of inhabiting a culturally distinct world remains, especially in newer generations.

Latinos are acknowledged—if at all—in a ghettoized cultural framework: as actors, film makers, musicians, and other kinds of artists; as a growing market with great promise if one caters to its cultural characteristics; perhaps as an "ethnic" electoral force—or, on the negative side, as immigrants who speak a "foreign" language and "swarm" across the border; as urban gangbangers with a culture of their own, órate Eddie Olmos! Even when these attitudes are not actively hostile, they are dehumanizing.

Does all this mean Latinos suffer for their culture and nationality, but not for their "race"? If we look at social conditions, at the actual experience of Latinos in the U.S., it makes more sense to conclude that the presence of national minority oppression doesn't signify the absence of racial oppression. It makes more sense to understand "racial" in terms of peoplehood and not only a supposed biology.

Social conditions affirm that combination of national, cultural, and racial oppression. The statistics for Latinos are grim: their national poverty rate (27%), high school drop-out rate (36%), and child poverty rate (42%) are even higher than for African-Americans, according to news reports on the 1990 Census. They are now reported to experience the most discrimination in housing markets of any U.S. population group (Lueck, 1991).

Life-endangering racism is not rare for Latinos in the Southwest, especially near the border, and especially for those who are poor and working class. For decades, Anglos in Texas, Arizona, and California have enslaved, tortured, and murdered Latinos because their victims were nonwhite "foreigners." Hundreds of Mexicans were lynched between 1847 and 1935, if not later.

On a recent visit, San Diego County in California felt to me for Mexicans and Central Americans like Mississippi felt for Blacks in the 1960s. Five years ago, in that county a pair of middle-class white youths spied two young, documented Latinos standing by the roadside; one shot them dead and later explained to the judge that he did it because he "didn't like Mexicans." Such attitudes are even more common in that county today. In urban areas Latinos number high among the victims of Los Angeles Police Department and Sheriff's Department brutality. It's far from chic to be a spic, as poet Gerardo Navarro rhymed it sardonically.

The borderlands remain the locus of the most intense oppression, for that is where Latinos are most vulnerable by virtue of nationality—with or without documents. Agents of the Border Patrol, the largest police force in the U.S., murder Latinos with impunity. Killing Latinos as they try to run back to Mexico, running them down with official vehicles, forcing them into the river to drown—all these seem to be favorite Border Patrol pastimes.

Women are among those most brutally abused at the border, their victimization has only recently attracted public attention. Officials rape and then sometimes murder Latinas trying to cross the border, at will. Latina women contracted in their home countries as housekeepers have been raped on the day of arrival here at a new job; worked 14 to 16 hours a day, seven days a week; never paid promised wages; and kept isolated from possible sources of assistance. What happens to young, "illegal" children has included separation from parents and being jailed.

Latino men, women, and children are victimized on the basis of nationality and culture, rendered vulnerable by their lack of documents and scant knowledge of English or of local institutions. More often than not, they are rendered additionally vulnerable by their skin color and other physical features. Nationality then combines with a nonwhite (though not Black) physical appearance to subject them to an oppression that is a form of racism. Even if a nonwhite appearance is lacking, however, nationality and culture create a separate personhood as the basis for oppression.

In a land where the national identity is white, nationality and race become interchangeable. We live today with a white definition of citizenship, which generates a racist dynamic. Think about our words, our codes, in the media and conversation. "Immigrants" today means only two things: Mexicans and Central Americans, or Asians. It doesn't mean French or Irish or Arabian people who have come to relocate (a nicer word than "immigrate").

A rigid line cannot be drawn between racial and national oppression when all victims are people of color. Both are racism, and in combination they generate new varieties of racism. All this suggests why we need to understand more than the Black/white model today.

RACISM EVOLVES

Racism evolves; as editor David Goldberg points out in his book *Anatomy of Racism,* it has no single, permanently fixed set of characteristics. New forms are being born today out of global events, in particular from the new international division of labor. He writes:

> . . . all forms of racism may be linked in terms of their exclusionary or inclusionary undertakings. A major historical shift has been from past racist forms defining and fueling expansionist colonial aims and pursuits to contemporary expressions in nationalist terms. Insistence on racial inferiority in the past fed colonial appetites and imperialist self-definition. Racism is taken now to be expressed increasingly in terms of isolationist nationalist self-image, of cultural differentiation tied to custom, tradition, and heritage, and of exclusionary immigration policies, anti-immigrant practices and criminality (Goldberg, 1990: xiv).

The increasing equation of racism with nationalism is spotlighted by the title of Paul Gilroy's provocative book, *There Ain't No Black in the Union Jack.* We need to look at that equation more closely here in the U.S. The challenge is to understand such new developments and to draw strength from our understanding. The challenge is to abandon a dead-end dualism that comprises two White Supremacist inventions: Blackness and Whiteness. The challenge is to extend a dialectical reach.

Black/white are real poles—but not the only poles. To organize against racism, as people in SNCC (the Student Nonviolent Coordinating Committee) used to say, Blackness is necessary but not sufficient. They were thinking of class, as I remember; today we can also think of other colors, other racisms. In doing so, we have to proceed with both boldness and infinite care. Talking race in these United States is an intellectual minefield; for every social observation, one can find three contradictions and four necessary qualifications. Crawling through the complexity, it helps to think: keep your eye on the prize, which is uniting against the monster.

Sitting on the porch of a Puerto Rican friend's beach cottage one warm evening about 20 years ago, my friend Jim Forman asked me the question. We had been working on his book, The Making of Black Revolutionaries, *about the years of fighting for Black civil rights and human rights. As Executive Secretary of SNCC, Jim had faced almost every danger and hardship; somehow he kept on pushing.*

With the surf crashing nearby under a million stars, Jim said: "We're all Black, don't you see? African people and Mexican people and Puerto Rican people, we are all Black in the eyes of racism. So we must come together as Black."

I thought to myself: there's sense in that. But Latinos also have their particularities. They don't want to give that up, it has meant survival. So I said nothing because the truth seemed to be somewhere between my thought and his, in a hidden place we had yet to find. Today it seems clearer that Jim's words were true at heart. He spoke not from a fortress looking down, but across borders that must be breached.

REFERENCES

Blauner, Robert, 1972, *Racial Oppression in America.* New York: Harper and Row: 165.

Goldberg, David Theo (ed.), 1990, *Anatomy of Racism.* Minneapolis: University of Minnesota Press.

Hayes-Bautista, David and Gregory Rodriguez, 1993, "Latinos Are Redefining Notions of Racial Identity." *Los Angeles Times* (January 15).

Lueck, T. J., 1991, "U.S. Study Finds Hispanic Minority Most Often Subject to Victimization." *New York Times* (November 3).

Martínez, Elizabeth, 1989, "A Certain Absence of Color." *Social Justice* 16.4.

Moraga, Cherríe, 1993, *The Last Generation.* Boston: South End Press (forthcoming).

Morrison, Toni, 1992, *Playing in the Dark: Whiteness and the Literary Imagination.* Cambridge: Harvard University Press.

Pastor, Manuel, Jr., 1993, *Latinos and the L.A. Uprising.* Tomas Rivera Center (TRC) Study, Occidental College, California.

Bisexuality and Deviant Identities

Mariana Valverde

It is interesting that although bisexuality, like homosexuality, is just another deviant identity, it also functions as a rejection of the norm/deviance model. People who are bisexual, and not just in a transition between heterosexuality and homosexuality, are people who have resisted both society's first line of attack and its second offensive, i.e. they have resisted both the institution of heterosexuality and of homosexuality. This means that every day they have to make specific choices about how they will appear, with whom they will flirt, what style they will express in clothes and mannerisms.

However, the flexibility and ambiguity inherent in bisexuality do not suffice to allow bisexuals to hover comfortably somewhere "above" the gay/straight split. Nobody can escape the social structures and ideologies that govern both gender formation and sexual-orientation formation, which have created hetero- and homosexuality as the main, institutionalized sexual identities. What bisexuals do is not so much escape the gay/straight split, but rather *manage* it. They are not above the fray, but participate in it by locating themselves at different points in the split according to the circumstances. Bisexuality is best seen not as a completely separate Third Option that removes itself from all the problems of both hetero- and homosexuality, but rather as a choice to combine the two lifestyles, the two erotic preferences, in one way or another.

This view of bisexuality as a combination of the two main sexual identities rather than a separate identity explains how there can be such huge differences among bisexuals. Homosexuals may be very different from each other—the closeted male politician who has secret affairs with boys does not have much in common with the lesbian feminist—but at the very least they all face a common social oppression and a marginalization into gay ghettoes. Bisexuals, on the other hand, do not have a common social experience upon which to build a specific *social* identity, although they do all share the problem of how to manage the gay/straight split and avoid feeling schizophrenic in the process.

Bisexuals who are unaware of the effects of heterosexism, and who see their situation as a purely individual choice with no significant social repercussions, often unwittingly reinforce, or at least go along with, heterosexist practices. If I have two lovers, one male and one female, it will not be easy to keep in mind that the heaps of social approval piled upon my "straight" relationship should be taken with a grain of salt. I will "naturally" tend to keep my lesbian relationship more private, without mentioning it to family and coworkers. I might also be more likely to tolerate faults and selfish habits in a man, because "you know how men are." For all my claims to gender blindness, I will have different expectations from men and from women, and society will treat my two relationships very differently. I might tend to differentiate myself from my lesbian lover, and assume that it will be she who will fight for gay rights, while I nod encouragingly from the sidelines. If I get some tolerance for my lesbian relationship, I might congratulate myself on having tolerant friends, without looking at the historic fight of gays and lesbians to *create* tolerance.

On the other hand, bisexuals who are aware of how gay oppression and heterosexism shape the contours of their own lives are in a good position to challenge these oppressive social forces, even as they make it clear that they are fighting as bisexuals, not as honorary gays or pseudo-gays. Those bisexuals who see themselves as sometimes benefiting from heterosexual privilege and at other times suffering gay oppression, and can see the different consequences of different ways of managing the gay/straight split are also those who tend to take up gay rights as a cause that affects them personally. They are the ones who do not vigorously protest when someone says, "Gee, I saw you going into a gay bar."

However, up until now the gay community has not been at all encouraging or even tolerant of bisexuals who have a commitment to resisting heterosexism and gay oppression. Gay people have traditionally dismissed bisexuals as deceitful, unreliable, and cowardly. This negative view has unfortunately been confirmed by the existence of many bisexuals who maintain a public heterosexual image while indulging in gay relationships in private, thus escaping gay oppression in a way that gay people can never do. Gay people do have a right to demand that bisexuals do not fall into the easy trap of being publicly straight and privately gay. However, there are now bisexuals, especially feminist women, who are resisting that traditional easy approach and who are increasingly willing to be public about their gay side. They have to be welcomed and treated with respect for their sexual choice. Gay people have to stop assuming that everyone who is bisexual is simply either afraid of coming out or is in transition to being fully gay. The transition theory assumes that those who call themselves bisexual are "really" gay, and this is as much an error as the belief that everyone is "really" bisexual. Both rely on the assumption that sexual orientation is an inner essence, an assumption known as "essentialism."

Because of our society's firmly entrenched belief in sexual essentialism, we are all more or less uncomfortable with people who are sexually ambiguous. We insist that everyone have a fixed gender identity and a fixed sexual orientation. When we see someone in the street and we cannot tell if it is a man or a woman, we get uneasy and go out of our way to get a second look. We do not rest until we have determined the correct gender of this person (who is otherwise completely unimportant to us). Now, sexual orientation is not as visible on a person as gender, but we all derive a certain satisfaction from investigating people's sexual identities and proceeding to label them as X or Y. Bisexuality is threatening partly because it seems to challenge our classification system, thus putting into question fundamental notions about sexuality and gender. Thus, even if some traditional bisexual behaviour patterns are questionable, and even though there is no such thing as an institutionalized bisexuality comparable to hetero- and homosexuality, I still think it is important to give sexual ambiguity a place in the sun of radical sexual thought. In other words, even though I share some of the gay skepticism about bisexuality, and am concerned to see bisexuals take a more active role in challenging heterosexism, I am also critical of the dogmatic view—found as much among gay people as among straight people—that bisexuals are inherently indecisive and immature. If the goals of feminism and gay liberation include the abolition of the gay/straight split, and its replacement by a social system which does not label and categorize people according to whom they are attracted, then bisexuality is an important part of the challenge to the status quo. Its role could involve vindicating and affirming sexual ambiguity, in a world which is presently extremely uncomfortable with any ambiguity. Bisexuality defies the experts' attempts to classify everything as either male or female, normal or deviant, good or bad.

Identity Politics, Coming Out, and Coming Together

Larry Gross

IDENTITY POLITICS

Like a streak of lightning, the phenomenon of outing illuminates a stormy landscape of contending ideologies and conflicting loyalties. At the root of much of the dispute about outing are unsettled and unsettling questions about the nature of sexual identity and the responsibilities, if any, that people who engage in homosexual relations have toward one another.

Beyond the failure to actively oppose bigotry or promote progress, the public officials, entertainment industry executives, celebrities, and journalists who have been targets of outing are also faulted for their unwillingness to publicly identify themselves with the gay community or show any solidarity with this still much oppressed group. Running through the articles on outing is the frequent invocation of comparisons between lesbian and gay people and other groups that have suffered and continue to suffer from oppression, specifically racial minorities and Jews. While David Geffen invoked blacks and Jews to imply that stereotypical portrayals are an unchangeable fact of life, his critics used the analogy in order to highlight the relative indifference of media executives to the problems faced by gay people: "certainly, record companies in 1990 wouldn't sign the Ku Klux Klan to do an album advocating genocide of Blacks and Jews" (Signorile 1990). But most frequently the comparison with other minorities is used to demand "the accountability by gays in high places to their own community, much the way that Blacks, Jews and women in high places are accountable to their respective communities" (ibid.).

The argument for outing is motivated by three related considerations. The primary stimulus that pushed outing from the realm of speculation into the public arena was . . . the realization of the costs of homophobia dramatically revealed by the AIDS epidemic and a rising tide of antigay violence. . . . The second impetus for outing is drawn from the initial structure of gay liberation: the political and the personal importance of coming out. The belief that "we'll never have the freedom and civil rights we deserve as human beings unless we stop hiding in closets" (Marotta 1981: 170) is as fervent today as when it was expressed during New York's first gay pride march in 1970. Public opinion research supports this belief with data:

> The polls show that gay activists have not been misguided in their campaign to "open the closet door": personal contact with people who are openly homosexual consistently produces greater tolerance for homosexuality. . . . [In a 1983 poll] among Americans nationwide who personally know an open homosexual, 35 percent were "negative" on [an attitudinal] index. Among those who did not know an open homosexual, the figure was much higher—61 percent. Knowing a homosexual also affected support for gay rights. Thirty-one percent of those who knew homosexuals—and 44 percent of those who did not—opposed gay rights, according to our index. What counted was knowing someone who was *openly* gay. Knowing a suspected homosexual made little difference. (Schneider and Lewis 1984)

In the early days of gay liberation it was often said that if all gay people turned lavender overnight, antigay oppression would end the next day. The sheer pervasiveness and distribution of gay people across all levels of society and within all ethnic, racial, and other groupings would, in this fantasy, overcome the biases that are born of the sense that gay people are fundamentally "other," not like us, not like anyone we already know, respect, love. The tactic of outing is thus a sort of selective "lavendering" of individuals who are already visible to mainstream society and therefore are known and often respected and even loved by millions who do not believe that they know any homosexuals. In the 1983 national survey cited by Schneider and Lewis in 1984, two-thirds of the respondents said they did not personally know anyone (family, friends, co-workers) who were "openly homosexual." It is likely that AIDS has lowered this percentage, just as it has vastly increased gay visibility in the media, but the majority of Americans would probably still answer the same way.

What has changed since 1970, obviously, is the conviction that the decision to come out must always be an individual choice. Outers argue that this choice can be made by others, for the greater good of the community. Those who wish to convince their fellow citizens that they do, in fact, know lesbian and gay people are faced with a formidable challenge. They can't very well simply go door-to-door all across the country and break the news individually—"Dear Sir or Madam: Did you know that your son/daughter/uncle/cousin/mother is gay/lesbian?" Using the media to bring to everyone at once the news that familiar and celebrated women and men are lesbian and gay is a way of short-circuiting this impossible individual task. Furthermore, outing proponents would argue that for media-fixated Americans, vicariously knowing openly gay celebrities would be the next best thing to personally knowing openly gay people. Some might even argue that it's better.

The third justification for outing rests on the dual claims that "those who engage in frequent, voluntary homosexual conduct, whatever their state of political awareness, are by definition gay" and that "gays are a real, inescapable minority marching towards increasing self-realization" (Rotello 1990: 52). These final contentions are the most far-reaching of the conceptual and political arguments made in the debate over outing, as they imply a set of assumptions about the nature of gay and lesbian identities and the lesbian and gay community. These contentions take a theoretical as well as a tactical position at one extreme of the "essentialist versus constructivist" dispute that has preoccupied much contemporary gay scholarship.[1]

ROLES OR REALITIES?

Briefly, what might be termed the *traditional* essentialist position assumes that homosexuals are a category of humanity existing in all cultures and throughout history:

> Homosexuality existed in ancient Egypt, in the Tigris-Euphrates Valley, in ancient China, and in ancient India. Many American Indian tribes had institutionalized homosexuality, at least the male variety, into the role of the *berdache* (the male woman), while other primitive groups have chosen their shamans from among them. Some societies in the past have idealized homosexual love, as did the ancient Greeks, while others have harshly condemned it, as did the ancient Jews. (Bullough 1979: 2)

There are two important components of this perspective on homosexuality: "For the essentialist, homosexuality is a universal, a form found across cultures and throughout

---

[1]The "essentialist versus social constructionist" debates raged throughout lesbian and gay scholarship for much of the past fifteen years (and have their analogues in feminist theory and theories of race as well; cf. Fuss 1989 and Spelman 1988). As someone who felt like a conscientious objector throughout the worst of the conflict—neither willing to accept the dominant social construction position in its full-blown excess, nor adhering to the often romantic and politically regressive alternative camp—I do not believe it is necessary to rehearse here the entire argument. For a comprehensive set of alternative positions, and some encouraging moves toward synthesis, see Stein 1992 (especially the chapters by Boswell, Epstein and Stein) and Roscoe 1988.

history: and the 'homosexual' of ancient Greece is directly comparable to the 'homosexual' of modern London" (Plummer 1981: 94). Writing in this tradition tends to celebrate the tracing of a continuous, if often hidden, thread that unites contemporary lesbian women and gay men with their counterparts across time and place. These celebrations have often been political, as in Jonathan Ned Katz's pioneering *Gay American History* (1976), which opens with these words:

> We have been the silent minority, the silenced minority—invisible women, invisible men. Early on, the alleged enormity of our "sin" justified the denial of our existence, even our physical destruction. . . . Our existence as a long-oppressed, long-resistant social group was not explored. We remained an unknown people, our character defamed. The heterosexual dictatorship has tried to keep us out of sight and out of mind; its homosexuality taboo has kept us in the dark. That time is over. The people of the shadows have seen the light; Gay people are coming out—and moving on—to organized action against a repressive society.[2]

These celebrations have also had a more spiritual focus, as in Judy Grahn's evocation of myths and language to connect past and present:

> The Gay culture I have set about to describe is old, extremely old, and it is continuous. The continuity is a result of characteristics that members teach each other so that the characteristics repeat era after era. I have found that Gay culture has its traditionalists, its core group, that it is worldwide, and that it has tribal and spiritual roots. Gay culture is sometimes underground, sometimes aboveground, and often both. . . .
>
> The position that Gay people take in society, the function we so often choose, is that of mediator between worlds. We transfer power, information, and understandings from one "world" or sphere of being to another. In a tribal environment, this means shape-shifting into wolves, birds, stones, the wind, and translating their wisdoms for the benefit of the people of the tribe. In a modern urban environment it may mean living in a port city, helping to absorb and translate new arrivals of all kinds; in the long patriarchal history that has gradually enveloped the world's people, the Gay function has been to make crossover journeys between gender-worlds, translating, identifying and bringing back the information that each sex has developed independently of the other. (1984: xiv, 269)

As might be imagined, objections have been made to these celebratory schools of lesbian and gay history, on grounds of both conceptual rigor and empirical evidence. The primary objections have come from sociologists and historians who describe themselves as social constructionists. These scholars argue that "there are no objective, culture-independent categories of sexual orientation—no one is, independent of a culture, a heterosexual or homosexual" (Stein 1992: 340). Therefore, in this view, homosexuality is not a transhistorical phenomenon that takes on somewhat differing form and coloration under varying local conditions. According to some social constructionists, the homosexuality that exists in the modern Western world is a conceptual product of the

---

[2]By 1983, when Katz published a sequel, *Gay/Lesbian Almanac,* he had become converted to social constructionism and now noted that he was adopting a "circumspect use of terms and concepts" in order to "correct my own earlier usage in *Gay American History* where the word 'homosexual' was employed in reference to phenomena of the early colonial era, and the specific historical character of early colonial 'sodomy' was thereby obscured" (1983: 14).

late nineteenth century, when "the spread of a capitalist economy and the growth of huge cities were allowing diffuse homosexual desires to congeal into a personal identity" (D'Emilio and Freedman 1988: 226). At this point, responding to "real changes in the social organization," medical writers came to describe homosexuality "not as a discrete, punishable offense, but as a description of the person, encompassing emotions, dress, mannerisms, behavior, and even physical traits" (ibid.). In the influential phrasing of Michel Foucault, "The sodomite had been a temporary aberration; the homosexual was now a species" (1978: 43).

Other social constructionists take a more extreme position, which Stein terms the "empty category version of constructionism," according to which it is inaccurate to talk about sexual orientations at all because they are merely figments of our society's need to categorize people. In illustration of this view Stein quotes Gore Vidal's statement that "there is no such thing as a homosexual, no such thing as a heterosexual. Everyone has homosexual and heterosexual desires and impulses and responses" (Stein 1992: 342). For this camp, the categories heterosexual and homosexual might be akin to the medieval category of witch: "There were people in the 17th century who were claimed (sometimes by others and sometimes by themselves) to be witches but we now know that there were no witches (i.e., there were no women with supernatural powers who had sex with the devil) and the category witch . . . did not properly apply to any person" (ibid.).

Whereas constructivist positions present a radically historicized view that emphasizes the *discontinuity* of socially defined roles and labels, what is termed the essentialist position suggests a contrasting focus on *similarities* of patterns of sexual attraction.[3] As John Boswell put it, in response to a constructivist view:

> Would it not be more economical to hypothesize that a percentage of human beings in all societies prefer their own gender sexually, that they are sometimes able to institutionalize this preference, and that the majority of human beings are sufficiently flexible to be able to derive sexual satisfaction from either gender under institutional pressure, whether or not that gender is their first choice? (quoted in Mass 1990: 220)

Boswell accepts the proposition that every person's experience, including sexuality, will be determined in a "largely irresistible way" by "the social matrix in which she or he lives," and that this includes "creating (or not creating) opportunities for sexual expression and possibly even awareness of sexual feelings and desires" (Boswell 1992: 135). Yet he points out that "agreeing on this, however, hardly begins to address the problematic underlying questions, such as whether society is itself responding to sexual phenomena that are generic to humans and *not created* by social institutions" (ibid.).

In contrast to the radical "empty category" social constructionists, the view proposed by Boswell might be analogous to pointing out that human beings in all cultures and periods have had blood types, even though the awareness and classification of blood

---

[3]I say it is termed the essentialist position because this is a characterization applied by its constructivist opponents. As John Boswell, a prominent scholar who has been so characterized, responded, "It seems to me that the common understanding of essentialist is a kind of stereotype presented by constructionists as a target rather than a position ever outlined by anyone who actually believes it" (Mass 1990: 213). As Charley Shively put it, essentialism is really a construction of the social constructionists (quoted in Stein 1992: 326).

types is a modern phenomenon. Identifying and naming blood types did not bring them into being and, in this analogy, there may have been people we might reasonably call homosexuals in the premodern past and in non-Western societies, even though we would acknowledge the vast variety of ways they would have experienced and described their own sexuality.

Many important theoretical and political differences flow from these two positions. Most crucial among them are their implications for the question obsessively asked (by heterosexuals): What causes homosexuality? (translation: What went wrong? Whose fault was it? How can it be prevented?). The strong versions of social constructionism that deny biology a role in the determination of sexuality would be seriously undermined by a demonstration that, say, "a predeliction for sexual activity with one gender could be shown to be innate in all humans or fixed in childhood in all (or even many) known cultures" (Boswell 1992: 138). Social constructionist David Halperin acknowledges that "if it turns out that there actually is a gene, say, for homosexuality, my notions about the cultural determination of sexual object-choice will—obviously enough—prove to have been wrong" (1990: 49). Thus, it was only to be expected that neuroscientist Simon LeVay's claim to have found evidence of biological determinants (or, at least, correlates) of sexual orientation (1991) would set off a barrage of counterattacks from the strict constructionists (cf. Gallagher 1991); similar responses awaited the publication of a study of twins by psychologist Michael Bailey and psychiatrist Richard Pillard (1991), purporting to show support for a genetic basis of homosexuality (Gessen and McGowan 1992).

In contrast to the suspicion voiced by many lesbian and gay scholars, the mass media loudly trumpeted the findings of these studies, proclaiming them as evidence for biological determination of sexual orientation and sex roles. The cover of a February 1992 issue of *Newsweek* featured a close-up photograph of a baby's face, over which is superimposed the stark headline "Is This Child Gay?" Whatever the status of the theoretical and empirical debates waged by researchers and theoreticians, the public discourse concerning sexuality and sexual orientation is overwhelmingly essentialist. That is, despite the tireless repetition of the fundamentalist jingle "God created Adam and Eve, not Adam and Steve," fewer and fewer people seem convinced by the argument that homosexuality is merely a perverse choice of "lifestyle" adopted in order to—what? Irritate our parents? Frighten the horses? The official media sex educators, Ann Landers, Dear Abby, Dr. Ruth, and their ilk, have long since abandoned the "it's a phase" and "perhaps she will meet the right man" phrases of comfort to worried parents and adopted such "liberal" alternatives as "they're born that way" and "sexual orientation is determined early in life, and is not a matter of choice." Likewise, the preponderance of lesbian and gay political rhetoric, both within the community and externally, reflects an essentialist position, insisting that one doesn't "choose" to be gay, but "recognizes and accepts" that one is.

In an important sense, however, both the constructionist and the essentialist positions assume that there *are* at present, in our society, persons who can be appropriately labeled homosexuals (and, conversely, heterosexuals)—whether they are seen as the latest metamorphoses of universally recurring orientations or as completely novel, "modern, Western bourgeois productions" (Halperin 1990: 8). That is, however these theoretical perspectives may vary in assigning ontological causes for the appearance of homosexuals in our midst, they both seem to agree that such people *do* exist here and now.

This brings us back to the claims made by the proponents of outing: first, that those who engage in "frequent, voluntary homosexual conduct, whatever their state of political awareness, are by definition gay"—an implicitly essentialist position; and second, that "gays are a real, inescapable minority marching towards increasing self-realization" (Rotello 1990: 52).[4] Whatever position one takes on the issue of the "reality" of homosexuality, the next question that must be addressed is whether the term "lesbian and gay community" (or lesbian and gay communities) has anything more than a convenient rhetorical status.

COMING OUT AND COMING TOGETHER

Sexual acts between members of the same sex occur in all societies, but only in some instances have they become the organizing principle for distinctive subcultures, and only in recent times have these subcultures achieved a level of public visibility comparable to ethnic and racial communities (Weeks 1981). The emergence of modern gay and lesbian subcultures (which are not necessarily or always the same) was made possible by the transformations and dislocations wrought by industrialization, which "brought rapid growth to the cities, often rupturing traditional family relations," and the movement toward "the privatization of sexuality, like religion, in the liberal philosophy of the growing bourgeoisie" (Adam 1978: 25). As unprecedented numbers migrated from rural to urban areas there grew up in these expanding cities a wide range of voluntary communities and forms of association:

> Homosexually inclined women and men, who would have been vulnerable and isolated in most pre-industrial villages, began to congregate in small corners of big cities. Most large nineteenth-century cities in Western Europe and North America had areas where men could cruise for other men. Lesbian communities seem to have coalesced more slowly and on a smaller scale. . . . Areas like these acquired bad reputations, which alerted other interested individuals of their existence and location. . . . By the late 1970s, sexual migration was occurring on a scale so significant that it began to have a recognizable impact on urban politics in the United States. (Rubin 1984: 286)

These are conditions for the emergence of deviant self-images, subcultural identities and argot. All of these have existed for centuries but have multiplied and become more widely visible in the past hundred years. At present most young lesbians and gay men get their first introduction to what it means to be gay, and how it's done, from mainstream mass media, as well as, for those with access, various gay publications, including pornography. This is one reason why the pervasive negative stereotyping of gay people in the mass media has been consistently singled out by the gay movement as a major source of oppression and self-oppression (see Dyer 1977; Russo 1987; Gross 1989).

---

[4]That these two claims are not identical can be illustrated by analogy with handedness: one can believe that left-handedness is a real attribute (i.e., not merely a form of laziness or recalcitrance) yet not wish to claim that left-handed people should constitute themselves as a minority on the model of an ethnic group, sharing a fundamental, encompassing identity.

Unlike ethnic or racial communities into which people are born and in which they are reared, sexual subcultures are joined much later in life. They are also joined secretly, at least at first. Most gay people believe, probably correctly, that those closest to them—family, friends, institutional authorities—will not be pleased to learn the truth about their sexual identity. This initial stage of "coming out" tends to be a private, individual recognition that often occurs long before any physical homosexual experience. It requires confronting the prejudices that everyone acquires as a member of a sexist and heterosexist society: "We learn to loathe homosexuality before it becomes necessary to acknowledge our own" (Hodges and Hutter 1974).

The next stages of coming out are more social and public, within the confines of whatever gay subculture the person can find and can muster the courage to join. At this point, there are skills to learn and codes to master: where to locate potential partners, how to identify likely candidates, how to negotiate with them, and, if successful, where and how to conduct these potentially dangerous activities (as of 1992 homosexual acts were illegal in 24 states and the District of Columbia; they are capital crimes in many countries).

Beyond coming out into a gay subculture are the stages John Alan Lee (1977) termed "going public," and these also can be categorized in phases, although there is no standard sequence followed by most people and few traverse the entire territory. Typically, the person who is going public begins by revealing his or her homosexuality to family, friends, and co-workers. Even within this relatively restricted public there are many variations and degrees of coming out. Because so many lesbian women and gay men move to large cities with concentrations of gay people, they may be quite out at work and where they live and yet still be closeted to their parents and others in their hometowns. Becoming associated with a lesbian and gay movement group and becoming an "activist" is often an important part of going public, although Lee's 1977 projection of at most 1 percent of Toronto's gay population is probably still a reasonable estimate of the proportion of lesbian and gay people who are active in such organizations. An even smaller number end up being publicly identified in the media—occasionally before filling in the typically prior step of coming out to family members: on more than a few television talk shows a guest who was asked, "Do your parents know that you're gay?" has answered, "They do now!"

Gay people who begin the process of coming out to the straight world often find themselves held back at the threshold by others. "I'm glad you've told me, and you know it won't make any difference to the way I feel about you," many a lesbian or gay person has been told by a parent, "but let's not tell your father (or mother, or grandparents). It would kill him (or her, or them)." Or, "I suppose it's better that you've told us, but please don't tell anyone else, or I don't know how we'll be able to face the neighbors." As a member of the organization Parents and Friends of Lesbians and Gays put it, gay people coming out of the closet meet their parents going in. An openly gay journalist recently wrote about his experience with his family in a way that many gay people would find familiar:

> The last time I went home, five years ago, it took a total of 32.7 seconds (I timed it) from the moment I left baggage claim to the moment when my uncle Luis asked if I was getting

married. So I came to this conclusion: As honesty is one of those moral imperatives that was instilled in me by my parents, whom I love, I decided to tell my Mom that, since having to lie about my life has led to the biggest traumas in it, I am not willing to do it again for her, or anyone else's, peace of mind. Simply put, if she is prepared for me to be completely honest when all of our relatives ask me why I haven't met "some nice girl" and gotten married, I will gladly go. If she isn't, it likely isn't me they want to see. (O'Neill 1991)

All of these responses, of course, merely reinforce the presumption that homosexuality is a dirty secret, best kept discreetly out of sight of those who, to paraphrase Jack Warner's "closeted" Jewish executive, think they don't like gay people and would be disconcerted to learn that someone they know, like, and perhaps even love, is gay.

The pre-Stonewall gay world had much of the flavor of a secret society—a fraternity (and a sorority) bound together by its common bond of reciprocal keeping of confidences. The dangers of this secretive existence also had their attendant pleasures. The in-group knowledge and solidarity of locations and codes, the excitement of shared risk, and the pleasures of gossip—all of these have been challenged and denigrated by a movement that insists on openness and visibility. The growth of something that might, with any semblance of accuracy, be called a gay community came about through the symbiotic processes of coming out and coming together: "Visibility was the precondition for the establishment of lesbian and gay communities that resembled the urban neighborhoods of the immigrant groups in the late nineteenth and early twentieth centuries" (Escoffier 1985: 145).

But concentrations of gay people in particular neighborhoods, along with businesses and organizations created for and by gay people, do not in themselves constitute a community to which all people who engage in homosexual relations can or will feel a sense of belonging or obligation. Going out to a gay bar, despite Congressman Gunderson's retort to Michael Petrelis ("I am out! I'm in this bar, aren't I?"), is not what the gay liberation movement means by coming out. Although the rhetoric of community is widely used by gay activists and their political allies, and often used by their opponents as well, its conceptual and practical fragility is also readily discernable. As one unfriendly observer put it:

I have to say that I've never really understood the definition of the "gay community." Presumably, some unemployed gay drug addict would be a member of this community. So would a wealthy gay polo-playing socialite. But other than how they choose to use their sexual appendages, I don't see that they have much in common, and it's unlikely the socialite would invite the gay drug addict to cocktails. So how close-knit a community can it be? (Royko 1990)

Association with other members of a "subaltern" group (Spivak 1988), including vicarious association with prominent figures, can provide the soil for the cultivation of a self-image that is less determined by the values of the dominant culture. But this requires an identification with the subaltern group, "the translation of commonality into community" (Adam 1978: 12). For many oppressed groups the experience of commonality is largely the commonality of their difference from, and oppression by, the dominant culture. Within the social construction paradigm, Foucault suggested that the labeling taxonomies elaborated by nineteenth-century professional "discourses on the species and subspecies of homosexuality . . . made possible the formation of a 'reverse' discourse: homosexuality began to speak in its own behalf" (1978: 101). Similarly, it has often been claimed that anti-Semitism may hold together a Jewish identity after religion and tradition are no longer experienced as part of one's selfhood. As Isaac Deutscher put it, "To me the Jewish community is still only negative. . . . Religion? I am an atheist. Jewish nationalism? I am an internationalist. In neither sense am I, therefore, a Jew. I am, however, a Jew by force of my unconditional solidarity with the persecuted and exterminated" (1968: 51).

The experience of Jews offers illuminating insights for understanding gay people because of their similar positions on a "rank order of visibility [which] may be constructed from almost entirely visible, e.g., women, through to almost entirely invisible (blacks through to Jews and gay people)" (Adam 1978: 14). Relative invisibility creates the possibility of *passing,* an option exercised by some people of color and Jews (and, as we've seen, often enforced by external institutions such as Hollywood studios).

The analogy of passing Jews or blacks with closeted lesbian women and gay men requires some critical qualifications, however. In contrast to the former category, as Richard Mohr points out, "it is not the passing gay person who is perceived as a major threat (since from gays who pass there is no fear of pollution through undetected miscegenation). Rather the normal-appearing person being out is a major threat and source of cultural anxiety. For that the normal can be queer means that anyone—father, brother, even you—may be gay" (1991: 26). In most cases passing is not a full-time or totally absorbing role. In fact, as we've seen, all gay people start out by passing, first unconsciously, as we rarely think of ourselves as gay early on, and then consciously, before deciding to come out. And most gay people pass some of the time, because no one can come out over and over, day after day, in opposition to the universal assumption of heterosexuality:

> The [person who is passing] is likely to be somewhat integrated into the subordinated community; his denial of identity continues on a part-time or ambivalent basis. To other inferiorized people, the [person] reveals a more "authentic" identity, discarding a pseudo-identity constructed for superordinate audiences. The former identity is experienced "at ease," the latter as inhibited—an act. (Adam 1978: 95–96)

Among assimilating Jews in turn-of-the-century Europe this strategy was characterized by the advice given by Hebrew poet Y. L. Gordon: "Be a Jew in your tent, and a man when you go out." But, as the private identity was a stigmatized one, the privilege acquired through the public identity was always fragile. As Theodor Herzl wrote, "The emancipated Jew lives in a ghetto of illusions."

Wealth and social position can insulate gay people from the costs associated with their stigmatized identity, as they were able to insulate many assimilated Jews from the cruder forms of anti-Semitism in pre-Nazi Germany. But even without the advent of an officially oppressive regime, the cost of this insulation could be counted in the form of self-denial and constriction. Writing in 1926, Richard Bernstein described the assimilated Jew in Weimar Germany, who "trembles for the revelation of his real origin; he keeps himself under constant observation lest he betray himself by a word, a gesture, a look; his life has no more than one aim and purpose: successful camouflage" (quoted in Adam 1978: 96).

Hodges and Hutter in the 1970s wrote about similarly assimilated gay people, who choose to see themselves as part of the "whole human race, refusing to be identified with just one small part of it. 'I'm not joining any liberation movement,' they cry, clambering on to the nigger end of the bus. 'I'm part of the wide, wide spectrum of humanity' " (1974: 36).

Passing also raises the difficult question of definition: who decides who is a member of a subordinate group, and on what basis? Despite the horrendous example of Nazi racial laws that determined that one Jewish grandparent was sufficient to constitute a death warrant, Israeli political parties have struggled mightily over the criteria for determining who is a Jew and thereby eligible for immediate citizenship, among other privileges. In the case of race, Americans have traditionally assumed that any black ancestry made a person black. As Gunnar Myrdal put it, "The definition of the 'Negro race' is thus a social and conventional, not a biological concept" (1964: 115).[5]

Gay identity is more fluid than racial or ethnic identity. As we have noted already, it is a realization one typically comes to as an adolescent, and coming out means abandoning the taken-for-granted heterosexual identity imposed on all infants by society. Thus, coming out has much of the flavor of a conversion experience. For many gay people it is both a confirmation of and an explanation for one's distance from the roles society expects everyone to adopt (this is sometimes labeled "gender nonconformity"). Coming out entails sacrifice and danger; it often means facing hostility, rejection, and even violence from family, friends, and total strangers. Thus, it is not surprising that many gay people strive to maintain membership in the dominant culture even while participating in the gay subculture. That is, they live double lives.

Often the ability as well as the desire to live in two worlds is a function of social class. In her account of gay male subcultures in Chicago and Kansas City in the mid-1960s, Esther Newton described two categories of homosexuals:

> The overts live their *entire* lives within the context of the community; the coverts live their entire *nonworking* lives within it. That is, the coverts are "straight" during working hours, but most social activities are conducted with and with reference to other homosexuals. These overts and coverts together form the core of the homosexual community. (1979: 21)

Newton's characterization of the two facets of the gay subculture of the 1960s parallels Leznoff and Westley's description of an urban Canadian subculture in the mid-1950s. In both instances the covert homosexuals occupied higher-status positions and had more to risk by being known to be homosexual, while the overt gays were in lower-status occupations "where the homosexual is tolerated . . . and confine[d] most of their social life to homosexual circles" (Leznoff and Westley 1956: 257). Not surprisingly, there was—and is—palpable tension between these two worlds. The overt gays derisively label the coverts "closet queens," while the secret gays are fearful of being too

---

[5]Under the apartheid system in South Africa, racial identification was a highly significant matter, and a special court existed to adjudicate requests for changes in people's official racial status.

visibly associated with their open counterparts. As one lawyer put it to Leznoff and Westley:

> I know a few people who don't care. They are really pitiful. They are either people who are in very insignificant positions or they are in very good positions but are independent. . . . I can't afford to know them very well, and I try to avoid them. . . . From their point of view it means living completely outside of society and they are no longer interested in people who they consider hypocrites. (ibid.: 259)

The primary tie that binds members of both groups together across the class and social divide is sexual activity itself: the search for sexual partners "forces the secret homosexual out into the open. . . . Thus it is the casual and promiscuous sexual contacts between the . . . secret and the overt . . . which weld the city's homosexuals into a community" (ibid.: 263). In Erving Goffman's dramaturgic terms, the members of both groups were all part of the same performance team. "Each teammate is forced to rely on the good conduct and behavior of his fellows, and they, in turn, are forced to rely on him. There is then, perforce, a bond of reciprocal dependence linking teammates to one another . . . [and] the mutual dependence created by membership in the team is likely to cut across structural or social cleavages . . . and thus provide a source of cohesion" (1959: 82).

Writing in the early 1970s, Newton acknowledged that the term "community" might not be appropriate to characterize gay people, though by the time she was preparing the 1979 edition she noted that "homosexuals are much closer to constituting a political force than they were in 1968," thanks to the emergence of the younger generation of gay activists (1979: 23n.8). But it is far from clear that the cohesion Goffman referred to has erased the distance between the upper and lower echelons of the gay community. The willingness of the young gay waiters and bartenders who were the objects of Malcolm Forbes's forays across the line dividing the covert and overt provinces of the gay world to divulge his secret in the interest of gay liberation does not suggest that two decades of post-Stonewall activism have done that much to erase that line.

REFERENCES

Adam, Barry. 1978. *The Survival of Domination: Inferiorization and Everyday Life.* New York: Elsevier.

Bailey, Michael, and Richard Pillard. 1991. "A Genetic Study of Male Sexual Orientation." *Archives of General Psychiatry,* December, 1089–96.

Boswell, John. 1992. "Concepts, Experience, and Sexuality." In *Forms of Desire,* edited by E. Stein, 133–73. New York: Routledge.

Bullough, Vern. 1979. *Homosexuality: A History.* New York: New American Library.

D'Emilio, John, and Estelle Freedman. 1988. *Intimate Matters: A History of Sexuality in America.* New York: Harper & Row.

Deutscher Isaac. 1968. *The Non-Jewish Jew and Other Essays.* New York: Oxford University Press.

Dyer, Richard. 1977. "Stereotyping." *In Gays and Film,* edited by Richard Dyer. London: British Film Institute.

Escoffier, Jeffrey. 1985. "Sexual Revolution and the Politics of Gay Identity." *Socialist Review,* September, 119–53.

Foucault, Michel. 1978. *The History of Sexuality.* Vol. 1, *An Introduction.* New York: Random House.

Fuss, Diana. 1989. *Essentially Speaking: Feminism, Nature and Difference.* New York: Routledge.

Gallagher, John. 1991. "Hypothalamus Study and Coverage of It Attract Many Barbs." *Advocate,* October 8, 14–15.

Gessen, Masha, and David McGowan. 1992. "Raiders of the Gay Gene." *Advocate,* March 24, 60–62.

Goffman, Erving. 1959. *The Presentation of Self in Everyday Life.* New York: Anchor.

Grahn, Judy. 1984. *Another Mother Tongue: Gay Words, Gay Worlds.* Boston: Beacon.

Gross, Larry. 1989. "Out of the Mainstream: Sexual Minorities and the Mass Media." In *Remote Control: Television, Audiences and Cultural Power,* edited by Ellen Seiter et al. London: Routledge.

Halperin, David. 1990. *One Hundred Years of Homosexuality.* New York: Routledge.

Hodges, Andrew, and David Hutter. 1974. *With Downcast Gays: Aspects of Homosexual Self Oppression.* Toronto: Pink Triangle.

Katz, Jonathan Ned. 1976. *Gay American History.* New York: Crowell.

———. 1983. *Gay/Lesbian Almanac.* New York: Harper.

Lee, John Alan. 1977. "Going Public: A Study in the Sociology of Gay Liberation." *Journal of Homosexuality* 3, no. 1, 49–78.

LeVay, Simon. 1991. "A Difference in Hypothalamic Structure Between Heterosexual and Homosexual Men." *Science,* August 30, 1034–37.

Leznoff, Maurice, and William Westley. 1956. "The Homosexual Community." *Social Problems,* 3, no. 4, 257–63.

Marotta, Toby. 1981. *The Politics of Homosexuality.* Boston: Houghton Mifflin.

Mass, Lawrence. 1990. "Sexual Categories, Sexual Universals: A Conversation with John Boswell." In *Homosexuality as Behavior and as Identity: Dialogues of the Sexual Revolution,* vol. 2. New York: Harrington Park.

Mohr, Richard. 1992. *Gay Ideas: Outing and Other Controversies.* Boston: Beacon.

Myrdal, Gunnar. 1964. *An American Dilemma.* New York: McGraw-Hill.

Newton, Esther. 1979. *Mother Camp.* Chicago: University of Chicago Press.

O'Neill, Cliff. 1991. "Cousin Lourdes Is Getting Married." *OutWeek,* February 20, 28.

Plummer, Ken. 1981. "Going Gay: Identities, Life Cycles and Lifestyles in the Gay Male World." In *The Theory and Practice of Homosexuality,* edited by John Hart and Diane Richardson, 93–110. London: Routledge and Kegan Paul.

Roscoe, Will. 1988. "Making History: The Challenge of Gay and Lesbian Studies." *Journal of Homosexuality.* 15, no. 3/4, 1–40.

Rotello, Gabriel. 1990. "Tactical Considerations." *OutWeek,* May 16, 52–53.

Royko, Mike. 1990. "Antsy Closet Crowd Should Think Twice." *Chicago Tribune,* April 2, 3.

Rubin, Gayle. 1984. "Thinking Sex." In *Pleasure and Danger,* edited by Carole Vance. Boston: Routledge and Kegan Paul.

Russo, Vito. 1987. *The Celluloid Closet: Homosexuality in the Movies.* New York: Harper & Row (revised edition).

Schneider, William, and I. A. Lewis. 1984. "The Straight Story on Gay Rights." *Public Opinion* 7, March, 16–20, 59–60.

Sciolino, Elaine. 1991. "Voice of the Pentagon Delivers Press Curbs with a Deftness Honed on TV." *New York Times,* February 8, A6.

Sedgwick, Eve. 1990. *The Epistemology of the Closet.* Berkeley: University of California Press.

———. 1991. "How to Bring Your Kids Up Gay." *Social Text,* no. 29, 18–27.

Seib, Charles. 1977. "How the Papers Covered the Cinema Follies Fire." *Washington Post,* October 30, C7.

Shewey, Don. 1991. "The Saint, the Slut, the Sensation . . . Madonna." *Advocate,* May 7, 42–51.

Shilts, Randy. 1982. *The Mayor of Castro Street: The Life and Times of Harvey Milk.* New York: St. Martin's.

———. 1987. *And the Band Played On.* New York: St. Martin's.

———. 1990a. "Is 'Outing' Gays Ethical?" *New York Times,* April 12, A19.

———. 1990b. "Naming Names." *GQ,* August.

———. 1991. "The Nasty Business of Outing." *Los Angeles Times,* August 7, 7.

Signorile, Michelangelo. 1990. "Gossip Watch." *OutWeek,* October 3, 47.

Spelman, Elizabeth. 1988. *The Inessential Woman: Problems of Exclusion in Feminist Thought.* Boston: Beacon.

Spivak, Gayatri. 1988. "Can the Subaltern Speak?" In *Marxism and the Interpretation of Culture,* edited by C. Nelson and L. Grossberg, 271–313. Urbana: University of Illinois Press.

Stein, Edward. 1992. "Conclusion: The essentials of constructionism and the construction of essentialism." In *Forms of Desire: Sexual Orientation and the Social Constructionism Controversy,* edited by E. Stein, 325–54. New York: Routledge.

Stein, Edward, ed. 1992. *Forms of Desire: Sexual Orientation and the Social Constructionism Controversy.* New York: Routledge.

Weeks, Jeffrey. 1981. *Sex, Politics and Society.* London: Longman.

Feeding Egos and Tending Wounds: Deference and Disaffection in Women's Emotional Labor

Sandra Lee Bartky

A number of feminist theorists have treated women's unequal provision of emotional caregiving to men as a zero-sum game: Men, they assume are empowered and women disempowered in proportion to the immediate emotional benefits—the feeding of egos, the tending of wounds—that men gain from an emotional service they do not fully reciprocate. Metaphors of filling and emptying are often used to describe this state of affairs: Women fill men with our energies; this filling strengthens men and depletes ourselves.[1] Moreover, the psychic benefits men gain from women's caregiving make them fitter to rule; in dispensing these benefits, women only make themselves fitter to obey.

There is no quarreling with the claim that men as a group receive direct psychological benefits from women's emotional sustenance: This seems obvious. But in my view, this standard view errs on two counts. First, I suspect that many feminist thinkers over-estimate the efficacy of female nurturance. I shall pursue the question of the extent and effect of female emotional support in the balance of this section. Second, I believe that the standard view underestimates the subjectively disempowering effects of unrecipro-cated caregiving on women themselves, quite apart from the question how and to what extent men may be psychologically empowered by receiving it. It may be the case that women's nurturance is not a zero-sum game, i.e., that, in many circumstances, women may disempower themselves more in the giving of emotional support than men are empowered in the getting of it. I shall examine the question of women's subjective dis-empowerment . . . [later].

One variant of what I have been calling the "standard view" is "the safety-valve the-ory." The claim is sometimes made that women's emotional caregiving does more than secure psychological benefits to individual men: This caregiving is said to shore up the patriarchal system as a whole by helping to stabilize the characteristic institutions of contemporary patriarchal society. These institutions, it is claimed, are marked by hier-archy, hence by unequal access to power, and by impersonality, alienated labor, and abstract instrumental rationality. Now men pay a heavy price for their participation in such a system, even though the system as such allows men generally to exercise more power than women generally. The disclosure of a person's deepest feelings is dangerous under conditions of competition and impersonality: A man runs the risk of displaying fear or vulnerability if he says too much. Hence, men must sacrifice the possibility of frank and intimate ties with one another; they must abandon the possibility of emotional release in one another's company. Instead, they must appear tough, controlled, and self-sufficient, in command at all times.

Now, so the argument goes, the emotional price men pay for participation in this sys-tem would be unacceptably high, were women not there to lower it. Women are largely excluded from the arenas wherein men struggle for prestige; because of this and by virtue of our socialization into patterns of nurturance, women are well situated to repair the emotional damage men inflict on one another. Women's caregiving is said to func-tion as a "safety valve" that allows the release of emotional tensions generated by a fun-damentally inhuman system. Without such release, these tensions might explode the set of economic and political relationships wherein they are now uneasily contained. Hence, women are importantly involved in preventing the destabilization of a system in which some men oppress other men and men generally oppress women generally.[2] Does this theory, the "safety-valve" theory of female nurturance, pinpoint what is chiefly disem-powering about the unbalanced provision of emotional sustenance? How persuasive is it anyhow?

Hegel says that no man may be a hero to his valet. Surely, though, many men are heroes to their wives. But consider the following: While it is good to have one's impor-tance affirmed, even by an underling, how valuable is it, in the last analysis, when such affirmation issues from one's social inferior? "Praise from Caesar is praise indeed"—but she isn't Caesar. Women, after all, are out of the action: Typically, we lack standing in the world. We have too little prestige ourselves to be a source of much prestige for men. Most men look to other men for the determination of their status and for an affirmation of personal worth that really counts. When such affirmation is not forthcoming, the tender concern of women must offer some consolation, but how much?

Moreover, we must remember that men are able to do without the emotional support of women for long periods of time, in prison, for example, or in the army. In an absorbing study of the current social and psychological dimensions of friendship, Lillian Rubin claims that even though men's relationships with other men do not typically exhibit the marks of intimacy—for her, verbal disclosure of feeling and significant emotional display—men are able nonetheless to bond with other men and that this bonding, in its own way, can become a significant source of emotional support. Men, she says,

> can live quite robustly without intimacy—an emotional connection that ties two people together in important and powerful ways. At the most general level, the shared experience of maleness—of knowing its differences from femaleness, of affirming those differences through an intuitive understanding of each other that needs no words—undoubtedly creates a bond between men. It's often a primitive bond, a sense of brotherhood that may be dimly understood, one that lives side by side with the more easily observable competitive strain that exists in their relations as well.[3]

Competition among men may not only *not* be a source of male emotional distress that requires female caregiving to "bind" its potentially destabilizing effects, but may itself be a powerful impetus to male bonding and a profound source of male self-esteem. One of her respondents has this to say about competition: "It's not that I don't feel comfortable with women, but I enjoy men in a special way. I enjoy competing with men. I don't like to compete with women: there's no fun in it."[4] When Rubin asks him what precisely he enjoys about competition, here is his reply:

> (Laughing) Only a woman would ask that. (Then more seriously) It's hard to put into words. I can strut my stuff, let myself go all the way. I really get off on that; its exciting. It doesn't make much difference whether it's some sport or getting an account, I'm playing to win. I can show off just how good I am.[5]

I am concerned in this paper with men who are capable of accepting emotional sustenance from women but who do not return what they are given. [Nonfiction] bestsellers . . . complain, to be sure, of inequalities in the provision of emotional suport, but they are much more exercized about men's emotional anemia—men's inexpressiveness and fear of self-disclosure, in a word, their *refusal* even to accept sustenance from their women. And this makes sense: Tough guys, confined since childhood to a narrow range of acceptable masculine emotion, cannot easily become emotionally expressive—even with a woman. But perhaps this way of formulating the situation is misleading, suggesting as it does a dualism of appearance and reality—the appearance of invulnerability without, the reality of a rich, suffering, and needy emotional life within. It is likelier that a taboo on the display of some emotion acts in effect as a refusal of permission to oneself even to feel it. Thus, there appear to be psychological mechanisms in men that tend, quite independently of female emotional nurturance, to "cool out" such potentially destabilizing emotions as resentment, grief, or frustration. Even if we assume that such emotions have not been anaesthetized, but are only simmering below the surface of a man incapable of sharing them with a woman, there is no evidence that emotionally inexpressive men are more rebellious than their less repressed counterparts. All kinds of men are rebels, the expressive and the inexpressive alike, men who take emotional sustenance from women without recompense, even the minority of men who know how to return what they are given. Nor is there evidence that in periods of political ferment, widespread resistance on the part of men to given conditions is correlated in any way with a breakdown or diminution in the provision of female nurturance—a correlation that the "safety-valve" theory would seem to suggest.

The better mental and physical health of married men is often cited as evidence that men receive very significant benefits from women's emotional caregiving. It has been assumed that the emotional support men receive from their wives may explain why married men live longer than single men and why they score lower on standard indices of psychopathology.[6] But even here, some scepticism may be in order. The greater longevity of married men, for example, may be due as much to better physical care (regular meals, better nutrition, more urging from the wife to seek medical help) as to wives' provision of emotional care. Moreover, it isn't clear whether the superior mental health of married men is due to female emotional caretaking or whether marriage as an institution selects men who are sufficiently stable to receive these benefits in the first place. And even in relationships of some duration, there are tragic cases in which every resource of a woman's loving attention is ineffective against what are arguably the effects of the stressful circumstances of her man's life—alcoholism, drug addiction, depression, or suicide. Contemplation of the scale on which these tragedies are repeated may generate, again, some scepticism as to the efficacy of female emotional sustenance.

All these considerations, I think, tell somewhat against the "safety-valve" theory of female caregiving. While there is no doubt that men receive benefits from women's provision of emotional sustenance, and while it is conceivable that this sustenance may to some extent keep the lid on male discontent, these effects may be neither as extensive nor as significant as the safety-valve theory suggests. I think it unlikely that women's disempowerment stands in any very direct proportion either to the concrete emotional benefits that men receive from our emotional labor, or to whatever stabilization men's psychological repair may lend to an oppressive political and economic system. I suggest instead that we look for a disempowerment that is more subtle and oblique, one that is rooted in the subjective and deeply interiorized effects *upon women ourselves* both of the emotional care we give and of the care we fail to get in return.

II

Love, affection, and the affectionate dispensing of emotional sustenance may seem to be purely private transactions that have nothing to do with the macrosocial domain of status. But this is false. Sociologist Theodore Kemper maintains that "a love relationship is one in which at least one actor gives (or is prepared to give) extremely high status to another actor."[7] "Status accord" he defines as "the voluntary compliance with the needs, wishes or interests of the other."[8] Now insofar as women's provision of emotional sustenance is a species of compliance with the needs, wishes and interests of men, such provision can be understood as a conferral of status, a paying of homage by the female to the male. Consider once again the bodily displays that are typical of women's intimate caregiving: the sympathetic cocking of the head; the forward inclination of the body; the frequent smiling; the urging, through appropriate vocalizations, that the man continue his recital, hence, that he may continue to commandeer the woman's time and attention. I find it suggestive that these behaviors are identical to common forms of deference display in hierarchies of status.[9] But status is not accorded mutually: Insofar as the emotional exchanges in question are contained within a gendered division of emotional labor that does not require of men what it requires of women, our caregiving, in effect, is a collective genuflection by women to men, an affirmation of male importance that is unreciprocated. The consistent giving of what we don't get in return is a performative acknowledgement of male supremacy and thus a contribution to our own social demotion. The implications of this collective bending of the knee, however, rarely enter consciousness. The very sincerity and quality of heartfelt concern that the woman brings to her man's emotional needs serves to reinforce in her own mind the importance of his little dramas of daily life. But he receives her attention as a kind of entitlement; by failing to attend to her in the same way she attends to him, he confirms for her and, just as importantly, for himself, her inferior position in the hierarchy of gender.

Women do not expect mutual recognition from the children we nurture, especially when these children are very young, but given the companionate ideal that now holds sway, we yearn for such recognition from the men with whom we are intimate. Its withholding is painful, especially so since in the larger society it is men and not women who have the power to give or to withhold social recognition generally. Wishing that he would notice; waiting for him to ask: how familiar this is to women, how like waiting for a sovereign to notice a subject, or a rich man, a beggar. Indeed, we sometimes find ourselves begging for his attention—and few things are as disempowering as having to beg.

Women have responded in a number of ways to men's refusal of recognition. A woman may merge with her man psychologically to such an extent that she just claims as her own the joys and sorrows he narrates on occasions of caretaking. She now no longer needs to resent his indifference to her doings, for his doings have just *become* her doings. After eight years of seeing it, we recall the picture easily: Ronald Reagan at the podium, Nancy, a bit behind her husband, fixing upon him a trancelike gaze of total admiration and utter absorption. Here is the perfect visual icon of the attempt to merge one's consciousness with the consciousness of the Other.

. . . Nancy Chodorow and Dorothy Dinnerstein have maintained that the relational style of women in matters of feeling and our more "permeable ego boundaries" are due to the fact that girls, unlike boys, are not required to sever in the same way their original identification with the maternal caretaker.[10] If this is true, the phenomenon that I am describing may be "overdetermined" by psychological factors. Nevertheless, it is worth asking to what extent the merging of the consciousness of the woman with the object of her emotional care may be a strategy adopted in adult life to avoid anger and the disruption of relationship, effects that might otherwise follow upon the refusal of recognition. Moreover, the successful provision of intimate caregiving itself requires a certain loss of oneself in the Other, whatever the infantile determinants of such merger and whatever the utility such merging may have in the management of anger or resentment. I shall return to this point later.

Women sometimes demand the performance of ritualized gestures of concern from men—the remembering of a birthday or anniversary, a Valentine's Day card—as signs of a male caring that appears to be absent from the transactions of everyday life. The ferocity with which women insist on these ritual observances is a measure, I believe, of our sense of deprivation. If the man forgets, and his forgetting issues in the absence of some object—a present, a Valentine—that cultural rituals have defined as visible and material symbols of esteem, a lack felt privately may be turned into a public affront. Women's preoccupation with such things, in the absence of an understanding of what this preoccupation means, has gained us a reputation for capriciousness and superficiality, a reputation that in itself is disempowering. "Why can't a woman be more like a man?" sings the exasperated Prof. Henry Higgins. "If I forgot your silly birthday, would you fuss? / . . . Why can't a woman be like us?"

Neither of these strategies—minimalism or merger—really works. The woman who accepts a ritualized gesture, performed at most a few times a year and often very perfunctorily, in exchange for the devoted caregiving she provides her man all the time, has made a bad bargain indeed, while the psychological overidentification I describe here is grounded in a self-deceived attempt to deny pain and to avoid the consequences of anger. To attempt such merger is to practice magic or to have a try at self hypnosis. A woman who is economically dependent on a man may find it natural to identify with his interests; in addition to the kind of merging I have described, such dependency itself feeds a tendency to overidentification. But given the generally fragile character of relationships today, the frequency of divorce, and the conflicts that arise even within ongoing relationships, prudence requires that a woman regard the coincidence of her interests with those of her partner as if they were merely temporary.

III

In this section, I shall argue that women run a risk that our unreciprocated caregiving may become both epistemically and ethically disempowering. In the course of her caretaking, a woman may be tempted to adopt morally questionable attitudes and standards of behavior or she may fall prey to a number of false beliefs that tend to mystify her circumstances.

First of all, there is the epistemic risk, i.e., the risk that the woman will accept uncritically "the world according to him" and that she will have corresponding difficulty in the construction of the world according to herself. How does this happen? To support and succor a person is, typically, to enter feelingly into that person's world; it is to see things from his point of view, to enter imaginatively into what he takes to be real and true. Nel Noddings expresses it well: To adopt a caring attitude toward another is to become "engrossed" in that other: it is "a displacement of interest from my own reality to the reality of the other," whereby "I set aside my temptation to analyze and to plan. I do not project; I receive the other into myself, and I see and feel with the other." Hence, caring "involves stepping out of one's own personal frame of reference into the other's."[11] Here is merger of another sort, one not motivated by a failure of recognition but by the very character of emotional caregiving itself.

Now a woman need not merge epistemically with the man she is sustaining on every occasion of caregiving; there are times when she will reject his version of things, either to his face or to herself. But if a caregiver begins *consistently* to question the values and beliefs of the one to whom she is supposed to be offering sustenance, her caregiving will suffer. She is caught in the following paradox: If she keeps her doubts to herself, she runs the risk of developing that sense of distance and falseness that . . . is a major mark of alienated caregiving in commercial settings. If she articulates her doubts, again consistently, likely as not she will be seen as rejecting or even disloyal. Either way, her relationship will suffer. Professional therapists are required to develop a "hermeneutic of suspicion"; our intimates are not. We have the eminently reasonable expectation that our friends and intimates will support our struggles and share our allegiances, rejoice in our victories and mourn our defeats, in a word, that they will see things—at least the big things in our lives—as we see them. And so, an "epistemic lean" in the direction of the object of her solicitude is part of the caregiver's job—of any caregiver's job—it comes, so to speak, with the territory.

"The world according to him": This is that ensemble of meanings that reflect a man's more privileged location in the social totality. Now the antagonism between men and women is only part of the complex system of antagonisms that structure the social order. Hence, there will be many occasions on which his version of things will be the same as her own best version, his picture of things as much a reflection of her interests as his own. For example, black women and men who struggle in common against racism must share, in large measure, an understanding of the society in which their struggle takes place. But unless we posit a *general* identity of interest between men and women, there will be occasions, indeed countless occasions, on which a man's version of what is real and true will reflect his more privileged social location, not hers.

We know from a variety of sources that women in our society lack epistemic authority.[12] The lack has many causes, not the least of which is the historic male monopoly of the means of social interpretation and communication, a monopoly that has only recently been challenged. We typically construe women's assimilation of masculinist ideology in too mechanical and intellectualist a fashion: Mystified and distorted ideas, we think, are transmitted from one location—say, the church or school—and received in another, the woman's mind. What is absent from this picture is women's own active role in the assimilation of men's ideas, our empathic, imaginative, and affective interiorization of a masculine perspective. Since we are dealing, once again, with a clear sexual division of labor, there is no corresponding affirmation, in intimacy, of the world according to *her*.

There is then, a risk for women's epistemic development in our unreciprocated caregiving. What are its risks for our ethical life? Hegel claimed that women's ethical perfectability lay in the family, a position that has been echoed by recent conservative Christian writers.[13] With more perspicacity, John Stuart Mill pointed to the patriarchal family as a source of moral corruption for both men and women: He saw lying, hypocrisy, and self-abasement as the principal dangers for women.[14] Mill's discussion of these dangers is unsurpassed. But I point to another danger still, one that involves neither lying nor self-abasement, one that arises from the sort of heartfelt and committed caregiving that is situated at the farthest reach from hypocrisy.

To affirm a man's sense of reality is at the same time to affirm his values. "Stand by your man": What else can this mean? . . . Tenderness requires compassion and forgiveness, clearly virtues under some circumstances and certainly excellences in a caregiver. But there are situations in which virtues such as forgiveness lead to moral blindness or outright complicity. . . .

[M]any of us, I suspect, have been morally silenced or morally compromised in small ways because we thought it more important to provide emotional support than to keep faith with our own principles. In such a situation, there is still a felt tension between our own commitments and what we find it prudent to express. More corrosive is a danger that inheres in the very nature of intimate caregiving—the danger of an "ethical lean" that, like the epistemic lean I mentioned earlier, may rob the caregiver herself of a place to stand.

The emotional caregiving provided by the "good wife" or her equivalent is similar in some ways to that furnished by the "good mother." But it is importantly different as well. Insofar as a mother is interested in the preservation, growth, and social acceptability of her child, she must be attentive to the child's moral development; she must, on occasion, show herself capable of "shaping a child according to moral restraints."[15] But a woman's adult partner is not a child, no matter how childishly he may behave; she will be judged by society more for her loyalty than for his morality. A husband—or lover—does not want and will not easily tolerate ethical training from his wife; what he wants instead is her approval and acceptance. . . . Women as well as men seek succor and repair in the sphere of intimacy, a "haven in a heartless world" where the damage that has been sustained elsewhere can be repaired. But here, as elsewhere, men's needs are not only likelier to be satisfied than women's needs but satisfied at women's expense. The epistemic and ethical dangers that, if I am correct, inhere in the heartfelt and successful provision of emotional sustenance in intimacy are borne disproportionately by women. Men get the benefits; women run the risks.

IV

Disempowerment, then, may be inscribed in the more prominent features of women's unreciprocated caregiving: in the accord of status and the paying of homage; in the scarcely perceptible ethical and epistemic "leaning" into the reality of one who stands higher in the hierarchy of gender. But this is only part of the story. In this section I want to identify some countertendencies, ways in which women's provision of emotional sustenance to men may *feel* empowering and hence contradict, on a purely phenomenal level, what may be its objectively disempowering character.

Tending to wounds: this is a large part of what it is to provide someone with emotional support. But this means that in one standard scenario of heterosexual intimacy, the man appears to his female caregiver as vulnerable and injured. Fear and insecurity: for many men, these are the offstage companions of competitive displays of masculinity, and they are aspects of men's lives that women know well. To the woman who tends him, this fellow is not only no colossus who bestrides the world, but he may bear little resemblance to the patriarchal oppressor of feminist theory. The man may indeed belong to a more powerful caste; no matter, this isn't what he *seems* to her at the moment. . . .

Why isn't every woman a feminist? . . . Feminism tells a tale of female injury, but the average woman in heterosexual intimacy knows that men are injured too, as indeed they are. She may be willing to grant, this average woman, that men in general have more power than women in general. This undoubted fact is merely a fact; it is *abstract,* while the man of flesh and blood who stands before her is *concrete:* His hurts are real, his fears palpable. And like those heroic doctors on the late show who work tirelessly through the epidemic even though they may be fainting from fatigue, the woman in intimacy may set her own needs to one side in order better to attend to his. She does this not because she is "chauvinized" or has "false consciousness," but because *this is what the work requires.* Indeed, she may even excuse the man's abuse of her, having glimpsed the great reservoir of pain and rage from which it issues. Here is a further gloss on the ethical disempowerment attendant upon women's caregiving: In such a situation, a woman may be tempted to collude in her own ill-treatment.[16]

Foucault has claimed that the practice of confession is disempowering to the one who confesses. Confession, as it is practiced in psychoanalysis or religion, is designed to lead the one confessing into the heart of a presumed "true" or "real" self, which he is ever after obligated to claim as his own. But there is no such self: The idea of such a self, says Foucault, is an illusion, a mere device whereby norms are inscribed in the one confessing that secure his subordination to the locus of power represented by the confessor.[17] But here is a counterexample to Foucault's claim: In the case of heterosexual intimacy, confession is disempowering not to the man who confesses but to the woman who hears this confession. How so? The woman is not the agent of any institutional power. She has no authority either to exact penance or to interpret the situation according to norms that could, in effect, increase the prestige of the institution she represents, hence her own prestige. Indeed, the exigencies of female tenderness are such as virtually to guarantee the man's absolution by the woman—not on her terms, but on his. Moreover, the man's confession of fear or failure tends to mystify the woman's understanding not only of the power dimensions of the relationship between herself and this particular man, but of the relations of power between men and women in general.

An apparent reversal has taken place: The man, her superior in the hierarchy of gender, now appears before the woman as the weaker before the stronger, the patient before his nurse. A source within the woman has been tapped and she feels flowing outward from herself a great power of healing and making whole. She imagines herself to be a great reservoir of restorative power. This feeling of power gives her a sense of agency and of personal efficacy that she may get nowhere else. . . .

While women suffer from our relative lack of power in the world and often resent it, certain dimensions of this powerlessness may seem abstract and remote. We know, for example, that we rarely get to make the laws or direct the major financial institutions. But Wall Street and the U.S. Congress seem very far away. The power a woman feels in herself to heal and sustain, on the other hand—"the power of love"—is, once again, concrete and very near: It is like a field of force emanating from within herself, a great river flowing outward from her very person.

Thus, a complex and contradictory female subjectivity is constructed within the relations of caregiving. Here, as elsewhere, women are affirmed in some ways and diminished in others, . . . this within the unity of a single act. The woman who provides a man with largely unreciprocated emotional sustenance accords him status and pays him homage; she agrees to the unspoken proposition that his doings are important enough to deserve substantially more attention than her own. But even as the man's supremacy in the relationship is tacitly assumed by both parties to the transaction, the man reveals himself to his caregiver as vulnerable and insecure. And while she may well be ethically and epistemically disempowered by the care she gives, this caregiving affords her the feeling that a mighty power resides within her being.

The situation of those men in the hierarchy of gender who avail themselves of female tenderness is not thereby altered: Their superordinate position is neither abandoned, nor their male privilege relinquished. The vulnerability these men exhibit is not a prelude in any way to their loss of male privilege or to an elevation in the status of women. Similarly, the feeling that one's love is a mighty force for good in the life of the beloved doesn't make it so. . . . The *feeling* of out-flowing personal power so characteristic of the caregiving woman is quite different from the *having* of any actual power in the world. There is no doubt that this sense of personal efficacy provides some compensation for the extra-domestic power women are typically denied: If one cannot be a king oneself, being a confidante of kings may be the next best thing. But just as we make a bad bargain in accepting an occasional Valentine in lieu of the sustained attention we deserve, we are ill advised to settle for a mere feeling of power, however heady and intoxicating it may be, in place of the effective power we have every right to exercise in the world.

Finally, a footnote to this discussion of the subjective gratifications of caregiving: In the tending of wounds, is there sometimes an unacknowledged *Schadenfreude*—a pleasure in the contemplation of another's distress—in the sight of the master laid so low? It may or may not be *this* man to whom she is forced to submit, but his vulnerability and dependency may in some sense represent for her the demotion of all men and she may find this symbolic demotion gratifying. Since there is no requirement that our emotional lives exhibit consistency, a mild, quite compensatory *Schadenfreude* may coexist with the most beneficent of motives. But the pleasures of revenge, like the pleasures of merger and self-loss, need to be foregone.

In the provision of emotional sustenance, then, as in the processes of narcissistic self-intoxication, conventional femininity reveals itself as profoundly seductive. . . . Here, as in other aspects of our lives, we are offered real and gratifying feminine satisfactions in return for what this same femininity requires that we renounce. Until alternative sources of gratification can be found, such pleasures may be indeed difficult to renounce.

V

Some concluding observations are now in order. We may think of relationships of emotional support as lying along a continuum. At one end are the perfunctory and routinized relationships of commercial caregiving in which the caregiver feels no genuine concern for the object of her attention and where, in the worst case, the doing of her job requires that she manipulate, suppress and falsify her own feeling life. At the other end of the continuum lies the caregiving of absolute sincerity; here there is neither an awareness of ulterior motive on the part of the caregiver nor any inner reservation that might compromise the total partisanship and wholehearted acceptance she directs toward the object of her solicitude. Most provisions of emotional support fall somewhere in between. I have chosen to focus on caregiving of the latter kind because I think that its risks have not been fully appreciated and because in most kinds of noncommercial caregiving we take *this* kind as a norm; we measure ourselves by it and blame ourselves when we fall short.[18] It is sobering to consider the extent to which the Victorian ideal of woman as "angel in the house" has survived even into the era of so-called postfeminism. The dispensing of "female tenderness"—by no means coupled with "unadulterated power"—is still seen, even by writers who declare themselves sympathetic to the aims of the women's movement, as crucial to the manifestation and enactment of femininity.

In regard to the dispensing of female tenderness, the claims of feminist theorists . . . have been vindicated. Women run real risks of exploitation in the transactions of heterosexual caregiving. . . . All too frequently, women's caregiving involves an unequal exchange in which one party to this exchange is disempowered by the particular inequalities that characterize the exchange itself. This disempowerment, I have argued, lies in women's active and affective assimilation of the world according to men; it lies too in certain satisfactions of caregiving that serve to mystify our situation still further. Such disempowerment, like the disempowerment of the wage worker, may be described as a species of alienation, i.e., as a prohibition on the development and exercise of capacities, the exercise of which is thought essential to a fully human existence. . . . The capacity most at risk here is not, as in the traditional Marxist theory of alienation, the capacity for creative labor; rather, it is the capacity, free from the subtle manipulation of consent, to construct an ethical and epistemic standpoint of one's own. Hence, Marxist categories of analysis—categories that have to do with exploitation, alienation, and the organization of the labor process—are by no means irrelevant to women's experience or, as some postmodernist feminists have maintained, do they invariably distort the nature of this experience.[19] Quite the contrary: Marxist questions, if we know how to follow out their answers, can lead us into the heart of female subjectivity.

Many feminist theorists have characterized this disempowerment in metaphors of filling and emptying: Women fill men with their energies, thereby strengthening them and depleting ourselves. I have argued not that there is no depletion, but that this depletion is to be measured not only in an increase of male energies, or—as the safety-valve theory maintains—in a reduction in male tensions, but in subtle affective and ideational changes in women ourselves that, taken *in toto,* tend to keep us in a position of subservience.

Conservatives argue, in essence, that women's caregiving may be properly exchanged for men's economic support. This view is not defensible. The classic bargain so lauded by conservatives—economic support in return for domestic and emotional labor—has broken down under the weight of economic necessity. Many millions of women must work outside the home. The continuing need of these women for men's economic patronage is a measure of the undervaluation of women's labor in the waged sector. To their superexploitation at work is added a disproportionate share of domestic labor, childcare, and emotional labor; women in this situation are quadruply exploited. Nor should we forget the growing number of single women, some single mothers as well, who give emotional support to men in relationships of shorter or longer duration, but receive absolutely no economic recompense at all. But even in the dwindling number of cases in which men are willing and able to offer economic patronage to women, it would be difficult to show how such support could compensate a woman for the epistemic decentering, ethical damage, and general mystification that put us at risk in unreciprocated caregiving.

Recently, conservatives have been joined by a number of feminist theorists in the celebration of female nurturance. The motives of these thinkers differ: Conservatives extol traditional female virtues in the context of a larger defense of the sexual *status quo;* feminist theorists, especially those who are drawn to the idea of an "ethics of care" based on women's traditional nurturant activities, want to raise women's status by properly valuing our emotional work and to see this quality of caring extended to the formal domains of commerce and politics. I applaud these aims. However, many feminist thinkers who extol women's nurturance, like most conservatives, have just ignored the possibility that women may suffer moral damage in the doing of emotional labor.[20] Clearly, the development of any ethics of care needs to be augmented by a careful analysis of the pitfalls and temptations of caregiving itself.

It may be true as feminist object relations theorists claim, that in the course of individuation, women have less need than men to sever our primary attachment to the maternal caretaker; this may account for our more "permeable" ego-boundaries and the relatively greater importance of attachment and relationship in our lives. But this is only part of the story. The exigencies of female psychological development alone are not responsible for our greater propensity to offer succor and support. Feminist object-relations theory, like a feminist ethics of care, stands in need of an analysis of the subjective effects of the labor we perform on a daily basis—including our emotional labor—and of the ways in which this labor structures the subjectivity both of those who perform it and of those whom it serves.

Female subjectivity is constructed through a continuous process, a personal "engagement in the practices, discourses, and institutions that lend significance (value, meaning, and affect) to the events of the world"[21]: A case in point is the discourse and practice of caregiving in heterosexual intimacy and the institution of domesticity (or its equivalent) that contains it. Insofar as we want to change ourselves and our lives, it is far easier to imagine, indeed, to enact changes in the way we accord status and in the kind of labor we perform on a daily basis than to undertake the restructuring of our basic patterns of psychological response. I am not suggesting that such a restructuring is impossible or that we should not support radical changes in the organization of early infant care, such as coparenting, that might help to develop similar patterns of relationality in men and women.[22] My point is a familiar one: In order to develop an effective politics of everyday life, we need to understand better than we do now not only the processes of personality development, but the "micropolitics" of our most ordinary transactions, the ways in which we inscribe and reinscribe our subjection in the fabric of the ordinary. The most prominent features and many of the subjective effects of this inscription can be grasped independently of any particular theory of personality formation. We need to locate our subordination not only in the hidden recesses of the psyche but in the duties we are happy to perform and in what we thought were the innocent pleasures of everyday life.

REFERENCES

1 See e.g. Shulamith Firestone, *The Dialectic of Sex* (New York: Bantam Books, 1971);
Ti-Grace Atkinson, "Metaphysical Cannibalism" in *Amazon Odyssey* (N.Y.: Links

Books, 1974, p. 53 and Marilyn Frye, *Politics of Reality* (Trumansburg, N.Y.: Crossing Press, 1983).

2 See Rosalind Coward, *Female Desires* (New York: Grove Press, 1983), p. 140; also Sheila Rowbotham, *Woman's Consciousness, Man's World* (Baltimore: Penguin Books, 1973) and *Politics of Sexuality in Capitalism* (London: Red Collective and Publications Distribution Cooperative, 1978), p. 46.

3 Lillian Rubin, *Just Friends* (New York: Harper and Row, 1985), p. 69.

4 Ibid., p. 90.

5 Ibid.

6 Jesse Bernard, "The Paradox of the Happy Marriage," in *Woman in Sexist Society,* ed. by Vivian Gornick and Barbara K. Moran (New York: Basic Books, 1971).

7 Theodore Kemper, *A Social Interactional Theory of Emotions* (New York: John Wiley and Sons, 1978), p. 285.

8 Ibid., p. 96. "Since giving and according status are, by definition, at the heart of love relationships and only one sex is particularly expected to be competent in the performance of this attribute—*although both sexes require it* if the mutuality of the relationship is to be maintained—it is likely that the deficit of affection and love given by men to women will have devastating effects on the relationship. Wives in troubled marriages do in fact report more often than their husbands a lack of demonstrated affection, tenderness and love. . . . This is precisely what we would have expected from an examination of the sex-linked differential in standards for status conferral that is an obvious feature of our culture." Kemper, *A Social Interactional Theory of Emotions,* p. 320.

9 See Arlie Hochschild, *The Managed Heart: The Commercialization of Human Feeling* (Berkeley, Calif.: University of California Press, 1983), p. 168. See also Nancy Henley, *Body Politics* (New York: Simon and Schuster, 1977), esp. Chapters 6, 9, and 10.

10 Dorothy Dinnerstein, *The Mermaid and the Minotaur* (New York: Harper and Row, 1977) and Nancy Chodorow, *The Reproduction of Mothering: Psychoanalysis and the Sociology of Gender* (Berkeley: University of California Press, 1978).

11 Nel Noddings, *Caring: A Feminine Approach to Ethics and Moral Education* (Berkeley: University of California Press, 1984), pp. 14, 30, 24.

12 See, for example, Mary Field Belenky, Blythe McVicker Clinchy, Nancy Rule Goldberger, and Jill Mattuck Garule, *Women's Ways of Knowing: The Development of Self, Voice and Mind* (New York: Basic Books, 1986).

13 Hegel, *The Phenomenology of Spirit,* trans. A. V. Miller (London: Oxford University Press, 1977), pp. 267–279; see also Judith M. Miles, *The Feminine Principle* (Minneapolis: Bethany Fellowship, 1975).

14 John Stuart Mill, "The Subjection of Women," in *Essays on Sex Equality,* ed. Alice S. Rossi (Chicago: University of Chicago Press, 1970).

15 Sara Ruddick, "Maternal Thinking," in *Women and Values: Readings in Recent Feminist Philosophy,* ed. Marilyn Pearsall (Belmont, Calif.: Wadsworth Publishing Co., 1986), p. 342.

16 I think that this may be true only for occasional or nonserious abuse. Women stay with chronic abusers either because of the serious emotional injury done them in long-term abusive situations—impairment of judgment, "learned helplessness," disablingly low self-esteem, or fear of worse abuse if they try to leave—or else for largely economic reasons. See Susan Schechter, *Women and Male Violence: The Struggles of the Battered Women's Movement* (Boston: South End Press, 1982).

17 Michel Foucault, *History of Sexuality,* Vol. I (New York: Random House/Vintage Books, 1980), pp. 58–62.

18 The risks to women will, of course, vary from one case to the next; they may be a function of a woman's age or her degree of economic or emotional dependency on the man or the presence or absence in her life of resources with which to construct a picture of the world according to herself.

19 See, for example, Jane Flax, "Postmodernism and Gender Relations in Feminist Theory," in Michelene R. Malson, Jean F. O'Barr, Sarah Westphal-Wihl and Mary Wyer, *Feminist Theory in Practice and Process* (Chicago: University of Chicago Press, 1989), p. 61.

20 Nell Nodding's otherwise impressive book contains no analysis of the effects on the moral agent of uncompensated caring. Nor is this a significant theme on the part of contributors to *Women and Moral Theory,* ed. Eva Feder Kittay and Diana T. Meyers (Totowa, N.J: Rowman and Littlefield, 1987), a book of essays on the philosophical implications of Carol Gilligan's research on gender differences in moral reasoning—research that has been a central source for theorizing about an ethics of care. Claudia Card's "Gender and Moral Luck" in *Identity, Character and Morality: Essays in Moral Psychology,* ed. Amelie Rorty and Owen Flanagan (Cambridge, MA: MIT Press, forthcoming, 1990) is a notable exception. Two classic papers on the wrongness of female deference that present approaches somewhat different than my own are Thomas E. Hill, Jr., "Servility and Self-Respect," *The Monist,* Vol. 57, No. 1, January 1973, pp. 87–104; and Marilyn Friedman, "Moral Integrity and the Deferential Wife," *Philosophical Studies,* Vol. 47, 1985, pp. 141–150.

21 Teresa de Lauretis, *Alice Doesn't* (Bloomington, Ind.: Indiana University Press, 1983), p. 159. Cited in Linda Alcoff, "Cultural Feminism versus Post-Structuralism: The Identity Crisis in Feminist Theory," in Malson, O'Barr, Westphal-Wihl and Wyer, *Feminist Theory in Practice and Process* (Chicago: University of Chicago Press, 1989), p. 313.

22 On the necessity for coparenting, see Isaac Balbus, *Marxism and Domination* (Princeton, N.J.: Princeton University Press, 1982).

The Uses of Anger: Women Responding to Racism

Audre Lorde

Every woman has a well-stocked arsenal of anger potentially useful against those oppressions, personal and institutional, which brought that anger into being. Focused with precision it can become a powerful source of energy serving progress and change. And when I speak of change, I do not mean a simple switch of positions or a temporary lessening of tensions, nor the ability to smile or feel good. I am speaking of a basic and radical alteration in those assumptions underlining our lives.

I have seen situations where white women hear a racist remark, resent what has been said, become filled with fury, and remain silent because they are afraid. That unexpressed anger lies within them like an undetonated device, usually to be hurled at the first woman of Color who talks about racism.

But anger expressed and translated into action in the service of our vision and our future is a liberating and strengthening act of clarification, for it is in the painful process of this translation that we identify who are our allies with whom we have grave differences, and who are our genuine enemies.

Anger is loaded with information and energy. When I speak of women of Color, I do not only mean Black women. The woman of Color who is not Black and who charges me with rendering her invisible by assuming that her struggles with racism are identical with my own has something to tell me that I had better learn from, lest we both waste ourselves fighting the truths between us. If I participate, knowingly or otherwise, in my sister's oppression and she calls me on it, to answer her anger with my own only blankets the substance of our exchange with reaction. It wastes energy. And yes, it is very difficult to stand still and to listen to another woman's voice delineate an agony I do not share, or one to which I myself have contributed.

. . .

We operate in the teeth of a system for which racism and sexism are primary, established, and necessary props of profit. Women responding to racism is a topic so dangerous that when the local media attempt to discredit this conference they choose to focus upon the provision of lesbian housing as a diversionary device—as if the Hartford *Courant* dare not mention the topic chosen for discussion here, racism, lest it become apparent that women are in fact attempting to examine and to alter all the repressive conditions of our lives.

Mainstream communication does not want women, particularly white women, responding to racism. It wants racism to be accepted as an immutable given in the fabric of your existence, like eveningtime or the common cold.

So we are working in a context of opposition and threat, the cause of which is certainly not the angers which lie between us, but rather that virulent hatred leveled against all women, people of Color, lesbians and gay men, poor people—against all of us who are seeking to examine the particulars of our lives as we resist our oppressions, moving toward coalition and effective action.

Any discussion among women about racism must include the recognition and the use of anger. This discussion must be direct and creative because it is crucial. We cannot allow our fear of anger to deflect us nor seduce us into settling for anything less than the hard work of excavating honesty; we must be quite serious about the choice of this topic and the angers entwined within it because, rest assured, our opponents are quite serious about their hatred of us and of what we are trying to do here.

And while we scrutinize the often painful face of each other's anger, please remember that it is not our anger which makes me caution you to lock your doors at night and not to wander the streets . . . alone. It is the hatred which lurks in those streets, that urge to destroy us all if we truly work for change rather than merely indulge in academic rhetoric.

This hatred and our anger are very different. Hatred is the fury of those who do not share our goals, and its object is death and destruction. Anger is a grief of distortions between peers, and its object is change. But our time is getting shorter. We have been raised to view any difference other than sex as a reason for destruction, and for Black women and white women to face each other's angers without denial or immobility or silence or guilt is in itself a heretical and generative idea. It implies peers meeting upon a common basis to examine difference, and to alter those distortions which history has created around our difference. For it is those distortions which separate us. And we must ask ourselves: Who profits from all this?

Women of Color in America have grown up within a symphony of anger, at being silenced, at being unchosen, at knowing that when we survive, it is in spite of a world that takes for granted our lack of humanness, and which hates our very existence outside of its service. And I say *symphony* rather than *cacophony* because we have had to learn to orchestrate those furies so that they do not tear us apart. We have had to learn to move through them and use them for strength and force and insight within our daily lives. Those of us who did not learn this difficult lesson did not survive. And part of my anger is always libation for my fallen sisters.

Anger is an appropriate reaction to racist attitudes, as is fury when the actions arising from those attitudes do not change. To those women here who fear the anger of women of Color more than their own unscrutinized racist attitudes, I ask: Is the anger of women of Color more threatening than the woman-hatred that tinges all aspects of our lives?

It is not the anger of other women that will destroy us but our refusals to stand still, to listen to its rhythms, to learn within it, to move beyond the manner of presentation to the substance, to tap that anger as an important source of empowerment.

I cannot hide my anger to spare you guilt, nor hurt feelings, nor answering anger; for to do so insults and trivializes all our efforts. Guilt is not a response to anger; it is a response to one's own actions or lack of action. If it leads to change then it can be useful, since it is then no longer guilt but the beginning of knowledge. Yet all too often, guilt is just another name for impotence, for defensiveness destructive of communication; it becomes a device to protect ignorance and the continuation of things the way they are, the ultimate protection for changelessness.

Most women have not developed tools for facing anger constructively. [Consciousness raising] groups in the past, largely white, dealt with how to express anger, usually at the world of men. And these groups were made up of white women who shared the terms of their oppressions. There was usually little attempt to articulate the genuine differences between women, such as those of race, color, age, class, and sexual identity. There was no apparent need at that time to examine the contradictions of self, woman as oppressor. There was work on expressing anger, but very little on anger directed against each other. No tools were developed to deal with other women's anger except to avoid it, deflect it, or flee from it under a blanket of guilt.

I have no creative use for guilt, yours or my own. Guilt is only another way of avoiding informed action, of buying time out of the pressing need to make clear choices, out of the approaching storm that can feed the earth as well as bend the trees. If I speak to you in anger, at least I have spoken to you: I have not put a gun to your head and shot you down in the street; I have not looked at your bleeding sister's body and asked, "What did she do to deserve it?" This was the reaction of two white women to Mary Church Terrell's telling of the lynching of a pregnant Black woman whose baby was then torn from her body. That was in 1921, and Alice Paul had just refused to publicly endorse the enforcement of the Nineteenth Amendment for all women—by refusing to endorse the inclusion of women of Color, although we had worked to help bring about that amendment.

The angers between women will not kill us if we can articulate them with precision, if we listen to the content of what is said with at least as much intensity as we defend ourselves against the manner of saying. When we turn from anger we turn from insight, saying we will accept only the designs already known, deadly and safely familiar. I have tried to learn my anger's usefulness to me, as well as its limitations.

For women raised to fear, too often anger threatens annihilation. In the male construct of brute force, we were taught that our lives depended upon the good will of patriarchal power. The anger of others was to be avoided at all costs because there was nothing to be learned from it but pain, a judgment that we had been bad girls, come up lacking, not done what we were supposed to do. And if we accept our powerlessness, then of course any anger can destroy us.

But the strength of women lies in recognizing differences between us as creative, and in standing to those distortions which we inherited without blame, but which are now ours to alter. The angers of women can transform difference through insight into power. For anger between peers births change, not destruction, and the discomfort and sense of loss it often causes is not fatal, but a sign of growth.

My response to racism is anger. That anger has eaten clefts into my living only when it remained unspoken, useless to anyone. It has also served me in classrooms without light or learning, where the work and history of Black women was less than a vapor. It has served me as fire in the ice zone of uncomprehending eyes of white women who see in my experience and the experience of my people only new reasons for fear or guilt. And my anger is no excuse for not dealing with your blindness, no reason to withdraw from the results of your own actions.

When women of Color speak out of the anger that laces so many of our contacts with white women, we are often told that we are "creating a mood of hopelessness," "preventing white women from getting past guilt," or "standing in the way of trusting communication and action." All these quotes come directly from letters to me. . . . One woman wrote, "Because you are Black and Lesbian, you seem to speak with the moral authority of suffering." Yes, I am Black and Lesbian, and what you hear in my voice is fury, not suffering. Anger, not moral authority. There is a difference.

To turn aside from the anger of Black women with excuses or the pretexts of intimidation is to award no one power—it is merely another way of preserving racial blindness, the power of unaddressed privilege, unbreached, intact. Guilt is only another form of objectification. Oppressed peoples are always being asked to stretch a little more, to bridge the gap between blindness and humanity. Black women are expected to use our anger only in the service of other people's salvation or learning. But that time is over. My anger has meant pain to me but it has also meant survival, and before I give it up I'm going to be sure that there is something at least as powerful to replace it on the road to clarity.

What woman here is so enamoured of her own oppression that she cannot see her heelprint upon another woman's face? What woman's terms of oppression have become precious and necessary to her as a ticket into the fold of the righteous, away from the cold winds of self-scrutiny?

I am a lesbian woman of Color whose children eat regularly because I work in a university. If their full bellies make me fail to recognize my commonality with a woman of Color whose children do not eat because she cannot find work, or who has no children because her insides are rotted from home abortions and sterilization; if I fail to recognize the lesbian who chooses not to have children, the woman who remains closeted because her homophobic community is her only life support, the woman who chooses silence instead of another death, the woman who is terrified lest my anger trigger the explosion of hers; if I fail to recognize them as other faces of myself, then I am contributing not only to each of their oppressions but also to my own, and the anger which stands between us then must be used for clarity and mutual empowerment, not for evasion by guilt or for further separation. I am not free while any woman is unfree, even when her shackles are very different from my own. And I am not free as long as one person of Color remains chained. Nor is any one of you.

I speak here as a woman of Color who is not bent upon destruction, but upon survival. No woman is responsible for altering the psyche of her oppressor, even when that psyche is embodied in another woman. I have suckled the wolf's lip of anger and I have used it for illumination, laughter, protection, fire in places where there was no light, no food, no sisters, no quarter. We are not goddesses or matriarchs or edifices of divine forgiveness; we are not fiery fingers of judgment or instruments of flagellation; we are women forced back always upon our woman's power. We have learned to use anger as we have learned to use the dead flesh of animals, and bruised, battered, and changing, we have survived and grown and, in Angela Wilson's words, we *are* moving on. With or without uncolored women. We use whatever strengths we have fought for, including anger, to help define and fashion a world where all our sisters can grow, where our children can love, and where the power of touching and meeting another woman's difference and wonder will eventually transcend the need for destruction.

For it is not the anger of Black women which is dripping down over this globe like a diseased liquid. It is not my anger that launches rockets, spends over sixty thousand dollars a second on missiles and other agents of war and death, slaughters children in cities, stockpiles nerve gas and chemical bombs, sodomizes our daughters and our earth. It is not the anger of Black women which corrodes into blind, dehumanizing power, bent upon the annihilation of us all unless we meet it with what we have, our power to examine and to redefine the terms upon which we will live and work; our power to envision and to reconstruct, anger by painful anger, stone upon heavy stone, a future of pollinating difference and the earth to support our choices.

We welcome all women who can meet us, face to face, beyond objectification and beyond guilt.

Some Disquiet about "Difference"[1]

Christine Sypnowich

That human beings, their cultures and identities, are heterogeneous, indeed perhaps as different from each other as they are alike, is not a novel idea. But the idea of "difference" has recently entered both intellectual and popular culture as a profound challenge to the assumptions and practices of politics. To take some striking contemporary examples, what had been thought to be two of the most stable and unified political systems, the former Soviet Union, bound together by a seemingly impregnable authoritarian system of control, and Canada, united around what seemed a harmonious social-democratic or liberal consensus, are now in the throes of fragmentation. The claims of various ethnic and regional identities have put into question the modern idea of citizenship as membership in a collective, universal entity which subsumes diversity and the particular. Moreover, the liberal and socialist complexions of such modern collectivities as Canada and the former USSR have been targeted in particular as sources of a false universalism. These processes of fragmentation in current affairs have been mirrored in philosophical inquiry with the rise to prominence of the idea of difference. Feminist and postmodern critics of liberal and Marxist theories of emancipation have been concerned to expose a myth of homogeneity and universalism in political thought since the Enlightenment. Instead of "the citizen," "the self," or even "the proletariat" or "Party," these critics posit human subjects who bear diverse and incommensurable identities that cannot be articulated within the confines of a single discourse. This paper assesses the importance of the idea of difference in contemporary political theory and practice. I argue that while an emphasis on difference is a useful antidote to the false universalism of many theories of emancipation, the significance of difference in any larger sense is more difficult to make out. In particular, I suggest grounds for disquiet about the role of difference in theories or movements which aspire to equality and justice.

THE METAPHYSICS OF SAMENESS: FROM THE ENLIGHTENMENT TO MARX

While the idea of difference is presented as an attack on the traditions of the Enlightenment, it may be argued that the idea of difference was unleashed by the Enlightenment itself. After all, both in its epistemic project of grounding rational understanding in the deductions or observations of the individual subject, and in its political project of assuring the individual agent some measure of liberty, the distinctiveness of individuals was the Enlightenment's starting point. In Descartes's preoccupations with the possibility of knowledge and Hobbes's argument for obligation based on self-interest there emerges the idea of the uniqueness of the individual perspective which cannot be subsumed under the authority of some community. Difference is inherent in the atomistic subject who doubts the authenticity of others' very existence, on Descartes's view, or who is at war with other self-interested subjects in Hobbes's war of all against all.[2] Difference persists in contemporary liberalism insofar as these considerations have generated a pluralism about values, where moral and political questions must be settled by the natural sympathies or personal choices of disparate selves behind a "veil of ignorance."[3] The market economy fits easily into this picture as the context within which disparate selves can pursue their diverse material interests.

However, for all its scope for diversity, the Enlightenment project had obvious homogenizing aspects. First, it assumes that the individual has certain immutable and universal characteristics, such as rationality, autonomy and self-interest. Indeed, the Cartesian subject is difficult to see as a particular person of any kind. Individuals are thus easily aggregated, however isolated they are from each other. Second, the individual was assumed to have a set of transhistorical concerns; individuals might put their liberty or property to different purposes, but it was supposed that all individuals valued liberty and property. Classical liberalism in particular was thus charged with generalizing from a model of the person specific to market societies, the possessive individual, to advance arguments about the nature of all human beings.[4] Liberal theories of rights, for example, were criticized for being derived from a false universalism; Marx in particular argued that the supposed "natural rights" proclaimed by the American and French revolutionaries were in fact the rights of "man as a bourgeois who is considered to be the *essential* and *true* man."[5]

This brings us to Marxism itself. One might expect that Marxism would not be prey to the false universalism of the liberal tradition. Certainly the Marxist critique of capitalism is also a critique of the abstract individualism of liberal thought. Marx argued that the image of the market and state as shaped by the free choices of individuals was an ideological illusion, masking the actual conflicting interests and struggle between classes.[6] Real differences, between historical periods, and between different persons, that is differences in interests and in power, were rendered opaque by the liberal model. For Marxists, true diversity was only possible in a society without the division of labor, private property and class divisions, where individuals might take on a variety of tasks and form a variety of attachments. Thus the famous description of Communism as a society where one can "hunt in the morning, fish in the afternoon, rear cattle in the evening, criticize after dinner . . . without ever becoming hunter, fisherman, shepherd or critic."[7]

Nevertheless, Marxism, too, could be said to be imprisoned in a metaphysics of sameness, a universalization of the particular, in three respects. First, in its preoccupation with the "universal laws" of capitalist oppression, Marxism excludes other kinds of oppression from its analysis, or simply deduces them from the logic of capitalist exploitation; thus Engels explains the subordination of women with reference to private property.[8] Second, this "economism" prompts Marxism to designate one agent with the task of human emancipation. Thus the working class, whose (real) interests lie in the overthrow of capitalism and its replacement by communism, is the world-historical or universal class that represents the interests of humanity as a whole. The third way in which difference is downplayed in the Marxist account is in the depiction of communism itself. Historically, of course, communist regimes such as that of Stalin or Mao imposed consensus by force. But Marxist *theory* also focuses on the ideal of social unity, considering it, however, as the natural and spontaneous consequence of the abolition of capitalism. The communist individual is a universal being who transcends particular identities or social definitions. Thus communism is a univocal, harmonious community, marking "the *genuine* resolution of the conflict between man and nature and between man and man."[9] We thus have the paradox in Marxist theory that the elimination of the division of labor not only makes it possible for the individual to enjoy a life of diversity, but also ensures that unanimity characterizes social relations as a whole.

"VIVE LA DIFFERENCE"

These images of universal emancipation, be they based on abstract individualism or the exclusivity of class, have come under attack from several quarters. Feminists in particular have taken issue with the Englightenment model of personal identity, although their critiques have implications for issues of race, ethnicity and a number of other cultural differences. On the face of it, Descartes's rationalism and Hobbes's contractualism look hospitable to a gender-neutral epistemology or politics. But feminists have argued, contra Descartes and Hobbes, that persons are not self-contained atoms, but embodied, intersubjective beings. In this, feminists have invoked, not abstract reason or hypothetical states of nature, but (among other things) empirical studies of early childhood development.[10] Introspective contemplation or the assertion of interests may validate the existence of the self, but relations of attachment with caring others, and attachment to one's own gendered body, bring diverse selves into existence. Poststructuralist feminists take the embodiedness of the subject further, arguing that the female body is the source of an alternative episteme.[11] It is concluded that the Cartesian or Hobbesian self refers, not to an abstract human nature, but to a particular, historically contingent, male nature.

In this, feminists join Marxists in suggesting that the idea of a universal human nature is ideological, camouflaging unequal relations of power. And indeed, feminists have long looked to Marxism for theoretical insights and frameworks to identify inequality between the sexes in liberal capitalist societies. Nonetheless, insofar as Marxism remains attached to a universalist model of philosophical anthropology and political emancipation, it is problematic for feminists. Marxist feminism has thus found itself on the defensive since the analysis of patriarchy as a unique form of oppression emerged in the 1970s. At best Marxism was blind to the specificities of sex; at worst, it placed women at the rear of the proletariat's march through history. The prospects of a partnership between such different emancipatory agendas looked bleak enough for feminists to decry the union of Marxism and feminism as an "unhappy marriage."[12]

However, having liberated itself from the imperialistic designs of liberal and Marxist theory, feminist theory has itself been accused of a homogenous account of oppression. Increasingly, issues of race, ethnicity and culture have prompted soul-searching among feminists about the extent to which the category "woman," introduced as an antidote to the false universalism of "man," also abstracts from important distinctions based on diverse identities. Feminists, like their counterparts elsewhere, were urged by black feminists in particular to "appreciate difference," to see that "there was no one strategy or formula for the development of political consciousness."[13]

The idea of a homogenous female identity was attractive for feminists in part because it seemed to promise an escape from the atomistic conception of the person in liberal political theories since Hobbes.[14] The idea that women acted on an "ethic of care" in their historical role as caretakers was the basis for this female ontology.[15] Paradoxically, while it insisted on the commonality among women, the ethic of care itself was commended for replacing the universal strictures of rules of justice with a concern for the particular needs of persons in specific contexts. Nonetheless, the emphasis on gender identity produced worries of an unrepresentative feminism focussed on the interests of the more privileged of women.[16] Like the liberalism it criticized, such "cultural feminisms" looked guilty of abstracting from diverse, historical reality to fashion a universal model of human agency: here the caring woman, rather than the atomistic individual.

These criticisms are not new, of course. Activists for other disempowered groups have accused feminism of elitism since the suffrage movement, when the vote for women was often pursued at the expense of alliances with workers or, in the United

States, the abolitionist cause. However, what is unique about these criticisms in the current context is their place in a wider disenchantment with the scope and aims of traditional emancipatory political projects, a disenchantment which has crystallized around the idea of difference. Old-style "grand narratives" of emancipation have been replaced by a plethora of new social movements spanning issues of personal and global politics, from sexual orientation to the arms race; it would appear that if political coalition is possible, it is perhaps now only on the terms of a self-conscious "rainbow coalition."

These political changes have found a theoretical context within post-modernism, in the writings of thinkers as diverse as Lyotard, Foucault, Rorty and Irigaray. They can be grouped together as "postmodern" insofar as they share a critique of fixity, certainty and unity. This critique undercuts the idea of progress so central to the modern age. Thus a foundation for knowledge, a transparent linguistic medium between world and self, an emancipatory political agent, humanist ideals of freedom or fraternity, the possibility of aesthetic judgement; all have been deconstructed with the idea that the individual subject is imprisoned within language or discourse, and so no archimedean point from which to perceive, let alone evaluate, the world is possible.

Whether or not the postmodern perspective is compatible with the liberatory projects of the constituents of the "rainbow coalition" is the subject of considerable debate.[17] But there is reason at least to be guarded on this score. Postmodernism's "breakdown of the grand narrative," Heller and Feher note, can take forms as diverse as "relativistic indifference of respective cultures to one another," or "the thoroughly inauthentic . . . 'third worldism' of first-world intellectuals."[18] Quietism seems a constant danger in the postmodern enterprise. Lyotard's "polytheism of values" means that political judgement can only be local and internal to the values themselves, thus suggesting a Burkean reverence for the deliverances of the community.[19] Rorty's critique of foundationalism has generated a self-conscious "bourgeois liberalism," which can only muster confidence in the trite injunction not to be cruel.[20] A feminist postmodernism might seem more likely to yield strategies of liberation. But here the critique of androcentrism is sometimes so thorough-going as to suggest a rejection of politics per se, and a focus on more amorphous modes of liberation, through poetic expression or dance.[21]

Foucault's preoccupation with power offers the most hope for an insurgent postmodern voice, which rouses "docile bodies" to challenge the oppression with which they have hitherto colluded. But Foucault suggests that discourse so determines the ground rules for its own unmasking that the prospects for an emancipatory viewpoint threaten to evaporate.[22] At times Foucault goes so far as to sneer at all previous liberatory projects as "the forms that made an essentially normalising power acceptable."[23] While Foucault's skepticism is certainly salutary, it threatens a paralysis that worries the social critic. As Donna Haraway notes, "for political people," postmodernism or social constructionism "cannot be allowed to decay into the radiant emanations of cynicism."[24]

DEMOCRACY AND DIFFERENCE

The possibility that the idea of difference might yield apolitical or worse, conservative, conclusions has been countered by some important efforts at uniting the postmodern framework with an emancipatory politics. Thus Iris Marion Young argues in her important and stimulating book, *Justice and the Politics of Difference* that attention to difference can "broaden and deepen" traditional socialist commitments to democracy and equality. Focussing on the specific identities which are produced by membership in oppressed groups, Young proposes a new approach to social justice, which eschews liberal ideas of impartiality and distributive fairness on the one hand, and communitarian ideas of unmediated community and "the good life" on the other. For Young, a more ambitious conception of justice is most likely to be realised if we recognize that the plethora of identities and oppressions in contemporary society requires that we scale down our ambitions for a single political criterion. Young thus proposes participatory democracy, affirmative action, group representation in political bodies and indeed, in order to eliminate prejudice, a cultural revolution involving "politicisation" of "habits, feelings and expressions of fantasy and desire," "a kind of social therapy."[25]

While Young's main target is the liberal-communitarian debates of mainstream political philosophy, a similar argument has been advanced within a "postMarxist" terrain by Ernesto Laclau and Chantal Mouffe. In their provocative and penetrating book, *Hegemony and Socialist Strategy,* they criticize the Marxist view of a universal emancipatory subject that emanates from a single set of social relations for being both incoherent in theory and oppressive in practice. They suggest nonetheless that certain Marxist tools, such as Althusser's idea of overdetermination and the Gramscian idea of hegemony, can contribute to a politics of diversity and openness which might disrupt the "logic of equivalence" which has thus far characterized egalitarian thought. On this basis they urge "articulatory practices" whereby diverse "subject positions" of class, race, occupation or sexuality can find expression in "floating signifiers" which do not predetermine or foreclose the political form but might crystallize into "nodal points" of common resistance. Social antagonisms can thus give rise to coalitions where the socialist struggle to abolish capitalism is complemented by other struggles in a "proliferation of radically new and different spaces."[26]

This vision of an open, democratic politics which includes the disenfranchised on their own terms is a compelling alternative to universalist discourses. One cannot help but be persuaded by the arguments of Young and Laclau and Mouffe that empowering dominated social groups should not mean their assimilation into institutions of domination, but rather, a recognition of their different identities that would challenge such institutions. How these different identities can come together, however, remains a thorny question. It might be argued that any effort to articulate a theory of social change whereby diverse social groups coalesce around common goals is susceptible to postmodern skepticism. On the postmodern view of difference, political projects can only aspire to the cohabitation of plural identities. Difference is thus bound to defeat the political theories which seek to emphasize and resolve it. With this danger in mind, I suggest we subject the idea of difference to more careful scrutiny.

BEGGING TO DIFFER

Simply from a practical point of view one might question the confidence of thinkers like Young or Laclau and Mouffe that difference is compatible with egalitarian politics. There seems to be good reason to think that if the distinctiveness of identities is taken seriously, then politics risks being stymied by differences which are ultimately irreconcilable. For example, the demands of gay and lesbian groups are not obviously compatible with those of black, aboriginal or other ethnic groups which seek the preservation of cultural traditions. The poor find themselves at odds with those who focus on regional autonomy. What is the likely outcome of such impasses?

Fearful of assessing the demands of any group with criteria which lie outside of it, politics may end up performing little more than a brokerage function, as was advocated by liberal theories of pluralism in the 1960s. At best, this produces a politics of compromise rather than one based on principles of justice. Worse, parochialism runs rampant or, as critics of interest-group theory have long argued, the most powerful (best financed) voices will tend to hold sway.[27] As Laclau has recently admitted, "if universalism does not necessarily lead in a democratic direction, particularism does not do so either." With the defeat of modernity's confidence in a rational ground of history, "exclusionary discourses" can develop which lead to intransigency and xenophobia.[28] Not justice or democracy, but paralysis, crisis or balkanization may thus be the consequences of the idea of difference, so long as external criteria by which to assess the claims of difference are excluded.[29]

It could be argued that the risks of difference are worth taking. After all, the critique of universalism suggested by the idea of difference underscores the extent to which the universal is in fact the particular—the propertied, men, or Caucasians, for example—camouflaged as the general. Xenophobia, it may be retorted, is no less rampant here, insofar as "the other" is excluded from and oppressed by the pseudo-universalist ontology, metaphysics and justice.

Nonetheless, there is a not unimportant distinction to be drawn between a universalism which fails to fulfil its promise and a particularism which repudiates the universal. Subjecting the claims of a purportedly inclusive social order to immanent critique to render it truly inclusive is thus important as both strategy and ideal. The contemporary nation-state, for all its bigotry and partiality, has within it the kernel of an emancipatory promise, the aspiration to unity in diversity, a universal order which, in its general guarantees of citizenship, is open to all. This aspiration should be struggled for and improved rather than rejected. Its full achievement would doubtless require far-reaching social change so that citizens are equal enough in resources to make good their citizenship. But the aspiration of citizenship is a useful target with which to guide such change. In Canada, it is this aspiration which sustains national welfare programs in the face of efforts by right-wing regional politicians to curtail them. It made possible the movement for desegregation in the United States. That members of diverse groups might embrace a more general identity as members of a larger society seems all the more important in our times, when conflict between particular identities threatens to destroy any possibility of community in societies as diverse as the former Soviet Union, a post-apartheid South Africa and contemporary Canada.

Another difficulty with the discussions of difference is the danger of uncritical acceptance of empirically given identities. If differences are born out of oppression, then it is not clear how libaratory the recognition of them can be. This idea has been the basis of criticism of the feminist ethic of care, since it could be argued that this ethic is a result of the stereotypical roles women have played in the home, and thus is unlikely to contribute to equality for women.[30] But it also applies to other group identities; in attending to difference we should be wary of making a virtue of oppression. The issue is complicated by the different ontological status of different differences, as it were. Some are wholly socially constructed (racism), some have important physical causes (as in the case of disabled people), some are complex combinations of various factors. This point does not go entirely unrecognized by Young. A significant part of her argument documents the multifarious ways material practices of oppression can construct the identity of the oppressed.[31] But Young's focus on "cultural imperialism" prompts her to advocate the inclusion of unmediated "heterogeneous and partial discourses" to combat racism, sexism and all the other "-isms" that are exclusionary, without considering the ways in which some discourses are more liberatory than others.

Laclau and Mouffe are more cognizant of the dangers of taking given identities as the basis for democratic politics; they therefore chart a progression of articulation from domination, where the dominated are unaware of their status, to subordination, which is recognized as such, culminating in oppression, which forms the basis of insurgency. However, the process of articulation is itself not much "articulated" in their theory; articulation ends up looking like little more than a promissory note that, in the absence of the old guarantees of vanguard party, universal agents, social contracts, etc., the good will win out. On the other hand, this distinction between levels of consciousness is rather difficult to square with Laclau and Mouffe's understandable suspicion of Marxist ideas of false consciousness and their insistence that radical democracy consists simply in a "polyphony of voices, each of which constructs its own irreducible discursive identity."[32]

At root the impulse to include difference is driven by a conviction that one's identity as the member of a race, sex, or linguistic culture should not disadvantage one in social life. Giving certain identities a voice may be one way of accomplishing this, but if power resides outside of those identities, and if the identities themselves are the products of oppression, then this strategy has limitations.[33] If we recognize that some differences are the fruits of injustice, then justice may require the elimination of difference, or at least the difference that difference makes.

From a philosophical point of view, it's not clear whether universalism of some kind is avoidable, in any case. After all, the fate that met feminists, who, having rejected the false universalism of androcentric discourse were then accused of false universalism in the face of race, class, etc., is a fate that can meet the assertions of identity that come after them; difference unleashes an endless cycle of accusations and inclusions. We are thus left reciting ever longer moralistic shopping lists of identities in a futile attempt to dam up the floods of interminable difference. Ultimately there are as many differences as selves, and thus our invocations of difference always risk essentialism, wherein we reify a certain identity and proclaim its immutable nature, without attention to the differences within the identity itself, or the damage done to the new "other" the reclaimed identity leaves in its wake.

In any case, why focus on the politics of difference? So that the different may be part of a "we" which is a source of social unity. The hope for commonality continues to drive the theories of Young and Laclau and Mouffe, for all their apparent disenchantment with the idea. We cannot do justice to the differences that characterize human beings, not just because of their infinite variations, but because the effort to "do justice" to them is to somehow mute their salience. The preoccupation with particular local identities emerges as a kind of "neo-foundationalism" to ward off the vertigo that besets radical thinkers who have been persuaded by the postmodern critique of foundations. In an impulse to restore the security of old forms of collectivism that the postmodern critique destroyed, difference is included in order for it to be tamed.[34]

These considerations suggest that a focus on the inclusion of difference *per se* is problematic; philosophically, the project risks incoherence, and politically, it risks an impotence in the face of oppression. We thus have grounds for being cautious about the role of difference in political theory. If we are to tackle injustice, which is after all the preoccupation of difference theorists, then we need a broader inquiry than that of difference itself. Is this possible, without being insensitive to difference and returning political philosophy to the false universalism of grand narratives?

DIFFERENCE'S DISCONTENTS

It may be suspected that my argument is simply the nostalgic lamentations of a has-been Marxist (I refuse the term post-Marxist!), one who cannot relinquish the ideals of fraternity and unity essential to the socialist project. Such lamentations should be countered by the astute diagnosis of the impulse for community as an impossible "Rousseauist dream" of a "unity of subjects with one another," as Young puts it, or what Laclau and Mouffe indict as the utopia of a transparent society embodied in the "Ideal City."[35]

There is no doubt that classical Marxism is shown to be inadequate by these kinds of arguments about the complexity of heterogenous identities in society. The fate of the Bolshevik project confirms the impossibility of simply incanting old theories in the wake of disturbing new events. As Eastern Europe abandons Marxism, Western Marxists cannot assume that they have the resources in some unrevised body of theory with which to correct the theoretical disasters with which Eastern Europeans have had to live in practice.[36] For Marxists in particular there is much to learn from the insights of the theory of difference about, among other things, the diversity of social injustices and the agents with which to counter them, the reality of micro-oppressions, the importance of a provisional and open approach in theory, and the inevitability of heterogenity in even the most ideal societies.

However, my misgivings about difference cannot be discounted simply as a communitarian antipathy to the reality of social divisions. These misgivings stem from a concern for how justice is to be achieved in the face of the competing claims of difference, since no clear political strategies follow from embracing identities as such. I have two, tentative proposals for meeting these concerns which, by taking us away from the focus on difference, can better remedy the injustice that is the consequence of issues of difference. These proposals are first, a consideration of how interests are articulated by the discourse of rights and second, a reassessment of the idea of impartiality.

RIGHTS AND IMPARTIALITY

Rights are an obvious means of instantiating diversity. Liberal political theories standardly employ rights to defend and resolve individual differences, and while rights originally referred to abstract liberties such as freedom to own property, they have been successively expanded to include political rights such as the right to vote, and social rights such as the right to health care. The achievements of rights discourse have prompted criticisms of the anti-rights thrust of Marxist theory, and the assumption that an ideal society would have no need of legal institutions is one bit of Marxist orthodoxy that must be abandoned once we understand the nature of difference.[37] The fantasy of a univocal, homogenous society which has no need of rights must be countered with a model of rights for articulating the claims of diverse social groups. Insofar as these claims are not merely the claims of abstract individuals, however, they require some revision of liberal theories. Young thus recognizes a role for rights in her theory, suggesting that "the specificity of each group requires a specific set of rights for each, and for some a more comprehensive system than for others."[38] For their part, Laclau and Mouffe emphasize that the liberal discourse of individual rights "permits different forms of articulation and redefinition which accentuate the democratic movement."[39]

However, it should be recognized that the discourse of rights does not map on to difference in any direct way. Rights cannot take the brute datum of diverse identities at face value. Rights are not the mere effluxes of identities, but politically contested claims that persons make to have their interests protected.[40] We thus must move from the identity of an agent to the interests to which identity gives rise. And having identified the agent's interests, we must then assess their legitimacy. Thus interests must, first, be capable of being formulated in general enough terms to count as rights, and, second, be capable of being recognized by others as worthy of the stature of rights. Rights require that difference be mediated by debate and consensus in order to assess competing claims in light of the demands of justice. Thus while difference will give rise to political activity about the terrain of rights, how that terrain is ultimately to be specified requires a reference outside of difference. Questions of human needs, the constituents of human dignity, the prerequisites for self-respect, these are universal ideals to which rights refer.

It must be emphasized, as Benhabib, after Habermas, argues against the abstraction of liberal theory, that rather than a hypothetical thought process, the constitution of rights must come from an "actual dialogue situation in which moral agents communicate with each other" about their needs.[41] Thus our understanding of justice need not be conceived as an eternal, ahistorical standard, an archimedean point beyond experience. Rights are inevitably constituted by evolving conceptions of justice, what Haraway calls "situated knowledges,"[42] which are constructed in the context of struggle and debate. The universalism of rights is thus to be understood in terms of the applicability of their ultimate ideals, rather than the fixity of their content.

The universalism of rights thus makes it possible for diverse groups to unite around a common political ideal. While rights discourse can be used to specify and meet particular needs—parents' rights to childcare, or aboriginal peoples' rights to land—it does so by reference to a consensus about a fulfilling or empowered life which is available to all.[43] By protecting different interests, rights give us grounds for a commitment to an entity outside of our disparate identities. In the context of Canada, the Charter of Rights has played a significant role, therefore, in debates about national unity. Indeed, the specification of a social charter has emerged as an important way of achieving consensus on the integrity of the Canadian polity.[44]

Rights are not typically seen as sources of unity, however. It must be admitted that rights can pit citizens against each other, as they seek the recognition of opposing interests. How are we to resolve the inevitable disputes that surround claims and counterclaims in terms of both the constitution and enforcement of rights? The idea of impartiality is the usual response in liberal theory, as the philosophical posture which establishes rights, and the legal mechanism to ensure rights are fairly enforced.

However, the idea of difference has been marshalled to discredit the idea of impartiality. For Young and Laclau and Mouffe, impartiality is both impossible, given the intractability of different identities, and undesirable, since it inevitably imposes one point of view on others.[45] This critique rests, however, on a caricature of the idea. No philosopher or judge can be impartial in the sense of devoid of perspective, interests or values. But the ideal of impartiality is just that, an ideal to which we should aspire. It would be a mistake to believe that any legal principle could succeed in making social life wholly predictable, but the impartial ideal embodied in the notion of the rule of law, for example, is able to enforce a degree of regularity in political and legal decision-making. Indeed, it is because the weighing of different claims inevitably requires value-judgments and policy decisions that we need some notion of procedural justice in order to prevent these normative processes from becoming wholly discretionary or arbitrary.

This is not to suggest that the status quo is in fact impartial. But our disillusion with the liberal capitalist state should cause us not to reject impartiality, but to demand it, and to point to the ways in which inequality prevents impartiality from being fully operable. The ideal of impartiality can thus figure as part of a struggle for social justice, and our demand for impartial treatment will thus cause us to challenge the unfairness of the advantages of property and social position. The discourses of rights and impartiality are, therefore, far from features of a false universalistic discourse, but are, rather, the means of struggling for that ever-elusive but nonetheless inspiring universalist ideal.

At the same time, essential to these discourses is a tolerance, and indeed protection, of diversity. Rights to privacy or autonomy, together with the rejection of discrimination or bias inherent in the ideal of impartiality, allow us to engage in different ways of living. It should be underlined that rights and impartiality do not make for total freedom and absolute neutrality; but they serve to keep Mill's "tyranny of the majority" at bay, so that the different are not treated as "the other." The challenge of our differences cannot be met by subsuming them within a new, multifarious "we"; rather, the only viable response must be a modest one, that of working towards a culture of openness.

CONCLUSION

The idea of difference provides an important reminder of the limitations of emancipatory political theory. Emancipation is not a likely prospect unless our political theories and practices stay open to other perspectives, take account of the diverse forms oppression can take, and remain consciously provisional and revisable. In our post-Communist age, these are important lessons. However, I have suggested that beyond this injection of caution into our political projects, it is not clear how the idea of difference in itself can shape political theory. Instead of identity itself, we should focus our attention on the interests that accrue from different identities and the extent to which they figure as claims for justice. This enterprise requires a central role for the institutions of rights and procedural fairness. Instead of jettisoning these institutions as the relics of a bygone false universalism, I suggest that we call upon them to express our aspirations for equality and democracy. If we are the bearers of incommensurable, diverse identities, we cannot expect political institutions to recognize and convert these identities into sources of unity and cohesion. What we can demand of our political institutions is that our differences do not give rise to injustice. Thus citizenship provides us with the abstract entitlement to political participation and adequate resources to remedy the inequalities of difference. Postmodernism has underscored the impossibility of bridging differences; but the ideals of liberalism and socialism need not be taken to be the pursuit of such universalist chimeras. Rather, we can live diversely in common only if inequality, not difference, becomes our focus.

NOTES

1 An earlier version of this paper was presented at a March 1992 conference on "Explorations in Difference" in Edmonton, Alberta. I am grateful to David Bakhurst, Don Carmichael, Stephen Andrews, and Jerry Bickenbach for helpful comments.

2 Descartes, *The Meditations,* in *Discourse on Method and the Meditations,* trans. F. E. Sutcliffe (Harmondsworth: Penguin, 1968), and Hobbes, *Leviathan,* ed. C. B. Macpherson (Harmondsworth: Penguin, 1968).

3 John Rawls, *A Theory of Justice* (Cambridge MA: Harvard University Press, 1972).

4 C. B. Macpherson, *Possessive Individualism* (Oxford: Clarendon, 1962).

5 Marx, "On the Jewish Question," *Marx and Engels Collected Works* (London: Lawrence and Wishart, 1975), 3: 164.

6 Marx and Engels, *German Ideology, Marx and Engels Selected Works* (Moscow: Progress, 1979), 68–76.

7 Ibid., 33–5.

8 Engels, *The Origin of the Family, Private Property and the State,* intro. and notes Eleanor Burke Leacock (New York: International Publishers, 1972).

9 Marx, "Economic and Philosophical Manuscripts," *Collected Works,* vol. 3, 298.

10 Nancy Chodorow, *The Reproduction of Mothering* (Berkeley: University of California Press, 1978), and Carol Gilligan, *A Different Voice* (Cambridge: Harvard University Press, 1982).

11 Luce Irigaray, *This Sex Which is Not One,* trans. Catherine Porter with Carolyn Burke (Ithaca: Cornell University Press, 1985). See selections by Irigaray and Julie Kristeva in Elaine Marks and Isabelle de Courtivron (ed. and introd.). *New French Feminisms* (New York: Schocken Books, 1988) and Judith Butler, *Gender Trouble* (New York: Routledge, 1990).

12 Heidi Hartmann, "The Unhappy Marriage of Marxism and Feminism: Toward a More Progressive Union," in L. Sargent, ed., *Women and Revolution* (Boston: South End Press, 1971).

13 bell hooks, "Sisterhood: Political Solidarity Between Women," in Ibid., and M. Lugones and E. Spelman, "Have We Got a Theory For You! Feminist Theory, Cultural Imperialism and the Demand for 'The Woman's Voice'," *Women's Studies* (1983).

14 I explore this in the context of contemporary debates in political theory in "Justice, Community and the Antinomies of Feminist Theory," *Political Theory* (forthcoming).

15 S. Ruddick, "Maternal Thinking," *Feminist Studies* 6: 2 (1980). E. Feder Kittay and D. Meyers, eds., *Women and Moral Theory* (Totowa, N.J.: Rowman and Littlefield, 1986).

16 Gayatri Spivak, "French Feminism in an International Frame," *In Other Worlds* (New York: Routledge, 1988).

17 See, for example, Jürgen Habermas, "Modernity versus Postmodernity," *New German Critique* 22 (1981); Charles Taylor, "Foucault on Freedom and Truth," *Philosophical Papers* vol. 2, (Cambridge: Cambridge University Press, 1982); Gad Horowitz, "The Foucaultian Impasse: No Sex, No Self, No Revolution," *Political Theory* 15: 1 (1987); selections by Scyla Benhabib and Nancy Hartsock in L. Nicholson, ed., *Feminism/Postmodernism;* Donna Haraway, *Symians, Cyborgs and Women* (New York: Routledge, 1991).

18 Agnes Heller and Ferone Feher, *The Postmodern Political Condition* (Oxford: Polity, 1988), 5.

19 Jean-Francois Lyotard, *The Postmodern Condition,* trans. G. Bennington and B. Massouri, foreword by F. Jameson (Minneapolis: University of Minnesota Press, 1984).

20 Richard Rorty, "Postmodern Bourgeois Liberalism," *Journal of Philosophy* 80 (1983) and *Contingency, Irony and Solidarity,* (Cambridge: Cambridge University Press, 1989).

21 See selections by Kristeva and Irigaray in *New French Feminisms,* and Spivak, "French Feminism in an International Frame."

22 So I argue in "Fear of Death: Mortality and Modernity in Political Philosophy," *Queen's Quarterly* (Fall, 1991).

23 Michel Foucault, *The History of Sexuality, Vol. I: An Introduction,* trans. R. Hurley (New York: Vintage), 144; but see also *Power/Knowledge,* ed. C. Gordon (New York: Pantheon, 1980).

24 Haraway, *Symians, Cyborgs and Women,* 184.

25 Iris Marion Young, *Justice and the Politics of Difference* (Princeton: Princeton University Press, 1990), 153.

26 Laclau and Mouffe, *Hegemony and Socialist Strategy: Towards a Radical Democratic Politics* (London: Verso, 1985), 176 81.

27 P. Bachrach and M. Baratz, "The Two Faces of Power," *American Political Science Review* 56 (1962); and S. Lukes, *Power: A Radical View* (London: Macmillan, 1974).

28 E. Laclau, "God Only Knows," *Marxism Today* (December, 1991): 57.

29 See also Alasdair MacIntyre's critique of liberal individualism in *After Virtue* (London: Duckworth, 1981).

30 See L. Segal, *Is the Future Female?* (London: Virago, 1987); N. Fraser and L. Nicholson, "Social Criticism without Philosophy," *Feminism/Postmodernism,* 32 3; Susan Moller Okin, *Justice, Gender and the Family* (New York: Basic Books, 1989). 15; Barbara Houston, "Rescuing Womanly Virtues" and Marilyn Friedman, "Beyond Caring," in M. Hanen and K. Nielsen, eds., *Science, Morality and Feminist Theory* (Calgary: University of Calgary Press, 1987), and my "Justice, Community and the Antinomics of Feminist Theory."

31 Young, *Justice and the Politics of Difference,* ch. 2.

32 Laclau and Mouffe, *Hegemony and Socialist Strategy,* 191. See the critiques of Norman Geras, "Post-Marxism?" *New Left Review* (1987): 163, and Peter Osborne, "Radicalism without Limit," in Osborne, ed., *Socialism and the Limits of Liberalism* (London: Verso, 1991).

33 Lynne Segal, "Whose Left? Socialism, Feminism and the Future," *New Left Review* (1991): 185.

34 I am grateful to David Bakhurst for this point.

35 Laclau and Mouffe, *Justice and the Politics of Difference,* 229–32, and *Hegemony and Socialist Strategy,* 176–93.

36 I make this argument in "The Future of Socialist Legality," *New Left Review* (1992): 193.

37 This is my argument in *The Concept of Socialist Law* (Oxford: Clarendon, 1990).

38 Young, *Justice and the Politics of Difference,* 183.

39 Laclau and Mouffe, *Hegemony and Socialist Strategy,* 176.

40 Thus Ronald Dworkin's idea of rights as "trumps" in *Taking Rights Seriously* (Cambridge, MA: Harvard University Press, 1978).

41 Seyla Benhabib, "The Generalised and the Concrete Other," in S. Benhabib and D. Cornell eds., *Feminism as Critique* (Oxford: Basil Blackwell, 1987), 93. See also Jürgen Habermas, *The Theory of Communicative Action* (Boston: Beacon Press, 1984), and, for an affirmation of this view against postmodern theories, *The Philosophical Discourse of Modernity* (Cambridge, MA: MIT Press, 1987).

42 Haraway, *Symians, Cyborgs and Women,* 191–6.

43 Thus Will Kymlicka advocates aboriginal rights as part of the liberal commitment of treating individuals as equals. See his *Liberalism, Community and Culture* (Oxford: Clarendon, 1989).

44 I develop this argument in "Rights, Community and the Charter," *British Journal of Canadian Studies* 6: 1 (1991).

45 Young, *Justice and the Politics of Difference,* 99–107; and Laclau and Mouffe, *Hegemony and Socialist Strategy,* 122–7. This argument has also been made by Critical Legal Theorists such as Duncan Kennedy. See his "Legal Formality." *Journal of Legal Studies* 2: 1 (1973).

FAMILY AND COMMUNITY

Misnaming is a common strategy of domination. Today in our society that strategy often centers on family and the values generally bound up with that institution. Those who misname family-related realities are less interested in families than in thwarting the moves toward sexual equality and human liberation in our society. Susan Faludi reports that

> By relabeling the terms of the debate over equality, [New Right men] discovered, they might verbally finesse their way into command. By switching the lines of power through a sort of semantic reversal, they might pull off a coup by euphemism. And in this case, words would speak louder than actions. Under this linguistic strategy, the New Right relabeled its resistance to women's newly acquired reproductive rights as "pro-life"; its opposition to women's newly embraced sexual freedom became "pro-chastity"; and its hostility to women's mass entry into the work force became "pro-motherhood." Finally, the New Right renamed itself—its regressive and negative stance against the progress of women's rights became "pro-family."[1]

Thus, "family values" now commonly equates with a renewal of the household patriarch's authority, a revalorization of heterosexual coupling, and a proprietary view of children. That circumstance makes writing about family at one and the same time singularly important and painfully difficult. Moreover, biological links with children seem to be mattering more of late than social-emotional bonds, at least judicially. That development exacerbates the challenge of showing that neither "home" nor "family" necessarily has anything to do with biology, male dominance, heterosexuality, or commodified children. Both arrays of lived experiences have everything to do, however, with what Anthony Giddens (following R. D. Laing) calls *ontological security,* which involves "an autonomy of bodily control within predictable routines."[2] Dignity presupposes ontological security, which is most firmly anchored in one's "family" and "community."

Delineating those arrays of lived experiences is no simple matter, though, especially now that they are contested notions. Despite the diversification of American families over the past several generations many Americans still use "family" with reference to husband, wife, and their biological children where the husband serves as the "head of the household." Often Americans see fit to note that the Smiths' children are adopted; they call the Joneses "a couple," not a family, because they have no children; they see Allison and Sandra with their children as a "household" at best or a "perversion" at worst. Overall, Americans still see "family" mostly in what fits the nuclear model typically predominating in school textbooks and on popular television shows. To that extent they fail to recognize and, therefore, cannot respect the family lives of many of the people around them. Indeed, they cannot lay hold of the meanings "family values" must include in order to honor the lived experiences of people whose ontological security is anchored in families far removed from the nuclear model.

Evelyn Fox Keller reminds us that naming is "the special business of science." She goes on to say, "Theories, models, and descriptions are elaborated names. In these acts of naming, the scientist simultaneously constructs and contains nature" and, one might add, social reality.[3] Part of theorists' cultural work, then, is to counteract the distortions of people's lived experiences propounded by movements such as the New Right. Yet because the social sciences treat realities already named in everyday life, naming can readily become misnaming unless great theoretical care is taken. In Alfred Schutz's terms social scientists can construct their technical "second-order concepts" by unscientifically appropriating commonsense "first-order concepts."[4] Nowhere is this likelier to happen than with profound commonplaces such as "family" and "community." Thus, this section begins with a reading focused on the responsibility of naming fairly and meaningfully. Anndee Hochman also weaves a tapestry of lived meanings that recent rhetoric about "family values" tries to unravel.

Hochman, who recognizes "family values" as a rhetorical "code aimed to halt a changing world" (p. 302), surveys the folds of language wherein we find words for the people who mean a great deal to us. Those folds, she finds, are often skimpy. Sometimes the available words are "quiet enforcers of the status quo" (p. 300); other times they are conspicuous for their absence. In any case Hochman speaks to how "The language of the nuclear family continues to sway our speech, crowd[ing] out equally valid models of living" (p. 301). By interrogating our vocabulary of intimacy, including our familial terms, Hochman takes us to the roots of the theoretical enterprise as well as to the roots of our social-emotional lives.

In the second reading, Bonnie Thornton Dill deals with roots torn assunder as the matrix of domination did its historical work in our society. We have already seen "race" theorized as an oppressive construction. Dill shows how its constructions set severe limits on what "family" could be among African Americans and Chinese Americans. She also shows how people nonetheless give their families whatever practical priority is necessary to sustain them against the odds. At the same time Dill illustrates that a variety of names are available for those "different" families and familial roles that members of these oppressed groups did manage to create. She mentions, for example, "paper sons," "split household families," and "sojourning husbands." Of interest is the theoretical, cultural, and political import of these terms. Are these terms of legitimacy or terms of illegitimacy? Do they function to construct "difference" or to underscore similarity?

Overall, Dill's selection implies that controlling people's family-making is tantamount to controlling their hearts. She points to the wrenching challenges oppressed people face when they try to make families under conditions their oppressors have intentionally made adverse, if not impossible. At a minimum such challenges include

> Keeping children alive, helping them to understand and participate in a system that exploited them, and working to ensure a measure—no matter how small—of cultural integrity. . . (p. 310).

Wives and mothers of color endured the further pains associated with their "double-bind situation," an inescapable fate given their positioning in the matrix of domination. These women had no choice but to work in the unenviable positions available to them in the labor force but in turn were "damned . . . as women, wives, and mothers because they did not confine their labor to the home" (p. 310). Neither their bodies nor their souls were uncontested. On the contrary, a vicious contest of dignity was set in long-term motion that made them constant contestants, never clear-cut winners.

The same broad brush strokes might paint a picture of family life among low-income, native-born people as well as among Euro-American and other immigrants with little schooling and few resources. Although differently nuanced, that picture would also illustrate the principles Dill delineates. In a nutshell those principles gravitate toward the stark generalization that respectable "family" life is an outcome hard won, continually contested, or practically denied to those members of our society who are "different." To that extent *the* American family—the one associated with long-term marriage, virtual monogamy, desexualized motherhood and disengaged fatherhood, a primary and a secondary earner, and nondelinquent kids more or less likely to go to college—is a white, middle-American, heterosexual institution more or less closed to people inhabiting other social territories. For "different" people, *the* American family is at once a challenge and an affront. Those members seeking respectability face it as a standing challenge; those seeking liberation, cultural integrity, or gender equality face it as an affront to their dignity.

In general, multicultural social theorists deconstruct "the" family so as to expose its regulatory functions. As Dill's selection shows, the familial institution has been used to keep women in their subordinate places, which vary with their race and ethnicity (among other circumstances), within and beyond their homes. Moreover, the same institution has historically been problematized for American women and men of color whose family-making was routinely undermined or even outlawed. Just as restricted reproductive rights regulate women's bodies, restricted familial rights regulate people's souls and the souls of those with whom they try to make families. As Dill shows, restricted familial rights usually also regulate women's bodies, if only by taxing them to the limit.

In the third reading Reva Landau deconstructs "the" family along other dimensions. Above all, she exposes the economic dependence—*not* interdependence—bound up with marriage and motherhood for many, many North American women. In order to document that state of affairs Landau presents waves of statistical data. Thereafter she launches a multifaceted interrogation of *the* family as envisioned in popular culture and the public imagination. Landau rejects the idea of encouraging women to think they can choose to work outside the home full- or part-time. She implies that women have no such meaningful choice in the standard marital situation unless one supposes that rational people sometimes choose financial dependence and, with it, a substantial risk of landing themselves and their children (if any) in poverty.

Landau's deconstruction of wives' and mothers' "choices" to work only in the home or work outside it only part-time discloses the financial reach of marriage. People's marital situations routinely affect not only their employment status but also their income, benefits, pensions, income taxes, and other material benefits, centrally including how much housekeeping and (if applicable) childcare service they get from their partner. That wives' and mothers' marital situations pervasively disadvantage them, long- and short-term, in ways that most people take for granted, strikes Landau as unacceptable. Thus, after deconstructing the "choice" many wives and mothers make to foreshorten their employment in one way or other, Landau delineates strategies for righting their situation. Those strategies revolve around legislating away "all incentives for men to have women provide housekeeping and childcare services for them" (p. 331).

Landau's paper offers a subtext on the ideology of romantic love in our culture. Taken out of a cultural context where that ideology holds sway, her paper makes it seem as if many wives and mothers are what Harold Garfinkel calls "judgmental dopes."[5] Why, otherwise, would they make woefully irrational choices? We know why. Encouraged to choose their partners when they are head-over-heels in love and walking on air, encouraged to stick it out in their marriages so as to be validated as worthwhile women, and encouraged to "feed egos and tend wounds" (see Bartky), women are commonly primed to choose, where possible, working primarily in the home where their children and husbands take refuge and find comfort. Given the familism pervading much of our society, women marry with the dice already stacked against the choices that might enhance their ontological security and advance their agency as wives, mothers, and co-homemakers. Landau (p. 326) makes the point well:

> As long as men who work outside the home are considered good fathers, while women who work outside the home are not considered to be good mothers, as long as it is considered to be the mother's duty, and not the father's duty, to take care of the children, to clean the house, to buy the clothes, to pick up the laundry, etc., etc., it can be doubted how much "choice" women have about their decision to work only in the home or work part-time.

Hers is thus a paper that suggests heterosexual women's consciousnesses have not been sufficiently problematized to see the regulatory side of the home-and-hearth institution they generally expect to center their emotional lives.

Paula Gunn Allen's selection bridges the matters of family and community. Assuming that "tribal consciousness . . . differs enormously from that of the contemporary western world," Allen explores a web of concepts inseparable in the former consciousness:

> The concept of family, the concept of community, the concept of women, the concept of bonding and belonging, and the concept of power were all distinctly understood in a tribal matrix; and those concepts were/are very different from those current in modern America (p. 335).

Indeed, the concepts differed enough from one to the other culture that as eminent an anthropologist as Bronislaw Malinowski did a good deal of misnaming in connection with American Indian households (p. 336). Allen implies that he needed to see what thinking, feeling people everywhere need to ponder carefully: "Among American Indians, spirit-related persons are perceived as more closely linked than blood-related persons" (p. 336). For many of us, such a formulation smacks of metaphor or exaggeration. Not only is such an interpretation a misrendering of American Indians' lived experiences, but it is also a measure of how much a kind of biological determinism still grips our consciousness. Such ethnocentrism may also make it hard for us to think about "community" not just as a set of "relationships that determine who can depend on whom for what" but *"sister* relationships that determine" the shape of such interdependence. (p. 338; my emphasis) While exploring "family," "community," "women," "bonding and belonging," and "power," Allen sketches a cultural context where being gay is positively, not negatively, sanctioned. Allen's selection thus brims over with theoretical and substantive richness. Hers is a narrative that shows particularly well how multicultural theorists grapple with issues such as conceptualization within the context of theorizing people's lived experiences. Put differently, I find it hard to imagine Allen as a metatheorist.

I face the same difficulty with William Wei. His concerns lie with weaving together theoretical and substantive issues so that their close connections with one another are rendered more apparent than in mainstream theory. Wei's selection ties community to cultural reclamation. He shows how community scholars and artists, acting locally as activists and advocates, have been laying the grounds for "countering the sense of 'otherness' " among Chinese Americans, Japanese Americans, Korean Americans, and Filipino Americans. Their work has spanned the visual and performing arts and also found expression in literary arts, including nonfiction as well as fiction. Characteristically using populist methods, such scholars and artists have involved community residents in their efforts. Over time their work, like that of feminist artists and Latino artists and artists from other marginalized groupings, raises questions about the proper mix of political and aesthetic elements in their art. Recall Wendy Rose's selection about whiteshamanism where she contrasts American Indian and other conceptions of art. Here might be a good point for returning to her paper and thinking about the close connections between community and the arts. Wei's treatment implies that even when they are narrowly aesthetic, the arts promote community. He subtly invites us to consider that building sustainable community without the arts may be nigh unto impossible.

Cheryl Townsend Gilkes implies the same conclusion, at least for oppressed groups of people. Her survey of "the tradition of resistance" (p. 369) anchored in African American women's "community work" cites as one dimension of such work "changing ideas, stereotypes, and images that keep a group perpetually stigmatized" (p. 362). Although formal schooling can be a vehicle of such change, the arts ranging from storytelling to sculpture are at least as significant a tool.

Gilkes observes, "Racial oppression takes up more time and creates extra work . . . for members of a victimized group" (p. 363). In that straightforward declaration she pinpoints an enormous frustration among members of marginalized and excluded groups. In addition to all the daily chores they face, oppressed people routinely face an extra drain on their energies in the form of snickers, putdowns, refusals of attention, and worse. Their dignity at issue, such individuals minimally face the challenge of overriding or using their hurt and anger enough to go on with the tasks at hand. As Gilkes emphasizes, many such individuals do a great deal more than that, both formally and informally. To her great credit Gilkes includes in "community work" all those activities that "combat racism and empower . . . communities to survive, grow, and advance in a hostile society" (p. 362). She says such work "consists of everything that people do to address oppression in their own lives, suffering in the lives of others, and their sense of solidarity or group kinship" (p. 362). Her formulations are embracing ones that point to the community-making inherent in resistance to group oppression. Out of people's localized resistance, she shows, comes the sociopolitical space wherein social movements and other vehicles of substantial change emerge and gain strength.

For oppressed groups, then, community cannot be built without some resistance to oppression. To suppose otherwise would be to suppose that people who feel overwhelmed, defeated, and lacking in agency can create and sustain strong ties with one another. It is to suppose that community can grow out of sharing a common fate imposed from above and outside rather than reshaping a common fate out of dialogue that takes intragroup diversity into sensitive account. To create viable community in the face of oppression means, Gilkes says, to dismiss "oppression as a normal and natural feature of human experience" (p. 364). Hers is thus a selection that illuminates the grounds of meaningful, sustainable community. At the same time hers is a selection showing that for oppressed people to experience their dignity and establish satisfying family lives they have to create communities supportive of those realities, which the matrix of domination continuously jeopardizes or even negates.

The final reading in this section is the only one in this volume treating environmentalism. In it Dorceta E. Taylor portrays a kind of community work increasingly necessary on the ravaged planet, especially in those areas where oppressed groups make their homes. Largely because of environmental racism in our society, the environmental justice movement emerged late in the 1980s. Taylor's selection characterizes its development. The environmental justice movement grows out of the "relationships among class, race, political power, and the exposure to environmental hazards" (p. 374) in our society. Given awareness of those relationships, its participants are creating a movement distinct from the older, more established environmental movement. Both demographically and ideologically, says Taylor, the newer movement is more inclusive. People of all races and ethnic groups visibly contribute, as do people from diverse social classes. Moreover, women's leadership is readily observable in the environmental justice movement. Ideologically, participants largely reject "NIMBYism" (p. 374) in favor of stances more respectful of communities and environmental well-being. The environmental justice movement "pays particular attention to questions of distributive justice, community empowerment, and democratic accountability" (p. 376).

That such a movement has emerged should come as no surprise. On the one hand, environmental racism has run rampant in our society; on the other hand, as Gilkes's selection shows, oppressed people have long done the kinds of community work now being put to the cause of environmental justice. This section thus ends with a selection that reminds us that our bodies, our families, our communities, our very future presuppose a viable environment. Taylor's selection also reminds us that lessons on how to make common cause with one another at the community level are probably best found among oppressed, not hyperprivileged, people. Implicitly, then, Taylor offers yet one more reason—and an eminently practical one at that—for familiarizing ourselves with multicultural theorizing and multicultural experiencing.

NOTES

1 Susan Faludi, *Backlash: The Undeclared War Against American Women,* Anchor Books, New York, 1991, p. 238.
2 Anthony Giddens, *The Constitution of Society: Outline of the Theory of Structuration,* University of California Press, Berkeley, 1984, p. 50.
3 Evelyn Fox Keller, *Reflections on Gender and Science,* Yale University Press, New Haven, 1985, p. 17.
4 Alfred Schutz, *Collected Papers II: Studies in Social Theory,* ed. by Arvid Brodersen, Nijhoff, The Hague, 1976, p. 59.
5 Harold Garfinkel, "Studies of the Routine Grounds of Everyday Activities" in David Sudnow (ed.), *Studies in Social Interaction,* Free Press, New York, 1972, p. 24.

What We Call Each Other

Anndee Hochman

My eighty-nine-year-old grandfather and I had covered all the routine subjects—the weather in Portland, the weather on the New Jersey shore (it was summer in both places). I'd thanked him for sending me a paperback copy of *The Joys of Yiddish.* Then he asked, "So, how's your lady friend?"

I gulped. It was possible he meant my roommate, Rachael, and "lady friend" was a quaint attempt to cover up the fact that he'd forgotten her name. But I'd never heard him use that phrase, with its tinge of old-fashioned, coy romance, to describe an acquaintance of mine.

Finally, I mumbled that she was just fine, thanks. There was no response. Later, I told my "lady friend" about the comment, and we both laughed. But I still don't know if my grandfather knew what he asked, if he grasped what he heard. Words are like that. They can swab the air clean of illusion, or they can fog the truth in a comfy, opaque veil.

So many of the words for romantic or sexual partners make women mere appendages of men, extend a long-standing power imbalance. What is the term to describe a relationship of equals, two adults trying to make a life together? I like "partner," with its hints of adventure and readiness, the idea of moving together through a love affair or a life. Most of my friends, gay or straight, use it to describe their romantic associates.

But even "partner" isn't perfect. For one thing, it conveys a sense of stability that doesn't apply to all relationships, especially brand new ones. Heterosexual couples have a whole vocabulary that hints at changing degrees of intimacy and intention. First "lovers" or "boyfriend/girlfriend"; then "fiancé/e"; finally "spouse." But unmarried or gay partners have no language to describe those shifts.

The words commonly used in such cases are designed to mask the truth rather than tell it. The euphemisms for gay and lesbian lovers—"constant companion" or "very special friend"—hide the true nature of the relationship under a cloak of decorum. But it's a cloak made to be seen through; everyone knows it's a cover for something else. It indicates that the real thing is too scandalous even for discourse; the word itself can't go out of doors unclad.

One lesbian couple I know dislikes "partner" for the same reasons I'm drawn to it—because it is democratic, gender-neutral. These women refer to each other as "girlfriends," refusing, even in casual conversation, to pass.

Slowly, slowly, names gather a new history; the weight of a word can shift. When lesbians and gay men appropriate the language of the mainstream, filling in their partners' names where government forms say "spouse," insisting that they deserve a "family" membership to the YMCA, they force others to reorder their mental maps. Those maps would change even faster if heterosexual couples boycotted marriage and its honorifics, if they, too combed the language for words that more precisely describe their bonds.

Girlfriend. Boyfriend. Mistress. Beau. Old man. Lady friend. Steady. Helpmate. Fiancé/e. Lover. Paramour. Spouse. Domestic partner. Soul mate. Significant other.

Homeslice. Sweetie. Co-habitant. Ally. Longtime companion. Live-in. Partner. Collaborator. Consort. Intimate. Confidant/e. Familiar. Alter ego. Mainstay. Second self. Complement. Mate.

Even words that don't carry a gender bias can be suspect, quiet enforcers of the status quo. I used the word "single" to describe women without intimate partners until the irony of the term struck me. I was writing about these women precisely because they'd built networks of support through work, friends, housemates, yet my easy description of them conveyed someone alone and unconnected, with no important social ties.

"Are you in a relationship?" people inquire euphemistically, when what they mean is "Are you sexually involved with someone?" The notion of *a* relationship—primary, intimate, more weighty than the rest—doesn't fit the lives of people who choose celibacy, or who are in non-monogamous relationships involving two or more significant "others."

Then there's "friend," which doesn't begin to cover enough ground. It describes everyone from the colleague I chat with once a month at a writers' meeting to the woman I've known since infancy but haven't seen for a decade, to Rachael, whom I lived with for more than five years. The word, forced to stand for such a range of connections, erases distinction, implies all friendships are the same.

Names wake us to the particulars of a thing. If I call Diana my mainstay, Pattie my soul mate, and Rachael my sister, I remember that these women have different qualities, that my friendship with each is unique.

I say Rachael is my "sister," and then pause. Why is that the only term that seems to fit? I struggle to describe closeness and am left holding a simile, a stand-in phrase that only gropes at description. "He's like a brother to me," we say, revealing not only the assumed potency of sibling bonds but the dearth of words to describe intense, nonsexual attachments.

There's a level of intimacy that "friend" seems too small to contain. Then we make it even smaller, often denigrating it with the qualifier "just." They're "just friends," we concede, as if friendship were automatic and uninteresting, less full of potential than any romantic pairing. In fact, the vast majority of people in our lives fall into that maligned category; friendship deserves a vocabulary of its own.

Acquaintance. Colleague. Buddy. Bosom-buddy. Sidekick. Chum. Amiga. Compadre. Homegirl. Mate. Pal. Sister. Fellow. Right-hand man. Companion. Compañera. Associate. Cohort. Crony. Aficionado. Compeer. Confrere. Ally. Comrade. Familiar. Accomplice. Mainstay. Primary. Neighbor. Friend.

I've wrestled, too, with "childless." It's a gender-weighted word—we don't refer, with quite the same sense of anomaly and pity, to "childless" men. And it assumes childbearing is the norm and *not* childbearing a lesser version of life; it defines an existence by what it lacks. "Nonparent" makes the same mistake.

I've seen women use "child-free," which seems tipped in the other direction—as though children were a burden and only people without them have liberty. Besides, many women who choose not to be parents include children in their lives as nieces and nephews, neighbors, clients, friends. I thought about words like "adult-based" or "adult-centered" for women who don't have much to do with children. But I've yet to find a term that expresses, without judgment, the facets of this complicated choice.

And there are relationships, existences we scarcely have language to describe. The words for an unmarried woman—maiden aunt, spinster—are all pejorative. "Old maid," in particular, holds layers of judgment—a woman who contradicts her own nature, at once old and young, a perpetual servant. Thanks to Mary Daly and others, feminists are reclaiming "spinster" as a source of creative pride; one woman I know named her sewing business "Spinster Textiles."

Few terms exist to describe former lovers who now are good friends, or nonbiological parents, or relationships between the childhood families of a gay couple. I've heard a woman explain to her child, conceived through alternative (as opposed to "artificial") insemination, that there are "seed daddies" as well as the kind of daddies who live at home, and a lesbian friend coined "sister-outlaws" to describe her lover's siblings.

The contemporary women's movement and gay and lesbian liberation helped prompt people to create new honorifics, such as "Ms.," and reclaim old names, taking them back from the domain of those who hate. Queer. Dyke. Crone. Cripple. Faggot. Fat person. Fairy. When we use these words for ourselves, we become powerful, filled with the awesome responsibility that is naming. We print the words on buttons, shout them in parades. We repossess the names and, in the process, repossess ourselves.

Language changes from the edges; new terms ripple back to the center. Gradually, I have seen "partner" replace "longtime companion" in news stories about gay men and lesbians. Several papers even have begun listing gay commitment ceremonies. As such events become more popular and public, terms unimagined as yet may enter the lexicon.

Coupling. Espousals. Union. Match. Bond. Pairing. Knot. Joining. Dovetailing. Commitment ceremony. Intentional. Dedication. Webbing. Mingling. Intertwining. Weaving. Blending. Braiding. Concord. Alignment. Alchemy. Convergence. Handfasting. Tryst.

What we call each other—how we refer to lovers and friends, partnerships and families—is more than a matter of etiquette. The words tell us who is owned and who is free, who really counts and who is merely secondary.

The language of the nuclear family continues to sway our speech, crowd out equally valid models of living. Homeless teenagers I worked with took the words of the families that failed them and applied them to each other. I heard them use "sister" and "brother" for their friends, but also "mother" and "kid," outlining large and intricate networks of street kin.

The actual people represented by those terms may have abused or abandoned these teenagers, but the words themselves seem to carry an infinitely renewable potency, a hope that someday someone will grow into the legend that is "mother," "sister," or "son."

"Blood family" itself carries that mythic power—"blood," with its symbolism of oath and source, a magical connection that cannot be undone. "Biological family" is less poetic but equally weighted. Married couples aren't related genetically, nor are adopted children. In families formed through remarriage, in foster families and extended families, "blood" connections have little to do with linkage.

I've toyed with "first family," "original family," and "childhood family" to describe the groups we grow up with, and "present family," "chosen family," or "adult family" for those we have now.

But the word "family" itself is loaded. The term can help justify secrecy ("let's keep it in the family") or serve as an argument for public hands-off ("that's a family matter"). And it is used disingenuously, as in "We're all one big happy family here" by businesses that want to promote childlike docility from employees and avuncular rule from bosses.

No mere noun, it's a way of categorizing society, even allocating resources, with "family" memberships and "family" fares on airlines and trains. "Family values" is political shorthand, evoking marriage, patriotism, and obedient children, a code aimed to halt a changing world.

Imagination is larger than language. The names claim who we already are and who we wish to become. We don't require them in order to live, but they make our living known, translatable, turn it into something we can talk about. There is room for more words, for the finest of distinctions, for as many possibilities as our minds can shape.

Someday, [my parents'] white house in New Jersey will be mine. I cannot imagine selling it. I want it to remain in the family. Families. Meaning me, my cousins, our parents, our children, if we have them. And more than that. The partners and compatriots, lovers and allies, cronies and intimates, all those who share the everyday acts of our lives.

I can see it. Someone will tap on the glass between the front stairs and the kitchen. I will look up, out the window, through the house and the window beyond it, straight out to the ocean we all come from. I will recognize the face, and I will wave.

Welcome, I might say, to my tribe. My group. Cabal. Circle. Club. Nucleus. Team. Neighborhood. Community. Affinity group. Kin. Karass. People. Coalition. League. Assemblage. Confederation. Gang. Clique. Coterie. Set. Crew. Crowd. Cadre. We-group. Affiliates. Relations. Folk. Household. Brood. Collection. Cronies. Network.

Welcome to my company, my clan.

Fictive Kin, Paper Sons: Women of Color and the Struggle for Family Survival

Bonnie Thornton Dill

Race has been fundamental to the construction of families in the United States since the country was settled. People of color were incorporated into the country and used to meet the need for cheap and exploitable labor. Little attention was given to their family and community life except as it related to their economic productivity. Upon their founding, the various colonies that ultimately formed the United States initiated legal, economic, political, and social practices designed to promote the growth of family life among European colonists. As the primary laborers in the reproduction and maintenance of families, White[1] women settlers were accorded the privileges and protection considered socially appropriate to their family roles. The structure of family life during this era was strongly patriarchal: denying women many rights, constraining their personal autonomy, and making them subject to the almost unfettered will of the male head of the household. Nevertheless, women were rewarded and protected within patriarchal families because their labor was recognized as essential to the maintenance and sustenance of family life.[2] In addition, families were seen as the cornerstone of an incipient nation, and thus their existence was a matter of national interest.

In contrast, women of color experienced the oppression of a patriarchal society but were denied the protection and buffering of a patriarchal family. Although the presence of women of color was equally important to the growth of the nation, their value was based on their potential as workers, breeders, and entertainers of workers, not as family members. In the eighteenth and nineteenth centuries, labor, and not the existence or maintenance of families, was the critical aspect of their role in building the nation. Thus they were denied the societal supports necessary to make their families a vital element in the social order. For women of color, family membership was not a key means of access to participation in the wider society. In some instances racial-ethnic families were seen as a threat to the efficiency and exploitability of the work force and were actively prohibited. In other cases, they were tolerated when it was felt they might help solidify or expand the work force. The lack of social, legal, and economic support for the family life of people of color intensified and extended women's work, created tensions and strains in family relationships, and set the stage for a variety of creative and adaptive forms of resistance.

AFRICAN AMERICAN SLAVES

Among students of slavery, there has been considerable debate over the relative "harshness" of American slavery, and the degree to which slaves were permitted or encouraged to form families. It is generally acknowledged that many slave owners found it economically advantageous to encourage family formation as a way of reproducing and perpetuating the slave labor force. This became increasingly true after 1807, when the importation of African slaves was explicitly prohibited. The existence of these families and many aspects of their functioning, however, were directly controlled by the master. Slaves married and formed families, but these groupings were completely subject to the master's decision to let them remain intact. One study has estimated that about 32 percent of all recorded slave marriages were disrupted by sale, about 45 percent by death of a spouse, about 10 percent by choice, and only 13 percent were not disrupted (Blassingame 1972). African slaves thus quickly learned that they had a limited degree of control over the formation and maintenance of their marriages and could not be assured of keeping their children with them. The threat of disruption was one of the most direct and pervasive assaults on families that slaves encountered. Yet there were a number of other aspects of the slave system that reinforced the precariousness of slave family life.

In contrast to some African traditions and the Euro-American patterns of the period, slave men were not the main providers or authority figures in the family. The mother-child tie was basic and of greatest interest to the slave owner because it was essential to the reproduction of the labor force.

In addition to the lack of authority and economic autonomy experienced by the husband-father in the slave family, use of rape of women slaves as a weapon of terror and control further undermined the integrity of the slave family.

> It would be a mistake to regard the institutionalized pattern of rape during slavery as an expression of white men's sexual urges, otherwise stifled by the specter of the white womanhood's chastity. . . . Rape was a weapon of domination, a weapon of repression, whose covert goal was to extinguish slave women's will to resist, and in the process, to demoralize their men. (Davis 1981: 23–24).

The slave family, therefore, was at the heart of a peculiar tension in the master-slave relationship. On the one hand, slave owners sought to encourage familiarities among slaves because, as Julie Matthaei (1982:81) states, "These provided the basis of the development of the slave into a self-conscious socialized human being." They also hoped and believed that this socialization process would help children learn to accept their place in society as slaves. Yet the master's need to control and intervene in the family life of the slaves is indicative of the other side of this tension. Family ties had the potential to become a competing and more potent source of allegiance than the master. Also, kin were as likely to socialize children in forms of resistance as in acts of compliance.

It was within this context of surveillance, assault, and ambivalence that slave women's reproductive labor[3] took place. They and their menfolk had the task of preserving the human and family ties that could ultimately give them a reason for living. They had to socialize their children to believe in the possibility of a life in which they were not enslaved. The slave woman's labor on behalf of the family was, as Angela Davis (1971) has pointed out, the only labor in which the slave engaged that could not be directly used by the slave owner for his own profit. Yet, it was crucial to the reproduction of the slave owner's labor force, and thus a source of strong ambivalence for many slave women. Whereas some mothers murdered their babies to keep them from being slaves, many sought autonomy and creativity within the family that was denied them in other realms of the society. The maintenance of a distinct African American culture is testimony to the ways in which slaves maintained a degree of cultural autonomy and resisted the creation of a slave family that only served the needs of the master.

Herbert Gutman (1976) gives evidence of the ways which slaves expressed a unique African-American culture through their family practices. He provides data on naming patterns and kinship ties among slaves that fly in the face of the dominant ideology of the period, which argued that slaves were immoral and had little concern for or appreciation of family life. Yet Gutman demonstrates that within a system that denied the father authority over his family, slave boys were frequently named after their fathers, and many children were named after blood relatives as a way of maintaining family ties. Gutman also suggests that after emancipation a number of slaves took the names of former owners in order to reestablish family ties that had been disrupted earlier. On plantation after plantation, Gutman found considerable evidence of the building and maintenance of extensive kinship ties among slaves. In instances where slave families had been disrupted, slaves in new communities reconstituted the kinds of family and kin ties that came to characterize Black family life throughout the South. The patterns included, but were not limited to, a belief in the importance of marriage as a long-term commitment, rules of exogamy that excluded marriage between first cousins, and acceptance of women who had children outside of marriage. Kinship networks were an important source of resistance to the organization of labor that treated the individual slave, and not the family, as the unit of labor (Caulfield 1974).

Another interesting indicator of the slaves' maintenance of some degree of cultural autonomy has been pointed out by Gwendolyn Wright (1981) in her discussion of slave housing. Until the early 1800s, slaves were often permitted to build their housing according to their own design and taste. During that period, housing built in an African style was quite common in the slave quarters. By 1830, however, slave owners had begun to control the design and arrangement of slave housing and had introduced a degree of conformity and regularity to it that left little room for the slaves' personalization of the home. Nevertheless, slaves did use some of their own techniques in construction, often hiding them from their masters.

> Even the floors, which usually consisted of only tamped earth, were evidence of a hidden African tradition: slaves cooked clay over a fire, mixing in ox blood or cow dung, and then poured it in place to make hard dirt floors almost like asphalt. . . . In slave houses, in contrast to other crafts, these signs of skill and tradition would then be covered over. (Wright 1981:48)

Housing is important in discussions of family because its design reflects sociocultural attitudes about family life. The housing that slave owners provided for their slaves reflected a view of Black family life consistent with the stereotypes of the period. While the existence of slave families was acknowledged, they certainly were not nurtured. Thus, cabins were crowded, often containing more than one family, and there were no provisions for privacy. Slaves had to create their own.

> Slave couples hung up old clothes or quilts to establish boundaries; others built more substantial partitions from scrap wood. Parents sought to establish sexual privacy from children. A few ex-slaves described modified trundle beds designed to hide parental lovemaking. . . . Even in one room cabins, sexual segregation was carefully organized. (Wright 1981:50)

Perhaps most critical in developing an understanding of slave women's reproductive labor is the gender-based division of labor in the domestic sphere. The organization of slave labor enforced considerable equality among men and women. The ways in which equality in the labor force was translated into the family sphere is somewhat speculative. Davis (1981:18), for example, suggests that egalitarianism between males and females was a direct result of slavery: "Within the confines of their family and community life, therefore, Black people managed to accomplish a magnificent feat. They transformed that negative equality which emanated from the equal oppression they suffered as slaves into a positive quality; the egalitarianism characterizing their social relations."

It is likely, however, that this transformation was far less direct than Davis implies. We know, for example, that slave women experienced what has recently been called the "double day" before most other women in this society. Slave narratives (Jones 1985; White 1985; Blassingame 1977) reveal that women had primary responsibility for their family's domestic chores. They cooked (although on some plantations meals were prepared for all the slaves), sewed, cared for their children, and cleaned house after completing a full day of labor for the master. John Blassingame (1972) and others have pointed out that slave men engaged in hunting, trapping, perhaps some gardening, and furniture making as ways of contributing to the maintenance of their families. Clearly, a gender-based division of labor did exist within the family, and it appears that women bore the larger share of the burden for housekeeping and child care.

In contrast to White families of the period, however, the division of labor in the domestic sphere was reinforced neither in the relationship of slave women to work nor in the social institutions of the slave community. The gender-based division of labor among the slaves existed within a social system that treated men and women as almost equal, independent units of labor.[4] Thus Matthaei (1982:94) is probably correct in concluding that

> whereas . . . the white homemaker interacted with the public sphere through her husband, and had her work life determined by him, the enslaved Afro-American homemaker was directly subordinated to and determined by her owner. . . . The equal enslavement of husband and wife gave the slave marriage a curious kind of equality, an equality of oppression.

Black men were denied the male resources of a patriarchal society and therefore were unable to turn gender distinctions into female subordination, even if that had been their desire. Black women, on the other hand, were denied support and protection for their roles as mothers and wives, and thus had to modify and structure those roles around the demands of their labor. Reproductive labor for slave women was intensified in several ways: by the demands of slave labor that forced them into the double day of work; by the desire and need to maintain family ties in the face of a system that gave them only limited recognition; by the stresses of building a family with men who were denied the standard social privileges of manhood; and by the struggle to raise children who could survive in a hostile environment.

This intensification of reproductive labor made networks of kin and fictive kin important instruments in carrying out the reproductive tasks of the slave community. Given an African cultural heritage where kinship ties formed the basis of social relations, it is not at all surprising that African American slaves developed an extensive system of kinship ties and obligations (Gutman 1976; Sudarkasa 1981). Research on Black families in slavery provides considerable documentation of participation of extended kin in child rearing, childbirth, and other domestic, social, and economic activities (Gutman 1976; Blassingame 1972; Genovese and Miller 1974).

After slavery, these ties continued to be an important factor linking individual household units in a variety of domestic activities. While kinship ties were also important among native-born Whites and European immigrants, Gutman (1976:213) has suggested that these ties

> were comparatively more important to Afro-Americans than to lower-class native white and immigrant Americans, the result of their distinctive low economic status, a condition

that denied them the advantages of an extensive associational life beyond the kin group and the advantages and disadvantages resulting from mobility opportunities.

His argument is reaffirmed by research on African American families after slavery (Shimkin et al. 1978; Aschenbrenner 1975; Davis 1981; Stack 1974). Niara Sudarkasa (1981:49) takes this argument one step further, linking this pattern to the African cultural heritage.

> Historical realities require that the derivation of this aspect of Black family organization be traced to its African antecedents. Such a view does not deny the adaptive significance of consanguineal networks. In fact, it helps to clarify why these networks had the flexibility they had and why they, rather than conjugal relationships, came to be the stabilizing factor in Black families.

In individual households, the gender-based division of labor experienced some important shifts during emancipation. In their first real opportunity to establish family life beyond the controls and constraints imposed by a slave master, Black sharecroppers' family life changed radically. Most women, at least those who were wives and daughters of able-bodied men, withdrew from field labor and concentrated on their domestic duties in the home. Husbands took primary responsibility for the fieldwork and for relations with the owners, such as signing contracts on behalf of the family. Black women were severely criticized by Whites for removing themselves from field labor because they were seen to be aspiring to a model of womanhood that was considered inappropriate for them. The reorganization of female labor, however, represented an attempt on the part of Blacks to protect women from some of the abuses of the slave system and to thus secure their family life. It was more likely a response to the particular set of circumstances that the newly freed slaves faced than a reaction to the lives of their former masters. Jacqueline Jones (1985) argues that these patterns were "particularly significant" because at a time when industrial development was introducing a labor system that divided male and female labor, the freed Black family was establishing a pattern of joint work and complementarity of tasks between males and females that was reminiscent of preindustrial American families. Unfortunately, these former slaves had to do this without the institutional supports given white farm families and within a sharecropping system that deprived them of economic independence.

CHINESE SOJOURNERS

An increase in the African slave population was a desired goal. Therefore, Africans were permitted and even encouraged at times to form families, as long as they were under the direct control of the slave master. By sharp contrast, Chinese people were explicitly denied the right to form families in the United States through both law and social practice. Although male laborers began coming to the United States in sizable numbers in the middle of the nineteenth century, it was more than a century before an appreciable number of children of Chinese parents were born in America. Tom, a respondent in Victor Nee and Brett de Bary Nee's book, *Longtime Californ'*, says: "One thing about Chinese men in America was you had to be either a merchant or a big gambler, have lot of side money to have a family here. A working man, an ordinary man, just can't!" (1973:80).

Working in the United States was a means of gaining support for one's family with an end of obtaining sufficient capital to return to China and purchase land. This practice of sojourning was reinforced by laws preventing Chinese laborers from becoming citizens, and by restrictions on their entry into this country. Chinese laborers who arrived before 1882 could not bring their wives and were prevented by law from marrying Whites. Thus, it is likely that the number of Chinese American families might have been negligible had it not been for two things: the San Francisco earthquake and fire in 1906, which destroyed all municipal records, and the ingenuity and persistence of the Chinese people, who used the opportunity created by the earthquake to increase their numbers in the United States. Since relatives of citizens were permitted entry, American-born Chinese (real and claimed) would visit China, report the birth of a son, and thus create an entry slot. Years later, since the records were destroyed, the slot could be used by a relative or purchased by someone outside the family. The purchasers were called "paper sons." Paper sons became a major mechanism for increasing the Chinese population, but it was a slow process and the sojourner community remained predominantly male for decades.

The high concentration of males in the Chinese community before 1920 resulted in a split household form of family. As Evelyn Nakano Glenn observes:

> In the split household family, production is separated from other functions and is carried out by a member living far from the rest of the household. The rest—consumption, reproduction and socialization—are carried out by the wife and other relatives from the home village. . . . The split household form makes possible maximum exploitation of the workers. . . . The labor of prime-age male workers can be bought relatively cheaply, since the cost of reproduction and family maintenance is borne partially by unpaid subsistence work of women and old people in the home village. (1983:38–39)

The Chinese women who were in the United States during this period consisted of a small number who were wives and daughters of merchants and a larger percentage who were prostitutes. Lucia Cheng Hirata (1979) has suggested that Chinese prostitution was an important element in helping to maintain the split household family. In conjunction with laws prohibiting intermarriage, it helped men avoid long-term relationships with women in the United States and ensured that the bulk of their meager earnings would continue to support the family at home.

The reproductive labor of Chinese women, therefore, took on two dimensions primarily because of the split household family. Wives who remained in China were forced to raise children and care for in-laws on the meager remittances of their sojourning husband. Although we know few details about their lives, it is clear that the everyday work of bearing and maintaining children and a household fell entirely on their shoulders. Those women who immigrated and worked as prostitutes performed the more nurturant aspects of reproductive labor, that is, providing emotional and sexual companionship for men who were far from home. Yet their role as prostitutes was more likely a means of supporting their families at home in China than a chosen vocation.

The Chinese family system during the nineteenth century was a patriarchal one and girls had little value. In fact, they were considered temporary members of their father's family because when they married, they became members of their husband's family.

They also had little social value; girls were sold by some poor parents to work as prostitutes, concubines, or servants. This saved the family the expense of raising them, and their earnings became a source of family income. For most girls, however, marriages were arranged and families sought useful connections through this process. With the development of a sojourning pattern in the United States, some Chinese women in those regions of China where this pattern was more prevalent would be sold to become prostitutes in the United States. Most, however, were married to men whom they saw only once or twice in the twenty- or thirty-year period during which he was sojourning in the United States. A woman's status as wife ensured that a portion of the meager wages her husband earned would be returned to his family in China. This arrangement required considerable sacrifice and adjustment by wives who remained in China and those who joined their husbands after a long separation.

Maxine Hong Kingston tells the story of the unhappy meeting of her aunt, Moon Orchid, with her husband, from whom she had been separated for thirty years: "For thirty years she had been receiving money from him from America. But she had never told him that she wanted to come to the United States. She waited for him to suggest it, but he never did" (1977:144). His response to her when she arrived unexpectedly was to say: " 'Look at her. She'd never fit into an American household. I have important American guests who come inside my house to eat.' He turned to Moon Orchid, 'You can't talk to them. You can barely talk to me.' Moon Orchid was so ashamed, she held her hands over her face" (1977:178).

Despite these handicaps, Chinese people collaborated to establish the opportunity to form families and settle in the United States. In some cases it took as long as three generations for a child to be born on U.S. soil.

> In one typical history, related by a 21 year old college student, great-grandfather arrived in the States in the 1890s as a "paper son" and worked for about 20 years as a laborer. He then sent for the grandfather, who worked alongside great-grandfather in a small business for several years. Great-grandfather subsequently returned to China, leaving grandfather to run the business and send remittance. In the 1940s, grandfather sent for father; up to this point, none of the wives had left China. Finally, in the late 1950s father returned to China and brought his wife back with him. Thus, after nearly 70 years, the first child was born in the United States. (Glenn 1981:14)

. . .

CONCLUSION

Reproductive labor for . . . women [of color] in the nineteenth century centered on the struggle to maintain family units in the face of a variety of assaults. Treated primarily as workers rather than as members of family groups, these women labored to maintain, sustain, stabilize, and reproduce their families while working in both the public (productive) and private (reproductive) spheres. Thus, the concept of reproductive labor, when applied to women of color, must be modified to account for the fact that labor in the productive sphere was required to achieve even minimal levels of family subsistence. Long after industrialization had begun to reshape family roles among middle-class White families, driving White women into a cult of domesticity, women of color were coping with an extended day. This day included subsistence labor outside the family and domestic labor within the family. For slaves, domestics, migrant farm laborers, seasonal factory workers, and prostitutes, the distinctions between labor that reproduced family life and labor that economically sustained it were minimized. The expanded workday was one of the primary ways in which reproductive labor increased.

Racial-ethnic families were sustained and maintained in the face of various forms of disruption. Yet the women and their families paid a high price in the process. High rates of infant mortality, a shortened life span, and the early onset of crippling and debilitating disease give some insight into the costs of survival.

The poor quality of housing and the neglect of communities further increased reproductive labor. Not only did racial-ethnic women work hard outside the home for mere subsistence, they worked very hard inside the home to achieve even minimal standards of privacy and cleanliness. They were continually faced with disease and illness that resulted directly from the absence of basic sanitation. The fact that some African women murdered their children to prevent them from becoming slaves is an indication of the emotional strain associated with bearing and raising children while participating in the colonial labor system.

We have uncovered little information about the use of birth control, the prevalence of infanticide, or the motivations that may have generated these or other behaviors. We can surmise, however, that no matter how much children were accepted, loved, or valued among any of these groups of people, their futures were precarious. Keeping children alive, helping them to understand and participate in a system that exploited them, and working to ensure a measure—no matter how small—of cultural integrity intensified women's reproductive labor.

Being a woman of color in nineteenth-century American society meant having extra work both inside and outside the home. It meant being defined as outside of or deviant from the norms and values about women that were being generated in the dominant White culture. The notion of separate spheres of male and female labor that developed in the nineteenth century had contradictory outcomes for the Whites. It was the basis for the confinement of upper-middle-class White women to the household and for much of the protective legislation that subsequently developed in the workplace. At the same time, it sustained White families by providing social acknowledgment and support to women in the performance of their family roles. For racial-ethnic women, however, the notion of separate spheres served to reinforce their subordinate status and became, in effect, another assault. As they increased their work outside the home, they were forced into a productive labor sphere that was organized for men and "desperate" women who were so unfortunate or immoral that they could not confine their work to the domestic sphere. In the productive sphere, racial-ethnic women faced exploitative jobs and depressed wages. In the reproductive sphere, they were denied the opportunity to embrace the dominant ideological definition of "good" wife or mother. In essence, they were faced with a double-bind situation, one that required their participation in the labor force to sustain family life but damned them as women, wives, and mothers because they did not confine their labor to the home.

Finally, the struggle of women of color to build and maintain families provides vivid testimony to the role of race in structuring family life in the United States. As Maxine Baca Zinn points out:

> Social categories and groups subordinate in the racial hierarchy are often deprived of access to social institutions that offer supports for family life. Social categories and groups elevated in the racial hierarchy have different and better connections to institutions that can sustain families. Social location and its varied connection with social resources thus have profound consequences for family life. (1990:74)

From the founding of the United States, and throughout its history, race has been a fundamental criterion determining the kind of work people do, the wages they receive, and the kind of legal, economic, political, and social support provided for their families. Women of color have faced limited economic resources, inferior living conditions, alien cultures and languages, and overt hostility in their struggle to create a "place" for families of color in the United States. That place, however, has been a precarious one because the society has not provided supports for these families. Today we see the outcomes of that legacy in statistics showing that people of color, compared with whites, have higher rates of female-headed households, out-of-wedlock births, divorce, and other factors associated with family disruption. Yet the causes of these variations do not lie merely in the higher concentrations of poverty among people of color; they are also due to the ways race has been used as a basis for denying and providing support to families. Women of color have struggled to maintain their families against all of these odds.

NOTES

Acknowledgments: The research in this study was an outgrowth of my participation in a larger collaborative project examining family, community, and work lives of racial-ethnic women in the United States. I am deeply indebted to the scholarship and creativity of members of the group in the development of this study. Appreciation is extended to Elizabeth Higginbotham, Cheryl Townsend Gilkes, Evelyn Nakano Glenn, and Ruth Zambrana (members of the original working group), and to the Ford Foundation for a grant that supported in part the work of this study.

1 The term "White" is a global construct used to characterize peoples of European descent who migrated to and helped colonize America. In the seventeenth century, most of these immigrants were from the British Isles. However, during the time period covered by this article, European immigrants became increasingly diverse. It is a limitation of this chapter that time and space do not permit a fuller discussion of the variations in the White European immigrant experience. For the purposes of the argument being made herein and of the contrast it seeks to draw between the experiences of mainstream (European) cultural groups and those of racial-ethnic minorities, the differences among European settlers are joined and the broad similarities emphasized.

2 For a more detailed discussion of this argument and the kinds of social supports provided these families, see an earlier version of this paper: "Our Mothers' Grief: Racial-Ethnic Women and the Maintenance of Families," *Journal of Family History* 13 (4) (1988): 415–431.

3 The term "reproductive labor" is used to refer to all of the work of women in the home. This includes, but is not limited to, the buying and preparation of food and clothing, provision of emotional support and nurturance for all family members, bearing children, and planning, organizing, and carrying out a wide variety of tasks associated with socialization. All of these activities are necessary for the growth of patriarchal capitalism because they maintain, sustain, stabilize, and reproduce (both biologically and socially) the labor force.

4 Recent research suggests that there were some tasks assigned primarily to males and some others to females. Whereas some gender-role distinctions with regard to work may have existed on some plantations, it is clear that slave women were not exempt from strenuous physical labor.

REFERENCES

Aschenbrenner, Joyce. 1975. *Lifelines: Black Families in Change.* New York: Holt, Rinehart, and Winston.

Baca Zinn, Maxine. 1990. "Family, Feminism and Race in America." *Gender and Society* 4 (1) (March): 68–82.

Blassingame, John. 1972. *The Slave Community: Plantation Life in the Antebellum South.* New York: Oxford University Press.

———. 1977. *Slave Testimony: Two Centuries of Letters, Speeches, Interviews, and Autobiographies.* Baton Rouge: Louisiana State University Press.

Caulfield, Mina Davis. 1974. "Imperialism, the Family, and Cultures of Resistance." *Socialist Review* 4 (2) (October): 67–85.

Davis, Angela. 1971. "Reflections on the Black Woman's Role in the Community of Slaves." *Black Scholar* 3 (4) (December): 2–15.

———. 1981. *Women, Race, and Class.* New York: Random House.

Genovese, Eugene D., and Elinor Miller, eds. 1974. *Plantation, Town, and County: Essays on the Local History of American Slave Society.* Urbana: University of Illinois Press.

Glenn, Evelyn Nakano. 1983. "Split Household, Small Producer, and Dual Earner: An Analysis of Chinese-American Family Strategies." *Journal of Marriage and the Family.* 45 (1) (February): 35–46.

Gutman, Herbert. 1976. *The Black Family in Slavery and Freedom, 1750–1925.* New York: Pantheon.

Hirata, Lucia Cheng. 1979. "Free, Indentured, Enslaved: Chinese Prostitutes in Nineteenth Century America." *Signs* 5 (Autumn): 3–29.

Jones, Jacqueline. 1985. *Labor of Love, Labor of Sorrow.* New York: Basic Books.

Kingston, Maxine Hong. 1977. *The Woman Warrior.* New York: Vintage Books.

Matthaei, Julie. 1982. *An Economic History of Women in America.* New York: Schocken Books.

Nee, Victor G., and Brett de Bary Nee. 1973. *Longtime Californ'.* New York: Pantheon Books.

Shimkin, Demetri, E. M. Shimkin, and D. A. Frate, eds. 1978. *The Extended Family in Black Societies.* The Hague: Mouton.

Stack, Carol S. 1974. *All Our Kin: Strategies for Survival in a Black Community.* New York: Harper & Row.

Sudarkasa, Niara. 1981. "Interpreting the African Heritage in Afro-American Family Organization." Pp. 37–53 in *Black Families,* edited by Harriette Pipes McAdoo. Beverly Hills, Calif.: Sage.

White, Deborah Gray. 1985. *Ar'n't I a Woman? Female Slaves in the Plantation South.* New York: W. W. Norton.

Wright, Gwendolyn. 1981. *Building the Dream: A Social History of Housing in America.* New York: Pantheon.

On Making "Choices"

Reva Landau

Feminists have long proclaimed the right of women to "have a choice," that is, to be able to choose between working at a career, or working only in the home, or doing both. One could argue that there were two valid arguments behind this reasoning. Denying the right of women to make the choice could alienate from the feminist movement the many women who do not work full-time outside the home. And stating that working only inside the home was a bad decision could hurt the feelings of the many women who had made a different choice.

But what has been the result of this decision? Feminists are still denounced as opposing stay-at-home mothers;[1] and women continue to make choices, and to encourage their daughters and granddaughters to make choices, that lead to poverty not only for themselves, and for their children, but for other women as well.

We are not doing anyone a favor by encouraging women to make the choice to work only in the home. We are encouraging a decision that hurts them, hurts their children, and hurts other women.

This paper examines how women do in fact participate (or not participate) in the outside-the-home work force, how the decision to work only in the home can hurt them, their children, and other women, and suggests strategies feminists should choose to promote awareness by women of the consequences of working only in the home, and to promote equal participation by men in housework and childcare.

PRESENT REALITY

Many women may be under the impression that this point is a non-issue, that almost all women currently work full-time outside the home. Unfortunately, that is not true. And, just as unfortunately, a current spate of articles is encouraging women to "drop out" for a few years, to work part-time, and to job-share. In other words, they are encouraging dropping out under a different name.

What Women Are Really Doing

The key point to realize is that women are still dropping out. Most women do NOT work year-round full-time outside the home. In 1992, while about 77% of Canadian women aged 25–44 worked outside the home,[2] only about 61% of Canadian women aged 25–44 worked FULL-TIME YEAR-ROUND outside the home, in contrast to 88% of men in this age group.[3] Only 52% of Canadian women aged 45–54 worked full-time year-round outside the home, again in contrast to about 84% of men in this age group.[4]

In the United States in 1992, while approximately 75% of women aged 25–44 worked outside the home, only 80% of these women worked full-time. Therefore, only about 60% of women 25–44 worked full-time outside the home, in contrast to 88% of men in this age group. Of women aged 45–54, 59% worked full-time, again in contrast to 87% of men in this age group.[5] This difference might be even more significant if, as will be discussed, we knew if some of the U.S. American female workers were employed for only part of the year.

The participation rate has undoubtedly gone up, but there is still a very significant difference between the full-time year-round participation rate of men and women. Participation rate figures can be very misleading if they ignore the fact that so many women work part-time or not year-round.

Another Canadian survey found that, in 1990, 60.1% of women with a youngest child under three worked outside the home but 31.3% worked part-time so that the full-time participation rate was only 41.8%. Similarly, while 66% with children 3–5 worked outside the home, only 70.7% worked full-time so the full-time participation rate was only 46.6%. Finally, even only 58% of women with a youngest child of 6–15 worked full-time.[6]

A summary of 1988 information found that of families with at least one child younger than 13, 41.1% of women worked full-time, 17.8% were employed part-time, 5.9% were unemployed, and 35.2% were not in the outside-the-home workforce. By comparison, 80.1% of men were employed full-time, NONE were employed part-time, 8.3% were unemployed, and 9.25% were not in the work force.[7]

Even when we consider married women under 55 without any children under 16, a 1984 Canadian study showed 54% worked full-time, 11% worked part-time, 7% were unemployed, and 27% did not work outside the home.[8] I could not find a more recent figure for Canadian married women under 55 with no children under 16 but the 59% figure earlier cited for Canadian women aged 45–54 indicates that the trend remains the same.

In the United States, a similar pattern appears. In 1988, 57.1% of married women with children under 6 were in the outside the home labor force, as were 72.5% of women with children 6–17.[9] Assuming only 80% worked full-time, that means only 45% of married women with children under 6 worked full-time, and only 57.2% of those with children aged 6–17 worked full-time.

If we examine a more detailed 1983 U.S. study, we see that even those who worked full-time may not have worked year-round. In Canada, anyone who does not work at least 49 weeks during the year is considered a part-time worker. But that does not necessarily seem to be true for U.S. statistics.

In 1983, of married women with at least one child under the age of three, only 58% worked outside the home at all (fairly close to the 1988 figures).[10] When the figures are examined more closely, we see that a significant number of these women worked part-time or not all the year-round. Only 16% worked full-time, 50–52 weeks during the year; 5% worked full-time, 40–49 weeks during the year; 10% worked part-time 40

developments and trends in her chosen profession, not contributing to her pension, not earning seniority credits, etc. That the woman does not plan to drop out forever, but only for a few years, does not diminish the impact of her decision during the years she has left the workforce. Nor does the fact that the woman who works part-time calls it "job-sharing" diminish the fact that she is working part-time while her husband works full-time.

As will be described in more detail, dropping out and working part-time have disastrous consequences for the woman herself, for her children, and for other women.

Harm Resulting to the Women Themselves

By now, it is almost a cliché that the living standard of divorced women falls by 73% in the first year of divorce while the living standard of divorced men rises by 42%.[20] Yet no one seems to question one of the major causes of this discrepancy: the decision by many married women to drop out or work part-time.

Obviously, an American married man working full-time with an average income of $38,407 a year in 1990[21] will be much better off than a married women earning nothing, or the average married woman working part-time (the average American part-time female worker who worked all year earned $9,229 in 1990).[22]

That the woman intends to drop out only for a few years does not change the consequences. While she is out of the paid labor force she is economically dependent on her husband, and may find it hard to leave a physically abusive husband. The only way a woman earning nothing a year and a man earning $38,000 a year could possibly be in the same position on marriage break-up would be if the woman were given sufficient assets that the interest from those assets made up the difference in work income. As will be discussed later, it is this sort of division, rather than an equal split based on the myth that husband and wife are partners, that stay-at-home wives should demand.

As most couples do not own anything near the amount of assets that would put a non-earning wife in the same position as an earning husband, the wife would still not be in the same position as the husband even if this principle were adopted. I am not even considering her husband's possible additional work benefits (health care, legal aid, etc.) or his future prospects (promotions, salary increases, etc.).

The inadequacy of alimony payments has also been well documented. The interesting point made by Lenore Weitzman in *The Divorce Revolution* was that, contrary to popular myth, women never received adequate maintenance. Only a small percentage of women were ever awarded alimony and it was rarely sufficient.[23] The reluctance of men to pay even the pitiful amounts awarded to their wives and children for maintenance has also been well-documented.

What must be remembered is that even if alimony payments were enforced, it would not make much difference. Only a small number of women are awarded alimony payments; most of these payments are small. In 1983, of the 17.1 million ever-divorced or currently separated women, only *14%* were even awarded alimony payments.[24] Of these, 77% received some percent of their award in 1983.[25] The average alimony received was $3,976.[26] This figure may not represent all the alimony awarded, but it does show that the alimony awarded is not a huge amount.

In other words, even if 100% of men, rather than 77% of men, made the alimony payments ordered, it would not make a great difference. Contrary to the general received opinion, the problem is not that men do not make alimony payments. The problem is that only a small percentage of women are awarded alimony payments, and that the alimony payments are small.

Far more divorced women receive child maintenance payments than alimony payments, and the issue of child maintenance will be discussed in far more detail. But what must be remembered is that when the maintenance payments for the child stop, the mother is then completely dependent on her own resources. If she has worked part-time or stayed at home to look after the child even after being divorced, she is then age 40–50 with very rusty skills, if any. Being dependent on maintenance payments for a child is no more reliable than being dependent on income from a husband.

That is not to say that women should not try to make men take responsibility for the support of women who have sacrificed their own careers in order to enable men to forward their own. But no system will put a woman who earns nothing in the same position as a man earning $38,000 a year, and leading women to believe that such a system could be devised is a cruel deception.

One of the saddest results of a woman being economically dependent is she may lose the very objects to whom she has devoted her life: her children. A man with a large income can, as courts have noted, give his children a better life than can his impoverished wife.[27] He can also afford to hire better lawyers. So not only may the work-only-in-the-home wife end up with no career, no income, and no security: she may also end up with no children.

Of course, women with an independent income may also lose their children. But at least they can better afford to hire a lawyer to defend themselves. And at least they have some income, some future prospects, and possibly an interesting job.

Encouraging women to think that they can drop out for a few years and then reenter the work force with no economic consequences is not doing women a favor.

Women with exceptional talents or exceptional connections might be able to drop out and in without much trouble. But the average woman will suffer consequences, just as the average man would.

Leaving aside the issue of discrimination, a legal secretary, a computer programmer, a teacher, who has not kept up with the latest developments for the last three or four (or even more if it is the last five to eight) years will not be able to command the same salary as someone who has been working over that period. In an area or a time when jobs are hard to get, the woman who has dropped out may even have trouble dropping back in, much less dropping back in at the same salary.

Moreover, if the woman becomes divorced, or separated, or deserted, or widowed, during what she planned as a temporary dropping out period, she is in basically the same position as a woman who had dropped out permanently. Her husband is earning $38,000 a year, and she is earning nothing. He has money to pay lawyers; she not only has no money to pay lawyers but is in so desperate an economic situation that she may accept a very inadequate settlement just in order to have money to pay the bills.

It could be argued that just because a woman works does not mean that she will earn the same amount as her husband. After all, the average income in the United States for a woman who worked full-time year-round was $23,238 in 1990 if she was married. The average income for a married man who worked full-time year-round was $38,407.[28] Therefore, even the woman who works full-time year-round is not going to earn as much as her husband.

While $23,328 is obviously not as much as $38,407 per year, it is a big improvement over no income per year, or over the average wage of a part-time worker. Moreover, as will be discussed, one of the reasons, though certainly not the only reason, that women, both married and single, earn so little is the perception that women will drop out, work part-time, etc.

The decision to drop out, work part-time, etc., seems to have some impact even on married women who have returned to working full-time year-round in the labor force. Married women who work full-time year-round do not seem to earn even as much as never-married women who work full-time year-round. I want to emphasize that the differential between single women and married women is not as significant as the differential between never-married women and married men. But the differential between never-married women and married women seems to suggest that there are other ways in which married women who returned to full-time year-round work have hurt themselves.

First of all, never-married women appear to be better educated than married women. A 1979 U.S. study revealed that 16% of never-married women aged 45–54 had 5 years or more of post-secondary education, in contrast to 6% of married women in the same age group.[29]

Various articles have been written showing that many young girls still see their future as being married and taking care of children. Even if they talk about jobs, it is a job they would drop out of for several years, while they take care of young children.[30]

Naturally, girls who do not see working as a major part of their future lives will not train or educate themselves in the same way as boys, who do see working as a major part of their future lives.

In addition, in some categories, this American study seemed to show that there was still a differential between never-married women and married women with the same years of education. This differential varied by educational category. There is practically no difference between never-married women and married women aged 45–54 with only an elementary education nor is there any significant differential between these two categories of women with 5 years or more of post-secondary education.

But, for example, married women with a high school education earned only 66% as much as never-married women aged 45–54 with the same education.[31] Without more information, one can only guess at possible explanations for this difference. Possibly married women, even those aged 45–54, are more likely to work part-time, which lowers their income. Possibly these women will not take on more demanding jobs because of their housekeeping responsibilities (most women aged 45–54 do not have children under the age of 6) or because of their husbands' resentment. Possibly the effect of dropping out means that they have less job experience and seniority, and therefore earn less money.

The differential between never-married and widowed or divorced women is much smaller. Divorced women earned, at a minimum, 88% as much as never-married women aged 45–54 with the same education; widowed women earned, at the minimum, 75%

as much. Thus, it appears much of the differential can be overcome once a woman no longer has the responsibilities of catering to her husband (childcare responsibilities remain, and possibly even increase, if one is divorced or widowed).

But these figures do seem to indicate that dropping out has a permanent effect on women's income even when they return to the labor force. The differential between never-married and married women is not nearly as significant as the differential between all women and married men. But, in view of the fact that women already have low incomes, they cannot afford to take actions that will further reduce this low income.

Making up for years of lost income and lost opportunity is not as easy as newspaper articles lead one to believe. For example, there have been several Canadian cases in which there was initially what appeared to be a satisfactory divorce settlement. Then the ex-wife became disabled. The courts ruled, on the face of it correctly, that her disablement was not the result of the marriage and that it was not such a "change in circumstances" that would justify increasing alimony payments.[32]

It is quite true that the disability had nothing to do with the marriage or divorce. But it is also true that if the wife had not dropped out during her marriage the disability might not have had the same impact on her. She might have been covered by disability insurance, provided either by her company or bought by herself. She might have acquired sufficient skills that she could have continued to be employed even after her disability. In other words, the impact of dropping out during one's potential peak earnings years has an impact that continues even after one has returned, or wishes to return, to work.

In real life, women who have dropped out find out too late that they will have trouble dropping in. But by the time these women find this out and write letters to Ann Landers, or give interviews to sympathetic book writers telling of the unhappy consequences of their decision to drop out,[33] it is too late.

Writing books about the tragic situation of women after divorce will not change anything. What we must start doing is telling women how to avoid, not being divorced, but suffering the devastating financial consequences.

Not all women who work only in the home end up as the 45% of Canadian single women, or the 54% of single Canadian women 65 or over, or the 39% of female heads of the family, who lived below the poverty line in 1988.[34] Some remain happily married and die still happily married; some become moderately well-off widows or divorcees; a few become rich widows or divorcees. One could argue that if women choose to risk poverty that is their business. But they should at least be told that they are risking poverty.

HOW THIS "CHOICE" HURTS CHILDREN

Numerous articles have been written about the children that live in poverty. Yet no one points out one common cause of child poverty: the decision by married women to drop out and who then end up living with their children below the poverty line. When women decide to work part-time or drop out, they are risking poverty not only for themselves but for their children.

Once again, relying on better enforcement of child maintenance payments will not change the situation.

In spring 1988, 9.4 million American women were living with children under 21 whose fathers were not living in the household; 59% of these women (74% of divorced women) had been awarded child support payments.[35]

Of those awarded child support payments, 51% received the full amount due; 25% received partial payment; 24% received nothing.[36] The mean amount of annual child support ordered for all women due payments in 1987 was $3,017. The mean amount actually received was $2,063.[37] About 68% of the total amount due was paid in 1987.

Again, certainly all measures that make men fulfill their responsibilities to their own children should be taken. But even if all fathers fulfilled their obligations, would it make much difference? Three thousand dollars annually is not an enormous amount on which to bring up a child. It is also significant that the higher a woman's income, the more likely she was both to be awarded child support payments, and to actually receive these payments.

For example, the average income of a woman receiving child support payments in 1983 was $10,791, not including the child support payments themselves. The average income of a woman awarded but *not* receiving child support payments was $8,433.[38] The average income of a woman who was not awarded any child payments at all was $7,389. In other words, a woman not awarded any child support payments had a total income only 68% of that of a woman awarded and receiving child support payments.

There could be various explanations for these figures. But one worth considering is that the higher a woman's own income, the better able she is to hire a lawyer and fight not only for herself but for her children.

It will be noted that a far higher percentage of divorced women are awarded child support payments than are awarded alimony: In 1987, 74% of divorced women were awarded child support payments versus 17% awarded alimony.[39]

But what must be remembered is that not only are such child support payments low, certainly not covering the cost of supporting a child, but they all generally cease anywhere from age 16 to 21, depending on the terms of the divorce and the various provincial or state regulations governing such terms as "Age of Majority," "child of the marriage," etc.[40] Thus, the husband's legal obligation to support the child may cease at precisely the moment when his aid is needed to allow the child to go on to higher education.

There is great concern professed about the number of children living in poverty. While there are some children who are poor because their fathers and mothers are both low-income earners, or because the father is disabled, the majority of poor children are poor because they are in families in which the head of the household is a woman. And while some of these women started out single, the majority are formerly married women who are now divorced, separated, deserted, or widowed—and poor.[41]

Women who make the choice to work only in the home are risking poverty not only for themselves, but for their children. Being concerned about poor children, and not recognizing one of the great causes of their poverty, is of no value. While greater efforts should be made to award reasonable child maintenance, and to enforce their maintenance, it is naive to think that any system is going to enable two households to live at the same standard as one on the same income. It is also naive to think that the household which will experience the drop in living standard is the household which is supplying the income.

And it is not only naive but dangerous to encourage women to think that the solution lies in better enforcement of child support payments rather than in women having sufficient income of their own to support themselves and their children.

HOW WORKING ONLY IN THE HOME HURTS ALL WOMEN

Women who work only in the home reinforce attitudes about how women should behave that hurt all women, including single women and women who do work full-time year-round outside the home.

A number of people have repeated the misleading statement that whereas married women earn about 60% as much as married men, never-married women earn as much, or almost as much, as never-married men.[42] The implication, though they never say so directly, is that single women earn a good salary and that married women earn so little only because they drop out of the workforce.

What they never say is that the reason single women earn so much compared to single men is that single men earn so little. The most comprehensive survey I have been able to find on this subject was done by the Bureau of the Census, based on 1979 statistics.

The survey compared the median earnings of persons aged 45–54 controlling for educational attainment, and marital status. Married females received $7,337; single (never-married) females received $11,070; single (never-married) males received $12,388; married males received $18,279.[43]

To put it another way, married females received 66% as much as single women, 60% as much as single men, and 40% as much as married men of the same age group. Never-married females earned 89% as much as single men, and 60% as much as married men. Obviously, married men do much better financially than either married women or never-married women.

When the educational attainment is factored in, the figures change considerably. When we control for education, the gap between single women and married women is much more variable, becoming insignificant for some categories. And the gap between never-married women and married men becomes much greater.

There is practically no difference in income between single women with just an elementary education and married women with a similar education, and between never-married and married women with 5 or more years of college. Single women with an elementary education earned $5,832; married women with an elementary education earned $5,655.[44]

On the other hand, never-married women with a 4-year college education received $15,329; married women with the same education earned $10,029.

Thus, married women earned, at the minimum, 65% as much as never-married women with the same education, and, at the most, 97% as much as never-married women with the same education. As explained earlier, part of the difference between never-married and married women may be explained by married women working part-time, not being willing to take on more responsible jobs, or the effect of lost years in the workforce.

The gap between never-married women and never-married men is steady at about 15%, in favor of single men.

But, of greater significance, never-married women earned, at the *most,* 62% as much as married men with the same education; and, at the lowest, only *45%* as much as married men with the same education. Never-married women with only an elementary education earned $5,832; married men with a similar education received $12,959.[45] Never-married women with a high school education received $11,074; married men with a similar education received $17,694. All the other groups were somewhere in between.

As stated above, unfortunately the 1979 statistics were the most recent I could find; I hope that a similar study will be done with the 1990 statistics. Even the annual Bureau of the Census *Money Income* report, which used to at least do a breakdown by marital status and age now puts all those in the same marital status over 18 in one category.

In Canada, a government survey showed that, in 1987, never-married women aged 35–44 earned $26,446, married women in the same age group earned $22,504, "other women" earned $23,309, never-married men in the same age group earned $29,187, and married men earned $36,291. To put it another way, married women aged 35–44 earned 85% as much as never-married women in the same age group, never-married women earned 90% as much as never-married men in the same age group, and never-married women earned 67% as much as married men in the same age group.[46]

These statistics appear to indicate that if we had the additional factor of education, the results would be fairly close to the U.S. 1979 results.

Both these groups of figures are significant. The effect of dropping out on the very women who do so has already been discussed. What will be discussed here is the effect on all women.

It can be safely assumed that never-married women have been steady members of the workforce. Certainly this could account for the difference in their income as compared to married women. So the difference between their income and that of married men cannot be explained by the drop-out factor. It also seems unlikely that a significant number of never-married women aged 45–54 would be working part-time.

One possible explanation is that the income differential is pure discrimination. But another explanation is that the expectation that all women will, or should, drop out or work part-time hurts all women, including women who do not drop out.

Thinking women are more likely to drop out than men, or to work part-time, is not discrimination. Discrimination is an *irrational* practice or prejudice. As we have seen, many more women than men do drop out, or work part-time. Moreover, many women are loudly proclaiming their continued right to do so and many articles are encouraging women to do so. So one cannot say that an employer's assumption that a female employee is more likely to drop out than a male employee, or to want to work part-time, is discrimination.

It is also simply common sense, and not discrimination, to prefer to train, give opportunities to, encourage, and promote people who will not drop out and be lost to your company. It can be argued that men can also switch jobs, switch careers, decided to travel around the world, follow their spouses to a new city, and so on. That certainly is true. But women can also do all the above, in addition to dropping out.

Therefore many employers who think that women are just as intelligent, as hard-working, and as generally able as men may promote men over women until the women have demonstrated that even after they have children they will return to the workforce after a maternity leave of four to six months.

Therefore, many employers are reluctant to promote any woman until she has either passed the prime years for childbearing or has demonstrated that she will continue working after she has had children. By the time the woman has demonstrated her intentions to go on working, she has been passed over for several promotions and chances at training.

There are, of course, many men who think that women *should* drop out to have children. Such men are encouraged in their views by the many women who do drop out and who say that women who do not drop out are bad mothers.

Thus women who drop out hurt not only themselves, but all women.

Therefore, while men are being promoted, women are being put on "hold." Even women who have no intention of dropping out or of working part-time will be placed on hold. After all, has there not been article after article about successful women, including professional women, who decided to drop out or work part-time?

Thus, this insistence on women having the right to make the choice hurts all women, not just women making this choice. Moreover, it helps perpetuate a vicious cycle. Women do not train themselves for lifetime jobs because they expect to drop out or work part-time. They are not promoted by employers who expect them to drop out. They then decide to drop out, partly because they are in dead-end jobs or because it "makes sense" as their husbands earn so much more.

Women who work only in the home are also hurting women who work outside the home in other ways.

A married man who, no matter how late he works, comes home to a hot meal, a made bed, clean clothes, and a clean house, will be able to work longer and later than a woman who comes home to make her own meals, clean her own clothes, and wash her own floors. Having a wife is a definite asset.

That married men earn approximately twice as much as single men in the same age group with the same education may not be the result of having a wife. But one thing is sure: being married is definitely not a disadvantage—to a man.

A married man who has a wife to iron shirts and shine shoes can set a higher standard of personal appearance at work than a woman who has to do these things for herself. Moreover, that some men have wives who work only in the home puts pressure on women who work outside the home to live up to these same standards. It is hard enough for single women who must do their own ironing, cleaning and cooking to work the same hours as men who have someone (who often works for less than minimum wage per hour) to do these jobs for them. How married women who not only must do their own cooking but must also cook for their husbands can manage is amazing.

Thus women who work only in the home hurt all women by giving their husbands an advantage. It is true that women who work outside the home also give their husbands an advantage over single women (and single men) if they provide their husbands with housekeeping and childcare services.

No women should give any man an advantage over other women by providing him with housekeeping and childcare services. But as long as there are women who work only in the home, there will be pressure on all women to provide their mates with housekeeping services. And at least women who also work outside the home are not providing an example of female behavior in the work force that can be used by men to hurt other women.

JOB-SHARING, WORKING PART-TIME AND OTHER WAYS OF AVOIDING THE ISSUE

The current spate of articles points out, quite correctly, that it is too much for most women to carry the double burden of housework, childcare, and a full-time job. The problem is not so much childcare during the day but the problem of taking the child to a childcare center, picking up the child, doing the shopping, doing the laundry, cleaning the home, and, of course, taking care of the children almost single-handedly during the evening and all weekends.

There are two solutions to this problem: one that will perpetuate women's unequal position in society, and one that will bring about true equality.

The proposals that perpetuate women's unequal position in society are those that assume women should go on carrying the double burden. As carrying the double burden is too much for most women, the only solution is FOR WOMEN to drop out, ostensibly for a few years, work part-time, or job-share.[47]

Unfortunately, flextime, job-sharing, part-time work, and so on are not only not solutions but treating them as solutions obscures the true problem.

The true problem is that as long as women do most of the housework and most of the childcare, women will continue to be unequal to men. Numerous surveys have shown that while there is more lip service paid to the fact that men should do housework, and some men may do slightly more housework than they used to, housework and childcare are still done mostly by women.[48]

There is no way a woman working part-time can earn as much as a similarly qualified man working full-time. Nor can she qualify for the same benefits, or build up the same seniority, or earn the same pension, or have either the same quantity or quality of experience. Nor, incidentally, can a woman on maternity leave be building up the same quality or quantity of experience, nor usually earning the same salary or the same pension benefits, as a man actually working at the job. If the maternity leave is for a relatively short period of time (4–6 months), this is irrelevant. But if the maternity, or so-called parental, leave is extended for several years and not split equally between both parents, the effect can be significant.

Similarly, job-sharing is basically working part-time under a different name. Job-sharing may be more likely to include benefits than working part-time, but the principle is the same. Again, if a woman "job-shares" and her husband works full-time, he is earning twice the salary, accumulating twice the pension, building up twice as much work experience, and is far more likely to be promoted.

There is nothing wrong with job-sharing, or working part-time, IF, and it is a big if, men job-share or work part-time to the same extent as women. If not, then there will continue to be great discrepancy between male and female income, not to mention in the number of men and women in positions of authority and decision-making.

In Sweden, the average salary of a woman working *full-time* is 80% of that earned by a man working full-time.[49] (The gap between higher-income earners and lower-income earners is generally much lower in Sweden than in Canada or the United States.) But the average salary of *all* female workers, including part-time workers, in 1989 was only 66% of the salary of all male workers, including part-time workers.[50] When we consider that about *40%* of all female workers, but only *7%,* of all male workers, work part-time,[51] the Swedish statistics become less surprising.

Similarly, in the United States, in 1990, while the average full-time year-round female worker 18 or over earned $23,404, the average year-round part-time worker earned only $9,229.[52]

Working part-time is not a solution as long as it is mostly women, and not men, who work part-time. A woman who works part-time, unless she has an exceptionally well-paying part-time job, is still dependent on her husband, may still feel financially unable to leave an abusive situation, and will not be able to pay for an expensive lawyer in case of divorce or separation.

Even if she is relatively well-paid, she is still not developing her career in the same way that her husband is. Working part-time is not a solution as long as it is only women who do it.

STRATEGIES

Once we have determined that working only in the home hurts women, we can determine the appropriate action to try to discourage women from making this "choice."

Do Not Mislead Women

The very first step should be not to go on advising women that either choice, to work only in the home or also outside it, is equally valid.

Both men and women are free, to paraphrase Proudhon, to work only in the home. What the right to work in the home is really about is approval and support for this decision. And what feminists must do is point out all the harmful consequences of this decision. And they must support measures that, as much as possible, do not encourage women to make this choice while still trying to minimize the suffering that often results from making it.

Naturally, the mere fact that feminists advise women not to work only in the home will not instantly stop them from doing so. And of course many women will object to this advice. But at least it is a first step.

As long as men who work outside the home are considered good fathers, while women who work outside the home are not considered to be good mothers, as long as it is considered to be the mother's duty, and not the father's duty, to take care of the children, to clean the house, to clean the clothes, to buy the clothes, to pick up the laundry, etc., etc., it can be doubted how much "choice" women have about their decision to work only in the home or work part-time.

It is no wonder that so many married women want to work part-time or drop out temporarily. But so-called "solutions" that just perpetuate a system that consolidates men's power should not be promoted. Instead we should refuse to praise as equally valid decisions that hurt women and decisions that help women.

As long as women continue to work only in the home, or to make the "double burden" manageable by working part-time or job-sharing, they are avoiding making men take responsibility for their share of housework and childcare. And men certainly will not take responsibility for housework and childcare unless women make them do so.

Most women who work outside the home also take most of the responsibility for childcare and housework. This is not a solution. That so many women work only inside the home, places pressure on all women to do most of the housework and childcare.

Working full-time year-round outside the home is not a sufficient condition for female equality. But it is a necessary condition for the next step—which is demanding that men take responsibility for half the housework and childcare.

Dropping out, working part-time, job-sharing: as long as these are choices made by women, and not by men, they can only perpetuate the pattern of female inequality. They can only perpetuate conditions that often hurt the women themselves, often hurt their children, and always hurt all women. Feminists should not encourage women to make these decisions.

We should stop writing articles about how hard it is to do it all, and suggesting temporary drop outs, or part-time work, or job-sharing as an answer. We should start writing articles about how the only solution is for men to do their share and how men will refuse to do their share until women go on strike. And by going on strike I mean refusing to live with, have sex with, have babies for, or do the housework for, men who do not do 50% of all the housework and childcare, including cleaning the toilet and taking responsibility for organizing.

Once we decide that our focus should be on making men take responsibility, rather than making it easier for women to carry the "double burden," then our strategies for dealing with marriage breakup and other events will change.

If feminists don't take the position that we should focus on making men carry their share, rather than encouraging women to go on carrying the man's share, then who will?

Realistic Pre-Nuptial Agreements

Once we decide that our strategy should be to make the man carry his fair share, then it becomes obvious that our present strategy of dealing with marriage breakup is wrong. Marriages in which both partners carried an equal burden should not be treated the same as marriages in which the wife carried an unequal share of the burden. Women should stop subscribing to the myth that marriage is a partnership in which both partners are entitled to share in the assets of the marriage by mere virtue of the fact that they were married.

Under some conditions, neither partner should be entitled to the assets of the other.

Under other conditions, for example, that one partner worked only in the home, this partner should be entitled to all the assets of the other. It is not the mere fact of being married that should determine division of assets, alimony, and maintenance payments for children; it is the sacrifices in terms of lost opportunities and the provision of house-keeping and childcare services that should determine this division.

Prenuptial agreements should state that provided each partner did an equal share of all housework and childcare, neither partner would be entitled to anything from the other partner aside from child maintenance. This provision would eliminate the absurd situation that sometimes develops in which a husband claims assets or even temporary alimony from his wife just because she has a higher income or more assets, even though the wife still did most of the childcare and/or housekeeping.

However, if one partner dropped out, or one partner worked part-time and the other worked full-time, then the partner who worked only in the home or only part-time would be entitled to all, not merely half, of the family assets up to the cutoff point.

The cutoff point would be where the nonworking partner's income from assets and job combined equalled the working partner's income from assets and job combined. After that, the assets should be split fifty-fifty.

The agreement should also provide that in the event of a divorce or separation, the children should go to the spouse who provided most of the childcare.

If both partners worked full-time, but one spent more time on housework and/or childcare than the other, then the assets of the spouse who did less housework should be adjusted to compensate the spouse who did more housework.

Such agreements would make it clear that entitlement to assets was based not on the mere fact of being married, but on providing compensation for housekeeping services and lost opportunity costs. They would also ensure that the children went to the spouse who had cared most for them during the marriage.

But, the reader will argue, such an agreement is obviously absurd. No man would ever sign an agreement which would give his nonworking spouse all the family and business assets. Even if he did, it would not benefit the average spouse because the assets of most families are so insignificant.

But urging women to get their spouses, or potential spouses, to sign such an agreement before they decide to work part-time or drop out would at least bring home the impact of such a decision on their financial stability. It would also bring home how questionable is their husbands' devotion to at-home childcare when it means it would be not just the wife, but the husband, who suffers the financial consequences.

Those Who Benefit Should Pay

A major problem has always been to protect women who do decide to drop out, or work part-time, in such a way as to encourage them to make this decision as rarely as possible.

If it costs men more to maintain women as full-time housekeepers, then they will be less likely to think having their wife work only in the home is such a terrific idea. Women should ensure that all payments made to women who sacrifice their own careers by working only part-time or not outside the home at all are made by the husbands or partners of these women, not by other women.

All survivors' benefits should be paid by charging husbands (or anyone who wants their survivor to be able to claim survivor benefits) higher premiums or by giving extra flat payments to anyone not claiming a survivor's benefit at retirement. (Some companies that have done this in England have refunded 20% of the premiums paid to single people at retirement).

Any tax benefits that accrue to married men whose wives work only in the home, or part-time, should be eliminated. The ability of a married man to considerably reduce his tax liability by filing jointly with a wife who has no income should be removed.

A married man filing jointly can claim what is estimated to be for 1993 a deduction of $6,200. A single filer can claim only $3,700.[53] Thus, a married man whose wife has no outside income can claim an extra $2,500. Moreover, the married man can also claim an extra $2,300 for his wife's exemption amount if his income is below the threshold point ($157,900 in 1993).[54] Therefore, a married man, especially a high-income earner, could find it financially beneficial for his wife not to work, because her deductions and exemptions reduce his high income. As an accountant who formerly practiced in the United States said, sometimes it is not worthwhile (at least to the husband) for the wife to work.

Thus the current tax system encourages men to keep their wives working only in the home. Moreover, inasmuch as this system means married men are paying less tax, it means that single women, single men, and married men and women who do not benefit from joint filing because they have roughly equal income, are paying more. The greater the inequality in income of husband and wife, the greater the advantages of filing jointly.[55]

Married men already receive the benefit of cheap housekeeping and childcare services. They certainly do not need additional tax benefits. Nor should they be encouraged to keep their wives working only in the home by such benefits.

Any "family benefits" should also be costed properly so that women do not subsidize married men. For example, a number of private and public employers pay all or part of the medical insurance for their employees. These employers often charge married men much less than double the amount they charge single people (or even nothing at all) for these benefits. For instance, most of the basic medical insurance plans available to City of New York employees provide basic medical coverage free, to both single people and families.

Again, this benefit is worth the most in households where only one spouse works. To the extent that more money spent on benefits for spouses of married men means less money available for other purposes, this policy amounts to a subsidy by working women of married men. "Family benefits" should be available only if they are costed on an actuarial basis.

It is bad enough that single women, and married women who work full-time outside the home, do not have the advantage of cheap cleaning, cooking, laundry and shopping services that married men have. To make women pay for the benefits married men enjoy by forcing women to subsidize survivors' benefits, tax exemptions and so on, is turning the knife in the wound.

Women who do not work full-time must be protected but the protection must be paid for by the men who benefit from their work in the home.

"Encouraging" Men to Choose Housework/Childcare

We can learn lessons from other countries, but unfortunately we seem to be learning the wrong ones.

The message from Sweden is that simply "allowing" men to take parental leave does not make men take parental leave. The Swedish parental system is very comprehensive and cannot possibly be covered in detail here. However, in summary, provided the parents qualify, a parent is entitled to a total of 450 days of parental leave, of which 270 days is paid at the same rate as the regular sickness benefit, and the remaining time at a smaller minimum level.[56]

The thirty days that can be taken before childbirth can be taken only by the mother; the rest of the time can be taken by either the father or the mother. This leave is available until the child is eight, and can be taken in half-days or quarter-days.[57]

As stated earlier, the average Swedish female full-time worker earns about 80% as much as the average male full-time worker. Yet, in spite of this relative equality of male and female earnings, in spite of the fact that the very generous Swedish benefit is available to both parents, in spite of the fact that this benefit has existed in one form or another from 1974, in 1990 fathers took only *7.4%* of all the above parental leave benefits.[58]

Either parent also has the right to work part-time until the child is eight. As discussed previously, while 40% of Swedish women work part-time, only 7% of Swedish men do so.

The old excuse that women drop out because it makes economic sense for them to do so does not apply so easily to Sweden. If Swedish women who work full-time earn 80% as much as men, then the reason women rather than men drop out and work part-time is not that men earn so much more than women that the family cannot afford to lose men's pay. Nor can it be argued that men do not have the right to parental leave benefits. Swedish women drop-out and work part-time because housework and childcare are considered women's responsibilities.

The Swedish example shows that no amount of parental leave or availability of part-time work, in itself, is going to change women's responsibilities for housework and childcare, even in progressive Sweden.

It is also worth noting that Canada has had paid maternity leave for a number of years, with women receiving the usual unemployment insurance benefit for 15 weeks, the benefit being 60% of their salary up to a maximum. The current criterion is the same as for other unemployment insurance, that is, twenty weeks of work out of the last fifty-two.[59] Yet the Canadian participation rate for women in the outside-the-home labor force is almost the same in Canada and the United States. Canada has recently changed its law so that the leave consists of 15 weeks' maternity leave and 10 weeks' parental leave which may be taken by either parent.[60] It will be interesting to see how many men take this leave now that it is available to them.

Fighting for better parental leave, better availability of part-time work, better daycare could indeed prove useful, PROVIDED we also fight to make men take equal responsibility for childcare and housework. Merely fighting for parental leave without also compelling men to take such leave might just reinforce the idea that childcare is women's responsibility.

What women must do is encourage the passage of legislation that not merely "allows" men to take parental leave, but penalizes them if they do not. For example, if one parent worked full-time throughout the marriage, while the other parent took some form of parental leave or worked part-time, then the parent who took parental leave should automatically get the children in a divorce or separation.

Similarly, any form of state-mandated parental leave should be split between both parents (except for single parents), with half the leave being lost if one parent did not take the leave. Perhaps there should be a financial penalty for the parent who did not take the available leave.

A number of alternatives could be discussed. The important point is for women to realize that legislation must remove all incentives for men to have women provide housekeeping and childcare services for them; and that it must provide penalties for men who do not take parental leave. Merely giving men the option of parental leave or part-time work is not sufficient.

CONCLUSION

Encouraging women to make choices about labor force participation that hurt them, their children, and other women is not doing anyone a favor. It is not helping women who have a good chance of living in poverty by the time they discover, too late, that they cannot drop back in to the workforce as easily as they have dropped out. It is not helping the children of such women who also stand a good chance of living in poverty. And it certainly does not help other women who are trying to persuade men that they should be trained or promoted because not all women drop out or work part-time.

Enough depressing books have been written about the sad state of women after they are divorced, or about women and children living in poverty. Let us start encouraging women to make choices that will not leave them dependent on men.

NOTES

1 Nicholas Davidson, *The Failure of Feminism* (Buffalo, N.Y.: Prometheus Press, 1988), 17.

2 Statistics Canada, Household Surveys Division, Cat. No. 71–001 *The Labour Force February 1992* (Ottawa, March 1992), Table 1, "Estimates by Age and Sex, Canada, February 1992," B–7.

3 Statistics Canada, *The Labour Force,* B–7; and Table 18, "Full-time and Part-time Employment by Sex and Age, Canada and Provinces, February 1992," B–33.

4 *Ibid.*

5 U.S. Department of Labor, Bureau of Labor Statistics, *Employment and Earnings* (Washington, May 1992), Table A–4, "Employment status of the civilian noninstitutional population by age, sex, and race," 10; and Table A–9, "Employed and unemployed full- and part-time workers by sex, age, and race," 18.

6 Statistics Canada, Health and Welfare Canada, Cat. No. 89–529E, Donna S. Lero, Hillel Goelman, Alan R. Pence, Lois M. Brockman and Sandra Nuttall, *Canadian National Child Care Study: Parental work patterns and child care needs* (Ottawa, 1992), 21.

7 *Ibid.,* Table 11, "Employment Status of Parents, by Gender, Families With At Least One Child Younger Than 13, Canada, 1988," 44.

8 Statistics Canada, Cat. No. 71–533, *Family Characteristics and Labour Force Activity: Annual Averages, 1977–84* (Ottawa, April 1986), Table 1, "Labour Force Status of Women by Presence of Husband and Children, 1984," 2.

9 U.S. Department of Commerce, Bureau of the Census, *Statistical Abstract of the United States 1990* (110th Edition) (Washington, 1990), Table 636, "Married, Separated, and Divorced Women—Labor Force Status by Presence and Age of Children: 1960 to 1988," 385.

10 U.S. Department of Labor, Bureau of Labor Statistics, *Employment in Perspective: Working Women,* Report 715 (Third Quarter 1984).

11 *Ibid.*

12 *Ibid.*

13 *Ibid.*

14 *Ibid.*

15 Statistics Canada, *The Labour Force,* B–7.

16 U.S. Department of Labor, *Employment and Earnings,* 10.

17 Terry Gilbert, "Women Find Maternal Instinct Overpowers Career Plan," *Toronto Star* (March 30, 1989): L–8.

18 Beverly Stephen, "Opting Out of the Rat Race," *New Woman* (October 1988): 107–111; Edith Fierst, "Careers And Kids," *Ms.* (May 1988): 62.

19 "A Mother's Choice," *Newsweek* (March 31, 1986): 46.

20 Lenore Weitzman, *The Divorce Revolution* (New York, N.Y.: The Free Press, 1985), 36. Notice that Susan Faludi, *Backlash* (New York, N.Y.: Crown Publishers, 1991), 20–21 disputes that the loss of income is so high.

21 Bureau of the Census, Current Population Reports, Consumer Income, Series P–60, No. 174, *Money Income of Households, Families, and Persons in the United States: 1990* (August 1991), Table 28, "Marital Status—Persons 18 Years Old and Over, by Total Money Income in 1990, Race, Hispanic Origin, Sex, and Work Experience in 1990," 124.

22 *Ibid,* Table 31, "Work Experience in 1990—Persons 15 Years Old and Over, by Total Money Earnings in 1990, Race, Hispanic Origin, and Sex," 160–162.

23 Weitzman, *The Divorce Revolution,* 144, stating that, in 1968, less than 20% of divorced wives received alimony and that the 1968 median was $98 a month.

24 Bureau of the Census, Current Population Reports, Special Studies, Series P–23, No. 148, *Child Support and Alimony: 1983* (1985), Table 3, "Award and Recipiency Status of Women—Alimony Payments in 1983, 1981, and 1978," 4. Note that a later study says that as of spring 1988, 17 percent of ever-divorced women were awarded alimony, but as this study does not say what percent received the alimony, it is not as useful. Bureau of the Census, Current Population Reports, Special Studies, Series P–23, No. 167, *Child Support and Alimony:* 1987 (June 1990), 1.

25 Bureau of the Census, *Child Support and Alimony:* 1983, 4.

26 *Ibid.*

27 *Porter v. Porter,* 274 N.W. 2d 235 (N.D. 1979).

28 Bureau of the Census, *Money Income of Households,* 124–126.

29 U.S. Department of Commerce, Bureau of the Census, *1980 Census of Population: Special Reports: Marital Characteristics,* Vol. 2 (March 1985), Table 8, "Years of School Completed and Earnings in 1979 of Persons 45–54 Years Old With Earnings in 1979 by Marital Status, Marital History, Race, Spanish origin, and Sex," 148.

30 "Study of teen girls unveils depressing view of future," *Toronto Star* January 18, 1986, A–9.

31 Bureau of the Census, *Marital Characteristics,* 148. It has also been reported in the Canadian press that a recent Canadian Department of Justice survey said that women who leave the work force for a decade or longer lose an average of more than $80,000 over the rest of their working careers, and that in some categories even a two-year break may mean lost earnings of $30,000. Jeff Sallot, "Career pause expensive for wives," *Globe and Mail,* July 7, 1992.

32 See, for example, *Tremblay v. Tremblay* (1989), 18 R.F.L. (3rd) 337 (Ont. H.C.)

33 Weitzman, *The Divorce Revolution,* 339–340; Ann Landers, "It's hard for older women to find work," *Toronto Star,* June 5, 1989, C–2.

34 Statistics Canada, Household Survey Division, Cat. No. 13–207, *Income Distributions by Size in Canada (1988)* (1989), Table A, "Incidence of Low Income Among Families, Unattached Individuals and Persons by Selected Characteristics, 1986, 1987 and 1988," 181. American statistics for 1988 state 37% of all households headed by women, 23% of single women and 20% of all single women over the age of 65 were living below the poverty line. Source is Bureau of the Census, Current Population Reports, Consumer Income, Series P–60, No. 166 *Money Income and Poverty Status in the United States: 1988* (October 1989), respectively, Table 18, "Poverty Status of Persons, by Family Relationship, Race and Hispanic Origin: 1959 to 1988," 58; Table 17, "Number, Poverty Rate and Standard Errors of Persons, Families and Unrelated Individuals Below the Poverty Level in 1988 and 1987," 57; Table F–7, "Selected Characteristics of Unrelated Individuals, by Race and Hispanic Origin and Poverty Status in 1988 (Poverty Thresholds based on CPI–U–X1): 144. Statistics reported use various measures of poverty. The American cut-off point seems to be much lower than the Canadian; for example, the CPI–U–X1 American Index has the poverty level for an individual at $5,478; the Canadian cut-off point goes from $8,759 in rural areas to $12,867 in cities of 500,000 or over.

35 Bureau of the Census, *Child Support and Alimony 1987,* 1.

36 *Ibid.,* 4.

37 *Ibid.,* 7.

38 Bureau of the Census, *Child Support and Alimony 1983,* Table 1, "Child Support Payments Agreed to or Awarded," 7.

39 Bureau of the Census, *Child Support and Alimony 1987,* 1.

40 *Hadican v. Hadican* (1984), 33 Sask R. 89 (Q.B.).

41 Bureau of the Census, *Child Support and Alimony 1987,* derived from Table A, "Women With Own Children Under 21 Years of Age Present from Absent Fathers, by Selected Characteristics," 2. 54% of women with children and absent fathers living below the poverty line had been married (including a small percent still married).

42 Sylvia Ann Hewlett, *A Lesser Life: The Myth of Women's Liberation in America* (New York, N.Y.: William Morrow, 1986): 82.

43 Bureau of the Census, *Marital Characteristics,* 147–148.

44 *Ibid.*

45 *Ibid.*

46 Statistics Canada, Housing, Family and Social Statistics Division, *Women in Canada: A Statistical Report,* 2nd ed. (February 1990), Table 30, "Average Earnings of earners, by work activity, marital status, age group, and sex, Canada, 1987," 99.

47 "Bank's Pilot Project May Signal New Approach to Flexible Work," *Toronto Star,* February 24, 1990, K–6.

48 National Council of Welfare, Minister of Supply and Services Canada, Cat. No. H68–25/1990, *Women and Poverty Revisited* (Ottawa 1990), 51–52; see also Jim Millar, "Women's Work Is Never Done," *Newsweek* (July 31, 1989): 65.

49 Statistics Sweden, *Statistical Abstract of Sweden 1988* (Stockholm 1987), Table 217, "Employees in the 20–64 age group by income of work, level of employment and sex," 203.

50 Statistics Sweden, *Statistical Yearbook of Sweden 1992* (Stockholm 1991), Table 220, "Income-earners by total income, sex and age," 194.

51 *Ibid.,* Table 188, "Employed and part-time employed," 163.

52 Bureau of the Census, *Money Income of Households,* 126, and 162.

53 Commerce Clearing House, Inc., *U.S. Master Tax Guide* (November 1992), (76th Ed. 1993), p. 87.

54 *Ibid,* 88.

55 *Ibid,* 95.

56 Sweden, National Social Insurance Board, Statistical Division, *Social Insurance Statistics Facts 1991* (Stockholm, 1991), 25.

57 The Swedish Institute, *Fact Sheets on Sweden* (Stockholm, 1984).

58 National Social Insurance Board, *Social Insurance Facts,* 27.

59 *Unemployment Insurance Act,* R.S.C. 1985, ch. U-1, s. 11.

60 *Unemployment Insurance Act,* S.C. 1990, c. 40, s. 9 revises s. 11.

Hwame, Koshkalaka, and the Rest: Lesbians in American Indian Cultures

Paula Gunn Allen

The lesbian is to the American Indian what the Indian is to the American—invisible. According to ethnographers' accounts, among the tribes there were women warriors, women leaders, women shamans, women husbands, but whether any of these were lesbians is seldom mentioned. On the few occasions lesbianism is referred to, it is with regard to a specific individual who is noted because she is a lesbian. This fosters the impression of uniform heterosexuality among Indian women except for a very few who deviate from that norm. It is an impression that is false.

In all the hundreds, perhaps thousands, of books and articles about American Indians that I have read while pursuing my studies or preparing for the variety of courses in American Indian studies that I have taught, I have encountered no reference to lesbians except one.[1] That one was contained in a novel by Fred Manfred, *The Manly-Hearted Woman,*[2] and though its protagonist dresses as a man and rejects her feminine role and though she marries a woman, the writer is very explicit: she and her wife do not share sexual intimacies, a possibility that seems beyond the writer's ability to envision. Indeed, the protagonist eventually falls in love with a rather strange young warrior who possesses enormous sexual prowess (given him by spirit power and a curious genetic circumstance). After the warrior's death the manly hearted woman divorces her wife and returns to woman's garb and occupation, discarding the spirit stone that has determined her life to that point. It seems that heterosexual love conquers all—even ritual tradition, custom, and spirit command.

Direct references to lesbians or lesbianism among American Indians are even more sparse than those about homosexual men (usually called hermaphrodites or berdache or, less often, transvestites), occurring almost outside the body of information about tribal life or included in ways that underscore white attitudes about tribes, Indians, and homosexuality. Consequently, much of my discussion of lesbians is necessarily conjectural, based on secure knowledge of American Indian social systems and customs that I have gathered from formal study, personal experience, and personally communicated information from other Indians as well as from my own knowledge of lesbian culture and practice.

My idea in this essay is to explore lesbianism within a larger social and spiritual tribal context as contrasted with its occurrence as an individual aberration that might show up on occasion but that has nothing to do with tribal life in general. Because tribal civilizations (like all others) function in entire gestalts and because they are based on the life-enhancing interconnectedness of all things, it is my contention that gayness, whether female or male, traditionally functions positively within tribal groups.

Certainly, the chances that aboriginal American women formed affectional alliances are enormous. Many tribes had marked tendency to encourage virginity or some version of chastity among pubescent women; this tendency rarely affected the sexual habits of married women, however, and it referred to intercourse with males. Nothing is said, to my knowledge, about sexual liaisons between women, except indirectly. It is equally likely that such relationships were practiced with social sanction, though no one is presently talking about this. The history of Native America is selective; and those matters pertaining to women that might contradict a western patriarchal world-view are carefully selected out.

Some suggestions about how things were in "time immemorial," as the old folks refer to pre-contact times, have managed to find their way into contemporary literature about American Indians. Many tribes have recorded stories concerning daughters born to spirit women who were dwelling alone on earth. These daughters then would become the mothers of entire tribes. In one such tale, First Mother was "born of the dew of the leaf of the beautiful plant."[3] Such tales point to a time prior to the advent of patriarchy. While historical and archeological evidence suggests that this time predated European contact in some regions of the western hemisphere, the change in cultural orientation was still proceeding. The tribes became more male-oriented and more male-dominated as acculturation accelerated. As this process continued, less and less was likely to be said by American Indians about lesbians among them. Indeed, less and less about women in any position other than that sanctioned by missionaries was likely to be recorded.

There are a number of understandings about the entire issue that will be important in my discussion of American Indian women, heterosexual or lesbian. It is my contention and belief that those two groups were not nearly as separate as modern lesbian and straight women are. My belief is based on my understanding of the cultures and social systems in which women lived. These societies were tribal, and tribal consciousness, with its attendant social structures, differs enormously from that of the contemporary western world.

This difference requires new understanding of a number of concepts. The concept of family, the concept of community, the concept of women, the concept of bonding and belonging, and the concept of power were all distinctly understood in a tribal matrix; and those concepts were/are very different from those current in modern America.

WOMEN AND FAMILY IN TRIBAL SOCIETIES

Among American Indians, Spirit-related persons are perceived as more closely linked than blood-related persons. Understanding this primary difference between American Indian values and modern Euro-Anglo-American Judeo-Christian values is critical to understanding Indian familial structures and the context in which lesbians functioned. For American Indian people, the primary value was relationship to the Spirit world. All else was determined by the essential nature of this understanding. Spirits, gods and goddesses, metaphysical/occult forces, and the right means of relating to them determined the tribes' every institution, every custom, every endeavor and pastime. This was not peculiar to inhabitants of the western hemisphere, incidentally; it was at one time the primary value of all tribal people on earth.

Relationship to the Spirit world has been of primary value to tribal people, but not to those who have studied them. Folklorists and ethnographers have other values that permeate their work and their understandings, so that most of what they have recorded or concluded about American Indians is simply wrong. Countless examples could illustrate this basic misunderstanding, but let me share just one, culled from the work of one of the most influential anthropologists, Bronislaw Malinowski. His massive study of the Keres Pueblo Acoma presumably qualified him as an authority on mother-right society in North America. In *Sex, Culture, and Myth* Malinowski wrote: "Patrilocal households are 'united households,' while 'split households' are the exclusive phenomena of matrilocal mother-right cultures."[4] While acknowledging that economic considerations alone do not determine the structure of marriage patterns, Malinowski fails to recognize marriage as a construct founded on laws derived from conversations with Spirits. The primary unit for a tribe is not, as he suggests, the household; even the term is misleading, because a tribal "household" includes a number of individuals who are clan rather than blood relatives. For nontribal people, "household" typically means a unit composed of a father, mother, and offspring—though contemporary living arrangements often deviate from that stereotyped conception. A tribal household might encompass assorted blood-kin, medicine society "kin," adoptees, servants, and visitors who have a clan or supernatural claim on membership although they are biologically unrelated to the rest of the household. Writing about tribal societies in Oceania, Malinowski wrote: "Throughout Oceania a network of obligations unites the members of the community and overrules the economic autonomy of the household."[5] To a tribal person, the very notion of the household's autonomy appears to be nonsensical. To exemplify his view of tribal practices, Malinowski cites the Trobriand Islanders' requirement that a man give approximately half of his produce to his sister(s) and another portion to other relatives, thus using only the remainder for "his own household" which, Malinowski concedes, is largely supported by the wife's brother(s) and other relatives. I mention this example from a tribe that is not American Indian because Malinowski himself encourages generalization: "Economic obligations," he continues, which "cut across the closed unity of the household could be quoted from every single tribe of which we have adequate information."[6]

Malinowski and other researchers have dismissed the household as an economic unit but have continued to perceive households from the viewpoint of the nuclear family—father, mother(s), and offspring. He remains within the accepted, biased European understanding of "household" when he states:

> The most important examples [of split households] come from the communities organised in extreme mother-right, where husband and wife are in most matters members of different households, and their mutual economic contributions show the character of gifts rather than of mutual maintenance.[7]

The case of matrifocal-matrilocal households seems extreme only when one defines "household" in terms that do not allow for various styles of bonding. Malinowski believes that this "extreme mother-right" method of housing people is exceptional. He does concede that it results from conditions found in high-level cultures rather than in "primitive" ones[8]—which is an extremely interesting observation. But in making it, he again relies on some assumptions that are not justified by available evidence.

If "household" signifies housing and food-provision systems, then the living arrangements of American Indians pose numerous problems, the matter of father-right versus mother-right being only one. In fact, Indians were inclined to live wherever they found themselves, if living signifies where you stash your belongings, where you take your meals, or where you sleep. Throughout North America, men were inclined to have little personal paraphernalia, to eat wherever they were when mealtime came, and to sleep in whatever spot was convenient when they were tired. Clan, band, and medicine-society affiliations had a primary bearing on these arrangements, as did the across-the-board separation of the sexes practiced formally or informally by most tribes.

Malinowski's view assumes that households may take various forms but that in any case they are unified to the extent that they may be spoken of as "mine" by a male who is husband to a woman and claims to be the father of her children. The "extreme" case of the "split household" occurs when a man who is identified as a woman's husband does not contribute to her economic life except by giving presents. This notion of "household" is quite removed from any held by tribal people with which I am familiar. Even among contemporary American Indians, a male who is identified as the husband of the lady of the house may not be (and often is not) the father of her children. But according to Malinowski, "The most important fact about such extreme matriarchal conditions [as among the Pueblo and several other groups cited] is that even there the principle of social legitimacy holds good; that though the father is domestically and economically almost superfluous, he is legally indispensable and the main bond of union between such matrilineal and matrilocal consorts is parenthood."[9]

Carefully examined, the foregoing observation makes no sense; even if it did, it suggests that although fatherhood is irrelevant in the home or office, a male remains indispensable because his presence (which may be very infrequent) confers legitimacy on something. Indeed.

Analyses like those of Malinowski can be explained only by the distorting function of cultural bias. A Pueblo husband is important because husbands are important. But I have known many "husbands" who had several "wives" and could claim that a number of women (who might or might not be claimed as wives) were the mothers of their children. And this remains the case despite some two to five hundred years of Christian influence. As an old Laguna woman has said in reference to these matters in the long ago, "We were very careless about such things then."

Actually, the legitimacy of motherhood was determined by its very existence. A woman who gave birth was a mother as long as she had a living child, and the source of a household's legitimacy was its very existence. American Indians were and are mystical, but they were and are a very practical people.

While there can be little question about the fact that most women married, perhaps several times, it is important to remember that tribal marriages often bore little resemblance to western concepts of that institution. Much that has been written about marriage as practiced among American Indians is wrong.

Among many tribes divorce was an easy matter for both women and men, and movement of individuals from one household to another was fluid and essentially unconstrained. There are many exceptions to this, for the tribes were distinct social groups; but many had patterns that did not use sexual constraint as a means of social control. Within such systems, individual action was believed to be directed by Spirits (through dreams, visions, direct encounter, or possession of power objects such as stones, shells, masks, or fetishes). In this context it is quite possible that lesbianism was practiced rather commonly, as long as the individuals cooperated with the larger social customs. Women were generally constrained to have children, but in many tribes, childbearing meant empowerment. It was the passport to maturity and inclusion in woman-culture. An important point is that women who did not have children because of constitutional, personal, or Spirit-directed disinclination had other ways to experience Spirit instruction and stabilization, to exercise power, and to be mothers.

"Family" did not mean what is usually meant by that term in the modern western world. One's family might have been defined in biological terms as those to whom one was blood kin. More often it was defined by other considerations; spiritual kinship was at least as important a factor as "blood." Membership in a certain clan related one to many people in very close ways, though the biological connection might be so distant as to be practically nonexistent. This facet of familial ordering has been much obscured by the presence of white Christian influence and its New Testament insistence that the term "family" refers to mother, father, and children, and those others who are directly related to mother and father. In this construct, all persons who can point to common direct-line ancestors are in some sense related, though the individual's distance from that ancestor will determine the "degree" of relationship to other descendants of that ancestor.

Among many American Indians, family is a matter of clan membership. If clan membership is determined by your mother, and if your father has a number of wives, you are not related to the children of his other wives unless they themselves happen to be related to your mother. So half-siblings in the white way might be unrelated in an Indian way. Or in some tribes, the children of your mother's sister might be considered siblings, while those of your father's brother would be the equivalent of cousins. These distinctions should demonstrate that the concept of family can mean something very different to an Indian than it does to a non-Indian.

In gynecentric systems, a unified household is one in which the relationships among women and their descendants and sisters are ordered; a split household is one in which this is not the case. A community, then, is an ordering of sister relationships that determine who can depend on whom for what. Male relationships are ordered in accordance with the maternal principle; a male's spiritual and economic placement and the attendant responsibilities are determined by his membership in the community of sisterhood. A new acquaintance in town might be asked, "Who is your mother?" The answer identifies the person and determines the ensuing relationship between the questioner and the newcomer.

Again, community in the non-Indian modern world tends to mean people who occupy a definable geographical area or who share a culture (lifestyle) or occupation. It can extend to include people who share an important common interest—political, avocational, or spiritual. But "community" in the American Indian world can mean those who are of a similar clan and Spirit; those who are encompassed by a particular Spirit-being are members of a community. In fact, this was the meaning most often given to the concept in traditional tribal cultures. So it was not impossible that members of a community could have been a number of women who "belonged" to a given medicine society or who were alike in that they shared consciousness of a certain Spirit.

WOMEN AND POWER

Any discussion of the status of women in general and of lesbians in particular cannot hope for accuracy if one misunderstands women's power in tribal societies. Indeed, in a recent random sampling of general ethnographies of several groups, I have noted that all matters of female life in the group under discussion can be found under the heading "Woman." This heading is divided into marriage, childbearing, childrearing, housekeeping, and, perhaps, menstruation. The discussions are neatly ordered according to middle-class white views about where women fit into social schemes, but they contain a number of false implications, not the least of which is that men don't marry, have children, or participate in childrearing.

It is clear, I think, that the ground we are exploring here is obscure: women in general have not been taken seriously by ethnographers or folklorists, and explorations that have been done have largely been distorted by the preconceptions engendered by a patriarchal world-view, in which lesbians are said not to exist and women are perceived as oppressed, burdened, powerless, and peripheral to interesting accounts of human affairs except in that they have babies.

In her discussion of the "universal" devaluation of women, Sherry Ortner cites the Crow, a matrilineal American Indian tribe that places women in high status. Crow Women, according to Ortner, were nevertheless required to ride "inferior" horses during menstruation and were prohibited from participating in ceremonies during their periods. She cites anthropologist Robert Lowie as stating that menstruation was seen as "a source of contamination, for [women] were not allowed to approach either a wounded man or men starting on a war party," and as a "threat to warfare, one of the most valued institutions of the tribe, one that is central to their [the tribe's] definition."[10] She interprets this evidence as proving that the Crow believed women inferior to men, even though many other aspects of their social structure and ritual life deny this assertion. But I think the vital question is why she interprets the evidence to demonstrate female inferiority and to mean that traditionally low status was woman's lot among them. She does not suggest that the present-day status of women among them might be attributable to the impact of colonization because she is attempting to prove that women have always and everywhere been oppressed by men. I contend that women have held a great deal of power in ritual cultures and that evidence supporting this contention is at least as massive as the evidence of our ignominy.

Ortner's conclusion that menstruation was perceived as dirty and contaminating by tribal people and that they saw it in the same light in which it was viewed by patriarchal peoples is simply wrong. Tribal people view menstruation as a "medicine" of such power that it can cause the death of certain people, such as men on the eve of combat, or pregnant women. Menstruating (or any other) Crow women do not go near a particularly sacred medicine bundle, and menstruating women are not allowed among warriors getting ready for battle, or those who have been wounded, because women are perceived to be possessed of a singular power, most vital during menstruation, puberty, and pregnancy, that weakens men's powers—physical, spiritual, or magical. The Crow and many other American Indians do not perceive signs of womanness as contamination; rather they view them as so powerful that other "medicines" may be canceled by the very presence of that power.

The Oglala Holy Man John (Fire) Lame Deer has commented that the Oglalas do not view menstruation, which they call isnati ("dwelling alone"), as "something unclean or to be ashamed of." Rather it was something sacred; a girl's first period was greeted by celebration. "But," he continues, "we thought that menstruation had a strange power that could bring harm under some circumstances. This power could work in some cases against the girl, in other cases against somebody else."[11]

Lois Paul has found similar attitudes in the context of a peasant culture. In her essay "Work and Sex in a Guatemalan Village," she discusses the power that menstruation, pregnancy, and menarche are believed to possess. She notes the belief of the peasant Pedranos in Guatemala that menstruating women can seriously impair a man's health or even kill him by stepping over him or putting menstrual blood in his food.[12]

Power among tribal people is not perceived as political or economic, though status and material possessions can and often do derive from it. Power is conceived of as being supernatural and paranormal. It is a matter of spirit involvement and destiny. Woman's power comes automatically, by virtue of her femaleness, her natural and necessary fecundity, and her personal acquaintance with blood. The Arapaho felt that dying in war and dying in childbirth were of the same level of spiritual accomplishment. In fact, there are suggestions in the literature on ritualism and tribal ceremony that warriors and male initiates into medicine societies gain their supernatural powers by imitating ritually the processes that women undergo naturally.

The power of women can be controlled and directed only by other women who possess power that is equal in magnitude but that is focused and under their control. A woman who is older is more cognizant of what that power entails, the kinds of destruction it can cause, and the ways in which it can be directed and used for good. Thus pubescent women are placed under the care of older women and are trained in manners and customs of modesty so that their powers will not result in harm to themselves or the larger community. Usually, a woman who has borne a child becomes an initiate into the mysteries of womanhood, and if she develops virtues and abilities beyond those automatically conferred on her by nature, she becomes a medicine woman. Often, the medicine woman knows of her destiny in early childhood; such children are watched very carefully so that they will be able to develop in the way ordained for them by the Spirits. Often these children are identified by excessive "sickliness," which leads them to be more reflective than other children and which often necessitates the added vigilance of adults around them.

Eventually, these people will enter into their true profession. How and when they do so will vary from tribe to tribe, but they will probably be well into their maturity before they will be able to practice. The Spirit or Spirits who teach and guide them in their medicine work will not appear for them until they have stabilized. Their health will usually improve, and their hormone-enzyme fluctuations will be regularized. Very often this stabilization will occur in the process of childbearing and nursing; this is one reason why women usually are not fully accepted as part of the woman's community until after the birth of a first child. Maternity was a concept that went far beyond the simple biological sense of the word. It was the prepotent power, the basic right to control and distribute goods, because it was the primary means of producing them. And it was the perfect sign of right spirit-human relationship. Among some modern American Indians this principle is still accepted. The Keres, for example, still recognize the Deity as female, and She is known as Thought Woman, for it is understood that the primary creative force is Thought.

LESBIANS AND TRIBAL LIFE

Simple reason dictates that lesbians did exist widely in tribal cultures, for they exist now. Because they were tribal people, the terms on which they existed must have been suited to the terms of tribal existence. The concepts of tribal cultures and of modern, western cultures are so dissimilar as to make ludicrous attempts to relate the long-ago women who dealt exclusively with women on sexual-emotional and spiritual bases to modern women who have in common an erotic attraction for other women.

This is not to make light of the modern lesbian but rather to convey some sense of the enormity of the cultural gulf that we must come to terms with when examining any phenomenon related to the American Indian. The modern lesbian sees herself as distinct from "society." She may be prone to believe herself somehow out of sync with "normal" women and often suffers great anguish at perceived differences. And while many modern lesbians have come to see themselves as singular but not sick, many of us are not that secure in our self-assessment. Certainly, however we come to terms with our sexuality, we are not in the position of our American Indian foresister who could find safety and security in her bond with another woman because it was perceived to be destined and nurtured by nonhuman entities, as were all Indian pursuits, and was therefore acceptable and respectable (albeit occasionally terrifying) to others in her tribe.

Spheres of influence and activity in American Indian cultures were largely divided between the sexes: there were women—goddesses, spirit-women, mothers, sisters, grandmothers, aunties, shamans, healers, prophets, and daughters; and there were men—gods, fathers, uncles, shamans, healers, diviners, brothers, and sons. What went on in one group was often unknown to the other.

There were points of confluence, of course, such as in matters pertaining to mundane survival. Family-band-clan groups interacted in living arrangements, in the procural or production of food, weaponry, clothing, and living space, and in political function. Men and women came together at certain times to perform social and ceremonial rituals or to undertake massive tasks such as hunts, harvests, or wars. They performed certain reciprocal tasks for one another. But in terms of any real sense of community, there were women and there were men.

Yet women who shared their lives with women did follow the usual custom of marrying. The duration of marriage and the bonding style of marriage differed among tribes. Many peoples practiced serial monogamy; others acknowledged the marriage bond but engaged in sexual activities outside of it. Women's adultery was not viewed with any particular alarm in most tribes, although some tribes did severely punish a woman who "transgressed" the marriage bonds, at least after they had some contact with Christian religious concepts.

But overall women spent a great deal of time together, outside the company of men. They had a whole array of women's rituals, only some of which were related to menstruation or childbearing. Together they spent weeks in menstrual huts; together women tilled their fields, harvested wild foods and herbs, ground grains, prepared skins, smoked or dried foodstuffs, and just visited. Women spent long periods together in their homes and lodges while the men stayed in men's houses or in the woods or were out on hunting or fishing expeditions. Young women were often separated from the larger groups for periods of months or years, as were young men. In such circumstances, lesbianism and homosexuality were probably commonplace. Indeed, same-sex relationships may have been the norm for primary pair-bonding. Families did not consist of nuclear units in any sense. There were clans and bands or villages, but the primary personal unit tended to include members of one's own sex rather than members of the opposite sex. It is questionable whether these practices would be identified as Lesbian by the politically radical lesbian community of today; for while sex between women probably occurred regularly, women also regularly married and raised children, often adopting children if they did not have any.

We should not see relationships among Indian women as being motivated primarily by opportunity. Lesbianism must be viewed in the context of the spiritual orientation of tribal life. It may be possible to distinguish between those women who took advantage of the abundant opportunities to form erotic bonds with other women and those women whose relationships with women were as much a matter of Spirit-direction as of personal preference (though the two were one in some senses).

It might be that some American Indian women could be seen as "dykes," while some could be seen as "lesbians," if one thinks of "dyke" as one who bonds with women to further some Spirit and supernatural directive and "lesbian" as a woman who is emotionally and physically intimate with other women. (The two groups would not have been mutually exclusive.)

The dyke (we might also call her a "ceremonial lesbian") was likely to have been a medicine woman in a special sense. She probably was a participant in the Spirit (intelligence, force field) of an Entity or Deity who was particularly close to earth during the Goddess period (though that Deity is still present in the lives of some American Indian women who practice Her ceremonies and participate actively and knowingly in Her reality). Signs of this Deity remain scattered all over the continent: Snake Mound in Ohio is probably one. La Virgin de Guadalupe is another. There are all sorts of petroglyphs, edifices, and stories concerning some aspect of Her, and Her signs are preserved in much of the lore and literature of many tribes.

Essentially a woman's spiritual way is dependent on the kind of power she possesses, the kind of Spirit to whom she is attached, and the tribe to which she belongs. She is required to follow the lead of Spirits and to carry out the tasks they assign her. For a description of one such rite, Fr. Bernard Haile's translation and notes on the Navajo Beautyway/Night chant is instructive. Such stories abound in the lore and literature of the American Indian people.[13] They all point to a serious event that results in the death of the protagonist, her visit to the Spirit realms from which she finally returns, transformed and powerful. After such events, she no longer belongs to her tribe or family, but to the Spirit teacher who instructed her. This makes her seem "strange" to many of her folk, and, indeed, she may be accused of witchcraft, though that is more likely to be charged at present than it was in the past. A dyke's initiation takes the same course as a male's: she is required to pass grueling physical tests, to lose her mundane persona, and to transform her soul and mind into other forms. (I might note here that among American Indians men are often accused of the same thing. Tales of evil sorcerers abound; in fact, in my reading, they seriously outnumber the tales about sorceresses.)

The Lakota have a word for some of these women, *koskalaka,* which is translated as "young man" or "woman who doesn't want to marry," in our terms, "dyke." These women are said to be the daughters (the followers/practitioners) of a Spirit/Divinity who links two women together making them one in Her power. They do a dance in which a rope is twined between them and coiled to form a "rope baby." The exact purpose or result of this dance is not mentioned, but its significance is clear. In a culture that values children and women because they bear them, two women who don't want to marry (a man) become united by the power of the Deity and their union is validated by the creation of a rope baby. That is, the rope baby signifies the potency of their union in terms that are comprehensible to their society, which therefore legitimizes it.

It is clear that the koskalaka are perceived as powerful, as are their presumed male counterparts, the *winkte.* But their power does not constitute the right "to determine [their] own and others' actions."[14] Rather, it consists of the ability to manipulate physical and nonphysical reality toward certain ends. When this power is used to determine others' actions, it at least borders on black magic or sorcery.

To clarify the nature of the power I am talking about, we can consider what Lame Deer says about the *winkte.* Lame Deer is inclined to speak rather directly and tends not to romanticize either the concept of power as it is understood and practiced by his people or the *winkte* as a person who has certain abilities that make him special.

He says that a *winkte* is a person who is a half-man and half-woman, perhaps even a hermaphrodite with both male and female organs. In the old days, *winktes* dressed like women and lived as women. Lame Deer admits that though the Lakotas thought people are what nature, or dreams, make them, still men weren't happy to see their sons running around with *winktes.* Still, he says that there are good men among the *winktes* and that they have special powers. He took Richard Erdoes (who was transcribing his conversation for their book *Lame Deer: Seeker of Visions*) with him to a bar to interview a *winkte.* He asked the man to tell him all about *winktes,* and the *winkte* told Lame Deer that "a *winkte* has a gift of prophecy and that he himself could predict the weather." The

Lakota go to a *winkte* for a secret name, and such names carry great power, though they are often off-color. "You don't let a stranger know [the secret name]," the *winkte* told them. "He would kid you about it."[15] A *winkte*'s power to name often wins the *winkte* great fame and usually a fine gift as well.

The power referred to here is magical, mysterious, and sacred. That does not mean that its possessors are to be regarded as a priestly pious people, for this is hardly the case. But it does mean that those who possess "medicine power," women and men, are to be treated with a certain cautious respect.

It is interesting to note that the story—one of the few reliable accounts of persons whose sexual orientation differs from the heterosexual—concerns a male, a *winkte*. The stories about *koskalaka* are yet to be told. It seems to me that this suppression is a result of a series of coincidental factors: the historical events connected with the conquest of Native America; the influence of Christianity and the attendant brutal suppression of medicine people and medicine practices; the patriarchal suppression of all references to power held by women; Christian notions of proper sexual behavior; and, recently, an attempt on the part of a number of American Indian men to suppress knowledge among their own people (and among Europeans and Americans) of the traditional place of woman as powerful medicine people and leaders in their own right, accompanied by a dismissal of women as central to tribal ritual life.[16]

Under the reign of the patriarchy, the medicine-dyke has become anathema; her presence has been hidden under the power-destroying blanket of complete silence. We must not allow this silence to prevent us from discovering and reclaiming who we have been and who we are. We must not forget the true Source of our being, nor her powerfulness, and we must not allow ourselves to be deluded by patriarchal perceptions of power that rob us of our true power, regardless of how many feathers those perceptions are cloaked in. As Indian women, as lesbians, we must make the effort to understand clearly what is at stake, and this means that we must reject all beliefs that work against ourselves, however much we have come to cherish them as we have lived among the patriarchs.

Womanculture is unregulated by males and is misperceived by ethnographers. Perhaps this is so because it is felt—at least among ethnographers' tribal informants—that it is wise to let "sleeping dogs lie." There may also be fear of what power might be unleashed if the facts about American Indian lesbianism were discussed directly. A story that has recently come to my attention might best clarify this statement.

Two white lesbians, feminists and social activists, were determined to expand their activities beyond the lesbian and feminist communities and to this end became involved in an ecological movement that centered on American Indian concerns. In pursuit of this course, they invited a Sioux medicine man to join them and arranged to pick him up from the small rural town he was visiting. When he saw them, he accused them of being lesbians and became very angry. He abused them verbally, in serious and obscene terms. They left him where he was and returned home, angry and confused.

A certain amount of their confusion was a result of their misperception of Indians and of this particular medicine man. I have friends in the primarily white lesbian community who seem to think that Indian men, particularly medicine men, are a breed apart who are "naturally just." Like other Americans, Indians are inclined to act in ways that are consistent with their picture of the world, and, in this particular Indian's picture, the world was not big enough for lesbians. The women didn't announce their sexual preference to him, by the way; but he knew a *koskalaka* when he saw one and reacted accordingly.

A friend who knew the women involved asked me about this encounter. She couldn't understand why the medicine man acted the way he had. I suspect that he was afraid of the lesbian's power, and I told her that. Another American Indian woman to whom I recounted the story had the same reaction. *Koskalaka* have singular power, and this medicine man was undoubtedly aware of it. The power of the *koskalaka* can (potentially, at least) override that of men, even very powerful medicine men such as the one in my story. I know this particular man, and he is quite powerful as a medicine man.

Not so long ago, the American Indians were clearly aware of the power that women possessed. Even now there are those among traditionals who know the medicine power of women. This is why a clear understanding of the supernatural forces and their potential in our lives is necessary. More than an interesting tour through primitive exotica is to be gained.

Before we worry about collecting more material from aborigines, before we join forces with those who are in a position to destroy us, and before we decide, like Sherry Ortner, that belief in ancient matriarchal civilization is an irrational concept born of conjecture and wish, let us adjust our perspective to match that of our foresisters. Then, when we search the memories and lore of tribal peoples, we might be able to see what eons and all kinds of institutions have conspired to hide from our eyes.

The evidence is all around us. It remains for us to *dis*cover what it means.

NOTES

1 I have read accounts that mention American Indian lesbians taken from a variety of sources, but those are all in publications that focus on gays and/or lesbians rather than on Native Americans.

2 Frederick Manfred, *The Manly-Hearted Woman* (New York: Bantam, 1978).

3 Natalie Curtis, *The Indians' Book* (New York: Dover, 1950), p. 4.

4 Bronislaw Malinowski, *Sex, Culture, and Myth* (New York: Harcourt, Brace & World, 1962), p. 12.

5 Malinowski, *Sex, Culture, and Myth,* p. 12.

6 Malinowski, *Sex, Culture, and Myth,* p. 12.

7 Malinowski, *Sex, Culture, and Myth,* p. 13.

8 Malinowski, *Sex, Culture, and Myth,* p. 13.

9 Malinowski, *Sex, Culture, and Myth,* p. 13.

10 Sherry B. Ortner, "Is Female to Male as Nature Is to Culture?" in *Woman, Culture and Society,* ed. Michelle Zimbalist Rosaldo and Louise Lamphere (Stanford: Stanford University Press, 1974), p. 70.

11 John (Fire) Lame Deer and Richard Erdoes, *Lame Deer, Seeker of Visions: The Life of a Sioux Medicine Man* (New York: Simon and Schuster, 1972), pp. 148–149.

12 Lois Paul, "Work and Sex in a Guatemalan Village," in Rosaldo and Lamphere, *Woman, Culture and Society,* pp. 293–298. Paul's article discusses these concepts in the frame-

work of a peasant culture, that is, one that exists in a pastoral, agriculture-centered environment and whose social structure is based on perceived relationship to the land. This type of culture occupies a niche that might be thought of as halfway between industrial urban society and tribal, ritual society.

13 See John Bierhorst, ed., *Four Masterworks of American Indian Literature: Quetzalcoatl/The Ritual of Concolence/Cuceb/The Night Chant* (New York: Farrar, Straus and Giroux, 1974). Fr. Bernard Haile's work is included in Leland C. Wyman, ed., *Beautyway: A Navajo Ceremonial,* Bollingen Series, 53 (New York: Pantheon, 1975).

14 As it is accurately put by Jane Fishburne Collier in "Women in Politics," in Rosaldo and Lamphere, *Woman, Culture and Society,* p. 90.

15 Lame Deer, *Lame Deer, Seeker of Visions,* p. 150.

16 Joan Bamburger, "The Myths of Matriarchy: Why Men Rule in Primitive Society," in Rosaldo and Lamphere, *Woman, Culture and Society,* pp. 260–271.

Reclaiming the Past and Constructing a Collective Culture

William Wei

RECLAIMING THE PAST

While refuting racial stereotypes has been a necessary part of forming an Asian American identity, so also has been learning what is accurate. An informed understanding has been even more important for Asian Americans themselves than for other people, since it has influenced their self-concepts and their children's. After all, what one was heavily influences what one is and will be. Historically voiceless, Asian Americans have needed to reclaim their history, find significance in it, and make it known to others. Through a more accurate understanding of their history, they hoped to find a voice, one that embodied a more meaningful and complex identity.

Community scholars and artists have been preserving Asian American heritage through local studies, documentaries, songs, posters, murals, plays, dances, historical societies, archival resources, ethnic museums, and other community-based projects. They brought to their task invaluable assets: scholars, their network of local informants and access to local records, resources that have taken a lifetime to develop; artists, an expressive media to illuminate and validate alternative representations of the Asian American experience. Both have been motivated by the belief that when people interact with information about their past, they can better interpret and understand the present and gain a feel for the future. The process affirms their individual and group identity, countering the sense of "otherness" that has marked the Asian American community; and, most significantly, it empowers them, freeing them from the dominant society's definition of who they are or should be. These scholars and artists see themselves as a vital link between the past and the future, their work a permanent memorial to earlier generations and a stable foundation for later ones.

Community scholars and artists have consciously involved local residents in documenting and interpreting their own history, an activity that engenders empathy and respect for others. They write social history from the bottom up, giving voice to the silent and educating the Asian American community about itself and answering explicitly the question of whose history scholars are reconstructing. Such efforts reflects the Movement's democratic thrust. A central activity has been to record, before they die, the recollections of the *lo wah kue* (a Cantonese expression for old overseas Chinese) of America's Chinatowns; the *issei* (first-generation Japanese Americans) who leased farmland in California and elsewhere in the American West; the *manong* (a Filipino term meaning "elder brother" that refers to all first-generation immigrants) who worked up and down the West Coast; and other early immigrants. It is a difficult task, since most of the elders are dead and those who are still alive are reticent about telling their story, which they consider private as well as insignificant. Community scholars and artists perceive such recordings to be an important task because these life stories constitute the building blocks of Asian American history and culture. Future listeners will learn about their roots and derive strength from that knowledge.

Community scholars are publishing their own studies, usually highly descriptive, in an effort to reconstruct the past, often for no reason other than its intrinsic value to the community. They focus their attention on specific Asian ethnic groups and research subjects that are integral to these communities: for Chinese Americans, the legacy of exclusion; for Japanese Americans, the trauma of the concentration camps; for Filipino Americans, the penurious and painful lives of Filipino migrant workers; for Korean Americans, their contribution to Korea's independence movement against Japan. These works often explore the human costs of racism in America. They demythologize the United States as *the* land of opportunity that welcomed the wretched of the earth to its shores and recapture the emotional aspects of the Asian American experience, which are often overlooked or treated abstractly in academic tomes.

Island: Poetry and History of Chinese Immigrants on Angel Island, 1910–40 is an example par excellence of community scholarship.[1] In the late 1970s, Him Mark Lai, a Bechtel Corporation engineer; Genny Lim, a housewife and nascent poet; and Judy Yung, a librarian in the Asian branch of the Oakland Public Library, felt that the story of the Chinese who passed through Angel Island, the harsh Ellis Island of the West, needed to be told. From 1882 to 1943, most Chinese were excluded from entering the country. The few who could enter had first to submit to intense questioning and scrutiny on Angel Island, where all aspiring immigrants were detained upon arrival. The core of *Island* is the poems that Chinese immigrants wrote and carved on the walls of their barrack prisons. . . . They are of significant literary value and constitute the beginnings of Asian American culture. Augmenting the translations are interviews with Chinese who had undergone the harsh treatment, and with immigration officials and social workers who once worked there. *Island* inspired a number of other artistic works: Felicia Lowe's docudrama, *Carved in Silence;* Genny Lim's play, *Paper Angels;* Loni Ding's film, *Island of Secret Memories;* and Betty Wong's musical narrative, "Bright Moon Rising," which was produced for Festival 2,000 in San Francisco.

Like the scholars, community artists have also been reconstructing a past that many Asian Americans have been silent about, preferring to repress the painful memories that they have lived with all their lives. For Japanese Americans, one of those memories is the internment camps of World War II. Loni Ding's film, *The Color of Honor: The Japanese American Soldier in WWII,* offers one of the most comprehensive looks at the internment. Inspired to make this feature-length documentary by the San Francisco hearings on redress for former internees, she felt that it was "extremely important to deal with the contradictions of battle and liberating towns when your family is locked up at home."[2]

In the film, Ding "recovers the voices of those who wrestled with the wrenching contradiction of being incarcerated by their own government, yet called to serve in its military."[3] What makes the work so significant for the Japanese American community, as well as others, is how she deals with the issue of honor. In addition to the men who served in the 442nd Regimental Combat Team, which became the most decorated unit in U.S. military history, and those who served in the Pacific Theater as members of the little-known Military Intelligence Service, which contributed decisively to the defeat of Japan, she discusses the thousands of draft resisters and army protesters who were willing to go to federal prisons in order to challenge the constitutionality of the concentration camps. As members of the Fair Play Committee at the Heart Mountain Relocation Center, they refused to serve in the military as long as their families remained imprisoned, becoming the largest group of Americans ever to resist the draft until the Vietnam War. As her film makes clear, this choice was as courageous and honorable as serving in the armed forces. For those who took this different path and have had to endure stigma and self-doubt ever since, the film is a vindication of their courageous choice.

Recovering the history of forgotten victims and unsung heroes is important work to be sure, but it can also be depressing. An exception to the focus on how Asian Americans have been victimized is Arthur Dong's *Forbidden City, USA,* a documentary about an internationally acclaimed Chinese nightclub in San Francisco. The film successfully preserves a piece of Asian American cultural history, but it does so in an entertaining way.[4] Dong was interested in portraying Asian Americans having fun. In this Asian American counterpart to the Cotton Club, Chinese American talent performed in all-American production numbers. These entertainers were rebels, for they had to face the Chinese community's opprobrium for dancing and singing in public, and at the same time challenge segregated show business, with its stereotype of Chinese as speaking only pidgin English, having bowed legs and no rhythm. Forbidden City was a unique club that "exploited and exploded stereotypes": It exploited them by promoting itself as an "exotic" form of entertainment and exploded them by providing a venue for Asian Americans who sang like Frank Sinatra and Sophie Tucker and danced like Fred Astaire and Ginger Rogers.

In his column in *Asian Week,* William Wong raised a query about these Chinese American performers that is germane to the development of Asian American culture in general: Were the Forbidden City performers "true to their ethnicities—somehow reflecting their root cultures, or were they " 'selling out' their cultural backgrounds simply for employment"?[5] It is a controversial question, one with which Asian American cultural activists have been grappling. The plight of Asian American actors, who must choose between playing roles they find objectionable or be unemployed, has even been the subject of a play: In *Yankee Dawg You Die,* Philip Kan Gotanda explores what it means to be an Asian American actor through the interaction between an older actor who has been forced to accept demeaning roles—"Ching Chong Chinamen houseboy, the stereotypical evil Japanese World War II general, the Fu Manchu villain from outer space"—in order to make a living, and a younger actor who will accept only "roles he thinks are correct, are dignified."[6] In the course of the play, both men peer into each other's personal and professional souls, becoming more understanding and tolerant in the process. Gotanda hopes that the play's audience will no longer look at an Asian American and see a stereotype; instead, he would like them to see the Asian American as "a complex human being who is also unique because he or she is an Asian-American in this country."[7]

In addition to local studies and creative works, community scholars and artists have helped found various community-based organizations dedicated to the preservation of the Asian American past. Three examples are the New York Chinatown History Project in New York City, the Japanese American National Museum in Los Angeles, and the Filipino American National Historical Society in Seattle, each on a "cultural rescue mission" to challenge the dominant society's implicit contention that Asian Americans led insignificant lives.[8]

The New York Chinatown History Project (NYCHP) is the only major Chinese American historical research group on the East Coast.[9] Officially incorporated in 1980, it actually traces its beginnings to the Basement Workshop, where its co-founders, Charlie Lai and John Kuo Wei Tchen, former student activists, had met four years earlier.[10] Like other people at the Basement, for a time *the* Asian American cultural organization on the East Coast, they wanted to contribute to the community in some significant way. But how? They had become skeptical about the efficacy of existing community activism and "constantly asked each other . . . Who are we organizing? . . . What makes us think that something *we* want is right for the community?"[11] Since much of the radical politics in the community at the time had degenerated into sophomoric sectarianism, they had to turn elsewhere. The Chinatown History Project proved to be the alternative that they were looking for.

In 1978, Tchen, who was serving as coordinator of Basement's Asian American Resource Center, applied for and received a grant from the New York Council for the Humanities to mount a major multimedia exhibition on Chinese in America called "Images from a Neglected Past: The Work and Culture of Chinese in America," which opened at the Chatham Square branch of the New York Public Library. According to Lai and Tchen, "the response was tremendous. Seniors would hike up those three steep flights to look at the exhibit. And many would begin to tell us their life stories. . . . It became very obvious that: one, there wasn't much publicly available material on the history of Chinatown; two, residents were deeply interested in the community's past; and three, those who have lived in the community are the real experts on the experience."[12] Inspired by this response, they decided "to establish an organization devoted to synthesizing the role of history with community-building"—the New York Chinatown History Project, which became, in effect, a vehicle for presenting a dissenting view of American society, that of the oppressed Chinese in America.[13]

Tchen and Lai decided that one of the things that the Chinatown community needed was a place—a physical and intellectual space—where people could come to raise and answer questions about themselves and the Chinatown community. They had a populist perspective, emphasizing the daily life of ordinary Chinese (as opposed to the elite), for they were convinced that working people had something significant to say. They assumed that the masses who lived and worked in Chinatown led "dynamic" rather than "passive" lives. They further believed that

> not only do all of us naturally look back to our personal past when we get older—something beautifully expressed in the traditional Chinese saying "falling leaves return to their roots"—but from a practical standpoint, we cannot improve the present unless we understand the past. Understanding the community's history, then, is not a luxury that should be left to the few who have the time and inclination, it is a necessity for all who wish to move positively into building a decent future.[14]

NYCHP is probably best known for its excellent exhibits on various aspects of community life, especially those less studied and understood, such as the lives of laundry and garment workers. In their own elliptical way, these exhibits have constituted an indictment of racial *and* class oppression. In December 1984, NYCHP opened its first exhibit, "Eight Pound Livelihood: History of Chinese Laundry Workers in the U.S.," which, as the title indicates, was about people who labored long hours in Chinese hand laundries. Mounting such an exhibit was difficult because many members of the community, including laundry workers themselves, would just as soon forget that racial barriers had forced them to enter such a low-esteem occupation and spend their lives doing such arduous work. . . . The ubiquitous laundries provided the major occupation of immigrants and thus played an important part in the social history of Chinese Americans. (The same could be said for the contemporary garment industry, which employs thousands of immigrant Chinese women and is the subject of NYCHP's "Both Sides of the Cloth: Chinese American Women in the New York City Garment Industry.") Over a dozen such exhibits, including ones on other Asian Americans, have "actively made public the validation of these experiences to the lifeblood of the community's history."[15]

Since its establishment in 1980, the NYCHP has developed an enviable reputation in the local community as a place where "personal possessions and stories can be transformed into a part of the collective memory."[16] In attempting to explore the complexity of the New York Chinese experience, the project has very deliberately placed it in the cultural pluralist context of the city. As Tchen pointed out:

> We've taken a strong cultural geographic approach of looking at how a space has had a succession of groups, often at the same time, making the streetscape a variety of homes for different cultures. We've deliberately resisted a straight cultural nationalist history and favored looking at history from a perspective of hierarchical segments and constructed experiences. Hence, the Chinese in New York are acknowledged to have multiple cultural influences and identities both within the Chinese experience (e.g. a Chinese cigar maker from Cuba, or a Chinese from Toishan who stayed in S.F. for years and then migrated to New York) and also cross-culturally (e.g. lots of early Chinese New York men, many of whom were sailors, married Irish women).[17]

In 1991, Fay Chew, the executive director, and the board of directors decided to broaden the scope of NYCHP and changed its name to the Chinatown History Museum (CHM).[18] It will be devoted to the Chinese diaspora in the Americas, extending its interest beyond the New York metropolitan area to include Chinese settlements throughout the Western hemisphere. In addition to its greater geographic scope, CHM will also be a "dialogue-driven" rather than a "collections-driven" facility, emphasizing collaboration with the intended audience and reflecting its needs, instead of basing its activities on what material is available in the collection, as is the case with many traditional museums. This concept came out of the project's effort to reflect on and improve its first ten years of work. With the change from NYCHP to CHM, it is becoming a permanent part of the community that it cares so much about.

At the same time that the Chinatown History Project was being established, on the other side of the country there was a concerted movement to found a relatively traditional museum dedicated to documenting and preserving the Japanese American experience.[19] That the impetus for this effort came from the *nisei* rather than the *sansei* probably explains, in part, its conservative character. In 1980, Bruce T. Kanji, president of the Merit Savings Bank, and other leaders in the *nikkei* (Japanese American) community "raised funds to commission a feasibility study for a 'National Museum of Japanese American History.' " Meanwhile, *nisei* veterans who had been responsible for bringing an exhibit on the Japanese American soldier in World War II to the Los Angeles Natural History Museum set up the 100th/442nd/MIS Museum Foundation to build a "Japanese American Heritage Museum." Since both groups shared similar goals, they decided to merge in 1985 as the "Japanese American National Museum" (JANM).

JANM had an auspicious beginning, receiving important assistance from various public agencies: Senator Art Torres introduced a California Senate bill that resulted in a state contribution of $750,000, the Community Redevelopment Agency provided a matching grant of $1 million, and the City of Los Angeles leased the historic Nishi Hongwanji Buddhist Temple in Little Tokyo to the museum for the sum of $1 a year. The temple was an ideal choice for the museum's permanent site. Besides providing 33,000 square feet of space, it has immeasurable symbolic value. Built in 1925, it is the oldest existing Buddhist temple in the city and an integral part of the Japanese American community. During World War II, it was used as a household storage facility for interned Japanese Americans; after the war, it served as a temporary hostel for many who returned from the concentration camps.

During the 1980s, when most community-based organizations were scrambling to survive, JANM's ability to acquire such significant support was remarkable, suggesting that the Los Angeles *nikkei* community has come a long way politically. The prospect of JANM enhancing Little Tokyo's attraction as a tourist spot probably played a role as well. But to become a reality, the museum needed much more money. For that, it had to depend on the resources of the *nikkei* community itself. Under the leadership of Irene Y. Hirano, the former director of T.H.E. Clinic for Women, JANM launched a sophisticated capital campaign to raise $24.1 million. Assisting in this endeavor were a succession of national campaign steering committees whose membership reads like a Who's Who of the Japanese American community and included Japanese executives such as Akio Morita, chairman of the Sony Corporation. During the first phase of the campaign, JAMN raised $10.2 million to renovate the temple, establish an initial exhibit area, and provide operating funds; during the second, it will try to raise $13.9 million to construct a pavilion that will add 65,000 square feet to the museum, placing it in the "world class" among historical and cultural museums; to expand exhibitions and public programs; and to establish a $5 million endowment to pay for general expenses.

Another national effort to preserve Asian American heritage is the Filipino American National Historical Society, a spin-off of the Seattle Demonstration Project for Asian Americans (DPAA), a community-based research/advocacy organization.[20] During the 1980s, DPAA focused on the history of Filipino and Korean Americans, two groups that had been overshadowed by the more numerous Chinese and Japanese Americans. It began the "Forgotten Asian Americans" project, a national oral history project supported by a $125,000 grant from the Division of Special Programs of the National Endowment for the Humanities. The DPAA is known nationally for its photographic exhibits of Filipino and Korean Americans and its publication *Filipinos: Forgotten Asian Americans,* by Fred Cordova. The latter is a pictorial essay that traces the history of Filipino Americans from 1763 to 1963 through rare photographs and oral histories.

When its application for a third year of funding for the DPAA was rejected, ostensibly because the project was too ambitious, the participants in DPAA decided to carry on without public assistance and finish transcribing the one hundred interviews they had conducted with Filipinos and Koreans. Meanwhile, the Filipino American participants wanted to continue building the new network of intellectuals they had developed, to return the results of their research to the community, and to record the history of Filipino Americans. In 1982, Dorothy L. Cordova,[21] a long-time community activist, conceived the idea of a national historical society to carry on the work of the project; hence the founding of the Filipino American National Historical Society (FANHS) three years later.

FANHS's mission is "to promote understanding, education, enlightenment, appreciation, and enrichment through the identification, gathering, preservation and dissemination of the history and culture of Filipino Americans."[22] It accomplishes this through a national office that serves as an information clearinghouse and depository of materials on Filipino Americans and provides various public services. Through its annual conferences, FAHNS has also nurtured future scholars for the field of Filipino American Studies by providing workshops and panels on how to do research. In 1987, FANHS focused its first meeting in Seattle on the theme "Who/What is a Filipino American." As Fred Cordova has observed, for Filipino Americans there is always an identity crisis.[23] Within the Movement, they feel like stepchildren and are ambivalent about identifying with other Asian Americans, who until recently were predominantly Chinese and Japanese Americans. As a "brown" people, they would have felt out of place at the Berkeley "Yellow Identity" conference; indeed, some Filipino Americans feel that they have more in common with Chicanos, with whom they share a Hispanic heritage and Catholic religion. Rather than continue to be "a minority within a minority,"[24] some of them feel that they should be an independent group, especially since their portion of the population is growing rapidly.

In 1988, to celebrate the 225th anniversary of Filipino settlement on the American continent, FANHS held its meeting in New Orleans, the locale of that settlement. Most people assume that Filipinos began arriving in the United States in the early twentieth century as agricultural laborers or later as professionals; in fact, as Marina Estrella

Espina has shown, as early as 1763 there were Filipinos (the so-called Manilamen) living in southeastern Louisiana.[25] They were the earliest Asians to cross the Pacific in the Spanish galleons that plied between Manila and Acapulco and the first to settle in what is now the continental United States.

In retrospect, it seems odd that NYCHP, JANM, and FANHS should have emerged during the 1980s, a difficult decade that saw decreasing federal support for nonprofit, community-based organizations. Within the context of the Asian American Movement and community, however, the 1980s was the right time. Since its inception, the Movement had instilled ethnic pride in individual Asian Americans and raised the ethnic consciousness of the entire community. A natural outcome was the conviction that the Asian American past was worth preserving for posterity. After twenty years of searching for their individual and collective identities, Asian Americans finally took steps to preserve and exhibit their recently recorded history.

CONSTRUCTING A COLLECTIVE CULTURE

Whereas Asian American activists have had little difficulty in accepting the need to refute stereotypes and reclaim history because challenging distorted images cleared away some of the psychological impediments to the development of an authentic Asian American identity, and recovering their history laid the foundation for a more authentic sense of themselves, they also realized the need to create an Asian American culture to give form and substance to that identity. But doing so has proven to be controversial, for within the Movement there have been two competing though interrelated approaches to Asian American culture: political and aesthetic.

During the early years of the Movement, the political approach to cultural development predominated, and it continues to have a strong following among activists. It was heavily influenced by Mao Tse-tung's "Talks at the Yenan Forum on Literature and Art" (May 1942), which defined the theoretical basis for artistic production in the People's Republic of China. Mao said in essence that art must meet first a political requirement and only secondarily aesthetic criteria. In the milieu of the late 1960s and early 1970s, the political approach had considerable appeal to newly politicized Asian American activists, many of whom thought that the long-awaited social revolution was imminent and wanted to be at the front of the anticipated changes rather than lag behind them. Any qualms they had about combining politics and culture were pushed aside by the urgent issues of the period—the vicious war in Vietnam and the malignant social conditions in Asian American communities.

The political approach emphasized the Asian American artist's moral responsibility to the community and the social purpose of an artist's work. For some cultural activists, this meant that Asian American writers (as well as other artists) should serve as "cultural ambassadors" and bear the burden of speaking for their people. Consequently, "their fictional characters must be shining role models. . . . And because the history of Asian Americans has gone largely untold for decades, some feel that Asian American writers have the artistic duty to shatter stereotypes and honor the historical record with religious fervor."[26] For others, it meant supporting the unity of the Asian American Movement and its struggle for social change and addressing community concerns. The political approach has resulted in vital and unvarnished works protesting the victimization of Asian Americans and celebrating their resistance to oppression.

. . .

Aion, the first Asian American magazine, was one of the earliest expression of the political approach to art. It was born in 1968 during the San Francisco State strike, but its two issues were published in 1970. According to Janice Mirikitani, who was radicalized by the antiwar movement, *Aion* was an effort "to combine the political consciousness of the day and Asian American culture, the things that the young people were into at that time."[27] Its purpose was to move readers from complacency, the seedbed for "cultural destruction," to participation in the "international movement to end the exploitation of all Third World peoples and work to create our own revolutionary culture in this country."[28] It offered readers a potpourri of essays, photographs, poems, and other socially informed works. Perhaps the most polemical was a statement by Alex Hing, minister of information of the Red Guard party, titled "The Need for an United Asian American Front."

Less rhetorical but more effective was A Grain of Sand, one of the first cultural groups to reflect the social and political issues of the Asian American Movement. It consisted of Chris Kando Iijima, Nobuko Joanne Miyamoto, and "Charlie" Chin, Asian American troubadours influenced by the social-protest music of the period.[29] . . .

The trio sang at Movement events across the country, at protest demonstrations, on college campuses, and at activities in support of community-based organizations. They inspired other Asian American cultural groups, such as Yokohama, California, on the West Coast. . . . In 1973, the trio recorded *A Grain of Sand: Music for the Struggle by Asians in America,* the first Asian American album. The dominant themes of the twelve songs on the album were the antiwar movement and Asian American identity.[30] Like others who have taken the political approach to Asian American culture, they made the social message of their songs explicit. A statement accompanying the record explained their perspective on the relationship of politics to culture: "Recently there has been a tendency to separate culture from politics, that one can have a "cultural" presentation without being "political." We believe that distinction is false. . . . Asian American culture in America must . . . move toward revolutionary culture; otherwise it moves toward reactionary culture."[31]

Soon after *A Grain of Sand* was released, the group disbanded; but its members have continued to make music, individually and sometimes together. "Charlie" Chin continued Asian American folk culture through one-man shows such as "ABC" (American Born Chinese), with songs and monologues about being Chinese American. In 1982, he and Iijima recorded *Back to Back,* an album in the tradition of "talk story" and folk music "that was shared in farm labor camps, around campfires along the Transcontinental Railroad, and under the stars that were looked at and dreamed upon by Asian Pacific people whether in Mother Asia and the Pacific, or here in the good old U.S. of A."[32] Miyamoto is the only one of the three who has made the performing arts central to her life. In 1978, she founded Great Leap, Inc., a nonprofit, community-based organization committed to presenting the experiences of Asian Americans "with shows that blend dance, music and drama."[33] Great Leap's most ambitious project has been *Talk Story: A Musical Odyssey of Asians in America,* a multi-media musical featuring short scenes that depict the life of Asians in America, from the early immigrants to the fourth generation.

During the middle 1970s, Asian American artists began to move away from the political and toward the aesthetic approach, a trend reinforced by the 1980s' obsessive preoccupation with ego and materialism. When the antiwar movement ended in the United States with the victory of the North Vietnamese and the South Vietnamese's National Liberation Front in 1975, the major political focus for cooperative activity among Asian American activists disappeared as well. The sense of crisis that had gripped them began to dissipate, and political activism began to decline. Without the implicit political constraints imposed by the exigencies of the late 1960s and early 1970s, Asian American artists no longer felt compelled to produce art that supported the struggle against various governments. They were tired of producing so-called politically correct art, or "socialist realist" art, which sought to propagate certain ideas in order to mobilize the masses behind a specific cause. Besides, even artists attracted to the idea of combining politics and art found it difficult to achieve such a goal in practice. And without the stirring social issues of the late 1960s and early 1970s, political art was difficult to justify.

The aesthetic approach is consciously individualistic, emphasizing the development of personal style and technique. To use the Maoist expression, it is "art for art's sake," rather than for politics' sake. Although aesthetic Asian American artists share the same themes (identity, cultural conflict, alienation, etc.) as political ones, they are less concerned with the political content of their work than with whether it fulfills their artistic vision and standards. They are also often more interested in exploring the universal rather than the particularistic aspects of these concerns and seek to make them recognizable to as wide an audience as possible, including non-Asian Americans. In recent years, being able to "cross over" to a general audience is considered a mark of artistic maturity as well as a means toward commercial success. Even if their works are based on their experiences as Asian Americans, as is usually the case, these artists try to speak to broad human concerns.

Among Asian American artists, writers have received the most attention.[34] Frank Chin, father of modern Asian American literature, pioneered in the development of Asian American culture, paving the way for the aesthetic approach. As an "angry young man," he decried and defined the dominant society's oppression of Asian American artists (though he was speaking specifically about writers). From the beginning, he assumed a "defiant stance . . . toward white assimilation, imitation, and paternalistic white racist evaluations of Asian American writing."[35] . . .

Chin has called for and written works that reflect Asian American history—a history that is a "valiant, vital part of the history of the American West," but one that Asian Americans "under the stress of white racism, have forgotten or wish to forget in their eagerness to be assimilated into the majority culture."[36] He also advocates a culture that reflects an Asian American sensibility, one that is neither Asian nor white. . . . In his writings, Chin believes he has, through the use of a distinctive Chinatown argot, "captured the rhythms and accents of Chinese America without which its culture cannot be truly represented."[37] Whether or not he has done that, it is at least certain that he has circumvented conventional literary and stylistic modes of expression and created one that he can call his own.

Chin's contribution to Asian American culture is incalculable. His provocative plays have achieved a number of "firsts." *Chickencoop Chinaman* was the first Asian American drama to be produced by the "legitimate" theater, and *The Year of the Dragon* was the first to be shown on national television.[38] His exploration of Asian American identity in his writings and his outspoken opposition to the exclusion of Asian Americans from American culture have inspired others to try their hand at creating unfettered literary works. But while Chin has achieved acclaim in the Asian American community, he has never been able to attain mainstream popularity. Much to his chagrin, this accomplishment was reserved for an Asian American woman—Maxine Hong Kingston.

In the history of Asian American culture, the 1976 publication of Maxine Hong Kingston's *The Woman Warrior: A Memoir of a Girlhood among Ghosts* was a watershed event. A critically acclaimed work, it became "the most widely taught book by a living author in U.S. colleges and universities."[39] In this work, Kingston intertwines myths and legends from traditional China with autobiographical reminiscences to dramatize a girl's struggle (presumably her own) to resolve her identity crisis as a Chinese American, that is, to mediate the demands of both traditional Chinese culture, as interpreted by her parents, and contemporary American culture. But as her verbal tapestry unfolds, it is evident that her identity cannot be divided simply into Chinese and American halves, even for analytical purposes. As one critic put it, "her identity in the book is not separable from culture and family, but knotted with the stories she has inherited from them and which she transforms in the retelling to suit her own needs as a Chinese American."[40] Kingston has written an engrossing and elegant narrative, one that has earned her an enviable reputation as one of the country's most original and provocative writers. She has attained national recognition, and her works are considered great novels about an Asian ethnic experience in America's pluralist society.

Unfortunately, Frank Chin has been engaged in a diatribe against Maxine Hong Kingston. It reflects the larger rift between cultural activists who advocate an Asian American artistic sensibility and look to Asian America as a source of inspiration and those they brand as assimilationists, "mostly academic artists, certified, trained and socialized in the prevailing European-dominated aesthetic and sensibility."[41] The roots of the conflict lie in Chin's apparent obsession with countering the image of Asian American men as emasculated, a result of their willingness to assimilate into the majority culture: "The white stereotype of the acceptable Asian is utterly without manhood. Good or bad, the stereotypical Asian is nothing as a man. At worst, the Asian-American is contemptible because he is womanly, effeminate, devoid of all the traditionally masculine qualities of originality, daring, physical courage, and creativity."[42] Dedicated to restoring the lost manhood of Asian American men, Chin is adamantly opposed to anyone who aids and abets their cultural castration. For him, the chief culprit in this process has been Kingston, whose very success condemns her, since in his eyes, only a person guilty of collaborating with the "enemy" can be accepted by them. He accuses her of being an "assimilationist who caters to all the stereotypes," calling her writing "border town whore talk" and those who enjoy her work (a phrase that more or less covers most of the reading public) "ignorant or racist or both."[43]

Kingston has conceded that her work may have been misunderstood and has been concerned about the "patronizing tone coming from white book reviewers . . . [who] left the impression that *Woman Warrior* was a tour guide's inside look at a strange, exotic people."[44] Nonetheless, she believes that what Chin and others like him are *really* saying is that Asian American women should not be writing at all.[45] It is the same problem that African American women writers, such as Alice Walker, author of *The Color Purple,* have had to face from their male counterparts.

Chin and Kingston have paid one another the literary compliment of satirizing each other: in the "Afterword" of his anthology of eight short stories, *The Chinaman Pacific & Frisco R.R. Co.,* Chin parodies Kingston with "Unmanly Warrior," who turns out to be Joan of Arc as a six-foot-four, 225-pound male homosexual; in Kingston's novel *Tripmaster Monkey: His Fake Book* the protagonist, Wittman Ah Sing, a would-be writer living in Berkeley during the 1960s, is modeled on Chin.[46]

The tense relationship between them notwithstanding, both Chin and Kingston have inspired other Asian American writers, who have been creating works of increasingly high quality and receiving literary accolades for them.[47] These later works have for the most part taken the aesthetic approach, showing "artistic vision and sophistication—a break from the angry writers of the '60s who often toed the 'correct' political line."[48] At the same time, they have been, in their own inimitable fashion, challenging stereotypes and creating "imaginative worlds in which they—not white culture—shape the language and motifs."[49] As the poet Li-Young Lee noted: "We still have to create literature without pandering or making it seem exotic. We still have to create art."[50] What has allowed them to escape literary ghettoization has been their ability to employ their ethnic sensibility to describe aspects of the Asian American experience that appeal to a common humanity.

The underlying impetus for the Asian American Movement was the search for identity and the creation of a new culture. Unlike European Americans, who could incorporate their ethnic identity into their sense of being American, Asian Americans had to create an entirely new identity: the Asian American. They resolved their "identity crisis" by directly challenging the distorted images that have diminished them as individuals and degraded them as a group, replacing them with more accurate ones based on historical knowledge about themselves, and creating a pan-Asian counterculture that reflects their values and experiences. In so doing, they instilled pride and self-esteem in their generation. This process in turn awakened ethnic sensibilities and led to a sense of cultural freedom that gave birth to their own forms of expression, enriching the multicultural mosaic that is America. Among these have been notable literary works equal to any produced by members of the dominant society. Given their history of marginalization, some people wonder whether this acknowledgment of Asian American literature is an example of cultural affirmative action or simply an aberration. Only time will tell. Meanwhile, Asian Americans have contributed significantly to the broadening of American culture.

An accompanying consequence of these changes was that Asian American women became aware of a second layer of their identity. As they fought side by side with men against racial injustice in America, they became aware of the equally pernicious problem of sexism. They realized that they suffered from an additional form of oppression, one that was particularly difficult to deal with because it was rooted in Asian patriarchal culture and nurtured in American sexist society. Moreover, raising the issue of gender inequality would and did give rise to accusations of disloyalty to the newly emergent Asian American community, distracting its members from the main conflict against racial inequality. . . . In spite of these impediments, women activists decided to start their own social movement for equality and empowerment within the larger Asian American Movement. In secure and supportive women's groups, they educated themselves about the relationship of racism, sexism, and class oppression in the Asian American community as well as the wider society.

NOTES

1 Him Mark Lai et al., *Island: Poetry and History of Chinese Immigrants on Angel Island, 1910–40* (San Francisco: HOC DOI Project, Chinese Culture Foundation of San Francisco, 1980).

2 Frances Leventhal, "Loni Ding Spent Five Years Making *Color of Honor,*" *Asian Week,* 13 January 1989. Several other documentaries on the internment of Japanese Americans have been produced recently, such as *Nisei Soldier, Unfinished Business, Family Gathering, and Days of Waiting.* Steven Okazaki's *Days of Waiting,* the story of Estelle Ishigo, a Caucasian woman who was voluntarily incarcerated with her *nisei* husband, is the best known, having won an Oscar for short documentary in 1991. There are even feature-length movies on the subject, such as *Farewell to Manzanar* and, most recently, *Come See the Paradise.* According to Keiko Ohnuma, " 'Paradise'—History But Not Art," *Asian Week,* 4 January 1991, the latter film is "destined to become part of the emerging canon of persecution pornography depicting the internment of Japanese Americans during World War II."

3 National Asian American Telecommunications Association, "CrossCurrent Media: 1990–91 Asian American Audiovisual Catalog," p. 7.

4 Unless otherwise noted, the discussion of *Forbidden City, U.S.A.* is based on Arthur Dong, interview, Los Angeles, 26 October 1989, and Gerrye Wong, "First Person: *Forbidden City* from Pen to Silver Screen," *Asian Week,* 24 November 1989.

5 William Wong's column, *Asian Week,* 26 January 1990.

6 Mervyn Rothstein, "Survival vs. Dignity in an Asian-American Play," *New York Times,* 7 June 1989.

7 Ibid.

8 The term "cultural rescue mission" was first used by J. Tevere MacFadyen, "Recording Chinatown's Past While It's Still There," *Smithsonian* 13, no. 10 (January 1983): 70–79, to describe the New York Chinatown History Project.

9 Him Mark Lai, "Chinese American Studies: A Historical Survey," *Chinese America: History and Perspectives, 1988,* provides information on other Chinese American historical societies, the earliest of which was the Chinese Historical Society of America, which was founded in San Francisco in January 1963.

10 Unless otherwise noted, the discussion of the New York Chinese History Project is based on: MacFadyen, "Recording Chinatown's Past"; Candace Floyd, "Chinatown," *History News* 39, no. 6 (June 1984): 6–11; John Kuo Wei Tchen, interview, New York City, 9 January 1990; and *Bu Gao Ban,* Summer 1984 to Winter 1991.

11 MacFayden, "Recording Chinatown's Past."

12 Ibid.

13 Joyce Yu, "Looking Backwards into the Future," *Bu Gao Ban* 7, no. 1 (Summer 1990).

14 Ibid.

15 John Kuo Wei Tchen, "Creating a Dialogic Museum: The Chinatown History Museum Experiment," in *Museums and Communities: The Politics of Public Culture,* ed. Ivan Karp et al. (Washington, D.C.: Smithsonian Institution Press, 1992), pp. 285–326.

16 Yu, "Looking Backwards into the Future."

17 Letter from John Wei Kuo Tchen to the author, 26 July 1991.

18 " 'Remembering New York Chinatown': Implementing Vehicles of Dialogue" (n.d.), pp. 1–22. Typewritten.

19 Unless otherwise noted, the discussion of the Japanese American National Museum is based on the *Japanese American National Museum Bulletin* 1, no. 2 (Fall 1986) to 6, no. 1 (Winter 1991); and "Japanese American National Museum Benefit Program," 1985.

20 Unless otherwise noted, the discussion of the Filipino American National Historical Society is based on Dorothy Laigo Cordova, telephone interview, 22 and 24 May 1991; and materials (newsletters, reports, conference programs, etc.) she sent to the author.

21 Bob Shimabukuro, "Dorothy Cordova," *International Examiner,* 19 June 1991, is an interview with Cordova, who won the newspaper's Community Voice Award.

22 Filipino American National Historical Society brochure.

23 Fred Cordova, "The Filipino American: There's Always an Identity Crisis," in Sue and Wagner, eds., *Asian-Americans: Psychological Perspectives,* pp. 136–139.

24 Nathaniel N. Wagner, "Filipinos: A Minority within a Minority," in Sue and Wagner, *Asian-Americans: Psychological Perspectives,* pp. 295–298.

25 Fred Cordova, *Filipinos: Forgotten Asian Americans* (Dubuque, Iowa: Kendall/Hunt, 1983).

26 Edward Iwata, "Hot Properties: More Asian Americans Suddenly Are Winning Mainstream Literary Acclaim," View section, *Los Angeles Times,* 11 September 1989.

27 Teri Lee, "An Interview with Janice Mirikitani," *Asian American Review,* Asian American Studies, Department of Ethnic Studies, University of California, Berkeley, 1976, pp. 34–44.

28 "Editorial," *Aion* 1, no. 1 (1970).

29 Unless otherwise noted, the discussion of A Grain of Sand and its individual members is based on "Charlie" Chin, interview, New York City, 31 May 1989; and Nobuko Miyamoto, interview, Los Angeles, 24 October 1989; and on Diane Mark, "Nobuko Miyamoto: The 'Mountain Moving Days' Continue," *Bridge* 10, no. 1 (Spring 1985): 15–19, 28, 29.

30 Nobuko Miyamoto, interview, Los Angeles, 24 October 1989.

31 "Statement," *A Grain of Sand.*

32 Chris Iijima and "Charlie" Chin, *Back to Back,* East/Wind Records, 1982, album cover.

33 Jon Woodhouse, "Bridging East and West: 'Talk Story' Shares Stories of New, Old Immigrants," *Maui News,* 15 November 1987.

34 Though less prominent, Asian Americans have been increasingly influential in film, video, and radio. From a variety of creative and critical perspectives, *Moving the Image:*

Independent Asian Pacific American Media Arts, ed. and intro. Russell Leong (Los Angeles: Asian American Studies Center, University of California at Los Angeles, and Visual Communications, 1991), explores their contribution over the last twenty years.

35 Fred Wei-Han Houn, "A Voice Is a Voice, But What Is It Saying," an unpublished review of Elaine Kim's *Asian American Literature,* 1984.

36 Dorothy Aitsuko McDonald, "Introduction," Frank Chin, *The Chicken-Coop Chinaman and The Year of the Dragon* (Seattle: University of Washington Press, 1981), p. ix.

37 Ibid., p. xviii.

38 Lawson Fusao Inada, "Introduction," in John Okada, *No-No Boy* (Seattle: University of Washington Press, 1976).

39 Stephen Talbot, "Talking Story: Maxine Hong Kingston Rewrites the American Dream," Image section, *San Francisco Examiner,* 24 June 1990, p. 8.

40 Bobby Fong, "Maxine Hong Kingston's Autobiographical Strategy in *The Woman Warrior," Biography* 12 (Spring 1989): 116–125.

41 Letter from Fred Ho (formerly Houn) to the author, 17 July 1991.

42 Chin et al., "An Introduction to Chinese- and Japanese-American Literature," p. 14.

43 Talbot, "Talking Story."

44 Edward Iwata, "Word Warriors," *Los Angeles Times,* 24 June 1990.

45 Talbot, "Talking Story."

46 Frank Chin, *The Chinamen Pacific & Frisco R.R. Co.* (Minneapolis: Coffee House Press, 1988); Maxine Hong Kingston, *Tripmaster Monkey: His Fake Book* (New York: Vintage, 1990). Kingston has publicly denied that Wittman Ah Sing is modeled on Frank Chin. During her visit to the University of Colorado at Boulder, she told the author that he was a composite of several people and that various individuals have thought they were the model, including her husband, Earl, who has been known to mimic a monkey just for the fun of it. Chin, however, is certain that Wittman Ah Sing is himself.

47 Iwata, "Hot Properties." Janice C. Simpson, "Fresh Voices above the Din," *Newsweek,* 3 June 1991, discusses new works by four writers who "splendidly illustrate the frustrations, humor and eternal wonder of the immigrant's life." The "Pacific Reader," Literary Supplement, *International Examiner,* 19 July 1989, provides critical reviews of some of the more recent books by Asian Americans.

48 Iwata, "Hot Properties."

49 Ibid.

50 Ibid.

"If It Wasn't for the Women . . .": African American Women, Community Work, and Social Change

Cheryl Townsend Gilkes

Many sociologists who studied the relationships between dominant and subordinate racial-ethnic groups in the 1960s and 1970s stress the creative ways in which individuals and groups enable communities to articulate their own needs and challenge oppressive structures in the wider society (Morris 1984). Other sociologists, such as Stanford

Lyman (1972), emphasize the historical experience of racial-ethnic groups in the data used for sociological interpretation. The Civil Rights Movement, the Black Power Movement, and the American Indian Movement, along with diverse movements within Asian American, Puerto Rican, and Chicano communities, challenged sociologists to explore historically rooted conflicts over power, labor, economic resources, and the appropriate strategies for achieving social change (Blauner 1972; Wilson 1973; Gilkes 1980).

Creative social conflict is inevitable and necessary if racial-ethnic, gender, and class inequities are to be eliminated and social justice achieved. When enterprising, caring members of oppressed communities become involved in public affairs, their actions often contribute to a creative cultural process that is a force for social change. This [paper] is about an aspect of that creative cultural process: enterprising women in African American communities who shape social change through their community work.

Women are vital to the creative cultural process of social change. African American women and their community work highlight the importance of a group's history and culture to the process of social change. The rise of the women's liberation movement and public concern about African American women, their families, and their position in the labor force (Cade 1970; King 1987; Gilkes 1990) generated a particular interest in their roles in the process of social change. Along with Asian American, Native American, and Latina women, African American women's work outside the home was recognized as a distinctive component in their family roles. Community work is part of this work outside the home. It is labor these women perform in addition to work in the household and the labor force.[1]

This [paper] describes the contemporary expression, historical foundations, and persistent activities of the community work of African American women. Community work includes a wide range of diverse tasks performed to confront and challenge racism as a total system. This work has historical foundations, and a historical perspective helps to highlight the areas of activity common to the work at different time periods. Community work consists of the women's activities to combat racism and empower their communities to survive, grow, and advance in a hostile society. The totality of their work is an emergent, dynamic, interactive model of social action in which community workers discover and explore oppressive structures, challenge many different structures and practices that keep their communities powerless and disadvantaged, and then build, maintain, and strengthen institutions within their community. These institutions become the basis for the community's political culture. The women generate an alternative organization and a set of commitments to group interests that are the basic elements of "community." They work for the community that they themselves re-create and sustain, a mutually reinforcing process.

During the late 1970s in a Northeastern city I gathered oral histories and observed the community activities of twenty-five African American women whom other African Americans had identified as those "who have worked hard for a long time for change in the Black community."[2] As these women talked about the ways in which they became involved in community work and the different kinds of organizations and activities in which they participated, I learned about the very intricate and diverse ways in which people make social change. I also learned about the many ways in which women experience racial oppression. Their family roles made them acutely conscious not only of their own deprivations but also of the suffering of their children and the men in their lives. Their insightful and enterprising responses to these many kinds of suffering led to their prominence in the community. They were responsible for maintaining a dynamic community life to create social change and an adaptive family system to foster survival in a hostile environment. Through community and family, these women generated a set of values and a social organization that persistently challenged and changed American society.

COMMUNITY WORK

Women in American society are expected to be good managers. They organize and coordinate diverse schedules and activities within their families, and among the organizations and institutions with which family members are involved. Work outside the home is often added to this responsibility. African American women usually work, manage their families, and, if they are community workers, participate in the struggles between the communities and the dominant society.

James Blackwell's (1985) definition of the African American community helps us to understand the context of their work. Blackwell argues that the community, although diverse, is held together by both internal and external forces. It is "a highly diversified set of interrelated structures and aggregates of people who are held together by the forces of white oppression and racism. Unity within the black community is a function of the strategies developed to combat white racism and to strengthen black social, economic, and political institutions for group survival and advancement" (1985: xi).

Community work consists of all tasks contained in strategies to combat racial oppression and to strengthen African American social, economic, and political institutions in order to foster group survival, growth, and advancement. Community work is focused on internal development and external challenge, and creates ideas enabling people to think about change. It is the work that opens doors to elected and appointed positions in the political power struggle, and demands and creates jobs in local labor markets and the larger economic system. Community work also focuses on changing ideas, stereotypes, and images that keep a group perpetually stigmatized. Sometimes this is done by demanding different textbooks in the schools or publicly criticizing newspapers and other media. At the same time, community workers may insist, rightly or wrongly, that community members change their behavior to avoid being treated in terms of prevailing stereotypes. Community work is a constant struggle, and it consists of everything that people do to address oppression in their own lives, suffering in the lives of others, and their sense of solidarity or group kinship.

Women participate in every part of a community's experience of racial oppression. Racial oppression is a phenomenon that not only singles out African Americans because of their heritage and color but also places the entire community in a colonial relationship, a relationship of powerlessness and dependency, within a dominant and dominating society. Robert Blauner (1972) calls this "internal colonialism," and it involves the subordination of an entire group of people in order to take away its land, to capture its labor, or to do both. Colonized people must be excluded from the political process and, by law, have few, if any, citizenship rights. Because the primary purpose of the group is to labor unceasingly for someone else, the other dimensions of its cultural life, such as family life, health, education, and religion, become difficult, if not impossible, to pursue.

During slavery African Americans had their children and spouses sold away from them. Their family lives were repeatedly disrupted and invaded by the sexual terrorism that was part of slavery. Teaching slaves to read and write in the antebellum South was illegal. During the last decades of slavery, religious worship outside of the supervision of white people was illegal as well. The health of African Americans was constantly threatened by the violence of white slave owners, through beatings and overwork. Because they were legally nonpersons, emancipation left African Americans overwhelmingly landless and still dependent upon white landowners for a livelihood. Political powerlessness through violence and denial of the vote increased that dependence. Racist stereotypes, ideologies, and actions continued to justify the dominant group's actions and the continued subordination of another group.[3] Racial oppression is a total phenomenon that combines cultural humiliation and destruction, political subordination, and economic exploitation to maintain a hierarchy that limits the life chances of a group of people.

The economic needs and organization of the society change. Slavery was abolished in 1865; African Americans moved to northern cities in large numbers during World Wars I and II; the Civil Rights Movement did away with Jim Crow laws. However, the racist hierarchy retained a life and meaning that survived massive changes in economic, legal, political, and social institutions. Although slavery ended, the society learned to associate low-paying, dirty work with Black people and higher-paying, clean work with White people. Contemporary racial stereotypes and media images perpetuate those images rooted in slavery.

Community work confronts this totality. Everett Hughes (1971:313) suggested that an important way to conceptualize "work" is to view it as a "bundle of several tasks." Racial oppression takes up more time and creates extra work, or more "bundles of tasks," for members of a victimized group.[4] People working for and with their communities involve themselves in activities surrounding the problems associated with jobs: labor union activities, creating access to jobs, teaching strategies to fight specific problems in work settings, and seeking legislation to protect occupations where group members are concentrated. One community worker had worked for the Urban League early in her career. She described recruiting other African American women for newly created jobs during World War II by visiting churches and women's clubs. She then organized discussion groups in order to teach these women how to confront the racial harassment they would encounter in unions and factories. Another woman described in great detail the way her women's club of the 1920s and 1930s taught fellow domestic workers how to demand the full wages their White female employers had promised. That same women's club, in the 1960s and 1970s, was involved in administering job training programs for homemakers *at the same time* they were lobbying for protective legislation for household workers. Community workers involved themselves in activities that confronted ideas as well as structures within and outside the community.

Education is a case in point. Issues of self-image and self-esteem are related to educational success at the same time that employment discrimination and racist attitudes in the educational system account for the lack of African American teachers. Educational failure locks many members of the community out of the economic system at the same time that political powerlessness through gerrymandering accounts for the lack of access to low-skilled but high-paying municipal jobs. One woman who had been quite prominent in challenging the public educational system talked about the importance of self-esteem for African American students. Another woman, an elected official, displayed publications she used for raising the racial self-esteem of teenagers and described the workshops she gave for parents in order to reduce the sense of intimidation they felt when confronting White teachers. Each of these problems presents a different "bundle of tasks," yet they are all manifestations of the totality of racial oppression.

Each woman interviewed described diverse and intricate daily schedules that reflected the complexity and connectedness of the social, political, and economic problems that pervade everyday life in minority communities. One woman, for example, described getting a group of adolescent males assigned to early morning jobs, going to court as a character witness for a teenager, meeting with a board of directors in another part of the city, and coordinating a public demonstration against that same board of directors before leaving for the meeting. While levels of confrontation and activity often vary, community work persistently rejects racial oppression as a normal and natural feature of human experience. Community work, encompassing issues of challenge as well as survival, is perhaps more complicated than the racial oppression that gives rise to it.

HISTORICAL FOUNDATIONS

Community workers' expectations and obligations represent a historical role. These women, through their public participation on so many levels, claim a prominent place in the community's history. This historical prominence often provides levels of prestige and influence unmatched in the lives of White women of similar class backgrounds.[5] All of the women were connected in some way to earlier generations of organizations, activists, and confrontations. What becomes visible to outsider observers as "social movements" are the most dramatic dimensions of an intergenerational tradition of community work. Bernice Johnson Reagon (1982:82–83) emphasizes this continuity:

> If we understand that we are talking about a struggle that is hundreds of years old, then we must acknowledge a continuance: that to be Black women is to move forward the struggle for the kind of space in this society that will make sense for our people. It is different today. Things have changed. The search for high levels of humanity and space to be who we know we are is the same. And if we can make sense of our people in this society, we will go a long way in making sense for the rest of the peoples who also live and suffer here.

The historical continuity of community work depends upon an intricate fit between many kinds of organizations and people. All of the women worked within traditional and nationally recognized groups, such as churches, the National Association for the Advancement of Colored People (NAACP), the Urban League, the Student Non-Violent Coordinating Committee (SNCC), the Young Women's Christian Association (YWCA), the National Association of Colored Women's Clubs, and the National Council of Negro Women. At the same time they formed local organizations that specialized in problems of job training, drug addiction, city services, welfare rights, or public education. People in the community actively encouraged these community workers to be leaders and, once the women responded to a community need, they organized whatever was necessary to see an activity through.

Such activities were not possible without intergenerational connections. When interviewing, I asked the women to identify their heroes and heroines. These women identified specific women within the local community as well as such notables as Mary McLeod Bethune. One woman remembered very clearly being impressed when Mrs. Bethune spoke at a local church for the Women's Day service. Several women identified Mrs. Burns,[6] who was also interviewed, as their heroine and local sponsor. One said, "I walked to Mrs. Burns when I was nine months old!" This elderly community worker identified Mrs. Bethune as a coworker in the National Association of Colored Women. Older community workers, as heroines and sponsors, were the critical connection to earlier generations of community workers or "Race" women. These women who remembered Mary McLeod Bethune and Mary Church Terrell, not only as "heroines" but also as living role models in club work and church work, were the links to an unbroken tradition of community work or working for "the Race" that could be traced directly to antebellum communities, both slave and free.

Working for "the Race" began during slavery. Within the slave community, women not only played key roles in the development of family, education, and religion but also developed a women's network that was a foundation of strength, leaders, and mutual aid (White 1985; Webber 1978). Deborah Gray White (1985) names midwives, nurses, and religious leaders as critical sources of survival. One religious leader, a prophet named Sinda, preaching the imminent end of the world, precipitated a strike by an entire plantation labor force. African American women in Northern free communities built churches and developed abolitionist, literary, mutual-aid, and missionary societies that provided poor-relief and insurance benefits for their communities (Perkins 1981; Sterling 1984). Women such as Maria Stewart and Frances Ellen Watkins Harper were militant antislavery crusaders and public lecturers. Stewart was the first woman of any race in the United States to lecture publicly and leave manuscripts that are still extant (Giddings 1984; Richardson 1987), and Harper was the first female public lecturer that many women, Black or White, ever saw and heard (Sterling 1984).

After emancipation, church women and teachers organized schools and churches throughout the South. Since male ministers also worked as teachers, male and female educators (preachers and teachers) became the vital source of leaders. With the rise of Jim Crow laws, women's public activism outside the church emerged in the form of an anti-lynching movement under the leadership of Ida B. Wells Barnett. This movement was the basis for the formation of the National Association of Colored Women, whose motto was "Lifting as We Climb." That club movement explored and confronted the way in which racism threatened or distorted every aspect of life.

In order to provide the leadership essential for their communities, African American women insisted upon their organizational autonomy while addressing their efforts to the condition of the entire community. In 1895, Josephine St. Pierre Ruffin wrote:

> Our woman's movement is a woman's movement in that it is led and directed by women for the good of women and men, for the benefit of all humanity. . . . We want, we ask the

active interest of our men; . . . we are not alienating or withdrawing, we are only coming to the front, willing to join any others in the same work . . . and inviting . . . others to join us. (Davis 1933:19)

The importance of these women's clubs was evident in the interviews with the elderly community workers, who described these organizations as places where they learned to lead and administer, and where they organized to win elections in organizations seemingly dominated by men, such as the NAACP and the Urban League.[7] The oldest surviving national African American political organizations are women's organizations whose founders and members also participated in organizing the NAACP, the Urban League,[8] the Association for the Study of Afro-American Life and History, and every other national African American organization. Emerging as one of the prominent leaders during the Depression, Mary McLeod Bethune created the National Council of Negro Women as a lobby for civil rights and working women. The clubs served as training stations for both middle-class and lower-class women leaders.

Several observers in the late nineteenth and early twentieth centuries noted the prestige associated with women's public participation and work for "the Race" (Perkins 1981; Lerner 1972). In urban communities, mothers clubs were organized to deal with childbirth at home, housework, and child care. As children grew older, these clubs became scholarship clubs. Clubs for the protection, cultural "uplift," and mutual aid of household workers were formed. Carter Woodson (1930) identified the significant role of washerwomen in financing and building associations that developed into the major Black insurance companies. He argued that this was one of many examples of the way in which African American working women not only supported their families but also contributed to the possibility of economic self-sufficiency in the entire community. Through such community work, Maggie Lena Walker became the first woman of any color to be a bank president in the United States (Brown 1989; Giddings 1983).

W. E. B. Du Bois (1975) observed that the club movement, lacking money as a resource, made its most substantial contribution through the web of affiliations it built, connecting and empowering Black people across class and status lines:

> . . . the women of America who are doing humble but on the whole the most effective work in the social uplift of the lowly, not so much by money as by personal contact, are the colored women. Little is said or known about it but in thousands of churches and social clubs, in missionary societies and fraternal organizations, in unions like the National Association of Colored Women, these workers are founding and sustaining orphanages and old folk homes; distributing personal charity and relief; visiting prisoners; helping hospitals; teaching children; and ministering to all sorts of needs. (1975:273)

The organizational history of these women is central to African American protest and survival history. They and their organizations have provided the space where contemporary community workers work as directors, managers, social workers, elected politicians, and advocates.

Because of the efforts of community workers, ideas and strategies change. People reflect on their successes and failures, and as new problems arise, these reflections contribute to new solutions or a change in ideology. Black Power activists, for instance, often accused older members of the community of complacency, accommodations, and do-nothingness. One community worker described a confrontation in which "young militants" challenged Mrs. Burns concerning what she had done for the community "lately," implying that she was an accommodationist and represented an old and useless style of leadership. Mrs. Burns reportedly replied, "I was out raising scholarship money to send you to college so you could come back here and give me sass!" When interviewed, Mrs. Burns mentioned things that she would have done differently in light of the logic of the Black Power Movement; she also named things that she was currently doing differently because of her own reflections on history. She told of one encounter with a Black federal official whom she lectured concerning his being used by his agency to steal ideas from her club rather than empowering the club to be the agency's subcontractor to teach the ideas to others. She claimed her feistiness came from her own reflections on a conflict during the 1920s when she accused another activist of "bringing Jim Crow" to her city by campaigning to build a Black hospital. Mrs. Burns conceded, in light of the late 1960s and early 1970s arguments for community control, that he had been right and she, although her view had prevailed then, had been wrong.

DISCOVERY, CHALLENGE, AND DEVELOPMENT: AN EMERGENT MODEL OF COMMUNITY WORK

The totality of racial oppression and the diversity of African American communities combine to make the tasks of community work so varied as almost to defy any kind of classification. Community work comprises both responses to and catalysts for change. Successful or not, it is the effort to make things better and to eliminate the problems and structures that make life difficult. Community work is the persistent effort across time to close the gap between Black and White life chances. The work is both immediate and long term, and its effects are cumulative. There is, however, an emergent model of action that is present in all of this. It is a model of discovery, challenge, and development that represents a multifaceted model of resistance.

Discovery that there is a problem is the first critical step. Community workers observe, discover, and explore the effects of oppressive practices and structures in their own and others' lives. They are the critical connection between the abrasions of personal experience and the social and political contexts that shape experience. It can be the simple act of sending one's daughter to the mailbox that leads to critical discovery. Describing this as the impetus for her neighborhood association, one worker said, "And simply because we wanted to get together and do things for the community and get the streets cleaned up and the garbage picked up and wanted a mailbox installed on the corner, things like that . . . and then we branched out into other things."

Personal discovery does not lead immediately to community action. The discovery process is complex and involves communicating with others about the reality and nature of community problems. Another worker, a Southern migrant whose community work addressed drug problems and public education, told of her "discovery" of school problems when comparing her son's homework with that of his cousin, who attended school in another, predominantly White, neighborhood. She went on to talk about the problem of transforming personal discovery into collective action, particularly in the North:

A lot is like shadow boxing. The problem is there, but you can't quite see it. We cover them a lot. But down South everything is out in the open. . . . You knew where you stood and everybody knew where the line was drawn, and actually you could deal with it better than here. First you've got to find the problem, then you've got to pull it out from under the covers, and then if somebody says it is a problem. . . . I remember when I came to Hamptonville, I thought there was discrimination in the schools *then* . . . when my kids were in school. . . . We [she and her sister-in-law] were discussing our children's work from school one day, and I looked at my son and his cousin [who were] in the same grade, and the entire curriculum was different. And I said, "What is this!" You know, they were in the same grade, and why is this curriculum so different . . . so when I questioned these things, I was really put down; I was bringing discrimination from the South. So I really kept quiet, but I've been looking at this thing for a long time.

The activity of discovery and exploration often overlaps with challenge, since discovery itself is subversive. The actions that follow from discovery, challenge oppressive structures and practices in a variety of ways. Challenge begins when community workers raise questions among their kin and neighbors, and eventually organize some kind of action. In order to do this they must argue, obstruct, organize, teach, lecture, demonstrate, sue, write letters, and so on. They communicate in such a way that they create a critical speech community around the problem—a group of people who share a point of view on a problem, acknowledging that it exists and that it is something on which public action is necessary.

These initial acts of challenge sometimes emerge into full-blown social movements. At other times, discovery and small-scale actions in one area—welfare rights, for instance—will bring a community worker to the attention of others and involve her in a related but quite different social movement. One woman, describing her involvement on the board of directors of a large human services agency outside of her neighborhood and her own community work focus, said, "The director of the program was having some trouble. . . . She knew that I had raised Hell over in [one neighborhood], so she figured that she needed some raised over in [another neighborhood]."

At the same time they are organizing confrontations with oppressive forces outside the community, community workers address needs within their communities that enable people to resist oppression and participate meaningfully in community life. In the struggle for voting rights, for example, civil rights organizations confronted voter registrars throughout the South with demonstrations and registration campaigns at the same time workers like Septima Clark organized schools to teach African Americans how to read and take the tests (Morris 1984). This is the task of internal development, the building and maintenance of organizations and institutions indigenous to the community.

One elected official argued that the most important problem African Americans faced was internal control: ". . . the way they can't have control over their lives. Although I am not a separatist, I feel as though until we can get into the mainstream of this society . . . we are going to be third- or fourth-class citizens." Trained in elementary education, she surprised me when she told me that she had no intention of teaching children. "I felt that even though I worked with a parents' group, that because I wasn't a teacher, no one took my words very seriously, and I decided that I was going to become a teacher, not to work in the classroom but to work with parents." For some community workers, internal development was so critical, it became their full-time vocation. They either found jobs in agencies that permitted them to do such work or they organized their own agencies.

In a society in which "integration" has become the dominant theme in the politics of race, internal community development can often be very controversial, implying separatism and inter-racial hostility. Mrs. Burns experienced such a conflict and found herself, fifty years later, an advocate for the kind of community control she had earlier labeled "bringing Jim Crow." Because of the power of the dominant society, failure to build and maintain community institutions is a problem. Carter Woodson (1933) labeled it "mis-education" and suggested that it could be solved by building alternative institutions. In my own research, community workers called this activity "building Black-oriented institutions."

What has been labeled a "retreat from integration" is actually the discovery of the internal development that was sometimes accomplished in disadvantaged, segregated, Southern schools. Because education was viewed as something akin to a religious mission, African American teachers, especially after 1915, taught African American history in Southern schools at least during the month of February. Aware of the aspirations of many fathers and mothers for their daughters' college educations, and also aware of the grim realities that governed women's opportunities, these teachers often insisted that their students learn classical subjects alongside trades and business subjects. In effect they refused to compound limited social opportunities with inflexible educational policies, now called tracking. Since Southern states made it illegal for White teachers to teach Black children, those children were inadvertently provided with important role models. Although African American teachers in segregated schools could be very assimilationist and Anglocentric in their outlook and thinking, their commitment to the community made a real difference. The teachers believed in and supported the students, who, in turn, observed educated African American women and men in positions of leadership.

The activities of discovery, challenge, and development are interrelated and together represent a tradition of resistance. This model of social action must be seen as dynamic and interactive. The women are agents of this tradition of resistance as both volunteers and professionals. Their persistent refusal to accept the discomfort of racial oppression is the conflicted connection between the individual and the society that contributes to the emergence of a social force for change. Commenting that "revolutions happen in the funniest ways," one worker whose agency specialized in developing women for jobs and finding jobs for women said: "It just started on a physical level. It really just shocked me that I was going to be physically inconvenienced for the simple reason that I was Black. You know? It was that simple, because I was Black. There were certain things that I was not going to be able to get physically, that was going to create conditions of security and warmth and feeling good." The diversity of their work again points to the totality of the pressure on African Americans as a group. When one accounts for the full range of the women's work, it becomes apparent that every question raised about the source of community afflictions contains the seeds of rebellion and social change.

CONCLUSION: IF IT WASN'T FOR THE WOMEN . . .

African American women's community work connects many "small pieces" of community life and contributes to the process of empowerment. The centrality of their work points to the need to examine the importance of women in any community resisting racial oppression. Racial oppression is a complex and interconnected phenomenon that shapes the lives of women and men. Most women of color are trapped in the worst and dirtiest sectors of the female labor market, providing the sole support of their families or supplementing the wages of their husbands, who are similarly trapped in male markets. Their families are not accorded the institutional and ideological supports that benefit White families. Additionally, African American, Asian, Latina, and Native American women also do community work. They find their historical role organized around the nurturance and defense and advancement of an oppressed public family. Women in a variety of community settings now and historically have demonstrated that it is safe to parallel the oft-repeated statement of African American church women that "If it wasn't for the women, you wouldn't have a church," to say, "If it were not for women of color, African American, Asian, Latino, and Native peoples would have far fewer alternatives and resources to maintain themselves and challenge a hostile social system."

African American women, and by extension Asian American, Native American, and Latina women, highlight the importance of women and their work for the creation of a just and more equitable society. Women bring three perspectives to community work that make them particularly rebellious. First, their consciousness is shaped by their experience in the society, especially in the labor force. Second, they see men's suffering and feel its effects in their own lives. These women observe and experience the effects of racism on the men of their community along with the effects of that racism in their own lives. The third and perhaps most important source of discontent is the effect of racial oppression in the lives of their children. Combating the damage to their children and attempting to fashion a more inclusive future for them was stated as the most important motivation for involvement. Community workers got involved "through my kids." It is in their roles as the principal caretakers of children that racial-ethnic women pose the largest political threat to the dominant society. Women and their children are the core around which group solidarity is constructed. Community workers are, in the words of Sadie Daniels, "women builders." Community work derives its character from the shared nature of the problems confronting all members of the community. The depths and complexities of racial oppression cannot be grasped without a thorough understanding of its expression in the lives of women and their children.

Although perspectives on women's roles are becoming a prominent part of the social science canon, this development has not incorporated the complex historical roles of women in powerless communities. These women must confront a politics that involves more than the politics implied by race or class or gender. When viewing the creative role of women in the simultaneous processes of social change and community survival, one must conclude that if it wasn't for the women, racially oppressed communities would not have the institutions, organizations, strategies, and ethics that enable the group not only to survive or to maintain itself as an integral whole, but also to develop in an alien, hostile, oppressive situation and to challenge it. In spite of their powerlessness, African American women and women of color generally have a dramatic impact within and beyond their communities. The translation of this historical role into real power and social justice is the ultimate goal of community work.

NOTES

1 The data for this chapter are taken from my larger study, "Living and Working in a World of Trouble: The Emergent Career of the Black Woman Community Worker." Similar stud-

ies of the Chinese American community (Yap 1983) and the Puerto Rican community (Uriarte-Gaston 1988) also identify the critical role of women community workers.

2 Earlier versions of this paper were presented to the Center for Research on Women, Memphis State University, Summer Research Institutes, 1983 and 1986.

3 Substantial insights for this discussion of racial oppression and internal colonialism are drawn from collaborative work with Bonnie Thornton Dill, Evelyn Nakano Glenn, Elizabeth Higginbotham, and Ruth Zambrana sponsored by the Interuniversity Working Group on Gender, Race, and Class.

4 The importance of the extra time and work cannot be overstated. Bettylou Valentine (1978), discussing the expanded time budgets of ghettoized African Americans, considers this to be part of the social cost of their combined poverty and racial oppression. She not only identifies "hustling" as the legal and extralegal strategies that Blackston residents used to produce and augment income, she also means the term to apply to the extra work, the extra hustle, that must be packed into each day because of poverty and racial oppression.

5 When I first began this research, people assumed I would be studying the African American equivalent of the Junior League. Although the twenty-three women who were employed full-time were in middle-class occupations, their class origins were as diverse as those of the larger community. Women with poor and working-class origins had usually experienced their upward mobility in the process of acquiring more education in order qualify for positions in human services that allowed them to do community work full-time, both as volunteers and as professionals. Calling it "going up for the oppressed," I explore this special kind of upward mobility in an earlier article (Gilkes 1983).

6 A pseudonym.

7 One Urban League consultant stated that women emerged as presidents of local Urban League and NAACP chapters as often as men, although they did not preside over the national bodies. She concluded that the role of women as local Urban League presidents combined with their roles in Urban League Guilds (women's clubs that raised money for the Urban League) showed the importance of the unacknowledged power of women in community affairs.

8 The Urban League was formed through the merger of two organizations, one male and one female.

REFERENCES

Balbus, Isaac. 1977. *The Dialectics of Legal Repression: Black Rebels Before the American Criminal Courts.* New Brunswick, N.J.: Transaction Books.

Blackwell, James. 1985. *The Black Community: Diversity and Unity.* Second edition. New York: Harper & Row.

Blauner, Robert. 1972. *Racial Oppression in America.* New York: Harper & Row.

Brown, Elsa Barkley. 1989. "Womanist Consciousness: Maggie Lena Walker and the Independent Order of Saint Luke." *Signs: Journal of Women in Culture and Society* 14 (3):610–633.

Cade, Toni, ed. 1970. *The Black Woman: An Anthology.* New York: Signet.

Cesaire, Aime. 1972. *Discourse on Colonialism.* New York: Monthly Review Press. (First published 1955).

Davis, Angela. 1971. "Reflections on the Black Woman's Role in the Community of Slaves." *Black Scholar* 3 (4):2–15.

———. 1981. *Women, Race, and Class.* New York: Random House.

Davis, Elizabeth Lindsey. 1933. *Lifting as They Climb: A History of the National Association of Colored Women.* Washington, D.C.: Moorland-Springarn Research Center.

Deloria, Vine. 1970. *We Talk, You Listen: New Tribes, New Turf.* New York: Dell.

Du Bois, W. E. B. 1975. *The Gift of Black Folk: Negroes in the Making of America* (1924). Millwood, N.Y.: Kraus-Thompson Organization.

Edelman, Marian Wright. 1987. *Families in Peril: An Agenda for Social Change.* Cambridge, Mass.: Harvard University Press.

Faris, Robert E. L. 1967. *Chicago Sociology, 1920–1932.* Chicago: University of Chicago Press.

Giddings, Paula. 1984. *When and Where I Enter: The Impact of Black Women on Race and Sex in America.* New York: William Morrow.

Gilkes, Cheryl Townsend. 1979. "Living and Working in a World of Trouble: The Emergent Career of the Black Woman Community Worker." Ph.D. dissertation, Northeastern University.

———. 1980. "The Sources of Conceptual Revolutions in the Field of Race Relations." pp. 7–31 in David Claerbaut, ed., *New Directions in Ethnic Studies: Minorities in America.* San Francisco: Century Twenty-One.

———. 1983. "Going up for the Oppressed: The Career Mobility of Black Women Community Workers." *Journal of Social Issues* 39 (3):115–139.

———. 1990. " 'Liberated to Work Like Dogs': Labeling Black Women and Their Work." Pp. 165–188 in Hildreth Y. Grossman and Nia Lane Chester, eds., *The Experience and Meaning of Work in Women's Lives.* Hillsdale, N.J.: Lawrence Erlbaum Associates.

Hughes, Everett C. 1963. "Race Relations and the Sociological Imagination." *American Sociological Review* 28 (6):879–890.

———. 1971. *The Sociological Eye: Selected Papers on Work, Self, and the Study of Society.* Chicago: Aldine-Atherton.

King, Mary. 1987. *Freedom Song: A Personal Story of the 1960s Civil Rights Movement.* New York: William Morrow.

Lerner, Gerda. 1972. *Black Women in White America: A Documentary History.* New York: Vintage Books.

Lyman, Stanford. 1972. *The Black American in Sociological Thought: A Failure of Perspective.* New York: G. P. Putnam.

Marable, Manning. 1983. *How Capitalism Underdeveloped Black America: Problems in Race, Political Economy, and Society.* Boston: South End Press.

Morris, Aldon. 1984. *The Origins of the Civil Rights Movement: Black Communities Organizing for Change.* New York: Free Press.

Perkins, Linda. 1981. "Black Women and Racial 'Uplift' Prior to Emancipation." pp. 317–334 in Filomina Chioma Steady, ed., *The Black Woman Cross-Culturally.* Cambridge, Mass.: Schenkman.

Reagon, Bernice Johnson. 1982. "My Black Mothers and Sisters or on Beginning a Cultural Autobiography." *Feminist Studies* 8 (1):81–96.

———. 1986. "African Diaspora Women: The Making of Cultural Workers." *Feminist Studies* 12 (1):77–90.

Richardson, Marilyn, ed. 1987. *Maria Stewart, America's First Black Woman Political Writer: Essays and Speeches.* Bloomington: Indiana University Press.

Sterling, Dorothy. 1984. *We Are Your Sisters: Black Women in the Nineteenth Century.* New York: W. W. Norton.

Uriarte-Gaston, Miren. 1988. "Organizing for Survival: The Emergence of a Puerto Rican Community." Ph.D. dissertation, Boston University.

Valentine, Bettylou. 1978. *Hustling and Other Hard Work: Life Styles in the Ghetto.* New York: Free Press.

Webber, Thomas L. 1978. *Deep like the Rivers: Education in the Slave Quarter Community, 1831–1865.* New York: W. W. Norton.

White, Deborah Gray. 1985. *Ar'n't I a Woman? Female Slaves in the Plantation South.* New York: W. W. Norton.

Wilson, William Julius. 1973. *Power, Racism, and Privilege: Race Relations in Theoretical and Sociohistorical Perspectives.* New York: Macmillan.

Woodson, Carter G. 1930. "The Negro Washerwoman." *Journal of Negro History* 15 (3):269–277.

——. 1933. *The Mis-Education of the Negro.* New York: Associated Publishers.

Yap, Stacey Guat Hong. 1983. "Gather Your Strength, Sisters: The Emergence of Chinese Women Community Workers." Ph.D. dissertation, Boston University.

Environmentalism and the Politics of Inclusion

Dorceta E. Taylor

Since at least the 1830s, European-American individuals and groups have championed the cause of the environment. In the early years, two concerns dominated this movement: natural resource conservation, and wilderness and wildlife preservation (Nash 1982; Paehlke 1989, pp. 4–22; Fox 1985; Devall and Sessions 1985; Pepper 1986; Bramwell 1990). While these two dominant perspectives often conflicted with each other, they also overlapped in their primary concern with the management of large, sparsely populated, public wildlands.

From the 1950s and 1960s onward, a third concern began to increasingly be seen as an essential aspect of modern environmentalism: human welfare ecology. As Robyn Eckersley notes, "The accumulation of toxic chemicals or 'intractable wastes'; the intensification of ground, air, and water pollution generally; the growth in new 'diseases of affluence' (e.g., heart disease, cancer); the growth in urban and coastal high rise development; the dangers of nuclear plants and nuclear wastes; the growth in the nuclear arsenal; and the problem of global warming and the thinning of the ozone layer have posed increasing threats to human survival, safety, and well-being" (Eckersley 1992, p. 36). It was on the basis of these concerns that the environmental movement finally emerged as a significant mass movement by the 1970s. Like its predecessors, however, this new wing of the modern environmental movement tended to operate without significant minority participation (Buttel and Flinn 1974; Lowe *et al.* 1980; Paehlke 1989; Fox 1985; Mohai 1990; Taylor 1989).

THE RISE OF AN INCLUSIVE ENVIRONMENTAL MOVEMENT

This pattern changed dramatically with the emergence of the multiracial environmental justice movement in the late 1980s. In recent years African Americans and other ethnic groups have organized around environmental issues at an unprecedented rate. New groups are constantly being formed, and older ones are continually expanding their agenda. Thousands of people of color have joined environmental groups, coalitions, and alliances in the United States (Bullard 1992). Hundreds have served as founders, leaders, organizers, researchers, academics, policymakers, board members, campaign managers, and environmental educators. The Citizens Clearinghouse for Hazardous Wastes estimates it works with over 7,000 community and grassroots groups nationwide. Just two years ago, CCHW's estimate was about 2,200 (Citizens' Clearinghouse for Hazardous Waste 1991; Suro 1989, p. 18; Collette 1987, pp. 44–45; Montague 1990; Ruffins 1990).

Like many people attracted to the modern environmental movement, activists of color were shocked when they learned of the dangers to their communities caused by acute and chronic exposures to toxins and other environmental hazards. As more and more communities woke up to find themselves suffering from chronic exposures to toxins, they started making connections between previously mysterious illnesses and environmental hazards. The environmental disasters at Love Canal (New York), Triana (Alabama), Institute (West Virginia), Warren County (North Carolina), and Emelle (Alabama)—along with research linking race and poverty to the siting of hazardous facilities—spawned a whole new breed of environmental activists.

These people looked directly at the relationships among class, race, political power, and the exposure to environmental hazards. They thus rejected conventional NIMBYism (Not In My Backyard campaigns). They refused to say "not in my backyard" without questioning or caring about whose backyard the problem ended up in. In addition to asking "why in my backyard?" they insisted that such hazards should not be located in anyone's backyard.

Herein lies a key distinction between the environmental justice movement and much of the white-dominated, well-to-do, community environmental organizations which have sought to protect their own neighborhoods from pollutants and hazardous wastes. Activists of color were more experientially equipped to perceive the injustice in the distribution of environmental hazards and envision a world where these burdens would be eliminated, reduced, or, where unavoidable, distributed equitably in the future.

As noted, research played a vital role in the growth of the environmental justice movement. In recent years, minority researchers have thoroughly documented the link between environmental hazards and race and poverty. They have also developed concepts such as "environmental blackmail," "environmental racism," and "environmental equity" to challenge and clarify the rest of the environmental movement's thinking.

As the research and discussion papers multiplied, conferences and roundtables were also convened to discuss and debate these issues. Notable among these conferences were the Urban Environmental Health Conference (1985), the Race and the Incidence of Environmental Hazards Conference (1990), and the first National People of Color Environmental Leadership Summit (1991). The Urban Environment Health Conference was particularly important. It was the first forum to raise the issue of toxic exposures on the job as well as in the community and pointed out how poor people and people of color were being forced to choose between their sources of income and their health and safety.

During these same years, several journals, magazines, and newsletters sprang up to cover environmental justice issues. Foremost among them are *Race, Poverty, and the Environment* (Earth Island Institute), *Toxic Times* (National Toxics Campaign), *Every-*

one's Backyard (Citizens' Clearinghouse for Hazardous Waste), *RACHEL's Hazardous Waste News* (Environmental Research Foundation), *Panna Outlook* (Pesticide Action Network), *Voces Unidas* (Southwest Organizing Project), *The Workbook* (Southwest Research and Information Center), and *The Egg: A Journal of Ecojustice* (Network Center for Religion, Ethics and Social Policy). In addition, other environmental magazines such as *Environmental Action* and *Green Letter* have carried substantial sympathetic coverage of environmental justice issues.

The most vital element in the rise of the environmental justice movement, however, was the emergence of grassroots activists willing to lay everything they have on the line. People with little previous knowledge of environmental issues or experience with political activism have been compelled to take radical action. For example, as we have seen in Warren County, North Carolina, African-American women, men, and children militantly stood and lay in front of trucks to prevent them from taking PCB-laced soil to the dump (Geiser and Waneck 1983; LaBalme 1988). Scenes like these have been repeated all over the country with people of various racial and ethnic groups participating. Increasingly distant are the days when communities of color would remain silent or refuse to question the nature of the new jobs promised them when companies manufacturing dangerous products moved into town, or when landfills, incinerators, or other toxic dumps were placed in their neighborhoods. While the more established sectors of the environmental movement were content to fight professional battles in quiet courtrooms and the lobbies of Congress, the participants of the grassroots environmental justice movement took much greater risks and made larger personal sacrifices.

This new movement has become well rooted throughout the country. According to Bullard (1991, pp. 6–10), 11 percent of the current multiracial environmental justice groups were formed prior to 1970, 24 percent between 1970 to 1980, and the rest during the 1980s and 1990s. For example, groups like Citizens for a Better America in Virginia and the Franklin Park Coalition in Boston (Roxbury) have been established for about 17 years. Citizens for a Better America is a multi-issue environmental group, and the Franklin Park Coalition is a park restoration and conservation group. Other groups like the Gulf Coast Tenants Organization (Baton Rouge, Louisiana), Southwest Organizing Project (New Mexico) have also been established for more than a decade.

While the issue has been highlighted in recent years, it would be a mistake to think that all minority environmental groups focus on community anti-toxins campaigns as do such grassroots groups such as Toxic Avengers, West Harlem Environmental Action, Mothers of East Los Angeles, Concerned Citizens of South Central Los Angeles, and Native Americans for a Clean Environment. Nor are the concerns of the environmental justice movement bounded by expanding the anti-toxins concern to include toxins on the job, as represented by such groups as the Labor/Community Strategy Center, the Michigan Association of Minority Environmental Services and Technologies, the Oil Chemical and Atomic Workers, and various local committees for occupational safety and health.

This diverse new movement actually includes professional networks (African American Environmental Association and the American Association of Blacks in Energy in Washington, D.C.); community gardens and farm cooperatives (Cambodian Gardens in Houston, Inner City Coop Farm in New Haven); business-environmental forums (Forum for Community Transformation in Portland, Oregon); Greens (African-American Black and Green Tendency in California); water and energy conservationists (Center for Environment, Commerce, and Energy in Washington, D.C.); wilderness activists (Flora, Folk and Fauna in Washington, D.C.); research, advocacy, and training organizations (Southwest Organizing Project, Gulf Coast Tenants Association, Center for Third World Organizing); environmental educators seeking access to the outdoors for inner city youths (Natural Guard in Connecticut); and groups combining an understanding of African-American history with an understanding of natural history (Underground Railroad in Kansas and Minnesota). Typically, environmental justice groups start off working on a single issue but quickly move on to multi-issue agendas and a diversity of strategies and tactics.

As this local activism has increased and national conferences and movement media have brought people together, a more coordinated, multi-issue national movement has emerged. Most early environmental justice groups engaged in solitary struggles. However, as the 1980s drew to a close and national clearinghouses, public information services, and regional networks (for information dissemination, training, testing, and organizing) were established, many of these groups started gathering together under one umbrella. Their approach also more and more distinguished itself from the other sectors of the environmental movement.

One key distinction, of course, is the racial diversity of the movement. Environmental justice groups range from those that are all, or primarily, African-American, Native-American, Puerto Rican, Latino, and Asian to multiracial coalitions, some including European Americans as members. For instance, the Labor/Community Strategy Center in Los Angeles is a multiracial coalition, while Mothers of East Los Angeles is all Latina, and Concerned Citizens of East Los Angeles is made up primarily of African Americans. Toxic Avengers is a Puerto Rican group in Brooklyn, while the People United for a Better Oakland (PUEBLO) is a multiracial group. A national conference of the environmental justice movement thus looks quite different from the national conferences of the Sierra Club or Friends of the Earth.

Women's leadership is also very strong in the environmental justice movement. In many instances women are founders or are the heads of these organizations. Native Americans for a Clean Environment, Mothers of East Los Angeles, and Concerned Citizens of South Central Los Angeles were all founded and headed by women and maintain primarily female memberships. In other instances, groups like Citizens for a Better America and West Harlem Environmental Action were co-founded by women along with men and their membership is more mixed. Women's participation in these organizations is still vital and valued, however.

The environmental justice movement is also more ideologically inclusive than more traditional ecology groups. It integrates both social and ecological concerns much more readily and pays particular attention to questions of distributive justice, community empowerment, and democratic accountability. It does not treat the problem of oppression and social exploitation as separable from the rape and exploitation of the natural world. Instead, it argues that human societies and the natural environment are intricately linked and that the health of one depends on the health of the other. It understands that if the human environment is poisoned, if there are no opportunities for economic survival or nutritional sustenance, or if there are no possibilities to be sheltered, then we have an inadequate environmental program. The environmental justice movement thus represents a revolution within the history of U.S. environmentalism.

IMPACT ON THE TRADITIONAL MOVEMENT

The environmental justice movement blasts apart the widely held myth within the traditional environmental movement that poor people and people of color are unconcerned with environmental issues. The fact that so many environmental groups of color have emerged and operate within the ideological framework of environmental justice demonstrates to the "mainstream" movement that people of color have always been interested in environmental issues. They simply remained outside the existing movement because of the ways in which environmental issues were framed, the kinds of issues which were focused on, and the ways those issues were strategically addressed.

Some white environmentalists dismiss this new sector of the environmental movement as radical social justice extremists and stubbornly ignore the potential insights to be gained by exploring their experience. For them, it is still business as usual. Others have sought to make just enough changes within their organizations to avoid charges of racism and negative press coverage. Still others have responded to this new sector of the movement by beginning to imagine more powerful and inclusive ways of furthering the environmental cause. The current impact of the environmental justice movement on the other sectors of the environmental movement is thus still inconclusive. But the seeds of change can be seen nearly everywhere. Directly or indirectly, the environmental justice movement has widened various debates, changed many of the terms of discussion, and altered the ways several issues are conceptualized and campaigns organized.

One example of this dynamic is the internal organizational policy changes that are underway. Several prominent environmental organizations, even some of those with the most conservative agendas, have felt compelled to racially diversify their staff, boards, and coalition partners. It has become increasingly hard to claim that there are not qualified people of color to sit on their boards, do research in their organizations, make policy, or teach environmental education. The environmental justice movement has begun to attract a growing number of people of color who are professors, researchers, policymakers, health and safety specialists, and environmental activists. People of color have become the members and volunteers that fuel the rapidly expanding environmental justice movement.

In light of this, several funding organizations are tying some of their funding to conventional environmental organizations to successful racial diversification efforts. We are increasingly seeing new opportunities for people of color to work and study within the environmental field. Today there are numerous minority internship programs, most notably those run by the Center for Environmental Intern Programs (CEIP). Other have launched collaborative efforts with minority environmental groups aimed at increasing the presence of people of color in the field. Greenpeace, for example, works closely with the Center for Environment, Commerce, and Energy to place interns.

While helpful, these efforts alone can not go very far beyond cosmetic tokenism. Hiring a few people of color can satisfy funders, the press, and liberal members, but it does

not necessarily address the deeper questions raised by the environmental justice movement or help the wider movement grow and win significant victories. Alliance-building
and logistical support are needed, not tokenism and cooptation.

One of the strengths of the multiracial environmental justice movement is that it provides the opportunity for people of color to lead instead of being led, to initiate and produce research instead of relying on someone else's, and to define the issues that are most
pressing to them instead of having their issues defined by others. While traditional environmental organizations should continue to racially diversify, they should also support
the new multiracial grassroots environmental organizations. For if recent trends hold,
people of color will continue flocking to the grassroots environmental justice movement
where they are immediately welcomed as contributing members. The chance for a
majoritarian movement for social and ecological renewal will be lost if the traditional
environmental movement does not develop respectful alliances with these new con-
stituencies and sources of political energy. This, of course, requires activists in the traditional movement to move beyond their often unconscious stance of white superiority.

The relationship between white and minority environmental groups has traditionally
been one of distrust, distance, discomfort, and misunderstanding. With a large number of
groups of color emerging with a radical politic, the relationship between minority and
nonminority environmental groups could easily get worse. However, both sides are now
expending considerable effort to achieve mutual understanding and find common
ground. They are working to identify the issues that keep them apart as well as the radical changes needed to bridge the distance.

PROSPECTS AND PROGNOSIS

Participation of people of color in the environmental justice movement will probably
continue to increase, but to reach the largest number of people possible will require
intense work by today's activists. First and foremost, they must meet the crying need
of their constituents for environmental education. This should begin early in people's
lives. Children in school need to be exposed to these issues so as to ensure that new
generations of environmental activists and specialists can be nurtured. Not only should
they be taught the basic facts and principles of the field, but they should also learn how
traditional fields such as medicine, law, education, or public health can be applied to
environmental work. Some Native Americans have already formed their own environmental law firms to handle their communities' legal battles.

Secondly, alliances need to be built between the environmentalists and labor activists.
Environmentalists and labor activists have often been at odds historically, a happy state
of affairs for big business. However, they can be a good allies for one another. Many
unions are fighting for worker health and safety. If environmentalists of color collaborate
with them and help create environmentally sound jobs and train people for them, the
animosity between the two movements will probably subside.

In addition, the environmental justice movement needs to continue to emphasize
community organizing. Militant environmental campaigns must be waged for access to
green space, toxic cleanup, inclusion of environmental issues in school curricula, pesticide reduction, clean air and water, healthier lifestyles among people of color, and a

reduction and redistribution of environmental risks. More active organizations of color are needed.

People of color have to be especially vigilant to prevent continued exposure of their communities to hazardous materials. It is estimated that the Defense Department alone will spend $22 billion over the next fifteen years on cleanup projects. In addition, between $25 and $50 billion will be spent to comply with the Clean Air Act through the installation of scrubbers and other smokestack devices. The Department of Energy estimates it will spend about $200 billion over the next 30 years to clean up 3,700 Superfund sites where nuclear materials are stored. In 1992 alone, more than $159 billion will be spent on all aspects of hazardous waste cleanups in the United States. This figure is expected to grow by about 10 percent a year as more sites are discovered. Yet, which sites will be targeted for cleanup? Where does the cleaned-up material go? Will the path of least resistance to dumping continue to lead polluters to minority communities?

Environmental justice groups also have to build alliances with other sectors of the social justice and environmental movements. The resources of these movements need to be combined to design and execute large-scale collaborative research projects, to create databanks on environmental health issues, and to build funding bases for future undertakings. Similarly, efforts to mount joint campaigns should be increased. More regional networks like the Southwest Network for Environmental and Economic Justice and the Southern Organizing Committee for Economic and Social Justice will enhance joint activities.

On another front, people of color should pressure the Congressional Black Caucus (CBC) and such formations to provide more high-profile leadership in these struggles. The CBC has already compiled one of the most outstanding and consistent environmental voting records in Congress. Yet, more needs to be done. The Caucus should let environmentalists know that it provides them their strongest congressional support and help further break down the myth that people of color have little interest in their relationship to the environment. Caucus members also need to make clear their support for these issues to their local communities. Caucus members should make environmental issues an even more prominent focus of their campaigns. Such legislative support will complement the efforts of grassroots groups.

People of color will also have to hold elected officials (regardless of their race) accountable for local environmental hazards. Those winning our support should champion the cause of environmental justice since their constituents have a better-than-average chance of being adversely affected by pollution. Those already elected should be held accountable for the factories, incinerators, landfills, etc., that they invite into communities to provide jobs. Activists should pursue elective office themselves to ensure that they have an actual say in the environmental health of their communities.

While the chances are good that many more groups of color will join the growing ranks of the environmental justice movement, these activists of color have an enormous task ahead of them. They have to continue the struggle for environmental justice, but also educate and organize their communities generally. In addition, they have to work closely with one another to increase funding for their projects and organizations, expand job-training and job-creation opportunities, enhance the political influence of their members, and ensure political accountability from elected officials. Finally, they must also find a way to link their local struggles with the larger ones in the national and international arenas.

REFERENCES

Bramwell, Anna. *Ecology in the 20th Century: A History.* New Haven: Yale University Press, 1989.

Bullard, Robert D. "Environmental Justice for All." *EnviroAction,* Environmental News Digest for the National Wildlife Federation (November 1991).

Bullard, Robert D. *Directory of People of Color Environmental Groups 1992.* Riverside, CA: University of California, Riverside, Department of Sociology, 1992.

Buttel, Frederick and Flinn, William, L. "The Structure and Support for the Environmental Movement 1968–1970." *Rural Sociology* 39 (1974):56–69.

Citizens' Clearinghouse for Hazardous Waste. *Everyone's Backyard* 9 (May 1991):2.

Collette, Will. "Institutions: Citizens Clearinghouse for Hazardous Waste." *Environment* 29 (September 1987):44–45.

Devall, Bill and Sessions, George. *Deep Ecology: Living as If Nature Mattered.* Salt Lake City, UT: Gibbs Smith, 1985.

Eckersley, Robyn. *Environmentalism and Political Theory: Toward an Ecocentric Approach.* Albany: State University of New York Press, 1992.

Fox, Stephen. *The American Conservation Movement: John Muir and His Legacy.* Madison, WI: University of Wisconsin Press, 1985.

Geiser, Ken and Gerry Waneck. "PCBs and Warren County." *Science for the People* 15 (1983):13–17.

LaBalme, Jenny. "Dumping on Warren County." In *Environmental Politics: Lessons from the Grassroots,* edited by Bob Hall, pp. 23–30. Durham, NC: Institute for Southern Studies, 1988.

Lowe, G.D.; Pinhey, T.K.; and Grimes, M.D. "Public Support for Environmental Protection: New Evidence from National Surveys." *Pacific Sociological Review* 23 (October 1980):423–445.

Mohai, Paul. "Black Environmentalism." *Social Science Quarterly* 71 (April 1990):744–765.

Montague, Peter. "What We Must Do: Grassroots Offensive Against Toxics in the 90's." *The Workbook* 19 (March 1990):90–114.

Nash, Roderick. *Wilderness and the American Mind.* 3rd ed. New Haven: Yale University Press, 1982.

Paehlke, Robert. *Environmentalism and the Future of Progressive Politics.* New Haven: Yale University Press, 1989.

Pepper, David. *The Roots of Modern Environmentalism.* London: Croom & Helm, Ltd., 1986.

Ruffins, Paul. "Blacks and Greens: What Can the Environmental Movement Do to Reach Out to Minorities?" *Race, Poverty and the Environment* 1 (February 1990):5.

Suro, Roberto. "Grass Roots Groups Show Power Battling Pollution Close to Home." *New York Times,* 2 July 1989:A1.

Taylor, Dorceta A. "Blacks and the Environment: Toward an Explanation of the Concern and Action Gap between Blacks and Whites." *Environment and Behavior* 21 (February 1989):175–205.

BEYOND SURVIVAL: SOCIAL CHANGE, DIGNITY, AND SOCIAL JUSTICE

In order to transform society in the interests of human dignity and social justice we need revitalized visions of selfhood, identity, consciousness, and community. Steven Seidman implies as much in the opening reading of this last section. Focusing on lesbian and gay people, Seidman first interrogates social constructionism and liberation theory and finds both wanting. His critique gains in force as he moves toward the conclusion that identity must be situated, both theoretically and pragmatically, "in a multidimensional social space" (p. 393). Using that theoretical mandate, issued in a rich context, Seidman sketches the possibilities of "a politics of resistance . . . guided by a transformative and affirmative social vision" (p. 393). By linking resistance, transformation, and affirmation, Seidman alludes to social justice, social change, and dignity. His is an open-ended, fluid vision centered on those three ends. Seidman thus announces the trifocal vision lending coherence to these last readings.

Institutionalized injustices must be undercut; our institutions must therefore change; human dignity will thereby be affirmed. These themes link Chicana/o, American Indian, feminist, lesbian/gay, Asian American, African American, and other multicultural social theorists. Their discourse, which takes shape around this trifocal vision, commonly invokes metaphors of exclusion. As we have seen, some such metaphors revolve around the insider/outsider dialectic that finds some theoretical resolution in Patricia Hill Collins's "outsider within." Other such metaphors illustrate a visible/invisible dialectic that may find some theoretical resolution in the feminist axiom: the personal is political. When feminists and other multicultural theorists challenge the public/private dualism that correlates with other oppressive dualisms in our culture, they transform the virtual invisibility of the private sphere into a political and cultural problematic. Think of domestic violence or queerness. Once barely present as flesh-and-blood realities in dominant discourses, they are now "visible," however haphazardly at this point.

Hand in hand with its concern over exclusion stands multiculturalists' concern with marginalization. Tokenism, second-class treatment, and grudging acceptance are scarcely the central issues here. Instead, margins are. The margins are the social and cultural spaces where power drops off in volume and reach, where status is ambiguous or incongruous, where authority is diminished, where resources thin due to having been repeatedly stretched to their limit. The margins are where contests of dignity are held, usually overseen from distant centers of power that elite members monopolize. Thus, the margins are also those social and cultural spaces where emancipatory scripts get written, where community-making gets serious priority, where anger gets put to transformative use, where ideology gets unmasked and knowledge gets its made-up face washed. The margins are where oppressed people resist the matrix of domination; the margins are where dignity asserts itself even at risk to life and limb. When multicultural social theorists refer to marginalization, then, they are meaning to focus attention on processes whereby groups get institutionally cheated of a fair chance or even a fighting chance. They mean by marginalization something insulting and damaging, something that in the interests of dignity must be addressed daily.

Besides its concern with exclusion and marginalization, multicultural discourse concerns itself with dualistic, hierarchical thinking. Prone to suspect the either/or associated with elitist worldviews and oppressive rhetorics, multicultural social theorists advocate consciousness attuned to subtleties, nuances, overlap, and fluidity. Above all, they advocate a suspicion of "difference" unattended by multiplicity and ambiguity. Thus, multicultural discourse commonly interrogates essentialist as well as dualistic thinking. By and large, it inveighs against what Seidman (p. 393) calls "a substantialist understanding of group life."

Similarly, multicultural discourse concerns itself with *lived* similarities and differences within a grouping such as women. Regardless of their other social positionings, women share certain experiences that make them prospective allies in struggles against heteropatriarchy. Routinely, for instance, women's right to privacy—even their right to the integrity of their experiences—comes under attack. As Naomi Scheman indicates,

> the interpretation of women's feelings and behavior is often appropriated by others, by husbands or lovers, or by various psychological "experts." Autonomy in this regard is less an individual achievement than a socially recognized right, and, as such, people with social power tend to have more of it.[1]

Although women do vary dramatically in the amount of autonomy they can reliably claim, within each social class they are entitled to less of it than their male counterparts; within most racial and ethnic groups, the same pattern holds; within most age groups, the same pattern holds. Similarly, as Elizabeth Kamarck Minnich observes,

> It is still the case today that a woman's relation to her sexuality is profoundly mediated by the hierarchy in a way that breaks through any neat divisions between women constructed in terms of class or race, however influential those *also* are. Consider that sexual abuse and violence, and harassment of all sorts, affect all women, as threat all the time, as actuality with stunning frequency.[2]

Citing the historian Gerda Lerner, Minnich observes more generally that even when we look at brothers and sisters of the same family, of the same race, of the same class, the relation of the siblings to the power hierarchy is *not* the same. Gender constructs them differently and keeps them different in important ways.[3]

Nevertheless, as Segura and Pesquera indicate, women's lived experiences often pit one dimension of their identity against another dimension of their identity. For people whose oppressive experiences derive from multiple parts of their identity, a hard-and-fast identification with only one basis of their oppression is unlikely. If one is oppressed because of one's sex *and* because of one's race/ethnicity *and* because of one's social class, as the Chicanas in Segura and Pesquera's study typically are, how could they be expected to become feminists but not cultural nationalists, cultural nationalists but not feminists, or feminists and cultural nationalists but not critics of the class structure?

Segura and Pesquera walk us through the "dialectical tension between [these women's] lives and the ideological configurations that dichotomize their experiences and exploit their political loyalties" (p. 395). In the process they show us what might also be shown about other groupings of heterosexual women whose ties to men of the same racial/ethnic group are often pragmatic and political as well as romantic and marital. In a nutshell they show us that "Chicanas and Chicanos share a collective identity" (p. 396). Both know the contempt of Anglos; both know the sting of employment discrimination; both are aware of the stereotypes portraying them as shiftless, devil-may-care individuals who, therefore, cannot get "ahead" in the world. They know one another's pain in ways that white heterosexual women and men seldom do, for white people share race privilege[4] and thus lack the grounds for making community together in and through their resistance to a clear-cut grouping of oppressors. Segura and Pesquera thus offer widely applicable lessons about how multiply oppressed people wend their way through the pains born of experiencing barriers, putdowns, and exclusion because they are two or three or more times the "wrong kind" of person. For such individuals then to face "loyalty tests" from feminists, Chicana/o activists, or any other grouping seeking their support is but one more measure of their multiple oppressions.

Segura and Pesquera further show how similarities and dissimilarities coexist within a specific grouping of women such as Chicana feminists. As they delineate the three voices they discerned among Chicana feminists, Segura and Pesquera bring the prospect of Chicana feminists' "common praxis" with one another to the fore. In the process they defeat "difference" as a sign of divisiveness. Segura and Pesquera show that it can make for a chorus of diversity.

R. W. Connell's selection also points to the prospect of common praxis, or what he calls "alliance politics" (p. 415). Like Segura and Pesquera, he appreciates the difficulties of achieving such a politics. Men, Connell emphasizes, are particularly prone to experience those difficulties in dislocating ways. To help disassemble the matrix of domination they must, each in his own social relationships and each within the context of his other social positionings, give up piece by piece the "patriarchal dividend" (p. 412) that has benefited them from the dawn of their consciousness. By surveying the various masculinities available in our society, Connell shows how men's other social positionings affect their advantages as men. At the same time he shows us that masculinity, like whiteness and heterosexuality, is pervasively promoted across the institutional spectrum. Connell notes, for instance, that

> Exalting technology over human relations . . . and exalting market forces over public responsibility are also ways of promoting masculinity, though they are not often recognized as such (p. 413).

Three additional observations merit attention in Connell's paper. First, he equates feminism with "mak[ing] a primary commitment to solidarity with women" (p. 410) and thus illuminates the problems Segura and Pesquera observed among Chicana feminists. At the same time Connell's position raises the question of what an inclusive definition of feminism might be, and he implicitly offers a response in his survey of various masculinities. No single definition will likely suffice. We need, he implies, to think in terms of feminism*s*. Second, he returns us to the environmental movement in the form of "green politics" where "men have worked productively with feminist women" (p. 414). His example raises the question, first implied perhaps in Dorceta Taylor's selection, of whether environmentalism might offer a ground where anti-elitists situated throughout the matrix of domination might make common cause with one another. Since environmentalism raises questions about equity, natural resources, population and reproduction, development, overdevelopment, and other multicultural matters, the question probably merits continuing theoretical attention.

Third, Connell sees dignity in social-justice undertakings. After citing strategies whereby men might help to advance feminist goals, Connell writes, "I find these strategies hopeful, not least because they offer some dignity to men involved in the highly undignified task of dismantling their own privileges" (p. 415). Thereby Connell underscores the centrality of voluntary action to dignity. Without their voluntary character, our projects become prisons—a virtual axiom of multicultural social theory.

Like her colleagues in this section, bell hooks emphasizes making common cause with one another across sexual, class, racial/ethnic, gender, and other lines drawn by the matrix of domination. Hers is a vision emphasizing inclusiveness and self-transformation interwoven with politicization and love. With her attention to love, Hooks goes to the core—the unromantic, compassionate center—of people's involvements in social-justice work. Their concern for their own and others' dignity and rights is strong enough to count as love.

Struggles against what hooks calls the "politics of domination" express people's love for themselves and others. Like Connell and Segura and Pesquera, though, hooks emphasizes, that "politicization—coming to critical consciousness—is a difficult, 'trying' process. . ." (p. 420). She says, "Women and men need to know what is on the other side of the pain experienced in politicization" (p. 421). Above all, what lies there is "the dignity and integrity of being that comes with revolutionary change" (p. 420). Willing to put feminism at the center of liberatory struggles, hooks emphasizes that it must be "part of the larger struggle to eradicate domination in all its forms." Thus, she reminds us that the various axes of the matrix of domination interlock so that disabling one axis alone is impossible. Thus, "feminist action" just as readily comprises assaults on racism as on sexism, critiques of the class structure as well as the sex/gender system, rejection of homophobia as well as misogyny.

In her critique of and support for feminism, hooks resounds a message central to multicultural social theory. In our theorizing and other practices we must understand that the same "ideological foundation" (p. 418) undergirds the institutionalized oppression of various groups in our society. When was the last time you met a misogynist who embraces racial diversity and gives no signs of severe homophobia? When was the last time you met a homophobe who enthusiastically supports women's rights and the advancement of people of color in American society? Although people's prejudices against and stereotypes of various groups vary in intensity and detail, they correlate with one another at or just beneath the interactional surface. To hooks's credit she drives that point home by insisting that each of us as persons needs to seek the

> transformation of self, of relationships, so that we might better be able to act in a revolutionary manner, challenging and resisting domination, transforming the world outside the self (p. 417).

In the end, hooks reminds us that caring about people seemingly unlike ourselves is the most revolutionary posture we can adopt as perpetrators/victims of the matrix of domination.

Finally, we come to Cornel West's selection, which brings us full circle by raising anew questions about what social theory is, what purposes it properly serves, and how we best make it. In his historically encompassing delineation of the "new cultural politics of difference" West puts the concerns of multicultural theorists on a huge stage whereon a community of cultural workers has labored and continue laboring on behalf of

> demoralized, demobilized, depoliticized and disorganized people in order to empower and enable social action and, if possible, to enlist collective insurgency for the expansion of freedom, democracy, and individuality (pp. 422).

West's essay weaves together the concerns common to all the readings in *Multicultural Experiences, Multicultural Theories*. It advocates that we serve as "critical organic analysts" availing ourselves of what is useful from mainstream culture while drawing inspiration from "affirming and enabling subcultures of criticism" (p. 435). West invites us to become

> intellectual freedom-fighters, that is, cultural workers who simultaneously position themselves within (or alongside) the mainstream while clearly aligned with groups who vow to keep alive potent traditions of critique and resistance (p. 436).

West's is ultimately an invitation to dignity, which he sees as a firm admixture of individuality, self-confidence, self-respect, and self-esteem (pp. 422, 429). It is an invitation, too, to grasp "the moral content of one's cultural identity" (p. 437) and make something fine of it in the world. West's is, then, an invitation to reread history in multicultural terms and to rewrite the future in multicultural scripts that give starring roles to all the groupings that make ours the vibrantly multicultural world it is. Thus, as "prophetic critics" we might appropriate formulations like Matthew Arnold's by twisting them to our own purposes: through multiculturalism seems to lie our way, not to perfection and perhaps not even to safety, but to honesty, meaning, and whatever chance we have for making a just world together.

NOTES

1 Naomi Scheman, *Engenderings: Constructions of Knowledge, Authority, and Privilege,* Routledge, New York, 1993, p. 28.
2 Elizabeth Kamarck Minnich, *Transforming Knowledge,* Temple University Press, Philadelphia, 1990, p. 60.
3 *Ibid.*
4 For a splendid survey of the privileges white people enjoy in our society, see Peggy McIntosh, "White Privilege and Male Privilege: A Personal Account of Coming to See Correspondences Through Work in Women's Studies" in Anne Minas (ed.), *Gender Basics: Feminist Perspectives on Women and Men,* Wadsworth Publishing Company, Belmont, CA, 1993, pp. 30–38.

The Politics of Subverting Identity and Foregrounding the Social

Steven Seidman

THE POLITICS OF SUBVERTING IDENTITY

Social constructionism recalls the standpoint of gay liberation. For example, by asserting the deeply social and historical character of sexuality, it encourages, at least implicitly, a culture of social activism. Sexual conventions can be changed through acts of social will. In addition, constructionism provides a language highlighting social differences that marginalized lesbians and gay men can appeal to in order to legitimate their demands for recognition.

Viewed from the standpoint of gay liberationism, however, social constructionism appears suspect. Unlike liberation theory that was closely aligned to the politics of the movement, constructionism is increasingly disconnected from the political impulses of the movement. Indeed, gay constructionism has been captured by primarily academic interests. The debate over constructionism has become a metaphysical one centered on unresolvable conflicts such as nature versus nurture or realism versus nominalism. Moreover, if the debates are not mired in a metaphysical quagmire, they are preoccupied with an equally sterile historical scholasticism that revolves around tracing the appearance of homosexual subcultures or dating the rise of a homosexual identity.

Furthermore, whereas liberation theory assumed an explicitly moral and political understanding of its own discourse, social constructionists are often wedded to scientistic presuppositions, claiming for their own approach an objectivity, value neutrality, and evidentiary-based truth. Indeed, many view a constructionist approach as superior precisely because it obtains true representations of reality in contrast to the ethnocentric distortions of essentialist conceptual strategies. While constructionists have uncovered ethnocentric bias in gay scholarship that universalizes present-centered, culture-bound perspectives, they have not applied the same suspicion to their own discourse. If categories of same-sex intimacies are marked by the sociocultural context of their origin, is not the same true of our categories of analysis? And, if representations are embedded in broad national environments, are they not likewise stamped by the more particular social traits of their producers, for example, their class, race, ethnicity, nationality, age, or gender? Gay social constructionists have been enthusiastic in taking over Foucault's historicism but decidedly less so when it comes to his understanding of human studies as a practical-moral social force.[1]

Many activists and intellectuals discontented with mainstream lesbian and gay male culture are looking back fondly to the agenda of gay liberation. Indeed, many who embrace the rhetoric of social constructionism do so, in part, because they see in it a warrant for radical social activism.

I share this discontent with mainstream lesbian and gay male cultural politics. I wish to recover the expansive social and political potential of liberation theory. Nevertheless, we need to be clear about its limitations. . . . Liberationists viewed their movement as one of sexual and gender liberation. Unfortunately, they understood emancipation as a release from homosexual/heterosexual and masculine/feminine roles. They challenged the dominant sexual/social regime by juxtaposing to it a polymorphous, androgynous ideal of a liberated—constraint-free—humanity. Wouldn't a liberated humanity, however, require stable identities, social roles, and normative constraints? Liberationists conflated the critique of rigid roles and identities with the critique of all identities and roles as signifying domination. In a word, liberationists projected a radically individualistic, utopian concept of emancipation. They lacked, moreover, a credible strategy to transform a stable, socially anchored gay/straight identity regime into a postidentity liberated order.

Liberationist theory emerged as a gay identity and community were coalescing. It assumed the social dominance of a system of mutually exclusive roles around sexual orientation and gender; it formed as an opposition movement to this regime but reinforced it by narrowing its agenda to abolishing this system.

Today lesbians and gay men find themselves in a very different situation. Our standpoint is that of an elaborated culture founded upon an affirmative identity. Many of us have built coherent and meaningful lives around this identity. Moreover, although we still encounter substantial opposition in the social mainstream, we have gained considerable social inclusion. The liberationist strategy of juxtaposing a postidentity model to current identities would seem to lack credibility today.

The present condition of communities organized around affirmative gay/lesbian identities yet exhibiting heightened conflicts around those very identities should be the starting point of contemporary gay theory and politics. Where gay liberation confronted a dialectic of identity and difference that revolved around straight/gay and man/woman polarities, currently these oppositions are multiplied a hundredfold as we introduce differences along the dimensions of race, ethnicity, gender, age, sexual act, class, lifestyle, and locale. Thus, the dominant liberationist opposition between gay/straight and gay/lesbian passes into divisions between, say, white/black gay, black/Latino gay, middle-class/working-class gay, or lesbian/lesbian S/M, and on and on. Contemporary gay culture is centered on social difference and the multiplication of identities.

A key issue we confront today is as follows: How can we theorize and organize politically our multiple differences in light of the suspicions surrounding the dominant mode of identity politics? One strategy has called for the abandonment or destabilization of identity as a ground of gay politics. In poststructuralist theorizing, we are urged to shift our focus from the politics of personal identity to the politics of signification, in particular, to the deconstruction of a hetero/homo code that structures the "social text" of daily life.[2]

Reflecting on the recent history of the exclusions and conflicts elicited around identity constructions, poststructuralists have abandoned efforts to defend or reconfigure identity politics by theorizing its multiple and interlocking character. Appealing to one's sexual, gender, or ethnic identity as the ground of community and politics is rejected because of its inherent instabilities and exclusions. Diana Fuss describes the Derridean understanding of identity as follows: "Deconstruction dislocates the understanding of identity as self-presence and offers, instead, a view of identity as difference. To the extent that identity always contains the specter of non-identity within it, the subject is always divided and identity is always purchased at the price of the exclusion of the

Other, the repression or repudiation of non-identity."[3] In other words, repudiating views of identity as essence or its effect, poststructuralists propose that the identity of an object or person is always implicated in its opposite. "Heterosexuality" has meaning only in relation to "homosexuality"; the coherence of the former is built on the exclusion, repression, and repudiation of the latter. These two terms form an interdependent, hierarchical relation of signification. The logic of identity is a logic of boundary defining which necessarily produces a subordinated other. The social productivity of identity is purchased at the price of a logic of hierarchy, normalization, and exclusion.[4]

Furthermore, gay identity constructions reinforce the dominant hetero/homo sexual code with its heteronormativity. If homosexuality and heterosexuality are a coupling in which each presupposes the other, each being present in the invocation of the other, and in which this coupling assumes hierarchical forms, then the epistemic and political project of identifying a gay subject reinforces and reproduces this hierarchical figure. Poststructuralists recommend that this discursive figure become the focus of a "deconstructive" analysis in place of the construction of the gay subject. In effect, poststructuralists urge an epistemic shift from the humanistic standpoint of the individual subject creating himself or herself to the standpoint of a "structural" order, in this case a signifying or cultural discursivity.

Some poststructuralists intend to move the analysis of homosexuality into the center of Western culture. Whereas identity political standpoints framed homosexuality as an issue of sexuality and minority politics, poststructuralists position hetero/homosexual symbolism at the very center of Western culture—as structuring the very core modes of thought and culture of Western societies. This is perhaps the chief contention of Eve Kosofsky Sedgwick, whose latest book begins with the declaration:

> *Epistemology of the Closet* proposes that many of the major nodes of thought and knowledge in twentieth-century Western culture as a whole are structured—indeed, fractured— by a chronic, now endemic crisis of homo/heterosexual definition. . . . The book will argue that an understanding of virtually any aspect of modern Western culture must be, not merely incomplete, but damaged in its central substance to the degree that it does not incorporate a critical analysis of modern homo/heterosexual definition.[5]

Sedgwick conjectures that the homo/heterosexual figure is the master cultural term marking not only sexual definitions but categorical pairings such as secrecy/disclosure, knowledge/ignorance, private/public, masculine/feminine, majority/minority, innocence/initiation, natural/artificial, same/different, health/illness, growth/decadence, urbane/provincial.[6] Poststructuralists urge an epistemic shift from the resisting gay subject to the analysis of the homo/hetero code and its pervasive structuring of modes of thought, knowledge, and culture whose themes are both sexual and non-sexual.

The surfacing of a poststructural standpoint is in response to the perceived impasse of current gay politics and theory. In particular, the movement of gay politics between radical separatism and assimilationism seems closely tied to its centering on identity. Poststructuralism aims to destabilize identity as a ground of politics and theory in order to open up alternative social and political possibilities; poststructuralists seem to be positioned as a sort of theoretical wing of Queer Nation, with its insistent opposition to normalizing, disciplining social forces; with its disruptive politics of subversion; and with its opposition to both the straight and gay mainstream.[7] Just as Queer Nation wishes to create a sort of unified block in opposition to global processes of domination and exclusion, poststructuralists, by repositioning homosexuality as a central social fact, intend to render their oppositional practices as broadly social and globally oppositional.

To what end is poststructural critique directed? If the premiere collection *Inside/Out* is exemplary of the poststructural turn, the chief domain of struggle is the multiple sites of cultural production, in particular, high-brow literary and popular culture.[8] The principal aim is to document the presence of the hetero/homo figure, to disclose its compelling discursive efficacy and culturally contagious character, and to deconstruct it by revealing the mutual dependency of the polar terms and the instability and susceptibility of the figure to be reversed and subverted. Underlying this politics of subversion is a vague notion that this will encourage new, affirmative forms of personal and social life, although poststructuralists are reluctant to name their social vision. The poststructural move seems troubling, moreover, to the extent that social practices are framed narrowly as discursive and signifying, and critical practice becomes deconstructive textual strategies. Insofar as poststructuralists narrow cultural codes into binary signifying figures, insofar as discursive practices are not institutionally situated, there is an edging toward textual idealism.

An additional doubt about the poststructural turn: Who is the agent or subject of the politics of subversion? The poststructuralist critique of the logic of identity ends in a refusal to name a subject. Indeed, I detect a disposition in the deconstruction of identity to slide into viewing identity itself as the fulcrum of domination and its subversion as the center of an anti-identity politic. For example, although Judith Butler often elaborates complex understandings of identity as both enabling and self-limiting, she, at times, conflates identity as a disciplining force with domination and a politics of subversion with a politics against identity. "If it is already true that 'lesbians' and 'gay men' have been traditionally designated as impossible identities, errors of classification, unnatural disasters within juridico-medical discourses, . . . then perhaps these sites of disruption, error, confusion, and trouble can be the very rallying points for a certain resistance to classification and to identity as such."[9] Butler's politics of subversion at times becomes little more than a kind of disruptive repetitive performance that works "sexuality *against* identity." But to what end?

The poststructural turn edges beyond an anti-identity politics to a politics against identity per se. Implicit in this subversion of identity is a celebration of liminality, of the spaces between or outside structure, a kind of anarchistic championing of "pure" freedom from all constraints and limits. A strong parallel with Queer Nation is, once again, apparent. Like the poststructural refusal of identity, under the undifferentiated sign of Queer are united all those heterogeneous desires and interests that are marginalized and excluded in the straight and gay mainstream. Queers are not united by any unitary identity but only by their opposition to disciplining, normalizing social forces. Queer Nation aims to be the voice of all the disempowered and to stand for the proliferation of social differences. In its resistance to social codes (sexual gender, race, class) that impose unitary identities, in rebelling against forces imposing a repressive coherence and order, Queer Nation affirms an abstract unity of differences without wishing to name and fix these. This positioning resembles the poststructural refusal to name the subject, as if any anchoring of the flux and abundant richness of experience marks the beginnings of conflict, domination, and hierarchy.

This very refusal to anchor experience in identifications ends up, ironically, denying differences by either submerging them in an undifferentiated oppositional mass or by blocking the development of individual and social differences through the disciplining compulsory imperative to remain undifferentiated. Poststructuralists, like Queer Nationals, hope to avoid the self-limiting, fracturing dynamics of identification by an insistent disruptive subversion of identity. Yet, their cultural positioning, indeed their subversive politics, presupposes these very identifications and social anchorings. Is it possible that underlying the refusal to name the subject (of knowledge and politics) is a utopian wish for a full, intact, organic experience of self and other?

I have noted a turn in poststructural gay theory beyond a critique of identity politics to a politics against identity. The latter seems driven by its centering on a politics of identity subversion and draws from both romantic and antinomian traditions for its cultural resonance. Its limit, if you will, is the continuing practical efficacy of the resisting gay subject. In other words, it fails to theoretically engage the practices of individuals organized around affirmative lesbian and gay identities. Although I am sure that poststructuralists would readily acknowledge that gay identities have developed in resistance to an administrative-juridico-medical institutional rendering of same-sex desires, acts, and social formations as a site of social oppression, their focus on subverting identity seems to abstract from this institutional struggle and the social origin and efficacy of identity politics.[10] Identity constructions are not disciplining and regulatory only in a self-limiting and oppressive way; they are also personally, socially, and politically enabling; it is this moment that is captured by identity political standpoints that seems lost in the poststructural critique.

If the issue is not identity versus nonidentity, if subjects and social formations cannot elude categories of identity, if, indeed, identity categories have enabling, self- and socially enriching qualities, then the issue is less their affirmation or subversion than analyzing the kinds of identities that are socially produced and their manifold social significance. In this regard, I would follow the poststructural move that recommends viewing identity as a site of ongoing social regulation and contestation rather than a quasi-natural substance or an accomplished social fact. Identities are never fixed or stable, not only because they elicit otherness but because they are occasions of continuing social struggle. Yet, I would not privilege, as many poststructuralists seem to, signifying practices and contestations but would connect these to institutional dynamics. I would, moreover, follow the poststructural turn in framing identities as social structuring forces or, to use Foucaultian terms, as disciplining forces whose consequences for the individual, social relations, and politics should be critically analyzed. However, to the extent that some poststructuralists reduce the regulating and disciplining force of identity constructions to modes of domination and hierarchy, I would object. This rendering edges toward a politics against identity, to a sort of negative dialectics. As disciplining forces, identities are not only self-limiting and productive of hierarchies but are enabling or productive of social collectivities, moral bonds, and political agency. Although the poststructural problematization of identity is a welcome critique of the essentialist celebration of a unitary subject and tribal politic, poststructuralism's own troubled relation to identity edges toward an empty politics of gesture or disruptive performance that forfeits an integrative, transformative politic.

The recent proliferation of critiques of identity politics, particularly under the guise of poststructuralism, gives expression to the sociopolitical assertion of difference. . . . In its critique of identity politics as normalizing and exclusionary, in its disruption of an illusory unity that masks difference and domination, in forcing us to view identities as political artifices, poststructuralism is valuable. To the extent, however, that poststructural critique edges toward an anti-identity or postidentity standpoint, to the extent that it folds into a politics of the disruptive gesture, it lacks coherence. At another level, insofar as poststructuralism encourages us to focus less on the formation of gay identities as grounds of an ethnic minority and urges us to analyze cultural codes, it pushes our inquiries beyond a sociology of a minority to a study of the structure and tensions of modern culture. Yet to the extent that poststructuralists reduce cultural codes to textual practice and to the extent that these practices are abstracted from institutional contexts, we come up against the limits of poststructuralism as social critique.

FOREGROUNDING THE SOCIAL: THE NEXT MOVE?

The limits of identity politics revolve around its thinking of identity as a unitary phenomenon, whether its unity is produced by nature or society. Positing a gay identity, no matter how it strains to be inclusive of difference, produces exclusions, represses difference, and normalizes being gay. Identity politics strains, as well, toward a narrow, liberal, interest-group politic aimed at assimilationism or spawns its opposite, a troubling ethnic-nationalist separatism. Poststructuralism is a kind of reverse or, if you wish, deconstructive logic; it dissolves any notion of a substantial unity in identity constructions leaving only rhetorics of identities, performances, and the free play of difference and possibility. Whereas identity politics offers a strong politics on a weak, exclusionary basis, poststructuralism offers a thin politics as it problematizes the very notion of a collective in whose name a movement acts.

I sense the battle over identity politics beginning to grow tiresome, or perhaps it's my own weariness. The terms of the discussion are in need of a shift. In both defenders of identity politics and its poststructural critics there is a preoccupation with the self and the politics of representation. Institutional and historical analysis and an integrative political vision seem to have dropped out. Perhaps as the politics of backlash comes to an end, we can begin to entertain broader, more affirmative social and political visions. Central to a renewal of political vision will be thinking issues of self, subject, and identity as a social positioning, as marking a social juncture in the institutional, administrative, juridical organization of society, and as an axis of social stratification. As much as race, sexuality, gender, or class mark a site of self-definition and therefore implicate us in a politics of identity and representation, these categories serve as social and political markers. Sexual orientational status positions the self in the social periphery or the social center; it places the self in a determinate relation to institutional resources, social opportunities, legal protections, and social privileges; it places the self in a relation to a range of forms of social control, from violence to ridicule. Locating identity in a multidimensional social space features its macrosocial significance; we are compelled to relate the politics of representation to institutional dynamics.

In framing identity as a social positioning we need to avoid assuming that all individuals who share a social location by virtue of their gender or sexual orientation share a common or identical history or social experience. The notion that a hetero/homosexual social positioning creates two antithetical unitary collectivities, the former positioned as one of privilege while the latter is positioned as an oppressed and resisting subject, lacks coherence. While appealing to a collective interest is a condition of political mobilization, it is unnecessary and undesirable to invoke a substantialist understanding of group life.

A major shortcoming of sociological essentialism is that it assumes that each axis of social constitution—gender, sexual orientation, ethnicity, class—can be isolated. However, as many feminist and gay people of color have argued, these axes of social positioning cannot be isolated in terms of a set of common attributes and experiences since they are always intersecting and mutually inflecting. Individuals experience sexual orientation in a particular class-, race-, or gender-mediated way, and only so. While we may wish, from time to time, to differentiate these axes of social positioning and identification for specific intellectual and practical reasons, we must avoid reifying what are analytical and political moves.

Unfortunately, I can do no more at this point than offer these rather sketchy proposals. However, the general direction of my thinking should be clear. Let me give a quick forward-looking résumé.

I urge a shift away from the preoccupation with self and representations characteristic of identity politics and poststructuralism to an analysis that embeds the self in institutional and cultural practices. I favor a politics of resistance that is guided by a transformative and affirmative social vision. This suggests an oppositional politic that intends institutional and cultural change without, however, being wedded to millennial vision. In a postmodern culture, anticipation of the "end of domination" or self-realization pass into local struggles for participatory democracy, distributive social justice, lifestyle choice, or reconfiguring knowledges. I prefer a pragmatic approach to social criticism. Conceptual and political decision making would be debated in terms of concrete advantages and disadvantages; the values guiding such pragmatic calculus would receive their moral warrant from local traditions and social ideals, not foundational appeals. In a pragmatically driven human studies, I imagine critical analyses that address specific conflicts, aim to detail the logics of social power, and do not shy away from spelling out a vision of a better society in terms resonant to policy makers and activists. In this regard, I am less patient with generalizing, systematizing "theories" in the tradition of Marxism or radical feminism; such efforts promote social hierarchy and an exclusionary politics. I favor social sketches, framed in a more narrative rather than analytical mode, as responses to specific social developments and conflicts with specific purposes in mind. I think for example of the writings, mostly essays with a strong narrative cast, most moving back and forth between the personal and the institutional, of Cherrie Moraga, Minnie Pratt, Audre Lorde, Gloria Anzaldúa, and Barbara Smith, as exemplary. This, however, is a topic for another occasion.

NOTES

I wish to thank Linda Nicholson, Rosemary Hennessey, and Michael Warner for their helpful comments on earlier drafts of this essay.

A note on terminology: When the term "gay" is used without further qualification, I intend to refer to both men and women. Although I have followed current conventions in speaking of lesbians, gay men, women, African-Americans, and so on, I mean by this only individuals who identify as, say, men or lesbians. My preference would be to speak of individuals who are gay-identified or African-American-identified, so as to convey the sociopolitical meaning of such identity constructs.

1 I urge that gay theory substitute postmodern for modernist premises. Standard modernist science justifies itself by its claims to objectivity and truth, the growth of knowledge, and its role as an agent of enlightenment. A postmodern perspective will describe modernist social science as itself a major force in the production of bodies, sexualities, institutional orders, and social hierarchies. It interprets the modernist language of truth, objectivity, value neutrality, and scientific and social progress as a symbolic, rhetorical code that conceals a will to power. All discourse is viewed as embedded in a specific social configuration and exhibiting a partial, value-laden, interested standpoint. The kind of postmodern approach I am recommending favors pragmatic, justificatory strategies that underscore the practical and rhetorical character of social discourse. Similarly, I urge abandoning grand theories and metanarratives in favor of genealogies, historical deconstructionist analyses, and local social narratives. On postmodern criticisms of conventional social science and the development of a distinctive postmodern social studies, see Linda Nicholson, ed., *Feminism/Postmodernism* (New York: Routledge, 1990); and Steven Seidman and David Wagner, *Postmodernism and Social Theory* (Oxford: Basil Blackwell, 1992).

2 On poststructural gay theory, see Diana Fuss, ed., *Inside/Out: Lesbian Theories, Gay Theories* (New York: Routledge, 1991); Ronald Butters et al., eds., *Displacing Homophobia* (Durham, N.C.: Duke University Press, 1989); Joseph Boone and Michael Cadden, eds., *Engendering Men* (New York: Routledge, 1990).

3 Diana Fuss, *Essentially Speaking* (New York: Routledge, 1989), 102–3.

4 See Fuss, "Introduction," *Inside/Out,* 1.

5 Eve Kosofsky Sedgwick, *Epistemology of the Closet* (Berkeley: University of California Press, 1990), 1.

6 Ibid., 11, 71–72.

7 See the symposium "Queer/Nation," *Out/Look* 11 (winter 1991).

8 See Fuss, ed., *Inside/Out.*

9 Judith Butler, "Imitation and Gender Insubordination," in *Inside/Out,* 16.

10 See the relevant comments by Michael Warner in his introduction to the present volume.

Beyond Indifference and Antipathy: The Chicana Movement and Chicana Feminist Discourse

Denise A. Segura and Beatriz M. Pesquera

Chicana feminism means working toward the liberation of Chicanas from the indifference of the Women's Movement, the antipathy among Chicanos/Latinos, and the fulfillment of their own dreams and capacities.

Faculty member, age 49

Feminism as an ideology and a movement has developed in response to women's need to overturn their historical subordination to men. By and large, the public discourse on feminism has been demarcated by white feminist scholars. Increasingly, women of Color,[1] both heterosexual and lesbian, are challenging the relevance of American feminism and the American Women's Movement of the 1960s and 1970s for evading varying, often competing interests among women.[2] They posit instead a unique feminism grounded in their experiences as women and as members of oppressed minority groups and classes.

In this article we explore the form and content of feminist discourse among a selected group of Chicanas[3] in higher education. We argue that their articulations of feminism reveals tension between Chicano cultural nationalism and American feminism. The ideology of Chicano cultural nationalism advocates racial/ethnic unity against Anglo American domination and idealizes traditional Mexican/Chicano culture.[4] Feminism, in the broadest sense, calls for female unity against patriarchy (a system of male domination and female subordination) in traditional cultural patterns. Each perspective is skewed in favor of race/ethnicity or gender. Neither addresses the unique situation of Chicanas whose life chances mirror the intersection of class, race/ethnicity, and gender. Chicana feminism reverberates with the dialectical tension between their lives and the ideological configurations that dichotomize their experiences and exploit their political loyalties.

We begin our analysis by examining Chicanas' perspectives of the American Women's Movement and the Chicano Movement of the late 1960s and early 1970s. This sets the stage for our analysis of the rise of the Chicana Movement and contemporary Chicana feminist discourse among a selected group of 101 Chicanas in higher education. This study elucidates the social context of Chicana feminism while contributing new evidence on the diverse expressions of feminism in the United States.

THE AMERICAN WOMEN'S MOVEMENT AND CHICANAS

The contemporary American Women's Movement emerged during the 1960s and evolved into two major branches—the "women's rights" branch and the "women's liberation" or "left" branch.[5] The women's rights branch concentrated on programs that would integrate women into the mainstream of American society.[6] The women's liberation branch, in contrast, called for a radical restructuring of society that would eliminate patriarchy, the system of male control and domination of women.[7] Although both branches of the Women's Movement advocated on behalf of women, the issues of women of Color were often overlooked.[8]

The Chicana Movement developed during the late 1960s. Organizationally, it shared some of the characteristics of the "left" or women's liberation branch of the Women's Movement. Chicanas formed caucuses within Chicano Movement organizations, started various groups to advocate a feminist agenda, began consciousness-raising groups, and organized conferences on *la mujer* [women]. Within the Women's Movement these activities often led to a separatist politic. When Chicanas engaged in these activities, however, they did not always articulate a separatist ideology or organizational strategy. When women formed Chicana organizations, they justified their actions under the rubric of the Chicano Movement. They insisted they were not "separate" but simply more focused on issues of *la mujer* thereby strengthening the Movement.

This stance makes sense if we consider that Chicanas' political consciousness is grounded in a fundamentally different reality than that of white feminists. Conquered in 1848, economically and culturally subordinated to Anglo American domination, Chicanas and Chicanos share a collective identity. Because of the historical racial/ethnic antagonisms between Anglos and Chicanos, Chicanas often feel a closer affinity to their Chicano brothers than their feminist sisters. At the same time, Chicanas share a physical, cultural, and material vulnerability to the dicta of men.

While Chicana activists recognized their gender-based oppression, they usually rejected the ideology of separatism and tried to find ways of integrating their concerns within Chicano Movement organizations.[9] These attempts were usually resisted by Chicano male activists, and to a lesser degree by some women. Therefore, Chicana activists committed to integrating gender into the race/class politic organized separate groups that responded to their needs as women and as members of an historically exploited racial/ethnic group and class.

Caught between the ideological pull of race/class unity and their subordination within the male-dominated Chicano left, Chicana activists articulated the seemingly contradictory position of advocating unity while forming separate organizations. Ideologically Chicanas adopted a "united front" stance. Adelaida del Castillo, editor of *Encuentro Femenil,* a Chicana feminist journal, voiced this perspective in 1974:

> We're not a separatist movement, that would be suicidal. We as Chicanas and Chicanos are oppressed. We're not going to ally ourselves to white feminists who are part of the oppressor. I mean, that would be a contradiction. It also hurts when Chicano men don't recognize the need for this specialization which is called "Chicana Feminism."[10]

Del Castillo rejected the politics of advancement advocated by the Women's Movement as a reform that would not change the social reproduction of inequality based on race/ethnicity, class, and gender. This perspective predominated among Chicanas of the late 1960s and early 1970s.[11]

CULTURAL NATIONALISM AND CHICANAS

Chicanas' critique of American feminism and the Women's Movement took shape during the heyday of Chicano cultural nationalism.[12] Ideologically, this perspective identified the primary source of Chicano oppression in the colonial domination of Mexican Americans following the annexation of Northern Mexico by the United States after the U.S.–Mexico War of 1846–48.[13] As part of the process of colonial domination, Chicanos had limited access to education, employment, and political participation. Thus, race/ethnicity rather than individual merit defined the life chances of Mexican Americans. Cultural differences between Anglos and Mexicans became the ideological basis that legitimized the unequal treatment and status of Mexicans in the United States.[14] In the Anglo American ideology, Mexicans were viewed as intellectually and culturally inferior.

Cultural nationalist ideology countered this pejorative perspective by celebrating the cultural heritage of Mexico in particular, indigenous roots, *la familia,* and political insurgency.[15] Politically, cultural nationalism called for self-determination including the maintenance of Mexican cultural patterns, culturally relevant education, and community control of social institutions.[16] The term "Chicano" arose as the symbolic representation of self-determination.[17] It conveys a commitment to struggle politically for the betterment of the Chicano community. Cultural nationalism became modified during the 1970s to incorporate a class analysis.[18] An analysis of gender as a base of oppression was and continues to be subsumed in the "larger" struggle against race or class-based domination.[19]

Cultural nationalism idealized certain patterns associated with Mexican culture (e.g., Spanish–English bilingualism, communalism, familism). Chicano Movement groups often organized around the ideal of *la familia.* Any critique of unequal gender relations within the structure of the family was discouraged. Chicanas who deviated from a nationalist political stance were subjected to many negative sanctions including being labeled *vendidas* (sell-outs), or *agabachadas* (white identified). Once labeled thus, they became subject to marginalization within Chicano Movement organizations. Martha Cotera points out that even the label "feminista" was a social control mechanism:

> We didn't say we were feminists. It was the men who said that. They said, "Aha! Feminista!" and that was a good reason for not listening to some of the most active women in the community.[20]

The severity of these sanctions rendered feminism an anathema to be avoided at almost any cost.

The ideological hegemony of cultural nationalism was exemplified in the first official position taken by the Chicana Caucus at the 1969 National Chicano Youth Conference in Denver, Colorado: "the Chicana woman does not want to be liberated."[21] This official statement belies the heated debate on gender oppression voiced by Chicana feminists that day.[22] While this debate was dropped from the official record, it acted as a catalyst to spur women to militant action to challenge the hegemonic sway of cultural nationalism.

Chicana writings and organizational activities of this period resounded with frustration over patriarchy in the Chicano Movement. Chicanas formed such groups as Hijas de Cuauhtémoc and founded alternative publications including *Encuentro Femenil* and *Regeneración.* For their organizations and publications, Chicanas adopted names rooted in Mexican revolutionary heritage. Hijas de Cuauhtémoc, a feminist organization founded in 1910 in Mexico City, opposed the dictatorship of Porfirio Díaz.[23] *Regeneración* was the official journal of the Partido Liberal Mexicano, a progressive Mexican political party.[24] These quintessential images of revolutionary struggle provided Chicanas with a means to frame their local agendas within a larger critique of race, class, and gender domination.

Chicanas sought various ways to reconcile their critique of male domination within the Chicano community to the Chicano Movement agenda. Numerous conferences on *la mujer* reverberated with tension between cultural nationalism and feminism—and whether or not a union between these ideologies was possible.

At the 1971 Conferencia de Mujeres por la Raza, in Houston, Texas, an ideological debate on "Chicana liberation" split participants into two opposing camps: "loyalists" and "feminists." Loyalists viewed Chicanas who called themselves feminists as allies of a middle-class Women's Movement who advocated individualistic upward mobility rather than struggle against race/class domination. Feminists, in contrast, argued that the struggle against male domination was central to the overall Chicana/o Movement for liberation.[25] Anna Nieto-Gómez, a prolific Chicana feminist writer of the late 1960s and early 1970s, articulates this position:

> What is a Chicana feminist? I am a Chicana feminist. I make that statement very proudly, although there is a lot of intimidation in our community and in the society in general against people who define themselves as Chicana feminists. It sounds like a contradictory statement, a Malinche statement—if you are a Chicana you're on one side, if you're a feminist, you must be on the other side. They say you can't stand on both sides—which is a bunch of bull.[26]

At the Houston conference, participants engaged in a hostile debate on reproductive rights. Loyalists argued that reproductive rights including birth control and abortions threatened *la familia.* They accused women who failed to support this position of betraying Chicano culture and heritage. Feminists, in turn, declared: "Our Culture Hell!" and sought to demystify the romanticization of Chicano culture which justified Chicanas' subordinate position by advocating a feminist agenda.[27] Alma García argues that the loyalist position continues to influence Chicanas' political consciousness.[28] It organizes oppression hierarchically, she claims, assigning primacy to the struggle against race, ethnicity and class domination. Within this formulation, feminism is nonrelevant and divisive to the "greater" Chicano struggle.

Early Chicana feminism viewed oppression as the simultaneous product of race, class, and gender subordination. Chicana feminists expressed a high level of frustration with both the Chicano Movement and the Women's Movement. They argued that freedom from race/class oppression would not eliminate sexual oppression. Similarly, freedom from sexual oppression would not eliminate oppression on the basis of race/ethnicity and class.

The extent to which Chicana feminists have adhered to American feminist ideologies is uncertain.[29] To gain insight into this issue we explore the views of a group of Chicanas in higher education. Based on their written responses to a mail survey, we discuss how the historical concerns of the Chicana/o community and feminism inform contemporary Chicana feminist discourse among these women. Specifically, we analyze the relationships among the Chicano Movement, the American Women's Movement, and the emergence of Chicana feminism. We end with a typology of the emergence of Chicana feminism.

THE WOMEN OF MALCS

In 1988 we mailed a questionnaire to women on the mailing list of MALCS (Mujeres Activas en Letras y Cambio Social), an organization of Chicana/Latina women in higher education. The organization's charter and activities demonstrate familiarity with Chicana concerns, a feminist orientation, and sensitivity to cultural concerns.

MALCS was founded in 1983 by Chicana faculty and graduate students as a support and advocacy group and a forum for sharing research interests. The founding declaration of MALCS states:

> We are the daughters of Chicano working class families involved in higher education. We were raised in labor camps and urban barrios, where sharing our resources was the basis of survival. . . . Our history is the story of working people—their struggles, commitments, strengths, and the problems they faced. . . . We are particularly concerned with the conditions women face at work, in and out of the home. We continue our mothers' struggle for social and economic justice.[30]

Drawing upon a tradition of struggle, MALCS members document, analyze, and interpret the Chicana/Latina experience in the United States.

A total of 178 questionnaires were mailed; 101 were completed and returned for a response rate of 57 percent. The questionnaire asked women to discuss their perceptions of the major features of the contemporary American Women's Movement, the major concerns of Chicanas today, and the extent to which the Women's Movement and feminist theory have addressed the needs of Chicana women. The questionnaire also contained a series of closed-ended questions about the respondents' familiarity with writings on the Women's Movement, their involvement with "feminist" and "women's" activities, and their socioeconomic status.

Nearly all who replied were associated with institutions of higher learning as faculty members (38.6 percent), graduate students (25.7 percent), undergraduate students (8.9 percent), or professional staff (8.9 percent). Eleven women were employed outside a university setting, and seven provided no information on their employment or education.

The women's ages ranged from 22 to 65 years, with a median age of 35 years and a mean age of 38.1 years. This age distribution means that a majority of the women were college-age (17–22) during the height of the Women's Movement (1967–76). Moreover, most of the women had activist backgrounds. Over three-fourths (78.2 percent) of the informants either belonged to or had previously been involved in women's organizations. Women overwhelmingly (83.2 percent) self-identified as "Chicana feminist."

Nearly three-fourths of the women said they were either *very familiar* or *somewhat familiar* with literature on the American Women's Movement. Over half also indicated they were either *very familiar* or *somewhat familiar* with feminist theoretical writings.[31]

This group of Chicanas does not represent all women of Mexican descent in the United States. They are academicians or highly educated women who inform the public discourse on feminism and women's issues. Moreover, as educated Chicanas they constitute one end of the continuum that forms the Chicana experience. Their perceptions, therefore, offer an excellent way to build knowledge on Chicanas and American feminism.

THE CHICANA MOVEMENT

Slightly over one-half of the women posit the existence of a Chicana Movement that is qualitatively distinct from the American Women's Movement and the Chicano Movement through a praxis based on the multifaceted dimension of Chicanas' experiences. That is, the Chicana Movement exposes class, race/ethnic and cultural contradictions that distinguish the Chicana Movement from the Women's Movement. For example:

> The Chicana Movement was a separatist movement which emerged out of the contradictions Chicanas found in white women's organizations and groups in practice and theory. It added the dimension of race and class. This movement was also largely working-class inspired while the WM [Women's Movement] was largely middle class.
>
> Graduate student, age 30

This perception, widely held among the informants and grounded in the relevant literature, argues that Women's Movement activists are predominantly middle-class white women who do not appreciate the nature of working-class and racial/ethnic oppression.

Some of the women emphasized that the Chicana Movement emerged in response to racism within the American Women's Movement:

> It has become clear that racism which has inhibited white women from sharing power with women of color has led to a distinct Chicana movement, however, weak.
>
> Graduate student, no age given

Chicanas also described the Chicana Movement as grounded in the unique cultural heritage of the Chicano/Mexicano people. They argued, moreover, that Chicanas are members of a colonized minority group with a cultural standard distinct from that of the white majority. Proponents of this viewpoint charged that white feminists are largely insensitive to Chicano culture and thereby exclude Chicana concerns from the Women's Movement.

When asked to describe the Chicana Movement vis-à-vis the Chicano Movement, women overwhelmingly proclaimed the Chicana Movement parted company with the Chicano Movement by challenging patriarchy. They attribute the political dissent that led to the development of a distinct Chicana feminist movement to the patriarchal relations within the Chicano Movement, the Chicano community, and the family:

The contemporary Chicana movement has its origins in the Chicano Movement and arose as a collective response to the *machismo* which surfaced among our compañeros to make menudo [tripe soup] while men talked strategy. In fact, I believe that one of the factors which precipitated the decline of the Chicano Movement was machismo.

Faculty member, age 33

Despite Chicanas' antagonism toward male domination within the Chicano Movement they still identify with the collective Chicano struggle:

Chicanos y [and] Chicanas share many of the same dreams and I feel that the Chicana movement has a greater affinity with the Chicano movement than with the Women's Movement.

Faculty member, age 33

Tension between Chicanas' need for racial/ethnic solidarity and their struggle for gender equality reverberates throughout the responses. Women who advocate a feminist agenda report being asked to prove their loyalty to *la causa* [the cause] by agreeing to defer the struggle against gender oppression until racial/ethnic domination is abolished. This "loyalty test" stems from the nationalist character of the Chicano Movement which identified race/ethnicity as the "primary contradiction" thereby producing an antagonistic climate for Chicana feminists. Within the Chicano Movement, labels were often used as mechanisms of social control to discredit Chicanas who articulated a feminist political agenda:

Overall the Chicano movement was great! But too many men (Chicano) became uptight when Chicanas began asking for and later demanding equality within the movement. Many of us were labeled as *agabachadas* [white-identified] or worse. Chicanas were seen more as a hindrance or decoration than as equal participants.

Faculty member, age 44

While all informants deplored sexism in the Chicano Movement, some acquiesced to a "we need to stay within the fold" perspective to maintain unity within the Movement:

It [Chicana Movement] has been distinct from the Chicano Movement because they did not deal with women's issues or even family issues. We could not split the movement— we had to sacrifice ourselves for the movement.

Graduate student, no age given

The informants explained the development of a Chicana Movement as irrevocably bound to Chicano cultural nationalism. This sentiment harkens back to the politic of the late 1960s and early 1970s wherein gender concerns were subsumed under the "larger struggle" against race/class oppression.

The perception of the MALCS survey respondents regarding the unique quality of the Chicana Movement in relation to the American Women's Movement and the Chicano Movement mirrors the sentiments of Chicana activists of the late 1960s and early 1970s. Like Chicana feminists of that period, MALCS survey informants reaffirmed that class, race/ethnicity and cultural differences distinguish the Chicana Movement from the American Women's Movement. The women argue that patriarchal relations within the Chicano Movement served as the primary catalyst for the emergence of a Chicana Movement.

Forty women who responded to the survey did not believe that a unique Chicana Movement exists. They indicated that although Chicanas shared social and political interests separate from other women and Chicano men, they had not coalesced on these issues either ideologically or organizationally. Instead, they claim Chicanas' struggle for equality is waged within small, dispersed groups.

CHICANA FEMINISM

Nearly all of the informants (83.2 percent) self-identified as Chicana feminists while seventeen eschew this label. Sixty-four discussed the meaning of Chicana feminism.[32]

Based on content analysis of the responses, three internally coherent and distinct voices emerged which depict different facets of Chicana feminism. To create a typology of Chicana feminism, we established three categories: *Chicana Liberal Feminism* (n = 28), *Chicana Insurgent Feminism* (n = 23), and *Cultural Nationalist Feminism* (n = 13). Each category expresses a collectivist orientation and is grounded in the material condition of the Chicana/o people. Women in each category articulate a commitment to improve the socioeconomic condition of Chicanas. Key differences emerge, however, with respect to the interpretation of social inequality and the preferred strategies to resist and redress Chicana subordination. Our typology captures a sense of the tension among liberal reformist, revolutionary, and nationalistic ideological positions.

Chicana liberal feminism centers on women's desire to enhance the well-being of the Chicano community, with a special emphasis on improving the status of women. Undergraduate students and staff were the most likely to articulate these views (80 percent). Almost one-third of Chicana faculty and graduate students also favored a liberal-reformist tradition (28.6 percent and 30 percent, respectively). Chicana empowerment—economic, social, and cultural—is a key theme in this category.

> Chicana [feminism means] living my personal and professional life in line with certain principles: equality, shared power, mutually reinforcing and empowering relationships among women and with men (when that is possible).
>
> Faculty member, age 37

Women described several strategies to empower Chicanas ranging from a personal approach (e.g., "support" other Chicanas) to a social reformist stance (e.g., "develop policy to meet Chicanas' needs").

> Only when we are able to improve our socio-economic level will we be able to determine policy in this country and gain access to the upper echelons of decision-making processes. We can't wait for THEM [her emphasis] (males or white females) to liberate us—no one will adequately address our issues except us.
>
> Faculty member, age 51

In general, respondents argued that Chicanas' lack of power emanates from at least two systems of stratification (race/ethnicity and gender) which are intertwined and which must be addressed simultaneously. They believe, however, that Chicana subordination can be redressed through institutional reforms that improve Chicanas' access to education, employment, and opportunity. They emphasize bringing Chicanas into the political and social mainstream.

> [The] term "Chicana" in itself represents a certain degree of feminism. She strives to understand the political, social, and economic state her people are in and actively seeks to make changes that will advance her raza [people].
>
> Graduate student, age 26

Women in this category advocate change within a liberal tradition similar to that of the women's rights branch of the American Women's Movement. This perspective reaffirms Chicanas' desires to develop a personal awareness of women's needs within the context of the social and economic situation of the Chicano community-at-large. Although critical of the low socioeconomic conditions of the Chicano people, the Chicana Liberal Feminist perspective adopts a political strategy that falls short of the more radical critique articulated by Chicanas who form the category identified as Insurgent Feminism.

Chicana Insurgent Feminism draws on a tradition of radical thought and political insurgency. Slightly over half of the graduate students (52.2 percent) and 42.9 percent of Chicana faculty expressed views consistent with these traditions. Women in this category were also slightly younger (33.1 years) than the average.

Chicana Insurgent Feminism emphasizes how Chicana inequality results from three interrelated forms of stratification—race/ethnicity, class, and gender:

> Chicana feminism means the struggle to obtain self-determination for all Chicanas, in particular that Chicanas can choose their own life course without contending with the pressure of racism, sexism and poverty. It means working to overcome oppression, institutional and individual. Chicana feminism is much more than the slogan: "the personal is political"; it represents a collective effort for dignity and respect.
>
> Faculty member, age 33

This perspective locates the source of Chicana oppression within the cultural expressions and social institutions of a hierarchically stratified society. Reminiscent of Chicano cultural nationalism, the informant cited above calls for Chicana self-determination which encompasses a struggle against both personal and institutional manifestations of racial discrimination, patriarchy, and class exploitation. She expands the "personal is political" position of the American Women's Movement beyond the individual woman to embrace the community of Chicana women, and the Chicano community-at-large. This informant did not call for revolutionary change, but it is implicit within her formulation of Chicana self-determination.

The intensity of Chicanas' articulations of insurgent feminism varies. Some call for revolutionary change to end all forms of oppression:

> I believe that the impact of sexism, racism and elitism, when combined result in more intensely exploitive, oppressive and controlling situations than when these conditions exist independently of one another. The status and quality of life of the Chicano community as a whole can only improve/change when that of women within that community

changes/improves. Any revolutionary change must include a change in relationships between men and women.

Faculty member, age 50

This woman argues that the cumulative effects of oppression are particularly pronounced for Chicanas. Like the previous informant, she connects the liberation of Chicanas to the overall struggle of the Chicano community. Her words, however, impart a more strident and uncompromising exposition of feminism which ties the liberation of the Chicano community to the struggle against patriarchy. Politically, she espouses a radical praxis advocating revolutionary change.

Other respondents extend insurgent feminism to include a critique of homophobia and solidarity with other oppressed peoples:

> It means that I am active and critical with respect to political, social and cultural manifestations of sexism, racism, Hispanophobia, heterosexism, and class oppression, and committed to working with others to create a more just society. It also means that I am moved by a sense of ethnic solidarity with Chicano, Mexican and other Latino people.
>
> Faculty member, age 40

This woman views political activism as a critical component of Chicana feminism. Like the other informants, she deplores the social subordination of Chicanas by race, class and gender. She and a small but vocal group of women call for the recognition of oppression on the basis of sexual orientation within Chicana feminism. This is one dimension of the Chicana experience has not been systematically incorporated into the agenda for Chicana liberation.

Chicana Insurgent Feminism advances what one woman referred to as "oppositional discourse" which challenges analytic frameworks that dichotomize the multiple sources of Chicana oppression while positing alternative frameworks grounded in their concrete experiences. Those in this category argue for theoretical-intellectual work that is not reactive but created from a Chicana-centered position taking into account the multiple sources of Chicana subjectivity. This includes an internal critique of Chicano/Mexicano culture to revitalize and empower the community. The more strident voices within Chicana Insurgent Feminism may reflect, in part, greater involvement with the feminist groups and higher levels of political activism within these groups vis-à-vis Chicana Liberal feminists or Chicana Nationalist feminists. For example, three-fourths of Chicanas in this category report either past or present membership in feminist groups compared with 61 percent of Liberal feminists and 54 percent of Nationalist feminists. When we presented respondents with six types of political activities (march, demonstration, sit-in, letter writing campaign, conference, and other), those women in the Chicana Insurgent Feminism category reported the highest levels of participation in the various activities (2.4 on the average).[33]

In general, Chicana Insurgent Feminism engages in a critique that calls for the radical restructuring of society. Chicanas voice commitment to developing alternative theories, empowerment through political insurgency, and social action to realize Chicana self-determination.

Finally, Cultural Nationalist Feminism includes a small group of women who identify as feminists but who are committed to a cultural nationalist ideology that emphasizes maintaining traditional cultural values. According to this view, a Chicana feminist politic must uphold Chicano/Mexicano culture:

> I want for myself and for other women the opportunities to grow and develop in any area I choose. I want to do this while upholding the values (cultural, moral) that come from my being a part of the great family of Chicanos.
>
> Graduate student, age 41

Reminiscent of the notion popularized within the Chicano Movement (that all Chicanos are members of the same family—*la gran familia de la raza*), Chicana Cultural Nationalist Feminism articulates a feminist vision within the ideological rubric of *la familia* and advocates struggle for justice and gender equality while adhering to Chicano cultural traditions, forms and ideologies:

> It involves the recognition that we must continue the struggle for women's rights and responsibilities within a cultural context.
>
> Faculty member, age 43

Chicana Cultural Nationalist Feminism overlooks the possibility that Chicano/Mexicano cultural traditions often uphold patriarchy. Caught between the need to reverse the historical subordination of Chicanas without challenging the patriarchal underpinnings of a cultural nationalist politic, Chicana nationalist feminists rarely articulate concrete strategies to realize their dual goals. Instead, they offer brief philosophical statements that reaffirm cultural values. This speaks to the difficulty of reconciling a critique of gender relations within the Chicano community while calling for the preservation of Chicano culture.

CONCLUSION

The Chicana Movement and Chicana feminist discourse emerged from the dialectical relationship between the ideology and politics of the Chicano Movement and the American Women's Movement of the late 1960s and early 1970s. They developed from Chicanas' desires to move beyond what they perceived as indifference to their racial/ethnic, cultural and class interests on the part of the American Women's Movement and the feminisms it advocated. They also felt compelled to counter the antipathy of the Chicano Movement toward a critique of gender relations and patriarchy in the Chicano community. Chicanas argued for an alternative discourse—one that would integrate the eradication of patriarchy in the Chicano community within a struggle against race/class domination.

Despite their criticism of American feminism, study informants overwhelmingly self-identified as Chicana feminists. However, the fact that more women identified as Chicana feminists (n = 84) than affirmed the existence of a distinct Chicana Movement (n = 54) suggests that the two phenomena are related to one another but are not mutually dependent. Informants may not be aware of sustained organizational activities that embrace a Chicana feminist political agenda. Or, women may interpret the *meaning* of a *distinct* Chicana movement in different ways. That is, women recognize the existence of small dispersed groups that advocate for Chicana rights but do not believe this constitutes a distinct Chicana Movement. Conversely, other women interpret Chicana feminist activities as comprising a distinct Chicana Movement.

Based on informants' descriptions of Chicana feminism we developed the following typology: Chicana Liberal Feminism, Chicana Insurgent Feminism, and Chicana Cultural Nationalist Feminism. Chicana Liberal Feminism centers on the conviction that Chicanas' life chances can be improved by modifying the existing structures of opportunity through both personal and political efforts. Chicana Insurgent Feminism vociferously critiques inequality by race/ethnicity, class, gender and sexual orientation and calls for a sustained political struggle to restructure society. Cultural Nationalist Feminism conveys the sentiment that women's interests must be expressed within a cultural maintenance framework.

Our discussion of the various perspectives of Chicana feminist voices poses critical questions for the future of Chicana feminism. While a concern with redressing the historical condition of Chicanas cuts across all three categories, the groups vary with respect to the centrality of gender oppression, the critique of Chicano culture, and the preferred political form of struggle. One question that comes to mind is whether or not differences among the perspectives portend a prominent role for ideological struggles in the future development of Chicana feminism. The relatively small number of Chicanas adopting a cultural nationalist ideology attests to its general decline in the Chicana/o community. The inherent contradictions within Chicana Nationalist Feminism and the lack of coherent political strategies make it unlikely that the sentiments articulated within this perspective will play a major role in the future of Chicana feminism.

On the other hand, future political agendas and preferred strategies may divide along liberal-reformist and more revolutionary lines. Women in both categories espoused distinct perspectives and strategies to realize Chicana liberation. Chicana Liberal Feminism accepts the premise that the life chances of Chicanas can be enhanced through programs aimed at incorporating them into all facets of existing social institutions while fostering changes through established political processes. Although women in this category advocate gender and race equality, they are not as likely to emphasize the struggle against all forms of patriarchy as women in the Chicana Insurgent Feminism category. Chicana Insurgent Feminism provides the most sweeping analysis of domination based on class, race/ethnicity, and sex/gender. Those who fall into this category question the value of social integration by offering a vision of society that requires a revolutionary transformation, placing gender liberation as a prerequisite to human liberation.

Another possibility is unity based on a commitment to Chicana liberation within the context of the overall liberation of the Chicana/o people. This goal could attenuate political differences and lead to a common praxis to redress class, race/ethnic, and gender oppression. Our analysis points to the viability of this scenario inasmuch as Chicana feminist discourse across all three categories affirms the significance of the Chicana struggle to the social and political struggles of the Chicano/Mexicano population.

NOTES

1 Several ethnic labels are used in this article. First, people of Color refers to Chicanos/Mexican Americans, Puerto Ricans, Native Americans, Asian Americans, and

African Americans, all of whom are native or colonized minorities (see A. Hurtado, "Relating to Privilege: Seduction and Rejection in the Subordination of White Women and Women of Color," *Signs: Journal of Women in Culture and Society* 14, 4 (1989):833. We find Hurtado's capitalization of the word, "Color," appropriate since it refers to specific racial/ethnic minority groups. Second, "women" of Color refers to women within each racial/ethnic minority group.

2 B. Thornton Dill, "Race, Class, and Gender: Prospects for an All-Inclusive Sisterhood," *Feminist Studies* 9 (1983):131–150; M. Baca Zinn, L. Weber Cannon, E. Higginbotham, and B. Thornton Dill, "The Costs of Exclusionary Practices in Women's Studies," *Signs: Journal of Women in Culture and Society* 11 (1986):290–303; Gloria Hull, Patricia Bell Scott, and Barbara Smith, *All Men Are Black, All Women Are White, but Some of Us Are Brave* (Old Westbury: Feminist Press, 1982); N. Alarcón, "Chicanas' Feminist Literature: A Revision Through Malintzin/or Malintzin: Putting Flesh Back on the Object," in Cherrie Moraga and Gloria Anzaldúa, eds., *This Bridge Called My Back: Writings by Radical Women of Color* (Watertown: Persephone, 1981); A. E. Quintana, "Chicana Motifs: Challenge and Counter-Challenge," in *Intersections: Studies in Ethnicity, Gender, and Inequality,* (Pullman: Washington State University Press, 1988), 197–217.

3 In social science literature, "Chicana" and "Chicano" typically refer respectively to women and men of Mexican descent residing in the United States. See M. Tienda, "The Mexican American Population," in A. H. Hawley and S. M. Mazie, eds., *Non-Metropolitan America in Transition,* (Chapel Hill: University of North Carolina Press, 1981), 502–548. "Chicano" is also a broad term that includes both males and females who claim Mexican heritage (e.g., the Chicano community). These labels offer an alternative to the more common ethnic identifiers "Mexican" and "Mexican American," see J. A. García " 'Yo Soy Mexicano . . .' Self-Identity And Socio-Demographic Correlates," *Social Science Quarterly* 62 (March 1981):88–98. These labels were popularized during the Chicano Movement to affix a political orientation that affirmed the need to struggle against the historical oppression of people of Mexican descent in the United States to an ethnic identifier. See Rodolfo Acuña, *Occupied America: A History of Chicanos,* 2d ed., (New York: Harper and Row, 1981) and A. Gutiérrez and H. Hirsch, "The Militant Challenge to the American Ethos: 'Chicanos' and 'Mexican Americans,' " *Social Science Quarterly* 53 (March 1973):830–845. See also F. Peñalosa, "Toward an Operational Definition of the Mexican American," *Aztlán: Chicano Journal of the Social Sciences and the Arts* 1 (1970):1–12. In recent years (post-1980s), the political dimension within the terms "Chicana" and "Chicano" has declined even as usage of the label "Hispanic" has grown. To maintain the integrity of the political and ethnic identification of this study's informants, we refer to the original political meaning of both "Chicana" and "Chicano."

4 Acuña, *Occupied America;* C. Muñoz, and M. Barrera, "La Raza Unida Party and the Chicano Student Movement in California," *Social Science Journal* 19 (April 1982):101–119.

5 This section summarizes the emergence of the "second wave" of the American Women's Movement that relates to our analysis of the emergence of the Chicana Movement and Chicana feminist discourse. For a more complete treatment of the Women's Movement, see Judith Hole and Ellen Levine, eds., *Rebirth of Feminism* (New York: Quadrangle Books, 1971) and J. Freeman, "The Women's Liberation Movement: Its Origins, Structure, Activities, and Ideas," in Jo Freeman, ed., *Women, a Feminist Perspective,* 3d ed. (Palo Alto: Mayfield Publishing Co., 1984):543–556.

6 Freeman, *Women;* Alison M. Jagger, *Feminist Politics and Human Nature* (Totowa, N.J.: Rowman and Allanheld, 1983).

7 Margaret L. Andersen, *Thinking About Women, Sociological Perspectives on Sex and Gender* 2d ed. (New York: Macmillan Co., 1988); Jagger, *Feminist Politics.*

8 Angela Y. Davis, *Women, Race and Class* (New York: Vintage Books, 1981); bell hooks, *Feminist Theory: From Margin to Center* (Boston: South End Press, 1984) and bell hooks, *Ain't I a Woman: Black Women and Feminism* (Boston: South End Press, 1981); Gloria Hull, Bell Scott, and Smith, *All Men Are Black;* Moraga and Anzaldúa, *This Bridge Called My Back.*

9 C. Nieto, "Chicanas and the Women's Rights Movements," *Civil Rights Digest* 4 (Spring):38–42; A. Nieto-Gómez, "La Feminista," *Encuentro Femenil* 1(1974):34–47. A. Sosa-Riddell, "Chicanas and El Movimiento," *Aztlán: Chicano Journal of the Social Sciences and the Arts,* 5 (Spring/Fall):155–165.

10 Adelaida del Castillo, "La Visión Chicana." *Encuentro Femenil* 2(1974):46–48, esp. 46.

11 Del Castillo, "La Visión Chicana"; Nieto-Gómez, "La Feminista"; E. Martínez," La Chicana," in *Third World Women,* (San Francisco: Third World Communications, 1972):130–132; Francisca Flores, "Equality," *Regeneración* 2 (1973):4–5.

12 This section, which reviews key facets of the Chicano Movement and Chicano cultural nationalism to contextualize the growth of Chicana feminism, is intended to be useful both to Chicano studies scholars as well as to readers wishing to gain more understanding of the topic.

13 Acuña, *Occupied America;* T. Almaguer, "Toward the Study of Chicano Colonialism," *Aztlán: Chicano Journal of the Social Sciences and the Arts* 2 (1971):7–22; M. Barrera, C. Muñoz, and C. Ornelas, "The Barrio as an Internal Colony," in *People and Politics in Urban Society, Urban Affairs Annual Review,* vol. 6, edited by Harlan H. Hahn (Beverly Hills, CA: Sage Publications, 1972):465–499; Robert Blauner, *Racial Oppression in America,* (New York: Harper and Row, 1972).

14 Blauner, *Racial Oppression;* Ronald T. Takaki, *Iron Cages: Race and Culture in Nineteenth-Century America* (New York: Albert A. Knopf, 1979); David Montejano, *Anglos and Mexicans in the Making of Texas, 1836–1986* (Austin: University of Texas Press, 1987).

15 Alfredo Mirandé, *The Chicano Experience: An Alternative Perspective* (Notre Dame: University of Notre Dame Press, 1985); J. R. Macías, "Nuestros Antepasados y el Movimiento," *Aztlán: Chicano Journal of the Social Sciences and the Arts* 5 (Spring/Fall 1974):143–153.

16 A. Navarro, "The Evolution of Chicano Politics" *Aztlán: Chicano Journal of the Social Sciences and the Arts* 5 (Spring/Fall 1974):57–84; Barrera, Muñoz, and Ornelas, "The Barrio"; R. Santillan, "The Politics of Cultural Nationalism: El Partido De La Raza Unida in Southern California, 1969–1978" (Ph.D. diss., Claremont College, 1978).

17 Chicano Coordinating Committee on Higher Education, *El Plan de Santa Barbara: A Chicano Plan for Higher Education* (Santa Barbara, CA: La Causa Publications, 1969); R. Alvarez, "The Unique Psychohistorical Experience of the Mexican American," *Social Science Quarterly* 52 (1971):15–29.

18 T. Almaguer, "Historical Notes on Chicano Oppression: The Dialectics of Racial and Class Domination in North America," *Aztlán: Chicano Journal of the Social Sciences and the Arts* 5 (Spring/Fall 1974):27–56; and Almaguer, "Class, Race and Chicano Oppression," *Socialist Revolution* 5 (1975); Mario Barrera, *Race and Class in the Southwest: A Theory of Racial Inequality* (Notre Dame: University of Notre Dame Press, 1979).

19 M. Baca Zinn, "Mexican-American Women in the Social Sciences," *Signs: Journal of Women in Culture and Society* 8 (1982):259–272; D. A. Segura, "Chicanas and Triple Oppression in the Labor Force," in Teresa Cordova et al., eds., *Chicana Voices: Inter-*

sections of Class, Race and Gender (Austin: Center for Mexican American Studies, The University of Texas at Austin, 1986), 47–76; A. M. García, "The Development of Chicana Feminist Discourse, 1970–1980," *Gender and Society* 3 (June 1989):217–238.

20 Martha P. Cotera, *The Chicana Feminist* (Austin: Information Systems Development, 1977), 31.

21 E. Longeaux y Vásquez, "The Mexican-American Woman," in Robin Morgan, ed., *Sisterhood Is Powerful* (New York: Vintage, 1970), 379.

22 M. Vidal, *Women: New Voice of La Raza* (New York: Pathfinder Press, 1971).

23 Anna Macías, *Against All Odds* (Westport: Greenwood Press, 1982).

24 Macías, *Against All Odds.*

25 Nieto-Gómez, "La Visión Chicana."

26 Nieto-Gómez, "La Visión Chicana," 34–47, esp. 39.

27 F. Flores, "Conference of Mexican Women: Un Remolino," *Regeneración* 1 (1971):1–4.

28 García, "The Development of Chicana Feminist Discourse."

29 García, "The Development of Chicana Feminist Discourse."

30 Adeljiza Sosa Riddell, ed., *Mujeres Activas en Letras y Cambio Social, Noticiera de M.A.L.C.S.* (Davis: University of California, Davis, Chicano Studies Program, 1983).

31 While both of these answers cannot be standardized (e.g., one woman's sense of being "very familiar" with literature on the American Women's Movement may differ substantially from that of another woman), we are confident that informants gave fairly accurate self-assessments. We base this evaluation on a content analysis of the different ways women describe the major agendas of the American Women's Movement and the relative ease with which they refer to various types of feminist theories (e.g., socialist feminism). Accordingly, women who indicated they were "very familiar" with either the American Women's Movement or feminist theoretical writing gave far more detailed and knowledgeable descriptions than women who indicated they were "slightly familiar" or "not familiar" with these writings.

32 Thirteen women provided nonspecific answers with no discernable pattern and seven women did not elaborate on the meaning of Chicana feminism.

33 Women who articulated liberal feminism reported an average of 1.8 activities and Chicano Nationalist feminists reported 2.1 activities. Between one-half and two-thirds of Chicanas in the Insurgent Feminist category had participated in marches and demonstrations compared with one-third of Nationalist feminists and Liberal feminists.

Men and the Women's Movement

R.W. Connell

What place should men have in feminist politics? Given the record of men's violence against women, abusive attitudes and speech, relentless sexism in high culture and the mass media, it's not hard to justify the notion that men have no place at all in the women's movement.

Yet, while we undeniably live in a sexist culture, men are far from monolithic in support of its sexism. There are significant resources among men that can be tapped for the resistance. Some men want to support feminism, and some men—not always the same ones—have been *useful* to feminism (for instance, in passing anti-discrimination laws, introducing women's studies programs in universities, and so on). Yet after a generation of continuous feminist mobilizing, men's support is erratic, contradictary, and mostly small-scale. Why, and what can be done about it?

NOT AN EASY RIDE

Anti-sexist politics for men is difficult at a personal level. Feminism (especially feminism concerned with violence) often reads to men as an accusation. If the accusation is accepted, the result is sometimes a paralyzing guilt. For sympathetic men, the encounter with feminism can easily be more disabling than energizing.

Nonetheless, some men do get energized—such as those who have gone to work with abusive men to reduce domestic violence. But for others, the encounter leads to a turn inward, in which men focus on reconstructing their own personalities and lose their impulse to reform social relations. There is a small but steady flow out of politics into therapy.

Men who do undertake action in support of feminism are not in for an easy ride. They are likely to be met with antagonism and derision from other men, picturing them as eunuchs, queers or sell-outs to "political correctness." They will not necessarily get warm support from feminists—some of whom are deeply suspicious of all men, most of whom are wary of men's power, and all of whom make a primary commitment to solidarity with women. An academic man teaching a feminist course, for instance, may be seen as taking resources away from women, and asserting men's cultural rights over all areas of knowledge, as often as being seen as an ally. One action, or a limited form of action, is hardly enough.

Taking on feminist principles means reconstructing personal relations as well as public life, and this offers endless opportunities for hurt, mistaken judgments, and mistrust. Indeed, it is often easier to acknowledge women's rights to fair and equal treatment in the public world than to confront sexism at the personal level. This is the response of some powerful men in the professions, in bureaucracies, in universities and in politics— liberal Democrats in the United States, Labor or Social Democratic leaders in countries like Australia and Sweden. Such men may find it easy to support equal opportunity and anti-discrimination programs, which correspond with their own agendas for efficiency and modernity. They are less likely to change the power structures of their own personal relationships.

WHAT ARE MEN AFRAID OF?

In 1989, a man massacred fourteen female students at the University of Montreal, in the process making abundantly clear that a hatred of "feminists" was his reason for shooting the women. He was, certainly, mad; but his madness was not random. It drew on a widespread sense of dislocation in gender relations, on a narrower but vehement ideology of men's supremacy, and on a festering fear of women's gains.

Why this fear? What are men afraid they will lose? In the early 1970s, it was argued that men had a lot to gain from women's liberation, which could lead to men being freed from their rigid sex roles too.

The problem is that rigidities of "sex roles" are far from the whole story. Men's dominant position in society has an economic pay-off. The statistics usually show women's incomes as a percentage of men's, but think of it the other way around—in terms of the dividend for men from current social arrangements. For full-time wage and salary earners in the United States, men's median earnings are 143 percent of women's (1989 figures). Taking all people with incomes in the US—including those doing part-time work and receiving welfare payments—men's mean incomes are a whopping 195 percent of women's (1988 figures). And more women than men have no income at all.

Of course, men do not do twice as much work as women. "Time budget" studies in modern economies suggest that men and women work about the same number of hours. But most of women's work hours are unpaid—housework, volunteer work, "caring" for children, family and friends. And much of this labor is work done for men: work that keeps men well-fed and properly clothed, their living spaces clean and functional, their social networks in good repair. On top of this labor comes the emotional attention and support that men expect from women, and often get, through marriage.

"Masculinity" is, to a large extent, formed around the psychological investment men make in this system of unequal power, income and respect. So any challenge to the system, any attempt to limit the power or reduce the dividend, is likely to be felt as an attack on masculinity. There are real reasons for men to fear feminism!

GENDER DIVISIONS AMONG MEN

All men do not benefit equally from this system, however, and all men do not derive from it the same concept of masculinity. A big employer may profit from the depressed wages of thousands of laboring women (as well as the ministrations of a wife and a secretary), while an unemployed inner-city 20-year-old may get little material gain from women's work, except his mother's. The poor person's practice of masculinity may thus be significantly different from the big employer's.

Race, too, is a factor. The history of masculinity is different for Black men and white men: comparing, for example, the free laborer with the slave, or considering how masculinity was shaped in communities terrorized by lynchings. Widespread unemployment, lower wages in employment, and endemic racism mean that Black men still get fewer of the benefits of patriarchy.

On the other hand, gay men, while often economically comfortable, pay another kind of penalty. They are the targets of discrimination, physical violence, and cultural abuse because of their sexuality. The young men who attack and sometimes kill gay men often accompany the beatings with abuse that clearly shows their preoccupation with defending masculinity. This is not to agree with the bashers that gay men are un-masculine. Rather, this is part of the evidence that there are different kinds of masculinity and important gender divisions among men. To understand this, consider for a moment into modern gender theory.

WHAT ARE "MASCULINITIES?"

The popular ideology of gender assumes that "masculinity" and "femininity" are unchanging, direct expressions of male and female bodies—male ones being strong and dominant, female ones being passive and nurturing. But there is overwhelming evidence, from anthropology and history, that this is not so. The meanings of male and female bodies differ from one culture to another, and change (even in our own culture) over time. There are cultures where it has been normal, not exceptional, for men to have homosexual relations. There have been periods in "Western" history when the modern convention that men suppress displays of emotion did not apply at all, when men were effusive to their (male) friends and demonstrative about their feelings.

Masculinities and femininities are constructed or accomplished in social processes such as child rearing, emotional and sexual relationships, work and politics—and bodies are involved in all this. We do experience gender in our bodies, in the ways we walk and sit, in our skills, in our reactions of sexual arousal and disgust—but not because bodies determine social life. Rather, bodies are drawn into social relations, become social actors, become engaged in constructing a social world. It is in this social world that inequality arises, that women are oppressed, that political struggle occurs.

In a patriarchal society, the dominant or hegemonic form of masculinity embodies a successful (that is to say, effective) strategy for subordinating women. In our society, hegemonic masculinity is heterosexual, aggressive and competitive, homo-social (excluding women from its social networks), emphasizes hierarchy and the capacity to dominate other men as well as women. This kind of masculinity (sometimes mislead-ingly called "the traditional male role") is not necessarily the reality most men live in. Few men are heavy hitters as corporate executives, or exemplars of masculinity as com-bat heroes, sport or film stars.

There are also subordinated masculinities, formed at the bottom of the gender hier-archy among men. The most obvious example in our culture is the masculinity of gay men, though effeminate straights may also be counted here. There are also the marg-inalized masculinities of oppressed ethnic groups such as Blacks in the United States. Here are found both alternatives to the hegemonic pattern, and specialized versions of it. Some Black men may be recruited to the position of masculine exemplar, while most Black men are denied authority or even respect. The resulting contradictions are visible in the lives of Mike Tyson and Clarence Thomas.

Finally, there are the forms of masculinity found among men who are complicit in the patriarchal system. They accept the patriarchal dividend, but are not directly involved in wielding power, in personal violence, or in displays of prowess. I suspect this is the largest group in contemporary gender politics.

Among these forms of masculinity, there are complex hierarchies, exclusions, alliances and oppressions. Recognizing the complexity of this picture goes a long way in explaining the variety in men's responses to feminist ideas. It also suggests that different politics can emerge in response to feminism as a movement. What kinds of politics emerge that make masculinities themselves an issue? Most have a base in one of these types of masculinity.

MASCULINITY POLITICS

The most conspicuous gender politics among men, in the United States at present, is found in the "men's movement." Robert Bly's mythopoetic groups are part of this, but not the whole. Drum-whacking and ho-shouting apart, what is going on here is a kind of 12-step recovery movement, addressed to the pain that heterosexual men feel and their uncertainties about masculinity. The core of this movement is the "complicit" masculinity just outlined.

The clients are mostly white, middle class, and in their middle decades. They feel they are in trouble but are not to blame. Different gurus offer rival diagnoses of their troubles: Bly thinks the problem is a failure by fathers to initiate their sons into true masculinity; others think it is a failure by women to recognize the true polarity between the sexes. As a result, this men's movement marginalizes, or simply ignores, inequality. The practical effect is to turn heterosexual men inward to contemplate their own troubles and withdraw energy from social change. It offers absolution from the guilt that feminism still seems to arouse.

Next there is a politics that exalts hegemonic masculinity, often by creating exemplary images or promoting the idea of male supremacy. Televised sports, Hollywood thrillers, video games, super-hero comics and airport-rack novels all insist on the physical superiority of men and their mastery of technology and violence. A tremendous wave of this material (with Sylvester Stallone movies at the crest) built up in the late 1970s and early 1980s. At the same time, the National Rifle Association was politicized after a right-wing takeover and turned into a mass campaign in support of gun use, and fundamentalist religion mobilized against the Equal Rights Amendment, women's abortion rights, and gay/lesbian/bisexual rights.

A politics of hegemonic masculinity is also built into the cult of the ruthless business entrepreneur. Exalting technology over human relations—from Star Wars to the Data Highway—and exalting market forces over public responsibility are also ways of promoting masculinity, though they are not often recognized as such. Men control technology and capital, while "economic rationality" and "competitiveness" have been used to roll back the kinds of public spending that most benefit women.

MEN FIGHTING SEXISM

The politics of subordinated masculinities is best seen in gay communities. Gay liberation began, twenty years ago, with a vigorous critique of both conventional masculinity and conventional stereotypes of gays. Urban gay communities since then have seen a revival of conventionally masculine styles—for instance, the "Castro Street clone"—and an enormous crisis in the form of the HIV epidemic. Gay men's politics have been reshaped around AIDS, which has obliged them to organize for prevention and care, put a premium on emotional support in the face of illness and death, and has reemphasized alliances (both with lesbians and with straight men in professions and government).

Some straight men, too, have contested patriarchy and supported feminism. In the 1970s, some men's "consciousness-raising" groups began in the United States and in Britain. Anti-sexist politics among men thrived for some years, declined in the 1980s, but still persists today. Left-wing men in Britain produced a lively and intelligent magazine called *Achilles Heel,* pooling anti-sexist men's experience, and discussing principles. The most impressive movement has been in Canada, in the wake of the Montreal killings of 1989. The "White Ribbon" movement about violence against women, which saw men campaigning alongside feminists, gained widespread support and had a considerable impact on mass media and conventional politics.

Since patriarchy works in "private" life as much as in public affairs, households and sexual relations also form a political arena. Some men have been part of the reconstruction of domestic life: sharing child care, cleaning and cooking, and decisionmaking. Among some groups of young people this is now common sense: a claim to precedence by men just because they are men would appear grotesque.

A few men have embraced feminism at a deeper emotional level, and have attempted to reconstruct their personality in total to escape conventional masculinity. This has elicited a variety of responses—becoming noncompetitive, taking a supportive rather than dominating position in conversations, engaging only in nonpenetrative sex, refusing careers and power in organizations. But the numbers trying in these ways to exit from mainstream masculinities are small, and it is difficult to see this approach becoming widely popular. Its emotional costs (at least in the short term) are high; it attracts ridicule from more conservative men and may not be attractive to women either.

A NEW GENDER ORDER

It does not require a complete demolition of hegemonic masculinity to democratize gender relations. The many forms of patriarchal ideology point to many ways of contesting it—in sexual life, in mass media, in the workplace, in formal politics, in conversation, in raising children. If conventional gender is, as sociologists call it, an "accomplishment"—something made by the way we conduct ourselves—then we can certainly accomplish something better.

This is happening in a number of settings where gay or straight men have worked productively with feminist women. Green politics, where there is a strong feminist presence, is perhaps the most obvious case. Similarly, in certain university departments, men have supported setting up and staffing feminist courses. In certain unions, men have allied themselves with militant women to break the traditions of exclusion and male dominance, and have worked for the needs of women workers—equal pay, work-based childcare, freedom from sexual harassment, and other issues.

In such work, men can find common cause with feminist women without falling into the "me-too" mold as the Men's Auxiliary To Feminism. What is required is not a yen for self-immolation, but, quite simply, a commitment to social justice. Under our current social arrangements women are, as a group, massively disadvantaged; and men as moral and political agents ought to be involved in changing that.

There are many ways men can do this. Share the care of young children equally, and change working hours to make this possible. Work to put women into office—until at least 50 percent of decision-making positions are held by women. Confront misogyny and homophobia in workplaces and media. Work for pay equity and women's employment rights, until women's earnings are equal to men's. Support the redistribution of wealth, and universal social security and health care. Talk among men to make domestic violence, gay bashing and sexual assault discreditable. Organize political and monetary support for battered women's shelters, rape crisis centers, domestic violence intervention. Change curricula in schools and colleges to include women's ideas and experiences, and to open up issues about men.

These are political strategies that can operate on a large scale, although they are based on particular workplaces, neighborhoods, and other settings. They offer a way past the general interest that men have in defending patriarchy by building on the specific interests particular groups of men share with women—as parents needing childcare, workers needing improved conditions, lesbians and gays fighting discrimination, for example. I find these strategies hopeful, not least because they offer some dignity to men involved in the highly undignified task of dismantling their own privileges.

In the long run, the democratization of gender will require profound social change, and the dismantling of conventional masculinities. Think, for instance, of the emotional consequences of full involvement in childcare. Many of the conventions of hegemonic masculinity such as restraining one's emotions and always trying to dominate in a conflict are outrageously inappropriate in the care of young children. We can recognize this, without expecting most men to swallow the dose in one gulp. The alliance politics that has begun to emerge in some settings has the possibility of making worthwhile gains in the short run, while building up the experience and imagination needed for the dangerous moves that finally have to be made.

Feminism: A Transformational Politic

bell hooks

We live in a world in crisis—a world governed by politics of domination, one in which the belief in a notion of superior and inferior, and its concomitant ideology—that the superior should rule over the inferior—effects the lives of all people everywhere, whether poor or privileged, literate or illiterate. Systematic dehumanization, worldwide famine, ecological devastation, industrial contamination, and the possibility of nuclear destruction are realities which remind us daily that we are in crisis. Contemporary feminist thinkers often cite sexual politics as the origin of this crisis. They point to the insistence on difference as that factor which becomes the occasion for separation and domination and suggest that differentiation of status between females and males globally is an indication that patriarchal domination of the planet is the root of the problem. Such an assumption has fostered the notion that elimination of sexist oppression would necessarily lead to the eradication of all forms of domination. It is an argument that has led influential Western white women to feel that feminist movement should be *the* central political agenda for females globally. Ideologically, thinking in this direction enables Western women, especially privileged white women, to suggest that racism and class exploitation are merely the offspring of the parent system: patriarchy. Within feminist movement in the West, this has led to the assumption that resisting patriarchal domination is a more legitimate feminist action than resisting racism and other forms of domination. Such thinking prevails despite radical critiques made by black women and other women of color who question this proposition. To speculate that an oppositional division between men and women existed in early human communities is to impose on the past, on these non-white groups, a world view that fits all too neatly within contemporary feminist paradigms that name man as the enemy and woman as the victim.

Clearly, differentiation between strong and weak, powerful and powerless, has been a central defining aspect of gender globally, carrying with it the assumption that men should have greater authority than women, and should rule over them. As significant and important as this fact is, it should not obscure the reality that women can and do participate in politics of domination, as perpetrators as well as victims—that we dominate, that we are dominated. If focus on patriarchal domination masks this reality or becomes the means by which women deflect attention from the real conditions and circumstances of our lives, then women cooperate in suppressing and promoting false consciousness, inhibiting our capacity to assume responsibility for transforming ourselves and society.

Thinking speculatively about early human social arrangement, about women and men struggling to survive in small communities, it is likely that the parent-child relationship with its very real imposed survival structure of dependency, of strong and weak, of powerful and powerless, was a site for the construction of a paradigm of domination. While this circumstance of dependency is not necessarily one that leads to domination, it lends itself to the enactment of a social drama wherein domination could easily occur as a means of exercising and maintaining control. This speculation does not place women outside the practice of domination, in the exclusive role of victim. It centrally names women as agents of domination, as potential theoreticians, and creators of a paradigm for social relationships wherein those groups of individuals designated as "strong" exercise power both benevolently and coercively over those designated as "weak."

Emphasizing paradigms of domination that call attention to woman's capacity to dominate is one way to deconstruct and challenge the simplistic notion that man is the enemy, woman the victim; the notion that men have always been the oppressors. Such thinking enables us to examine our role as women in the perpetuation and maintenance of systems of domination. To understand domination, we must understand that our capacity as women and men to be either dominated or dominating is a point of connection, of commonality. Even though I speak from the particular experience of living as a black woman in the United States, a white-supremacist, capitalist, patriarchal society, where small numbers of white men (and honorary "white men") constitute ruling groups, I understand that in many places in the world oppressed and oppressor share the same color. I understand that right here in this room, oppressed and oppressor share the same gender. Right now as I speak, a man who is himself victimized, wounded, hurt by racism and class exploitation is actively dominating a woman in his life—that even as I speak, women who are ourselves exploited, victimized, are dominating children. It is necessary for us to remember, as we think critically about domination, that we all have the capacity to act in ways that oppress, dominate, wound (whether or not that power is institutionalized). It is necessary to remember that it is first the potential oppressor within that we must resist—the potential victim within that we must rescue—otherwise we cannot hope for an end to domination, for liberation.

This knowledge seems especially important at this historical moment when black women and other women of color have worked to create awareness of the ways in which racism empowers white women to act as exploiters and oppressors. Increasingly this fact is considered a reason we should not support feminist struggle even though sexism and sexist oppression is a real issue in our lives as black women (see, for example, Vivian Gordon's *Black Women, Feminism, Black Liberation: Which Way?).* It becomes necessary for us to speak continually about the convictions that inform our continued advocacy of feminist struggle. By calling attention to interlocking systems of domination—sex, race, and class—black women and many other groups of women acknowledge the diversity and complexity of female experience, of our relationship to power and domination. The intent is not to dissuade people of color from becoming engaged in feminist movement. Feminist struggle to end patriarchal domination should be of primary importance to women and men globally not because it is the foundation of all other oppressive structures but because it is that form of domination we are most likely to encounter in an ongoing way in everyday life.

Unlike other forms of domination, sexism directly shapes and determines relations of power in our private lives, in familiar social spaces, in that most intimate context—home—and in that most intimate sphere of relations—family. Usually, it is within the family that we witness coercive domination and learn to accept it, whether it be domination of parent over child, or male over female. Even though family relations may be, and most often are, informed by acceptance of a politic of domination, they are simultaneously relations of care and connection. It is this convergence of two contradictory impulses—the urge to promote growth and the urge to inhibit growth—that provides a practical setting for feminist critique, resistance, and transformation.

Growing up in a black, working-class, father-dominated household, I experienced coercive adult male authority as more immediately threatening, as more likely to cause immediate pain than racist oppression or class exploitation. It was equally clear that experiencing exploitation and oppression in the home made one feel all the more powerless when encountering dominating forces outside the home. This is true for many people. If we are unable to resist and end domination in relations where there is care, it seems totally unimaginable that we can resist and end it in other institutionalized relations of power. If we cannot convince the mothers and/or fathers who care not to humiliate and degrade us, how can we imagine convincing or resisting an employer, a lover, a stranger who systematically humiliates and degrades?

Feminist effort to end patriarchal domination should be of primary concern precisely because it insists on the eradication of exploitation and oppression in the family context and in all other intimate relationships. It is that political movement which most radically addresses the person—the personal—citing the need for transformation of self, of relationships, so that we might be better able to act in a revolutionary manner, challenging and resisting domination, transforming the world outside the self. Strategically, feminist movement should be a central component of all other liberation struggles because it challenges each of us to alter our person, our personal engagement (either as victims or perpetrators or both) in a system of domination.

Feminism, as liberation struggle, must exist apart from and as a part of the larger struggle to eradicate domination in all its forms. We must understand that patriarchal domination shares an ideological foundation with racism and other forms of group oppression, that there is no hope that it can be eradicated while these systems remain intact. This knowledge should consistently inform the direction of feminist theory and practice. Unfortunately, racism and class elitism among women has frequently led to the suppression and distortion of this connection so that it is now necessary for feminist thinkers to critique and revise much feminist theory and the direction of feminist movement. This effort at revision is perhaps most evident in the current widespread acknowledgement that sexism, racism, and class exploitation constitute interlocking systems of domination—that sex, race, and class, and not sex alone, determine the nature of any female's identity, status, and circumstance, the degree to which she will or will not be dominated, the extent to which she will have the power to dominate.

While acknowledgement of the complex nature of woman's status (which has been most impressed upon everyone's consciousness by radical women of color) is a significant corrective, it is only a starting point. It provides a frame of reference which must serve as the basis for thoroughly altering and revising feminist theory and practice. It challenges and calls us to re-think popular assumptions about the nature of feminism that have had the deepest impact on a large majority of women, on mass consciousness. It radically calls into question the notion of a fundamentally common female experience which has been seen as the prerequisite for our coming together, for political unity. Recognition of the inter-connectedness of sex, race, and class highlights the diversity of experience, compelling redefinition of the terms for unity. If women do not share "common oppression," what then can serve as a basis for our coming together?

Unlike many feminist comrades, I believe women and men must share a common understanding—a basic knowledge of what feminism is—if it is ever to be a powerful mass-based political movement. In *Feminist Theory: from margin to center,* I suggest that defining feminism broadly as "a movement to end sexism and sexist oppression" would enable us to have a common political goal. We would then have a basis on which to build solidarity. Multiple and contradictory definitions of feminism create confusion and undermine the effort to construct feminist movement so that it addresses everyone. Sharing a common goal does not imply that women and men will not have radically divergent perspectives on how that goal might be reached. Because each individual starts the process of engagement in feminist struggle at a unique level of awareness, very real differences in experience, perspective, and knowledge make developing varied strategies for participation and transformation a necessary agenda.

Feminist thinkers engaged in radically revisioning central tenets of feminist thought must continually emphasize the importance of sex, race and class as factors which *together* determine the social construction of femaleness, as it has been so deeply ingrained in the consciousness of many women active in feminist movement that gender is the sole factor determining destiny. However, the work of education for critical consciousness (usually called consciousness-raising) cannot end there. Much feminist consciousness-raising has in the past focussed on identifying the particular ways men oppress and exploit women. Using the paradigm of sex, race, and class means that the focus does not begin with men and what they do to women, but rather with women working to identify both individually and collectively the specific character of our social identity.

Imagine a group of women from diverse backgrounds coming together to talk about feminism. First they concentrate on working out their status in terms of sex, race, and class using this as the standpoint from which they begin discussing patriarchy or their particular relations with individual men. Within the old frame of reference, a discussion might consist solely of talk about their experiences as victims in relationship to male oppressors. Two women—one poor, the other quite wealthy—might describe the process by which they have suffered physical abuse by male partners and find certain commonalities which might serve as a basis for bonding. Yet if these same two women engaged in a discussion of class, not only would the social construction and expression of femaleness differ, so too would their ideas about how to confront and change their circumstances. Broadening the discussion to include an analysis of race and class would expose many additional differences even as commonalities emerged.

Clearly the process of bonding would be more complex, yet this broader discussion might enable the sharing of perspectives and strategies for change that would enrich rather than diminish our understanding of gender. While feminists have increasingly given "lip service" to the idea of diversity, we have not developed strategies of communication and inclusion that allow for the successful enactment of this feminist vision.

Small groups are no longer the central place for feminist consciousness-raising. Much feminist education for critical consciousness takes place in Women's Studies classes or at conferences which focus on gender. Books are a primary source of education which means that already masses of people who do not read have no access. The separation of grassroots ways of sharing feminist thinking across kitchen tables from the spheres where much of that thinking is generated, the academy, undermines feminist movement. It would further feminist movement if new feminist thinking could be once again shared in small group contexts, integrating critical analysis with discussion of personal experience. It would be useful to promote anew the small group setting as an arena for education for critical consciousness, so that women and men might come together in neighborhoods and communities to discuss feminist concerns.

Small groups remain an important place for education for critical consciousness for several reasons. An especially important aspect of the small group setting is the emphasis on communicating feminist thinking, feminist theory, in a manner that can be easily understood. In small groups, individuals do not need to be equally literate or literate at all because the information is primarily shared through conversation, in dialogue which is necessarily a liberatory expression. (Literacy should be a goal for feminists even as we ensure that it not become a requirement for participation in feminist education.) Reforming small groups would subvert the appropriation of feminist thinking by a select group of academic women and men, usually white, usually from privileged class backgrounds.

Small groups of people coming together to engage in feminist discussion, in dialectical struggle make a space where the "personal is political" as a starting point for education for critical consciousness can be extended to include politicization of the self that focusses on creating understanding of the ways sex, race, and class together determine our individual lot and our collective experience. It would further feminist movement if many well known feminist thinkers would participate in small groups, critically reexamining ways their works might be changed by incorporating broader perspectives. All efforts at self-transformation challenge us to engage in ongoing, critical self-examination and reflection about feminist practice, about how we live in the world. This individual commitment, when coupled with engagement in collective discussion, provides a space for critical feedback which strengthens our efforts to change and make ourselves new. It is in this commitment to feminist principles in our words and deeds that the hope of feminist revolution lies.

Working collectively to confront difference, to expand our awareness of sex, race, and class as interlocking systems of domination, of the ways we reinforce and perpetuate these structures, is the context in which we learn the true meaning of solidarity. It is this work that must be the foundation of feminist movement. Without it, we cannot effectively resist patriarchal domination; without it, we remain estranged and alienated from one another. Fear of painful confrontation often leads women and men active in feminist movement to avoid rigorous critical encounter, yet if we cannot engage dialectically in a committed, rigorous, humanizing manner, we cannot hope to change the world. True politicization—coming to critical consciousness—is a difficult, "trying" process, one that demands that we give up set ways of thinking and being, that we shift our paradigms, that we open ourselves to the unknown, the unfamiliar. Undergoing this process, we learn what it means to struggle and in this effort we experience the dignity and integrity of being that comes with revolutionary change. If we do not change our consciousness, we cannot change our actions or demand change from others.

Our renewed commitment to a rigorous process of education for critical consciousness will determine the shape and direction of future feminist movement. Until new perspectives are created, we cannot be living symbols of the power of feminist thinking. Given the privileged lot of many leading feminist thinkers, both in terms of status, class, and race, it is harder these days to convince women of the primacy of this process of politicization. More and more, we seem to form select interest groups composed of individuals who share similar perspectives. This limits our capacity to engage in critical discussion. It is difficult to involve women in new processes of feminist politicization because so many of us think that identifying men as the enemy, resisting male domination, gaining equal access to power and privilege is the end of feminist movement. Not only is it not the end, it is not even the place we want revitalized feminist movement to begin. We want to begin as women seriously addressing ourselves, not solely in relation to men, but in relation to an entire structure of domination of which patriarchy is one part. While the struggle to eradicate sexism and sexist oppression is and should be the primary thrust of feminist movement, to prepare ourselves politically for this effort we must first learn how to be in solidarity, how to struggle with one another.

Only when we confront the realities of sex, race, and class, the ways they divide us, make us different, stand us in opposition, and work to reconcile and resolve these issues will we be able to participate in the making of feminist revolution, in the transformation of the world. Feminism, as Charlotte Bunch emphasizes again and again in *Passionate Politics,* is a transformational politics, a struggle against domination wherein the effort is to change ourselves as well as structures. Speaking about the struggle to confront difference, Bunch asserts:

> A crucial point of the process is understanding that reality does not look the same from different people's perspective. It is not surprising that one way feminists have come to understand about differences has been through the love of a person from another culture or race. It takes persistence and motivation—which love often engenders—to get beyond

one's ethnocentric assumptions and really learn about other perspectives. In this process and while seeking to eliminate oppression, we also discover new possibilities and insights that come from the experience and survival of other peoples.

Embedded in the commitment to feminist revolution is the challenge to love. Love can be and is an important source of empowerment when we struggle to confront issues of sex, race, and class. Working together to identify and face our differences—to face the ways we dominate and are dominated—to change our actions, we need a mediating force that can sustain us so that we are not broken in this process, so that we do not despair.

Not enough feminist work has focussed on documenting and sharing ways individuals confront differences constructively and successfully. Women and men need to know what is on the other side of the pain experienced in politicization. We need detailed accounts of the ways our lives are fuller and richer as we change and grow politically, as we learn to live each moment as committed feminists, as comrades working to end domination. In reconceptualizing and reformulating strategies for future feminist movement, we need to concentrate on the politicization of love, not just in the context of talking about victimization in intimate relationships, but in a critical discussion where love can be understood as a powerful force that challenges and resists domination. As we work to be loving, to create a culture that celebrates life, that makes love possible, we move against dehumanization, against domination. In *Pedagogy of the Oppressed,* Paulo Freire evokes this power of love, declaring:

> I am more and more convinced that true revolutionaries must perceive the revolution, because of its creative and liberating nature, as an act of love. For me, the revolution, which is not possible without a theory of revolution—and therefore science—is not irreconcilable with love . . . The distortion imposed on the word "love" by the capitalist world cannot prevent the revolution from being essentially loving in character, nor can it prevent the revolutionaries from affirming their love of life.

That aspect of feminist revolution that calls women to love womanness, that calls men to resist dehumanizing concepts of masculinity, is an essential part of our struggle. It is the process by which we move from seeing ourselves as objects to acting as subjects. When women and men understand that working to eradicate patriarchal domination is a struggle rooted in the longing to make a world where everyone can live fully and freely, then we know our work to be a gesture of love. Let us draw upon that love to heighten our awareness, deepen our compassion, intensify our courage, and strengthen our commitment.

The New Cultural Politics of Difference

Cornel West

In these last few years of the 20th century, there is emerging a significant shift in the sensibilities and outlooks of critics and artists. In fact, I would go so far as to claim that a new kind of cultural worker is in the making, associated with a new politics of difference. These new forms of intellectual consciousness advance reconceptions of the vocation of critic and artist, attempting to undermine the prevailing disciplinary divisions of labor in the academy, museum, mass media and gallery networks, while preserving modes of critique within the ubiquitous commodification of culture in the global village. Distinctive features of the new cultural politics of difference are to trash the monolithic and homogeneous in the name of diversity, multiplicity and heterogeneity; to reject the abstract, general and universal in light of the concrete, specific and particular; and to historicize, contextualize and pluralize by highlighting the contingent, provisional, variable, tentative, shifting and changing. Needless to say, these gestures are not new in the history of criticism or art, yet what makes them novel—along with the cultural politics they produce—is how and what constitutes difference, the weight and gravity it is given in representation and the way in which highlighting issues like exterminism, empire, class, race, gender, sexual orientation, age, nation, nature, and region at this historical moment acknowledges some discontinuity and disruption from previous forms of cultural critique. To put it bluntly, the new cultural politics of difference consists of creative responses to the precise circumstances of our present moment—especially those of marginalized First World agents who shun degraded self-representations, articulating instead their sense of the flow of history in light of the contemporary terrors, anxieties and fears of highly commercialized North Atlantic capitalist cultures (with their escalating xenophobias against people of color, Jews, women, gays, lesbians and the elderly). The thawing, yet still rigid, Second World ex-communist cultures (with increasing nationalist revolts against the legacy of hegemonic party henchmen), and the diverse cultures of the majority of inhabitants on the globe smothered by international communication cartels and repressive postcolonial elites (sometimes in the name of communism, as in Ethiopia) or starved by austere World Bank and IMF policies that subordinate them to the North (as in free-market capitalism in Chile) also locate vital areas of analysis in this new cultural terrain.

The new cultural politics of difference are neither simply oppositional in contesting the mainstream (or *male*stream) for inclusion, nor transgressive in the avant-gardist sense of shocking conventional bourgeois audiences. Rather, they are distinct articulations of talented (and usually privileged) contributors to culture who desire to align themselves with demoralized, demobilized, depoliticized and disorganized people in order to empower and enable social action and, if possible, to enlist collective insurgency for the expansion of freedom, democracy and individuality. This perspective impels these cultural critics and artists to reveal, as an integral component of their production, the very operations of power within their immediate work contexts (i.e., academy, museum, gallery, mass media). This strategy, however, also puts them in an inescapable double bind—while linking their activities to the fundamental, structural overhaul of these institutions, they often remain financially dependent on them (so much for "independent" creation). For these critics of culture, theirs is a gesture that is simultaneously progressive *and* co-opted. Yet without social movement or political pressure from outside these institutions (extra-parliamentary and extra-curricular actions like the social movements of the recent past), transformation degenerates into mere accommodation or sheer stagnation, and the role of the "co-opted progressive"—no matter how fervent one's subversive rhetoric—is rendered more difficult. There can be no artistic breakthrough or social progress without some form of crisis in civilization—a crisis usually generated by organizations or collectivities that convince ordinary people to put their bodies and lives on the line. There is, of course, no guarantee that such pressure will yield the result one wants, but there is a guarantee that the status quo will remain or regress if no pressure is applied at all.

The new cultural politics of difference faces three basic challenges—intellectual, existential and political. The intellectual challenge—usually cast as methodological debate in these days in which academicist forms of expression have a monopoly on intellectual life—is how to think about representational practices in terms of history, culture and society. How does one understand, analyze and enact such practices today? An adequate answer to this question can be attempted only after one comes to terms with the insights and blindnesses of earlier attempts to grapple with the question in light of the evolving crisis in different histories, cultures and societies. I shall sketch a brief genealogy—a history that highlights the contingent origins and often ignoble outcomes—of exemplary critical responses to the question. This genealogy sets forth a historical framework that characterizes the rich yet deeply flawed Eurocentric traditions which the new cultural politics of difference build upon yet go beyond.

THE INTELLECTUAL CHALLENGE

An appropriate starting point is the ambiguous legacy of the Age of Europe. Between 1492 and 1945, European breakthroughs in oceanic transportation, agricultural production, state-consolidation, bureaucratization, industrialization, urbanization and imperial dominion shaped the makings of the modern world. Precious ideals like the dignity of persons (individuality) or the popular accountability of institutions (democracy) were unleashed around the world. Powerful critiques of illegitimate authorities—of the Protestant Reformation against the Roman Catholic Church, the Enlightenment against state churches, liberal movements against absolutist states and feudal guild constraints, workers against managerial subordination, people of color and Jews against white and gentile supremacist decrees, gays and lesbians against homophobic sanctions—were fanned and fuelled by these precious ideals refined within the crucible of the Age of Europe. Yet the discrepancy between sterling rhetoric and lived reality, glowing principles and actual practices loomed large.

By the last European century—the last epoch in which European domination of most of the globe was uncontested and unchallenged in a substantive way—a new world seemed to be stirring. At the height of England's reign as the major imperial European power, its exemplary cultural critic, Matthew Arnold, painfully observed in his "Stanzas From the Grand Chartreuse" that he felt some sense of "wandering between two worlds, one dead/the other powerless to be born." Following his Burkean sensibilities of cautious reform and fear of anarchy, Arnold acknowledged that the old glue—religion—that had tenuously and often unsuccessfully held together the ailing European regimes could not do so in the mid-19th century. Like Alexis de Tocqueville in France, Arnold saw that the democratic temper was the wave of the future. So he proposed a new conception of culture—a secular, humanistic one—that could play an integrative role in cementing and stabilizing an emerging bourgeois civil society and imperial state. His famous castigation of the immobilizing materialism of the declining aristocracy, the vulgar philistinism of the emerging middle classes and the latent explosiveness of the working-class majority was motivated by a desire to create new forms of cultural legitimacy, authority and order in a rapidly changing moment in 19th century Europe.

For Arnold, (in *Culture and Anarchy,* [1869]) this new conception of culture

> *. . . seeks to do away with classes; to make the best that has been thought and known in the world current everywhere; to make all men live in an atmosphere of sweetness and light . . .*

> *This is the* social idea *and the men of culture are the true apostles of equality. The great men of culture are those who have had a passion for diffusing, for making prevail, for carrying from one end of society to the other, the best knowledge, the best ideas of their time, who have laboured to divest knowledge of all that was harsh, uncouth, difficult, abstract, professional, exclusive; to humanize it, to make it efficient outside the clique of the cultivated and learned, yet still remaining the best knowledge and thought of the time, and a true source, therefore, of sweetness and light.*

As an organic intellectual of an emergent middle class—as the inspector of schools in an expanding educational bureaucracy, Professor of Poetry at Oxford (the first non-cleric and the first to lecture in English rather than Latin) and an active participant in a thriving magazine network—Arnold defined and defended a new secular culture of critical discourse. For him, this discursive strategy would be lodged in the educational and periodical apparatuses of modern societies as they contained and incorporated the frightening threats of an arrogant aristocracy and especially of an "anarchic" working-class majority. His ideals of disinterested, dispassionate and objective inquiry would regulate this new secular cultural production, and his justifications for the use of state power to quell any threats to the survival and security of this culture were widely accepted. He aptly noted, "Through culture seems to lie our way, not only to perfection, but even to safety."

This sentence is revealing in two ways. First, it refers to "our way" without explicitly acknowledging who constitutes the "we." This move is symptomatic among many bourgeois, male Eurocentric critics whose universalizing gestures exclude (by guarding a silence around) or explicitly degrade women and peoples of color. Second, the sentence links culture to safety—presumably the safety of the "we" against the barbaric threats of the "them," i.e., those viewed as different in some debased manner. Needless to say, Arnold's negative attitudes toward British working-class people, women and especially Indians and Jamaicans in the Empire clarify why he conceives of culture as, in part, a weapon for bourgeois male European "safety."

For Arnold the best of the Age of Europe—modeled on a mythological mélange of Periclean Athens, late Republican/early Imperial Rome and Elizabethan England—could be promoted only if there was an interlocking affiliation among the emerging middle classes, a homogenizing of cultural discourse in the educational and university networks, and a state advanced enough in its policing techniques to safeguard it. The candidates for participation and legitimation in this grand endeavor of cultural renewal and revision would be detached intellectuals willing to shed their parochialism, provincialism and class-bound identities for Arnold's middle-class-skewed project: ". . . Aliens, if we may so call them—persons who are mainly led, not by their class spirit, but by a general *humane* spirit, by the love of human perfection." Needless to say, this Arnoldian perspective still informs much of the academic practices and secular cultural attitudes today—dominant views about the canon, admission procedures and collective self-definitions of intellectuals. Yet Arnold's project was disrupted by the collapse of 19th century Europe—World War I. This unprecedented war brought to the surface the crucial role and violent potential not of the masses Arnold feared but of the state he heralded. Upon the ashes of this wasteland of human carnage—some of it the civilian European population—T.S. Eliot emerged as the grand cultural spokesman.

Eliot's project of reconstituting and reconceiving European highbrow culture—and thereby regulating critical and artistic practices—after the internal collapse of imperial Europe can be viewed as a response to the probing question posed by Paul Valéry in "The Crisis of the Spirit" after World War I,

> *This Europe, will it become* what it is in reality, *i.e., a little cape of the Asiatic continent? or will this Europe remain rather what it seems, i.e., the priceless part of the whole earth, the pearl of the globe, the brain of a vast body?*

Eliot's image of Europe as a wasteland, a culture of fragments with no cementing center, predominated in postwar Europe. And though his early poetic practices were more radical, open and international than his Eurocentric criticism, Eliot posed a return to and revision of tradition as the only way of regaining European cultural order and political stability. For Eliot, contemporary history had become, as James Joyce's Stephen declared in *Ulysses* (1922), "a nightmare from which he was trying to awake"— "an immense panorama of futility and anarchy" as Eliot put it in his renowned review of Joyce's modernist masterpiece. In his influential essay, "Tradition and the Individual Talent," (1919) Eliot stated

> *Yet if the only form of tradition, of handing down, consisted in following the ways of the immediate generation before us in a blind or timid adherence to its successes, "tradition" should positively be discouraged. We have seen many such simple currents soon lost in the sand; and novelty is better than repetition. Tradition is a matter of much wider significance. It cannot be inherited, and if you want it you must attain it by great labour.*

Eliot's fecund notion of tradition is significant in that it promotes a historicist sensibility in artistic practice and cultural reflection. This historicist sensibility—regulated in Eliot's case by a reactionary politics—produced a powerful assault on existing literary canons (in which for example Romantic poets were displaced by the Metaphysical and Symbolist ones) and unrelenting attacks on modern Western civilization (such as the liberal ideas of democracy, equality and freedom). Like Arnold's notion of culture, Eliot's idea of tradition was part of his intellectual arsenal, to be used in the battles raging in European cultures and societies.

Eliot found this tradition in the Church of England, to which he converted in 1927. Here was a tradition that left room for his Catholic cast of mind, Calvinistic heritage, puritanical temperament and rebullient patriotism for the old American South (the place of his upbringing). Like Arnold, Eliot was obsessed with the idea of civilization and the horror of barbarism (echoes of Joseph Conrad's Kurtz in *Heart of Darkness*) or more pointedly, the notion of the decline and decay of European civilization. With the advent of World War II, Eliot's obsession became a reality. Again unprecedented human carnage (50 million dead)—including an indescribable genocidal attack on Jewish people—throughout Europe as well as around the globe, put the last nail in the coffin of the Age of Europe. After 1945, Europe consisted of a devastated and divided continent, crippled by a humiliating dependency on and deference to the USA and USSR.

The second historical coordinate of my genealogy is the emergence of the USA as *the* world power. The USA was unprepared for world power status. However, with the recovery of Stalin's Russia (after losing 20 million dead), the USA felt compelled to make its presence felt around the globe. Then with the Marshall plan to strengthen Europe against Russian influence (and provide new markets for U.S. products), the 1948 Russian takeover of Czechoslovakia, the 1948 Berlin blockade, the 1950 beginning of the Korean War and the 1952 establishment of NATO forces in Europe, it seemed clear that there was no escape from world power obligations.

The post-World War II era in the USA, or the first decades of what Henry Luce envisioned as "The American Century," was not only a period of incredible economic expansion but of active cultural ferment. In the classical Fordist formula, mass production required mass consumption. With unchallenged hegemony in the capitalist world, the USA took economic growth for granted. Next to exercising its crude, anti-communist, McCarthyist obsessions, buying commodities became the primary act of civic virtue for many American citizens at this time. The creation of a mass middle class—a prosperous working class with a bourgeois identity—was countered by the first major emergence of subcultures of American non-WASP intellectuals: the so-called New York intellectuals in criticism, the Abstract Expressionists in painting and the BeBop artists in jazz music. This emergence signaled a vital challenge to an American male WASP elite loyal to an older and eroding European culture.

The first significant blow was dealt when assimilated Jewish Americans entered the higher echelons of the cultural apparatuses (academy, museums, galleries, mass media). Lionel Trilling is an emblematic figure. This Jewish entree into the anti-Semitic and patriarchal critical discourse of the exclusivistic institutions of American culture initiated the slow but sure undoing of the male WASP cultural hegemony and homogeneity. Lionel Trilling's project was to appropriate Matthew Arnold for his own political and cultural purposes—thereby unraveling the old male WASP consensus, while erecting a new post-World War II liberal academic consensus around cold war, anti-communist renditions of the values of complexity, difficulty, variousness and modulation. In addition, the post-war boom laid the basis for intense professionalization and specialization in expanding institutions of higher education—especially in the natural sciences that were compelled to somehow respond to Russia's successful ventures in space. Humanistic scholars found themselves searching for new methodologies that could buttress self-images of rigor and scientific seriousness. For example, the close reading techniques of New Criticism (severed from their conservative, organicist, anti-industrialist ideological roots), the logical precision of reasoning in analytic philosophy and the jargon of Parsonian structural-functionalism in sociology helped create such self-images. Yet towering cultural critics like C. Wright Mills, W.E.B. DuBois, Richard Hofstadter, Margaret Mead and Dwight MacDonald bucked the tide. This suspicion of the academicization of knowledge is expressed in Trilling's well-known essay "On the Teaching of Modern Literature"

> . . . can we not say that, when modern literature is brought into the classroom, the subject being taught is betrayed by the pedagogy of the subject? We have to ask ourselves whether in our day too much does not come within the purview of the academy. More and more, as the universities liberalize themselves, turn their beneficent imperialistic gaze upon what is called life itself, the feeling grows among our educated classes that little can be experienced unless it is validated by some established intellectual discipline. . . .

Trilling laments the fact that university instruction often quiets and domesticates radical and subversive works of art, turning them into objects "of merely habitual regard." This process of "the socialization of the anti-social, or the acculturation of the anti-cultural, or the legitimization of the subversive" leads Trilling to "question whether in our culture the study of literature is any longer a suitable means for developing and refining the intelligence." Trilling asks this question not in the spirit of denigrating and devaluing the academy but rather in the spirit of highlighting the possible failure of an Arnoldian conception of culture to contain what he perceives as the philistine and anarchic alternatives becoming more and more available to students of the 60's—namely, mass culture and radical politics.

This threat is partly associated with the third historical coordinate of my genealogy— the decolonization of the Third World. It is crucial to recognize the importance of this world-historical process if one wants to grasp the significance of the end of the Age of Europe and the emergence of the USA as a world power. With the first defeat of a western nation by a non-western nation—in Japan's victory over Russia (1905), revolutions in Persia (1905), Turkey (1908), China (1912), Mexico (1911–12) and much later the independence of India (1947) and China (1948) and the triumph of Ghana (1957)—the actuality of a decolonized globe loomed large. Born of violent struggle, consciousness-raising and the reconstruction of identities, decolonization simultaneously brings with it new perspectives on that long festering underside of the Age of Europe (of which colonial domination represents the *costs* of "progress," "order" and "culture"), as well as requiring new readings of the economic boom in the USA (wherein the Black, Brown, Yellow, Red, female, elderly, gay, lesbian and White working class live the same *costs* as cheap labor at home as well as in US-dominated Latin American and Pacific rim markets).

The impetuous ferocity and moral outrage that motors the decolonization process is best captured by Frantz Fanon in *The Wretched of the Earth* (1961).

> Decolonization, which sets out to change the order of the world, is obviously, a program of complete disorder . . . Decolonization is the meeting of two forces, opposed to each other by their very nature, which in fact owe their originality to that sort of substantification which results from and is nourished by the situation in the colonies. Their first encounter was marked by violence and their existence together—that is to say the exploitation of the native by the settler—was carried on by dint of a great array of bayonets and cannons . . .

> In decolonization, there is therefore the need of a complete calling in question of the colonial situation. If we wish to describe it precisely, we might find it in the well-known words:

"The last shall be first and the first last." Decolonization is the putting into practice of this sentence.

The naked truth of decolonization evokes for us the searing bullets and bloodstained knives which emanate from it. For if the last shall be first, this will only come to pass after a murderous and decisive struggle between the two protagonists.

Fanon's strong words, though excessively Manichean, still describe the feelings and thoughts between the occupying British Army and colonized Irish in Northern Ireland, the occupying Israeli Army and subjugated Palestinians on the West Bank and Gaza Strip, the South African Army and oppressed Black South Africans in the townships, the Japanese Police and Koreans living in Japan, the Russian Army and subordinated Armenians and others in the Southern and Eastern USSR. His words also partly invoke the sense many Black Americans have toward police departments in urban centers. In other words, Fanon is articulating century-long heartfelt human responses to being degraded and despised, hated and hunted, oppressed and exploited, marginalized and dehumanized at the hands of powerful xenophobic European, American, Russian and Japanese imperial countries.

During the late '50s, '60s and early '70s in the USA, these decolonized sensibilities fanned and fueled the Civil Rights and Black Power movements, as well as the student anti-war, feminist, gray, brown, gay, and lesbian movements. In this period we witnessed the shattering of male WASP cultural homogeneity and the collapse of the short-lived liberal consensus. The inclusion of African Americans, Latino/a Americans, Asian Americans, Native Americans and American women into the culture of critical discourse yielded intense intellectual polemics and inescapable ideological polarization that focused principally on the exclusions, silences and blindnesses of male WASP cultural homogeneity and its concomitant Arnoldian notions of the canon.

In addition, these critiques promoted three crucial processes that affected intellectual life in the country. First is the appropriation of the theories of post-war Europe—especially the work of the Frankfurt school (Marcuse, Adorno, Horkheimer), French/Italian Marxisms (Sartre, Althusser, Lefebvre, Gramsci), structuralisms (Lévi-Strauss, Todorov) and post-structuralisms (Deleuze, Derrida, Foucault). These diverse and disparate theories—all preoccupied with keeping alive radical projects after the end of the Age of Europe—tend to fuse versions of transgressive European modernisms with Marxist or post-Marxist left politics and unanimously shun the term "post-modernism." Second, there is the recovery and revisioning of American history in light of the struggles of white male workers, women, African Americans, Native Americans, Latino/a Americans, gays and lesbians. Third is the impact of forms of popular culture such as television, film, music videos and even sports, on highbrow literate culture. The Black-based hip-hop culture of youth around the world is one grand example.

After 1973, with the crisis in the international world economy, America's slump in productivity, the challenge of OPEC nations to the North Atlantic monopoly of oil production, the increasing competition in hi-tech sectors of the economy from Japan and West Germany and the growing fragility of the international debt structure, the USA entered a period of waning self-confidence (compounded by Watergate) and a nearly contracting economy. As the standards of living for the middle classes declined, owing to runaway inflation, and the quality of living fell for most, due to escalating unemployment, underemployment and crime, religious and secular neo-conservatism emerged with power and potency. This fusion of fervent neo-nationalism, traditional cultural values and "free market" policies served as the ground work for the Reagan-Bush era.

The ambiguous legacies of the European Age, American preeminence and decolonization continue to haunt our postmodern moment as we come to terms with both the European, American, Japanese, Soviet, and Third World *crimes against* and *contributions to* humanity. The plight of Africans in the New World can be instructive in this regard.

By 1914 European maritime empires had dominion over more than half of the land and a third of the peoples in the world—almost 72 million square kilometers of territory and more than 560 million people under colonial rule. Needless to say, this European control included brutal enslavement, institutional terrorism and cultural degradation of Black diaspora people. The death of roughly seventy-five million Africans during the centuries-long transatlantic slave trade is but one reminder, among others, of the assault on Black humanity. The Black diaspora condition of New World servitude—in which they were viewed as mere commodities with production value, who had no proper legal status, social standing or public worth—can be characterized as, following Orlando Patterson, natal alienation. This state of perpetual and inheritable domination that diaspora Africans had at birth produced the *modern Black diaspora problematic of invisibility and namelessness.* White supremacist practices—enacted under the auspices of the prestigious cultural authorities of the churches, printed media and scientific academics—promoted Black inferiority and constituted the European background against which Black diaspora struggles for identity, dignity (self-confidence, self-respect, self-esteem) and material resources took place.

An inescapable aspect of this struggle was that the Black diaspora peoples' quest for validation and recognition occurred on the ideological, social and cultural terrains of other non-Black peoples. White supremacist assaults on Black intelligence, ability, beauty and character required persistent Black efforts to hold self-doubt, self-contempt and even self-hatred at bay. Selective appropriation, incorporation and re-articulation of European ideologies, cultures and institutions alongside an African heritage—a heritage more or less confined to linguistic innovation in rhetorical practices, stylizations of the body in forms of occupying an alien social space (hair styles, ways of walking, standing, hand expressions, talking) and means of constituting and sustaining comraderie and community (e.g. antiphonal, call-and-response styles, rhythmic repetition, risk-ridden syncopation in spectacular modes in musical and rhetorical expressions)—were some of the strategies employed.

The modern Black diaspora problematic of invisibility and namelessness can be understood as the condition of *relative lack of Black power to represent themselves to themselves and others as complex human beings, and thereby to contest the bombardment of negative, degrading stereotypes put forward by White supremacist ideologies.* The initial Black response to being caught in this whirlwind of Europeanization was to resist the misrepresentation and caricature of the terms set by uncontested non-Black norms and models and fight for self-representation and recognition. Every modern Black person, especially cultural disseminators, encounters this problematic of invisibility and namelessness. The initial Black diaspora response was a mode of resistance that was *moralistic in content* and *communal in character.* That is, the fight for representation and recognition highlighted moral judgments regarding Black "positive" images over and against White supremacist stereotypes. These images "re-presented" monolithic and homogeneous Black communities, in a way that could displace past misrepresentations of these communities. Stuart Hall has talked about these responses as attempts to change "the relations of representation."

These courageous yet limited Black efforts to combat racist cultural practices uncritically accepted non-Black conventions and standards in two ways. First, they proceeded in an *assimilationist manner* that set out to show that Black people were really like White people—thereby eliding differences (in history, culture) between Whites and Blacks. Black specificity and particularity was thus banished in order to gain White acceptance and approval. Second, these Black responses rested upon a *homogenizing impulse* that assumed that all Black people were really alike—hence obliterating differences (class, gender, region, sexual orientation) between Black peoples. I submit that there are elements of truth in both claims, yet the conclusions are unwarranted owing to the basic fact that non-Black paradigms set the terms of the replies.

The insight in the first claim is that Blacks and Whites are in some important sense alike—i.e., in their positive capacities for human sympathy, moral sacrifice, service to others, intelligence and beauty, or negatively, in their capacity for cruelty. Yet the common humanity they share is jettisoned when the claim is cast in an assimilationist manner that subordinates Black particularity to a false universalism, i.e., non-Black rubrics or prototypes. Similarly, the insight in the second claim is that all Blacks are in some significant sense "in the same boat"—that is, subject to White supremacist abuse. Yet this common condition is stretched too far when viewed in a *homogenizing* way that overlooks how racist treatment vastly differs owing to class, gender, sexual orientation, nation, region, hue and age.

The moralistic and communal aspects of the initial Black diaspora responses to social and psychic erasure were not simply cast into simplistic binary oppositions of positive/negative, good/bad images that privileged the first term in light of a White norm so that Black efforts remained inscribed within the very logic that dehumanized them. They were further complicated by the fact that these responses were also advanced principally by anxiety-ridden, middle-class Black intellectuals, (predominantly male and heterosexual) grappling with their sense of double-consciousness—namely their own crisis of identity, agency and audience—caught between a quest for White approval and acceptance and an endeavor to overcome the internalized association of Blackness with inferiority. And I suggest that these complex anxieties of modern Black diaspora intellectuals partly motivate the two major arguments that ground the assimilationist moralism and homogeneous communalism just outlined.

Kobena Mercer has talked about these two arguments as the *reflectionist* and the *social engineering* arguments. The reflectionist argument holds that the fight for Black representation and recognition must reflect or mirror the real Black community, not simply the negative and depressing representations of it. The social engineering argument claims that since any form of representation is constructed—i.e., selective in light of broader aims—Black representation (especially given the difficulty of Blacks gaining access to positions of power to produce any Black imagery) should offer positive images of themselves in order to inspire achievement among young Black people, thereby countering racist stereotypes. The hidden assumption of both arguments is that we have unmediated access to what the "real Black community" is and what "positive images" are. In short, these arguments presuppose the very phenomena to be interrogated, and thereby foreclose the very issues that should serve as the subject matter to be investigated.

Any notions of "the real Black community" and "positive images" are value-laden, socially-loaded and ideologically-charged. To pursue this discussion is to call into question the possibility of such an uncontested consensus regarding them. Stuart Hall has rightly called this encounter "the end of innocence or the end of the innocent notion of the essential Black subject . . . the recognition that 'Black' is essentially a politically and culturally *constructed* category." This recognition—more and more pervasive among the postmodern Black diaspora intelligentsia—is facilitated in part by the slow but sure dissolution of the European Age's maritime empires, and the unleashing of new political possibilities and cultural articulations among ex-colonialized peoples across the globe.

One crucial lesson of this decolonization process remains the manner in which most Third World authoritarian bureaucratic elites deploy essentialist rhetorics about "homogeneous national communities" and "positive images" in order to repress and regiment their diverse and heterogeneous populations. Yet in the diaspora, especially among First World countries, this critique has emerged not so much from the Black male component of the left but rather from the Black women's movement. The decisive push of postmodern Black intellectuals toward a new cultural politics of difference has been made by the powerful critiques and constructive explorations of Black diaspora women (e.g. Toni Morrison). The coffin used to bury the innocent notion of the essential Black subject was nailed shut with the termination of the Black male monopoly on the construction of the Black subject. In this regard, the Black diaspora womanist critique has had a greater impact than the critiques that highlight exclusively class, empire, age, sexual orientation or nature.

This decisive push toward the end of Black innocence—though prefigured in various degrees in the best moments of W.E.B. DuBois, Anna Cooper, C.L.R. James, James Baldwin, Claudia Jones, the later Malcolm X, Frantz Fanon, Amiri Baraka and others—forces Black diaspora cultural workers to encounter what Hall has called the "politics of representation." The main aim now is not simply access to representation in order to produce positive images of homogeneous communities—though broader access remains a practical and political problem. Nor is the primary goal here that of contesting stereotypes—though contestation remains a significant though limited venture. Following the model of the Black diaspora traditions of music, athletics and rhetoric, Black cultural workers must constitute and sustain discursive and institutional networks that deconstruct earlier modern Black strategies for identity-formation, demystify power relations that incorporate class, patriarchal and homophobic biases, and construct more multivalent and multi-dimensional responses that articulate the complexity and diversity of Black practices in the modern and postmodern world.

Furthermore, Black cultural workers must investigate and interrogate the other of Blackness–Whiteness. One cannot deconstruct the binary oppositional logic of images of Blackness without extending it to the contrary condition of Blackness/Whiteness itself.

However, a mere dismantling will not do—for the very notion of a deconstructive social theory is oxymoronic. Yet social theory is what is needed to examine and *explain* the historically specific ways in which "Whiteness" is a politically constructed category parasitic on "Blackness," and thereby to conceive of the profoundly hybrid character of what we mean by "race," "ethnicity," and "nationality." For instance, European immigrants arrived on American shores perceiving themselves as "Irish," "Sicilian," "Lithuanian," etc. They had to learn that they were "White" principally by adopting an American discourse of positively-valued Whiteness and negatively-charged Blackness. This process by which people define themselves physically, socially, sexually and even politically in terms of Whiteness or Blackness has much bearing not only on constructed notions of race and ethnicity but also on how we understand the changing character of U.S. nationalities. And given the Americanization of the world, especially in the sphere of mass culture, such inquiries—encouraged by the new cultural politics of difference—raise critical issues of "hybridity," "exilic status" and "identity" on an international scale. Needless to say, these inquiries must traverse those of "male/female," "colonizer/colonized," "heterosexual/homosexual," et al., as well.

In light of this brief sketch of the emergence of our present crisis—and the turn toward history and difference in cultural work—four major historicist forms of theoretical activity provide resources for how we understand, analyze and enact our representational practices: Heideggerian *destruction* of the western metaphysical tradition, Derridean *deconstruction* of the western philosophical tradition, Rortian *demythologization* of the western intellectual tradition and Marxist, Foucaultian, feminist, anti-racist or anti-homophobic *demystification* of western cultural and artistic conventions.

Despite his abominable association with the Nazis, Martin Heidegger's project is useful in that it discloses the suppression of temporality and historicity in the dominant metaphysical systems of the West from Plato to Rudolph Carnap. This is noteworthy in that it forces one to understand philosophy's representational discourses as thoroughly historical phenomena. Hence, they should be viewed with skepticism as they are often flights from the specific, concrete, practical and particular. The major problem with Heidegger's project—as noted by his neo-Marxist student, Herbert Marcuse—is that he views history in terms of fate, heritage and destiny. He dramatizes the past and present as if it were a Greek tragedy with no tools of social analyses to relate cultural work to institutions and structures or antecedent forms and styles.

Jacques Derrida's version of deconstruction is one of the most influential schools of thought among young academic critics. It is salutary in that it focuses on the political power of rhetorical operations—of tropes and metaphors in binary oppositions like white/black, good/bad, male/female, machine/nature, ruler/ruled, reality/appearance—showing how these operations sustain hierarchal world views by devaluing the second terms as something subsumed under the first. Most of the controversy about Derrida's project revolves around this austere epistemic doubt that unsettles binary oppositions while undermining any determinate meaning of a text, i.e., book, art-object, performance, building. Yet, his views about skepticism are no more alarming than those of David Hume, Ludwig Wittgenstein or Stanley Cavell. He simply revels in it for transgressive purposes, whereas others provide us with ways to dissolve, sidestep or cope with skepticism. None, however, slide down the slippery, crypto-Nietzschean slope of sophomoric relativism as alleged by old-style humanists, be they Platonists, Kantians or Arnoldians.

The major shortcoming of Derrida's deconstructive project is that it puts a premium on a sophisticated ironic consciousness that tends to preclude and foreclose analyses that guide action with purpose. And given Derrida's own status as an Algerian-born, Jewish leftist marginalized by a hostile French academic establishment (quite different from his reception by the youth in the American academic establishment), the sense of political impotence and hesitation regarding the efficacy of moral action is understandable—but not justifiable. His works and those of his followers too often become rather monotonous, Johnny-one-note rhetorical readings that disassemble texts with little attention to the effects and consequences these dismantlings have in relation to the operations of military, economic and social powers.

Richard Rorty's neo-pragmatic project of demythologization is insightful in that it provides descriptive mappings of the transient metaphors—especially the ocular and specular ones—that regulate some of the fundamental dynamics in the construction of self-descriptions dominant in highbrow European and American philosophy. His perspective is instructive because it discloses the crucial role of narrative as the background for rational exchange and critical conversation. To put it crudely, Rorty shows why we should speak not of History, but histories, not of Reason, but historically constituted forms of rationality, not of Criticism or Art, but of socially constructed notions of criticism and art—all linked but not reducible to political purposes, material interests and cultural prejudices.

Rorty's project nonetheless leaves one wanting owing to its distrust of social analytical explanation. Similar to the dazzling new historicism of Stephen Greenblatt, Louis Montrose and Catherine Gallagher—inspired by the subtle symbolic-cum-textual anthropology of Clifford Geertz and the powerful discursive materialism of Michel Foucault—Rorty gives us mappings and descriptions with no explanatory accounts for change and conflict. In this way, it gives us an aestheticized version of historicism in which the provisional and variable are celebrated at the expense of highlighting who gains, loses or bears what costs.

Demystification is the most illuminating mode of theoretical inquiry for those who promote the new cultural politics of difference. Social structural analyses of empire, exterminism, class, race, gender, nature, age, sexual orientation, nation and region are the springboards—though not landing grounds—for the most desirable forms of critical practice that take history (and herstory) seriously. Demystification tries to keep track of the complex dynamics of institutional and other related power structures in order to disclose options and alternatives for transformative praxis; it also attempts to grasp the way in which representational strategies are creative responses to novel circumstances and conditions. In this way, the central role of human agency (always enacted under circumstances not of one's choosing)—be it in the critic, artist or constituency and audience—is accented.

I call demystificatory criticism "prophetic criticism"—the approach appropriate for the new cultural politics of difference—because while it begins with social structural analyses it also makes explicit its moral and political aims. It is partisan, partial, engaged and crisis-centered, yet always keeps open a skeptical eye to avoid dogmatic traps, premature closures, formulaic formulations or rigid conclusions. In addition to social structural analyses, moral and political judgments, and sheer critical consciousness, there indeed is evaluation. Yet the aim of this evaluation is neither to pit art-objects against one another like racehorses nor to create eternal canons that dull, discourage or even dwarf contemporary achievements. We listen to Ludwig Beethoven, Charlie Parker, Luciano Pavarotti, Laurie Anderson, Sarah Vaughan, Stevie Wonder or Kathleen Battle, read William Shakespeare, Anton Chekhov, Ralph Ellison, Doris Lessing, Thomas Pynchon, Toni Morrison or Gabriel García Márquez, see works of Pablo Picasso, Ingmar Bergman, Le Corbusier, Martin Puryear, Barbara Kruger, Spike Lee, Frank Gehry or Howardena Pindell—not in order to undergird bureaucratic assents or enliven cocktail party conversations, but rather to be summoned by the styles they deploy for their profound insight, pleasures and challenges. Yet all evaluation—including a delight in Eliot's poetry despite his reactionary politics, or a love of Zora Neale Hurston's novels despite her Republican party affiliations—is inseparable from, though not identical or reducible to, social structural analyses, moral and political judgments and the workings of a curious critical consciousness.

The deadly traps of demystification—and any form of prophetic criticism—are those of reductionism, be it of the sociological, psychological, or historical sort. By reductionism I mean either one factor analyses (i.e., crude Marxisms, feminisms, racialisms, etc.) that yield a one-dimensional functionalism, or a hyper-subtle analytical perspective that loses touch with the specificity of an art work's form and the context of its reception. Few cultural workers of whatever stripe can walk the tightrope between the Scylla of reductionism and the Charybdis of aestheticism—yet demystificatory (or prophetic) critics must.

THE EXISTENTIAL CHALLENGE

The existential challenge to the new cultural politics of difference can be stated simply: how does one acquire the resources to survive and the cultural capital to thrive as a critic or artist? By cultural capital (Pierre Bourdieu's term), I mean not only the high-quality skills required to engage in critical practices but, more important, the self-confidence, discipline and perseverance necessary for success without an undue reliance on the mainstream for approval and acceptance. This challenge holds for all prophetic critics, yet it is especially difficult for those of color. The widespread modern European denial of the intelligence, ability, beauty and character of people of color puts a tremendous burden on critics and artists of color to "prove" themselves in light of norms and models set by white elites whose own heritage devalued and dehumanized them. In short, in the court of criticism and art—or any matters regarding the life of the mind—people of color are guilty, i.e., not expected to meet standards of intellectual achievement, until "proven" innocent, i.e., acceptable to "us."

This is more a structural dilemma than a matter of personal attitudes. The profoundly racist and sexist heritage of the European Age has bequeathed to us a set of deeply-ingrained perceptions about people of color including, of course, the self-perceptions that people of color bring. It is not surprising that most intellectuals of color in the past exerted much of their energies and efforts to gain acceptance and approval by "white normative gazes." The new cultural politics of difference advises critics and artists of color to put aside this mode of mental bondage, thereby freeing themselves to both interrogate the ways in which they are bound by certain conventions and to learn from and build on these very norms and models. One hallmark of wisdom in the context of any struggle is to avoid knee-jerk rejection and uncritical acceptance.

Self-confidence, discipline and perseverance are not ends-in-themselves. Rather they are the necessary stuff of which enabling criticism and self-criticism are made. Notwithstanding inescapable jealousies, insecurities and anxieties, one telling characteristic of critics and artists of color linked to the new prophetic criticism should be their capacity for and promotion of relentless criticism and self-criticism—be it the normative paradigms of their white colleagues that tend to leave out considerations of empire, race, gender and sexual orientation or the damaging dogmas about the homogeneous character of communities of color.

There are four basic options for people of color interested in representation—if they are to survive and thrive as serious practitioners of their craft. First, there is the Booker T. Temptation, namely the individual preoccupation with the mainstream and its legitimizing power. Most critics and artists of color try to bite this bait. It is nearly unavoidable, yet few succeed in a substantive manner. It is no accident that the most creative and profound among them—especially those with staying power beyond mere flashes in the pan to satisfy faddish tokenism—are usually marginal to the mainstream. Even the pervasive professionalization of cultural practitioners of color in the past few decades has not produced towering figures who reside within the established White patronage system that bestows the rewards and prestige for chosen contributions to American society.

It certainly helps to have some trustworthy allies within this system, yet most of those who enter and remain tend to lose much of their creativity, diffuse their prophetic energy and dilute their critiques. Still, it is unrealistic for creative people of color to think they can sidestep the White patronage system. And though there are indeed some White allies conscious of the tremendous need to rethink identity politics, it's naive to think that being comfortably nested within this very same system—even if one can be a patron to others—does not affect one's work, one's outlook and, most important, one's soul.

The second option is the Talented Tenth Seduction, namely, a move toward arrogant group insularity. This alternative has a limited function—to preserve one's sanity and sense of self as one copes with the mainstream. Yet it is, at best, a transitional and transient activity. If it becomes a permanent option it is self-defeating in that it usually reinforces the very inferior complexes promoted by the subtly racist mainstream. Hence it tends to revel in a parochialism and encourage a narrow racialist and chauvinistic outlook.

The third strategy is the Go-It-Alone option. This is an extreme rejectionist perspective that shuns the mainstream and group insularity. Almost every critic and artist of color contemplates or enacts this option at some time in their pilgrimage. It is healthy in that it reflects the presence of independent, critical and skeptical sensibilities toward perceived constraints on one's creativity. Yet it is, in the end, difficult if not impossible to sustain if one is to grow, develop and mature intellectually; as some semblance of dialogue with a community is necessary for almost any creative practice.

The most desirable option for people of color who promote the new cultural politics of difference is to be a critical organic catalyst. By this I mean a person who stays attuned to the best of what the mainstream has to offer—its paradigms, viewpoints and methods—yet maintains a grounding in affirming and enabling subcultures of criticism. Prophetic critics and artists of color should be exemplars of what it means to be intellectual freedom-fighters, that is, cultural workers who simultaneously position themselves within (or alongside) the mainstream while clearly aligned with groups who vow to keep alive potent traditions of critique and resistance. In this regard, one can take clues from the great musicians or preachers of color who are open to the best of what other traditions offer yet are rooted in nourishing subcultures that build on the grand achievements of a vital heritage. Openness to others—including the mainstream—does not entail wholesale co-optation, and group autonomy is not group insularity. Louis Armstrong, W.E.B. DuBois, Ella Baker, Jose Carlos Mariatequi, M.M. Thomas, Wynton Marsalis, Martin Luther King, Jr., and Ronald Takaki have understood this well.

The new cultural politics of difference can thrive only if there are communities, groups, organizations, institutions, subcultures and networks of people of color who cultivate critical sensibilities and personal accountability—without inhibiting individual expressions, curiosities and idiosyncrasies. This is especially needed given the escalating racial hostility, violence and polarization in the USA. Yet this critical coming-together must not be a narrow closing-ranks. Rather it is a strengthening and nurturing endeavor that can forge more solid alliances and coalitions. In this way, prophetic criticism—with its stress on historical specificity and artistic complexity—directly addresses the intellectual challenge. The cultural capital of people of color—with its emphasis on self-confidence, discipline, perseverance and subcultures of criticism—also tries to meet the existential requirement. Both are mutually reinforcing. Both are motivated by a deep commitment to individuality and democracy—the moral and political ideals that guide the creative response to the political challenge.

THE POLITICAL CHALLENGE

Adequate rejoinders to intellectual and existential challenges equip the practitioners of the new cultural politics of difference to meet the political ones. This challenge principally consists of forging solid and reliable alliances of people of color and white progressives guided by a moral and political vision of greater democracy and individual freedom in communities, states and transnational enterprises, e.g. corporations, information and communications conglomerates.

Jesse Jackson's Rainbow Coalition is a gallant yet flawed effort in this regard—gallant due to the tremendous energy, vision and courage of its leader and followers, yet flawed because of its failure to take seriously critical and democratic sensibilities within its own operations. In fact, Jackson's attempt to gain power at the national level is a symptom of the weakness of U.S. progressive politics, and a sign that the capacity to generate extra-parliamentary social motion or movements has waned. Yet given the present organizational weakness and intellectual timidity of left politics in the USA, the major option is that of multi-racial grass-roots citizens' participation in credible projects in which people see that their efforts can make a difference. The salutary revolutionary developments in Eastern Europe are encouraging and inspiring in this regard. Ordinary people organized can change societies.

The most significant theme of the new cultural politics of difference is the agency, capacity and ability of human beings who have been culturally degraded, politically oppressed and economically exploited by bourgeois liberal and communist illiberal status quos. This theme neither romanticizes nor idealizes marginalized peoples. Rather it accentuates their humanity and tries to attenuate the institutional constraints on their life-chances for surviving and thriving. In this way, the new cultural politics of difference shuns narrow particularisms, parochialisms and separatisms, just as it rejects false universalisms and homogeneous totalisms. Instead, the new cultural politics of difference affirms the perennial quest for the precious ideals of individuality and democracy by digging deep in the depths of human particularities and social specificities in order to construct new kinds of connections, affinities and communities across empire, nation, region, race, gender, age and sexual orientation.

The major impediments of the radical libertarian and democratic projects of the new cultural politics are threefold: the pervasive processes of objectification, rationalization and commodification throughout the world. The first process—best highlighted in Georg Simmel's *The Philosophy of Money* (1900)—consists of transforming human beings into manipulable objects. It promotes the notion that people's action have no impact on the world, that we are but spectators not participants in making and remaking ourselves and the larger society. The second process—initially examined in the seminal works of Max Weber—expands bureaucratic hierarchies that impose impersonal rules and regulations in order to increase efficiency, be they defined in terms of better service or better surveillance. This process leads not only to disenchantment with past mythologies but also to deadening, flat, banal ways of life. The third and most important process—best examined in the works of Karl Marx, Georg Lukács and Walter Benjamin—augments market forces in the form of oligopolies and monopolies that centralize resources and powers and promote cultures of consumption that view poeple as mere spectatorial consumers and passive citizens.

These processes cannot be eliminated, but their pernicious effects can be substantially alleviated. The audacious attempt to lessen their impact—to preserve people's agency, increase the scope of their freedom and expand the operations of democracy— is the fundamental aim of the new cultural politics of difference. This is why the crucial questions become: What is the moral content of one's cultural identity? And what are the poltical consequences of this moral content and cultural identity?

In the recent past, the dominant cultural identities have been circumscribed by immoral patriarchal, imperial, jingoistic and xenophobic constraints. The political consequences have been principally a public sphere regulated by and for well-to-do White males in the name of freedom and democracy. The new cultural criticism exposes and explodes the exclusions, blindnesses and silences of this past, calling from it radical libertarian and democratic projects that will create a better present and future. The new cultural politics of difference is neither an ahistorical Jacobin program that discards tradition and ushers in new self-righteous authoritarianism nor a guilt-ridden leveling anti-imperialist liberalism that celebrates token pluralism for smooth inclusion. Rather, it acknowledges the uphill struggle of fundamentally transforming highly objectified, rationalized and commodified societies and cultures in the name of individuality and democracy. This means locating the structural causes of unnecessary forms of social misery (without reducing all human suffering to historical causes), depicting the plight and predicaments of demoralized and depoliticized citizens caught in market-driven cycles of therapeutic release—drugs, alcholism, consumerism—and projecting alternative visions, analyses and actions that proceed from particularities and arrive at moral and political connectedness. This connectedness does not signal a homogeneous unity or monolithic totality but rather a contingent, fragile coalition building in an effort to pursue common radical libertarian and democratic goals that overlap.

In a world in which most of the resources, wealth and power are centered in huge corporations and supportive political elites, the new cultural politics of difference may appear to be solely visionary, utopian and fanciful. The recent cutbacks of social service programs, business takebacks at the negotiation tables of workers and management, speedups at the workplace and buildups of military budgets reinforce this perception. And surely the growing disintegration and decomposition of civil society—of shattered families, neighborhoods and schools—adds to this perception. Can a civilization that evolves more and more around market activity, more and more around the buying and selling of commodities, expand the scope of freedom and democracy? Can we simply bear witness to its slow decay and doom—a painful denouement prefigured already in many poor black and brown communities and rapidly embracing all of us? These haunting questions remain unanswered yet the challenge they pose must not remain unmet. The new cultural politics of difference tries to confront these enormous and urgent challenges. It will require all the imagination, intelligence, courage, sacrifice, care and laughter we can muster.

The time has come for critics and artists of the new cultural politics of difference to cast their nets widely, flex their muscles broadly and thereby refuse to limit their visions, analyses and praxis to their particular terrains. The aim is to dare to recast, redefine and revise the very notions of "modernity," "mainstream," "margins," "difference," "otherness." We have now reached a new stage in the perennial struggle for freedom and dignity. And while much of the First World intelligentsia adopts retrospective and conservative outlooks that defend the crisis-ridden present, we promote a prospective and prophetic vision with a sense of possibility and potential, especially for those who bear the social costs of the present. We look to the past for strength, not solace; we look at the present and see people perishing, not profits mounting; we look toward the future and vow to make it different and better.

To put it boldly, the new kind of critic and artist associated with the new cultural politics of difference consists of an energetic breed of New World *bricoleurs* with improvisational and flexible sensibilities that sidestep mere opportunism and mindless eclecticism; persons from all countries, cultures, genders, sexual orientations, ages and regions with protean identities who avoid ethnic chauvinism and faceless universalism; intellectual and political freedom-fighters with partisan passion, international perspectives, and, thank God, a sense of humor that combats the ever-present absurdity that forever threatens our democratic and libertarian projects and dampens the fire that fuels our will to struggle. Yet we will struggle and stay, as those brothers and sisters on the block say, "out there"—with intellectual rigor, existential dignity, moral vision, political courage and soulful style.